Third Edition

RHETORICAL CRITICISM

Third Edition

RHETORICAL CRITICISM

Exploration & Practice

Sonja K. Foss
University of Colorado at Denver

WAVELAND

PRESS, INC.

Long Grove, Illinois

For information about this book, contact:
Waveland Press, Inc.
4180 IL Route 83, Suite 101
Long Grove, IL 60047-9580
(847) 634-0081
info@waveland.com
www.waveland.com

Contents

8   Ideological Criticism   239

9   Metaphor Criticism   299

12 Generative Criticism   411

Preface

Rhetorical criticism is not a process confined to a few assignments in a rhetorical or media criticism course. It is an everyday activity we can use to understand our responses to symbols of all kinds and to create symbols of our own that generate the kinds of responses we intend. I hope this book not only provides guidelines for understanding and practicing critical analysis but also conveys the excitement and fun that can characterize the process.

I am grateful to a number of people who have assisted me throughout my work on this project. Ernest G. Bormann, Cindy L. Griffin, D. Lynn O'Brien Hallstein, Kellie Hay, and Debian L. Marty read portions of the manuscript and provided invaluable suggestions that significantly improved the work. William J. C. Waters's ideas were instrumental in creating the steps of generative criticism in chapter 12. Karen A. Foss, Robert Trapp, and Richard L. Johannesen read the entire manuscript of the first edition, which formed the basis for this version, and Karen A. Foss read the entire manuscript of this edition. Their gifts of time, energy, and support are particularly appreciated.

Many others contributed in other significant ways to the book. Diana Brown Sheridan, Xing Lu, Laura K. Hahn, and Michelle A. Holling provided research support and assistance with bibliographies with competence, care, and efficiency. My thanks to Karen A. Foss, Bernard J. Armada, and Robert Trapp for providing me with excellent samples of their students' work. I also appreciate the willingness of the scholars whose work I have included to share their work; their excellent models of criticism both enrich and clarify the approaches they illustrate. Kimberly C. Elliott pursued permissions for copyrighted material with delight, perseverance, technological wizardry, and creativity. My publishers, Carol Rowe and Neil Rowe, provided their usual enthusiastic support, amazing freedom, and just the right amount of prodding to produce this revision. Finally, this book is also a product of the questions, insights, and essays of criticism of the students in my rhetorical criticism courses at the University of Denver, the University of Oregon, Ohio State University, and the University of Colorado at Denver. Special thanks go to my husband, Anthony J. Radich, a superb rhetorical critic, who contributed to this project entertaining antics, constant good humor, and love.

Part I

INTRODUCTION

The Nature of
Rhetorical Criticism

We live our lives enveloped in symbols. How we perceive, what we know, what we experience, and how we act are the results of the symbols we create and the symbols we encounter in the world. We watch movies and television, we listen to speeches by political candidates, we read advertisements on billboards and buses, we choose furniture and works of art for our apartments and houses, and we talk with friends and family. As we do, we engage in a process of thinking about symbols, discovering how they work, and trying to figure out why they affect us. We choose to communicate in particular ways based on what we have discovered. This process is called *rhetorical criticism*, and this book provides an opportunity for you to develop skills in the process and to explore the theory behind it.

RHETORIC

A useful place to start in the study of rhetorical criticism is with an understanding of what rhetoric is. Many of the common uses of the word *rhetoric* have negative connotations. The term commonly is used to mean empty, bombastic language that has no substance. Political candidates and governmental officials often call for "action not rhetoric" from

3

their opponents or from the leaders of other nations. In other instances, *rhetoric* is used to mean flowery, ornamental speech laden with metaphors and other figures of speech. Neither of these conceptions is how rhetoric is used in rhetorical criticism, and neither is how the term has been defined throughout its long history as a discipline dating back to the fifth century B.C. In these contexts, rhetoric is defined as the human use of symbols to communicate. This definition includes three primary dimensions: (1) humans as the creators of rhetoric; (2) symbols as the medium for rhetoric; and (3) communication as the purpose for rhetoric.

Humans as the Creators of Rhetoric

Rhetoric involves symbols created and used by humans. Some people debate whether or not symbol use is a characteristic that distinguishes humans from all other species of animals, pointing to research with chimpanzees and gorillas in which these animals have been taught to communicate using signs. As far as we know, humans are the only animals who create a substantial part of their reality through the use of symbols. Every symbolic choice we make results in seeing the world in one way rather than in another, and in contrast to animals, human experience is different because of the symbols we use to frame it. Thus, *rhetoric* is limited to human rhetors as the originators or creators of messages.

Symbols as the Medium for Rhetoric

A second primary concept in the definition of rhetoric is that rhetoric involves symbols rather than signs. A symbol is something that stands for or represents something else by virtue of relationship, association, or convention. Symbols are distinguished from signs by the degree of direct connection to the object represented. Smoke is a sign that fire is present, which means that there is a direct relationship between the fire and the smoke. Similarly, the changing color of the leaves in autumn is a sign that winter is coming because the color is a direct indicator of a drop in temperature. A symbol, by contrast, is a human construction connected only indirectly to its referent. The word *cup*, for example, has no natural relationship to an open container for beverages. It is a symbol invented by someone who wanted to refer to this kind of object. A *cup* could have been labeled a *fish*, for example, and the selection of the word *cup* to refer to a particular kind of container is arbitrary.

The distinction between a symbol and a sign can be seen in a tennis match involving someone who does not exercise regularly and who plays tennis for the first time in many years. Following the match, he tells his partner that he is out of shape and doesn't have much stamina. The man is using symbols in an effort to explain to his partner how he is feeling, to suggest the source of his discomfort, and perhaps to rationalize his poor performance. The man also experiences an increased heart rate, a red face, and shortness of breath, but these changes in his bodily condition are not conscious choices. They communicate to his partner, just as his words do, but they are signs directly connected to his physical shape. They thus are not rhetorical. Only his conscious use of symbols to communicate a particular condition is rhetorical.

That signs and symbols often intertwine is typical of human communication. For instance, a tree standing in a forest is not a symbol. It does not stand for something else; it simply is a tree. The tree could become a symbol, however, if it is used by someone to communicate an idea. It could be used in environmental advocacy efforts as a symbol of the destruction of redwood forests, for example, or as a symbol of Jesus's birth when it is cut for use as a Christmas tree. Humans use all sorts of nonrhetorical objects in rhetorical ways, turning them into symbols in the process.

Although rhetoric often involves the deliberate and conscious choice of symbols to communicate with others, actions not deliberately constructed by rhetors also can be interpreted symbolically. Humans often choose to interpret something rhetorically that the sender of the message did not intend to be symbolic. In this case, someone chooses to give an action or an object symbolic value, even though the sender does not see it in symbolic terms. Often, in such cases, the meaning received is quite different from what the creator of the message intends. When the United States deploys an aircraft carrier off the coast of North Korea to warn its government not to continue with the development of nuclear weapons, the United States has performed a rhetorical action that is designed to be read symbolically by both sides, and there is no doubt about the meaning of the message. If a United States reconnaissance plane accidentally strays over North Korea without the purpose of communicating anything to North Korea, however, the pilot is not engaged in rhetorical action. In this case, however, the North Koreans can choose to interpret the event symbolically and take retaliatory action against the United States. Any action, whether intended to communicate or not, can be taken as symbolic by those who experience or encounter those actions.

The variety of forms that symbols can assume is broad. Rhetoric is not limited to written and spoken discourse; in fact, speaking and writing make up only a small part of our rhetorical environment. Rhetoric, then, includes nondiscursive or nonverbal symbols as well as discursive or verbal ones. Speeches, essays, conversations, poetry, novels, stories, comic books, television programs, films, art, architecture, plays, music, dance, advertisements, furniture, automobiles, and dress are all forms of rhetoric.

Communication as the Purpose of Rhetoric

A third component of the definition of rhetoric is that its purpose is communication. Symbols are used for communicating with others or with oneself. For many people, the term *rhetoric* is synonymous with *communication*. The choice of whether to use the term *rhetoric* or the term *communication* to describe the process of exchanging meaning is largely a personal one, often stemming from the tradition of inquiry in which a scholar is grounded. Individuals trained in social scientific perspectives on symbol use often prefer the term *communication*, while those who study symbol use from more humanistic perspectives tend to select the term *rhetoric*.

Rhetoric functions in a variety of ways to allow humans to communicate with one another. In some cases, we use rhetoric in an effort to persuade others—to encourage others to change in some way. In other instances, rhetoric is an invitation to understanding—we offer our perspectives and invite others to enter our worlds so they can understand us and our perspectives better. Sometimes, we use rhetoric simply as a means of self-discovery or to come to self-knowledge. We may articulate thoughts or feelings out loud to ourselves or in a journal or diary and, in doing so, come to know ourselves better and perhaps make different choices in our lives.

Another communicative function that rhetoric performs is that it tells us what reality is. Reality is not fixed but changes according to the symbols we use to talk about it. What we count as real or as knowledge about the world depends on how we choose to label and talk about things. This does not mean that things do not really exist—that this book, for example, is simply a figment of your imagination. Rather, the symbols through which our realities are filtered affect our view of the book and how we are motivated to act toward it. The frameworks and labels we choose to apply to what we encounter influence our perceptions of what we experience and thus the kinds of worlds in which we live. Is someone an *alcoholic* or *morally depraved?* Is a child *misbehaved* or *suffering from ADD?* Is an unexpected situation a *struggle* or an *adventure?* Is a coworker's behavior *irritating* or *eccentric?* The choices we make in terms of how to approach these situations are critical in determining the nature and outcome of the experiences we have regarding them.

RHETORICAL CRITICISM

The process you will be using for engaging in the study of rhetoric is rhetorical criticism. It is a qualitative research method that is designed for the systematic investigation and explanation of symbolic acts and artifacts for the purpose of understanding rhetorical processes. This definition includes three primary dimensions: (1) systematic analysis as the act of criticism; (2) acts and artifacts as the objects of analysis in criticism; and (3) understanding rhetorical processes as the purpose of criticism.

Systematic Analysis as the Act of Criticism

We are responding to symbols continually, and as we encounter symbols, we try to figure out how they are working and why they affect us as they do. We tend to respond to these symbols by saying "I like it" or "I don't like it." The process of rhetorical criticism involves engaging in this natural process in a more conscious, systematic, and focused way. Through the study and practice of rhetorical criticism, we can understand and explain why we like or don't like something by investigating the symbols themselves—we can begin to make statements about these messages rather than statements about our feelings. Rhetorical criticism, then, enables us to become more sophisticated and discriminating in explaining, investigating, and understanding symbols and our responses to them.

Acts and Artifacts as the Objects of Criticism

The objects of study in rhetorical criticism are symbolic acts and artifacts. An act is executed in the presence of a rhetor's intended audience—a speech or a musical performance presented to a live audience, for example. Because an act tends to be fleeting and ephemeral, making its analysis difficult, many rhetorical critics prefer to study the artifact of an act—the text, trace, or tangible evidence of the act. When a rhetorical act is transcribed and printed, posted on a Web site, recorded on film, or preserved on canvas, it becomes a rhetorical artifact that then is accessible to a wider audience than the one that witnessed the rhetorical act. Both acts and artifacts are objects of rhetorical criticism. But because most critics use the tangible product as the basis for criticism—a speech text, a building, a sculpture, a recorded song, for example—the term *artifact* will be used in this book to refer to the object of study. The use of the term is not meant to exclude acts from your investigation but to provide a consistent and convenient way to talk about the object of criticism.[1]

Understanding Rhetorical Processes as the Purpose of Criticism

The process of rhetorical criticism often begins with an interest in understanding particular symbols and how they operate. A critic may be interested in a particular kind of symbol use or a particular rhetorical artifact—the Holocaust Museum in Washington, D.C., or Eminem's music, for example—and engages in criticism to deepen appreciation and understanding of that artifact. Critics of popular culture such as restaurant, television, theatre, film, and music critics are these kinds of critics—they tend to be most interested in understanding the particular experience of the restaurant or CD they are reviewing. But criticism undertaken primarily to comment on a particular artifact tends not to be "enduring; its importance and its functions are immediate and ephemeral."[2] Once the historical situation has been forgotten or the rhetor—the creator of the artifact—is no longer the center of the public's attention, such criticism no longer serves a useful purpose if it has been devoted exclusively to an understanding of a particular artifact.

In contrast to critics of popular culture, rhetorical critics don't study an artifact for its qualities and features alone. Rhetorical critics are interested in discovering what an artifact teaches about the nature of rhetoric—in other words, critics engage in rhetorical criticism to make a contribution to rhetorical theory.[3] *Theory* is a tentative answer to a question we pose as we seek to understand the world. It is a set of general clues, generalizations, or principles that explains a process or phenomenon and thus helps to answer the question we asked. We are all theorists in our everyday lives, developing explanations for what is happening in our worlds based on our experiences and observations. If a friend never returns your phone calls or e-mail messages, for example, you might come to the conclusion—or develop the theory—that the friendship is over. You have asked yourself a question about the state of the friendship, collected some evidence (made phone calls and sent e-mail messages and observed that they were not returned), and reached a tentative conclusion or claim (that the other person no longer wishes to be your friend).

In rhetorical criticism, the theorizing that critics do deals with explanations about how rhetoric works. A critic asks a question about a rhetorical process or phenomenon and how it works and provides a tentative answer to the question. This answer does not have to be fancy, formal, or complicated. It simply involves identifying some of the basic concepts involved in a rhetorical phenomenon or process and explaining how they work. Admittedly, the theory that results is based on limited evidence—in many cases, one artifact. But even the study of one artifact allows you to step back from the details of a particular artifact to take a broader view of it and to draw some conclusions about what it suggests concerning some process of rhetoric.

The process of rhetorical criticism does not end with a contribution to theory. Theories about rhetorical criticism enable us to develop a cumulative body of research and thus to improve our practice of communication. The final outcome of rhetorical criticism is a contribution to the improvement of our abilities as communicators. As a rhetorical critic, you implicitly suggest how more effective symbol use may be accomplished. In suggesting some theoretical principles about how rhetoric operates, you provide principles or guidelines for those of us who want to communicate in more self-reflective ways and to construct messages that best accomplish our goals.[4] As a result of our study of these principles, we should be more skilled, discriminating, and sophisticated in our efforts to communicate in talk with our friends and families, in the decoration of our homes and offices, in the choices we make about our dress, and in our efforts to present our ideas at school or at work.

Knowledge of the operation of rhetoric also can help make us more sophisticated audience members for messages. When we understand the various options available to rhetors in the construction of messages and how they function together to create the effects they produce, we are able to question the choices others make in the construction of acts and artifacts. We are less inclined to accept existing rhetorical practices and to respond uncritically to the messages we encounter. As a result, we become more engaged and active participants in shaping the nature of the worlds in which we live.

Notes

[1] This distinction is suggested by Kathleen G. Campbell, "Enactment as a Rhetorical Strategy/Form in Rhetorical Acts and Artifacts," Diss. University of Denver 1988, pp. 25–29.

[2] Karlyn Kohrs Campbell, "Criticism: Ephemeral and Enduring," *Speech Teacher*, 23 (January 1974), p. 11.

[3] More elaborate discussions of rhetorical criticism as theory building can be found in: Roderick P. Hart, "Forum: Theory-Building and Rhetorical Criticism: An Informal Statement of Opinion," *Central States Speech Journal*, 27 (Spring 1976), 70–77; Richard B. Gregg, "The Criticism of Symbolic Inducement: A Critical-Theoretical Connection," in *Speech Communication in the 20th Century*, ed. Thomas W. Benson (Carbondale: Southern Illinois University Press, 1985), pp. 42–43; and Campbell, "Criticism," pp. 11–14.

[4] Discussions of rhetorical criticism to increase the effectiveness of communication can be found in: Robert Cathcart, *Post Communication: Criticism and Evaluation* (Indianapolis: Bobbs-Merrill, 1966), pp. 3, 6–7, 12; and Edwin Black, *Rhetorical Criticism: A Study in Method* (Madison: University of Wisconsin Press, 1978), p. 9.

Doing Rhetorical Criticism

The definitions of *rhetoric* and *rhetorical criticism* in chapter 1 have provided a starting place for understanding rhetorical criticism. Knowledge about what rhetorical criticism *is* does not automatically translate into the ability to *do* criticism, however. This chapter is designed to provide an overview of the actual process of producing an essay of criticism. At the end of the chapter is a discussion of the standards used to evaluate essays of criticism.

Because this textbook is a first experience with rhetorical criticism for many of you, you probably will feel more comfortable initially practicing rhetorical criticism using specific methods. Using these methods enables you to begin to develop your critical skills and to learn the language and basic procedures of criticism. This chapter, then, provides you with information about how to do criticism when your starting point is a formal method of criticism. A variety of these methods are presented in chapters 3 through 11. In chapter 12, a different way of approaching criticism is presented—generative criticism—an approach you probably will want to try as your skills as a critic grow. Using this approach, you will create a method or framework for analyzing an artifact from the data of the artifact itself.

Your starting place, then, is with a method of criticism—either one you have chosen or one selected for you by your professor. You know, for example, that you will be writing an essay of criticism using the cluster or the fantasy-theme method of criticism. When you begin with a particular method, the process of rhetorical criticism involves four steps:

11

(1) selecting an artifact; (2) analyzing the artifact; (3) formulating a research question; and (4) writing the essay.

SELECTING AN ARTIFACT

Your first step is to find an artifact to analyze that is appropriate for the method you will be applying. The artifact is the data for the study—the rhetorical act, event, or product you are going to analyze. It may be any instance of symbol use that is of interest to you and seems capable of generating insights about rhetorical processes—a song, a poem, a speech, a work of art, or a building, for example. What you probably will find is that particular artifacts interest you because there is something about them that you cannot explain, even if what you cannot explain is why you like the artifact as much as you do.

An artifact is appropriate for a method in two ways. It first must contain the kinds of data that are the focus of the units of analysis of the method. Units of analysis focus attention on certain dimensions of an artifact and not others. A critic cannot possibly examine all of the features of an artifact, so units of analysis serve as a vehicle or lens for you to use to examine the artifact. They are scanning devices for picking up particular kinds of information about an artifact, directing and narrowing the analysis in particular ways, revealing some things and concealing others. Units of analysis are things like strategies, types of evidence, values, word choice, or metaphors. If you are using the narrative method, for example, you will need an artifact that is a narrative or story or that includes a story within it. If you are using metaphor criticism, you will need an artifact that contains some metaphors.

A second criterion to use in selecting an artifact is that it should be one where whatever intrigues, baffles, or excites you about that artifact might be able to be explained by the units of analysis the method supplies. The kinds of explanations that methods can supply are different, so you want your artifact to be able to be explained by the method. For example, if you are puzzled by a song and cannot understand why you like it, the method should have the potential to provide an explanation for or address your confusion about that artifact. The cluster method, for example, which asks you to look for key terms in the artifact and the terms that cluster around them to discover the meaning an artifact has for its creator, might provide you with the means to understand it. If, for example, you are intrigued by the many instances of religious discourse that are appearing in the political realm, you probably would not find the feminist method, which focuses on the construction of gender, to be very useful in helping you understand what is going on. You probably would do well to use those religious artifacts as your data when you are asked to write an essay of generic criticism, where the method allows critics to discover patterns across different artifacts. Similarly, if you are interested in the gender roles of characters on a television show, you probably would find that the feminist method works better for analyzing this artifact than does the cluster method. If what intrigues you about an artifact is not something that the method is likely to be able to address, the artifact probably is not an appropriate one to use for practicing that method.

Beyond its appropriateness for your method, the artifact you choose should be something you really like or really dislike, something that puzzles or baffles you, or something that you cannot explain. We have such responses to the artifacts around us all the time—we love a particular song, we cannot understand why a singer has the appeal that she does, we marvel at the artistry involved in a quilt, or we cannot figure out what the message of a building is supposed to be. Let your interest in your daily encounters with artifacts guide you in your selection of an artifact. Your interest in, passion for, and curiosity about an artifact are important initial ingredients for writing an essay of criticism.

ANALYZING THE ARTIFACT

The second step in the process of criticism is to code or analyze your artifact using the procedures of the method. Each method of criticism has its own procedures for analyzing an artifact, and at this step you apply the units of analysis provided by the method. If you are applying metaphor analysis, for example, you will be involved in coding your artifact for metaphors. If you are applying the cluster method, you will be identifying key terms in the artifact and finding the terms that cluster around them. This is the step in which you engage in a close and systematic analysis of the artifact and become thoroughly familiar with whatever dimensions of the artifact are highlighted by your method.

An easy way to do the coding of your artifact is to write or type your notes about the artifact in a list, leaving some space between each "code" or observation that you make. Physically cut the observations you have made apart so that each idea or observation is on a separate strip of paper. Then group the strips that are about the same thing and put them in one pile. Group the strips that are about something else and put them in another pile. What is in these piles will depend on the method of criticism you are using—perhaps different fantasy themes, different metaphors, or different elements of narratives, for example. Play around with different ways to organize your piles. The strips of paper allow you to group your codings in different ways into different categories and encourage you to try out all sorts of ways of conceptualizing your data.

⟩ FORMULATING A RESEARCH QUESTION

The research question is what you want to find out about rhetoric by studying an artifact. It suggests what your study contributes to our understanding of how rhetorical processes work—your contribution to rhetorical theory. Although you probably will not state your research question as an actual question in your essay, you want to be able to articulate what your research question is in your mind because it encourages you to be very clear about your objective in your analysis. Research questions are questions such as: "How does an ambiguous artifact persuade?" "What strategies can help people regain credibility after they have been humiliated?" "What strategies do marginalized groups use to challenge a dominant perspective?" or "How does a political leader construct a nation as an enemy?"

To create a research question, use the principle behind *Jeopardy* and create a question for which the analysis you have just completed is the answer. Use your findings to discover what is most significant, useful, or insightful about your artifact and make that focus into a research question. If your analysis reveals, for example, that an artifact is making a highly controversial topic seem normal, your research question might be something like, "What rhetorical strategies facilitate the normalization of a controversial perspective?"

Research questions tend to be about four basic components of the communication process—the rhetor, the audience, the situation, and the message. If you are having trouble developing a research question, identifying the arena in which your study belongs might help you formulate your question.

1. *Rhetor.* Some research questions deal with the relationship between rhetors and their rhetoric. Questions that focus on the rhetor might be concerned with the motive of the rhetor, the worldview of the rhetor, or how the rhetoric functions for the rhetor. "How do cowboy references function in the rhetoric of politicians?" is a research question that has the rhetor as a focus.

2. *Audience.* Some research questions are concerned with the relationship between an artifact and an audience. Although rhetorical criticism does not allow you to answer questions about the actual effects of rhetoric on an audience, you can ask questions about the kind of audience an artifact constructs as its preferred audience or how an artifact functions to facilitate the development of certain values or beliefs in an audience. A research question centered on audience is: "What is the ideal audience constructed by and for reality TV shows?"

3. *Situation.* Other research questions deal with the relationship between an artifact and the situation or context in which the arti-

fact is embedded. Such questions might deal with the impact of a situation on an artifact, the rhetor's definition of a situation in an artifact, or whether the artifact adequately addresses an exigence in a particular situation. Research questions in which situation is central are: "How do political leaders define exigencies following a national crisis?" "What is the impact of those definitions on perceptions of the crisis?"

4. *Message.* Most research questions in rhetorical criticism deal with the message. The focus here is on the specific features of the artifact that enable it to function in particular ways. Such questions might deal with the kinds of arguments constructed, the types of metaphors used, the key terms used, or a combination of rhetorical strategies and characteristics that create a particular kind of artifact. Research questions that focus on method are questions such as: "What are the features of effective apologies?" or "How does rhetoric generate support for propositions that are contrary to cultural norms?"

When you formulate your research question, try to avoid three mistakes that beginning critics sometimes make as they create research questions. One is to make the question too broad and generic. A question such as "How does political rhetoric about war function?" is too broad and unfocused to answer through the rhetorical analysis of one or even several artifacts. Try to narrow the scope of the question by paying attention to the specific features of the artifact that are most interesting to you. You then might narrow the question to one such as "What rhetorical strategies do political leaders use to justify unpopular wars?"

A second problem that can occur with research questions is that the wording of the questions does not allow much of interest to be explained. Yes-or-no questions, which typically begin with *do*, are these kinds of questions. "Do political leaders justify unpopular wars?" is such a question. Not only do these kinds of questions require simple yes-or-no answers, but the answers to them are usually obvious—of course political leaders try to justify unpopular wars. An easy way to make sure your research question is one that takes advantage of the interesting and useful insights your analysis has produced is to begin your question with words and phrases such as *How? In what way? What are the rhetorical processes used in?* or *What are the rhetorical strategies used to?*

There is one more thing to avoid as you develop your research question. Do not include your specific artifact or data in your research question. Although there are exceptions with some methods of criticism (such as the ideological approach), the question usually should be larger than the artifact you are analyzing. You should be able to use any number of artifacts to answer the question and not only the one you have analyzed for this study. Turn the question that fits the analysis of your artifact into a more general one by making the elements of the question more abstract. Instead of a question such as, "How did George W. Bush reassure citizens after the terrorist attacks of September 11?," your question could be, "What rhetorical strategies do political leaders use to reassure citizens after catastrophic events?" Instead of a question such as, "How does the National Rifle Association make its ideology palatable to resistant audiences?," your question could be, "How do organizations with strong ideologies construct messages that appeal to normally resistant audiences?"

WRITING THE ESSAY

After you have analyzed your artifact, you are ready to write your essay of criticism. Think of doing the analysis and writing the essay as two separate processes. All of the thinking you have done and the steps you have gone through to conduct your analysis are not included in your essay. What you want to put on paper is the end result of your analysis so that you produce a coherent, well-argued essay that reports your insights. An essay of criticism includes five major components: (1) an introduction, in which you discuss the research question, its contribution to rhetorical theory, and its significance; (2) a description of your artifact and its context; (3) a description of your method of analysis; (4) a report of the findings of the analysis; and (5) a discussion of the contribution your analysis makes to rhetorical theory. These components do not need to be discussed in separate sections or identified with headings, but you want to include these topics in your essay in some way.

Introduction

Your task in the introduction to the essay is the task of the introduction of any paper. You want to orient the reader to the topic and present a clear statement of purpose that organizes the essay. In the introduction, identify the research question the analysis answers, although you probably will not state the question as an actual question in your essay. It usually is stated as the purpose statement in your essay, using words such as "I will argue," "I will suggest," or "I will explore." If the research question you have formulated, for example, is "What are the functions of reality-television shows for audiences?," you may want to state it in your essay in this way: "In this essay, I will explore the functions of reality-television shows for their audiences to try to discover the appeal of such programs."

A major purpose of the introduction is to generate interest so that your readers will want to read your essay, even if they have no initial concern or curiosity about your artifact. One way to invite them into the essay is by suggesting that they will learn something about something they care about. Explain why the analysis of the artifact is important or significant to them. If possible, think of some real-life examples of rhetorical processes with which your readers have had experience that relate to your analysis. If you are analyzing a speech by an NRA member to gun-control supporters, for example, you might provide common examples where individuals want to or must try to persuade those who hold views that are hostile to theirs. If you are analyzing a speech in which a rhetor attempts to synthesize two polarized positions, you might argue that this artifact is a model of how rhetors can create identification between opposing positions. Knowledge about how to do this, you can suggest, is important for managing conflict effectively between other opposing factions.

Another way to generate interest is by providing information about other studies that have been done on the artifact you are analyzing that are incomplete, inadequate, or do not provide a satisfactory explanation for it. You also can suggest that your study is important because it extends, elaborates on, builds on, or in some way adds to knowledge that already exists concerning a particular rhetorical process. When you discuss why the knowledge about the rhetorical process to which you are contributing is important, you are addressing the "so what?" question in research. This question asks you to consider why the reader should care about the topic and continue to read the essay.

Description of the Artifact

If the readers of your essay are to understand your analysis of an artifact, they must be somewhat familiar with the artifact itself. To acquaint readers with the artifact, provide a brief overview or summary of the artifact near the beginning of the essay. Give readers whatever information they need to understand the artifact and to be able to follow your analysis. If you are analyzing a film, for example, provide an overview of the plot, the major characters, and significant technical features of the film. If you are analyzing a speech, include in the description of the artifact the major arguments presented by the rhetor and any significant features of the rhetor's delivery, the occasion, and the response of the audience. You also want to provide the context for the artifact, locating it within the social, political, and economic arrangements of which it is a part. If, for example, you are analyzing a Harry Potter book or movie, give a brief explanation of the Harry Potter phenomenon—tell who the author of the books is, the number of books in the series, the number of books sold, the amount of money generated at the box office by the films, and the controversies the phenomenon has generated among some religious groups.

Your description of the artifact is, to some extent, an interpretation of the artifact. You cannot tell the reader everything about the artifact, so you must make decisions about what to feature in the description. In this process, you want to describe and thus to highlight aspects of the artifact that are most important for and relevant to the analysis that will follow. Do not describe the artifact in too much detail here. You will reveal a great deal about what the artifact is like as you present the findings of your analysis, so details that will emerge later in your analysis do not need to be given in your introduction. This is the place to provide a broad overview of the artifact, knowing that readers will become much more familiar with your artifact later.

In the description of the artifact, also provide a justification for why that artifact is a particularly appropriate or useful one to analyze in order to answer the research question. Many different artifacts can be used for answering the same research question, so provide an explanation as to why analyzing your artifact is a good choice for explaining the rhetorical process your research question addresses. Many kinds of reasons can be used to justify your artifact. You might provide historical context that suggests the artifact is important within that context. Perhaps the artifact represents a larger set of similar texts that are culturally significant. Perhaps the artifact you are analyzing has won many prestigious awards or has been highly successful in generating money. Perhaps the artifact has reached large numbers of people or created an unusual response. Perhaps the rhetorical techniques used in the artifact warrant exploration.

Description of the Method

You need to cover one more topic to complete readers' understanding of what will happen in the essay—a description of the method used to analyze the artifact. Identify the method you are using, explain who created the method (if one person is identifiable with the method), define its key concepts, and briefly lay out its basic tenets or procedures. If you are using the fantasy-theme method of criticism, for example, your description might include mention of its creator, Ernest Bormann; a definition of its basic terms, *fantasy theme* and *rhetorical vision*; and a brief explanation of the method's assumptions.

Report of the Findings of the Analysis

The report of the findings of your analysis constitutes the bulk of the essay. In this section, lay out for readers the results of your analysis of the artifact. Tell what you discovered from an application of the method of criticism to the artifact and provide support for your discoveries from the data of the artifact. If you used pentadic analysis as your method, for example, you would identify the terms of act, purpose, agent, agency, and scene for your artifact. If you analyzed the artifact using the fantasy-theme method, this section would be organized around the fantasy themes of settings, characters, and actions evident in your artifact and the rhetorical vision they create.

Bring in relevant literature as you explain your findings to elaborate on or extend your ideas. Be sure that you feature your ideas in your analysis section, making the thesis statements of your paragraphs about *your* ideas and not echoes of the ideas of others. Any theories or concepts you believe are relevant to your analysis should be used to support, elaborate on, and extend your ideas rather than letting the ideas of others subsume yours.

If you used the technique of cutting apart your observations on individual strips of paper in the coding step, you have available to you a very easy way to write up your analysis. Organize the piles in the order in which you want to talk about the components of your findings. As you are ready to write a section of your analysis, take the pile relevant to the topic of the section and sort the strips of paper within it, laying out the pieces in the order in which you want to discuss ideas and examples and eliminating those you do not want to include in your essay. Write through the pile of pieces of paper, connecting the strips with transitions, previews, summaries, and interpretations.

Using this approach, your essay is easy to write for a number of reasons. You have the freedom to write the sections of the analysis in any order—you do not have to begin with the first component of the schema because each pile contains all of your ideas relevant to a section. You do not need to see what happens in one section to be able to write the next. Another advantage of this system is that you cannot lose track of where you are because the ideas of your conceptual schema are clear to you, and all the content you want to discuss is already known to you and waiting in the piles to be written.

Contribution to Rhetorical Theory

Your essay ends with a discussion of the contribution your analysis makes to rhetorical theory. This contribution is your answer to your research question. At this point in the essay, move away from your specific artifact or data and answer your research question more generally and abstractly. Transcend the specific data of your artifact to focus on the rhetorical processes with which you are concerned. Suggest to your readers how your analysis of your artifact provides an answer to the larger issue with which your essay is concerned, discussing the implications or significance of the contribution you mentioned in the introduction. Perhaps you also can suggest how the new knowledge you have generated can make human communication better in some way.

Your contribution to rhetorical theory is likely to be made in one of two ways: identifying new concepts or new relationships among concepts. These are the two basic elements of theories. Concepts are the components, elements, or variables the theory is about. The concepts tell what you are looking at and what you consider important. Statements of relationship are explanations about how the concepts are related to one another. They identify patterns in the relationships among variables or concepts, and they tell how concepts are connected. One rhetorical theory concerning the process of credibility, for example, suggests that, to be credible, a rhetor must demonstrate intelligence, moral character, and good will toward the audience. The concepts of the theory are intelligence, moral character, and good will, and the theory posits that all three of these concepts, interacting together and displayed in an artifact itself, contribute to an audience's perception that the rhetor is credible; this is a statement of relationship. Your analysis can contribute to rhetorical theory, then, by identifying important concepts in a rhetorical process or by suggesting how concepts relate to one another or both.

Although you cannot generalize your findings to other artifacts like yours or to artifacts characterized by similar rhetorical processes to make a contribution to rhetorical theory, you can make a contribution without moving beyond the particular artifact you have studied. David Zarefsky calls this kind of contribution a "theory of the particular case" and suggests that your analysis of your artifact—the particular case—allows you to suggest a theory that "more fully encompasses the case than do the alternatives." You are able to provide an initial general understanding of some aspect of rhetoric on the basis of the necessarily limited evidence available in the artifact.[1]

The idea that you can and should make a contribution to rhetorical theory in an essay of criticism makes many beginning rhetorical critics uncomfortable. You may feel as though you are not expert enough to develop a theory or to contribute to our understanding of how rhetoric works, or you may feel that you have not yet earned the right to make such contributions. You are an expert, however, in your way of seeing—in the application of your perspective on the world. This is a perspective that belongs to no one else. You will see things in an artifact that no one else sees, and making a contribution to rhetorical theory is the way in which you can share with us your unique perspective and offer a new understanding of an artifact. Also remember that the perspective you share with others is not coming out of thin air—you will have the backing of the careful and systematic analysis you have completed as the basis on which to make your contribution to rhetorical theory.

STANDARDS OF EVALUATION FOR CRITICAL ESSAYS

What makes one essay of criticism better than another? By what standards is an essay of criticism judged? Rhetorical criticism is a different kind of research from quantitative research, so it is not judged by the standards that are used for such research. In quantitative research, the basic standards of evaluation are validity—whether researchers are measuring what they claim they are measuring—and reliability—replicability of results if the same set of objects is measured repeatedly with the same or comparable measuring instruments.

The standards used in rhetorical criticism to judge analyses of artifacts are rooted in two primary assumptions. One assumption is that objective reality does not exist. As discussed in chapter 1, those of us who study rhetoric believe that reality is constituted through the rhetoric we use to talk about it; it is a symbolic creation. Thus, the artifact you are analyzing does not constitute a reality that can be known and proved. You cannot know what the artifact "really" means because there are as many realities about the artifact as there are vocabularies from which to conduct inquiry about it. A second assumption on which the standards of rhetorical criticism are built is very much related to the first: A critic can know an artifact only through a personal interpretation of it. You cannot be objective, impartial, and removed from the data because you bring to the critical task particular values and experiences that are reflected in how you see and write about an artifact. As a result of these assumptions, your task as a critic is to offer one perspective on an artifact—one possible way of viewing it. You are not concerned with finding the true, correct, or right interpretation of an artifact. Consequently, two critics may analyze the same artifact, ask the same research question, and come up with different conclusions, and the essays they write both can be excellent essays of criticism.

The primary standard used in judging an essay of criticism is justification—the argument made by a critic.[2] You must be able to justify what you say or offer reasons in support of the claims you make in your report of your findings. All of the ways in which we judge arguments, then, apply to judgments about the quality of a critical essay. You must have a claim—the conclusion of the argument you are seeking to justify. The claim is the answer to the question, "Where are we going?" You must provide evidence to support the claim you are making and have sufficient evidence from the artifact to back up your claim. This evidence constitutes the grounds of your argument—the data from the artifact on which the argument is based. Grounds provide the answer to the question, "What do we have to go on?" The easiest way for us to see that the artifact is as you say it is is to use ample quotations from a discursive artifact and ample descriptions of the dimensions of a visual one. You also must quote the evidence accurately, and the evidence you cite should be representative of the artifact as a whole. This standard of adequate, accurate documentation requires that what you say exists in an artifact is, in fact, there.

A second standard by which arguments are judged and that also applies to essays of criticism is reasonable inference. What this means is that you must show how you moved from the data of the artifact to the claims you are making. As you write your essay, you must show the reader how the claims you make reasonably can be inferred from your data. If, for example, you suggest that the straight lines on a building suggest rigidity, you would want to explain how you inferred rigidity from straight lines—perhaps because of their "straight-and-narrow" nature or their visual lack of variation and deviation. What you are doing here is explicating the warrants of your claim. The warrant authorizes movement from the grounds to the claim and answers the question, "How do we justify the move from these grounds to that claim?"[3] Although your readers must be able to follow you from the data to your claims, they do not have to agree with those claims. They do not have to come up with the same claims that you did to judge your essay to be rigorous or excellent. Each critic brings a unique framework and biases to the process, so complete agreement on the interpretation of an artifact is not likely. Your readers, however, should be able to see and appreciate how you arrived at your claims.

A third criterion by which essays of rhetorical criticism are judged is coherence. You must order, arrange, and present your findings so they are congruent and consistent. Congruence means that your findings do not contradict one another and are internally consistent. It also means that all of the major dimensions of the artifact are included in the schema or theory you present of your findings—nothing major is left hanging, unable to be explained. Parallel constructs and labels for your findings create coherence as well—the labels should be parallel in terms of level of abstraction and language. If your findings include three major strategies, those strategies should be equally concrete or abstract, equally specific or general, and their wording should match one another in length, tone, and type of vocabulary. For example, labels for the three strategies of *using rhetoric to make oneself suffer, pleading*, and *a rhetor's development of a new plan to convince a teenage audience* are at different levels of abstraction and use different voice and language forms. More parallel labels for these strategies might be *suffering, pleading*, and *innovating*.

Coherence also requires that a critic has done sufficient analysis of the findings to present them in an insightful and useful way to the reader. If you are doing a metaphor analysis, for example, you could report your findings as a list of the metaphors used by the rhetor in the artifact. To satisfy the criterion of coherence, however, you would engage in an additional act of analysis. You would want to organize the metaphors into categories and provide an interpretation of those categories in a coherent framework. Simply the act of presenting your findings in a coherent way usually provides many more insights into your data.

The criteria for evaluating an essay of criticism point to the essence of rhetorical criticism as an art, not a science. In rhetorical criticism, artifacts are dealt with more as the artist deals with experience than as the scientist does. As a rhetorical critic, you are required to bring a variety of creative abilities to bear throughout the process of rhetorical criticism—writing in a way that is not dull, helping the reader envision and experience an artifact as you do, conveying your interest in and perhaps passion for an artifact, persuading readers to view the artifact's contribution to rhetorical theory as you do, and offering a compelling invitation to readers to experience some aspect of the world in a new way.[4]

▌ WHAT COMES NEXT

The chapters that follow are designed to provide additional guidelines for you as a rhetorical critic. They provide formal methods of rhetorical criticism that will give you practice developing your skills in the art of rhetorical criticism. To help you become comfortable with the critical process and to learn to produce excellent criticism, the chapters include four components, each offering a different opportunity for exploring the method and the kinds of insights it can produce for an artifact.

Each chapter begins with a theoretical overview of the critical method, including a discussion of its origins, assumptions, and units of analysis the method offers. The second part of the chapter details the procedures or steps for applying the method to an artifact. This is followed by sample essays in which the method has been used. Some of the sample essays were written by students who were just learning about criticism, as you are, and some were written by seasoned rhetorical critics. If you are a beginning critic with no experience in rhetorical criticism, you probably will find the essays by the students shorter, simpler, and more accessible, but all of the essays were selected because they model the application of a method with particular clarity. Each chapter ends with a list of additional samples of essays in which the method that is the subject of the chapter has been used. These lists of samples are not exhaustive; they are designed simply to serve as places to start if you wish to locate other samples of the method.

The chapters are organized alphabetically: cluster, fantasy-theme, feminist, generic, ideological, metaphor, narrative, and pentadic criticism. The steps in the process of rhetorical criticism discussed in this chapter are repeated in each of the following chapters to provide a basic framework for criticism that remains constant regardless of your method, artifact, or research question. The chapters on neo-Aristotelian criticism and generative criticism are not alphabetized with the nine chapters that present the different methods of criticism. Neo-Aristotelian criticism is the first of these chapters because it was the first method of criticism developed in the communication field and served as an exigence to which the other formal methods responded. It differs from the others in that it dictates a particular end for criticism, and it is rarely used by rhetorical critics today. A chapter on generative criticism concludes the book because it involves a different process for doing criticism than the process presented in the other chapters. In the generative approach, a critic generates a method or an explanatory schema from the data of the artifact itself. Generative criticism also is an advanced approach to criticism that you will be ready to try after you have gained practice in criticism by using some of the formal methods of criticism.

You are about to embark on an exciting adventure that will engage and stimulate your critical thinking skills and challenge you to develop more sophisticated writing skills. If you are like most rhetorical critics, you will find yourself engaged, intrigued, inspired, and sometimes frustrated and baffled as you work through critical methods and develop analyses of artifacts. The process of rhetorical criticism is demanding and difficult, but it is also fun, and it is a skill that will enable you to analyze the worlds others have created and to choose more deliberately the symbolic worlds that you yourself inhabit.

Notes

[1] David Zarefsky, "The State of the Art in Public Address," in *Texts in Context: Critical Dialogues on Significant Episodes in American Political Rhetoric*, ed. Michael C. Leff and Fred J. Kauffeld (Davis, CA: Hermagoras, 1989), pp. 22–23.

[2] A good discussion of the role of argument in rhetorical criticism is provided by Wayne Brockriede, "Rhetorical Criticism as Argument," *Quarterly Journal of Speech*, 60 (April 1974), 165–74. Barbara A. Larson suggests that Stephen Toulmin's model of argument can be used to connect data and claims in rhetorical criticism in "Method in Rhetorical Criticism: A Pedagogical Approach and Proposal," *Central States Speech Journal*, 27 (Winter 1976), 297–301.

[3] Claims, grounds, and warrants are components of the layout of an argument suggested by Stephen Toulmin. For more detail on his model of argument, see: Stephen Toulmin, *The Uses of Argument* (Cambridge, UK: Cambridge University Press, 1958); Stephen Toulmin, Richard Rieke, and Alan Janik, *An Introduction to Reasoning* (New York: Macmillan, 1984); and Sonja K. Foss, Karen A. Foss, and Robert Trapp, *Contemporary Perspectives on Rhetoric*, 3rd ed. (Prospect Heights, IL: Waveland, 2002), chpt. 5.

[4] For more detailed discussions of standards for judging rhetorical criticism, see: Sonja K. Foss, "Criteria for Adequacy in Rhetorical Criticism," *Southern Speech Communication Journal*, 48 (Spring 1983), 283–95; and Philip Wander and Steven Jenkins, "Rhetoric, Society, and the Critical Response," *Quarterly Journal of Speech*, 58 (December 1972), 441–50.

3

Neo-Aristotelian Criticism
Genesis of Rhetorical Criticism

The first formal method of rhetorical criticism developed in the communication field is called the *neo-classical*, *neo-Aristotelian*, or *traditional* method of criticism. The central features of the neo-Aristotelian method first were suggested in 1925 by Herbert A. Wichelns in "The Literary Criticism of Oratory."[1] Until Wichelns's essay, no specific guidelines for criticism were used by critics, and no clear understanding existed of what rhetorical criticism was. Because Wichelns's essay provided "substance and structure to a study which heretofore had been formless and ephemeral . . . it literally *created* the modern discipline of rhetorical criticism."[2] As Donald C. Bryant explained, the impact Wichelns's essay had on the practice of rhetorical criticism was significant: it "set the pattern and determined the direction of rhetorical criticism for more than a quarter of a century and has had a greater and more continuous influence upon the development of the scholarship of rhetoric and public address than any other single work published in this century."[3]

In his essay, Wichelns began by distinguishing literary criticism from rhetorical criticism, asserting that rhetorical criticism "is not concerned with permanence, nor yet with beauty," as is literary criticism. Rather, it "is concerned with effect. It regards a speech as a communication to a specific audience, and holds its business to be the analysis and appreciation of the orator's method of imparting his ideas to his hearers."[4] Wichelns's concern with this distinction reflects the origins of the communication discipline in departments of English. Early theorists in communication wanted to develop their field as a separate and legitimate discipline.

Wichelns's major contribution to the development of neo-Aristotelianism was that he listed the topics that should be covered in the study of a speech. A critic, he suggested, should deal with these elements: the speaker's personality, the public character of the speaker or the public's perception of the speaker, the audience, the major ideas presented in the speech, the motives to which the speaker appealed, the nature of the speaker's proofs, the speaker's judgment of human nature in the audience, the arrangement of the speech, the speaker's mode of expression, the speaker's method of speech preparation, the manner of delivery, and the effect of the discourse on the immediate audience and its long-term effects.[5]

Although Wichelns did not discuss how a critic should analyze these topics, they were many of the same topics discussed by Aristotle in the *Rhetoric* and by other classical rhetoricians such as Cicero and Quintilian. Thus, critics turned to classical sources for elaboration of Wichelns's guidelines and began to use as units of analysis the classical canons of rhetoric—invention, arrangement, style, delivery, and memory—and named the approach *neo-Aristotelianism*. They used as their framework for criticism the topics covered and the perspectives taken on them by the ancient rhetorical theorists.

Wichelns's suggested approach to rhetorical criticism was solidified in numerous critical studies that followed. The widespread use of neo-Aristotelianism was particularly evident in the two-volume *A History and Criticism of American Public Address*, edited by William Norwood Brigance and published in 1943.[6] In the studies included in this work, authors used either the Aristotelian pattern alone or in combination with those of other classical rhetoricians to guide their critical efforts. Wichelns's method became more firmly fixed in 1948 with the publication of *Speech Criticism*, in which Lester Thonssen and A. Craig Baird presented an elaborate system for the practice of rhetorical criticism based on the topics suggested by Wichelns and the writings of classical rhetoricians.[7]

As a consequence of the adoption of neo-Aristotelianism as virtually the only method of rhetorical criticism in the early years of the communication field, the practice of rhetorical criticism was limited in subject matter and purpose. Rhetorical criticism became the study of speeches because the approach required that a critic determine the effect of rhetoric on the immediate audience. Neo-Aristotelianism thus was not used to study written discourse or nondiscursive rhetoric. Neo-Aristotelianism also led to the study of single speakers because the sheer number of topics to cover relating to the rhetor and the speech made dealing with more than a single speaker virtually impossible. Thus, various speeches by different rhetors related by form or topic were not included in the scope of rhetorical criticism.[8]

The single speakers who were the focus of study were limited further in that they tended to be individuals of the past—generally elite men—who had made significant contributions in the realm of public affairs. A critic was required to determine a number of details about the speaker's life, public character, and the audience for the speech at the time. Such data were only available for famous people because their speeches were the ones that were saved and archived.

Neo-Aristotelian criticism was virtually unchallenged as the method to use in rhetorical criticism until the 1960s, when the orthodoxy that had developed in rhetorical criticism began to be criticized on a number of grounds. One criticism was that the work on which neo-Aristotelianism was based, Aristotle's *Rhetoric*, was not intended as a guide for critics. The *Rhetoric* and other classical works that were being used to guide the critic were designed to teach others how to speak well. Nothing in them suggested they were to be used to appraise discourse.[9]

The concern with effects that derived, in part, from an emphasis on teaching effective speech led to another problem with neo-Aristotelianism. An exclusive concern with effects does not always produce significant criticism, critics of neo-Aristotelianism argued. "Did the speech evoke the intended response from the immediate audience?" and "Did the rhetor use the available means of persuasion to achieve the desired response?" are not always the most appropriate questions to ask about a rhetorical artifact. These questions also do not always produce significant insights into an artifact. As Otis M. Walter pointed out, a critic who is studying Jesus's Sermon on the Mount using the neo-Aristotelian approach asks whether Jesus used the means of persuasion available to him. But this question may not produce a significant answer. More interesting might be questions such as, "Were Jesus's means of persuasion consistent with his ethical doctrines?" or "What changes in Old Testament morality did Jesus present?"[10] But neo-Aristotelian criticism does not allow a critic to explore these questions. As Karlyn Kohrs Campbell explained, neo-Aristotelianism excludes "all *evaluations* other than the speech's potential for evoking intended response from an immediate, specified audience."[11]

Still others objected to neo-Aristotelianism on the grounds that the works on which it was based—Aristotle's *Rhetoric* and other classical writings—were written at a time and in the context of cultures that were different in values, orientation, and knowledge from ours. Yet, critics using the neo-Aristotelian mode of criticism assumed that what were believed to be ideal rhetorical principles in ancient Greek and Roman cultures are the same today. In other words, critics of neo-Aristotelianism suggested, rhetorical principles have undergone change since their formulation in classical Greek and Roman times, and later cultures have modified or extended those principles.[12] To use only classical tenets of rhetoric as units of analysis in criticism was to ignore a large body of new scholarship about rhetorical principles.

Yet another criticism of neo-Aristotelianism concerned its rational bias. As Campbell explained, a basic assumption of the approach was that our unique attribute is the capacity to be rational, and humans are able to engage in persuasion and be subject to it only because they are rational beings. Thus, rhetoric was seen as the art of reasoned discourse or argumentation. Emotional and psychological appeals exist and affect persuasion, neo-Aristotelianism suggests, but they are secondary to judgments resulting from rational means of persuasion. One consequence, explained Campbell, was that "'true' or 'genuine' rhetoric" became "the art by which men are induced to act in obedience to reason in contrast to 'false' or 'sophistic' rhetoric which uses any and all means to produce acquiescence."[13] Critics and theorists operating out of this approach either had to denigrate or ignore nonrational appeals and attempt, generally fruitlessly, to distinguish between rational and nonrational appeals.

Another criticism of neo-Aristotelianism as the presiding method of criticism was that it encouraged the mechanical application of categories to rhetoric, with the result that the work that critics did sometimes was unimaginative and self-fulfilling. Critics set out to find the particular rhetorical techniques suggested by classical rhetoricians in the artifacts they were studying—techniques such as logical argument and emotional appeals—and, indeed, did find them being used in the speeches they were analyzing. But rather than helping a critic understand and illuminate the speeches using these units of analysis, neo-Aristotelianism sometimes became "a mechanical accounting or summing up of how well" a speech fit "an *a priori* mold."[14]

Today, critics who use the neo-Aristotelian approach to analyze rhetoric are few, and essays that feature the method rarely find their way into the journals and convention programs of the communication field. Criticisms of how the neo-Aristotelian framework limited the potential of criticism led, in the 1960s, to pluralism in critical approaches. As evident in the remaining chapters of this book, a wide variety of approaches now characterize rhetorical criticism. Discussions and defenses of neo-Aristotelianism ended largely in the early 1970s.[15]

As the first critical approach developed in the communication field, neo-Aristotelianism served to differentiate the discipline from literature and literary criticism and helped to legitimize it by focusing on its classical roots. While you may not choose to use this approach in critical essays, understanding its basic components will facilitate your understanding of the approaches discussed in the remainder of the book, for they were developed largely in response to both the strengths and limitations of neo-Aristotelian criticism.

PROCEDURES

Using the neo-Aristotelian method of criticism, a critic analyzes an artifact in a four-step process: (1) selecting an artifact; (2) analyzing the artifact; (3) formulating a research question; and (4) writing the essay.

Selecting an Artifact

The neo-Aristotelian method of criticism was developed to analyze speeches, so speeches are particularly good artifacts to select for this method of criticism. If you are not interested in analyzing a speech, selecting a discursive text rather than an entirely visual one will maximize the insights your criticism produces because most of the units of analysis of neo-Aristotelianism deal with linguistic dimensions of rhetoric. Because the method includes an investigation of the rhetor, you also want to select an artifact produced by a rhetor about which some biographical information is available.

Analyzing the Artifact

Neo-Aristotelian criticism involves three basic steps: (1) reconstructing the context in which the artifact occurred; (2) application of the five canons to the artifact; and (3) assessing the impact of the artifact on the audience.[16]

Reconstructing the Context

Connecting the rhetorical artifact with its context helps a critic discover how various components of the context affected the rhetoric that was formulated. A critic investigates three major components of the context—the rhetor, the occasion, and the audience.

A critic begins by discovering information about the rhetor. The aim of this inquiry is not to develop a typical biography of the individual's life. Rather, the purpose is to study the individual as a rhetor and to discover links between rhetorical efforts and the rhetor's history, experience, and character. For example, you may want to seek information about early environmental influences on the rhetor's attitudes, motivation, and communication skills. Other areas to investigate include whether the rhetor had formal training in the rhetorical medium selected for expression, the rhetor's previous experience with the subject and the medium, the rhetor's rhetorical philosophy or principles, and methods of rhetorical preparation. Finally, try to discover the motivating forces of the rhetor—why the rhetor chose to produce this rhetoric on this particular occasion and what the rhetor sought to accomplish.

After investigating the background of the rhetor to discover its effects on the rhetorical artifact, a critic turns to an examination of the occasion on which the rhetoric was presented. The rhetorical act is affected by factors in the occasion, so your task here is to determine the elements in the occasion that influenced the rhetor in choice of subject and approach or the peculiar demands of the time and place of the rhetoric. Pay attention to the historical antecedents of the rhetoric, the specific events that gave rise to and followed it, and the social and cultural attitudes toward the topic of the rhetoric.

A critic completes the examination of the context by looking at the audience for the rhetoric. The rhetor constructs rhetoric to accomplish a particular goal for a specific individual or group. Knowing about the audience, then, helps you understand why the rhetor selected particular strategies. The same forces that helped to shape the occasion for the rhetor also affect the audience, so you probably already know something about the audience through investigating the occasion. Additional lines of inquiry to pursue are the composition of the audience, the rhetor's reputation for this audience, and the listeners' knowledge about and attitudes toward the rhetor's subject.

Applying the Canons

The second component of neo-Aristotelian criticism is the analysis of the artifact itself using the five canons of classical rhetoric. In classical Greek and Roman times, when the study of rhetoric began, rhetoric was divided into five parts. These five parts of or canons of rhetoric are the steps that go into the process of public speaking.[17] They are: (1) invention, the location and creation of ideas and materials for the speech; (2) organization, the structure or arrangement of the speech; (3) style, the language of the speech; (4) memory, mastery of the subject matter, which may include the actual memorizing of the speech; and (5) delivery, management of the voice and gestures in the presentation of the speech.

Invention.   A critic's concern in applying the canon of invention is with the speaker's major ideas, lines of argument, or content. Invention is based on two major forms of proof. External or inartistic proofs are those the rhetor uses from other sources but does not create, including the testimony of witnesses and documents such as contracts and letters. Internal or artistic proofs, those that the rhetor creates, fall into three categories: (1) *logos* or logical argument; (2) *ethos* or the appeal of the rhetor's character; and (3) *pathos* or emotional appeal.

Logos deals with the logical or rational elements of the rhetoric and with the effect of these elements on the audience. In discovering the rhetor's use of logical appeals, a critic identifies the argument or thesis the rhetor is presenting and determines how that thesis is developed and supported. The evidence presented to enforce or support the point is evaluated in terms of the beliefs of the audience and the context of the rhetoric. Whether the evidence is the quoting of experts, statistical summaries, personal experience, or some other form, a critic examines it to see whether it is relevant to the thesis being developed, whether the evidence is consistent, and whether sufficient evidence has been supplied to make the point.

A rhetor cannot simply present evidence to the audience; something must be done with the evidence to encourage the audience to come to some conclusion based on it. This is the process of reasoning, which assumes two major forms—inductive and deductive. In inductive reasoning, a series of specific examples is used to draw a general conclusion. Six cases in which individuals who talked on cell phones while driving were involved in serious accidents could be used by a rhetor, for example, to make the point that people should not simultaneously drive and talk on cell phones. Deductive reasoning, in contrast, begins with a generalization that is acceptable to the audience, and the rhetor then applies the generalization to a specific case. A rhetor who begins with the generalization that smoking and lung cancer are linked may conclude, using deductive reasoning, that those in the audience who smoke are in danger of developing the disease. A critic, then, assesses both the evidence and the reasoning used by the rhetor to develop the thesis.

The second form of artistic proof, *ethos*, is what we today call *credibility*. It deals with the effect or appeal of the speaker's character on the audience. Your concern in analyzing *ethos* is with how the rhetor's character, as known to the audience prior to the speech and as presented to the audience during the speech, facilitates the acceptance of belief on the part of the audience. Credibility is demonstrated by a rhetor largely through the display of three qualities in the rhetorical act: (1) moral character or integrity, achieved by linking the message and rhetor with what the audience considers virtuous; (2) intelligence, evident in a display of common sense, good taste, and familiarity with current topics and interests; and (3) good will, the establishment of rapport with the audience through means such as identifying with the audience members or praising them.

The third form of artistic proof, *pathos*, concerns appeals designed to generate emotions in the audience. Here, a critic identifies the emotions generated by the speech—perhaps fear, shame, or pity—and explains how those emotions put the listeners in a particular frame of mind to react favorably to the rhetor's purpose.

Organization. The second major area of the rhetorical artifact a critic analyzes using the neo-Aristotelian method is its arrangement or structure. Your task here is to determine the general pattern of arrangement adopted for the rhetoric—for example, a chronological order, where material is divided into time units, or a problem-solution order, where a discussion of a problem is followed by suggested solutions to it. Determine which aspects of the content are given emphasis in the rhetoric through the structure and the various functions the parts of the artifact perform. Emphasis can be determined by discovering which parts of the rhetoric are given greater weight through their placement at the beginning or end, the topic on which the rhetor spends the most time, and the ideas the rhetor repeats. Your task is also to assess the results of the arrangement of the discourse in its entirety to discover if the organization of the speech is consistent with the subject and purpose of the discourse and is appropriate for the audience.

Style. The canon of style deals with the language used by the rhetor. A critic assesses how particular kinds of words or other symbols are used by the rhetor to create varying effects and how the symbols are arranged to form larger units such as sentences, figures of speech, images, and so on. Analysis of style involves determining the general effect that results—common and ordinary, forceful and robust, or stately and ornate, for example. In general, a critic's concern in examining style is with whether the language style contributes to the accomplishment of the rhetor's goal and helps to create the intended response.

Delivery. The canon of delivery is concerned with the speaker's manner of presentation. In the application of this canon, a critic investigates the influence of delivery on the success of the rhetorical artifact. In a public speech, delivery involves the rhetor's mode of presentation—whether the speech is delivered impromptu, from memory, extemporaneously, or by reading from a manuscript. The bodily action of the rhetor while delivering the rhetoric—posture, movement, gestures, and eye contact—and how the appearance and physical characteristics of the rhetor affected the audience are also part of your examination of delivery. Assessment of the vocal skill of the rhetor, including how articulation, pronunciation, rate of speech, and pitch contributed to the audience's acceptance of the message—if that information is available—completes your analysis of delivery.

Memory. Although memory also is among the five classical canons of rhetoric, it was not dealt with systematically by Aristotle. Partly for this reason and also because many speeches are not memorized (and memory is irrelevant to most nondiscursive forms of rhetoric), this canon often is not applied by the neo-Aristotelian critic. When it is, it deals with the rhetor's control of the materials of the speech and the relation of memory to the mode of presentation selected.

Assessing the Effects

At the conclusion of criticism using neo-Aristotelianism, a critic judges the effects of the rhetoric. Because the rhetoric was designed to accomplish some goal—the rhetor sought a response of some kind—your task is to determine whether or not this goal was met or what happened as a result of the rhetoric. There is no single measure of effectiveness, and how you choose to assess the effects depends on the characteristics of the rhetorical artifact itself, the rhetor's intention, the audience to which the rhetoric is addressed, and the context in which the rhetoric is presented. The effectiveness of a speech frequently is judged by the immediate and/or long-term response of the audience—either those changes immediately visible in the audience or those that emerge at a later time.

Formulating a Research Question

The research question asked about artifacts in neo-Aristotelian criticism is: "Did the rhetor use the available means of persuasion to evoke the intended response from the audience?"

Writing the Essay

After completing the analysis, you are ready to write your essay, which includes five major components: (1) an introduction, in which you discuss the research question, its contribution to rhetorical theory, and its significance; (2) a description of the artifact and its context; (3) a description of the method of criticism—in this case, neo-Aristotelian criticism; (4) a report of the findings of the analysis, in which you explicate the rhetor's choices through application of the five canons to your artifact; and (5) a discussion of the contribution the analysis makes to rhetorical theory.

SAMPLE ESSAYS

The two essays that follow demonstrate the neo-Aristotelian approach to criticism. Forbes Hill's essay on a speech by Richard Nixon not only provides an illustration of neo-Aristotelian criticism but also an assessment of the value of this critical approach. Gary W. Brown uses neo-Aristotelian criticism to analyze the rhetoric of Saddam Hussein during the Persian Gulf War in 1991. The research question guiding both analyses is: "Did the rhetor select the best rhetorical options available to him to evoke the intended response from the audience?"

Notes

[1] Herbert A. Wichelns, "The Literary Criticism of Oratory," in *Studies in Rhetoric and Public Speaking in Honor of James A. Winans*, ed. A. M. Drummond (New York: Century, 1925), pp. 181–216. A more accessible source for the essay is Herbert A. Wichelns, "The Literary Criticism of Oratory," in *Methods of Rhetorical Criticism: A Twentieth-Century Perspective*, ed. Bernard L. Brock and Robert L. Scott, 2nd ed. (Detroit: Wayne State University Press, 1980), pp. 40–73.

[2] Mark S. Klyn, "Toward a Pluralistic Rhetorical Criticism," in *Essays on Rhetorical Criticism*, ed. Thomas R. Nilsen (New York: Random House, 1968), p. 154.

[3] Donald C. Bryant, ed., *The Rhetorical Idiom: Essays in Rhetoric, Oratory, Language, and Drama* (Ithaca: Cornell University Press, 1958), p. 5.

[4] Wichelns, in Brock and Scott, p. 67.

[5] Wichelns, in Brock and Scott, pp. 69–70.

[6] William Norwood Brigance, ed., *A History and Criticism of American Public Address*, 2 vols. (New York: McGraw-Hill, 1943). A third volume was published in 1955: Marie Kathryn Hochmuth, ed., *A History and Criticism of American Public Address, III* (New York: Longmans, Green, 1955).

[7] Lester Thonssen and A. Craig Baird, *Speech Criticism* (New York: Ronald, 1948). In the second edition of the book, a third author was added: Lester Thonssen, A. Craig Baird, and Waldo W. Braden, *Speech Criticism*, 2nd ed. (New York: Ronald, 1970).

[8] G. P. Mohrmann and Michael C. Leff point out that neo-Aristotelianism itself does not preclude the study of discourse larger than a single speech; in fact, Aristotle discusses oratorical genres—deliberative or political speaking, forensic or legal speaking, and epideictic or ceremonial speaking. The notion of genres was not incorporated into the neo-Aristotelian approach because of Wichelns's determination that the purpose of rhetorical criticism is to uncover effects on the specific audience. See G. P. Mohrmann and Michael C. Leff, "Lincoln at Cooper Union: A Rationale for Neo-Classical Criticism," *Quarterly Journal of Speech*, 60 (December 1974), 463.

[9] Edwin Black, *Rhetorical Criticism: A Study in Method* (Madison: University of Wisconsin Press, 1978), p. 33; and Otis M. Walter, "On the Varieties of Rhetorical Criticism," in *Essays in Rhetorical Criticism*, ed. Thomas R. Nilsen (New York: Random, 1968), p. 162.

[10] Walter, pp. 162–65.

[11] Karlyn Kohrs Campbell, "The Forum: 'Conventional Wisdom—Traditional Form': A Rejoinder," *Quarterly Journal of Speech*, 58 (December 1972), 454.

[12] Black, p. 124.

[13] Karlyn Kohrs Campbell, "The Ontological Foundations of Rhetorical Theory," *Philosophy and Rhetoric*, 3 (Spring 1970), 98.

[14] Douglas Ehninger, "Rhetoric and the Critic," *Western Speech*, 29 (Fall 1965), 230.

[15] See, for example: J. A. Hendrix, "In Defense of Neo-Aristotelian Rhetorical Criticism," *Western Speech*, 32 (Fall 1968), 216–52; Forbes I. Hill, "Conventional Wisdom—Traditional Form: The President's Message of November 3, 1969," *Quarterly Journal of Speech*, 58 (December 1972), 373–86; Campbell, "The Forum," pp. 451–54; Forbes I. Hill, "The Forum: Reply to Professor Campbell," *Quarterly Journal of Speech*, 58 (December 1972), 454–60; and Mohrmann and Leff, pp. 459–67.

[16] The summary of these procedures is brief. Much more detail about them is available in Thonssen, Baird, and Braden.

[17] Although these canons were formulated to apply to public speaking and neo-Aristotelian criticism originally was applied to speeches, the canons can be applied to rhetorical acts and artifacts of various kinds. Admittedly, in such an application, the canons and neo-Aristotelian criticism must be stretched. For an example of this kind of expansion of the canons, see Nancy Harper, *Human Communication Theory: The History of a Paradigm* (Rochelle Park, NJ: Hayden, 1979), pp. 181–261.

Conventional Wisdom—
Traditional Form—
The President's Message of November 3, 1969

Forbes Hill

More than one critique of President Nixon's address to the nation on November 3, 1969 has appeared,[1] which is not remarkable, since it was the most obvious feature of the public relations machine that appears to have dammed back the flood of sentiment for quick withdrawal of American forces from Southeast Asia. To be sure, the dike built by this machine hardly endured forever, but some time was gained—an important achievement. It seems natural, then, that we should want to examine this obvious feature from more than one angle.

Preceding critiques have looked at Nixon's message from notably nontraditional perspectives. Stelzner magnified it in the lens of archetypal criticism, which reveals a non-literary version of the quest story archetype, but he concluded that the President's is an incomplete telling of the story that does not adequately interact with the listeners' subjective experiences. Newman condemned the message as "shoddy rhetoric" because its tough stance and false dilemmas are directed to white, urban, uptight voters. Campbell condemned it on the basis of intrinsic criticism because though its stated purposes are to tell the truth, increase credibility, promote unity, and affirm moral responsibility, its rhetoric conceals truth, decreases credibility, promotes division, and dodges moral responsibility. Then, stepping outside the intrinsic framework, she makes her most significant criticism: the message perpetuates myths about American values instead of scrutinizing the real values of America.

I propose to juxtapose these examinations with a strict neo-Aristotelian analysis. If it differs slightly from analyses that follow Wichelns[2] and Hochmuth-Nichols,[3] that is because it attempts a critique that reinterprets neo-Aristotelianism slightly—a critique guided by the spirit and usually the letter of the Aristotelian text as I understand it. What the neo-Aristotelian method can and should do will be demonstrated, I hope, by this juxtaposition.

Neo-Aristotelian criticism compares the means of persuasion used by a speaker with a comprehensive inventory given in Aristotle's *Rhetoric*. Its end is to discover whether the speaker makes the best choices from the inventory to get a favorable decision from a specified group of auditors in a specific situation. It does not, of course, aim to discover whether or not the speaker actually gets his favorable decision; decisions in practice are often upset by chance factors.[4] First the neo-Aristotelian critic must outline the situation, then specify the group of auditors and define the kind of decision they are to make. Finally he must reveal the choice and disposition of three intertwined persuasive factors—logical, psychological, and characterological—and evaluate this choice and disposition against the standard of the *Rhetoric*.

From *Quarterly Journal of Speech*, 58 (December 1972), 373–86. Used by permission of the Speech Communication Association [National Communication Association] and the author.

THE SITUATION

The state of affairs for the Nixon Administration in the fall of 1969 is well known. The United States had been fighting a stalemated war for several years. The cost in lives and money was immense. The goal of the war was not clear; presumably the United States wanted South Viet Nam as a stable non-Communist buffer state between Communist areas and the rest of Southeast Asia. To the extent that this goal was understood, it seemed as far from being realized in 1969 as it had been in 1964. In the meantime, a large and vocal movement had grown up, particularly among the young, of people who held that there should have been no intervention in Viet Nam in the first place and that it would never be possible to realize any conceivable goal of intervention. The movement was especially dangerous to the Administration because it numbered among its supporters many of the elements of the population who were most interested in foreign policy and best informed about it. There were variations of position within the peace movement, but on one point all its members were agreed: the United States should commit itself immediately to withdraw its forces from Viet Nam.

The policy of the Nixon Administration, like that of the Johnson Administration before it, was limited war to gain a position of strength from which to negotiate. By fall 1969 the Administration was willing to make any concessions that did not jeopardize a fifty-fifty chance of achieving the goal, but it was not willing to make concessions that amounted to sure abandonment of the goal. A premature withdrawal amounted to public abandonment and was to be avoided at all costs. When the major organizations of the peace movement announced the first Moratorium Day for October 15 and organized school and work stoppages, demonstrations, and a great "March on Washington" to dramatize the demand for immediate withdrawal from Viet Nam, the Administration launched a counterattack. The President announced that he would make a major address on Viet Nam November 3. This announcement seems to have moderated the force of the October moratorium, but plans were soon laid for a second moratorium on November 15. Nixon's counterattack aimed at rallying the mass of the people to disregard the vocal minority and oppose immediate withdrawal; it aimed to get support for a modified version of the old strategy: limited war followed by negotiated peace. The address was broadcast the evening of November 3 over the national radio and television networks.

THE AUDITORS AND THE KIND OF DECISION

An American President having a monopoly of the media at prime time potentially reaches an audience of upwards of a hundred million adults of heterogeneous backgrounds and opinions. Obviously it is impossible to design a message to move every segment of this audience, let alone the international audience. The speaker must choose his targets. An examination of the texts shows us which groups were eliminated as targets, which were made secondary targets, and which were primary. The speaker did not address himself to certain fanatical opponents of the war: the ones who hoped that the Viet Cong would gain a signal victory over the Americans and their South Vietnamese allies, or those who denied that Communist advances were threats to non-Communist countries, or those against any war for any reason. These were the groups the President sought to isolate and stigmatize. On the other hand, there was a large group of Americans who would be willing to give their all to fight any kind of Communist expansion anywhere at any time. These people also were not a target group: their support could be counted on in any case.

The speaker did show himself aware that the Viet Cong and other Communist decision-makers were listening in. He represented himself to them as willing and anxious to negotiate and warned them that escalation of the war would be followed by effective retaliation. The Communists constituted a secondary target audience, but the analysis that follows will make plain that the message was not primarily intended for them.

The primary target was those Americans not driven by a clearly defined ideological commitment to oppose or support the war at any cost. Resentment of the sacrifice in money and lives, bewilderment at the stalemate, longing for some movement in a clearly marked direction—these were the principal aspects of their state of mind assumed by Nixon. He solicited them saying "tonight—to you, the great silent majority of my fellow Americans—I ask for your support."[5]

His address asks the target group of auditors to make a decision to support a policy to be continued in the future. In traditional terms, then, it is primarily a deliberative speech. Those who receive the message are decision-makers, and they are concerned with the past only as it serves as analogy to future decisions. The subjects treated are usual ones for deliberation: war and peace.[6]

DISPOSITION AND SYNOPSIS

The address begins with an enthymeme that attacks the credibility gap.[7] Those who decide on war and peace must know the truth about these policies, and the conclusion is implied that the President is going to tell the truth. The rest of the *proem* is taken up by a series of questions constructing a formal partition of the subjects to be covered. The partition stops short of revealing the nature of the modification in policy that constitutes the Nixon plan. The message fits almost perfectly into the Aristotelian pattern of *proem*, narrative, proofs both constructive and refutative, and epilogue. Just as *proem* has served as a general heading for a synoptic statement of what was done in the first few sentences, so the other four parts will serve us as analytical headings for a synopsis of the rest.

The narrative commences with Nixon's statement of the situation as he saw it on taking office. He could have ordered immediate withdrawal of American forces, but he decided to fulfill "a greater obligation . . . to think of the effect" of his decision "on the next generation, and on the future of peace and freedom in America, and in the world." Applicable here is the precept: the better the moral end that the speaker can in his narrative be seen consciously choosing, the better the *ethos* he reveals.[8] An end can hardly be better than "the future of peace and freedom in America, and in the world." The narrative goes on to explain why and how the United States became involved in Viet Nam in the first place. This explanation masquerades as a simple chronological statement—"Fifteen years ago . . ." but thinly disguised in the chronology lie two propositions: first, that the leaders of America were right in intervening on behalf of the government of South Viet Nam; second, that the great mistake in their conduct of the war was over-reliance on American combat forces. Some doubt has been cast on the wisdom of Nixon's choice among the means of persuasion here. The history, writes one critic, "is a surprising candidate for priority in any discussion today. . . . The President's chief foreign policy advisors, his allies on Capitol Hill, and the memorandum he got from the Cabinet bureaucracy all urged him to skip discussions of the causes and manner of our involvement. Yet history comes out with top billing."[9] This criticism fails to conceive the rhetorical function of the narrative: in the two propositions the whole content of the proofs that follow is foreshadowed, and foreshadowed in the guise of a non-controversial statement about the historical facts. Among traditional orators this use of the narrative to foreshadow proofs is common, but it has seldom been handled with more artistry than here.

Constructive proofs are not opened with an analytical partition but with a general question: what is the best way to end the war? The answer is structured as a long argument from logical division: there are four plans to end American involvement; three should be rejected so that the listener is left with no alternative within the structure but to accept the fourth.[10] The four plans are: immediate withdrawal, the consequences of which are shown at some length to be bad; negotiated settlement, shown to be impossible in the near future because the enemy will not negotiate in earnest; shifting the burden of the war to the Vietnamese with American withdrawal on a fixed timetable, also argued to have bad consequences; and shifting the burden of the war to the Vietnamese with American withdrawal on a flexible schedule, said to have good consequences, since it will eventually bring "the complete withdrawal of all United States *combat ground* forces," whether earnest negotiations become possible or not. Constructive proofs close with one last evil consequence of immediate withdrawal: that it would lead eventually to Americans' loss of confidence in themselves and divisive recrimination that "would scar our spirit as a people."

As refutative proof is introduced, opponents of the Administration are characterized by a demonstrator carrying a sign, "Lose in Viet Nam"; they are an irrational minority who want to decide policy in the streets, as opposed to the elected officials—Congress and the President—who will decide policy by Constitutional and orderly means. This attack on his presumed opponents leads to a passage which reassures the majority of young people that the President really wants peace as much as they do. Reassuring ends with the statement of Nixon's personal belief that his plan will succeed; this statement may be taken as transitional to the epilogue.

The epilogue reiterates the bad consequences of immediate withdrawal—loss of confidence and loss of other nations to totalitarianism—it exhorts the silent majority to support the plan, predicting its success; it evokes the memory of Woodrow Wilson; then it closes with the President's pledge to meet his responsibilities to lead the nation with strength and wisdom. Recapitulation, building of *ethos*, and reinforcing the right climate of feeling—these are what a traditional rhetorician would advise that the epilogue do,[11] and these are what Nixon's epilogue does.

Indeed, this was our jumping-off place for the synopsis of the message: it falls into the traditional paradigm; each frame of the paradigm contains the lines of argument conventional for that frame. The two unconventional elements in the paradigm—the unusual placement of the last evil consequence of immediate withdrawal and the use of the frame by logical division for the constructive proofs—are there for good rhetorical reasons. That last consequence, loss of confidence and divisive recrimination, serves to lead into the refutation which opens with the demonstrator and his sign. It is as if the demonstrator were being made an example in advance of just this evil consequence. The auditor is brought into precisely the right set for a refutation section that does not so much argue with opponents as it pushes them into an isolated, unpopular position.

Because of the residues-like structure, the message creates the illusion of proving that Vietnamization and flexible withdrawal constitute the best policy. By process of elimination it is the only policy available, and even a somewhat skeptical listener is less likely to question the only policy available. Approaching the proposal with skepticism dulled, he perhaps does not so much miss a development of the plan. In particular, he might not ask the crucial question: does the plan actually provide for complete American withdrawal? The answer to this question is contained in the single phrase, "complete withdrawal of all United States *combat ground* forces." It is fairly clear, in retrospect, that this phrase concealed the intention to keep in Viet Nam for several years a large contingent of air and support forces. Nixon treats the difference between plan three, Vietnamization and withdrawal on a fixed schedule, and plan four, Vietnamization and withdrawal on a flexible schedule, as a matter of whether or not the schedule is announced in advance. But the crucial difference is really that plan three was understood by its advocates as a plan for quick, complete withdrawal; plan four was a plan for partial withdrawal. The strategic reason for not announcing a fixed schedule was that the announcement would give away this fact. The residues structure concealed the lack of development of the plan; the lack of development of the plan suppressed the critical fact that Nixon did not propose complete withdrawal. Although Nixon's message shows traditionally conventional structure, these variations from the traditional show a remarkable ability at designing the best adaptations to the specific rhetorical situation.

LOGICAL AND PSYCHOLOGICAL PERSUASIVE FACTORS

Central to an Aristotelian assessment of the means of persuasion is an account of two interdependent factors: (1) the choice of major premises on which enthymemes[12] that form "the body of the proof" are based, and (2) the means whereby auditors are brought into states of feeling favorable to accepting these premises and the conclusions following from them. Premises important here are of two kinds: predictions and values. Both kinds as they relate to good and evil consequences of the four plans to end American involvement, will be assessed. The first enthymeme involving prediction is that immediate withdrawal followed by a Communist takeover would lead to murder and imprisonment of innocent civilians. This conclusion follows from the general predictive rule: the future will resemble the past.[13] Since the Communists murdered and imprisoned opponents on taking over North Viet Nam in 1954 and murdered opponents in the city of Hue in 1968, they will do the same when they take over South Viet Nam. Implied also is an enthymeme based on the value premise that security of life and freedom from bondage are primary goods for men;[14] a Communist takeover would destroy life and freedom and therefore destroy primary goods for men.

Presumably no one would try to refute this complex of enthymemes by saying that life and freedom are not primary goods, though he might argue from more and less;[15] more life is lost by continuing the war than would be lost by a Communist takeover, or American-South Vietnamese political structures allow for even less political freedom than the Communist alternatives. Nixon buries these questions far enough beneath the surface of the message that probably auditors in the target group are not encouraged to raise them. One could also attack the predictive premise: after all, the future is not always the past writ over again. But this kind of refutation is merely irritating; we know that the premise is not universally true, yet everyone finds it necessary to operate in ordinary life as if it were. People on the left of the target group, of course, reject the evidence—North Viet Nam and Hue.

A related prediction is that immediate withdrawal would result in a collapse of confidence in American leadership. It rests on the premise that allies only have confidence in those who both have power and will act in their support.[16] If the United States shows it lacks power and will in Viet Nam, there will be a collapse of confidence, which entails further consequences: it would "promote reckless-ness" on the part of enemies everywhere else the country has commitments, i.e., as a general premise, when one party to a power struggle loses the confidence of its allies, its enemies grow bolder.[17] The conclusion is bolstered by citations from former presidents Eisenhower, Johnson, and Kennedy: the statement of the "lib-eral saint," Kennedy, is featured.

It is difficult to attack the related premises of these tandem arguments. They rest on what experience from the sandbox up shows to be probable. The target group consists of people with the usual American upbringing and experience. Someone will question the premises only if he questions the worldview out of which they develop. That view structures the world into Communist powers—actual or potential enemies—and non-Communist powers—allies. America is the leader of the allies, referred to elsewhere as the forces of "peace and freedom" opposed by "the forces of totalitarianism." Because of its association with free-dom, American leadership is indisputably good, and whatever weakens confi-dence in it helps the enemies. Only a few people on the far left would categori-cally reject this structure.

The foregoing premises and the worldview fundamental to them are even more likely to be accepted if the auditors are in a state of fear. Fear may be defined as distress caused by a vision of impending evil of the destructive or painful kind.[18] This message promotes a state of fear by the nature of the evil conse-quences developed—murder and imprisonment of innocents, collapse of leader-ship in the free world, and reckless aggressiveness of implacable enemies. America is the prototype of a nation that is fearful; her enemies are watching their opportunities all over the globe, from Berlin to the Middle East, yes even in the Western Hemisphere itself. The enemies are cruel and opposed to American ide-als. They are strong on the battlefield and intransigent in negotiations. Conditions are such that America's allies may lose confidence in her and leave her to fight these enemies alone. But these circumstances are not too much amplified: only enough to create a state of feeling favorable to rejecting immediate withdrawal, not so much as to create the disposition for escalation.

Nixon claims to have tried hard to make a negotiated settlement, but he could not make one because the Communists refused to compromise. The evidence that they would not compromise is developed at length: public initiatives through the peace conference in Paris are cited, terms for participation of the Communist forces in internationally supervised elections offered, and promises made to nego-tiate on any of these terms. Then there were private initiatives through the Soviet Union and directly by letter to the leaders of North Viet Nam, as well as private efforts by the United States ambassador to the Paris talks. These efforts brought only demands for the equivalent of unconditional surrender. The citation of evidence is impressive and destroys the credibility of the position that negotiations can bring a quick end to the war.

Nixon does not explicitly predict that the plan for negotiated settlement will not work ever; on the contrary, he says that he will keep trying. But if the auditor believes the evidence, he finds it difficult to avoid making his own enthymeme with the conclusion that negotiated settlement will never work; the major premise is the same old rule, the future will be like the past. Nixon gives another reason, too: it will not work while the opposite side "is convinced that all it has to do is to wait for our next concession, and our next concession after that one, until it gets everything it wants." The major premise—no power convinced that victory is probable by forcing repeated concessions will ever compromise—constitutes a commonplace of bargaining for virtually everyone.

Peace is seen in these arguments as almost an unqualified good. Although compromise through bargaining is the fastest way to peace, the other side must make concessions to assure compromise. Reasons for continuing the war, such as an ideological commitment, are evil. There is no glory in war and prolonging it is not justified by political gains made but only by a commitment to higher values like saving lives and preserving freedom. Prolonging the war is also justified as avoiding future wars by not losing Southeast Asia altogether and not promoting the spirit of recklessness in the enemies. "I want," states Nixon, "to end it [the war] in a way which will increase the chance that their [the soldiers'] younger brothers and their sons will not have to fight in some future Vietnam . . . ."

A listener is prone to reject the likelihood of a negotiated peace if he is angry with his opponents. Anger is a painful desire for revenge and arises from an evident, unjustified slight to a person or his friends.[19] People visualizing revenge ordinarily refuse compromise except as a temporary tactic. Nixon presents the American people as having been slighted: they value peace, and their leaders have with humility taken every peace initiative possible: public, private, and secret. The Communist powers wish to gain politically from the war; they have rebuffed with spite all initiatives and frustrated our good intentions by demanding the equivalent of unconditional surrender. Frustration is, of course, a necessary condition of anger.[20] Again, Nixon does not go too far—not far enough to create a psychological climate out of which a demand for escalation would grow.

Nixon announces that his plan for Vietnamization and American withdrawal on a flexible timetable is in effect already. Its consequences: American men coming home, South Vietnamese forces gaining in strength, enemy infiltration measurably reduced, and United States' casualties also reduced. He predicts: policies that have had such consequences in the past will have them in the future, i.e., the future will be like the past. Again, the undisputed value that saving lives is good is assumed. But in this case the argument, while resting on an acceptable premise, was, at the time of this speech, somewhat more doubtful of acceptance by the target group. The evidence constitutes the problem: obviously the sample of the past since the policy of Vietnamization commenced was so short that no one could really judge the alleged consequences to be correlated with the change in policy, let alone caused by it. There is, then, little reason why that audience should have believed the minor premise—that the consequences of Vietnamization were good.

A temporizing and moderate policy is best presented to auditors who while temporarily fearful are basically confident. Nothing saps the will to accept such a proposal as does the opposite state, basically fearful and only temporarily confident. Confidence is the other side of the coin from fear: it is pleasure because destructive and painful evils seem far away and sources of aid near at hand.[21] The sources of aid here are the forces of the Republic of South Viet Nam. They have continued to gain in strength and as a result have been able to take over combat responsibilities from American forces. In contrast, danger from the enemy is receding—"enemy infiltration . . . over the last three months is less than 20 per cent of what it was over the same period last year." Nixon assures his auditors that he has confidence the plan will succeed. America is the "strongest and richest nation in the world"; it can afford the level of aid that needs to be continued in Viet Nam. It will show the moral stamina to meet the challenge of free world leadership.

For some time rumors about gradual American withdrawal from Viet Nam had been discounted by the peace movement. The only acceptable proof of American intentions would be a timetable showing withdrawal to be accomplished soon. Thus the third plan: withdrawal on a fixed timetable. Nixon predicts that announcing of a timetable would remove the incentive to negotiate and reduce flexibility of response. The general premise behind the first is a commonplace of bargaining: negotiations never take place without a *quid pro quo*; a promise to remove American forces by a certain date gives away the *quid pro quo*. For most Americans, who are used to getting things by bargaining, this premise is unquestionable. Only those few who think that the country can gain no vestige of the objective of the war are willing to throw away the incentive. The premises behind the notion of flexibility—that any workable plan is adaptable to changes in the situation—is a commonplace of legislation and not likely to be questioned by anyone. Nixon adds to this generally acceptable premise a specific incentive. Since withdrawal will occur more rapidly if enemy military activity decreases and the South Vietnamese forces become stronger, there is a possibility that forces can be withdrawn even sooner than would be predicted by a timetable. This specific incentive is illusory, since it is obvious that one can always withdraw sooner than the timetable says, even if he has one; it is hard to see how a timetable actually reduces flexibility. Everyone makes timetables, of course, and having to re-make them when conditions change is a familiar experience. But the average man who works from nine to five probably thinks that the government should be different: when it announces a timetable it must stick to it; otherwise nothing is secure. This argument may seem weak to the critic, but it is probably well directed to the target group. The real reason for not announcing a timetable has already been noted.[22]

One final prediction is founded on the preceding predictions—whenever a policy leads to such evil consequences as movement of Southeast Asia into alliance with the enemy and a new recklessness on the part of enemies everywhere, it will eventually result in remorse and divisive recrimination which will, in turn, result in a loss of self-confidence. Guiltlessness and internal unity, the opposites of remorse and recrimination, are here assumed as secondary goods leading to self-confidence, a primary good. The enthymeme predicting loss of self-confidence consequent on immediate withdrawal is summary in position: it seems to tie together all previous arguments. It comes right after a particularly effective effort at *ethos* building—the series of statements developed in parallel construction about not having chosen the easy way (immediate withdrawal) but the right way. However, it rests on the assumption that the long term mood of confidence in the country depends on the future of Southeast Asia and the recklessness of our enemies. Since these two factors are only an aspect of a larger picture in which many other events play their parts, it is surely not true that they alone will produce a loss of confidence. The enthymeme based on this assumption, placed where it is, however, does not invite questioning by the target group. Doubtful though it may look under searching scrutiny, it has an important function for the structure of psychological proof in this message. It reinforces the vague image of the danger of facing a stronger enemy in a weakened condition: America itself would be less united, less confident, and less able to fight in the future if this consequence of immediate withdrawal were realized.

Other things being equal, the more commonplace and universally accepted the premises of prediction in a deliberative speech, the more effective the speech. This is especially true if they are set in a frame that prepares the auditor psychologically for their acceptance. There is almost no doubt that given the policy of the Nixon Administration—Vietnamization and partial withdrawal on a flexible schedule not announced in advance—the message shows a potentially effective choice of premises. In some cases it is almost the only possible choice. Likewise the value structure of the message is wisely chosen from materials familiar to any observer of the American scene: it could be duplicated in hundreds of other messages from recent American history.

Several additional value assumptions are equally commonplace. Betraying allies and letting down friends is assumed to be an evil, and its opposite, loyalty to friends and allies the virtue of a great nation. This premise equates personal loyalty, like that a man feels for his friend, with what the people of the whole nation should feel for an allied nation. Many people think this way about international relations, and the good citizens of the target group can be presumed to be among them.

Policies endorsed by the people they are supposed to help are said to be better policies than those not endorsed by them. This statement undoubtedly makes a good political rule if one expects participation in the execution of policy of those to be helped. Policies that result from the operation of representative government are good, whereas those made on the streets are bad. This value is, of course, an essential of republican government: only the most radical, even of those outside the target group, would question it. Finally, Nixon assumes that the right thing is usually the opposite of the easy thing, and, of course, *he* chooses to do the right thing. Such a value premise does not occur in rhetorics by Aristotle or even George Campbell; it is probably a peculiar product of Protestant-American-on-the-frontier thinking. Its drawing power for twentieth-century urban youngsters is negligible, but the bulk of the target group probably is made up of suburbanites in the 30–50 category who still have some affinity for this kind of thinking.

Some shift from the traditional values of American culture can be seen in the tone of Nixon's dealing with the war: the lack of indication that it is glorious, the muted appeal to patriotism (only one brief reference to the first defeat in America's history), the lack of complete victory as a goal. But nowhere else does the culture of the post-atomic age show through; by and large the speech would have been applauded if delivered in the nineteenth century. That there has been a radical revolution of values among the young does not affect the message, and one might predict that Nixon is right in deciding that the revolution in values has not yet significantly infected the target group.

CHARACTEROLOGICAL AND STYLISTIC FACTORS

Nixon's choice of value premises is, of course, closely related to his *ethos* as conveyed by the speech. He promises to tell the truth before he asks the American people to support a policy which involves the overriding issues of war and peace—phraseology that echoes previous Nixonian messages. He refrains from harsh criticism of the previous administration; he is more interested in the future America than in political gains; such an avowal of disinterestedness is the commonest topic for self-character building.

Nixon is against political murders and imprisonments and active pushing initiatives for peace. He is flexible and compromising, unlike the negotiators for the enemy. He chooses the right way and not the easy way. He is the champion of policy made by constitutional processes; his opponents conduct unruly demonstrations in the streets. But he has healthy respect for the idealism and commitment of the young; he pledges himself in the tradition of Woodrow Wilson to win a peace that will avoid future wars. He has the courage to make a tasteful appeal to patriotism even when it's unpopular. Such is the character portrait drawn for us by Richard Nixon: restrained not hawkish, hard-working and active, flexible, yet firm where he needs to be. He seems an American style democrat, a moral but also a practical and sensitive man. The message is crowded with these overt clues from which we infer the good *ethos* of political figures in situations like this. Any more intensive development of the means of persuasion derived from the character of the speaker would surely have been counter-productive.

The language of Nixon's message helps to reinforce his *ethos*. His tone is unbrokenly serious. The first two-thirds of the message is in a self-consciously plain style—the effort is clearly made to give the impression of bluntness and forthrightness. This bluntness of tone correlates with the style of deliberative argumentation:[23] few epideictic elements are present in the first part of the speech. Everything seems to be adjusted to making the structure of residues exceedingly clear.

About two-thirds of the way through, the message shifts to a more impassioned tone. The alternative plans are collapsed into two, thus polarizing the situation: either immediate withdrawal or Nixon's plan for Vietnamization and unscheduled withdrawal. From here on parallel repetitions are persistent, and they serve no obvious logical function, but rather function to deepen the serious tone. There is, in short, an attempt to rise to a peroration of real eloquence. The qualities aimed at in the last third of the message seem to be gravity and impressiveness more than clarity and forthrightness. The effort seems to tax the speechwriter's literary skill to the limit, and the only new phrases he comes up with are the "silent majority" and the description of the energies of the young as "too often directed to bitter hatred against those they think are responsible for the war." All else is a moderately skillful pastiche of familiar phrases.

GENERAL ASSESSMENT

A summary answer can now be given to the question, how well did Nixon and his advisors choose among the available means of persuasion for this situation? The message was designed for those not ideologically overcommitted either to victory over Communism or to peace in any case while frustrated by the prolonged war. It operates from the most universally accepted premises of value and prediction; it buries deep in its texture most premises not likely to be immediately accepted. Enough of the means for bringing auditors into states of fear, anger, and confidence are used to create a psychological climate unfavorable to immediate withdrawal and favorable to Vietnamization. The goals—life, political freedom, peace, and self-confidence—are those shared by nearly all Americans, and connections of policies to them are tactfully handled for the target group. The structure is largely according to tradition: it can best be seen as falling into the four parts, and the right elements are contained in each of the parts. Two minor variations from the traditional are artfully designed to realize evident psychological ends. Conventional wisdom and conventional value judgments come dressed in conventional structure. The style of the narrative and proofs reflects adequately Nixon's reliance on clearly developed arguments from accepted premises; the style of the latter part of the message shows a moderately successful attempt at grandeur. In choice and arrangement of the means of persuasion for this situation this message is by and large a considerable success.

Neo-Aristotelian criticism tells a great deal about Nixon's message. It reveals the speechwriter as a superior technician. It permits us to predict that given this target group the message should be successful in leading to a decision to support the Administration's policies. It brings into sharp focus the speechwriter's greatest technical successes: the choice of the right premises to make a version of the domino theory plausible for these auditors and the creation of a controlled atmosphere of fear in which the theory is more likely to be accepted. Likewise, the choice of the right means of making success for peace negotiations seems impossible and the building of a controlled state of anger in which a pessimistic estimate of the chances for success seems plausible. Also the finely crafted structure that conceals exactly what needs to be concealed while revealing the favored plan in a context most favorable to its being chosen.

What neo-Aristotelianism does not attempt to account for are some basic and long-run questions. For instance, it does not assess the wisdom of the speaker's choice of target audience as does Newman, who wanted the President to alleviate the fears of the doves. All critics observe that Nixon excludes the radical opponent of the war from his audience. Not only is this opponent excluded by his choice of policy but even by the choice of premises from which he argues: premises such as that the Government of South Viet Nam is freer than that of North Viet Nam, or that the right course is the opposite of the easy one. Radical opponents of the war were mostly young—often college students. The obvious cliché, "they are the political leadership of tomorrow," should have applied. Was it in the long run a wise choice to exclude them from the target? An important question, but a neo-Aristotelian approach does not warrant us to ask it. There is a gain, though, from this limitation. If the critic questions the President's choice of policy and premises, he is forced to examine systematically all the political factors involved in this choice. Neither Newman nor Campbell do this in the objective and systematic fashion required by the magnitude of the subject. Indeed, would they not be better off with a kind of criticism that does not require them to do it?

Nor does the neo-Aristotelian approach predict whether a policy will remain rhetorically viable. If the critic assumes as given the Nixon Administration's choice of policy from among the options available, he will no doubt judge this choice of value and predictive premises likely to effect the decision wanted. To put it another way, Nixon's policy was *then* most defensible by arguing from the kinds of premises Nixon used. It seems less defensible at this writing, and in time may come to seem indefensible even to people like those in the target group. Why the same arguments for the same policy should be predictably less effective to people so little removed in time is a special case of the question, why do some policies remain rhetorically viable for decades while others do not. This question might in part be answered by pointing, as was done before, to the maturing of the students into political leadership. But however the question might be answered, neo-Aristotelianism does not encourage us to ask it. As Black truly said, the neo-Aristotelian comprehends "the rhetorical discourse as tactically designed to achieve certain results with a specific audience on a specific occasion,"[24] in this case that audience Nixon aimed at on the night of November 3, 1969.

Finally, neo-Aristotelian criticism does not warrant us to estimate the truth of Nixon's statements or the reality of the values he assumes as aspects of American life. When Nixon finds the origin of the war in a North Vietnamese "campaign to impose a Communist government on South Vietnam by instigating and supporting a revolution," Campbell takes him to task for not telling the truth. This criticism raises a serious question: are we sure that Nixon is not telling the truth? We know, of course, that Nixon oversimplifies a complex series of events—any speaker in his situation necessarily does that. But will the scholar of tomorrow with the perspective of history judge his account totally false? Campbell endorses the view that basically this is a civil war resulting from the failure of the Diem government backed by the United States to hold elections under the Geneva Agreements of 1954. But her view and Nixon's are not mutually exclusive: it seems evident to me that both the United States and the Communist powers involved themselves from the first to the extent they thought necessary to force an outcome in their favor in Viet Nam. If a scientific historian of the future had to pick one view of the conflict or the other, he would probably pick Nixon's because it more clearly recognizes the power politics behind the struggle. But I am not really intending to press the point that Campbell commits herself to a wrong view, or even a superficially partial one. The point is that she espouses here a theory of criticism that requires her to commit herself at all. If anyone writing in a scholarly journal seeks to assess the truth of Nixon's statements, he must be willing to assume the burden of proving them evidently false. This cannot be done by appealing to the wisdom of the liberal intellectuals of today.[25] If the essential task were accomplished, would the result be called a *rhetorical* critique? By Aristotle's standards it would not, and for my part I think we will write more significant criticism if we follow Aristotle in this case. To generalize, I submit that the limitations of neo-Aristotelian criticism are like the metrical conventions of the poet—limitations that make true significance possible.

Notes

[1] Robert P. Newman, "Under the Veneer: Nixon's Vietnam Speech of November 3, 1969," *Quarterly Journal of Speech*, 56 (Apr. 1970), 168–178; Hermann G. Stelzner, "The Quest Story and Nixon's November 3, 1969 Address," *Quarterly Journal of Speech*, 57 (Apr. 1971), 163–172; Karlyn Kohrs

Campbell, "An Exercise in the Rhetoric of Mythical America," in *Critiques of Contemporary Rhetoric* (Belmont, CA: Wadsworth, 1972), pp. 50–58.

[2] Herbert A. Wichelns, "The Literary Criticism of Oratory," in Donald C. Bryant, ed., *The Rhetorical Idiom: Essays in Rhetoric, Oratory, Language, and Drama* (1925; rpt. Ithaca: Cornell Univ. Press, 1958), pp. 5–42.

[3] Marie Hochmuth [Nichols], "The Criticism of Rhetoric," in *A History and Criticism of American Public Address* (New York: Longmans, Green, 1955) III, 1–23.

[4] Aristotle, *Rhetoric* I. 1. 1355b 10–14. "To persuade is not the function of rhetoric but to investigate the persuasive factors inherent in the particular case. It is just the same as in all other arts; for example, it is not the function of medicine to bring health, rather to bring the patient as near to health as is possible in his case. Indeed, there are some patients who cannot be changed to healthfulness; nevertheless, they can be given the right therapy." (Translation mine.) I understand the medical analogy to mean that even if auditors chance to be proof against any of the means of persuasion, the persuader has functioned adequately as a rhetorician if he has investigated these means so that he has in effect "given the right therapy."

[5] Text as printed in *Vital Speeches*, 36 (15 Nov. 1969), 69.

[6] Aristotle *Rhetoric* I. 4. 1359b 33–1360a 5.

[7] Aristotle *Rhetoric* III. 14. 1415a 29–33. Here Nixon functions like a defendant in a forensic speech. "When defending he will first deal with any prejudicial insinuation against him . . . it is necessary that the defendant when he steps forward first reduce the obstacles, so he must immediately dissolve prejudice."

[8] See Aristotle *Rhetoric* III. 16. 1417a 16–36.

[9] Newman, p. 173.

[10] See Aristotle *Rhetoric* II. 23. 1398a 30–31. This basic structure is called method of residues in most modern argumentation textbooks.

[11] Aristotle *Rhetoric* III. 19. 1419b 10–1420a 8.

[12] For the purpose of this paper the term enthymeme is taken to mean any deductive argument. Aristotle gives a more technical definition of enthymeme that fits into the total design of his organon; in my opinion it is not useful for neo-Aristotelian criticism.

[13] Remarkably enough Aristotle does not state this general rule, though it clearly underlies his treatment of the historical example, *Rhetoric* II. 20.

[14] See Aristotle *Rhetoric* I. 6. 1362b 26–27 for life as a good; I. 8. 1366a for freedom as the object of choice for the citizens of a democracy.

[15] The subject of *Rhetoric* I. 7. Chaim Perelman and L. Olbrechts-Tyteca, commenting on this chapter, indicate that there is usually a consensus on such statements as 'life is good'; the dispute is over whether life is a greater good than honor in this particular situation. See *The New Rhetoric: A Treatise on Argumentation*, trans. John Wilkinson and Purcell Weaver (Notre Dame: Univ. of Notre Dame Press, 1969), pp. 81–82.

[16] See Aristotle *Rhetoric* II. 19. 1393a 1–3.

[17] This principle follows from *Rhetoric* II. 5. 1383a 24–25.

[18] Aristotle *Rhetoric* II. 5. 1382a 21–22. Aristotle treated the *pathe* as states of feeling that a man enters into because he draws certain inferences from the situation around him: he sees, for example, that he is the type of man who experiences pity when faced with this type of victim in these circumstances. The means of getting a man to draw inferences are themselves logical proofs; hence *pathos* does not work apart from the logical proofs in a message but through them. See Aristotle *Rhetoric* II. 1. 1378a 19-28 and my explication in James J. Murphy, ed. *A Synoptic History of Classical Rhetoric* (New York: Random House, 1972).

[19] Aristotle *Rhetoric* II. 2. 1378a 30–32.

[20] Aristotle *Rhetoric* II. 2. 1379a 10–18.

[21] Aristotle *Rhetoric* II. 5. 1383a 16–19.

[22] Since he gave this speech Nixon has made a general timetable for American withdrawal, thus, presumably, showing that he was not utterly convinced by his own argument. But he has never quite fixed a date for complete withdrawal of all American support forces from Viet Nam; he has been consistent in maintaining that withdrawal as a bargaining point for negotiation with the Viet Cong and North Vietnamese.

[23] See Aristotle *Rhetoric* III. 12. 1414a 8–19.

[24] Edwin B. Black, *Rhetorical Criticism: A Study in Method* (New York: Macmillan, 1965), p. 33.

[25] Richard H. Kendall, writing a reply to Newman, "The Forum," *Quarterly Journal of Speech*, 56 (Dec. 1970), 432, makes this same point, particularly in connection with Newman's implication that ex-President Johnson was a fraud. "If so, let us have some evidence of his fraudulent actions. If there is no evidence, or if there is evidence, but an essay on the rhetoric of President Nixon does not provide proper

scope for a presentation of such evidence, then it seems to me inclusion of such a charge (or judgment) may fall into the category of gratuitous." Newman in rejoinder asks, "Should such summary judgments be left out of an article in a scholarly journal because space prohibits extensively supporting them? Omission might contribute to a sterile academic purity, but it would improve neither cogency nor understanding." I would certainly answer Newman's rhetorical question, yes, and I would go on to judge that view of criticism which encourages such summary judgments not to be a useful one.

Vietnamization Speech
Richard Nixon
November 3, 1969

Good evening, my fellow Americans: Tonight I want to talk to you on a subject of deep concern to all Americans and to many people in all parts of the world—the war in Vietnam.

I believe that one of the reasons for the deep division about Vietnam is that many Americans have lost confidence in what their Government has told them about our policy. The American people cannot and should not be asked to support a policy which involves the overriding issues of war and peace unless they know the truth about that policy.

Tonight, therefore, I would like to answer some of the questions that I know are on the minds of many of you listening to me.

How and why did America get involved in Vietnam in the first place?

How has this administration changed the policy of the previous administration?

What has really happened in the negotiations in Paris and on the battlefront in Vietnam?

What choices do we have if we are to end the war?

What are the prospects for peace?

Now, let me begin by describing the situation I found when I was inaugurated on January 20.

- The war had been going on for 4 years.
- 31,000 Americans had been killed in action.
- The training program for the South Vietnamese was behind schedule.
- 540,000 Americans were in Vietnam with no plans to reduce the number.
- No progress had been made at the negotiations in Paris and the United States had not put forth a comprehensive peace proposal.
- The war was causing deep division at home and criticism from many of our friends as well as our enemies abroad.

In view of these circumstances there were some who urged that I end the war at once by ordering the immediate withdrawal of all American forces.

From a political standpoint this would have been a popular and easy course to follow. After all, we became involved in the war while my predecessor was in office.

I could blame the defeat which would be the result of my action on him and come out as the peacemaker. Some put it to me quite bluntly: This was the only way to avoid allowing Johnson's war to become Nixon's war.

But I had a greater obligation than to think only of the years of my administration and of the next election. I had to think of the effect of my decision on the next generation and on the future of peace and freedom in America and in the world.

Let us all understand that the question before us is not whether some Americans are for peace and some Americans are against peace. The question at issue is not whether Johnson's war becomes Nixon's war.

The great question is: How can we win America's peace?

Well, let us turn now to the fundamental issue. Why and how did the United States become involved in Vietnam in the first place?

Fifteen years ago North Vietnam, with the logistical support of Communist China and the Soviet Union, launched a campaign to impose a Communist government on South Vietnam by instigating and supporting a revolution.

In response to the request of the Government of South Vietnam, President Eisenhower sent economic aid and military equipment to assist the people of South Vietnam in their efforts to prevent a Communist takeover. Seven years ago, President Kennedy sent 16,000 military personnel to Vietnam as combat advisers.

Four years ago, President Johnson sent American combat forces to South Vietnam.

Now, many believe that President Johnson's decision to send American combat forces to South Vietnam was wrong. And many others—I among them—have been strongly critical of the way the war has been conducted.

But the question facing us today is: Now that we are in the war, what is the best way to end it?

In January I could only conclude that the precipitate withdrawal of American forces from Vietnam would be a disaster not only for South Vietnam but for the United States and for the cause of peace.

For the South Vietnamese, our precipitate withdrawal would inevitably allow the Communists to repeat the massacres which followed their takeover in the North 15 years before.

- They then murdered more than 50,000 people and hundreds of thousands more died in slave labor camps.
- We saw a prelude of what would happen in South Vietnam when the Communists entered the city of Hue last year. During their brief rule there, there was a bloody reign of terror in which 3,000 civilians were clubbed, shot to death, and buried in mass graves.
- With the sudden collapse of our support, these atrocities of Hue would become the nightmare of the entire nation—and particularly for the million and a half Catholic refugees who fled to South Vietnam when the Communists took over in the North.

For the United States, this first defeat in our Nation's history would result in a collapse of confidence in American leadership, not only in Asia but throughout the world.

Three American Presidents have recognized the great stakes involved in Vietnam and understood what had to be done.

In 1963, President Kennedy, with his characteristic eloquence and clarity, said: "we want to see a stable government there, carrying on a struggle to maintain its national independence."

"We believe strongly in that. We are not going to withdraw from that effort. In my opinion, for us to withdraw from that effort would mean a collapse not only of South Vietnam, but Southeast Asia. So we are going to stay there."

President Eisenhower and President Johnson expressed the same conclusion during their terms of office.

For the future of peace, precipitate withdrawal would thus be a disaster of immense magnitude.

- A nation cannot remain great if it betrays its allies and lets down its friends.
- Our defeat and humiliation in South Vietnam without question would promote recklessness in the councils of those great powers who have not yet abandoned their goals of world conquest.
- This would spark violence wherever our commitments help maintain the peace—in the Middle East, in Berlin, eventually even in the Western Hemisphere.

Ultimately, this would cost more lives.

It would not bring peace; it would bring more war.

For these reasons, I rejected the recommendation that I should end the war by immediately withdrawing all of our forces. I chose instead to change American policy on both the negotiating front and battlefront.

In order to end a war fought on many fronts, I initiated a pursuit for peace on many fronts.

In a television speech on May 14, in a speech before the United Nations, and on a number of other occasions I set forth our peace proposals in great detail.

- We have offered the complete withdrawal of all outside forces within 1 year.
- We have proposed a cease-fire under international supervision.
- We have offered free elections under international supervision with the Communists participating in the organization and conduct of the elections as an organized political force. And the Saigon Government has pledged to accept the result of the elections.

We have not put forth our proposals on a take-it-or-leave-it basis. We have indicated that we are willing to discuss the proposals that have been put forth by the other side. We have declared that anything is negotiable except the right of the people of South Vietnam to determine their own future. At the Paris peace conference, Ambassador Lodge has demonstrated our flexibility and good faith in 40 public meetings.

Hanoi has refused even to discuss our proposals. They demand our unconditional acceptance of their terms, which are that we withdraw all American forces immediately and unconditionally and that we overthrow the Government of South Vietnam as we leave.

We have not limited our peace initiatives to public forums and public statements. I recognized, in January, that a long and bitter war like this usually cannot be settled in a public forum. That is why in addition to the public statements and negotiations I have explored every possible private avenue that might lead to a settlement.

Tonight I am taking the unprecedented step of disclosing to you some of our other initiatives for peace—initiatives we undertook privately and secretly because we thought we thereby might open a door which publicly would be closed. I did not wait for my inauguration to begin my quest for peace.

- Soon after my election, through an individual who is directly in contact on a personal basis with the leaders of North Vietnam, I made two private offers for a rapid, comprehensive settlement. Hanoi's replies called in effect for our surrender before negotiations.
- Since the Soviet Union furnishes most of the military equipment for North Vietnam, Secretary of State Rogers, my Assistant for National Security Affairs, Dr. Kissinger, Ambassador Lodge, and I, personally, have met on a number of occasions with representatives of the Soviet Government to enlist their assistance in getting meaningful negotiations started. In addition, we have had extended discussions directed toward that same end with representatives of other govern-

ments which have diplomatic relations with North Vietnam. None of these initiatives have to date produced results.

- In mid-July, I became convinced that it was necessary to make a major move to break the deadlock in the Paris talks. I spoke directly in this office, where I am now sitting, with an individual who had known Ho Chi Minh [President, Democratic Republic of Vietnam] on a personal basis for 25 years. Through him I sent a letter to Ho Chi Minh.

I did this outside of the usual diplomatic channels with the hope that with the necessity of making statements for propaganda removed, there might be constructive progress toward bringing the war to an end. Let me read from that letter to you now.

> Dear Mr. President
>   I realize that it is difficult to communicate meaningfully across the gulf of four years of war. But precisely because of this gulf, I wanted to take this opportunity to reaffirm in all solemnity my desire to work for a just peace. I deeply believe that the war in Vietnam has gone on too long and delay in bringing it to an end can benefit no one—least of all the people of Vietnam . . . .
>   The time has come to move forward at the conference table toward an early resolution of this tragic war. You will find us forthcoming and open-minded in a common effort to bring the blessings of peace to the brave people of Vietnam. Let history record that at this critical juncture, both sides turned their face toward peace rather than toward conflict and war.

I received Ho Chi Minh's reply on August 30, 3 days before his death. It simply reiterated the public position North Vietnam had taken at Paris and flatly rejected my initiative. The full text of both letters is being released to the press.

- In addition to the public meetings that I have referred to, Ambassador Lodge has met with Vietnam's chief negotiator in Paris in 11 private sessions.
- We have taken other significant initiatives which must remain secret to keep open some channels of communication which may still prove to be productive.

But the effect of all the public, private, and secret negotiations which have been undertaken since the bombing halt a year ago and since this administration came into office on January 20, can be summed up in one sentence: No progress whatever has been made except agreement on the shape of the bargaining table.

Well now, who is at fault?

It has become clear that the obstacle in negotiating an end to the war is not the President of the United States. It is not the South Vietnamese Government.

The obstacle is the other side's absolute refusal to show the least willingness to join us in seeking a just peace. And it will not do so while it is convinced that all it has to do is to wait for our next concession, and our next concession after that one, until it gets everything it wants.

There can now be no longer any question that progress in negotiation depends only on Hanoi's deciding to negotiate, to negotiate seriously.

I realize that this report on our efforts on the diplomatic front is discouraging to the American people, but the American people are entitled to know the truth—the bad news as well as the good news—where the lives of our young men are involved.

Now let me turn, however, to a more encouraging report on another front.

At the time we launched our search for peace I recognized we might not succeed in bringing an end to the war through negotiation. I, therefore, put into effect another plan to bring peace—a plan which will bring the war to an end regardless of what happens on the negotiating front.

It is in line with a major shift in U.S. foreign policy which I described in my press conference at Guam on July 25. Let me briefly explain what has been described as the Nixon Doctrine—a policy which not only will help end the war in Vietnam, but which is an essential element of our program to prevent future Vietnams.

We Americans are a do-it-yourself people. We are an impatient people. Instead of teaching someone else to do a job, we like to do it ourselves. And this trait has been carried over into our foreign policy.

In Korea and again in Vietnam, the United States furnished most of the money, most of the arms, and most of the men to help the people of those countries defend their freedom against Communist aggression.

Before any American troops were committed to Vietnam, a leader of another Asian country expressed this opinion to me when I was traveling in Asia as a private citizen. He said: "When you are trying to assist another nation defend its freedom, U.S. policy should be to help them fight the war but not to fight the war for them."

Well, in accordance with this wise counsel, I laid down in Guam three principles as guidelines for future American policy toward Asia:

- First, the United States will keep all of its treaty commitments.
- Second, we shall provide a shield if a nuclear power threatens the freedom of a nation allied with us or of a nation whose survival we consider vital to our security.
- Third, in cases involving other types of aggression, we shall furnish military and economic assistance when requested in accordance with our treaty commitments. But we shall look to the nation directly threatened to assume the primary responsibility of providing the manpower for its defense.

After I announced this policy, I found that the leaders of the Philippines, Thailand, Vietnam, South Korea, and other nations which might be threatened by Communist aggression, welcomed this new direction in American foreign policy.

The defense of freedom is everybody's business not just America's business.

And it is particularly the responsibility of the people whose freedom is threatened.

In the previous administration, we Americanized the war in Vietnam. In this administration, we are Vietnamizing the search for peace.

The policy of the previous administration not only resulted in our assuming the primary responsibility for fighting the war, but even more significantly did not adequately stress the goal of strengthening the South Vietnamese so that they could defend themselves when we left.

The Vietnamization plan was launched following Secretary Laird's visit to Vietnam in March. Under the plan, I ordered first a substantial increase in the training and equipment of South Vietnamese forces.

In July, on my visit to Vietnam, I changed General Abrams' orders so that they were consistent with the objectives of our new policies. Under the new orders, the primary mission of our troops is to enable the South Vietnamese forces to assume the full responsibility for the security of South Vietnam.

Our air operations have been reduced by over 20 percent.

And now we have begun to see the results of this long overdue change in American policy in Vietnam.

- After 5 years of Americans going into Vietnam, we are finally bringing American men home. By December 15, over 60,000 men will have been withdrawn from South Vietnam—including 20 percent of all of our combat forces.
- The South Vietnamese have continued to gain in strength. As a result they have been able to take over combat responsibilities from our American troops.

Two other significant developments have occurred since this administration took office.

- Enemy infiltration, infiltration which is essential if they are to launch a major attack, over the last 3 months is less than 20 percent of what it was over the same period last year.
- Most important—United States casualties have declined during the last 2 months to the lowest point in 3 years.

Let me now turn to our program for the future.

We have adopted a plan which we have worked out in cooperation with the South Vietnamese for the complete withdrawal of all U.S. combat ground forces, and their replacement by South Vietnamese forces on an orderly scheduled timetable. This withdrawal will be made from strength and not from weakness. As South Vietnamese forces become stronger, the rate of American withdrawal can become greater.

I have not and do not intend to announce the timetable for our program. And there are obvious reasons for this decision which I am sure you will understand. As I have indicated on several occasions, the rate of withdrawal will depend on developments on three fronts.

One of these is the progress which can be or might be made in the Paris talks. An announcement of a fixed timetable for our withdrawal would completely remove any incentive for the enemy to negotiate an agreement. They would simply wait until our forces had withdrawn and then move in.

The other two factors on which we will base our withdrawal decisions are the level of enemy activity and the progress of the training programs of the South Vietnamese forces. And I am glad to be able to report tonight progress on both of these fronts has been greater than we anticipated when we started the program in June for withdrawal. As a result, our timetable for withdrawal is more optimistic now than when we made our first estimates in June. Now, this clearly demonstrates why it is not wise to be frozen in on a fixed timetable.

We must retain the flexibility to base each withdrawal decision on the situation as it is at that time rather than on estimates that are no longer valid. Along with this optimistic estimate, I must—in all candor—leave one note of caution.

If the level of enemy activity significantly increases we might have to adjust our timetable accordingly.

However, I want the record to be completely clear on one point. At the time of the bombing halt just a year ago, there was some confusion as to whether there was an understanding on the part of the enemy that if we stopped the bombing of North Vietnam they would stop the shelling of cities in South Vietnam. I want to be sure that there is no misunderstanding on the part of the enemy with regard to our withdrawal program.

We have noted the reduced level of infiltration, the reduction of our casualties, and are basing our withdrawal decisions partially on those factors.

If the level of infiltration or our casualties increase while we are trying to scale down the fighting, it will be the result of a conscious decision by the enemy.

Hanoi could make no greater mistake than to assume that an increase in violence will be to its advantage. If I conclude that increased enemy action jeopardizes our remaining forces in Vietnam, I shall not hesitate to take strong and effective measures to deal with that situation.

This is not a threat. This is a statement of policy, which as Commander in Chief of our Armed Forces, I am making in meeting my responsibility for the protection of American fighting men wherever they may be.

My fellow Americans, I am sure you can recognize from what I have said that we really only have two choices open to us if we want to end this war.

- I can order an immediate, precipitate withdrawal of all Americans from Vietnam without regard to the effects of that action.

- Or we can persist in our search for a just peace through a negotiated settlement if possible, or through continued implementation of our plan for Vietnamization if necessary—a plan in which we will withdraw all of our forces from Vietnam on a schedule in accordance with our program, as the South Vietnamese become strong enough to defend their own freedom.

I have chosen this second course.

It is not the easy way.

It is the right way.

It is a plan which will end the war and serve the cause of peace—not just in Vietnam but in the Pacific and in the world.

In speaking of the consequences of a precipitate withdrawal, I mentioned that our allies would lose confidence in America.

Far more dangerous, we would lose confidence in ourselves. Oh, the immediate reaction would be a sense of relief that our men were coming home. But as we saw the consequences of what we had done, inevitable remorse and divisive recrimination would scar our spirit as a people.

We have faced other crises in our history and have become stronger by rejecting the easy way out and taking the right way in meeting our challenges. Our greatness as a nation has been our capacity to do what had to be done when we knew our course was right.

I recognize that some of my fellow citizens disagree with the plan for peace I have chosen. Honest and patriotic Americans have reached different conclusions as to how peace should be achieved.

In San Francisco a few weeks ago, I saw demonstrators carrying signs reading: "Lose in Vietnam, bring the boys home."

Well, one of the strengths of our free society is that any American has a right to reach that conclusion and to advocate that point of view. But as President of the United States, I would be untrue to my oath of office if I allowed the policy of this Nation to be dictated by the minority who hold that point of view and who try to impose it on the Nation by mounting demonstrations in the street.

For almost 200 years, the policy of this Nation has been made under our Constitution by those leaders in the Congress and the White House elected by all of the people. If a vocal minority, however fervent its cause, prevails over reason and the will of the majority, this Nation has no future as a free society.

And now I would like to address a word, if I may, to the young people of this Nation who are particularly concerned, and I understand why they are concerned, about this war.

I respect your idealism.

I share your concern for peace.

I want peace as much as you do.

There are powerful personal reasons I want to end this war. This week I will have to sign 83 letters to mothers, fathers, wives, and loved ones of men who have given their lives for America in Vietnam. It is very little satisfaction to me that this is only one-third as many letters as I signed the first week in office. There is nothing I want more than to see the day come when I do not have to write any of those letters.

- I want to end the war to save the lives of those brave young men in Vietnam.
- But I want to end it in a way which will increase the chance that their younger brothers and their sons will not have to fight in some future Vietnam someplace in the world.
- And I want to end the war for another reason. I want to end it so that the energy and dedication of you, our young people, now too often directed into bitter hatred against those responsible for the war, can be turned to the great challenges of peace, a better life for all Americans, a better life for all people on this earth.

I have chosen a plan for peace. I believe it will succeed.

If it does succeed, what the critics say now won't matter. If it does not succeed, anything I say then won't matter.

I know it may not be fashionable to speak of patriotism or national destiny these days. But I feel it is appropriate to do so on this occasion.

Two hundred years ago this Nation was weak and poor. But even then, America was the hope of millions in the world. Today we have become the strongest and richest nation in the world. And the wheel of destiny has turned so that any hope the world has for the survival of peace and freedom will be determined by whether the American people have the moral stamina and the courage to meet the challenge of free world leadership.

Let historians not record that when America was the most powerful nation in the world we passed on the other side of the road and allowed the last hopes for peace and freedom of millions of people to be suffocated by the forces of totalitarianism.

And so tonight—to you, the great silent majority of my fellow Americans—I ask for your support.

I pledged in my campaign for the Presidency to end the war in a way that we could win the peace. I have initiated a plan of action which will enable me to keep that pledge.

The more support I can have from the American people, the sooner that pledge can be redeemed, for the more divided we are at home, the less likely the enemy is to negotiate at Paris.

Let us be united for peace. Let us also be united against defeat. Because let us understand: North Vietnam cannot defeat or humiliate the United States. Only Americans can do that.

Fifty years ago, in this room and at this very desk, President Woodrow Wilson spoke words which caught the imagination of a war-weary world. He said: "This is the war to end war." His dream for peace after World War I was shattered on the hard realities of great power politics and Woodrow Wilson died a broken man. Tonight I do not tell you that the war in Vietnam is the war to end wars. But I do say this: I have initiated a plan which will end this war in a way that will bring us closer to that great goal to which Woodrow Wilson and every American President in our history has been dedicated—the goal of a just and lasting peace.

As President I hold the responsibility for choosing the best path to that goal and then leading the Nation along it.

I pledge to you tonight that I shall meet this responsibility with all of the strength and wisdom I can command in accordance with your hopes, mindful of your concerns, sustained by your prayers.

Thank you and goodnight.

The Power of Saddam Hussein's
War Rhetoric

Gary W. Brown

In January, 1991, the United States and its allies, Great Britain, France, and Saudi Arabia, initiated a war with Iraq in response to Iraq's invasion of Kuwait in August of that year. Although the United States and its allies won the war quickly, another less destructive—yet equally important—war was being fought while the air and ground campaigns occurred. This was a war of words that involved campaigns by the two sides to instill public support for the war and their respective causes. In sharp contrast to the clear victory that the United States and its allies obtained as a result of the air and ground campaign, the outcome of the war of the rhetoric that occurred during the conflict proved to be less decisive.

From a Western perspective, Saddam Hussein was a ruthless tyrant who would stop at nothing to conquer the world and to eliminate any opposition to him. His rhetoric during the war, usually disseminated through radio addresses, often was discredited by the Western listener. Yet, how was Hussein's rhetoric viewed from the perspective of his own people or of the people of Iraq's neighboring nations? That is the question I wish to address in this essay.

Using neo-Aristotelian criticism, I will examine how influential Saddam Hussein's war rhetoric was for those in his own country and neighboring countries using as my artifact five daily radio addresses Hussein presented during February, 1991. The tapes of the short-wave radio addresses used for my analysis were obtained by a classmate whose boyfriend was stationed in Saudi Arabia during the war. These tapes contained Hussein's speeches in Arabic, which I translated into English. I lived in Kuwait and had taken two years of intensive Arabic language classes as a requirement for graduating from the American School of Kuwait, the high school I attended. I will proceed, in my analysis, by examining the context in which the speeches were presented, analyzing the speeches by applying the five canons of rhetoric, and assessing the success of Hussein's rhetoric for its intended audience.

CONTEXT

I will examine three areas that will help provide the context for the artifact: Hussein as a rhetor, the occasions on which the rhetoric was presented, and the audience to whom the rhetoric was addressed.

Information about Hussein's background helps to explain the motives for and nature of his war rhetoric. First, Hussein is Muslim, and his rhetoric was directed at a Muslim audience, which means his rhetoric was not typical of rhetorics that embody Western ideologies. Rather, his speeches deal with philosophies and background experiences that are completely foreign to us. In most of his speeches, he devoted a great deal of time to praising Allah, for example. Thus, in order to criticize the war rhetoric of Hussein effectively, my examination of the artifact

This essay was written while Gary W. Brown was a student in Karen A. Foss's rhetorical criticism class at Humboldt State University in 1991. Used by permission of the author.

must take place, as far as is possible, through the eyes of a Muslim rather than those of a Westerner.

At the time he gave the speeches, Hussein was the political as well as the military leader of Iraq. This position had an impact on the way he addressed his people as well as on the flavor and tone of his rhetoric. Hussein was interested in maintaining his power and prestige, and his rhetoric reflected a desire for dominance and authority.

Although Hussein was the military leader of Iraq as well as its political leader, curiously, he never served in the military. Not until he became the leader of Iraq did he have any extensive training in military strategy and tactics. This factor may have affected audiences' assessment of his war rhetoric. Military leaders from both his and other countries may not have responded favorably to his war rhetoric simply because of his lack of a military background. This lack of military experience, however, may have been of less importance to the average listener with little or no military background. Thus, Hussein's rhetoric probably was targeted to the untrained military public rather than to the trained military.

In terms of the occasion for the radio addresses, an all-out confrontation between the United States and its allied forces and Iraq was underway. Baghdad, Iraqi military targets, and Iraqi troops constantly were being bombed by the allies. Because of this heavy air assault, I assume that morale in Iraq was low. In an attempt to increase morale and public support for Iraq, Hussein made irregularly timed addresses over short-wave radio to inform his people of war-worthy news such as allied "defeats." These radio addresses came at a time when the leader of Iraq was under severe criticism by both his own people and many other nations around the world.

The intended audiences for these radio broadcasts consisted primarily of the people of Iraq and the neighboring "friendly" nations that border Iraq. Evidence for these as his intended audience comes first from the fact that the addresses were spoken in the Arabic language. In addition, the common, ordinary words and phrases he used seemed to be directed at the average Arab citizen. Very little effort was made to discuss sophisticated and technical specifications about war strategies or the like. In fact, very little, if any, time was spent by Hussein in dealing with such topics. Rather, he chose to read scriptures from the Koran and to denounce the evil Western societies, strategies that seemed designed to motivate and strengthen general Arab public opinion in support of Hussein.

The Arabic audiences to which Hussein's speeches were addressed were, like Hussein, Muslim. They shared the same background philosophies and ideologies as Hussein, and they all possessed a certain amount of national and racial pride about their heritage. There also existed a high degree of tension and animosity toward Western societies, especially the United States, which probably heightened the Arab audiences' national pride.

Another hidden audience that could have been a target audience that Hussein was trying to reach was the Western societies themselves. Such descriptions as "the allies will drown in their own pools of blood" or "the holy mother war to end all wars and bring the downfall of Western societies" were presented with a possible intent to scare Western audiences and encourage the allied forces to move back due to a lack of Western public support.

ANALYSIS OF HUSSEIN'S RHETORIC

I now will examine Hussein's rhetoric itself by applying the five canons of rhetoric to the radio addresses. I will examine how Hussein used (1) invention; (2) organization; (3) style; (4) memory; and (5) delivery in order to create a rhetoric that was effective for his audience.

Invention

In terms of invention, the major sources on which Hussein depended for logical proof was the Koran, the holy book of Muslims; traditional Arab tribal laws; and Arab unity against evil Western societies. In his speeches, every movement he made, such as the initial attack on Kuwait, was justified by the Koran and Allah. In Arab society and culture, if an individual is able to perform an action with little or no opposition, then, in God's eyes, that person is assumed to be correct and that individual's action is justified by Allah. Because Hussein's military was successful in conquering Kuwait in a matter of days with very little resistance, Arab logic dictated that Hussein must have been right in Allah's eyes.

Using this logic, Hussein was able to justify his action to the Arab people. In all five radio broadcasts I analyzed, Hussein justified his right to take over Kuwait. In his first public radio announcement shortly after the air raids began, for example, he stated, "God has given us the strength and power to rid Kuwait of its corrupt and sinful leaders." Thus, Hussein used the logic that Allah had given him the power to conquer Kuwait to set it straight; he removed the responsibility for the action from himself and attributed it to God. In this way, Hussein tried to establish his *ethos* among the people of his nation and those of other neighboring Arab countries.

In addition, Kuwait always has been considered part of Iraq by the Iraqis. This idea can be traced back to tribal conflicts, when the Bedouins migrated around the Middle East during the different seasons. Part of the land now found in Kuwait, as far as the Iraqis are concerned, belongs to members of tribes whose descendants currently inhabit Iraq. Thus, in their minds, Kuwait actually belongs to Iraq, a belief that aided Hussein in justifying his conquering of Kuwait.

Hussein's third major argument, which remained consistent throughout the radio addresses, was the appeal to other Arabic nations to help Iraq fight off the "evil" Western societies that interfered with Arab business. He developed this argument in two ways: (1) He sought to instill or reinforce a sense of racial prejudice; and (2) He sought to draw attention away from the Kuwait issue by trying to involve Israel in the conflict.

In several radio addresses before and during the air and ground campaign, Hussein called upon other "Arab brothers" to help Iraq "conquer and humiliate" the United States and its allies. Hussein developed this argument by employing *logos, ethos,* and *pathos*. He relied on the logic that Arab "brothers must stick together to fight off evil Bush and his minions." The logic assumed that all Arab brothers would converge together regardless of past conflicts that may have occurred: "You are all, in the eyes of Allah, Arab brothers. We all need to come together to rid ourselves of the evil menace that infects our lands."

Hussein also was trying to establish his *ethos* in the speeches. He accomplished this by indicating repeatedly that all the Arab people were "brothers" as well as Muslims who must fight together for a common cause. By referencing his identity as a Muslim as well as an Arab and showing that the majority of the inhabitants of the allied nations were neither, he provided a reason to support his war efforts. This argument also showed signs of *pathos* for similar reasons. Because Hussein and the residents of Iraq were both Muslim and Arab, he hoped to stir up emotions to sway other Muslims and Arabs to help Iraq fight.

Hussein also developed his appeal to fight evil Western societies by taking the focus off of the Kuwait conflict and placing it on the Palestinian issue. He tried to pull other Arab nations into the conflict by addressing an issue that was a political "hot potato" in the Arab culture's eyes. Perhaps Hussein realized the reservations that other nations possessed about entering into his "holy war." Bringing up Iraq's commitment to help the Palestinians regain the land from Israel that was "rightfully theirs" was a means Hussein used to encourage other Arab nations to fight on the side of Iraq in the war. As a consequence of this argument, Hussein could be seen as a leader who was attempting to settle the Palestinian dispute, thus contributing to his *ethos*. He could be perceived as a leader who was fighting for the good of all Arab people because he was addressing an issue close to the hearts of all Arabs.

Organization

An examination of the organization of Hussein's radio addresses reveals a consistent pattern. Each speech began with a quote or paraphrase from the Koran, the holy book of the Muslim faith. This was followed by praise for the strength and courage of the Iraqi citizens who were enduring constant air raids by allied forces. He also reassured his people that Iraq would prevail and would be victorious in the war. Hussein concluded the speeches by criticizing the Western allied nations. He used such descriptive terms as "evil corrupt society" or "evil President Bush" to help instill emotional hatred of the allies. Finally, he again appealed to other Arabs to join the fight that Iraq entered in order to help the Palestinian cause.

Style

The style of speech Hussein used during his addresses also played a critical role in their effectiveness. Hussein used the classical Arabic dialect rather than any other dialect of Arabic, a style that helped give him authority. Classical Arabic is used as both the diplomatic and religious languages of Iraq. Thus, simply using classical Arabic promotes an image of prestige and grace. To use an example of how effective this style of Arabic is, let me use an example of how this dialect might apply to Western languages. The President of the United States, when addressing the nation, would not use slang terms. Rather, he or she purposely would use a somewhat formal style because it would be appropriate for a leadership role. The same argument can be made for the use of classical Arabic. In the minds of Arabs, a leader who uses this dialect of the language is both eloquent and appropriate.

By using classical Arabic, Hussein also was assured that every Arab citizen was able to understand his speech. Many different dialects exist in the Arab language, and I know from my own experience in Kuwait that if I attempted to speak a different dialect of Arabic to an individual unfamiliar with it, that person would have no idea what I was saying. Because classical Arabic is the dialect taught in the schools of Arab nations, however, all Arabs would have been able to understand the words of Hussein regardless of their local dialects.

Because the classical Arabic style is used as the written language of the Koran, Hussein's use of this form also contributed to his credibility as a religious authority. Hussein had declared this war a holy war, and by using the holy language, Hussein reinforced this image. In essence, Hussein used the classical Arabic to establish himself as a religious leader protected by Allah.

Delivery

The delivery of Hussein's addresses also helped to promote a sense of authority and control for his listeners. Hussein's style of delivery was dynamic and energetic, particularly when he read from the Koran. His delivery style, in fact, helped to create the impression that he was passionate about the cause.

I believe that Hussein's speeches were prepared much earlier than the dates on which they were delivered. Most of the wording in the speech was carefully chosen so as not to insult any potential allies of Iraq. Also, the vividness of the descriptive language used to condemn the United States (such as "let them lie drowning in their own pools of blood for their persistence" or "Allah sheds the dust upon the evil machines [the war machines used by the allies] to protect the true followers of Muhammad") suggests that much preparation went into the speeches before they were delivered.

Memory

The last canon I will use to analyze the effectiveness of Hussein's radio addresses is memory. As I have suggested, I believe the speeches were prepared prior to their delivery. I also believe the speeches were written in manuscript form and read over the radio. On occasion, Hussein seemed to stumble on certain words, after which he quickly corrected himself. I suspect this was due to misreading his script.

ASSESSMENT OF EFFECTS

The creation of memorable speeches constituted only part of the purpose of Hussein's rhetoric. The other part is how effective the rhetoric was in meeting its objectives. In spite of the outcome of the military campaign, I argue that his rhetoric was successful. Although many Arab nations did not go to the aid of Iraq, Hussein was successful in obtaining some sympathy from Muslim nations as well as other nations around the world. The most memorable example of such a case occurred when the United States bombed a "public residence." When Hussein sharply accused the United States of intentionally killing innocent citizens, many Arab nations announced their agreement with his position and suggested their disgust with the United States' action. Hussein's attempts to address the Palestinian issue as well as Iraq's attempt to sign a peace treaty with Russia also contributed to the speeches' effectiveness. All these attempts by Iraq to address political problems and peaceful solutions to issues concerning the Arab community helped create a feeling of sympathy for Iraq.

Hussein's speeches did help to promote Arab pride. As reports from CNN and other network news stations illustrated, many Arabs felt that the Iraqi leader's attempt to address the Palestinian issue, as well as to fight the allies for the good "of the Arab people," was a valiant attempt on Hussein's part. They argued that the Palestinian issue had become public once again and had helped to establish a sense of Arab "brotherhood" and unity. If the military campaign had not been so one-sided in favor of the allies, I believe that stronger Arab unity eventually would have created problems for the allied forces.

Finally, Hussein was successful in reaching his intended audience, evidenced in the fact that many Arabs from nations other than Iraq were willing to join the Iraqi army and fight for Hussein. Once again, the concept of Arab "brotherhood" was a strong political theme that Hussein used to his advantage.

The allied nations may have won the military campaign, but I am less sure that they achieved such a decisive victory from a rhetorical standpoint. If the Iraqi forces had been more successful in fighting off the allies, I believe that, given time, Hussein would have proved to be a deadly rhetorical weapon by influencing other Arab nations to fight for his cause. In fact, Hussein was successful in achieving many of the goals he set out to accomplish through the use of his rhetoric. In addition, after the victory by the allied nations, Hussein remained in power. Potentially, Hussein could have suffered defeat and been forced to resign as the Iraqis' leader, but this did not occur. This may not have been the case had he not used rhetoric effectively to bring Arabs together in a spirit of unity and pride.

Withdrawal from Kuwait

Saddam Hussein
February 26, 1991

In the name of God, the merciful, the compassionate. O great people, O stalwart men in the forces of jihad and faith, glorious men of the Mother of Battles, O zealous, faithful, and sincere people in our glorious nations, and among all Muslims and all virtuous people in the world, O glorious Iraqi women, in such circumstances and times, it is difficult to talk about all that should be talked about, and it is difficult to recall all that has to be recalled. Despite this, we have to recall what has to be recalled, and say part—a principal part—of what should be said.

We start by saying that on this day, our valiant armed forces will complete their withdrawal from Kuwait. And on this day, our fight against aggression and the ranks of infidelity, joined in an ugly coalition comprising 30 countries, which officially entered war against us under the leadership of the United States of America—our fight against them would have lasted from the first month of this year, starting with the night of 16–17 January, until this moment in the current month, February. It was an epic duel which lasted for two months, which came to confirm clearly a lesson that God has wanted as a prelude of faith, impregnability, and capability for the faithful, and a prelude to an abyss, weakness, and humiliation which God almighty has wanted for the infidels, the criminals, the traitors, the corrupt and the deviators.

To be added to this is the military and nonmilitary duel, including the military and the economic blockade, which was imposed on Iraq and which lasted throughout 1990 until today, and until the time God almighty wishes it to last. Before that, the duel lasted in other forms for years before this time. It was an epic struggle between right and wrong; we have talked about this in detail on previous occasions.

It gave depth to the age of the showdown for the year 1990, and the already elapsed part of the year 1991. Hence, we do not forget because we will not forget this great struggling spirit, by which men of great faith stormed the fortifications and the weapons of deception and the Croesus' [Kuwaiti rulers] treachery on the honorable day of the call. They did what they did within the context of legitimate deterrence and great principled action.

All that we have gone through or decided within its circumstances, obeying God's will and choosing a position of faith and chivalry is a record of honor, the significance of which will not be missed by the people and nation and the values of Islam and humanity. Their days will continue to be glorious, and their past and future will continue to relate the story of a faithful, jealous, and patient people who believed in the will of God and in the values and stands accepted by the Almighty for the Arab nation in its leading role and for the Islamic nation in the essentials of its true faith and how they should be. These values—which had their effect in all those situations, offered the sacrifices they had offered in the struggle, and symbolized the depth of the faithful character in Iraq—will continue to leave their effects on souls. They will continue to reap their harvest, not only in terms of direct targets represented in the slogans of their age—whether in the conflict between the oppressed poor and the unjust and opportunist rich, or between faith and blasphemy, or between injustice, deception, and treachery on the one hand and fairness, justice, honesty, and loyalty on the other—but also the indirect targets as well. This will shake the opposite ranks and cause them to collapse after everything has become clear. This will also add faith to the faithful, now that the minds and eyes have been opened and the hearts are longing for what the principles, values, and stances should long for and belong to.

The stage that preceded the great day of the call on 2 August 1990 had its own standards, including dealing with what is familiar and inherited during the bad times, whether on the level of relations between the ruler and the ruled, or between the leader and the people he leads. The relations between the foreigners among the ranks of infidelity and oppression and among the region's states and the world had their own standards, effects, and privileges that were created by the Arab homeland's circumstances, and which were facilitated by propaganda, which no one could expose more than it has now been exposed. The conflict was exacerbated by the vacuum that was created by the weakness of one of the two poles that used to represent the two opposite lines in the world. After 2 August 1990, however, new concepts and standards were created. This was preceded by a new outlook in all walks of life, in relations among peoples, relations among states, the relations between the ruler and the ruled, and by standards of faith and positions; patriotism, pan-Arabism, and humanitarianism; jihad, faith, Islam, fear and non-fear; restlessness and tranquility; manhood and its opposite; struggle, jihad, and sacrifice; and readiness to do good things and their opposite.

When new measures spring forth and the familiar, failed, traitorous, subservient, corrupt [people] and tyrants are rejected, then the opportunity for the cultivation of the pure soil will increase in its scope, and the seeds of this plant will take root deep in the good land, primarily the land of the Arabs, and the land of revelation and the messages, and the land of prophets. God says: "Like a goodly tree, whose root is firmly fixed, and its branches reach to the heavens. It brings forth its fruit at all times, by the leave of its Lord" [Koranic verse].

Then, everything will become possible on the road of goodness and happiness that is not defiled by the feet of the invaders or by their evil will or the corruption of the corrupt among those who have been corrupted and who spread corruption in the land of the Arabs. Moreover, the forces of plotting and treachery will be defeated for good. Good people and those who are distinguished by their faith and by their faithful, honorable stands of jihad will become the real leaders of the gathering of the faithful everywhere on earth, and the gathering of the corruption, falsehood, hypocrisy, and infidelity will be defeated and meet the vilest fate. The earth will be inherited, at God's order, by His righteous slaves. "For the earth is God's to give as a heritage to such of His servants as He pleaseth; and the end is best for the righteous" [Koranic verse].

When this happens, the near objectives will not only be within reach, available and possible, but also the doors will be open without any hindrance which might prevent the achievement of all the greater, remoter, and more comprehensive objectives to the Arabs, Muslims, and humanity at large.

Then, also, it will be clear that the harvest does not precede the seeding and that the threshing floor and the yield are the outcome of a successful seeding and a successful harvest.

The harvest in the Mother of Battles has succeeded. After we have harvested what we have harvested, the greater harvest and its yield will be in the time to come, and it will be much greater than what we have at present, in spite of what we have at present in terms of the victory, dignity, and glory that was based on the sacrifices of a deep faith which is generous without any hesitation or fear. It is by virtue of this faith that God has bestowed dignity upon the Iraqi mujahidin and upon all the depth of this course of jihad at the level of the Arab homeland and at the level of all those men whom God has chosen to be given the honor of allegiance, guidance, and honorable position, until He declares that the conflict has stopped or amends its directions and course and the positions in a manner which would please the faithful and increase their dignity.

O valiant Iraqi men, O glorious Iraqi women, Kuwait is part of your country and was carved from it in the past. Circumstances today have willed that it remain in the state in which it will remain after the withdrawal of our struggling forces from it. It hurts you that this should happen.

We rejoiced on the day of the call when it was decided that Kuwait should be one of the main gates for deterring the plot and for defending all Iraq from the plotters. We say that we will remember Kuwait on the great day of the call, on the days that followed it, and in documents and events, some of which date back 70 years.

The Iraqis will remember and will not forget that on 8 August 1990 Kuwait became part of Iraq legally, constitutionally, and actually. They remember and will not forget that it remained throughout this period from 8 August 1990 until last night, when withdrawal began, and today we will complete withdrawal of our forces, God willing. Today, certain circumstances made the Iraqi Army withdraw as a result of the ramifications which we mentioned, including the combined aggression by 30 countries. Their repugnant siege had been led in evil and aggression by the machine and the criminal entity of America and its major allies.

These malicious ranks took the depth and effectiveness of their aggressiveness not only from the aggressive premeditated intentions against Iraq, the Arab nation, and Islam, but also from the position of those who were deceived by the claim of international legitimacy. Everyone will remember that the gates of Constantinople were not opened before the Muslims in the first struggling attempt, and that the international community consigned dear Palestine's freedom and independence to oblivion.

Whatever the suspect parties try, by virtue of the sacrifices and struggle of the Palestinians and Iraqis, Palestine has returned anew to knock at the doors closed on evil.

Palestine returned to knock on those doors to force the tyrants and the traitors to a solution that would place it at the forefront of the issues that have to be resolved—a solution that would bring dignity to its people and provide better chances for better progress.

The issues of poverty and richness, fairness and unfairness, faith and infidelity, treachery and honesty and sincerity have become titles corresponding to rare events and well-known people and trends that give priority to what is positive over what is negative, to what is sincere over what is treacherous and filthy, and to what is pure and honorable over what is corrupt, base, and lowly. The confidence of the nationalists and the faithful mujahidin and the Muslims has grown bigger than before, and hope grew more and more. Slogans have come out of their stores to occupy strongly the facades of the pan-Arab and human jihad and struggle. Therefore, victory is great, now and in the future, God willing.

Shout for victory, O brothers, shout for your victory and the victory of all honorable people, O Iraqis. You have fought 30 countries, and all the evil and the largest machine of war and destruction in the world that surrounds them. If only one of these countries threatens anyone, this threat will have a swift and direct effect on the dignity, freedom, or life of this or that country, people, and nation.

The soldiers of faith have triumphed over the soldiers of wrong. O stalwart men, your God is the one who granted your victory. You triumphed when you rejected, in the name of faith, the will of evil which the evildoers wanted to impose on you to kill the fire of faith in your hearts. You have chosen the path you have chosen, including acceptance of the Soviet initiative, but those evildoers persisted in their path and methods, thinking that they can impose their will on Iraq, as they imagined and hoped. This hope of theirs may remain in their heads, even after we withdraw from Kuwait. Therefore, we must be cautious, and preparedness to fight must remain at the highest level.

O you valiant men, you have fought the armies of 30 states and the capabilities of an even greater number of states which supplied them with the means of aggression and support. Faith, belief, hope, and determination continue to fill your chests, souls, and hearts. They have even become deeper, stronger, brighter, and more deeply rooted. God is great, God is great, may the lowly be defeated. Victory is sweet with the help of God.

Note: This speech by Saddam Hussein was given during the time of the speeches analyzed by Gary W. Brown, but it is not necessarily one of the speeches he analyzed.

Additional Samples of Neo-Aristotelian Criticism

Anderson, Jeanette. "Man of the Hour or Man of the Ages? The Honorable Stephen A. Douglas." *Quarterly Journal of Speech*, 25 (February 1939), 75–93.

Bauer, Marvin G. "Persuasive Methods in the Lincoln-Douglas Debates." *Quarterly Journal of Speech*, 13 (February 1927), 29–39.

Brigance, William Norwood, ed. *A History and Criticism of American Public Address*. Vol. I. New York: McGraw-Hill, 1943, numerous essays, pp. 213–500.

Brigance, William Norwood, ed. *A History and Criticism of American Public Address*. Vol. II. New York: McGraw-Hill, 1943, numerous essays, pp. 501–992.

Casmir, Fred L. "An Analysis of Hitler's January 30, 1941 Speech." *Western Speech*, 30 (Spring 1966), 96–106.

Dell, George W. "The Republican Nominee: Barry M. Goldwater." *Quarterly Journal of Speech*, 50 (December 1964), 399–404.

Hochmuth, Marie Kathryn, ed. *A History and Criticism of American Public Address*. Vol. III. New York: Longmans, 1955, numerous essays, pp. 24–530.

McCall, Roy C. "Harry Emerson Fosdick: Paragon and Paradox." *Quarterly Journal of Speech*, 39 (October 1953), 283–90.

Miller, Joseph W. "Winston Churchill, Spokesman for Democracy." *Quarterly Journal of Speech*, 28 (April 1942), 131–38.

Mohrmann, G. P., and Michael C. Leff. "Lincoln at Cooper Union: A Rationale for Neo-Classical Criticism." *Quarterly Journal of Speech*, 60 (December 1974), 459–67.

Peterson, Owen. "Keir Hardie: The Absolutely Independent M. P." *Quarterly Journal of Speech*, 55 (April 1969), 142–50.

Reid, Ronald F. "Edward Everett: Rhetorician of Nationalism, 1824–1855." *Quarterly Journal of Speech*, 42 (October 1956), 273–82.

Stelzner, Hermann G. "The British Orators, VII: John Morley's Speechmaking." *Quarterly Journal of Speech*, 45 (April 1959), 171–81.

Thomas, Gordon L. "Aaron Burr's Farewell Address." *Quarterly Journal of Speech*, 39 (October 1953), 273–82.

Thomas, Gordon L. "Benjamin F. Butler, Prosecutor." *Quarterly Journal of Speech*, 45 (October 1959), 288–98.

Wills, John W. "Benjamin's Ethical Strategy in the New Almaden Case." *Quarterly Journal of Speech*, 50 (October 1964), 259–65.

Wilson, John F. "Harding's Rhetoric of Normalcy, 1920–1923." *Quarterly Journal of Speech*, 48 (December 1962), 406–11.

Part II

CRITICAL APPROACHES

4

Cluster Criticism

The rhetorical theorist and critic who probably has had the greatest impact on rhetorical criticism as it is practiced today is Kenneth Burke. A "specialist in symbol-systems and symbolic action,"[1] Burke's interdisciplinary work crosses the disciplines of philosophy, literature, linguistics, rhetoric, sociology, and economics. Burke spent his life exploring language and its nature, functions, and consequences in books such as *Permanence and Change, Counter-Statement, Attitudes Toward History, The Philosophy of Literary Form, A Grammar of Motives*, and *A Rhetoric of Motives*.[2]

Burke defines rhetoric as "the use of words by human agents to form attitudes or to induce actions in other human agents."[3] The inducement that characterizes rhetoric takes place, Burke suggests, through the process of identification. Individuals form selves or identities through various properties or substances, which include such things as physical objects, occupations, friends, activities, beliefs, and values. As they ally themselves with various properties or substances, they share substance with whatever or whomever they associate and simultaneously separate themselves from others with whom they choose not to identify. Burke uses the term *consubstantial* to describe this association. As two entities are united in substance through common ideas, attitudes, material possessions, or other properties, they are consubstantial.[4] Two artists are consubstantial, for example, in that they share an interest in art. Roommates are consubstantial in that they share living space and a lease agreement.

Burke uses the term *identification* synonymously with *consubstantiality*. Shared substance constitutes an identification between an individual and some property or person: "To identify A with B is to make A 'consubstantial' with B."[5] Burke also equates *persuasion* with *consubstantiality*, seeing persuasion as the result of identification: "You persuade a man only insofar as you can talk his language by speech, gesture, tonality, order, image, attitude, idea, *identifying* your ways with his."[6]

Identification cannot be understood apart from division, which Burke sometimes calls *alienation* or *dissociation*. Human beings are inevitably isolated and divided from one another as a result of their separate physical bodies. The *"individual centrality of the nervous system"* requires that what "the body eats and drinks becomes its special private property; the body's pleasures and pains are exclusively its own pleasures and pains."[7] Although, in the process of identification, "A is 'substantially one' with a person other than himself . . . he remains unique, an individual locus of motives. Thus he is both joined and separate, at once a distinct substance and consubstantial with another."[8]

In division lies a basic motive for rhetoric: people communicate in an attempt to eliminate division. Burke asserts that if individuals were "not apart from one another, there would be no need for the rhetorician to proclaim their unity."[9] Only because of their separation or division do individuals communicate with one another and try to resolve their differences. Paradoxically, then, identification is rooted in division.[10]

One of the ways in which rhetors attempt to create identification is by naming or defining situations for audiences. A speech or a poem, for example, is "a *strategy for encompassing a situation*, an answer to the question posed by the situation.[11] A rhetor sizes up a situation and names its structure and outstanding ingredients. The Constitution of the United States, for example, names a situation concerned with political governance. Calling a person a *friend* or naming the admission standards to a school *rigorous* tells the qualities of the situation that the rhetor deems important.

Rhetoric does not simply provide a name for a situation, however. It also represents a creative strategy for dealing with that situation or for solving the problems inherent in it. Rhetoric offers commands or instructions of some kind, helping individuals maneuver through life and helping them feel more at home in the world. Because rhetoric is a rhetor's solution to perceived problems, it constitutes "equipment for living"[12]—a chart, formula, manual, or map that an audience may consult in trying to decide on various courses of action.

A rhetorical act or artifact provides assistance to its audience in a number of ways. It may provide a vocabulary of thoughts, actions, emotions, and attitudes for codifying and thus interpreting a situation. It may encourage the acceptance of a situation that cannot be changed, or it may serve as a guide for how to correct a situation. In other instances, it may help rhetors justify their conduct, turning actions that seem to be unethical or absurd into ones considered virtuous or accurate. Rhetoric, then, provides an orientation in some way to a situation and provides assistance in adjusting to it.[13]

At the same time that artifacts are functioning to provide equipment for living for audiences, they are revealing the worldview or what Burke calls the *terministic screen*s of the rhetors who created them. The terms we select to describe the world constitute a kind of screen that directs attention to particular aspects of reality rather than others. Our particular vocabularies constitute a reflection, selection, and deflection of reality.[14] Many of our observations, then, *"are but implications of the particular terminology in terms of which the observations are made.* In brief, much that we take as observations about 'reality' may be but the spinning out of possibilities implicit in our particular choice of terms."[15] There are as many different terministic screens as there are people. As Burke suggests, "We can safely take it for granted that no one's 'personal equations' are quite identical with anyone else's" because they are the product of the "peculiar combination of insights associated" with their idiosyncratic combinations of experiences.[16] From the infinite terms available to rhetors, they put together components of rhetoric in a way that reflects who they are, the subjects about which they are engrossed, and the meanings they have for those subjects.

Rhetorical critics can gain insights into rhetors by analyzing the terministic screens evidenced in their rhetoric. Critics can *"track down the kinds of observation implicit in the terminology"* a rhetor has chosen, whether the *"choice of terms was deliberate or spontaneous."*[17] Burke explains the basic approach: "If a writer speaks of life on a mountain, for instance, we start with the impertinent question, 'What is he talking about?' We automatically assume that he is not talking about life on a mountain (not talking *only* about that). Or if he gives us a long chapter on the sewers of Paris, we ask: 'Why that?'—and no matter how realistic his account of the locale may be, we must devote our time to a non-realistic interpretation of his chapter."[18] Cues to rhetors' worldviews and meaning are available by charting the important ingredients of their terministic screens and "noting what follows what."[19]

Burke offers many critical approaches to help a critic discover rhetors' worldviews through an investigation of the rhetoric that constitutes their terministic screens. His notions of identification,[20] representative anecdote,[21] perspective by incongruity,[22] motivational orders,[23] form,[24] and redemption[25] have been used as critical methods for this purpose. Two samples of Burkean methods are included in this book to illustrate the kinds of insights Burkean criticism produces. Cluster criticism is the focus of this chapter, and pentadic criticism is the subject of chapter 11.

In cluster criticism, the meanings that key symbols have for a rhetor are discovered by charting the symbols that cluster around those key symbols in an artifact. Burke explains the central idea of cluster analysis: "Now, the work of every writer [rhetor] contains a set of implicit equations. He uses 'associational clusters.' And you may, by examining his work, find 'what goes with what' in these clusters—what kinds of acts and images and personalities and situations go with his notions of heroism, villainy, consolation, despair, etc."[26] In other words, the task of a critic using this method is to note "what subjects cluster about other subjects (what images *b, c, d* the poet [rhetor] introduces whenever he talks with engrossment of subject *a*)."[27] Burke provides a simple example of how terms that cluster around key terms can illuminate the meanings the rhetor has for those key terms. Speaking about a man with a tic who spasmodically blinks his eyes when certain subjects are mentioned, Burke suggests that if "you kept a list of these subjects, noting what was said each time he spasmodically blinked his eyes, you would find what the tic was 'symbolic' of."[28]

The equations or clusters that a critic discovers in a rhetor's artifact generally are not conscious to the rhetor. As Burke explains, although a rhetor is "perfectly conscious of the act of writing, conscious of selecting a certain kind of imagery to reinforce a certain kind of mood, etc., he cannot possibly be conscious of the interrelationships among all these equations."[29] As a result, the clusters manifest in someone's rhetoric can "reveal, beneath an author's 'official front,' the level at which a lie is impossible. If a man's virtuous characters are dull, and his wicked characters are done vigorously, his art has voted for the wicked ones, regardless of his 'official front.' If a man talks dully of *glory*, but brilliantly employs the imagery of *desolation*, his *true subject* is desolation."[30] A cluster analysis, then, provides "a survey of the hills and valleys" of the rhetor's mind,[31] resulting in insights into the meanings of key terms and thus a worldview that may not be known to the rhetor.

PROCEDURES

Using the cluster method of criticism, a critic analyzes an artifact in a four-step process: (1) selecting an artifact; (2) analyzing the artifact; (3) formulating a research question; and (4) writing the essay.

Selecting an Artifact

Both discursive and nondiscursive artifacts are appropriate for application of the cluster method of criticism. Because the method requires you to identify key terms and the terms that cluster around them, select an artifact that is long enough and complex enough to contain several terms that cluster around the key terms in the artifact. An advertisement with only a few lines of text or a short poem, for example, may not provide enough data for a cluster analysis.

Analyzing the Artifact

Cluster analysis involves three basic steps: (1) identifying key terms in the artifact; (2) charting the terms that cluster around the key terms; and (3) discovering an explanation for the artifact.

Identifying Key Terms

The first step in cluster criticism is to select the key terms in the artifact. Generally, try to select no more than five or six terms that appear to be the most significant for the rhetor. The task of analysis becomes more complex with each term you add.

Significance of terms is determined on the basis of frequency or intensity. A term that is used over and over again by a rhetor is likely to be a key term in that person's thought and rhetoric, so if one term frequently appears in the artifact, that term probably should be selected as one of the rhetor's key terms. In Martin Luther King, Jr.'s speech, "I Have a Dream," for example, *dream* is such a term. A second criterion to use in selecting the rhetor's key terms is intensity. A term may not appear very often in a rhetor's work, but it may be critical because it is central to the argument being made, represents an ultimate commitment, or conveys great depth of feeling. It is a term whose removal would change the nature of the text significantly. In many of George W. Bush's speeches dealing with the aftermath of the terrorist attacks of September 11, *evil* was a key term because it was used as the starting point for many of his arguments and was the focus of the conclusion of many of his speeches. Its intensity suggests that *evil* was a key term for him in these speeches.

Often, the terms that are key for rhetors function as god and devil terms. God terms are ultimate terms that represent the ideal for a rhetor, while devil terms represent the ultimate negative or evil for a rhetor.[32] In the speeches of many politicians, for example, *welfare* and *work* are key terms, with *welfare* a devil term and *work* a god term.

If the artifact you are analyzing is nondiscursive, such as a work of art, the key terms are not words but visual elements. Colors, shapes, or images can serve as key terms. The key terms of the Vietnam Veterans Memorial in Washington, D.C., for example, are its black color, its V shape, and its listing of the names of those who died in Vietnam by date of death.

Charting the Clusters

After you have identified the key terms in the artifact, chart the clusters around those key terms. This process involves a close examination of the artifact to identify each occurrence of each key term and identification of the terms that cluster around each key term. Terms may cluster around the key terms in various ways. They simply may appear in close proximity to the term, or a conjunction such as *and* may connect a term to a key term. A rhetor also may develop a cause-and-effect relationship between the key term and another term, suggesting that one depends on the other or that one is the cause of the other.

A paragraph from Supreme Court Justice Clarence Thomas's speech to the National Bar Association in 1998 illustrates the process of identifying the terms that cluster around a key term—in this case, the term of *criticism*:

> Of course there is much **criticism** of the court by this group or that, depending on the court's decisions in various highly publicized

cases. Some of the **criticism** is profoundly uninformed and unhelpful. And all too often, uncivil second-guessing is not encumbered by
the constraints of facts, logic or reasoned analysis. On the other
hand, the constructive and often scholarly **criticism** is almost always
helpful in thinking about or rethinking decisions. It is my view that
constructive **criticism** goes with the turf, especially when the stakes
are so high and the cases arouse passions and emotions, and, in a free
society, the precious freedom of speech and the strength of ideas. We
at the court could not possibly claim exemption from such **criticism**.
Moreover, we are not infallible, just final.[33]

In this speech, *criticism* is a key term. Terms that cluster around the key
term of *criticism* in this paragraph are: *court, group, decisions, uninformed,
unhelpful, constructive, helpful, turf, scholarly, constructive, cases, (no) exemption,* and *not infallible.*

Discovering an Explanation for the Artifact

At this step of the process, a critic attempts to find patterns in the
associations or linkages discovered in the charting of the clusters as a
way of making visible the worldview constructed by the rhetor. If a
rhetor often or always associates a particular word or image with a key
term, that linkage suggests that the key term's meaning for the rhetor is
modified or influenced by that associated term. If the terms *surveillance*
and *violation of privacy,* for example, usually appear with *freedom* in a
rhetor's speeches, you may speculate that the rhetor's view of freedom is
constrained by these terms associated with security. Security is necessary
to ensure freedom, this rhetor appears to believe, and, as a result, freedom is not a feeling of being unbound and unrestrained. Although you
would want to chart all of the clustering terms around *criticism* before
you looked for patterns in the clusters of Clarence Thomas's speech, the
analysis of the one paragraph begins to suggest that, for Thomas, criticism is a group activity (it involves the court, scholars, and groups), and
it is about standards of judgment, whether those standards are about
who is subject to criticism or what types of criticism are appropriate.

At this point, an agon analysis may help you discover patterns in the
clusters you have identified. Agon analysis is the examination of opposing
terms and involves looking for terms that oppose or contradict other terms
in the rhetoric. Note whether key terms emerge in opposition to other key
terms because such a pattern may suggest a conflict or tension in the
rhetor's worldview or may make explicit the allies and enemies or the god
and devil terms in the rhetor's world. In the contexts surrounding the key
terms, look for opposing terms that cluster around a key term—perhaps
suggesting some confusion or ambiguity on the part of the rhetor about
that term. If *freedom* and *surveillance* are both terms that cluster around
patriotism, for example, you might surmise that, for this rhetor, a conflict
exists between freedom and restriction in the meaning of patriotism.

As a result of your charting of the terms that cluster around the key
terms, you have a dictionary of sorts for the rhetor's key terms. This dic-

tionary suggests the meanings of the key terms for the rhetor and lays out any relationships that emerged among key terms or clustering terms. Your task now is to identify which of the clusters are most interesting and significant and have the most explanatory value for your artifact. You probably chose to analyze your artifact because there is some aspect of the artifact that doesn't fit or that you cannot explain. Perhaps you like the artifact and cannot explain its appeal for you. Perhaps it disturbs you, but you don't know why. Perhaps it seems unusual in some way. The clusters you have identified around key terms can provide an explanation for your initial reactions.

Once again, use the principles of frequency and intensity to discover what is significant about the artifact and can provide an explanation for it. If you discover that many similar terms cluster around all or most of the rhetor's key terms, frequency—a pattern you observe in which the same feature recurs—suggests an important insight into the rhetor's worldview. A major revelation also might emerge from just one of the key terms and its clusters—an insight based on intensity—and you might choose this as your focus in explaining the artifact.

Formulating a Research Question

Knowing the meanings of key terms for a rhetor can be the basis for understanding many different rhetorical processes, so the research questions asked by critics using the cluster method of criticism vary widely. The explanations you develop for your artifact from charting its clusters can suggest questions about, for example, the strategies that are used to accomplish particular objectives, the kinds of meaning that are being communicated, or the implications of particular constructions of meaning for rhetorical processes or public controversies.

Writing the Essay

After completing the analysis, you are ready to write your essay, which includes five major components: (1) an introduction, in which you discuss the research question, its contribution to rhetorical theory, and its significance; (2) a description of the artifact and its context; (3) a description of the method of criticism—in this case, cluster criticism; (4) a report of the findings of the analysis, in which you explain the key terms, the terms that cluster around them, and the meanings for the key terms suggested by the clustered terms; and (5) a discussion of the contribution the analysis makes to rhetorical theory.

SAMPLE ESSAYS

In the sample essays that follow, the cluster method of criticism is used to answer various research questions. Kathaleen Reid analyzes a nondiscursive text, a painting by Hieronymus Bosch, as a way to answer the question: "How do viewers establish the meanings of ambiguous messages?" In "A Cluster Analysis of Enron's *Code of Ethics*," Kimberly C. Elliott analyzes the ethics manual for the failed Enron corporation to answer the question: "How do organizations use new meanings to persuade their members to adhere to prescribed organizational values?" Kristin Nowlen, Shannon Jensen, Deborah A. Gibbs, Robert E. Murphy, Michael R. Taylor, and Wei Wang analyze George W. Bush's "State of the Union" speech of 2003, asking the question: "How do political leaders use rhetoric to induce the public to view another country as an enemy?"

Notes

[1] William H. Rueckert, *Kenneth Burke and the Drama of Human Relations*, 2nd ed. (Berkeley: University of California Press, 1982), p. 227.

[2] For an overview of Burke's rhetorical theory, see Sonja K. Foss, Karen A. Foss, and Robert Trapp, *Contemporary Perspectives on Rhetoric*, 3rd ed. (Prospect Heights, IL: Waveland, 2002), pp. 187–232.

[3] Kenneth Burke, *A Rhetoric of Motives* (1950; rpt. Berkeley: University of California Press, 1969), p. 41.

[4] Substance is discussed in: Burke, *A Rhetoric of Motives*, pp. 20–24; and Kenneth Burke, *A Grammar of Motives* (1945; rpt. Berkeley: University of California Press, 1969), pp. 21–23, 57.

[5] Burke, *A Rhetoric of Motives*, p. 21.

[6] Burke, *A Rhetoric of Motives*, p. 55.

[7] Burke, *A Rhetoric of Motives*, p. 130.

[8] Burke, *A Rhetoric of Motives*, p. 21.

[9] Burke, *A Rhetoric of Motives*, p. 22.

[10] For additional discussions of division, see Burke, *A Rhetoric of Motives*, p. 150; and Kenneth Burke, *The Philosophy of Literary Form: Studies in Symbolic Action* (1941; rpt. Berkeley: University of California Press, 1973), p. 306.

[11] Burke, *The Philosophy of Literary Form*, p. 109.

[12] Burke, *The Philosophy of Literary Form*, pp. 293–304.

[13] Burke discusses the ways in which rhetoric functions to provide assistance in orientation and adjustment in Kenneth Burke, *Counter-Statement* (1931; rpt. Berkeley: University of California Press, 1968), pp. 154–56; and Burke, *The Philosophy of Literary Form*, pp. 64, 294, 298–99.

[14] Kenneth Burke, *Language as Symbolic Action: Essays on Life, Literature, and Method* (Berkeley: University of California Press, 1966), p. 45.

[15] Burke, *Language as Symbolic Action*, p. 46.

[16] Burke, *Language as Symbolic Action*, p. 52.

[17] Burke, *Language as Symbolic Action*, p. 47.

[18] Kenneth Burke, *Attitudes Toward History* (1937; rpt. Berkeley: University of California Press, 1984), p. 191.

[19] Burke, *Attitudes Toward History*, p. 191.

[20] See, for example, Chester Gibson, "Eugene Talmadge's Use of Identification During the 1934 Gubernatorial Campaign in Georgia," *Southern Speech Journal*, 35 (Summer 1970), 342–49.

[21] Barry Brummett explores this notion as a critical tool in "Burke's Representative Anecdote as a Method in Media Criticism," *Critical Studies in Mass Communication*, 1 (June 1984), 161–76.

[22] An example is James L. Hoban, Jr., "Solzhenitsyn on Detente: A Study of Perspective by Incongruity," *Southern Speech Communication Journal*, 42 (Winter 1977), 163–77.

23 See, for example, Karen A. Foss, "Singing the Rhythm Blues: An Argumentative Analysis of the Birth-Control Debate in the Catholic Church," *Western Journal of Speech Communication*, 47 (Winter 1983), 29–44.

24 An example is Jane Blankenship and Barbara Sweeney, "The 'Energy' of Form," *Central States Speech Journal*, 31 (Fall 1980), 172–83.

25 For an example, see Barry Brummett, "Burkean Scapegoating, Mortification, and Transcendence in Presidential Campaign Rhetoric," *Central States Speech Journal*, 32 (Winter 1981), 254–64.

26 Burke, *The Philosophy of Literary Form*, p. 20.

27 Burke, *Attitudes Toward History*, p. 232.

28 Burke, *The Philosophy of Literary Form*, p. 20.

29 Burke, *The Philosophy of Literary Form*, p. 20.

30 Burke, *Attitudes Toward History*, p. 233.

31 Burke, *Attitudes Toward History*, pp. 232–33.

32 Burke, *A Grammar of Motives*, p. 74; Burke, *A Rhetoric of Motives*, pp. 298-301; and Richard M. Weaver, *The Ethics of Rhetoric* (South Bend, IN: Regnery/Gateway, 1953); pp. 211–32.

33 Clarence Thomas, "I am a Man, a Black Man, an American," speech to the National Bar Association, Memphis, Tennessee, July 29, 1998. Available at http://douglass.speech.nwu.edu/thom_b30.htm.

The Hay-Wain
Cluster Analysis in Visual Communication
Kathaleen Reid

The popularity of the fifteenth-century painter Hieronymus Bosch has fluctuated dramatically over the last five centuries. This fluctuation is due, in part, to his surrealistic style; his paintings are executed in brilliant colors and with bold presentation, which was a major deviation from the style typical of the fifteenth century. Also contributing to his on-again, off-again popularity were his apparently mystical statements about humanity's plight here on earth. The paintings depict torment, suffering and unearthly terrors.

Art historians have debated the meaning behind Bosch's visions, but few of their methods have unraveled successfully the cloud of mystery that still envelops his work. What is of concern in this paper is how a rhetorical methodology can be used to understand forms of visual communication such as the painting of Bosch. Also of concern are further issues that apply both to traditional visual media (such as painting) and to modern technological media (such as photography and video): the fixed versus fleeting nature of visual communication (e.g., photographs versus film) and the transition of meaning (including shifts of meaning that occur within a culture as a result of time) through visual images.

The Hay-Wain by Bosch is an example of medieval visual communication designed specifically for use by the public, functioning in ways similar to contemporary mass communication. Originally a triptych, a three-part altar piece, this painting depicts the medieval story of the creation, the fall, and the potential redemption or destruction of humankind. Placed in a cathedral where the populace would have congregated on a regular basis, the triptych would have been viewed simultaneously by all individuals attending worship services. The audience would have been composed of rich and poor, noble and simple, scholars and tradesmen, clergy and laymen. In this way, the painting would function as a form of public visual communication for a diverse audience; therefore, such a painting as this might be considered a predecessor of contemporary mass communication.[1]

The Hay-Wain and other such paintings designed specifically for public audiences provide contemporary public communication scholars with an opportunity to examine early forms of visual communication in which the author of the work presents a narrative through full control over the manipulation of the materials, the ideas, and the representations of objects found within the work. Thus, these early paintings like contemporary narrative film can present stories that may have highly subjective simultaneous representations of natural, supernatural and ideological worlds.

This juxtaposition of the natural and supernatural may result in potentially more ambiguous, difficult messages in both film and traditional media. A rhetorical methodology such as Burke's cluster analysis may aid viewers in establishing the meanings of ambiguous messages. Applying the methodology to a piece of

From *Journal of Communication Inquiry,* 14 (Summer, 1990), 40–54. Used by permission of the Iowa Center for Communication Study and the author.

visual communication such as *The Hay-Wain* simplifies the task of attributing meaning, since the static nature of the painting eliminates the dimensions of movement and time that add complexities to study of film and video.

The Hay-Wain by Hieronymus Bosch, 1485–1490.

In this paper, the visual communication of Bosch's painting—*The Hay-Wain*—has been analyzed in order to: (1) test the applicability of a rhetorical methodology to visual communication and (2) demonstrate how such a methodology can help the audience derive meaning from a highly subjective visual communication such as *The Hay-Wain*, which is often assessed as being so idiosyncratic that its meaning must remain a mystery.

BACKGROUND

Hieronymus Bosch Van Aeken was born around 1450 in southern Holland. His family originally may have been from Aachen, but Bosch was born in a quiet town in the central lowlands called 's Hertogenbosch, which was less than two days' journey from the Dutch artistic capitals of Haarlem and Delft. Bosch was a member of a highly puritanical, nonclerical organization called the Brotherhood of Our Lady, whose staunch religious *Weltanschauung* may have influenced Bosch's artistic visions. He married into a wealthy family, and he had no children. Little else is known of his personal life, except that he died in 1516.

Several attempts have been made to understand Bosch's work, efforts made particularly difficult because of the lack of information about Bosch. Charles de

Tolnay (1965) has made the most complete catalog of Bosch's work, dividing it into three major periods (early, middle, and late). Bosch became more esoteric throughout his career, de Tolnay asserts, moving from traditional approaches to Biblical topics to a more introspective view of creation, redemption, and damnation.

Another of Bosch's chroniclers, Max Friedlander (1969), has sought to find explanations of the artist's unique style and themes in his personal characteristics. He attempts to link what was known about Bosch as a person with the subject matter and themes of his work and suggests that Bosch's idiosyncratic personality explains his divergence from the mainstream of art during the fifteenth century. Friedlander never explains fully, however, what impact Bosch's personality might have had on his individual works.

Still other theories exist to explain why Bosch painted as he did. Cuttler (1968) and Combe (1946) have suggested that belief in alchemy and superstition could have influenced the artistry of someone like Bosch. Bax (1979) suggests that popular folklore and contemporary prose seem an integral part of Bosch's work.

A RHETORICAL PERSPECTIVE

As the above scholarship indicates, Bosch's paintings have been interpreted most often from one of two perspectives: (1) as a product of his personality, or (2) as a product of his environment. Since neither of these deductive methods seems to explain satisfactorily his motive and uniqueness, another approach that may be more adequate is the analysis of a single work without allowing either his personality or history to overshadow its content. Thus, the critic could move from the painting to the man rather than moving from the man to the communication.

One potentially useful perspective for analyzing the meaning behind a form of visual communication, especially work as complex as that of Bosch, is derived from rhetoric. In the past, rhetoric was limited to the study of discursive communication, but, recently, a broader definition has expanded the arena for rhetorical criticism to include non-discursive communication. These non-discursive forms of communication function in a way that is similar to discourse in that they transmit information and evoke some response from the audience. Here the non-discursive form being examined is visual communication, defined as communication through visual forms such as painting, photography, videography, and film.

That such human activity is within the purview of rhetorical criticism was suggested by the Committee on the Advancement and Refinement of Rhetorical Criticism (Sharf, 1979), which reported that the rhetorical critic "studies his subject in terms of its suasory potential or persuasive effect. So identified, rhetorical criticism may be applied to any human act, process, product or artifact" (Sharf 1979, p. 21). Karlyn Kohrs Campbell echoed this sentiment by asserting that "if criticism is to fulfill its function, the rhetorical critic must proclaim: Nothing that is human symbolization is alien to me" (1974, p. 14).

Foss and Radich suggest that art is a form of visual communication that is within the scope of rhetoric because it is a "conscious production to evoke a response" (1980, p. 47). Burke lends further credence to the view that a painting is a visual communicative act when he states:

> For when an art object engages our attention, by the sheer nature of the case we are involved in at least as much of a communicative relationship as prevails between a pitchman and a prospective customer. (1964, p. 106)

Thus, visual communication such as painting can be defined in a way that is similar to verbal communication based on its ability to engage our attention to evoke responses.

This basic parallel between visual and verbal rhetoric—that both convey information and evoke some response from an audience—can be found in the aesthetics studies of art history. Egbert notes that the artist "is intent on expressing something which he feels can best be said through the medium of his art . . ." (1944, p. 99). Gombrich stresses the importance of good articulation in the rhetorical process. When commenting on the works of artists like Constable, he says, "All human communication is through symbols, through the medium of a language [he includes the visual arts in his notion of language] and the more articulate that language the greater the chance for the message to get through" (1960, p. 385).

Just as others use words to describe things, "the artist uses his categories of shapes and color to capture something universally significant in the particular" (Arnheim, 1971, p. vi). Kleinbauer states that "an artist may deliberately or even unconsciously conceal or transfigure his intention, thoughts and experience in his work" (1971, p. 68). These and other theorists indicate that the artist uses his or her techniques as a medium of rhetoric for expressing ideas and experiences just as verbal rhetoric functions to express the experiences of the speaker.

Schools such as the Prague Structuralists reinforce the phenomenological position that both verbal and visual rhetoric function as social artifacts in the communication process. They study how the relationships between creator of the artifact and the interpreter function in forming our society. Their work, especially that of Lotman and Mukarovsky, presents both verbal and visual communication as part of the communication process that constitutes our entire social system (Lotman 1976; Mukarovsky 1977; Morawsky 1974; Lucid 1977; Bailey, Matejka, and Steiner 1980).

METHODOLOGY FOR THE ANALYSIS OF BOSCH'S WORKS

Perhaps one key to unraveling the mystery of Bosch lies in his use of symbolic counterpoint—the juxtaposition of various elements within a single setting.

> Simultaneously attracted by the joys of the flesh and seduced by the promises of asceticism, too much a believer to fall into heresy, but too clear-sighted not to see through the short-comings of the clergy and the evils of the world, dazzled by the beauty and wonders of nature and unwilling to recognize their divine or human value, contenting himself with the *docta ignorantia*, Bosch lays bare the contradictions of his age and makes them the subject of his artistic production. (De Tolnay, 1965, p. 49)

If the juxtaposition of elements is viewed as basic to the structure of his works, then a method to describe this structure may be of value in understanding Bosch.

Burke contends that a communicator consciously or unconsciously juxtaposes ideas within a communication act, showing how he or she sees the meaning of terms. This process of clustering of ideas gives evidence of the communicator's motive for the rhetorical act or work. Burke asserts that the motive and the form of a rhetorical act are inseparable.

In *A Grammar of Motives*, Burke states, "There must . . . be some respect in which the act is a *causa sui*, a motive of itself" (1945, p. 66) and that when one is searching for motives of the communicator, "the thinker will in effect locate the motive under the head of the Act itself" (1945, p. 69). So each act has within it some measure of motive directing the communicator. Duncan clarifies Burke's position: ". . . as we think about human motives, it becomes increasingly obvious that they depend on the forms of communication available to us . . ." (1954, p. xvii).

In order to reveal this motive, Burke develops, in *Attitudes Toward History*, a methodology for discovering what elements are associated with what other elements in the mind of the communicator (1937, p. 233). This methodology is called "cluster analysis," which he clarifies in later essays (Burke, 1954, 1957). Cluster analysis asks "what follows what?" and is concerned with the examination of elements that are linked together by the communicator.

The methodology consists of three steps. The first is the selection of key terms, or the important elements used in the rhetoric. The key terms are selected because of their high frequency and/or high intensity of use (Rueckert 1963, p. 84). Frequency refers to how often the term is repeated, and intensity refers to how significant the term appears to be in the work. Wong (1972) discusses principles of design and notes that the main elements of design in a painting consist of color, line, form, value, texture, rhythm, balance, repetition, similarity, and other design elements. These are used as key terms in this analysis.

The second step is to identify what clusters around each key term each time it appears in painting. This is a description of what elements are adjacent to or in close radius to each key term.

The third step is interpretation of the clusters. In this step, each cluster is analyzed to reveal what potential messages are being presented by the communicator. The interpretations revealed then are examined as a whole to determine an overall interpretation of the painting and a possible explanation of the communicator's motive for creating the work.

While cluster analysis generally has been applied to written discourse, such as Berthold's (1976) analysis of Kennedy's Presidential speeches, it also should provide valuable insights into visual communication.

THE HAY-WAIN

One aspect of Burke's method of cluster analysis is that each communication act is in itself a microcosm of an individual's motives. Thus, to assess these motives, the critic can survey, in detail, a single communicative act to derive understanding of motive. Because Bosch's paintings universally contain contradictory elements I have narrowed the scope of this investigation to a single work—*The Hay-Wain*. Not only is it one of Bosch's most recognizable works, but many art historians have selected it as highly representative of his paintings in general. The work is a triptych—composed of three panels—and is attributed to the start of Bosch's middle period, painted sometime around 1485–1490.

The central panel of the painting shows a hay wagon overflowing with hay and drawn by a team of minotaur-like creatures. The wagon is surrounded by peasants clamoring to grab pieces of hay, while other peasants are crushed beneath the wheels. Common interpretation suggests that this scene was taken from a Flemish proverb that says that the world is a haystack from which each person plucks what he or she can. Behind the wagon is a procession headed by clerical figures who look down upon the melee from horseback with stoic aloofness. On top of the hay are lovers, flanked by an angel and a demon. This central, frantic scene is counterpointed by the depiction of everyday activities—such as a woman changing a baby's diaper, another cooking food, and a patient being tended by a medieval physician in the foreground. Above hovers a large cloud containing the Christ figure, with His hands raised in a blessing.

The left panel is a traditional visualization of the story of creation and follows Adam and Eve from their "birth" to their expulsion from the Garden. Executed mainly in tranquil blues and greens, this panel portrays a peaceful environment except for three elements: rebellious angels being cast from the heavens, the serpent tempting the couple inside the Garden, and the archangel with drawn sword guarding the entrance to the Garden.

In stark contrast to the left panel, the right panel is a scene of unearthly horrors, with demons attacking naked humans in front of a tower. The whole panel is crowned with violent reds and oranges, representing fire and smoke. Colors are flat and bold. The figures seem to bathe in the light, turning them shades of pink and orange, totally different from the jaundiced skin of those in the center panel and from the skin tones provided by the blues and greens of the left panel.

KEY ELEMENTS

The figures in this painting appear small and somewhat weightless as they engage in numerous activities. Still dominant is Bosch's concern with color. The golden mass of hay on the wagon is the central focus and part of the first and most striking key term—gold color. In *The Hay-Wain*, the use of the bright golden color dominating the central panel is a significant design element. By its dominance— via size and intensity or brightness—it attracts the eye more rapidly than other important, yet less significant design elements. By its eminence and brightness, the gold color shows high intensity; therefore, it is considered a major key term.

While the golden color was the most dominant and intense design element, repetition and similarity were the major criteria for choosing the other key terms. These were the arch shape, ladders, clerics, couples, fish, and the boar. Similarity was a strong criterion for choosing the two arches as key elements. They are of the same elongated form and both serve the same function as portals or entry ways. The same is true of the ladders. Two ladders are parallel in structure, length, and usage.

The other key terms—clerics, couples, fish, and boars—were chosen because of frequency; they each occur in the painting three or more times. Clerics are presented in three places. Four couples—as prototypes of the original Adam and Eve—appear. The fish or variations of the fish appear three times and the same is true for the boar. Because the image of the boar is connected to that of the fish in two places, the boar and the fish are treated as one unit.

CLUSTERS AROUND KEY ELEMENTS

Gold Color. The golden-yellow color that pervades the painting is one of its most striking elements. The two golden clouds that float in the blue sky contain the figure of God as judge and the figure of Christ. The God-judge figure is surrounded by the rebellious angels who are being cast from heaven. Their blue and light-red tones contrast with the bright yellow of the cloud in which they are placed. The golden cloud is matched by a similar one in the upper portion of the center panel. Within this cloud, Christ is isolated from others. His hands, with their bleeding wounds, are raised as if in blessing, and the light-red drapery surrounding His pierced body is similar in color to the clothing of the God-judge figure.

Most of the gold color is found in the central panel. Creating a large golden triangle, the large patch of color includes the majority of the center ground and has as its central focus the hay wagon. Within this golden triangle are many scenarios: people fighting, others scrambling to grab a piece of hay, a woman tending an injured man, peasants being crushed by the wagon, a boar's head and a fish roasting over a fire, and anthropomorphic creatures such as the boar-like demonic figure pulling the wagon toward hell. At the apex of the triangle is a soberly clad pilgrim. Standing with his staff, he carries a small child on his shoulders and is accompanied by an adolescent. The small trio seems separated from the crowd; yet, they are a part of life on earth as they stand adjacent to women involved in everyday activities.

Ladders. Bosch has incorporated two similar ladders in *The Hay-Wain*. These are parallel in design and structure, one resting against the wagon in the center panel and the other leaning against the tower in the right panel. The ladder of the center panel is held by a member of the crowd, apparently attempting to climb toward the couple on top. The ladder of the right panel holds a demon who is climbing it in order to work on building the tower. Members of the clergy and nobility are next to the center ladder. At the base of the ladder in the right panel, a group of demons in animalistic form leads a naked human toward the tower.

Arches. Two arches are significant elements. These two key terms are similar not only in size and shape but also similar in function and location within the painting. The similar function is that they are both entry ways, one in the left panel and one in the right. The left-panel arch is the entrance into the pastoral Garden of Eden, which is barred by the archangel who threatens the now-guilty Adam and Eve. The other arch symmetrically positioned in the right panel is filled with blackness. Before it cowers a figure reminiscent of Adam, who is being pushed toward the portal by a demon with a staff.

Couples. Bosch has included several couples in *The Hay-Wain*, all of whom have either a good or evil supernatural figure near them. Adam and Eve are shown in a number of vignettes: in one, depicting the creation, God as creator is standing with them; the fall of humankind is depicted in the vignette containing the couple and the serpent. The most prominent pair are being thrown out of the Garden by the archangel, and their flight leads the viewer directly into the center panel with all of its banality and travail. The second prominent couple sits on top of the hay wagon, flanked by an angel and a demon. This pair enjoys the music of a lute player, and they are oblivious to the turmoil just below their feet. They do not display the anguish of those who struggle to attain the heights of the wagon, but they are equally unaware that the wagon is being dragged toward damnation.

Fish and Boar. A fish appears on the spit by the fire in the center panel, waiting to serve as nourishment for the humans around it. The immediate environment suggests the humdrum of everyday life, with the fish being just one more artifact of human existence. In the same panel, however, the fish symbol begins to change. It becomes a demonic half-fish, half-human creature that is helping pull the wagon into hell. In the right panel, the fish symbol is perverted even more, so that now the fish feeds upon the human rather than the opposite. This scene also is surrounded by activities, but these are the activities of hell, such as an emaciated black-hooded demonic priest carrying a human on a spit, animals attacking men, and other grotesque torture of humans.

Because of the similarity of their treatment, the boar is placed in the same cluster as the fish. The boar's head, along with the fish, is being roasted over the open fire. It, too, will serve as part of a meal for the women around the fire. Boar-headed creatures also are found pulling the wagon toward hell. Unlike the fish, the boar is not as clearly found in the right panel—though some demonic faces are reminiscent of a boar.

Clerics. Church figures appear in opposite corners of the center panel. In the upper left, prelates mounted on horses observe the anguish of the peasants as they fight around the wagon. In the lower right corner, nuns carry hay to a priest who calmly sits oblivious to what is happening around him. These people are outside the flow of action but have potentially significant positions. In the right panel, directly across from the black-hooded priest located in the central panel, is a black-hooded demonic priest who carries a human thrust upon a spit-like staff. This demonic cleric is a mocking replica of the priest sitting amongst the nuns in the center panel.

INTERPRETATION OF CLUSTERS

Examination of the clusters in *The Hay-Wain* reveals a common theme—that of transition. Whether the symbols in each cluster reveal a physical transition such as the moving hay wagon or a more esoteric transition such as the moral transition of Adam and Eve, this theme is suggested in each cluster.

Gold Color. While the golden-color cluster is the most dominant key term and gives an underlying commonality to the diverse elements contained within the cluster, it is also the most confusing. Contained within this large cluster are terms of both good and evil. Because it represents warmth, prosperity, and power in most cultures, it lends a positive atmosphere to the cluster. This positiveness is offset somewhat by such negative elements as greed and conflict as people struggle for handfuls of hay.

The God-judge figure in the gold cluster immediately and visually transmits the concept of transition as the rebellious angels are forced to leave the heavens. The second element, Christ with hands raised, does not indicate transition visually; yet, traditionally in the Christian religion, Christ represents the greatest of all transitions. He descends from heaven to earth and ascends back to heaven. He was God who became human and the One who moved from life to death, from immortal to mortal and from temporal to eternal. Via Him, humans also may attain these characteristics, thereby moving the individual past human limitations.

With the hay wagon in the gold-color cluster, Bosch presents the viewer with both a physical transition—the journey along the earthly trail—and an esoteric transition—the journey of greed that takes a person from life on earth to life in hell. The pilgrim shares this same duality, both a physical and an esoteric transition. Physically, the pilgrim is on a journey through the plane containing the mob surrounding the hay wagon. Also, by definition, a pilgrim refers to a wayfarer on a spiritual journey as he or she seeks to make the transition from a mundane plateau to a more holy place.

Ladders. The first prominent ladder in this painting speaks of an important transition, for the individual may follow the ladder in the central panel to the false plateau atop the hay wagon, or he or she may continue in an upward direction toward Christ. The parallel ladder in the right panel allows the person ascending to reach the top of the tower, while the viewer's eye again allows for a transition from the bottom of the ladder to the ladder's ultimate direction—into the depths of hell where the fire burns the brightest.

Arches. The two major arches function as portals, openings leading from one setting to another. The concept of transition is found in the left panel, as the arch is the doorway from earthly life to paradise. The interior side of the portal is smooth and straight, seemingly indicating an easy movement from paradise to outside, while movement in the opposite direction is much more difficult because of the archangel guarding the rough-hewn facade on the outer side of the portal. Although some light flows through the archway, the rocky exterior, irregular and rugged, seems to denote this as a portal from God's grace into the travails of humanity. In contrast, the corresponding archway in the right panel is smooth and sleek. This architecturally precise portal makes entrance into the black interior easy, while the demon holding a wooden beam seems to block anything trying to exit the interior of the tower. The darkness of the interior of a building that has no roof speaks of a transition into an unnatural, black void.

Couples. Major transitional aspects can be noted among the couples. In the left panel, Adam and Eve make both moral and immortal-mortal transitions as they succumb to the temptation presented by the serpent in the garden. The transition from one life to another is presented in the couple's removal from a perfect garden, which required no work, to a life of toil outside the gates of paradise. Both physical and spiritual journeys are presented in the couple on the wagon in the center panel. Physically, they are being transported, while spiritually they are continuing in a destructive, even if entertaining, direction. Thus, when the couples are followed through the narrative via the composition leading from one vignette to the next, we can note the idea of transition on both physical and metaphoric levels.

Fish and Boar. Both the fish and boar representations suggest a transition of power. Both are presented in a traditional fashion such as food being prepared for a household. The next appearance of a fish and boar is in anthropomorphic form, human legs with either a boar or fish head, and they are part of the power that pulls the loaded wagon toward hell. The right panel, while not clearly presenting the boar, does present the fish in its final form—a red-eyed monster that has human legs instead of fins. But more grotesque than its form is its action: it is swallowing a human being. This is the ultimate transition in power. Instead of the fish functioning as nourishment for the humans who control the animals, the fish now feasts upon the humans whom they now control.

Clerics. Even if it has not actually occurred yet, the prelates astride their horses seem to present the transition of the church from an organization that is deeply involved in the concerns of the people to an organization of clerics who merely observe, not prevent, the people moving in the direction of damnation. The group of nuns is located at the entrance of hell, and although they are not as compositionally active in carrying the eye from the center panel to the right as are the half-humans pulling the wagon, they are still part of the visual transition into hell. That they are part of the transition seems incongruous with their role as representatives of religion. Perhaps more fascinating is Bosch's placement of the black-hooded demon immediately adjacent to the black-hooded priest. Though located in separate panels, their physical proximity causes the viewer to recognize immediately the similarity between the two figures. This presents the illusion of a transition from an easy-going priest to a sadistic ogre.

In summary, the two major themes derived from this interpretation center around transition. The first theme deals with the transition of life from that which is good and innocent to that which eventually may be and most often is destructive. Only two of the transitions are positive: the Christ figure, who offers salvation through a transition from mortal to immortal life, and the pilgrim, who seeks to attain a higher spiritual being. Except for the pilgrim, no other human on earth seems exempt from a destructive transition, and even the success of the pilgrim is questioned since the path appears difficult to follow. The second theme is the transition of power from the humans to outside forces, whether they are supernatural animals that become masters of human beings or the Christ figure as master when the individual chooses the difficult route along with the pilgrim.

In numerous ways the transitions suggest the loss of the "autonomous" individual. In each vignette of couples, supernatural figures such as imps and angels can be found, and power over the individual shifts to those beings. The center panel demonstrates the loss of power as individuals strive to control each other as they fight one another for the hay. The major and final transition of power to others outside of the self is shown in the right panel. While the center panel shows that humans have delusions of power in their attempts to control each other and the animals (roasting the fish and boar, prelates riding on horses), the right panel illustrates the final, most tragic transition of power: the animals mutilate and torture the humans, who had controlled them in the center panel.

Bosch seems to be motivated in *The Hay-Wain* by an over-riding pessimism that indicates that all the world is doomed for destruction. He does provide a limited amount of optimism by placing the Christ figure and the pilgrim within the gold cluster suggesting warmth, prosperity, power and security. That touch of optimism, however, seems largely overshadowed by the sweeping movement of the entire painting toward hell. Thus, Bosch seems motivated to shove people out of their complacent acceptance of life viewed only from a single perspective, although he seems to doubt his ability to produce change in the perspectives and direction of most individuals.

Also revealed in the analysis were four important presuppositions. These reinforce Bosch's motive for persuading individuals to consider the transitions of their lives. As the painting indicates, he is predominantly concerned with the spiritual and moral transitions, not the physical.

The Ambiguity of Human Existence. Ambiguity, uncertainty of a symbol's meaning, is one of the first presuppositions generally noted about the paintings of Bosch. In one place, a symbol has one meaning and in another place, its counterpart has an opposite meaning. This is demonstrated, for example, by his use of the arch shape, where one arch leads into a beautiful garden and the other into a tower of punishment for humans. Duality also is seen in the ladder symbol, where one ladder leads to Christ and salvation, and the other points toward blackness, fire, and eternal torture.

Such contradictions with their resulting ambiguity suggest that Bosch understood the reflexive nature of symbols. The reflexivity that he demonstrated using the arch, ladder, and fish illustrates his consciousness of the complexity of the many facets of life. As a result, Bosch perceived life as being ambiguous, with the artifacts of life drawing meaning from their surroundings; their meanings are not fixed. These artifacts can fall on the side of good or evil, and Bosch's placement of elements seems to state his recognition of right and wrong. He seems to believe that anything can be an instrument of salvation or perdition.

Demonstration of the Reality of the Supernatural. The supernatural elements are not treated as dreams or figments of the imaginations of the individuals within the painting; rather, they are treated the same way as the human, earthly figures. This can be seen with clusters surrounding the couples and, in particular, with the archangel guarding the entrance to the garden. The archangel with drawn sword is truly there, as he refuses to allow Adam and Eve to reenter the garden. The couples in the garden also are in a pastoral setting that is treated as natural and real. One couple is seated above the hay wagon happily singing with the angel and demon perched near their shoulders being as clearly and naturally depicted as the couple.

Further evidence of this treatment of the supernatural as the natural can be seen in the gold-color cluster. The Christ figure's physical portrayal is as accurate as the painting of the pilgrim at the apex of the golden triangle. Also within the golden cluster are the anthropomorphic figures that are pulling the wagon. In particular, the boar-headed creatures are as real as the boar's head roasting over the fire near the everyday activities of the women in the foreground. This portrayal of anthropomorphic creatures as being as real as the people in the crowd makes this painting gruesome. The strife and death shown in the golden triangle are mere forerunners of that which follows in the right panel, where humans suffer eternal torture.

Bosch shows the viewer a hideousness that is a tangible, real entity. His view of hell is as real in his mind and in this painting as is the common daily life portrayed in the center panel. This is indeed no dream, but rather a *wakeful reality* in which humans must overcome depravity just as surely as they must overcome the trials of earthly existence.

Choice in Life. Bosch made clear that one must select a path of salvation or destruction and that one must seek guidance in order to complete the journey successfully. He depicts the people with decisions to be made; decisions that have direct impact upon their current lives. They choose to fight or not fight for the hay, for example, and for their eternal destiny. These are illustrated by the clusters around the gold color. Only the pilgrim seems to have the strength to make the difficult choice. At the apex of the triangle, he must choose one of two paths. One of those paths is difficult; it goes against the cultural customs and norms such as grabbing pieces of the hay. The pilgrim must traverse through the crowd and climb higher than those around him. He must not stop on the false plateau atop the hay wagon, where the couple sits. Rather, he must continue toward the next golden cloud of color—toward Christ, who acts as intercessor for the pilgrim on the long, difficult journey.

Questioning the Role of the Church. In this painting, the clergy are not acting in their traditional role of "priests for confession"; instead, Church officials are following the wagon of destruction. The other members of the Church are now nuns, whose interaction with people outside the Church is limited to the one playing cat's cradle. This lack of interaction seems to indicate more concern with internal problems than with caring for those around them in dire need of help. Bosch does not want to exclude the Church from the life drama of salvation, but he has difficulty justifying the excesses of the clergy that infected the Church of the fifteenth century. He could not bring himself to give the clergy a key role, but neither could he bring himself to exclude them, depicting them as he viewed their lack of effectiveness in aiding humanity.

On the basis of these four indicators, the basic motive of *The Hay-Wain* is reinforced. It seems to be that Bosch had a high level of concern for his fellow human beings who cannot act alone and who must eventually face the reality of perdition if they continue in their current direction.

This motive is enhanced further by noting the relationships of the indicators to each other. The high levels of ambiguity in the painting generally confuse viewers and lead them to conclude that Bosch is either inconsistent or a mystic who follows his own rules of logic. However, if we take that ambiguity as simply an indicator of his recognition that things are not always as they first appear, and that there are two sides to a coin, then internal consistency demands that Bosch note both sides and that he question whether or not something is always as good as it first seems.

The second indicator, demonstration of the supernatural as real, takes this ambiguity into a level that incorporates the earthly and the supernatural. It explains why so many seemingly harmless things on earth can have a flip side that is detrimental for people. For example, a common wagon becomes an instrument of destruction for the people snatching at the hay. It suggests the potential of a greed that can destroy totally and the supernatural forces that affect the individual's decisions.

If Bosch held these presuppositions, as *The Hay-Wain* indicates, then he would be highly concerned about the plight of those around him. He deals with these presuppositions by illustrating the difficulty of choosing the right path. This is accomplished by placing the pilgrim at a distance from the Christ-figure, who can provide salvation. Yet he gives hope by placing Christ in a bright golden cloud that the pilgrim can keep in sight as he traverses the tumultuous path on earth.

Another way in which Bosch acts upon these presuppositions is to question the role of the Church. This questioning is natural since traditionally the Church's major responsibility is for the spiritual and physical lives of the people. Therefore, Bosch would seek to evaluate how well the Church's representatives were performing, since failure on their part could have severe consequences for individuals.

The basic motivation of concern for others, which I have derived, may seem too simple and too obvious. However, Bosch's complexity of design and his mixing of cues (i.e., a nun playing cat's cradle instead of binding the wounds of the injured) confuses the casual observer who then questions what his true stance and motive might have been. This cluster analysis, which began by examining clusters of elements around key symbols of the painting, shows that Bosch indeed did hold and express a consistent perspective regarding human life on earth.

CONCLUSION

The purposes of this paper were to: (1) discover whether highly subjective visual communication such as the work of Bosch can be deciphered; and (2) to test whether a rhetorical methodology such as Burke's cluster analysis can be applied to visual communication. Although, by its nature, cluster analysis permits the discovery and analysis of the structure of a form of visual communication first and foremost, it also suggests dimensions of the communicator's character. This methodology has revealed enough insights to affirm that Bosch was not so idiosyncratic that he cannot be understood.

The cluster analysis reveals repeated patterns of elements within the painting that had high levels of consistency. While the consistency found may be the result of the critic's biases, I propose that enough clarity exists to suggest that Bosch, though intricate and complex, is not as bewildering as many observers assume. The consistencies found through cluster analysis support the idea that this work is not simply a private language of a communicator who cannot be understood except by his contemporaries. For through an analysis such as this, the critic can examine the underlying framework of the paintings, "what goes with what," and determine what synonyms and metaphors Bosch has expressed in his communication.

The cluster analysis reveals one of the major conflicts in Bosch's work that accounts for much of the confusion surrounding his work regarding intended meaning. The conflict is defined as the point at which traditional cultural images such as the figure of Christ meet and clash with incongruities. Such conflict is found in the distant figure of Christ, seemingly isolated from others, in *The Hay-Wain*. Bosch takes the traditional and places it in a context that at first is confusing: Why is the figure of Christ so distant? Why is Christ not interacting with those in the groups around Him? Perhaps, Bosch is asking the viewer, as well as himself, to contemplate the role of traditional Christian spirituality in the midst of the fluctuating Western world of the fifteenth and early sixteenth centuries.

Whether this questioning reflects Bosch's own private skepticism and doubt or whether it is a rhetorical tool to push viewers to face issues regarding their psychological and physical destiny cannot be determined by this study. Whichever is the case, this painting by Bosch has continued through the years as a rhetorical device that challenges the observer to question his or her own understanding of the issues portrayed in the process of trying to understand Bosch.

The primary purpose of the paper, to test whether a rhetorical methodology can be applied to visual communication, however, raises a number of issues that should be considered. Cluster analysis is based on the assumption that the connotative meaning of a term can be known by examining the context of that element. Questions arise as to how those connotative meanings are derived and interpreted when cluster analysis is applied to visual communication.

One area of concern is with the data—the paintings by Bosch. The nature of this form of communication is fixed rather than fleeting. An important distinction between visual communication such as painting and photography and other types of communication is that the forms within painting and photography are "fixed."[2] The advantage is that there is no need to halt a process as when "freezing" a frame in film or when using recordings. While cluster analysis could be applied to fleeting communication (incorporating paralinguistics and other aspects of the spoken word) perhaps it is most easily applied to fixed data where the structure and context of elements can be more easily examined, collected, and interpreted.

Another issue is to what extent we should treat the visual communication as a language. If, in using cluster analysis, we do indeed treat visual images as language, we ignore differences between the images and full language systems. In other words, we need to examine to what extent Burke's methodological procedures are grounded in his understanding of language systems and are at least partially ruled by those presuppositions.

Like other forms of nonverbal communication that are not full language systems, some basic questions may need to be asked: (1) Is there a given rule structure governing how visual symbols should be put together, just as there is a full rule structure for use of verbal language? (2) Based on Burke's ideas of the distinction between verbal and nonverbal communication, can visual communication reference the negative (communicate absence of joy, absence of pain)? (3) Can the visual communications be self-reflective—talk about themselves as in verbal language, when Mary says that Joe says that Bill says that Janie says? (4) We know that visual communication is not time bound in the sense that it can depict events of yesterday and today as well as project scenes into the future. But does visual communication have full ability to indicate past, present, and future tense? Can it depict present perfect, past perfect, or future perfect tense? What about the subjunctive mood?[3] Perhaps these four areas are not crucial for the use of cluster analysis and interpretation; however, these are ways in which visual communication may differ from verbal communication that could present potential problems if we treat the two in the same manner.

Still another issue revealed in this application of cluster analysis to visual communication concerns methodology. A major drawback to examining a painting or photograph rather than discourse is that the critic is presented with a more limited number of symbols. A comparison to clarify my point would be to look at the difference between a short poem by e. e. cummings as compared to a lengthy address by President J. F. Kennedy. Social artifacts such as paintings, photographs, and poems that contain fewer elements may create problems in generating sufficient material to study when using the methodology of cluster analysis.

A final issue in this kind of application involves interpretation. A major problem here concerns the high level of reflexivity found in visual communication. While written and spoken language is reflexive, it expresses as much by what is between words as by the words themselves; there is even more reflexivity in visual communication, since elements such as those found in paintings are not always as specific as words for describing the communicator's intentions. This high level of reflexivity allows for more multiple realities than do words. The extent to which the visual communicator and viewer have similar interpretations is based on the extent of their shared knowledge and understanding of the elements (Merleau-Ponty 1964, 1968).

Despite these issues that arise from the application of cluster analysis, the rhetorical perspective helps open the door for more research regarding visual communication. However, further research needs to be done in order to establish more clearly the boundaries of cluster analysis and how it might relate to contemporary media such as film and video that have a fleeting rather than fixed nature. I hope this application of cluster analysis can challenge and encourage others within the field of communication to apply this method to "fleeting" communication and to explore further the issues raised.

Notes

[1] The distinction that often is made between fine arts, mass mediated and applied arts is subject to much debate. Dondis (1973), for instance, suggests that the dichotomy between fine and applied

arts is false. He notes the varying historical perspectives, emphasizing that groups such as the Bauhaus made no distinctions. Painting, architecture, photography, all were assumed to have similar communicative functions. Dondis further emphasizes his point by noting that "The idea of a 'work of art' [fine art] is a modern one, reinforced by the concept of the museum as the ultimate repository of the beautiful. . . . This attitude removes art from the mainstream, gives it an aura of being special and petty, reserves it for an elite, and so negates the true fact of how it is struck through our lives and our world. If we accept this point of view, we abdicate a valuable part of our human potential. We not only become consumers with not very sharp criteria, but we deny the essential importance of visual communication both historically and in our own lives" (1973, p. 6). Contemporary critics who view Bosch's *Hay-Wain* in the art museum must remember that the current setting was not its original. It was not designed with the purpose of being simply a work of fine art; rather, its form and function was one of public communication.

2 This characteristic is based on Ricoeur's (1971, p. 528) notion of fleeting versus fixed communication. He notes that spoken language is fleeting, and the written text is fixed. The major distinction between them is their temporal aspects. Fleeting communication is the "instance of discourse," while fixed communication exists and continues over time in the form originally intended by the communicator.

3 For further elaboration of these concepts see Burgoon and Saine (1978, pp. 18–20). In addition to these four questions by Burgoon and Saine, other works that question similarities and differences among visual art and other forms of rhetoric include Barthes (1977, pp. 32–51) and Eco (1976, pp. 190–216).

References

Arnheim, R. (1971). *Art and Visual Perception*. Berkeley: University of California.

Bailey, R. W., Matejka, L., and Steiner, P. ([1978] 1980). *The Sign: Semiotics around the World*. Reprint. Ann Arbor, MI: Slavic Publications.

Barthes, R. (1977). *Image Music Text*. New York: Hill and Wang.

Bax, D. (1979). *Hieronymus Bosch: His Picture-Writing Deciphered*. Montclair, NJ: Abner Schram.

Berthold, C. A. (1976). "Kenneth Burke's Cluster-Agon Method: Its Development and an Application." *Central States Speech Journal*, 27, 302–09.

Burgoon, J. K. and Saine, T. (1978). *The Unspoken Dialogue*. Boston: Houghton Mifflin.

Burke, K. (1945). *A Grammar of Motives*. New York: Prentice-Hall.

Burke, K. (1954). "Fact, Inference, and Proof in the Analysis of Literary Symbolism," in Bryson, L. (ed.), *Symbols and Values: An Initial Study* (pp. 283–306). New York: Harper and Brothers.

Burke, K. (1957). *Philosophy of Literary Form*. rev. ed. New York: Vintage.

Burke, K. ([1937] 1961). *Attitudes Toward History*. Reprint. Boston: Beacon Press.

Burke, K. (1964). On Form. *Hudson Review*, 17, 106.

Campbell, K. K. (1974). Criticism: Ephemeral and Enduring. *Speech Teacher*, 23, 14.

Combe, J. (1946). *Jheronimus Bosch*. Paris, France: Pierre Tisne.

Cuttler, C. D. (1968). *Northern Painting from Puccelle to Bruegel/Fourteenth, Fifteenth, and Sixteenth Centuries*. New York: Holt, Rinehart and Winston.

De Tolany, C. (1965). *Hieronymus Bosch*. New York: Reynal.

Dondis, D. A. (1974). *A Primer of Visual Literacy*. Cambridge: Massachusetts Institute of Technology.

Duncan, H. D. (1954). Introduction to *Performance and Change*, by K. Burke. Indianapolis: Bobbs-Merrill.

Eco, U. (1976). *A Theory of Semiotics*. Bloomington: Indiana University Press.

Egbert, D. D. (1944). "Foreign Influences in American Art," in Bowers, D. F. (ed.), *Foreign Influences in American Life: Essays and Critical Bibliographies* (pp. 99–126). Princeton: Princeton University Press.

Foss, S. K. and Radich, A. J. (1980). The Aesthetic Response to Nonrepresentational Art: A Suggested Model. *Review of Research in Visual Arts Education*, 12(4), 40–49.

Friedlander, M. J. ([1937] 1969). *Early Netherlandish Painting*. Vol. 5, *Geertgen tot Sint Jans and Jerome Bosch*. Reprint, with translation by H. Norden. New York: Frederick Praeger.

Gombrich, E. H. (1960). *Art and Illusion: A Study in the Psychology of Pictorial Representation*. New York: Pantheon Books.

Guillaud, J. and M. (in collaboration with Isabel Matco Gomez) (1989). *Hieronymus Bosch: The Garden of Earthly Delights*. Ian Robson, Translator. New York: Clarkson N. Potter.

Kleinbauer, W. E. (1971). *Modern Perspectives in Western Art History*. New York: Holt, Rinehart and Winston.

Lotman, Y. (1976). *Analysis of the Poetic Text*. Ed. D. B. Johnson. Ann Arbor: Ardis.

Lucid, D. P., ed. (1977). *Soviet Semiotics*. Baltimore: Johns Hopkins University Press.

Merleau-Ponty, M. (1964). *Signs*. Evanston: Northwestern University Press.

Merleau-Ponty, M. (1968). *The Visible and the Invisible*. Ed. C. Lefort. Evanston: Northwestern University Press.

Morawsky, S. (1974). *Inquiries into the Fundamentals of Aesthetics*. Cambridge: Massachusetts Institute of Technology.

Mukarovsky, J. (1977). *The Word and Verbal Art*. Ed. J. Burbank and P. Steiner. New Haven: Yale University Press.

Reid-Nash, K. (1984). *Rhetorical Analysis of the Paintings of Hieronymus Bosch*. University of Denver.

Ricoeur, P. (1971). The Model of the Text: Meaningful Action Considered as a Text. *Social Research*, 38, 529–62.

Rueckert, W. H. (1963). *Kenneth Burke and the Drama of Human Relations*. Minneapolis: University of Minnesota Press.

Sharf, B. F. (1979). Rhetorical Analysis of Nonpublic Discourse. *Communication Quarterly*, 21(3), 21–30.

Wong, W. (1972). *Principles of Two-dimensional Design*. New York: Van Nostrand Reinold.

A Cluster Analysis of Enron's *Code of Ethics*
Kimberly C. Elliott

Enron is a name known worldwide for American corporate corruption, ethical failure, executive misconduct, and financial collapse. Most anyone told of Enron's *Code of Ethics* responds with surprise that the company even had one. The published *Code,* once distributed to all Enron employees, became such a curiosity after the company's failure that the Smithsonian Institution acquired a copy of the document for display. Indeed, a common understanding of the meaning of *ethics* coupled with even a cursory understanding of how Enron operated suggests that ethics had little bearing upon Enron's operations.

In his book *The Words We Live By*, Brian Burrell explains, "a code [of ethics] must address questions involving moral choice—what people ought to do, as opposed to what they are required to do. Any set of rules that is made mandatory, therefore, cannot be about ethics." A code of ethics, then, "cannot properly be about ethics unless it restricts its scope to ideals, suggestions, goals, and general principles. What is ethical is clearly and easily distinguishable from what is merely required." [1]

If Enron's ethics are listed in their entirety within its *Code of Ethics*, then Burrell's description of ethics validates a common perception: Enron had virtually no ethics. Cluster analysis of the *Code* reveals Enron's consistent equation of legal requirements and ethics. Far from distinguishing between what is *merely required* and what is ethical, the company implies that they are one and the same. By doing so, the company assigns what Kenneth Burke calls a "new meaning" to the word *ethics*. With new meanings, Burke explains, we are asked to "alter our orientations." [2]

Enron's new meaning of *ethics* suggests some explanation for its now-legendary organizational ethical failure wherein many individual employees seemed to have lost or suspended any basic understanding of what is right or wrong. With this cluster analysis, I will seek some insight into how an organization might use *new meanings* to persuade its members to set aside their own values and judgments in favor of adhering to prescribed organizational values and rules.

BACKGROUND

On December 2, 2001, Enron Corp. filed for Chapter 11 bankruptcy protection following a failed merger attempt, massive financial losses, a swift and precipitous fall in its market value, the launch of a Securities and Exchange Commission investigation into some of its activities and amid emerging reports of staggering executive misconduct that included personal enrichment. Not only was Enron's bankruptcy filing the largest in U.S. history, but the failure of Enron launched a severe crisis of confidence in corporate America's ethics. Three months later, a company publication dated July, 2000, entitled the *Enron Code of Ethics*, was a top-selling item in eBay's online auctions, commanding up to $225 per copy. One former employee offered a copy in perfect condition, stating that it had "never

This essay was written while Kimberly C. Elliott was a student in Sonja K. Foss's rhetorical criticism class at the University of Colorado at Denver in 2003. Used by permission of the author.

been read." Observers might have concluded that Enron's ethical void grew from employee indifference to the *Code of Ethics*. My analysis of the document suggests otherwise. Close adherence to the *Enron Code of Ethics* would not have yielded ethical employee behavior because the document is not about ethics.

At Enron, ethics were defined by and limited to laws. Cluster analysis of the company's *Code of Ethics* suggests that Enron's leadership either mistook legal compliance and protection of company assets for ethical conduct or simply applied the *Code of Ethics* title to its legal compliance manual after writing it. The result is either an unlikely title for the document's content or unlikely content for the document's title.

Previously published analyses of the document have assumed the *Code of Ethics* was about ethics. In other words, reliance was placed upon the title rather than its incongruous contents. Ethical theorists and business journalists have discussed various reasons that simply having a code of ethics does not ensure ethical behavior, neglecting to discuss what having a code of ethics that does not address ethics might cause. Evaluations consistently have concluded that the company's "ethical lapses" resulted from disregard for its own *Code of Ethics*. Few writers have made any reference at all to the contents of the document. Comments appear to have been guided instead by writers' own notions of what a code of ethics is rather than what Enron's *Code of Ethics* was. They ascribed their own meaning to *ethics* rather than Enron's *new meaning*.

Those writers who did reference the *Code's* contents tended to focus on five particular pages, which differ significantly from the document's other 59 pages. Page 2 presents a letter from Kenneth L. Lay, Chairman and Chief Executive Officer, to the document's intended audience, "officers and employees of Enron Corp." Page 3, entitled "How to Use this Booklet," explains that employees must sign a "Certificate of Compliance," assuring the company they will "comply with the policies stated herein." Pages 4, 5, and 6 comprise a multi-purpose section entitled "Principles of Human Rights." Writers have noted repeatedly the irony of Lay's stated interest in the company's reputation given that he was subsequently faulted for leading the company into extreme disrepute. Some writers have commented on the four "values" stated in the "Principles of Human Rights" section. I have not yet found an existing reference to the *Enron Code of Ethics* that acknowledges the final 59 pages of the document, which outline various laws and internal policies that regulate employee behavior and the consequences for failure to abide by them.

METHOD

Cluster analysis was developed by Kenneth Burke as a method for gaining insight into a rhetor's worldview. The critic selects the target artifact's key terms and observes those terms that cluster around them for the purpose of learning more about how the rhetor associates particular concepts. In this analysis, I have selected the key terms *ethics, laws, the Company,* and *employees* to analyze Enron's *Code of Ethics*.

Some question may arise regarding the identity of the rhetor in this artifact. The Enron *Code of Ethics* is unattributed, as is customary of such corporate documents. Any discussion of its authorship is therefore speculative. Although I have no company-provided information regarding its authorship, the *Code of Ethics* appears to have been written by more than one person. Its tone and language use vary dramatically among sections, significantly undermining the consistency of the document. For example, the "Principles of Human Rights" section repeatedly uses the term *we* to refer to employees, managers, and directors. The section concerned with insider trading labels employees *personnel, employees*, and *you*, forsaking the term *we*. The "Use of Communication and Services Equipment" section labels employees *users* of services and equipment.

If the *Code of Ethics* were written by more than one author, any attempt to gain insight into the author's worldview might be fruitless as any number of worldviews may be represented. Within this analysis, I will attribute any emerging worldview to the company rather than to the individual or individuals who wrote the document. Although such personification of a corporation may be problematic, I think one can treat a widely distributed document issued under a company's name and the signature of its CEO as a representation of the company's position.

ANALYSIS

In the Enron *Code of Ethics*'s foreword, CEO Kenneth L. Lay does not even mention ethics or the title of the document. Instead, he describes the contents of "this booklet" as "certain policies" approved by the Board of Directors and intended to "keep [the company's] reputation high." The instructions for "How to Use this Booklet" describe it as "a set of written policies dealing with rules of conduct" rather than a code of ethics. The only section of the document that even aspires to anything resembling ethics is the three-page section subtitled "Principles of Human Rights." Even Enron's discussion of human rights outlines laws, crimes, and punishments. The section contains the company's *vision*, a term often used synonymously elsewhere with *mission statement* and *values*. "Principles of Human Rights" apparently was considered an appropriate heading under which to publish the company's *vision* and *values* because "Enron's Vision and Values are the platform upon which our human rights principles are built." This statement suggests that "Principles of Human Rights" is Enron's name for "conduct that will help us achieve our mission in accordance with our values." This is hardly a common application suggested by the term "Principles of Human Rights." It is more likely a *new meaning*.

The "Principles of Human Rights" section includes Enron's *vision*; four *values*; a rephrased version of the Golden Rule ("at Enron, we treat others as we expect to be treated ourselves"); a toothless "belief" in non-discrimination that offers no expansion upon federal non-discrimination laws; an assertion of dedication to obey "all applicable laws and regulations including, but not limited to, the U.S. Foreign Corrupt Practices Act"; a commitment to safety through compliance with various laws; a belief in "playing an active role in every community in which we operate"; a belief in "fair compensation" for employees; and an assertion that all of the aforementioned comprise "principles." Those "principles" are then distilled into "policies and procedures," which are equated with "written guidelines" that mandate "compliance with the law" under threat of "disciplinary action, which may include termination." By the conclusion of the "Principles of Human Rights" section on page 6 of the document, the company has issued its first threat of severance to employees and dramatically challenged any preconceived notion readers may have of "Human Rights."

The four stated *values* are the only items in the document that may be construed to be ethics. They are *respect, integrity, communication,* and *excellence. Respect* is a second reiteration of the Golden Rule. *Integrity* is described as honest behavior pertaining specifically to "customers and prospects." The *communication* value states that "we have an obligation to communicate." The value of *excellence* at Enron means "the very best in everything we do." Individuals familiar with a wider range of values will note the frugality of Enron's collection. Some also might find *new meanings* in Enron's version of those definitions. Readers may observe that the remainder of the stated "Principles of Human Rights" does not necessarily have any obvious connection to the four *values*, despite the company's assertion that the values are the *platform* upon which the *principles* are built. Six pages into this document, one senses that its authors built upon a hill of sand rather than a platform of any sort. The remaining 90% of the text, however, shores up the structure by attaching it to rigid laws, rules, regulations, and policies.

KEY TERM: *ETHICS*

Lay's foreword describes employee responsibility to conduct "the affairs of the companies in accordance with all applicable laws and in a moral and honest manner." This is the sole appearance of the word *moral* in the document. Because many rhetors use the words *moral* and *ethical* interchangeably, this cluster analysis notes that the terms *applicable laws* and *honest* cluster around the sole appearance of the word *moral* in this document. One may gain some insight into Lay's notion of ethics from both his usage of the word *moral* and his reference to the company's *Code of Ethics* as "certain policies" and "this booklet" rather than by its title.

Accordingly, the *Enron Code of Ethics* makes little mention of ethics. The word *ethics* and its adjective form *ethical* appear only seven times in the 64-page document. This contrasts with the word *laws* (or *law*), which appears more than 100 times. Nevertheless, this document was presented by virtue of its title as a *Code of Ethics* rather than a *Legal Compliance Manual*, so the document's treatment of the word *ethics* is central to this analysis.

The words *ethics* and *ethical* are surrounded by legal and compliance matters in all but one instance. One mention of *ethical* concerns the company's reputation rather than any legal compulsion for ethical conduct. The terms clustering around *ethics* and *ethical* include *laws and regulations, policies, guidelines, standards, violations, disciplinary action, legal obligations,* and *legal uses*. The *Code* references ethics in conjunction with such terms as *the law and ethical standards, principles and business ethics,* and *ethical and legal uses*.

Primary assertions often pertain to laws, with mentions of ethics serving as afterthoughts. The *Code* states, for example, "we are dedicated to conducting business according to all applicable local and international laws and regulations, including, but not limited to, the U.S. Foreign Corrupt Practices Act, and with the highest professional and ethical standards." The terms clustered around *ethics* strongly suggest that the company equates legal compliance with ethical conduct. This view of ethics finds value in what employees must do under the law and threat of punishment rather than what they ought to do because it is the right thing to do.

KEY TERM: *LAWS*

The document names 11 federal laws and several types of unnamed laws and the punishments the company and its employees may face for noncompliance. The terms *moral, honest, ethical,* and *values* cluster around the words *law* and *laws* to suggest strongly the equation of laws with ethics. Other terms, including *compliance, in accordance, commitment, faithfully,* and *obey* signal unconditional acceptance of the authority of law. For example, the *Code* asserts, "laws, regulations, and standards are designed to safeguard the environment, human health, wildlife, and natural resources. Our commitment to observe them faithfully is an integral part of our business and of our values." In one succinct statement, the *Code* claims, "laws and regulations affecting the Company will be obeyed." Lay's foreword tells officers and employees, "we are responsible for conducting the business affairs of the companies in accordance with all applicable laws and in a moral and honest manner."

Other terms clustered around the key term *law* recognize the consequences of failure to comply with laws, including *violations, abuses, consequences,* and *penalties.* The words *company* and *employee* also cluster around the words *law* and *laws,* indicating both who must obey the laws and who suffers from disobedience. At Enron, "compliance with the law and ethical standards are conditions of employment, and violations will result in disciplinary action, which may include termination."

KEY TERM: *THE COMPANY*

The words clustering around the term *the Company,* which is always thus capitalized, and *Enron Corp.* often demonstrate esteem for *the Company* through words like *honest, proud, respected, important, integrity, excellence,* and *quality.* Far more prevalent, however, are terms indicating a desire to protect the company from harm imposed by employees and their potential failures to comply with various laws and internal policies. Such words clustered around *the Company* include *trade secrets, proprietary information, interests, confidentiality, unique assets, valuable, property,* and *reputation,* all things the company seeks to protect.

An example of such clustering is "employees will maintain the confidentiality of the Company's sensitive or proprietary information." Another part of Enron's *Code of Ethics* explains that all products of employees' work are "the sole and exclusive property of the Company." Further, "the Company's confidential and proprietary information could be very helpful to suppliers and the Company's competitors, to the detriment of the Company." One might surmise that protecting company information is the highest priority by noting that 22 of the 64 pages of the *Code of Ethics* mandate specific employee behaviors surrounding company information. The plan for implementing that protection shows up in other terms clustering around *the Company,* including *policies, rules of conduct, applicable laws, standards, laws, regulations, regulatory requirements,* and *rights.*

KEY TERM: *EMPLOYEES*

The *Code of Ethics* lists and describes dozens of ways that employees can harm both themselves and the company. This document, which proclaims such extensive company vulnerability to employee misdeeds, is heavily populated with terms clustered around references to employees that describe employee misbehavior in terms of criminal conduct. Employees are referenced as *you, we, personnel, employees,* and *users* within the *Code of Ethics.* The terms of criminal conduct that cluster around those labels include *violate, illegal behavior, not authorized, infringe, unauthorized disclosure, misappropriation, counterfeit, failure to comply, abusing, criminal offense, criminal conduct, wrongdoers, harassment,* and *intimidation.* Clusters indicate that the company approves of employee efforts to *avoid actions, abide by the letter and spirit of laws, maintain confidentiality, refrain, honor obligations, laws, rules, regulations, standards, compliance,* and *duty.*

The word *employee* is also often surrounded by terms describing consequences for failure to behave as prescribed. These terms include *sanction, corrective action, losing privileges, disciplinary action, suspend, dismiss, termination, prosecuted to the full extent of the law, criminal penalties, civil penalty, criminal fine, jail term, prosecution, will not tolerate,* and *liable.* In one mention, for example, "any breach of this policy may subject employees to criminal penalties." One statement in the code proclaims in an enlarged, all-caps font, "FAILURE TO ABIDE BY THESE RESTRICTIONS MAY SUBJECT EMPLOYEES TO CIVIL AND/OR CRIMINAL PROSECUTION."

The last sentence of the document is a final, exponentially redundant threat issued to employees: "An employee who violates any of these policies is subject to disciplinary action including but not limited to suspension or termination of employment, and such other action, including legal action, as the Company believes to be appropriate under the circumstances." Cluster analysis reveals that the company considers employees to pose grave danger to both themselves and the company. Further, the company's attempt to mitigate that perceived danger is revealed as the invocation of threats to employees' continued employment, personal freedom, and financial security. In short, the company attempts to scare employees into the legal compliance that it equates with ethical conduct.

CONCLUSION

Kenneth Burke explains that, "if we change our ways of acting to bring them more into accord with the new meanings (rejecting old means and selecting new means as a better solution for the problem as now rephrased), we shall bring ourselves and our group nearer to the good life."[3] If Enron were to preface its *Code of Ethics* by paraphrasing Burke to suit its application, it might have said, "if you change your ways to behave according to *The Company's Code of Ethics*, both you and *The Company* will achieve more success." The original problem of ethics is to answer the question, "What is the right thing to do?" The rephrased problem at Enron was, "What will the law permit us to do?"

Cluster analysis reveals a *new meaning* assigned to the word *ethics* at Enron. By publishing a 64-page *Code of Ethics* that contains only a trace of codified ethics, Enron effectively announced that it had no ethics to anyone rejecting the *new meaning* offered within the document. Rejection of the *new meaning* was unlikely, however, among the *Code of Ethics's* intended audience members—the company's employees—because their success in the organization required them to subjugate their own values and judgment to *The Company's* ethics. The prescribed behavior masqueraded as the right thing to do by wearing the title *Code of Ethics.* The document therefore carried a moral imperative for employees in addition to requiring compliance in order to avoid being fired, fined, or imprisoned.

Enron frames individual employees as inherently dangerous, unruly, and unimportant entities capable of becoming and being safe, ethical, and validated through compliant membership in the inherently good, valuable, and ethical organization. Presenting this formula for success as an Enron employee under the title *Code of Ethics* suggests that success comes through ethical behavior at Enron. Acceptance of the *new meaning* of *ethics* is framed as the key to employee redemption within the organization.

With its *Code of Ethics*, Enron demonstrates a bold attempt to assign a *new meaning* to *ethics*. This analysis revealed a variety of methods used to gain acceptance of the *new meaning*: (1) the lures of success and continued membership in the organization; (2) a moral imperative and the implied threat of being judged unethical; and (3) the overt threats of sanction, severance from the organization, criminal penalties, and civil penalties. Cluster analysis of the document offers some insight into how one organization used *new meanings* to persuade its members to accept a prescribed definition of *ethics* over their own preexisting definitions.

Notes

[1] Brian Burrell, *The Words We Live By: The Creeds, Mottoes, and Pledges That Have Shaped America* (New York: Free, 1997), p. 98.

[2] Kenneth Burke, *Permanence and Change: An Anatomy of Purpose,* 3rd ed. (Berkeley: University of California Press, 1984), p. 81.

[3] Burke, p. 81.

Construction of an Enemy in George W. Bush's State of the Union Speech

Kristin Nowlen, Shannon Jensen, Deborah A. Gibbs, Robert E. Murphy, Michael R. Taylor, and Wei Wang

Enemies are not naturally occurring. To have an enemy, a person, group, or nation must impute malicious intent to and interpret actions by another as hostile. Those parties who perceive others in these ways usually have other rhetorical options. They can choose to see the "hostile" actions as, for example, unintentional, accidental, misguided, comic, or irrelevant. Given such a wide array of options, the construction of an enemy is a deliberate rhetorical choice, and it is a significant one. Construction of an enemy creates major divisions between parties, usually leads to limited and dysfunctional communication between them, and often leads to an escalation of conflict. Understanding the rhetorical process by which enemies are constructed, then, is important. Such understanding can help rhetors see the process as a rhetorical one in which they have choice. It can suggest strategies for resolving conflicts that arise from such constructions, and it may be able to prevent such conflicts in the first place.

We seek to contribute to an understanding of the process by which enemies are rhetorically constructed by analyzing the State of the Union address by President George W. Bush on January 28, 2003. Although the president addresses both domestic and international affairs in the speech, for the purposes of this paper, our analysis will be focused only on the portion of the speech that pertains specifically to relations between the United States and Iraq. This is the portion of the speech in which Bush actively constructs an enemy and thus is the relevant part for the purposes of this analysis.

Following the terrorist attacks on the United States on September 11, 2001, the American public viewed the al-Qaeda network as an enemy. Fewer Americans believed that Saddam Hussein, the leader of Iraq, posed a similar threat to the United States. As a means to gain support for his desire to invade Iraq and depose Hussein, Bush sought in this speech to construct Hussein as an enemy. The speech thus represents an example of rhetoric designed to create an enemy for a country.

Admittedly, tensions had been high between the United States and Saddam Hussein since the end of the Gulf War in 1991. At that point, Hussein was allowed to maintain political power by signing a treaty agreeing to disarm. Following September 11, the United Nations passed Defense Council Resolution 1441, which gave Iraq guidelines for disarmament. In his State of the Union address, Bush set out to prove that Iraq had committed a material breach of Resolution 1441 by continuing to possess weapons of mass destruction. Although Hussein had made no efforts to attack others or to use weapons of mass destruction since the Gulf War, Bush sought to make Hussein into a threat that was perceived as immediate and as dangerous as al-Qaeda.

This essay was written while Kristin Nowlen, Shannon Jensen, Deborah A. Gibbs, Robert E. Murphy, Michael R. Taylor, and Wei Wang were students in Sonja K. Foss's rhetorical criticism class at the University of Colorado at Denver in 2003. Used by permission of the authors.

Our method for analyzing Bush's speech is cluster analysis, a method developed by Kenneth Burke as a way to provide insights into rhetors' worldviews. In cluster analysis, key terms that appear often in the artifact or are of high intensity are selected for analysis. Once the key terms have been selected, a tally is taken of the other terms in the artifact that cluster immediately around the key terms. Identification of the clustering terms around the key terms can be used by a critic to interpret the links among all the terms to produce a theory about the rhetor's perceptions and worldview.

ANALYSIS

Four key terms emerge from the portion of the State of the Union speech dealing with international relations: *Saddam Hussein*, *Iraq*, *United States/America*, and *Iraqi people*. The clustered terms around all of these key terms can be categorized into three sub-clusters—character, tools, and actions.

Around the term *Hussein* are clustered terms such as *deceived*, *dominated*, and *intimidate*, all of which relate to character. These words serve to portray Hussein as a morally unfit leader. Two types of terms that cluster around *Hussein* are related to tools. Some are tools formed by humans themselves, such as *terrorist*, *hijackers*, and *Al Qaeda*; others are the mechanical tools of *biological weapons* and *nuclear weapons*. These terms show Hussein's willingness to use mechanical and sentient assets to create terror in the world. Four terms that cluster around *Hussein* can be categorized as action terms—*kill*, *war*, *death*, and *hiding*. These clustered terms help paint a picture of Hussein as a devil-like leader, unconcerned with the affairs of others and willing to commit any act of atrocity.

The second key word in the speech is *Iraq*. Three terms in the speech cluster around *Iraq* are related to character—*evil*, *enemy*, and *dictator*. The terms in this category all point to Iraq, as a country, possessing the same character traits as its leader. Bush also uses a substitute term to define the difference between most world governments and Iraq. Part way through the speech, Bush begins to use the word *regime* instead of *government* to refer to Iraq's leadership. Due to its negative connotations, *regime* is a powerful word to use to describe the government of a fellow member of the United Nations. In the category of tools, two types of tools are again established—physical weapons and war crimes. Physical weapons include the terms *biological weapon* and *illegal weapon*. The tool of war crimes is developed from the terms *burning*, *rape*, *mutilation*, and *electric shock*. The actions category of terms around Iraq consists of *not disarm*, *denying*, *blocking*, and *intimidating*. Bush uses *not disarm* in place of *unarmed* because of the negative modifier, which serves to make the word more powerful. Again, the effect of Bush's choice of words is that Iraq is portrayed as a devil-like entity. By describing Iraq in much the same way as he describes Hussein, Bush is able to muddy the distinction between war on Hussein and war on Iraq.

The third key term in Bush's speech is *United States/America*. Within the character category, Bush uses the terms *honorable*, *resolute*, *strong*, *free*, *brave*, and *innocent* as clustering terms. These words depict the United States as on the other end of the moral scale from Iraq. Each term is something that most persons and nations would like others to say about them. Tools are divided into two groups once again—physical weapons and support. The physical weapons chosen are *armed forces*, *military*, and *power*. The support category consisted of the terms *God*, *allies, friends,* and *U.N.* Actions the United States is willing to do to achieve its goals are developed through the clustering terms of *battle, force, risk,* and *peace.* Bush chooses words that would link the United States with the goodness and power of God, "placing our confidence in the loving God behind all life." While Bush openly uses the word *God* in close proximity to the word *U.S.,* he never uses the word *devil* in the address. Bush relies upon the strength of the devil terms describing Iraq to make the suggestion implicitly.

A final key term that emerges in Bush's speech is *Iraqi people.* The character terms that cluster around this term are *brave, oppressed,* and *refugee.* These terms are used to portray the Iraqi people as worthy of compassion and aid. Clustering around this key term is also a group of tools created by the terms *food, medicine,* and *supplies.* All of these terms are things to which the Iraqi people will have access if the United States is allowed to remove Hussein from power. The actions category of clustering terms contains the terms *freedom* and *liberation.* In the speech, Bush speaks directly to the Iraqi people to assure them of the United States's ability and desire to be of help: "The liberty we prize is not America's gift to the world, it is God's gift to humanity." Bush uses positive language to link the Iraqi people to the United States to add the weight of compassion to his argument. In addition, the use of the word *God* furthers the god-devil relationship he is depicting between the United States and Iraq.

Conclusion

In the State of the Union speech, Bush uses rhetoric to persuade the people of the United States that Iraq and Hussein are indeed viable threats. Bush's clustered terms around *Iraq* and *Hussein* show that he associates them with the devil. These devil terms are used to create an aura of evil associated with Iraq and Hussein. In comparison, Bush associates god-like terms with the United States and the Iraqi people.

The dichotomy between god and devil is reinforced even more by the types of terms Bush uses to create these associations. They are terms that create a particular character and suggest the actions the character will take and the tools that will be used to implement or execute the actions. As a result, Bush creates an image of a live person, an action figure, someone who is ready to spring into action at a moment's notice. By constructing Hussein and Iraq in such ways, he increases the sense of urgency to the threat. His answer to the threat, of course, is an action-oriented United States, ready and even eager to respond to the threat.

Bush's State of the Union address suggests a number of effective rhetorical strategies for the creation of enemies. One is to cluster terms around key terms that create images of the devil and the evil with which it is associated as prominent in the minds of the audience. Another is to create, through the particular type of clustering terms selected, an image of a person ready to engage in speedy and dramatic action. Such a depiction helps to create a sense of urgency and a strong exigence to which the rhetor and the audience members are more likely to believe they must respond.

State of the Union Speech
George W. Bush
January 28, 2003

[Included here is the concluding portion of the address,
which was analyzed in the sample essay.]

. . . Our war against terror is a contest of will in which perseverance is power. In the ruins of two towers, at the western wall of the Pentagon, on a field in Pennsylvania, this nation made a pledge, and we renew that pledge tonight: Whatever the duration of this struggle, and whatever the difficulties, we will not permit the triumph of violence in the affairs of men—free people will set the course of history. Today, the gravest danger in the war on terror, the gravest danger facing America and the world, is outlaw regimes that seek and possess nuclear, chemical, and biological weapons. These regimes could use such weapons for blackmail, terror, and mass murder. They could also give or sell those weapons to terrorist allies, who would use them without the least hesitation.

This threat is new; America's duty is familiar. Throughout the 20th century, small groups of men seized control of great nations, built armies and arsenals, and set out to dominate the weak and intimidate the world. In each case, their ambitions of cruelty and murder had no limit. In each case, the ambitions of Hitlerism, militarism, and communism were defeated by the will of free peoples, by the strength of great alliances, and by the might of the United States of America.

Now, in this century, the ideology of power and domination has appeared again, and seeks to gain the ultimate weapons of terror. Once again, this nation and all our friends are all that stand between a world at peace, and a world of chaos and constant alarm. Once again, we are called to defend the safety of our people, and the hopes of all mankind. And we accept this responsibility.

America is making a broad and determined effort to confront these dangers. We have called on the United Nations to fulfill its charter and stand by its demand that Iraq disarm. We're strongly supporting the International Atomic Energy Agency in its mission to track and control nuclear materials around the world. We're working with other governments to secure nuclear materials in the former Soviet Union, and to strengthen global treaties banning the production and shipment of missile technologies and weapons of mass destruction.

In all these efforts, however, America's purpose is more than to follow a process—it is to achieve a result: the end of terrible threats to the civilized world. All free nations have a stake in preventing sudden and catastrophic attacks. And we're asking them to join us, and many are doing so. Yet the course of this nation does not depend on the decisions of others. Whatever action is required, whenever action is necessary, I will defend the freedom and security of the American people.

Different threats require different strategies. In Iran, we continue to see a government that represses its people, pursues weapons of mass destruction, and supports terror. We also see Iranian citizens risking intimidation and death as they speak out for liberty and human rights and democracy. Iranians, like all people, have a right to choose their own government and determine their own destiny—and the United States supports their aspirations to live in freedom.

On the Korean Peninsula, an oppressive regime rules a people living in fear and starvation. Throughout the 1990s, the United States relied on a negotiated framework to keep North Korea from gaining nuclear weapons. We now know that that regime was deceiving the world, and developing those weapons all along. And today the North Korean regime is using its nuclear program to incite fear and seek concessions. America and the world will not be blackmailed.

America is working with the countries of the region—South Korea, Japan, China, and Russia—to find a peaceful solution, and to show the North Korean government that nuclear weapons will bring only isolation, economic stagnation, and continued hardship. The North Korean regime will find respect in the world and revival for its people only when it turns away from its nuclear ambitions.

Our nation and the world must learn the lessons of the Korean Peninsula and not allow an even greater threat to rise up in Iraq. A brutal dictator, with a history of reckless aggression, with ties to terrorism, with great potential wealth, will not be permitted to dominate a vital region and threaten the United States.

Twelve years ago, Saddam Hussein faced the prospect of being the last casualty in a war he had started and lost. To spare himself, he agreed to disarm of all weapons of mass destruction. For the next 12 years, he systematically violated that agreement. He pursued chemical, biological, and nuclear weapons, even while inspectors were in his country. Nothing to date has restrained him from his pursuit of these weapons—not economic sanctions, not isolation from the civilized world, not even cruise missile strikes on his military facilities.

Almost three months ago, the United Nations Security Council gave Saddam Hussein his final chance to disarm. He has shown instead utter contempt for the United Nations, and for the opinion of the world. The 108 U.N. inspectors were not sent to conduct a scavenger hunt for hidden materials across a country the size of California. The job of the inspectors is to verify that Iraq's regime is disarming. It is up to Iraq to show exactly where it is hiding its banned weapons, lay those weapons out for the world to see, and destroy them as directed. Nothing like this has happened.

The United Nations concluded in 1999 that Saddam Hussein had biological weapons sufficient to produce over 25,000 liters of anthrax—enough doses to kill several million people. He hasn't accounted for that material. He's given no evidence that he has destroyed it.

The United Nations concluded that Saddam Hussein had materials sufficient to produce more than 38,000 liters of botulinum toxin—enough to subject millions of people to death by respiratory failure. He hadn't accounted for that material. He's given no evidence that he has destroyed it.

Our intelligence officials estimate that Saddam Hussein had the materials to produce as much as 500 tons of sarin, mustard and VX nerve agent. In such quantities, these chemical agents could also kill untold thousands. He's not accounted for these materials. He has given no evidence that he has destroyed them.

U.S. intelligence indicates that Saddam Hussein had upwards of 30,000 munitions capable of delivering chemical agents. Inspectors recently turned up 16 of them—despite Iraq's recent declaration denying their existence. Saddam Hussein has not accounted for the remaining 29,984 of these prohibited munitions. He's given no evidence that he has destroyed them.

From three Iraqi defectors we know that Iraq, in the late 1990s, had several mobile biological weapons labs. These are designed to produce germ warfare agents, and can be moved from place to place to evade inspectors. Saddam Hussein has not disclosed these facilities. He's given no evidence that he has destroyed them.

The International Atomic Energy Agency confirmed in the 1990s that Saddam Hussein had an advanced nuclear weapons development program, had a design for a nuclear weapon and was working on five different methods of enriching uranium for a bomb. The British government has learned that Saddam Hussein recently sought significant quantities of uranium from Africa. Our intelligence sources tell us that he has attempted to purchase high-strength aluminum tubes suitable for nuclear weapons production. Saddam Hussein has not credibly explained these activities. He clearly has much to hide.

The dictator of Iraq is not disarming. To the contrary; he is deceiving. From intelligence sources we know, for instance, that thousands of Iraqi security personnel are at work hiding documents and materials from the U.N. inspectors, sanitizing inspection sites and monitoring the inspectors themselves. Iraqi officials accompany the inspectors in order to intimidate witnesses.

Iraq is blocking U-2 surveillance flights requested by the United Nations. Iraqi intelligence officers are posing as the scientists inspectors are supposed to interview. Real scientists have been coached by Iraqi officials on what to say. Intelligence sources indicate that Saddam Hussein has ordered that scientists who cooperate with U.N. inspectors in disarming Iraq will be killed, along with their families.

Year after year, Saddam Hussein has gone to elaborate lengths, spent enormous sums, taken great risks to build and keep weapons of mass destruction. But why? The only possible explanation, the only possible use he could have for those weapons, is to dominate, intimidate, or attack.

With nuclear arms or a full arsenal of chemical and biological weapons, Saddam Hussein could resume his ambitions of conquest in the Middle East and create deadly havoc in that region. And this Congress and the America people must recognize another threat. Evidence from intelligence sources, secret communications, and statements by people now in custody reveal that Saddam Hussein aids and protects terrorists, including members of al Qaeda. Secretly, and without fingerprints, he could provide one of his hidden weapons to terrorists, or help them develop their own.

Before September the 11th, many in the world believed that Saddam Hussein could be contained. But chemical agents, lethal viruses and shadowy terrorist networks are not easily contained. Imagine those 19 hijackers with other weapons and other plans—this time armed by Saddam Hussein. It would take one vial, one canister, one crate slipped into this country to bring a day of horror like none we have ever known. We will do everything in our power to make sure that that day never comes.

Some have said we must not act until the threat is imminent. Since when have terrorists and tyrants announced their intentions, politely putting us on notice before they strike? If this threat is permitted to fully and suddenly emerge, all actions, all words, and all recriminations would come too late. Trusting in the sanity and restraint of Saddam Hussein is not a strategy, and it is not an option.

The dictator who is assembling the world's most dangerous weapons has already used them on whole villages—leaving thousands of his own citizens dead, blind, or disfigured. Iraqi refugees tell us how forced confessions are obtained—by torturing children while their parents are made to watch. International human rights groups have catalogued other methods used in the torture chambers of Iraq: electric shock, burning with hot irons, dripping acid on the skin, mutilation with electric drills, cutting out tongues, and rape. If this is not evil, then evil has no meaning.

And tonight I have a message for the brave and oppressed people of Iraq: Your enemy is not surrounding your country—your enemy is ruling your country. And the day he and his regime are removed from power will be the day of your liberation.

The world has waited 12 years for Iraq to disarm. America will not accept a serious and mounting threat to our country, and our friends and our allies. The United States will ask the U.N. Security Council to convene on February the 5th to consider the facts of Iraq's ongoing defiance of the world. Secretary of State Powell will present information and intelligence about Iraqi's illegal weapons programs, its attempt to hide those weapons from inspectors, and its links to terrorist groups.

We will consult. But let there be no misunderstanding: If Saddam Hussein does not fully disarm, for the safety of our people and for the peace of the world, we will lead a coalition to disarm him.

Tonight I have a message for the men and women who will keep the peace, members of the American Armed Forces: Many of you are assembling in or near the Middle East, and some crucial hours may lay ahead. In those hours, the success of our cause will depend on you. Your training has prepared you. Your honor will guide you. You believe in America, and America believes in you.

Sending Americans into battle is the most profound decision a President can make. The technologies of war have changed; the risks and suffering of war have not. For the brave Americans who bear the risk, no victory is free from sorrow. This nation fights reluctantly, because we know the cost and we dread the days of mourning that always come.

We seek peace. We strive for peace. And sometimes peace must be defended. A future lived at the mercy of terrible threats is no peace at all. If war is forced upon us, we will fight in a just cause and by just means—sparing, in every way we can, the innocent. And if war is forced upon us, we will fight with the full force and might of the United States military—and we will prevail.

And as we and our coalition partners are doing in Afghanistan, we will bring to the Iraqi people food and medicines and supplies—and freedom.

Many challenges, abroad and at home, have arrived in a single season. In two years, America has gone from a sense of invulnerability to an awareness of peril; from bitter division in small matters to calm unity in great causes. And we go forward with confidence, because this call of history has come to the right country.

Americans are a resolute people who have risen to every test of our time. Adversity has revealed the character of our country, to the world and to ourselves. America is a strong nation, and honorable in the use of our strength. We exercise power without conquest, and we sacrifice for the liberty of strangers.

Americans are a free people, who know that freedom is the right of every person and the future of every nation. The liberty we prize is not America's gift to the world, it is God's gift to humanity.

We Americans have faith in ourselves, but not in ourselves alone. We do not know—we do not claim to know—all the ways of Providence, yet we can trust in them, placing our confidence in the loving God behind all of life, and all of history.

May He guide us now. And may God continue to bless the United States of America.

Additional Samples of Cluster Criticism

Berthold, Carol A. "Kenneth Burke's Cluster-Agon Method: Its Development and an Application." *Central States Speech Journal*, 27 (Winter 1976), 302–09.

Cooks, Leda, and David Descutner. "Different Paths from Powerlessness to Empowerment: A Dramatistic Analysis of Two Eating Disorder Therapies." *Western Journal of Communication*, 57 (Fall 1993), 494–514.

Corcoran, Farrel. "The Bear in the Back Yard: Myth, Ideology, and Victimage Ritual in Soviet Funerals." *Communication Monographs*, 50 (December 1983), 305–20.

Courtright, Jeffrey L. "'I Am a Scientologist': The Image Management of Identity." In *Public Relations Inquiry as Rhetorical Criticism: Case Studies of Corporate Discourse and Social Influence*. Ed. William N. Elwood. Westport, CT: Praeger, 1995, pp. 69–84.

Crowell, Laura. "Three Sheers for Kenneth Burke." *Quarterly Journal of Speech*, 63 (April 1977), 152–67.

Foss, Sonja K. "Women Priests in the Episcopal Church: A Cluster Analysis of Establishment Rhetoric." *Religious Communication Today*, 7 (September 1984), 1–11.

Heinz, Bettina, and Ronald Lee. "Getting Down to the Meat: The Symbolic Construction of Meat Consumption." *Communication Studies*, 49 (Spring 1998), 87–99.

Lee, Sang-Chul, and Karlyn Kohrs Campbell. "Korean President Roh Tae-Woo's 1988 Inaugural Address: Campaigning for Investiture." *Quarterly Journal of Speech*, 80 (February 1994), 37–52.

Marston, Peter J., and Bambi Rockwell. "Charlotte Perkins Gilman's `The Yellow Wallpaper': Rhetorical Subversion in Feminist Literature." *Women's Studies in Communication*, 14 (Fall 1991), 58–72.

Mechling, Elizabeth Walker, and Jay Mechling. "Sweet Talk: The Moral Rhetoric Against Sugar." *Central States Speech Journal*, 34 (Spring 1983), 19–32.

Pullum, Stephen J. "Common Sense Religion for America: The Rhetoric of the Jewish Televangelist Jan Bresky." *Journal of Communication and Religion*, 15 (March 1992), 43–54.

5

Fantasy-Theme Criticism

The fantasy-theme method of rhetorical criticism, created by Ernest G. Bormann, is designed to provide insights into the shared worldview of groups.[1] Impetus for the method came from the work of Robert Bales and his associates in their study of communication in small groups. Bales discovered the process of group fantasizing or dramatizing as a type of communication that occurs in groups.[2] He characterized fantasizing communication in this way: "The tempo of the conversation would pick up. People would grow excited, interrupt one another, blush, laugh, forget their self-consciousness. The tone of the meeting, often quiet and tense immediately prior to the dramatizing, would become lively, animated, and boisterous, the chaining process, involving both verbal and nonverbal communication, indicating participation in the drama."[3] In contexts larger than small groups, fantasizing or dramatizing occurs when individuals find some aspect of a "message that catches and focuses their attention until they imaginatively participate in images and actions stimulated by the message."[4] Bormann extended the notion of fantasizing discovered by Bales into a theory (symbolic convergence theory) and a method (fantasy-theme criticism) that can be applied not only to the study of small groups but to all kinds of rhetoric in which themes function dramatically to connect audiences with messages.

Symbolic convergence theory is based on two major assumptions. One is that communication creates reality. As chapter 1 describes, reality is not fixed but changes as our symbols for talking about it change. A second assumption on which symbolic convergence theory is based is that symbols not only create reality for individuals but that individuals' meanings for symbols can converge to create a shared reality or community consciousness. Convergence, in the theory, refers "to the way two or more private symbolic worlds incline toward each other, come more closely together, or even overlap during certain processes of communication." Convergence also means consensus or general agreement on subjective meanings, as Bormann explains: "If several or many people develop portions of their private symbolic worlds that overlap as a result of symbolic convergence, they share a common consciousness and have the basis for communicating with one another to create community, to discuss their common experiences, and to achieve mutual understanding."[5] Meanings are not all that are shared in symbolic convergence. Participants "have jointly experienced the same emotions; they have developed the same attitudes and emotional responses to the personae of the drama; and they have interpreted some aspect of their experience in the same way."[6]

Evidence of symbolic convergence can be discerned through frequent mention of a theme, a narrative, or an analogy in a variety of messages in different contexts. The war on drugs discussed by many politicians exemplifies such a theme. Widespread appeal of an advertising theme also may indicate a convergence. The "Got milk?" advertising campaign by the National Dairy Council, for example, caught the imagination of the American public and has chained out in various ways. In the Denver International Airport, for example, travelers leaving the security area encounter a sign, "Got laptop?" A Kinko's copy shop has a sign on its recycling bin that asks "Got trees?" A catalog advertises a doormat featuring an image of a cat and the words "Got mouse?," and a book of cookie recipes is titled *Got Milk?* All of these are evidence that the slogan has chained out because it is easily recognized and resonates with many people in a number of different contexts.

Evidence of the sharing of fantasies includes cryptic allusions to symbolic common ground. When people have shared a fantasy theme, they have charged that theme with meanings and emotions that can be set off by an agreed-upon cryptic symbolic cue. This may be a code word, phrase, slogan, or nonverbal sign or gesture. These serve as allusions to a previously shared fantasy and arouse the emotions associated with that fantasy. Among a group of college students who lived together in a dorm, for example, *sweet red grape* might serve as a symbolic cue that evokes fond memories of dorm parties where they drank cheap red wine.

The basic unit of analysis of symbolic convergence theory and fantasy-theme criticism is the fantasy theme. *Fantasy*, in the context of symbolic convergence theory, is not used in its popular sense—as something imaginary and not grounded in reality. Instead, *fantasy* is "the creative and imaginative interpretation of events,"[7] and a *fantasy theme* is the means through which the interpretation is accomplished in communication. A fantasy theme is a word, phrase, or statement that interprets events in the past, envisions events in the future, or depicts current events that are removed in time and/or space from the actual activities of a group. The term *fantasy* is designed to capture the constructed nature of the theme. Fantasy themes tell a story about a group's experience that constitutes a constructed reality for the participants.

A fantasy theme depicts characters, actions, and settings that are removed from an actual current group situation in time and place. Bormann distinguishes between a dramatic situation that takes place in the immediate context of a group and a dramatized communication shared by a group: "If, in the middle of a group discussion, several members come into conflict, the situation would be dramatic, but because the action is unfolding in the immediate experience of a group it would not qualify as a basis for the sharing of a group fantasy. If, however, a group's members begin talking about a conflict some of them had in the past or if they envision a future conflict, these comments would be dramatizing messages."[8]

In addition to their dramatic nature, fantasies are characterized by their artistic and organized quality. While experience itself is often chaotic and confusing, fantasy themes are organized and artistic. They are designed to create a credible interpretation of experience—a way of making sense out of experience. Thus, fantasy themes are always ordered in particular ways to provide compelling explanations for experiences. All fantasy themes involve the creative interpretation of events, but the artistry with which the fantasies are presented varies. Some groups construct fantasies "in which cardboard characters enact stereotyped melodramas," while others participate in "a social reality of complexity peopled with characters of stature enacting high tragedies."[9]

A close relationship exists between fantasies and argumentation in that shared fantasies provide the ground for arguments or establish the assumptive system that is the basis for arguments. Argumentation requires a common set of assumptions about the proper way to provide good reasons for arguments, and fantasy themes provide these assumptions. Bormann provides an example of the connection between fantasy themes and arguments:

> For instance, the Puritan vision gave highest place to evidence not of the senses but to revelations, from God. The assumptive system undergirding the Puritan arguments was a grand fantasy type in which a god persona revealed the ultimate truth by inspiring humans to write a sacred text. Supplementing this core drama was the fantasy type in which the god persona inspired ministers to speak the truth when preaching and teaching. These fantasy types provided the ultimate legitimization for the Bible as a source of revealed knowledge and for the ministers as the proper teachers of biblical truths.[10]

Other shared fantasies provide different kinds of assumptions for argumentation than did the Puritan vision. Scientists, for example, assume that argument is based on the careful observation of facts, while lawyers use precedent or past experience as the basis for argument. These groups share different fantasy themes as the basis for their construction of arguments.

The fantasy themes that describe the world from a group's perspective are of three types, corresponding to the elements necessary to create a drama: setting themes, character themes, and action themes. Statements that depict where the action is taking place are setting themes. They not only name the scene of the action but also may describe the characteristics of that scene. Character themes describe the agents or actors in the drama, ascribe characteristics and qualities to them, and assign motives to them. Often, some characters are portrayed as heroes, while others are villains; some are major characters, while others are supporting players. Action themes, which also can be called *plotlines*, deal with the actions of the drama. The actions in which the characters engage comprise action themes.

When similar scenarios involving the same setting themes, character themes, and action themes are shared by members of a community, they form a fantasy type. A fantasy type is a stock scenario that encompasses several related fantasy themes. Once a fantasy type has developed, rhetors do not need to provide an audience with details about the specific fantasy themes it covers. They simply state the general story line of the fantasy type or refer to one of the fantasy themes in the scenario, and the audience is able to call up the specific details of the entire scenario. If a fantasy type has formed, a student in a university community can say, for example, "Students are fed up with professors who are so busy with their own research that they don't have time for students," and an entire scenario is called up among audience members. The success of the type shows that audience members have shared specific fantasies about teachers who are unprepared for class, who do not hold office hours, and who return exams and papers late if at all.

Fantasy types encourage groups to fit new events or experiences into familiar patterns. If a new experience can be portrayed as an instance of a familiar fantasy type, the new experience is brought into line with a group's values and emotions and becomes part of its shared reality. If the members of a university community, for example, share a fantasy type that the State Board of Higher Education does not support a university, the forced retirement of the university's president by the Board may be interpreted as a continued lack of support for the school and incorporated into the group's reality.

The second primary unit of analysis in fantasy-theme criticism is the rhetorical vision. A rhetorical vision is a "unified putting together of the various shared fantasies"[11] or a swirling together of fantasy themes to provide a particular interpretation of reality. It contains fantasy themes relating to settings, characters, and actions that together form a symbolic drama or a coherent interpretation of reality. A rhetorical vision shared by college students at many state institutions, for example, might include hostile legislators as character themes, the legislature as a setting theme, and cutting funds to the university as an action theme.

The presence of a rhetorical vision suggests that a rhetorical community has been formed that consists of participants in the vision or members who have shared the fantasy themes.[12] The people who participate in a rhetorical vision, then, constitute a rhetorical community. They share common symbolic ground and respond to messages in ways that are in tune with the rhetorical vision: "They will cheer references to the heroic persona in their rhetorical vision. They will respond with antipathy to allusions to the villains. They will have agreed-upon procedures for problem-solving communication. They will share the same vision of what counts as evidence, how to build a case, and how to refute an argument."[13]

The motives for action for a rhetorical community reside in its rhetorical vision. Each rhetorical vision contains as part of its substance the motive that impels the participants. As Bormann explains: "Motives do not exist to be expressed in communication but rather arise in the expression itself and come to be embedded in the drama of the fantasy themes that generated and serve to sustain them."[14] Bormann provides some examples of how participation in a rhetorical vision motivates individuals to particular action: "The born-again Christian is baptized and adopts a life-style and behavior modeled after the heroes of the dramas that sustain that vision. . . . Likewise the convert to one of the countercultures in the 1960s would let his hair and beard grow, change his style of dress, and his method of work, and so forth."[15] Actions that make little sense to someone outside of a rhetorical vision make perfect sense when viewed in the context of that vision because the vision provides the motive for action. The willingness of terrorists to die in support of a cause, for example, may seem absurd to most of us. Once we discover the rhetorical vision in which these terrorists participate, however, we have a much better idea of why they are motivated to sacrifice their lives as they do.

PROCEDURES

Using the fantasy-theme method of criticism, a critic analyzes an artifact in a four-step process: (1) selecting an artifact; (2) analyzing the artifact; (3) formulating a research question; and (4) writing the essay.

Selecting an Artifact

The artifact you select for a fantasy-theme analysis should be one where you have some evidence that symbolic convergence has taken place—that people have shared fantasy themes and a rhetorical vision. Any artifact that is popular—an advertisement, a song, a book, or a film, for example—is likely to show evidence of such symbolic convergence.

So is an artifact produced by a major public figure, such as a U.S. president's speech or a commencement address by a talk-show host. Both discursive and nondiscursive artifacts can be used with the fantasy-theme method of criticism.

Analyzing the Artifact

Analysis of an artifact using fantasy-theme analysis involves two steps: (1) coding the artifact for setting, character, and action themes; and (2) constructing the rhetorical vision(s) from the fantasy themes.

Coding for Fantasy Themes

The first step in the fantasy-theme method of criticism is to code the artifact for fantasy themes. This involves a careful examination of the artifact, sentence by sentence in a verbal text or image by image in a visual artifact. Pick out each reference to settings, characters, and actions. This coding process can be illustrated in a verse from Don McLean's song "American Pie":

> Helter-skelter in the summer swelter the birds flew off with a fall-out shelter
>
> Eight miles high and fallin' fast, it landed foul on the grass
>
> The players tried for a forward pass, with the jester on the sidelines in a cast
>
> Now the half-time air was sweet perfume while the sergeants played a marching tune
>
> We all got up to dance but we never got the chance
>
> 'Cause the players tried to take the field, the marching band refused to yield
>
> Do you recall what was revealed
>
> The day the music died
>
> We started singin' . . .[16]

The setting themes you would code in this passage are: *summer, swelter, grass, sidelines, half-time, field,* and *day the music died*. They suggest where the action takes place or characteristics of the places in which the action occurs. Character themes to code are: *birds, players, jester, sergeants, we, marching band, you,* and *music*. In this case, two non-human entities are coded as characters—*birds* and *music*. Any person or object shown engaging in human-like action is coded as a character. Code the actions in which the characters are shown engaging as action themes, noting the character to whom the action is linked: *flew off* (birds), *tried for a forward pass* (players), *played a marching tune* (sergeants), *got up to dance* (we), *tried to take the field* (players), *refused to yield* (marching band), *recall* (you), *started singin'* (we), and *died* (music). If more than one setting is presented, note which characters appear in which settings.

At this preliminary stage of the coding, you may not always be sure if a theme belongs in one category or another—settings, characters, or actions. A word such as *America,* for example, may function both as a setting and a character. If the appropriate category is unclear, code it in both categories initially. Decisions you make in the next step of looking for patterns as you construct the rhetorical vision will determine in which category the word or phrase best belongs.

Constructing the Rhetorical Vision

Your second step in a fantasy-theme analysis is to look for patterns in the fantasy themes and to construct the rhetorical vision from the patterns. Begin by determining which of the fantasy themes appear to be major and minor themes. Those that appear most frequently are major themes that become the subject of the analysis, and those that appear only once or infrequently are discarded as not important parts of the rhetorical vision. In "American Pie," for example, the birds may appear only once, while the jester may appear several times. The jester would be considered a character in the vision, but the birds would not.

Your next task is to construct the rhetorical vision from the patterns of fantasy themes you discovered. This involves looking at the major setting themes identified and linking them with the characters who are shown depicted in those settings and the actions those characters are shown performing. There may be more than one rhetorical vision in your artifact. Some rhetorical communities participate in numerous dramas, with each one developed around a different topic. By linking setting themes with the appropriate characters and actions, you can discover if more than one rhetorical vision exists. If two setting themes appear in the artifact—America and Iraq, for example—the characters of good citizens engaged in the art of working to support their families would be combined with the setting of America to create one rhetorical vision. The characters of an evil dictator harming innocent Iraqis would combine with the Iraq setting to form another vision.

Formulating a Research Question

Knowing the rhetorical vision of an artifact can be the basis for understanding many different rhetorical processes, so the research questions asked by critics using fantasy-theme analysis vary widely. You can ask questions, for example, about strategies used to accomplish particular objectives, the kinds of messages that are being communicated through particular rhetorical visions, the functions of particular rhetorical visions, or the implications of particular rhetorical visions for rhetorical processes or social controversies.

Writing the Essay

After completing the analysis, you are ready to write your essay, which includes five major components: (1) an introduction, in which you discuss the research question, its contribution to rhetorical theory, and its significance; (2) a description of the artifact and its context; (3) a description of the method of criticism—in this case, fantasy-theme analysis; (4) a report of the findings of the analysis, in which you reveal the fantasy themes and rhetorical vision(s) identified in your analysis; and (5) a discussion of the contribution the analysis makes to rhetorical theory.

SAMPLE ESSAYS

The sample essays that follow illustrate applications of fantasy-theme analysis to various kinds of artifacts. The research question that guides Ana Garner, Helen M. Sterk, and Shawn Adams's analysis of sexual etiquette in teenage magazines is, "What messages do popular teen magazines carry for young women about social and cultural norms for sex and sexual relationships?" In Kelly Mendoza's analysis of the song "One Tree Hill" by U2, fantasy-theme criticism is used to explore the question, "What strategies does a rhetor use to cope emotionally with the loss of sudden death?" Kimberly A. McCormick and David Weiss analyze a mural in the parking lot of a Planned Parenthood clinic in Albuquerque, New Mexico, to explore the question, "How can a subversive art form articulate socially acceptable views of controversial issues?"

Notes

[1] Overviews of fantasy-theme criticism are provided by Bormann in: Ernest G. Bormann, "Fantasy and Rhetorical Vision: The Rhetorical Criticism of Social Reality," *Quarterly Journal of Speech*, 58 (December 1972), 396–407; Ernest G. Bormann, "Symbolic Convergence Theory: A Communication Formulation," *Journal of Communication*, 35 (Autumn 1985), 128–38; and Ernest G. Bormann, John F. Cragan, and Donald C. Shields, "In Defense of Symbolic Convergence Theory: A Look at the Theory and Its Criticisms After Two Decades," *Communication Theory*, 4 (November 1994), 259–94. For other information on and samples of the fantasy-theme approach, see John F. Cragan and Donald C. Shields, *Applied Communication Research: A Dramatistic Approach* (Prospect Heights, IL: Waveland, 1981). For a critique of and a defense of the usefulness of fantasy-theme criticism, see: G. P. Mohrmann, "An Essay on Fantasy Theme Criticism," *Quarterly Journal of Speech*, 68 (May 1982), 109–32; Ernest G. Bormann, "Fantasy and Rhetorical Vision: Ten Years Later," *Quarterly Journal of Speech*, 68 (August 1982), 288–305; and G. P. Mohrmann, "Fantasy Theme Criticism: A Peroration," *Quarterly Journal of Speech*, 68 (August 1982), 306–13. Additional critiques of fantasy-theme analysis include: Stephen E. Lucas, rev. of *The Force of Fantasy: Restoring the American Dream*, by Ernest G. Bormann, *Rhetoric Society Quarterly*, 16 (Summer 1986), 199–205; and Charles E. Williams, "Fantasy Theme Analysis: Theory vs. Practice," *Rhetoric Society Quarterly*, 17 (Winter 1987), 11–20.

[2] Robert Freed Bales, *Personality and Interpersonal Behavior* (New York: Holt, Rinehart and Winston, 1970), pp. 136–55.

[3] Bormann, "Fantasy and Rhetorical Vision," p. 397.

[4] Ernest G. Bormann, Roxann L. Knutson, and Karen Musolf, "Why Do People Share Fantasies? An Empirical Investigation of a Basic Tenet of the Symbolic Convergence Communication Theory," *Communication Studies*, 48 (Fall 1997), 255.

[5] Ernest G. Bormann, "Symbolic Convergence: Organizational Communication and Culture," in *Communication and Organizations: An Interpretive Approach*, ed. Linda L. Putnam and Michael E. Pacanowsky (Beverly Hills: Sage, 1983), p. 102.

[6] Bormann, "Symbolic Convergence Theory," p. 104.

[7] Ernest G. Bormann, "How to Make a Fantasy Theme Analysis," unpublished essay, p. 4.

[8] Ernest G. Bormann, *The Force of Fantasy: Restoring the American Dream* (Carbondale: Southern Illinois University Press, 1985), pp. 4–5.

[9] Bormann, *The Force of Fantasy*, p. 10.

[10] Bormann, *The Force of Fantasy*, pp. 16–17.

[11] Bormann, "Symbolic Convergence Theory," p. 114.

[12] Bormann, *The Force of Fantasy*, p. 8.

[13] Bormann, "Symbolic Convergence Theory," p. 115.

[14] Bormann, "Fantasy and Rhetorical Vision," p. 406.

[15] Bormann, "Fantasy and Rhetorical Vision," pp. 406–07.

[16] Don McLean, "American Pie" (Mayday Music, Inc. and The Benny Bird Co., 1971, 1972).

Narrative Analysis of Sexual Etiquette in Teenage Magazines

Ana Garner, Helen M. Sterk, and Shawn Adams

Enormously popular and highly successful, women's magazines represent the largest segment of the U.S. consumer magazine industry. Circulations range from 500,000 to more than 1 million. Containing advice on everything from diets and exercise, to how to dress and use make-up, to how to attract men, women's magazines play a socializing function through the stories they tell in columns, features, and advertising. Readers encounter and then may imitate cultural myths of identity. Women's magazines fill in the contours and colors of what it means to be a woman and how women should relate to men. According to Kellner (1995), "media stories provide the symbols, myths, and resources through which we constitute a common culture and through the appropriation of which we insert ourselves into this culture" (p. 5). Magazines constitute part of the media stories that shape both society's sense of culture and our sense of self in culture.

Researchers have argued that women's magazines play a role in the acculturation of women (e.g., Durham, 1996; Ferguson, 1983; May, 1988; McCracken, 1993; McRobbie, 1991; Peirce, 1990, 1993, 1995; Steiner, 1995; Wolf, 1991). Our concern is with the acculturating rhetoric of a segment of this industry, namely, magazines aimed at teenage girls. The five most popular of these are *YM* (*Young and Modern*), *'Teen*, *Seventeen*, *Glamour*, and *Mademoiselle*. Each has over 1.5 million in circulation (*Standard Rate and Data*, 1995). Ironically, only a few studies have attended specifically to magazines directed at this market (Duffy & Gotcher, 1996; Duke, 1995; Evans, Rutberg, Sather, & Turner, 1991; Frazer, 1987; McCracken, 1993; McRobbie, 1991; Peirce, 1990, 1993, 1995; Pool, 1990). Not surprisingly, these studies, like those for their adult counterparts, found that teen magazines work to shape women into enthusiastic consumers who pump money into capitalistic enterprises. Taking it as a given, then, that their latent function is to acculturate readers into consumers, we found ourselves intrigued by the kind of story teen girls' magazines tell about a narrow, but extremely interesting and crucial part of life—sexuality.

Studies have shown that teens rank the media just behind peers and parents as sources of information and influence on attitudes and behaviors, including sexuality (Strasburger, 1995, p. 41). Fine's (1988) study of adolescent females' sexual education found that "public schools have rejected the task of sexual dialogue and critique, or what has been called 'sexuality education'" (p. 30). Peer influence (Fine, 1988) and the popular media (Moore & Rosenthal, 1993; Thompson, 1995) fill in gaps left by schools and parents. As Thompson (1995) noted, "teenage girls still spend several billion dollars a year and untold hours following the advice of friends and teen magazines to 'fit in but be themselves'" (p. 51). Furthermore, Finders (1997) claimed that junior high school girls appropriated the experiences reported in teen magazines as their own and the "zines [sic] served as [their] handbook" (pp. 59–60). The girls said that "the advertisements and articles were 'just like me'" (p. 61), and "talked as if each [article or ad] carried an implicit com-

From *Journal of Communication*, 48 (Autumn 1998), 59–78. Used by permission of Oxford University Press and the authors.

mand that one must follow in order to achieve high status" (p. 62). They treated the magazine's content as a ruler for judging the behavior, values, and opinions of themselves and other girls (p. 65). DeFleur and Ball-Rokeach (1982) suggested that people are most dependent upon a given medium when that medium offers the most direct information and when people lack experiences and interpersonal advice required to serve their informational needs.

Clearly, sexual education for teens is not limited to one site or one source. Parents, peers, and the media all offer advice. For teenage girls, it could be argued that magazines are one of the most accessible, inexpensive, and readily available media for information about sexuality. Magazines allow for private, repeated readings. They are easily purchased in stores, are free in libraries, and are passed along from friends or relatives. Further, magazines can give more explicit kinds of information to readers. As Strasburger (1995) noted, print media are more likely than electronic media to discuss birth control and to advertise birth control products (p. 46).

In this study, we looked for the story of women's sexuality, both emerging (in magazines directed at younger teens) and maturing (in magazines directed at older teens and women in their early 20s). We asked this question: What messages do the highly popular teen magazines carry for young women about social and cultural norms for sex and sexual relationships?

WOMEN'S MAGAZINES AS TRAINING GROUNDS FOR TRADITION

Paging through contemporary teen magazines, readers may be struck by the seeming "hipness" of the images. The pictures feature pert, smiling, predominately White, middle-class, young women dressed in the latest fashions. The teenage models look confident and in control. In short, they imply agency, the ability to do as they choose. However, this image is at odds with the messages carried in the magazines.

The slight body of research available on teenage girls' magazines suggests that they construct a traditional, advertiser-influenced style of female sexuality, which features pleasing men through enhancing beauty and sexual availability. In a study of *Jackie*, a best-selling British teen magazine, McRobbie (1991) found the magazine scripted for young women a sexually competitive world in which other girls were positioned as adversaries in the quest for connection with a man. Similar findings marked Evans, Rutberg, Sather, and Turner's (1991) study, which noted that "articles and advertisements mutually reinforced an underlying value that the road to happiness is attracting males for successful heterosexual life by way of physical beautification" (p. 110). Peirce (1990) also found that traditional socialization messages (e.g., "finding a man to take care of her") dominated more feminist messages (e.g., self-reliance), even when influences from the feminist movement of the late 1960s and 1970s were taken into account. Duffy and Gotcher (1996) argued that *YM* provided a "rhetorical vision that permeates the magazine lead[ing] the viewer to believe that beauty, costuming, popularity, and romance are the keys to female success" (p. 44). The end result was a "distorted world view . . . where success is determined by meeting the needs and expectations of males, and a world view free of consequences for sexual activity" (p. 45).

Although these studies addressed issues of sexuality, sexuality was neither their main focus nor purpose. We found no studies focusing specifically on the overt sexual advice given in regular columns. Only one brief, intriguing article, found in the popular press, spoke directly to the nature of sexual advice in teen magazines. The *Utne Reader* ran a short feature, written by *Sassy* staff member Elizabeth Larsen (1990), which allowed an inside glimpse into the dynamics of the coverage of sexuality in teen magazines. *Sassy's* initial editorial policy focused on questions teenage girls asked them, writing columns and features in response, "to let girls know that whatever choices they made about their sexuality weren't shameful as long as they were responsible about safe sex, birth control, and emotional self-care" (p. 97). Shortly after they began publication, *Sassy* was boycotted by Women Aglow, an evangelical women's group. Advertising revenue dropped precipitously, until "*Sassy* had lost nearly every ad account and we were publishing what we jokingly called *The Sassy Pamphlet*" (p. 97). After the magazine reluctantly removed "'controversial content'" (p. 97), *Sassy's* advertisers returned. In 1994, *Sassy* was purchased by Peterson Publishers, who also own *'Teen* magazine, called "a more traditional and middle-of-the-road publication for teen-age girls" by the *New York Times* (Carmody, 1994). Anecdotal though it may be, this glimpse inside the workings of a popular teen magazine shows that advice that treats women as relatively autonomous decision-makers is controversial. Significantly, Women Aglow did not boycott magazines whose columns advised women to act according to more traditional heterosexual norms.

Previous scholarship has revealed that messages about sexuality are present, but researchers have not examined the columns that advise young women about issues of sexuality with the explicit intent of understanding the sexual discourse presented in teen magazines. Our purpose is to expand both the focus and range of previous work by examining the explicit sexual advice popular teen magazines have presented to young girls over the past 20 years. We begin by developing a base founded on Bormann's (1972, 1985a) symbolic convergence theory.

Symbolic Convergence: Merging Narrative and Culture

Mediated messages symbolically reflect and shape attitudes and values. Fisher's (1987) paradigm suggests that narratives act symbolically to create meaning for "those who live, create, or interpret them" (p. 58). Narrative, whether persuasive or literary, packages information, inferences, attitudes, and values. Narratives invite audiences to identify with the characters; they suggest motives as reasonable and as working for these characters. They encourage imitation. Symbolic convergence theory, originally applied to small-group interaction (Bales, 1970) and later elaborated as a theory of public discourse (Bormann, 1972, 1985a, 1985b), allows discovery of both long-term social and cultural impact of mediated messages, and analysis of the narrative elements found within those messages.

Symbolic convergence theory is based upon two major assumptions. First, communication creates reality. Second, individuals' meaning for symbols can converge to create a shared reality for participants. According to this perspective, people construct reality through inductive and intuitive forms, such as narrative. People do not deduce their reality from abstract symbols, rather they create reality based upon interpretation, intuition, and shared messages. The power of symbolic convergence theory stems from dynamic narrative, through which people understand events in terms of characters with certain personality traits and motivations, making decisions, taking actions, and causing things to happen. Narrative can shape what people see as possible, even as real, if it is attractive enough and repeated enough.

"Fantasy theme criticism" (the method of charting symbolic convergence) can be used in media analysis and evaluation. *Fantasy* refers to the creative or imaginative interpretation of events. *Fantasy theme* refers to the verbal or nonverbal means through which a particular interpretation of reality appears (i.e., a word, phrase, statement, or image). Filling a rhetorical need to explain experience, fantasy themes use words, phrases, statements, or images to interpret events in the past, envision events in the future, or depict current events that are removed in time or space from the actual activities of the group. Fantasy themes tell a story that accounts for the group's experience and shapes group members' understanding of what is real.

Just like drama, fantasy can be analyzed through use of elements of the scene, character, and action (Bales, 1970; Bormann, 1972, 1985b). *Setting themes* depict where the characters act out their roles or where the action takes place. The elements of the scene are closely integrated with characters and action and are given presence through them. *Character themes* describe the agents or actors in the drama, ascribe qualities to them, assign motives to them, and portray them as having certain characteristics (Bormann, 1985b). *Action themes*, or plotlines, deal with characters' actions within the drama (Bormann, 1985b). The action of the drama gives meaning to the fantasy theme. Within the drama, motives are personified within actions that converge in a unified vision.

Symbolic convergence encourages group members to be caught up in the drama. Those who share the fantasy act it out (Bales, 1970; Bormann, 1985b). The psychological process of being caught up in the narrative helps group members interpret some aspects of common experience, enabling symbolic convergence on that issue. That convergence creates a coherent rhetorical vision of some aspect of their social reality (Bormann, 1985a). The rhetorical vision is a shared image of what the world is like and how people fit into the world. People who share the vision become a rhetorical community, knit together by a common sense of purpose, agency, motivation, and action.

METHOD

We surveyed five magazines aimed at teenage girls for their advice on sex: *YM*, *'Teen*, and *Seventeen* aimed at a younger (12–19) audience, and *Glamour* and *Mademoiselle*, whose audience, although older (18–24), includes teenage readers. According to *Standard Rate and Data* (1995), each has been published for at least 20 years and has a circulation over 1.5 million.

Even though the demographics of *Glamour* and *Mademoiselle* suggest an older audience, we included them for three reasons. First, their messages of sexuality continue themes sounded in magazines for younger women. Given that "by the time they are 20 years old, 70% of girls and 80% of boys have engaged in sexual intercourse" (Greenberg, Brown, & Buerkel-Rothfuss, 1997, p. 1), these magazines may be sought for information and guidance. Second, according to Teenage Research Unlimited (1991), *Mademoiselle* and *Glamour* captured 14.4% and 18.3%, respectively, of the 12- to 19-year-old market. *Mademoiselle* reported that 20% of its readers are between 12 and 19 years of age and *Glamour* reported that 14.5% of its readers fall within this age group (S. Martin, personal communication, March 2,

1993). Third, although their targeted audience may be older, younger and midrange teens find easy access to them in older sisters' rooms, libraries, and store shelves.

Focusing on the editorial part of the magazines that gave direct sexual or relationship advice to young women, we analyzed health, sex, and relationship columns, as well as any directly related feature articles or stories in the April and October issues from 1974, 1984, and 1994. We selected these years because we wanted to see if the advice changed over time, and reflected the impact of AIDS. We chose advice columns and features because they provide readers the clearest possible picture of what sex and sexual relationships should be like; this is information supported by the prescriptive advice of the "experts" who author the articles. The 30 issues provided us with 175 articles for analysis. April and October issues were used because we wanted months that would not be influenced by holidays (e.g., Christmas) or special events (e.g., proms and summer vacations).

Relying on categories of analysis drawn from Bormann's symbolic convergence theory, we mapped the narrative of appropriate sexual conduct and expression created by the material as a whole. Within this interpretive frame, we looked specifically for sexual metaphors, phrases, and sentences as they relate to setting, character, and action. Following the guidelines of Silverman (1993), the three primary authors and two other researchers read all the advice columns and stories in all the magazines and interpreted the material. Each independently made his or her own lists of sexual metaphors, key words, phrases, and sentences. Each recorded interpretations and whether he or she thought items related to setting, character, or action. The descriptive lists were collated. As a group, we discussed the emerging themes and patterns (major, minor, and conflicting ones) and came to agreement on the content and its implications. Differences were resolved by reexamining and discussing the text in question.

THE STORY OF SEX

In 1974, only 'Teen, Glamour, and Mademoiselle directly and openly addressed the issue of sexual activity and sexuality through such topics as sex and the single scene, infidelity, pregnancy and abortion, venereal disease, "his body," and bust exercises. Coverage in YM and Seventeen was more implicit, focusing on the dating game, dating etiquette, abusive boyfriends, kissing, love letters, going steady, surviving a breakup, and being a loser on the dating scene. By 1984, all more openly addressed male-female sexuality and sexual relations. Coverage in YM and Seventeen was not as extensive, but it was as definitive. Seventeen, for example, carried articles on teen pregnancy and masturbation, abortion, and sexual double standards. Mademoiselle and Glamour continued their unabashed approach to sexuality by talking about subjects such as ejaculations, male attitudes toward their penis, and talking too much while lovemaking. By 1994, the differences in treatment of sexuality among magazines were slim. Whereas Glamour and Mademoiselle talked about erotic dreams with lesbians, satisfying sex with an older man, penis enlargements, last minute flings, and so forth, YM, Seventeen, and 'Teen discussed wanting babies, boyfriends wanting virgins (and she's not), sex with cousins, sexual abuse, sex between juveniles and adults, chastity belts, whether a guy can tell if you're a virgin, and being addicted to love. In sum, over time we saw a shift in the range and explicitness of topics relating to sexuality. This finding is consistent with Strasburger's (1995) observation that contemporary magazines, like television, reflect a trend away from "naive or innocent romantic love" to "increasingly clinical concerns about sexual functioning" (p. 46). We did not see, however, any significant change over time or magazine in how women's sexuality was framed. We decided, therefore, to treat the material primarily in a paradigmatic (stressing content-based categories) rather than syntagmatic (stressing change over time) way. We will, however, discuss changes over time that we did observe.

Setting Themes

The setting for the sexual relationship dance between male and female teenagers was rarely named or described in teen magazines. Sex appeared to occur whenever and wherever possible. Teenage sexual activities and relationships took place wherever teens could find a private space at home, parties, or even school. The magazines, however, did not show sexual activity taking place on vacation, at home, or within bedrooms, sites where adults typically engage in sexual activity. This lack of focus on the physical setting was in marked contrast with adult magazines. A cursory review of more adult-directed women's magazines, such as *Cosmopolitan*, *Elle*, and *Harper's Bazaar*, revealed the importance of place for adults by providing articles that focused on subjects like decorating the bedroom or bathroom to make it more romantic or suitable for lovemaking, creating the most romantic picnics for two, and discovering the most romantic vacation hideaways. The question, then, is why was there no clear physical setting for the sexual drama?

The most obvious answer is that parents control the "normal" sex setting. Rules forbidding members of the opposite sex in a daughter's or son's bedroom are not uncommon. This makes sexual activity difficult within the home, especially the bedroom. A less obvious answer is that to focus directly on setting assumes an established knowledge level most, or many, teens do not have. Young teens do not ask sophisticated questions, such as where can I have sex, or what is the most romantic hideaway for sex. Rather, they ask such questions as should I have sex, and if I do, "how do I kiss," "give oral sex," or must I have "anal sex if I don't want to?" (Lever & Schwartz, 1994b, p. 69). The scene of the story, then, is not of primary importance. Reducing adolescent uncertainty about the basic nature of sex is.

Character Themes

Finders (1997) found that teen magazines help young women identify the nature of their new adult community, as well as the other actors. In the magazines we surveyed, there were two actors in this sexual drama: the "guy," or boyfriend, and the "girl." The most prevalent questions were these: What are guys like? What do guys want from girls? How should I behave around guys? Overall, men or "guys" were characterized as users and controllers within the community, whereas women or "girls" were characterized as negotiators of their own use.

Girls

In teen magazines, girls were assumed to be, quite simply, in the process of "becoming." Girls were never right just as they were. This vision takes on added importance in light of the Gilligan, Lyons, and Hanmer (1987) finding that adolescent girls see themselves as becoming someone in relation to other important persons in their lives (e.g., their mothers or teachers). Gilligan et al. (1987) argued that many girls submerge their individuality and sense of identity in favor of becoming what someone else wants them to be. They found that it was the rare girl who maintained her sense of self if it conflicted with what she perceived to be the sense of self promoted by important others. Our analysis revealed that teen magazines encouraged girls to become what significant others, in particular, guys, wanted them to be.

Health and relationship advice columns, supplemented and complemented by fictional stories and features on sexual issues, encouraged young women to become sexual objects whose lives were not complete unless sexually connected with a man. Girls could earn a man, first, by recognizing traditional interests ("affection" and "company") and training of women (to be "ladylike," "neat," and "polite"; Rubis, 1984), and, second, through the changing of self as they negotiated their way through sexual encounters and relationships. Young women achieved the latter by being better informed than guys about male and female physiology and psychology; by attracting guys through good-looking hair, beautiful clothes, and thin bodies; and by developing sex and relationship skills. According to *Seventeen*, "If you see someone you like or who seems interested in you, let yourself glow. Take a chance. Bring yourself to flirt. Play a little. That's what flirting really is: part of a game between men and women" (Wood, 1974, p. 58). According to *YM*, it also helps if they possess the quality of innocence.

> Do you know the one quality boys can't resist? It's innocence. They refer to it by many terms ("cute," "sweet," "adorable," "charming," etc.), but what really attracts boys is innocence. That's why an actress like Brooke Shields is so alluring; she projects childlike, wide-eyed naiveté into her roles. (Rubis, 1984, p. 47)

This innocence was especially evident in the 1974 issues of *YM* and *Seventeen*, where the girls were, implicitly, virgins looking for tips on being a good kisser and proper dating etiquette. "My question is short and sweet: Is it or is it not considered proper to call a boy these days?" (Borchart, 1974, p. 38). Not all the younger teens were virgins, however, as evidenced by articles in *'Teen* on venereal disease ("The Truth Behind VD," 1974) and "his body" ("You, Your Parents," 1974), and in *Mademoiselle* about "getting laid," infidelity, and abortion (Baudry & Weiner, 1974; Durbin, 1974a, 1974b). By 1984, girls were told, both subtly and directly, that they should focus primarily on understanding the "guy," and meeting or dealing with his constant sexual desire and readiness. Even in articles focusing on a young woman's emerging sexuality, such as in the April 1984 issue of *'Teen*, "Sexual Involvement: The Experts Answer Your Questions," young women were warned that they could expect to be pressured into sex and experience painful emotional and sexual scars from male-female relationships (Soria, 1984a). *'Teen*'s October 1994 issue stated:

> That's not to say that guys don't value girls as people, but chances are they may have some sexual agenda as well. Girls often get physically involved with a guy to feel close emotionally. Guys are more apt to separate the emotional from the physical. Girls, therefore, can be more vulnerable to getting hurt after getting physical. ("Why Guys Do What They Do," 1994, p. 34)

To survive the presumably inherently animalistic traits of men, the October 1974 issue of *Seventeen* advised girls to be patient, as, "like most boys, your friend simply doesn't want to make a big display of his emotions, especially in school"

(Borchart, 1974, p. 36). In 1984, it advised that, when guys "make these lame non-committal offers, we're also trying to gauge your reaction. If you respond with a friendly smile and a sincere 'that would be great,' we just might come through for once and say exactly what we mean when we make that promised call" (Schwartz, 1984a, p. 104). In 1984 *Glamour* cautioned girls to avoid the tendency to be "pushy," "bossy," or to act like "mom" (Naifeh & Smith, 1984). "The other mistake women make is to show their 'independence' by being demanding" (Naifeh & Smith, 1984, p. 291). In *Seventeen* and *YM*, girls were told to fight the "desperate" urge to get pregnant (Duncan, 1994; Fuller, 1994). In *'Teen* they were told to fight the urge to "pin guys down" or to push for "commitments" before guys are ready ("Why Guys Do What They Do," 1994).

Guys

In teen magazines, guys simply "are." Guys need to know only themselves and, because they "are," they need not worry about "becoming" men or achieving power or status; they already have it. According to *'Teen*, because they possess these qualities, guys are "allowed to be wild," have "fewer restrictions," and focus more on "impressing buddies" and "group bonding" than on relationship and communication skills ("Why Guys Do What They Do,"1994, pp. 32–34).

Whether looking at teen magazines from 1974, 1984, or 1994, we found that guys lacked relationship skills and proved unable to express themselves verbally or emotionally. Any presentation of women's sexuality also involved a treatment of men's sexuality. Over the 20 years, men's sexuality was narrowly portrayed as animalistic and self-centered, and the sexual advice became more explicit and graphic. In 1974, guys were difficult to talk to, used girls, made them feel like losers, and cheated on them sexually (only in *Mademoiselle* was this explicitly stated, see Durbin, 1974a). By 1984, guys did all these things, *and* they were primarily motivated by sex and self-interest. Guys "don't learn [about sex] from talking with the guys. [They] learn from hands-on training with girls." Their training, however, was inherently unsuccessful, because they only knew the basic mechanics of sex (Nelson, 1984, p. 157). Nonetheless, according to *'Teen*, guys pushed girls beyond their level of sexual readiness (e.g., beyond kissing) or used excuses to pressure girls into sexual intercourse.

> Are guys really in pain if they are sexually aroused, then don't have sexual intercourse? . . . It's important to be aware that this "pain" is sometimes used as a tactic to pressure a girl into more sexual activity than she's ready for. For example, if a guy says, "If you loved me, you wouldn't want to see me in pain." This line should be a warning to you that this person puts his own physical satisfaction above your emotional welfare. (Soria, 1984a, pp. 9–10)

Younger teens were told by *Seventeen* that guys kiss you and then call you "stupid" (Schwartz, 1984b, p. 68). They were told by *'Teen* that guys start going "out a lot" and "stop coming around" when you get pregnant (Soria, 1984b, p. 91). They were told by *YM* that guys marry only virgins (Clifford, 1994, p. 37), and by *'Teen*, again, that guys toy with your emotions or "act mean," because they "want to be cool in front of friends" (Nguyen, 1994, p. 30). Older teens were warned by *Mademoiselle* that guys deceive you sexually and emotionally (Durbin, 1974a). They were told by *Glamour* that guys demand that you "make [yourself] irresistible to other men" as a means of measuring your worth and his own (Barbasch, 1984, p. 325). They were warned by *Mademoiselle* that guys ask you to do things like join in a threesome with your best friend (Vernon, 1994, p. 74).

Ironically, these male ways of being, although depicted as regrettable, were not shown as lacking worth. Although the advice columns overtly guided young women to accept men as they were, further guidance came from other parts of the magazine, in particular, the celebrity biography and photo spread. In teen magazines guys were set up as ideals or poster boys meant to be treated by young women as icons—someone to placate, adore, and manipulate. This ideal, two-dimensional male was presented as the type of "guy" who could fulfill the "girl's" dream, standing in for all men for young women trying to understand and know men's wishes, needs, and behaviors.

> Warning: "TV Turn-ons," our tear-out-and-tape-it-to-your-wall story, may be damaging to your social life. Once you get a look at our favorite guys from the new fall shows, you'll be tempted to stay home every night and glue yourself to the couch in front of the tube. ("TV Turn-Ons," 1994, p. 10)

Young women, encouraged to "study" these icons as if they were the enemy, read about "guy" qualities and characteristics to survive within the community.

Action Themes

The narrative clarified the elements of sexual advice and told the reader which elements were the most important. It stressed the kind of character, and person, the young woman should strive to be within the community. Three central action themes emerged from our analysis. All presumed sexual activity on the part of young women, suggesting how they should adapt themselves to sex, as young men want it. We should be clear, these magazines encouraged women to be self-reliant and to defend themselves and their desires for better treatment within a relationship. The women were not told to be patsies or to let men walk all over them. Independence and emotional strength were touted in all the magazines. These messages, however, were usually not tied to the woman's own sexuality. Instead, the predominant themes included presenting oneself as sexually desirable (not desiring), developing the skills of sexual therapy (designed to enhance men's sexual pleasure and performance), and becoming a communication teacher (to help guys become better relational partners).

Woman as Sex Object

As members of the adolescent, sexually active community, young women were told to be sexually desirable and ready for sexual activity. This is not to say the advice columns, like those in *Seventeen* and *YM*, did not tell young women to "wait" until they are emotionally (Kent, 1994) or legally "ready" (Clifford, 1994; Lee, 1994). They repeatedly cautioned young women about engaging in sex before they were ready. However, woven into these cautions was the underlying assumption that readers are, or soon will be, engaging in sexual activity. The presumption was that sexual intercourse would happen before marriage. The only questions were where, when, and with whom.

Magazines told young women to be ready and willing through standard articles and advertisements on "sexy outfits," "sexy hair he'll love," and "passionate fingernails." They encouraged girls to "shape-up" for that "sexy swimsuit he'll love," and to eat right for that "healthy" and "sexy" glow. Through advice columns, like those in *Mademoiselle*, older teens read questions from other teens about whether it was safe to have sex if your boyfriend had cold sores ("he says not to worry"; Rosenbaum, 1984, p. 50), whether sex was better when your bladder was full (Vernon, 1994, p. 78), or whether getting pregnant to "tie a man down" was ever successful (Baudry & Wiener, 1974, p. 34). Older teens could also read in *Glamour* about how to deal with the sexual activities men desire of women. "I've been seeing a guy for a couple of months. Our sex life is great, but lately he's been asking me to perform oral sex on him. I'd love to—but I don't even know how to begin. Please tell me" (Lever & Schwartz, 1994a, p. 76). Through discourse such as this, younger women were told that others within their community were actively engaging in sex, and that others achieved success and status within their community through sexual intimacy.

This sense of a sexually active community was especially evident in the 1994 magazines geared toward the younger teens. Here, young girls wrote to *YM* about having sex with their 18-year-old boyfriends when they were 14 years old (Lee, 1994), or to *'Teen* about sex when they were 13 years old ("Ask Juli," 1994b), or to *Seventeen* about their desire to have a baby (Duncan, 1994). In *YM* one girl wrote: "I'm a 15-year-old girl and I want a baby—in fact, I've always wanted a baby. I've been going out with the guy for about seven months . . . . I've agreed to wait, but it hurts really badly—I want a child so much" (Fuller, 1994, p. 28).

In 1984, the sexual activity of the younger women was addressed more implicitly in these same magazines through articles on sexual involvement (Soria, 1984a), pregnancy (Graeber, 1984; Kellogg, 1984), and premature parenthood (Soria, 1984b). In 1974, only *'Teen* magazine acknowledged sexual activity beyond kissing, through its discussion of venereal disease ("The Truth Behind VD"). This shift, over time, in content acknowledging sexual activity seemingly corresponded with increased teen sexual activity noted by Greenberg et al. (1997) and the editorial trend cited by Strasburger (1995). Regardless, these articles and columns for younger and older teens rarely addressed the teen's own sexual needs and concerns. The one exception was the "Sex and Your Body" column in *Seventeen* (McCoy, 1984) entitled "Masturbation: Normal or Not." Even more importantly in the age of AIDS, young girls were rarely told how to protect themselves.

Over time, in the advice columns to younger teens, young women who were not ready for sex or were having problems getting dates were encouraged to employ self-analysis for possible emotional or behavioral problems—for example, is she "not getting enough love from [her] own parents" (Fuller, 1994, p. 28), or is she "too dependent on him"? ("Whoa!," 1994, p. 46). Young women were advised to let their "shyness" work for them, and stop being "flirts [and] social butterflies" because "boys like to feel special. They love it when you shower them with [selective] attention" (Rubis, 1984, p. 47). According to *Seventeen*, if you are a "loser" because you "can't bring [yourself] to flirt the way some girls do because it seems so fake," you should examine your own anger and hidden feelings and reconsider "the other old saw: A boy runs after a girl until she catches him!" (Wood, 1974, p. 58).

Self-analysis is also a way young women can determine what may be going "wrong" in a relationship. The "Dear Jill" column in *'Teen* (October 1984) suggested:

> Next, it may help to examine how you're acting around guys, to make sure you're not sending out the wrong signals. For example, do you act naturally

around guys? Some girls get caught up in acting according to how they think a "popular" girl would act, rather than how they feel most comfortable. This often appears phony. Are you too complimentary? Sincere compliments seem insincere when they're dished out excessively. Do you tend to talk too much around guys? (p. 24)

Is the girl "ask[ing] him questions about himself," just filling "the dead space with tales about [her]self," or "cornering him into a commitment" ("Dating Dilemmas," 1994, p. 18)? Questions such as these encourage several assumptions on the part of young women: (a) Relationship problems are the fault and responsibility of women, (b) women must subjugate self for the sake of the relationship, and (c) women who do not make men the center of the relationship will not succeed as members of the community. This self-analysis, and the self-help culture that promotes the continued social and emotional subordination of women, have been well studied (e.g., May, 1988; Simonds, 1992; Tavris, 1992), but the sites of study have been adult women's magazines and self-help books. These cultural messages begin much earlier.

Because guys are "inconsiderate," "manipulative," and "possessive," girls can expect to be treated like "dirt." Teen magazines provided explanations and potential solutions or warnings for this "guy" behavior. According to 'Teen, for example, "guys" act "kind of mean because they want to act cool in front of their friends." The solution is to "be nice to him—suggest swapping phone numbers" (Nguyen, 1994, p. 30). YM told young women that

> if it's hearts and flowers you're looking for, try to initiate some romance yourself. . . . If your boyfriend is like most guys, he should take the hint and start doing nice things for you. But don't expect him to change overnight; some guys can be really thickheaded about picking up clues. (Blanchard, 1994, p. 37)

The implication was that their behavior can be changed eventually. Other solutions, offered by *Seventeen*, included reassuring guys of their worth and changing guy behavior (e.g., dating other girls) through the sharing of feelings (Borchart, 1974; Schwartz, 1984b). Conversely, YM warned girls that guys who didn't want a "used tire" (i.e., a nonvirgin) should be dumped (Blanchard, 1994, p. 37). It should also be noted that the advice given by YM in this latter situation included one of the few references we found about AIDS: "He, as your new partner, has the right to know your sexual history—what with AIDS and other sexually transmitted diseases" (Blanchard, 1994, p. 37). Significantly, the woman was not encouraged to press him for information about his sexual history. In fact, and in contrast to Strasburger's (1995) claim that print media are more informative about birth control, we found only eight overt mentions of birth control and nine references to sexually transmitted diseases or AIDS; all but two appeared in the 1994 issues of YM, *Seventeen*, *Mademoiselle*, and *Glamour*.

Women as Sex Therapists

Not only must young women adapt themselves to male-defined sexual expression, they must also teach men their own needs and how to satisfy them. Although this theme did not appear overtly in the 1974 sample, it was foreshadowed in its grooming of young women to communicate well with men, on their terms. By 1984, however, whether the magazines targeted younger or older teens, the sex therapist character theme was clear—it is the job of women to teach men how to be good lovers and to adapt themselves to male desires and needs. The explicitness of the messages, especially those from 1994, reflected more graphic sexual content rather than sexual agency on the part of women. Overall, male pleasure oriented and drove the advice.

On one level, teen magazines encouraged young women to think of themselves and their needs (e.g., to be independent, assertive, self-assured, and confident of their body image). Young women were told to move at their own pace and respect themselves by standing up to guys and avoiding male pressure to engage in activities that made them feel uncomfortable. *Seventeen* advised: "In terms of sexual activity, it's always possible to slow down, and anyone can choose to go from intercourse to kissing or anywhere in between. What you do—and don't do—is entirely up to you" (Kent, 1994, p. 114). Magazines aimed at younger teens encouraged them to refuse unwanted sexual moves, even if they had been active in the past: "Though you may have been sexually involved in the past, this doesn't mean that you are obligated to continue to be sexually active. . . . Let him know that it's not acceptable for him to pressure you. You said no, and you mean it" ("Ask Juli," 1994a, p. 6). Girls were also urged to "reconsider staying in a relationship" that's making them "unhappy" or where guys engage in unkind "macho" behavior (Schwartz, 1984b, p. 69).

However, once they have crossed the threshold of intercourse, the magazines sought to persuade girls to act as sex therapists in the male-female relationship. This was especially true in the 1984 and 1994 magazines directed toward older teens, who were told sexual issues were their responsibility through articles and advice on how to deal with male sexual desires such as the desire for a ménage à trois (Vernon, 1994) or anal sex (Lever & Schwartz, 1994b). The magazines also provided a guide for dealing with sexual problems such as waning sexual desire (Markowitz, 1994), and premature ejaculation or male impotency (Nelson, 1984). Young women were encouraged to help their "guys" through these problems by directly addressing the problem (Rosenbaum, 1984) or looking for "love boosts" to get them out of a dull routine (Volchok, 1984). The predominate focus, however, was not on the young woman's own sexual needs, or even how to train a man to please her or to enjoy sex more.

Women as Communication Teachers

Across the spectrum, from younger to older markets, teen magazines encouraged young women to teach men emotional intimacy by acting as communication teachers and therapists. The best example was an article in the April 1984 issue of *Glamour*. Entitled "Men and Intimacy: How to Get Your Man to Open Up," the article noted that a man can't help himself because "He's paralyzed by his fears— of rejection, of dependence, and that he's not the man he ought to be. He needs a woman's help" (Naifeh & Smith, p. 290). The article then provided "five ways to help him open up" and "ten ways to get him talking." Younger teens were counseled by *YM* to:

> Remember that boys are human, too. They're sensitive (some experts say more so than girls), they need comforting, and they have feelings, thoughts, worries, dreams, just as you do. Work hard to see this side of boys, and respond to it. (Rubis, 1984, p. 48)

Rarely, however, were young women encouraged to discuss issues of pregnancy, birth control, or AIDS with the guys; the one exception was found in *YM* (Blanchard, 1994).

In teen magazines a young woman's primary schema, goal, or responsibility was presented as developing a working heterosexual relationship. *'Teen* advised that, "If you want to understand a guy, it's important to look at his actions. That way you'll be better able to understand the language he's been taught—the language of action" ("Why Guys Do What They Do," 1994, p. 34). According to *Glamour*, she must:

> Teach a man—by example and encouragement; learn to listen more closely to the sometimes muted and indirect ways he may express his feelings; and try to understand the value of nonverbal forms of communication. "There is a male and female code of expression," says one psychiatrist, "and you have to know how to translate feelings and ideas into each other's language. Since it's not very likely that a man will try to learn the female code of expression on his own, a woman's going to have to make the effort to teach him her language." (Naifeh & Smith, 1984, p. 355)

In other words, she must, "in a sense, tutor the guy" by example ("Why Guys Do What They Do," 1994, p. 34). She can do this by "being open herself," "accepting his foibles," "not forcing the issue," and "seeing the problem from his side" (Naifeh & Smith, 1984, pp. 354–355). Young women were advised to put the guy and his problems first. This was illustrated in advice that if she must complain, a "girl" should first "validate" her boyfriend's feelings. In the time-honored tradition of wife meeting weary warrior husband, she must put her boyfriend's needs first and foremost.

A RHETORICAL VISION OF CONTAINMENT

Teen magazines' columns, stories, and features on sex and heterosexual relationships present a simple, clear rhetorical vision: The sexual community belongs to men, and women survive by containing themselves and by adapting and subjugating themselves to male desires. This drama or fantasy is comprised of three types: setting, character, and action. The setting for the sexual drama is everywhere and nowhere. The characters are heterosexual men and women, each with their own characteristics. In teen magazines, man is depicted as animal (not self-conscious), and woman is depicted as animal trainer. That is demeaning to men, given their role in the creation of ethical, moral, philosophical, and religious systems, and to women, who are given only private and no public power. This persona is not very different from the one projected in advertising and other media. Strasburger (1995) and Greenberg et al. (1997) found that, although sexual content in television and music videos has increased in quantity and explicitness, traditional depictions of men as sexually powerful and aggressive and women as sexually weak and submissive are pervasive. Cross-culturally, van Zoonen (1994) found that, despite their extensive spiritual and intellectual training, geishas are perceived by Western males, especially, as objects and providers of male sexual desires (p. 80). Similar negation of intellectual worth and promotion of erotic fantasies have been held about African women (p. 82). In teen magazines, the fantasy action for young White women perpetuates the Victorian idea of woman as the keeper of the flame of male-defined culture. She becomes the keeper by developing a self-denying, male-affirming persona that is shaped, influenced, and determined by the hegemonic sexuality of the drama.

The rhetorical community developed through the working out of this vision is impoverished, as well. By implication, the community of people bound together by this common vision is made up of young, White, heterosexually active men and women who have no fear of, or concerns about, AIDS, other sexually transmitted diseases, or pregnancy. Over time and magazine, the characters within the community have not changed. The fantasy actions, however, have changed somewhat. Younger girls are assumed to be more openly and explicitly engaging in sexual relations with men; older teens are doing the same (plus also serving as sexual therapists). *Mademoiselle* and *Glamour* were most explicit, but the other magazines were not far behind. There were few virgins, no gay men or lesbian women, no men interested in learning how to love women, no women who thought as highly of themselves as they did of men. There were just sexually experienced guys and girls. Whether young girls' real-world experiences enable them to critique these actions adequately, along with the overwhelming sense that everyone else is "doing it," remains to be explored.

Other than brief mentions of masturbation in *Seventeen* (McCoy, 1984), lesbian dreams in *Mademoiselle* (Vernon, 1994), bisexual men who put their female partners at risk in *Glamour* (Lever & Schwartz, 1994a), and one story in *Mademoiselle* about a woman trying to save a gay man from being gay (Scott, 1984), we found no representations that homosexuality or masturbation can be appropriate expressions of sexuality. Although there was nothing that condemned these sexual expressions, their absence can be seen as very limiting or isolating to young women with these interests. The question, then becomes: Although the male-centered, heterosexual focus of the magazines may be regrettable, is it not also an accurate depiction of our culture? Are these magazines not realistic in their fantasy themes and the community that is developed? The answer is, predominately, "yes," but that does not make the presentation any less problematic. Certainly, the goal, as presented in these magazines, of pleasing one's sexual partner is desirable, but at what expense? Although young girls in teen magazines are given agency to say no, that agency is overwhelmed by the message that their prime goal should be to please men and not give offense.

Within this vision, young women are told that they must lose weight, learn about sophisticated sexual techniques, apply makeup well, dress in a sexy manner, and engage in self-analysis when (not if) their real world does not fit with the world depicted. This serves the magazines' purpose of selling advertising. Female deficiency is needed to maintain advertising sufficiency. Editorial content that promotes knowledge about issues such as AIDS, abortion, and pregnancy do not fit advertisers' profiles of deficient women (Steinem, 1990). As *Sassy* and *Ms.* found out, magazines that put women first do not prosper with advertisers. They do not fit the vision or the community.

Far from presenting a modern and up-to-date image of women, one that might enhance young women's sense of their own sexual worth, contemporary teenage girls' magazines sound the same themes sounded for years in women's magazines and home economics textbooks—how to meet successfully the needs and desires of men. Josephine Morris (1913), for example, noted for young women attending the Kirksville, Missouri, Normal Practice School the following: "But the mother or home maker is expected to be unfailingly pleasant, cheerful, and patient, and to smooth out all difficulties, no matter how worn or tired she may be" (pp. 221–222). Similarly, the 1960s Amy Vanderbilt Success Program for Women provided advice that began: "A man arrives at his own door with the day's atmosphere—good or bad—still clinging to him. A sensitive wife greets him warmly and waits to take her cue from him" (Fischer, 1964, p. 43).

In essence, the rhetorical vision presented in teen magazines, and these earlier quotes for successful female life, is one of containment, in which women fit themselves into a subordinate, male-defined sexual role. May (1988) noted that containment was the "overarching principle" that guided post-World War II Americans in their personal and political lives. May added that "much of [society's] anxiety focused on women, whose economic and sexual behavior seemed to have changed dramatically" (p. 93). Working women, and women who expressed their own sexuality outside of the home, were seen as socially deviant and dangerous to home and country (pp. 94–100). Popular culture and social and psychological "experts" joined the bandwagon and encouraged women to stay at home and adhere to family values. If women were unhappy with this arrangement, they were encouraged to look to themselves for the source of their displeasure and to consult the many self-help books and magazines available to reduce their discomfort (May, 1988; Simonds, 1992; Tavris, 1992; Wolf, 1991). As Simone de Beauvoir observed, "Once again women are being defined in terms of 'the other,' once again they are being made into the 'second sex'" (quoted in Schwartzer, 1984, p. 103). That view, as well as that of May, appears to still be true—at least in teen magazines. The story they tell of female sexuality leaves little room for oppositional readings and little space for young women who might want to find out how to please themselves or teach men how to please them, or who might desire discussion of sexually transmitted diseases, of sexual abstinence, of masturbation, or of same-sex relationships.

Ehrenreich and English (1978) noted that 19th-century feminists such as Charlotte Perkins Gilman and Olive Schreiner realized, "the problem in the middle to upper classes was that marriage had become a 'sexuo-economic relation' in which women performed sexual reproductive duties for financial support" (p. 95). The training manuals or primers noted above guided young women to accept a reduced situation in the early and mid-20th century. We argue a similar, but not identical, guiding function is fulfilled by the containment rhetoric of teenage girls' magazines. Brumberg (1997) pointed out that, at least in the past, women could count on men taking care of them. "Although girls now mature sexually earlier than ever before, contemporary American society provides fewer social protections for them, a situation that leaves them unsupported in their development and extremely vulnerable to the excesses of popular culture and to pressure from peer groups" (p. xvii). Although earlier cultural training manuals promised economic stability, if not advancement, to women who fulfilled their character roles, modern teen magazines offer little to women in return for their sexual and relational involvement with men. Indeed, these magazines tell young women not to nag, not to push for commitment, but to simply wait for whatever men wish to give them.

Magazines marketed to young men, such as *GQ* and *Esquire*, offer a message that complements those given to young women. As Ehrenreich (1996) observed,

"The masculine ideal of popular culture has long since ceased to be the man in the grey flannel suit, trudging dutifully between office and home. It has become the millionaire hoop star with a stable of interchangeable gal pals" (p. 36). When stories of heterosexual relations are told in men's magazines, they are stories of sexual conquest or of surviving demanding women (*Esquire*, June 1995).

The combination of stories may well be a potent one, reinforcing the cultural assumption that young teen males are fine just as they are, and that the world is both oriented to and dominated by men. If young people take these messages to heart, they will continue to enact a vision in which men are the citizens of the world and women are citizens of the world of men. Ultimately showing little change in story dynamic from the primers of yesterday, little influence from the feminist movement or 20 years of political conservatism, and virtually no influence from the presence of AIDS in American society, teen magazines present young women with a limited rhetorical vision of the world. This vision of women as sex objects, sex therapists, and interpersonal communication teachers rather than friends, partners, lovers, and mothers, promotes the subordination of self for others and encourages young women to become contained.

References

Ask Juli. (1994a, October). '*Teen*, *38*, 10.

Ask Juli. (1994b, April). '*Teen*, *38*, 6.

Bales, R. F. (1970). *Personality and interpersonal behavior*. New York: Holt, Rinehart, & Winston.

Barbasch, A. (1984, October). The ghost of your first love. *Glamour*, *82*, 325–327.

Baudry, F., & Wiener, A. (1974, April). A woman's choice: Pregnancy or abortion. *Mademoiselle*, *80*, 34, 42.

Blanchard, K. (1994, October). His side. *YM*, *42*, 37.

Borchart, D. (1974, October). Relating. *Seventeen*, *33*, 36, 38.

Bormann, E. G. (1972). Fantasy and rhetorical vision: The rhetorical criticism of social reality. *Quarterly Journal of Speech*, *68*, 288–305.

Bormann, E. G. (1985a). Symbolic convergence theory: A communication formulation. *Journal of Communication*, *35*(4), 128–138.

Bormann, E. G. (1985b). *The force of fantasy: Restoring the American dream*. Carbondale: Southern Illinois University Press.

Brumberg, J. J. (1997). *The body project: An intimate history of American girls*. New York: Random House.

Carmody, D. (1994, December 8). Peterson will restart *Sassy* with push for older readers. *New York Times*, p. D19.

Clifford, C. (1994, April). Dear Katie. *YM*, *42*, 37.

Dating dilemmas. (1994, April). '*Teen*, *38*, 18.

Dear Jill. (1984, October). '*Teen*, *28*, p. 24.

DeFleur, M., & Ball-Rokeach, S. (1982). *Theories of mass communication* (4th ed.). New York: Longman.

Duffy, M., & Gotcher, M. J. (1996). Crucial advice on how to get the guy: The rhetorical vision of power and seduction in the teen magazine *YM*. *Journal of Communication Inquiry*, *20*(1), 32–48.

Duke, L. (1995, August). *From Seventeen to Sassy: Teen magazines and the construction of the "model" girl*. Paper presented at the annual conference of the Association for Education in Journalism and Mass Communication, Washington, DC.

Duncan, S. (1994, October). Sex + body. *Seventeen*, *53*, 100–101.

Durbin, K. (1974a, April). The intelligent woman's guide to sex. *Mademoiselle*, *80*, 94.

Durbin, K. (1974b, October). The intelligent woman's guide to sex. *Mademoiselle*, *80*, 70.

Durham, G. (1996). The taming of the shrew: Women's magazines and the regulation of desire. *Journal of Communication Inquiry, 20*(1), 18–31.

Ehrenreich, B., & English, D. (1978). *For her own good.* Garden City, NY: Anchor Press.

Ehrenreich, B. (1996, May 6). Whose gap is it anyway? *Time, 147,* 36.

Evans, E. D., Rutberg, J., Sather, C., & Turner, C. (1991). Content analysis of contemporary teen magazines for adolescent females. *Youth and Society, 23*(1), 99–120.

Ferguson, M. (1983). *Forever feminine: Women's magazines and the cult of femininity.* London: Heinemann.

Finders, M. J. (1997). *Just girls: Hidden literacies and life in junior high.* New York: Teachers College Press.

Fine, M. (1988). Sexuality, schooling, and adolescent females: The missing discourse of desire. *Harvard Educational Review, 58*(1), 28–53.

Fischer, N. (1964). *How to help your husband get ahead.* Garden City, NY: Doubleday.

Fisher, W. (1987). *Human communication as narration: Toward a philosophy of reason, value, and action.* Columbia: University of South Carolina Press.

Frazer, E. (1987). Teenage girls reading Jackie. *Media, Culture and Society, 9,* 407–425.

Fuller, B. (1994, April). Love crisis. *YM, 42,* 28.

Gilligan, C., Lyons, N. P., & Hanmer, T. J. (1990). *Making connections: The relational worlds of adolescent girls at Emma Willard School.* Cambridge, MA: Harvard University Press.

Graeber, L. (1984, April). Teen pregnancy: "It couldn't happen to me." *YM, 32,* 46–48, 76–77.

Greenberg, B. S., Brown, J. D., & Buerkel-Rothfuss, N. L. (1997). *Media, sex and the adolescent.* Cresskill, NJ: Hampton Press.

Kellner, D. (1995). Cultural studies, multiculturalism and media culture. In G. Dines & J. M. Humez (Eds.), *Gender, race and class in media: A text-reader* (pp. 5–17). London: Sage.

Kellogg, M. A. (1984, October). How two teens faced pregnancy: "I had an abortion"/"I kept my baby." *Seventeen, 43,* 144–146.

Kent, D. (1994, April). Sex body. *Seventeen, 53,* 112–113.

Larsen, E. (1990, July). Censoring sex information: The story of "*Sassy.*" *Utne Reader, 40,* 96–97.

Lee, S. (1994, October). Love crisis. *YM, 42,* 38.

Lever, J., & Schwartz, P. (1994a, April). Sex & health. *Glamour, 92,* 76–78.

Lever, J., & Schwartz, P. (1994b, October). Sex & health. *Glamour, 92,* 69.

Markowitz, L. (1994, April). Cycles of desire. *Glamour, 92,* 226–227, 281–283.

May, E. T. (1988). *Homeward bound: American families in the cold war era.* New York: Basic Books.

McCoy, K. (1984, October). Sex and your body. *Seventeen, 43,* 12–14.

McCracken, E. (1993). *Decoding women's magazines: From Mademoiselle to Ms.* Houndmills, UK: Macmillan.

McRobbie, A. (1991). *Feminism and youth culture: From Jackie to just seventeen.* Boston: Unwin Hyman.

Moore, S., & Rosenthal, D. (1993). *Sexuality in adolescence.* New York: Routledge.

Morris, J. (1913). *Household science and arts.* New York: American Book.

Naifeh, S., & Smith, G. W. (1984, April). How to get your man to open up. *Glamour, 82,* 290–293, 354–357, 363–365.

Nelson, P. (1984, October). Growing up the hard way. *Mademoiselle, 90,* 156–157, 254, 256.

Nguyen, M. (1994, April). Teen to teen. *'Teen, 38,* 30.

Peirce, K. (1990). A feminist theoretical perspective on the socialization of teenage girls through "Seventeen." *Sex Roles, 23,* 491–500.

Peirce, K. (1993). Socialization of teenage girls through teen-magazine fiction: The making of a new woman or an old lady? *Sex Roles, 29,* 59–68.

Peirce, K. (1995). Socialization messages in *Seventeen* and *'Teen* magazines. In C. M. Lout (Ed.), *Women and media: Content/careers/criticism* (pp. 79–86). Belmont, CA: Wadsworth.

Pool, G. (1990). Magazines in review. *Wilson Library Bulletin, 95*(4), 131–135.

Rosenbaum, M. B. (1984, October). Body and soul. *Mademoiselle, 90,* 50.

Rubis, S. (1984, October). 10 ways to be popular with boys. *YM*, *32*, 46–48, 76.

Schwartz, G. (1984a, April). Boy's-eye view. *Seventeen*, *43*, 104.

Schwartz, G. (1984b, October). Boy's-eye view. *Seventeen*, *43*, 68.

Schwartzer, A. (1984). *After "The second sex": Conversations with Simone de Beauvoir*. New York: Pantheon.

Scott, J. (1984, April). I loved a gay man. *Mademoiselle*, *90*, 272–279.

Silverman, D. (1993). *Interpreting qualitative data: Methods for analysing talk, text and interaction*. Thousand Oaks, CA: Sage.

Simonds, W. (1992). *Women and self-help culture: Reading between the lines*. New Brunswick, NJ: Rutgers University Press.

Soria, S. S. (1984a, April). Sexual involvement: The experts answer your questions. *'Teen*, *28*, 9–12, 100.

Soria, S. S. (1984b, October). Premature parenthood: Coping with the consequences. *'Teen*, *28*, 10–11, 91–93.

Standard rate and data: Consumer magazine and agri-media source. (1995, January). U.S. Consumer Magazines. Willmette, IL: Standard Rate and Data Service.

Steinem, G. (1990, July/August). Sex, lies & advertising. *Ms.*, *1*, 18–28.

Steiner, L. (1995). Would the real women's magazine please stand up . . . for women. In C. M. Lout (Ed.), *Women and media: Content/careens/criticism* (pp. 99–110). Belmont, CA: Wadsworth.

Strasburger, V. (1995). *Adolescents and the media: Medical and psychological impact*. Thousand Oaks, CA: Sage.

Tavris, C. (1992). *The mismeasure of woman*. New York: Simon & Schuster.

Teenage Research Unlimited. (1991). *Seventeen research*. New York: Author.

The truth behind the VD scare. (1974, October). *'Teen*, *18*, 26–30.

Thompson, S. (1995) *Going all the way: Teenage girls' tales of sex, romance and pregnancy*. New York: Hill & Wang.

TV Turn-ons. (1994, October). *YM*, *42*, p. 78–83.

van Zoonen, L. (1994). *Feminist media studies*. Thousand Oaks, CA: Sage.

Vernon, B. (October, 1994). Sex. *Mademoiselle*, *100*, 78.

Volchok, S. M. (1994, April). Love boosts: How to rev up a relationship that's slipped into the doldrums. *Glamour*, *92*, 208–215.

Whoa! Stop boyfriend woes. (1994, April). *'Teen*, *38*, 44–47.

Why guys do what they do. (1994, October). *'Teen*, *38*, 32–34.

Wolf, N. (1991). *The beauty myth: How images of beauty are used against women*. New York: Anchor Books.

Wood, A. (1974, April). Relating. *Seventeen*, *33*, 58, 62.

You, your parents and "his body." (1974, October). *'Teen*, *33*, 18–20.

Coping with Loss
U2's "One Tree Hill"
Kelly Mendoza

On July 3, 1986, a drunk driver killed Greg Carroll, roadie and assistant to U2, in an accident in Dublin, Ireland. Bono, the singer of U2, was devastated by Carroll's sudden death. On July 10, he spoke and sang at Carroll's funeral in Wanganui, New Zealand, and two days later wrote lyrics to "One Tree Hill" in honor of his friend Carroll. The song, a response to the extremely painful experience of grieving and loss, suggests strategies that individuals may use to cope with the mysterious and difficult subject of death. In this essay, I analyze "One Tree Hill" to explore the strategies a rhetor uses to cope emotionally with the loss of sudden death.

"One Tree Hill" is on U2's *The Joshua Tree* album, released in 1987. The lyrics to the song appear to be written for a funeral because noted under the lyrics on the album insert are the words, "Greg Carroll's Funeral, Wanganui, New Zealand, 10th July 1986" (although the lyrics actually were written *after* Carroll's funeral). On the last page of the album insert is the text, "To the Memory of Greg Carroll 1960–1986." The song "One Tree Hill" refers to the highest of the volcanic hills that overlook Aukland, New Zealand, and Bono apparently knew this place was very special to Carroll. The song itself is neither extremely slow nor sad; in fact, it has an upbeat melody (unlike many songs that deal with death and dying). Bono sings the song in a loud and strong voice.

The critical method I use to explore "One Tree Hill" is fantasy-theme criticism, developed by Ernest G. Bormann to investigate a shared worldview among a group of individuals. There are two units of analysis in fantasy-theme criticism. The first is the fantasy theme, an interpretation through communication that is organized and artistic and assumes the form of settings, characters, and actions. The second unit of fantasy-theme criticism is the rhetorical vision, the grouping together of several shared fantasy themes to create a worldview.

RHETORICAL VISION

Identification of the character, action, and setting themes of "One Tree Hill" reveals two primary categories of fantasy themes in the song. One set involves violence and the other nonviolence. Below are the individual fantasy themes in each of these categories:

Violence

The fantasy themes connected to violence are as follows:

Characters	Actions	Settings
day	begs	
(your) sun	leaves no shadows	
scars	carved into stone	face of earth
(our) world		firezone, heart of darkness
poets	speak their hearts	
poets	bleed for (speaking)	

This essay was written while Kelly Mendoza was a student in Sonja K. Foss's rhetorical criticism class at the University of Colorado at Denver in 2000. Used by permission of the author.

Characters	Actions	Settings
Jara	sang his song	hands of love
(Jara's) blood	still cries	ground
bullets	rape the night	
stars	fall	

In the category of fantasy themes concerned with violence, non-human characters (*day, sun, scars, world, blood, bullets,* and *stars*) perform somewhat violent actions, such as *begs for mercy, leaves no shadows, carved, cries, rape,* and *fall.* The *bullets* perform the most extreme and sudden violence—the act of *rape.* These actions reveal a nature that is unpredictable and unforgiving. In contrast, whenever human characters (*poets* and *Jara*) speak or sing, they get hurt—both of them *bleed.*

Raging heat exists in the war zone of nature. For example, the *sun* is so *bright* that it seems to scorch the earth, the *sun leaves no shadows,* and the *day begs the night for mercy.* The *firezone* setting describes a fiery war zone because when poets speak here, their *hearts bleed.* After *Jara sang his song* (his *weapon*), his *blood cried* from the *ground.* This category illustrates a hot and dry desert of nature's violent and war-like elements and bloodshed that exists only on earth. Humans, however, have no violent influence here.

Nonviolence

The fantasy themes connected to nonviolence are as follows:

Characters	Actions	Settings
we	turn away to face	cold, enduring chill
moon	is up and over	One Tree Hill
we	see the sun go down	your eyes
you	ran like a river	sea
you	know	
it	runs like a river	sea
	(runs) like a river	sea
I	don't believe	red
moon	has turned red	One Tree Hill
we	run like a river	sea
	(run) like a river	sea

The category of nonviolence is submissive and calm. The human characters (*I, we,* and *you*) do not perform violent actions or even try to fight against the violence of nature but *run, turn away,* or *see* the violence nature performs. The moon character acts with the same passivity as the human characters because it goes *up and over* and *has turned.* Because the *moon* looks over earth and is separate from earth, it is not a part of earth's violent nature. The *moon,* like human characters, observes the violence going on and, unlike the *sun,* it cannot *carve scars* onto the *face of earth.*

In contrast to the heat and war featured in the category of violence, the prevailing image of the category of nonviolence is coolness and calmness. The actions that the humans and the moon perform in this category are passive. To add to the calmness of the actions, the water of the *river* and the *sea* are a part of this category. In these waters exist a coolness and a flowing that are in extreme contrast to the dry heat of nature's *firezone.* The coolness *runs like a river* to the wide body of calmness—the *sea.*

The setting of one tree on a hill represents the only part of the violent earth that is passive, barren, neutral, and safe. The *moon* performs its actions only around One Tree Hill, suggesting that this place is calm and cool. Perhaps the one tree is a metaphor for a person (possibly Carroll) on the hill, and this is the only place on earth that is not violent where a person can stand (but must stand alone in death).

The two different patterns created by the fantasy themes in the song—violence and nonviolence—create an overall rhetorical vision. Bono's rhetorical vision or worldview is that humans ultimately find some sort of balance, comfort, understanding, and commonality (*we run like a river to the sea*) in the face of a violent, unfair, and unpredictable nature that kills. This vision also suggests that humans should not try to fight against the extreme forces of nature but accept them with passivity.

Because of the circumstances of Carroll's accident—he was hit by a drunk driver—one might expect Bono's rhetorical vision to blame drunk drivers and the careless actions of human beings. Instead, Bono associates death with the harshness and unpredictability of nature. The rhetorical vision of the song is antithetical to a stereotypical blaming of humans for causing tragic events. The rhetor surrenders to and accepts the force of nature's laws as an explanation for his friend's death.

A fantasy-theme analysis of Bono's lyrics in "One Tree Hill" suggests rhetorical strategies that are available to any individual who seeks to cope with the death of a loved one. The construction of a world in which elements of nature (over which humans have no control) are given agency for death removes the blame and guilt many humans feel regarding a loved one's death. By removing the agency from human actions, mourners may find comfort in the fact that they cannot prevent death. The violent picture created in this song suggests a relentless war, with death seeming to provide a relief from the heat, fire, and violence. These dramatic images encourage mourners to let go of a loved one in an act of relief. Another strategy for coping with the loss of death is the depiction of the human actions in the song. Humans are shown as passive and accepting, viewing death as a natural process that requires no opposing action. Typical responses to death of resistance and rage are not presented as useful options because they serve only to perpetuate the violence that death involves. Bono recommends instead a peaceful acquiescence to a very normal event.

One Tree Hill
Bono and U2

We turn away to face the cold, enduring chill
As the day begs the night for mercy
Your sun so bright it leaves no shadows, only scars
Carved into stone on the face of earth
The moon is up and over One Tree Hill
We see the sun go down in your eyes
You ran like a river to the sea
Like a river to the sea
And in our world a heart of darkness, a firezone
Where poets speak their hearts, then bleed for it
Jara sang his song a weapon, in the hands of love
You know his blood still cries from the ground
It runs like a river to the sea
Like a river to the sea
I don't believe in painted roses or bleeding hearts
While bullets rape the night of the merciful
I'll see you again when the stars fall from the sky
And the moon has turned red over One Tree Hill
We run like a river to the sea
Like a river to the sea

The Sociopolitical Messages of Graffiti Art
Kimberly A. McCormick and David Weiss

Public art, graffiti included, is a raw yet emotional demonstration of world-views. Although graffiti artists frequently are viewed as anti-establishment, their art, paradoxically, can represent established or mainstream views. Often, as McCormick (2002) noted, graffiti artists express dominant values, such as life-affirming or religious ideals, through icons that offer a multitude of interpretations. Frequently, however, these expressions are not analyzed for their implicit messages; the illegal form or placement of the art becomes the focus for many viewers rather than the societally compatible content of its message. As a result, graffiti tends to be assessed primarily as a rebellious, vandalistic, selfish expression of territoriality (e.g., Gomez, 1993; Grant, 1996); an expression of frustration or resistance (e.g., Boland & Hoffman, 1983; Bruno & Kelso, 1980); or the expression of negative components of identity (e.g., Bowen, 1999; Grant, 1999).

Our goal in this essay is to investigate the means by which a subversive art form can articulate socially acceptable views of controversial issues. We believe that graffiti can serve positive societal functions, such as constructing ideal visions of society, affirming the identities of viewers, offering perspectives on social issues, and facilitating pride in viewers. We seek to discover the rhetorical means by which graffiti can be interpreted positively in such ways by viewers.

To discover how a subversive art form can articulate socially acceptable views of controversial issues, we explicate the rhetorical vision of a subversive culture by uncovering the characteristics of a work of art: an outdoor graffiti-style mural. The mural is spray painted on a 100-foot-long, five-foot-high privacy wall of cinder block that forms the western perimeter of the parking lot of a Planned Parenthood clinic in a lower income commercial area of Albuquerque, New Mexico. The clinic serves as the northern boundary of the lot and the far right end of the mural. The wall, parking lot, and clinic are located directly off busy, gritty San Mateo Boulevard, clearly visible to passing cars and pedestrians. Visitors to the clinic have no choice but to see the wall. While not technically "graffiti" in that Planned Parenthood commissioned the art, the person who painted the mural, "Sug," is a local Albuquerque artist best known for his illegal graffiti art. The mural contains a number of standard elements of the graffiti genre: the use of spray paint, the primacy and style of the artist's signature, bold outlining of words and letters, the contrasting size of words within set phrases, the anthropomorphizing of animal figures, and the splitting of quotations into separate word strings.

Because the wall is so much longer than it is high, there is an inescapable horizontality to the mural. An observer's eye moves from left to right across the wall rather than up and down. Further, because the Planned Parenthood clinic is adjacent to the right end of the wall (at the mural's "conclusion" rather than at its "beginning"), an observer—particularly a client of Planned Parenthood—may experience the mural as a comment on the clinic, a preparation for a visit, or a post-visit endorsement of the clinic's functions and philosophies.

This essay was written while Kimberly A. McCormick and David Weiss were students in Karen A. Foss's rhetorical criticism class at the University of New Mexico in 2002. Used by permission of the authors.

We describe the elements of the artifact from left to right. The mural's first element is a piece (the graffiti term for *masterpiece*), a stylized signature, in which the artist has rendered his alias, *SUG*, in bold sky-blue illegible letters. A stone-gray background shaped like a hill that spans the height of the wall is visible behind the piece. A ribbon of royal blue water extends to the right from the hill across the length of the mural, serving as a literal link visually connecting the mural's disparate foreground elements.

To the right of the hill is a small symbol painted in black. The symbol, shaped like a mirror image of the letters *OK,* is the Chinese character *hé,* which means peace. To its right, a saguaro cactus extends from the base of the wall to its top. Sitting in the "elbow" of the saguaro's left "arm" is a small gray bird with an open beak. The river flows to the right across the earth, past the cactus and a buzzard wearing a brown short-sleeved garment with beige stripes. Extending from its arms and from behind its head are feathers in the style of a Native American headdress.

The river flows behind the buzzard into a gray mountain strewn with watermelons. A second river runs below it, coursing into the next visual element, the word *FIRST,* rendered in bold capitals. Beneath it is the word *AMENDMENT* in plain black uppercase letters. From the right of *FIRST,* the river flows into a second cactus hosting a bird. This cactus resembles a prickly-pear bush, and the bird is large and brown with powerful-looking wings. Three more watermelons sit on the mountainside to the right of the cactus and bird.

Leaning against the side of the mountain is the next figure. Unlike the birds and cacti, which are painted in bold colors and convey three dimensionality, this next figure is flat and black, like a cut-out paper doll. It is Kokopelli, the legendary Hopi character who appears in petroglyphs throughout the Southwest. As is the case with most renditions of Kokopelli, this one is holding a flute to his mouth. Unlike most, however, this one has the word *TOLERANCE* flowing on a pennant from the flute.

To the right of *TOLERANCE* is the sloping edge of the next mountain. Superimposed over this mountain's face is another creature: a gray-green dragon. It is mostly torso and head, the latter little more than a long snout open to reveal sharp white teeth. Its pointy, blood-red tongue protrudes menacingly from its mouth. A flame shoots out from the creature's right ear, while other flames descend from the open snout and flicker around the dragon's head. A red apple sits on the mountain to the right of the dragon's claw. It is partially obscured by another blue-and-gray *FIRST* below a plain black *AMENDMENT.* The upper river flows behind *FIRST,* then re-emerges near a group of apples and from there into the next figure: a dark-brown-skinned woman wearing a red, yellow, green, and black turban.

In an angle formed by the edge of the river and the slope of the mountain is another section of text: *ONE'S PHILOSOPHY, ONE'S EXPERIENCES, ONE'S EXPOSURE TO THE RAW EDGES OF HUMAN EXISTENCE . . . .* An arrow at the end of the text points to a large stylized sun drawn in the manner of the Zia symbol, in yellow with black outlines. This Zia is a circle from which four "wings"— curved like the blades of a fan—radiate. The river flows under the Zia, then re-emerges as three separate, parallel tributaries. Between the upper and middle branches is a continuation of the earlier text: *ONE'S RELIGIOUS TRAINING, ONE'S ATTITUDE TOWARD LIFE AND FAMILY AND THEIR VALUES, AND THE.* Beneath the middle branch, the text continues: *MORAL STANDARDS ONE*

ESTABLISHES AND SEEKS TO. Finally, below the lower branch, the text concludes with *OBSERVE ARE LIKELY TO COLOR ONE'S THINKING AND CONCLUSIONS.... —JUSTICE BLACKMUN.*

FANTASY THEMES

To illuminate the rhetorical vision characterized by the mural, we use the fantasy-theme method of criticism. Fantasy-theme analysis, derived from Bormann's (1972) symbolic convergence theory, applies the central metaphor of drama to examine an artifact in terms of its settings, characters, and actions. Although characters are the most evident thematic components of the mural, we first describe its settings to provide the context for the characters and the actions they perform.

Settings

While the actions presented in the mural take place in a literal (that is, geographical) setting—New Mexico—the settings that more effectively establish the rhetorical vision are temporal: past, present, and future. The mural, however, is not a triptych; there are not clear visual divisions of past, present, and future. Further, visual movement from left to right does not necessarily correlate with the passage of time. Rather, elements of the three temporal settings are strewn throughout the work, suggesting a blurring of time boundaries or perhaps a spatio-temporal location that simultaneously comprises components of different eras.

Helping the viewer sort out this pastiche is the river. Its blue horizontal bands move continuously rightward, touching or approaching nearly every discrete element of the mural and providing a visual link across time. As it moves from left to right, it variously connects with or nears "past" components (Kokopelli, the words *FIRST AMENDMENT*, the traditionally dressed buzzard, the dragon, the dark-skinned woman); "present" or timeless components (mountains, cacti, watermelons, apples, the gray and brown birds, the Zia sun); and "future" components (the dragon, which represents past as well as future, and the word *TOLERANCE*). The elements connected by the river, however, are not arranged linearly from left to right to suggest an orderly chronology from past to present.

Characters

As described above, the mural contains a multiplicity of visual and lexical characters. We see these components not as an army of characters but as traits of two primary character themes—New Mexico and the Director.

A variety of traits, which can be classified as geographical, botanical, zoological, spiritual, and cultural, represent the character of New Mexico. The geographical elements are the mountains, river, and desert-region earth tones. The presence of watermelons and apples on the mountains locate them specifically in the Albuquerque region because *watermelon* in Spanish is *sandia* and *apple* is *manzano*; the Sandias and the Manzanos are the two mountain ranges forming Albuquerque's eastern boundary. The Manzano Mountains were named for the apple orchards located in their foothills, while the Sandia range was named for the mountains' watermelon-like color at sunset. Because the mountains note the location as Albuquerque, the river running through the mural is the Rio Grande. Light brown, the dominant New Mexican earth tone, represents the region's desert landscape. Botanical elements of New Mexico include cacti and the apples, and indigenous birds—a buzzard, a roadrunner, and a hawk—reference the zoological traits of New Mexico.

There are two spiritual aspects of New Mexico in the mural. The first is the Zia sun, an ancient symbol of universal harmony that was originated by New Mexico's indigenous Zia Pueblo Indians; it is now the sole visual element of the state flag. The second spiritual figure is Kokopelli, an early Hopi symbol of fertility, harmony, and peace.

Finally, the cultural elements of the mural represent New Mexico's diversity, both historical and idealized. The artist's signature piece, *SUG*, alludes to his urban, graffiti-art subculture. The Chinese character *hé* represents not only peace and harmony but also New Mexico's Asian peoples. The buzzard's blanket and decorative feathers symbolize the Mexican and Native American cultures central to New Mexico's history. The dark-skinned woman and her red, yellow, green, and black turban reference New Mexico's early African heritage.

The second character theme is the Director of the drama, giving instructions to New Mexico. Viewers do not actually see the Director. Rather, they infer his or her "off-stage" presence from the visual manifestation of four elements, one visual and three lexical. The presence of the dragon makes visible the Director's warning to New Mexico about the ever-present danger to the state posed by nuclear war. The reference here is to the scientists who worked on the Manhattan Project in Los Alamos in the 1940s, who referred to the process of armoring the first atomic bomb as "tickling the dragon's tail." But the presence of atomic energy in New Mexico can be found even closer to the mural's site than Los Alamos; sizable portions of America's nuclear stockpile were stored beneath the Manzano Mountains from 1952 to 1992. The "music" emanating from Kokopelli's flute literally illustrates the Director's demand for tolerance. The prominence and repetition of the words *FIRST AMENDMENT* evidence the value the Director places on American freedoms. Finally, the Director imposes his or her philosophy on New Mexico through the excerpt from Justice Harry Blackmun's *Roe v. Wade* opinion.

Actions

New Mexico's action themes are primarily narrative. As if painting a visual autobiography, New Mexico discloses its history and describes its present. The disclosure of history is accomplished through the symbolic portrayal of the various cultures that have contributed to the region. Mexico is recalled by the buzzard's clothing. The Zia sun, the fluting Kokopelli, and the buzzard's decorative feathers represent indigenous Native nations. The black woman's presence affirms the part Africans and African Americans played in the state's very early history. New Mexico hails its present primarily through its presentation of the natural world. Mountains, cacti, birds, and the river, while obviously also part of the state's past, are still very much a part of its present.

Although perhaps redundant, the Director's role is precisely that: to direct the other character in the drama. To a limited degree, the Director points out to New Mexico the glories and tragedies of its past and sets standards of behavior for its present. But this character's more important action is forecasting and guiding, creating or modeling a vision of the future for New Mexico. The Director cautions New Mexico about the evil lurking within its own borders, the danger of nuclear proliferation. This brings to the forefront of New Mexico's consciousness the destruction wrought in its own past as well as an ongoing threat. The menacing dragon gives visual form to the voice of contemporary anti-nuclear discourse and also predicts what the future might tragically hold should nothing be done to change the current course of events.

The Director orchestrates Kokopelli's "music," the piping of the word TOL-ERANCE. This is a condition not yet achieved (and therefore neither a past nor present reality) but potentially achievable in the future. Finally, the Director provides a guiding philosophy for New Mexico through the recitation of the excerpt from Blackmun's *Roe v. Wade* opinion. This action has ramifications for past, present, and future. The decision was written in the 1970s; is still part of present U.S. law, albeit tenuously; and, ideally, represents a standard that can be upheld in the future.

RHETORICAL VISION

The fantasy themes in the mural establish a rhetorical vision of a sociopolitical utopia. The utopian worldview is motivated by a need to eradicate ignorance, which is manifested by intolerance, the flouting of First Amendment principles, a lack of appreciation for history, complacency in the face of ever-present nuclear danger, and a lack of respect for basic human rights. In the rhetorical vision, the setting themes and action themes support the dominant, although not overwhelming, character themes. Within the temporal setting, past and present serve as an important prologue to the future, the temporal "location" of the utopian vision's realization. Within the character and action themes, New Mexico establishes history and context, while the Director articulates prescriptions for the future.

The artist of the mural illustrates New Mexico's past and present through the repeated inclusion of established features of the state: its landscape, flora and fauna, indigenous cultures, and spiritual symbols. By using these familiar elements, the rhetor allows the participants in the rhetorical vision to situate themselves in a current place and time upon first approaching the artifact. These temporal and geographic benchmarks serve as a necessary foundation for the yet-to-be established sociopolitical utopia. The visual references to *sandias* (watermelons) and *manzanos* (apples) even can be seen as an inside joke by those New Mexicans and other Spanish speakers who recognize the visual pun as an allusion to the names of the local mountain ranges. The images of Kokopelli and Zia, long-revered Native American symbols, similarly call out to present-day members of local Native cultures as well as to members of those cultures who have arrived more recently in New Mexico. Even New Mexican population groups as numerically underrepresented as African Americans and Asian Americans are included in the rhetorical vision, thanks to the presence of the turbaned woman and the Chinese *hé* symbol. The blue stream gives life and movement to all aspects of the mural, just as the Rio Grande has given life and movement to all of New Mexico's cultures and, should it be allowed to survive, would be a critical element of a New Mexican utopian future.

The rhetor locates the Director peripherally in the past and present and centrally in the future. With the dragon, the Director addresses controversial aspects of New Mexico's nuclear past—specifically the Manhattan Project—as well as current concerns about the state's reliance on the nuclear energy industry, as epitomized by Los Alamos and Sandia National Laboratories. The dragon is clearly a threatening manifestation. In addition to breathing fire, it has a deformed, grotesque body, sharp teeth, and a protruding red tongue. While "tickling the dragon" may have been a tongue-in-cheek allusion to tampering with nuclear weapons in the 1940s, the dragon's present and future roles in the rhetorical vision articulated by the Director are anything but humorous.

For the most part, however, the Director's contributions to the present and future aspects of the rhetorical vision are positive. Through the Director, the mural telegraphs the rhetorical vision's valuation of core American freedoms with the words *FIRST AMENDMENT*. With only two boldly painted words, the rhetor reminds viewers of their rights in a multiplicity of domains: religion, speech, the press, peaceable assembly, and protest. The words *FIRST AMENDMENT,* however, are not a mere reminder of the role these rights have played in the collective past. They are also a call to action, an announcement of the need to foreground First Amendment rights in the present and—perhaps even more important—to establish the future sociopolitical utopia upon the principles embodied by the Amendment.

Mural by Sug at Planned Parenthood clinic, Albuquerque, New Mexico, 2002. Photograph by David Weiss.

With *TOLERANCE*, the Director links all three of the temporal settings of the rhetorical worldview. Tolerance is another foundational element of the utopian future; surely, the rhetor is not claiming that tolerance has been practiced in the past or is an actual lived ideal of the present. Yet, by having the word *TOLERANCE* emanate from the flute of Kokopelli, perhaps the most omnipresent symbol of this region's ancient past, the Director is able to suggest that tolerance is or should be a timeless New Mexican value.

The excerpt from Justice Blackmun's *Roe v. Wade* opinion also links the three temporal settings but does so in a way that subtly spells out tensions between present reality and the vision of a utopian future. The section of the Blackmun text included in the mural concerning one's philosophy and experiences ends with an ellipsis. The actual Blackmun quotation, however, ends with the words *about abortion*, which are omitted from the mural's text. The incomplete Blackmun sentence on the mural wall and the Planned Parenthood abortion clinic located immediately adjacent to the wall serve as an enthymeme: members of the rhetorical community must mentally fill in the blanks, supplying the words that are only hinted at by the ellipsis.

By including almost all of a key passage from the *Roe v. Wade* decision and purposely omitting the two words that encapsulate the nature of that decision—it was about abortion, after all—the Director and rhetor underscore the critical difference between the temporal settings of present and future articulated in the rhetorical vision. In the present, the word *abortion* and the phrase *right to abortion* are highly politicized and inevitably polarizing. They are often omitted from contemporary discourse, euphemized or obliquely referred to as *choice, reproductive freedom,* or *control over one's fertility.* Consequently, the ellipsis at the end of the Blackmun quotation signals the present setting of the mural's rhetorical vision, a time during which certain bold truths cannot be safely uttered. In the rhetorical vision's future, however, to rely on enthymeme will not be necessary. In the sociopolitical utopia of the rhetorical worldview, a time and place in which tolerance and respect for First Amendment rights are foundational, there will be safety to make such bold statements directly and completely.

CONCLUSION

The graffiti artist's worldview, often inaccurately characterized by society as subversive, actually may converge with the values and motives of the dominant culture. The revulsion much of society claims to have for graffiti art may stem from the inability to recognize that the art can reflect rather than contradict society's own worldviews. Hence, graffiti art can articulate socially acceptable views of sociopolitically controversial issues, such as tolerance for diversity, demand for universal freedoms, recognition of past and possible future mistakes, diligence in protecting lands and peoples, and a command for the freedom and respect to make choices about our lives in much the same way as expressions offered by any other artist or thoughtful individual: by describing and prescribing what the world would look like if we could grasp and enact all of these ideals.

Different elements motivate characters to perform actions within a drama. Beauty, religion, family, money, love, hatred, and myriad other ideas and emotions motivate people. However, the prospect of a perfect place, ideal in its social, political, and moral aspects—a utopia—can motivate even the most skeptical, subjugated, cynical, disconfirmed individuals. The ideologies of those who normally do not have a voice or whose voices are not often recognized—voices included in the mural—may be the voices necessary to create such a utopia.

References

Bales, R. (1970). *Personality and interpersonal behavior.* New York: Rinehart and Winston.

Boland, R., & Hoffman, R. (1983). Humor in a machine shop: An interpretation of symbolic action. In L. Pondy, P. Frost, G. Morgan, & T. Dandridge (Eds.), *Organizational symbolism* (pp. 187–198). Greenwich, CT: JAI.

Bormann, E. (1972). Fantasy and rhetorical vision: The rhetorical criticism of social reality. *Quarterly Journal of Speech, 58,* 396–407.

Bowen, T. E. (1999). Graffiti art: A contemporary study of Toronto artists. *Studies in Art Education, 41,* 22–40.

Bruner, E., & Kelso, J. (1980). Gender differences in graffiti: A semiotic perspective. *Women's Studies International Quarterly, 3,* 239–252.

Gomez, M. (1993). The writing on our walls: Finding solutions through distinguishing graffiti art from graffiti vandalism. *University of Michigan Journal of Law Reform, 26,* 633–707.

Grant, C. (1996). Graffiti: Taking a closer look. *FBI Law Enforcement Bulletin, 65,* 11–15.

McCormick, K. (2002, June). *A content analysis of graffiti in Albuquerque.* Paper presented at the annual meeting of the Hawaii International Conference on Social Sciences, Honolulu, HI.

Rodriguez, A., & Clair, R. (1999). Graffiti as communication: Exploring the discursive tensions of anonymous texts. *Southern Communication Journal, 65,* 1–15.

Additional Samples of Fantasy-Theme Criticism

Benoit, William L., Andrew A. Klyukovski, John P. McHale, and David Airne. "A Fantasy Theme Analysis of Political Cartoons on the Clinton-Lewinsky-Starr Affair." *Critical Studies in Media Communication*, 18 (December 2001), 377–94.

Bishop, Ronald. "The World's Nicest Grown-Up: A Fantasy Theme Analysis of News Media Coverage of Fred Rogers." *Journal of Communication*, 53 (March 2003), 16–31.

Bormann, Ernest G. "A Fantasy Theme Analysis of the Television Coverage of the Hostage Release and the Reagan Inaugural." *Quarterly Journal of Speech*, 68 (May 1982), 133–45.

Bormann, Ernest G. "Fetching Good Out of Evil: A Rhetorical Use of Calamity." *Quarterly Journal of Speech*, 63 (April 1977), 130–39.

Bormann, Ernest G. "The Eagleton Affair: A Fantasy Theme Analysis." *Quarterly Journal of Speech*, 59 (April 1973), 143–59.

Bormann, Ernest G. *The Force of Fantasy: Restoring the American Dream*. Carbondale: Southern Illinois University Press, 1985.

Brown, William R. "The Prime-Time Television Environment and Emerging Rhetorical Visions." *Quarterly Journal of Speech*, 62 (December 1976), 389–99.

Cragan, John F. "Rhetorical Strategy: A Dramatistic Interpretation and Application." *Central States Speech Journal*, 26 (Spring 1975), 4–11.

Cragan, John F., and Donald C. Shields. *Applied Communication Research: A Dramatistic Approach*. Prospect Heights, IL: Waveland, 1981, several essays.

Doyle, Marsha Vanderford. "The Rhetoric of Romance: A Fantasy Theme Analysis of Barbara Cartland Novels." *Southern Speech Communication Journal*, 51 (Fall 1985), 24–48.

Duffy, Margaret. "High Stakes: A Fantasy Theme Analysis of the Selling of Riverboat Gambling in Iowa." *Southern Communication Journal*, 62 (Winter 1997), 117–32.

Edwards, Janis L., and Chen, Huey-Rong. "The First Lady/First Wife in Editorial Cartoons: Rhetorical Visions Through Gendered Lenses." *Women's Studies in Communication*, 23 (Fall 2000), 367–91.

Endres, Thomas G. "Rhetorical Visions of Unmarried Mothers." *Communication Quarterly*, 37 (Spring 1989), 134–50.

Ford, Leigh Arden. "Fetching Good Out of Evil in AA: A Bormannean Fantasy Theme Analysis of *The Big Book* of Alcoholics Anonymous." *Communication Quarterly*, 37 (Winter 1989), 1–15.

Foss, Karen A., and Stephen W. Littlejohn. "*The Day After*: Rhetorical Vision in an Ironic Frame." *Critical Studies in Mass Communication*, 3 (September 1986), 317–36.

Foss, Sonja K. "Equal Rights Amendment Controversy: Two Worlds in Conflict." *Quarterly Journal of Speech*, 65 (October 1979), 275–88.

Glaser, Susan R., and David A. Frank. "Rhetorical Criticism of Interpersonal Discourse: An Exploratory Study." *Communication Quarterly*, 30 (Fall 1982), 353–58.

Haskins, William A. "Rhetorical Vision of Equality: Analysis of the Rhetoric of the Southern Black Press During Reconstruction." *Communication Quarterly*, 29 (Spring 1981), 116–22.

Hensley, Carl Wayne. "Rhetorical Vision and the Persuasion of a Historical Movement: The Disciples of Christ in Nineteenth Century American Culture." *Quarterly Journal of Speech*, 61 (October 1975), 250–64.

Hubbard, Rita C. "Relationship Styles in Popular Romance Novels, 1950 to 1983." *Communication Quarterly*, 33 (Spring 1985), 113–25.

Huxman, Susan Schultz. "Perfecting the Rhetorical Vision of Woman's Rights: Elizabeth Cady Stanton, Anna Howard Shaw, and Carrie Chapman Catt." *Women's Studies in Communication*, 23 (Fall 2000), 307–36.

Ilkka, Richard J. "Rhetorical Dramatization in the Development of American Communism." *Quarterly Journal of Speech*, 63 (December 1977), 413–27.

Kidd, Virginia. "Happily Ever After and Other Relationship Styles: Advice on Interpersonal Relations in Popular Magazines, 1951–1973." *Quarterly Journal of Speech*, 61 (February 1975), 31–39.

King, Andrew A. "Booker T. Washington and the Myth of Heroic Materialism." *Quarterly Journal of Speech*, 60 (October 1974), 323–27.

Koester, Jolene. "The Machiavellian Princess: Rhetorical Dramas for Women Managers." *Communication Quarterly*, 30 (Summer 1982), 165–72.

Kroll, Becky Swanson. "From Small Group to Public View: Mainstreaming the Women's Movement." *Communication Quarterly*, 31 (Spring 1983), 139–47.

Nimmo, Dan, and James E. Combs. "Fantasies and Melodramas in Television Network News: The Case of Three Mile Island." *Western Journal of Speech Communication*, 46 (Winter 1982), 45–55.

Porter, Laurinda W. "The White House Transcripts: Group Fantasy Events Concerning the Mass Media." *Central States Speech Journal*, 27 (Winter 1976), 272–79.

Putnam, Linda L., Shirley A. Van Hoeven, and Connie A. Bullis. "The Role of Rituals and Fantasy Themes in Teachers' Bargaining." *Western Journal of Speech Communication*, 55 (Winter 1991), 85–103.

Swartz, Omar. *The View from* On the Road: *The Rhetorical Vision of Jack Kerouac*. Carbondale: Southern Illinois University Press, 1999.

6

Feminist Criticism

Feminist criticism has its roots in a social and political movement, the feminist or women's liberation movement, aimed at improving conditions for women. Although *feminism* has negative connotations for many people, the term is much more complex than the negative connotations suggest because many different kinds of feminisms exist. One common definition of feminism features the concept of equality, exemplified in definitions such as the belief that women and men should have equal opportunities for self-expression. Another such definition is "movement towards creating a society where women can live a full, self-determined life."[1] Some definitions feature the idea of oppression and ways to end it, as does a definition that conceptualizes feminism as "the theoretical study of women's oppression and the strategical and political ways that all of us, building on that theoretical and historical knowledge, can work to end that oppression."[2] A similar definition is "the struggle to end sexist oppression"—the effort to change existing power relations between women and men.[3] For some, feminism is larger than issues of gender and is defined as "a struggle to eradicate the ideology of domination that permeates Western culture on various levels."[4]

The diversity among definitions of feminism also characterizes the goals and objectives of feminists. One way to summarize the diversity of the perspectives that exist within feminism is to conceptualize feminism in three waves or stages.[5] The first wave of feminism in the United States, a wave that took place from the middle of the nineteenth century through 1920, was focused on securing the right to vote for women.

151

Second-wave feminism is the feminism many people think about when they hear the term *feminist* today. Often seen as originating with the publication of Betty Friedan's *A Feminine Mystique* in 1963 and ending in the early 1980s (although many individuals who became feminists during the second wave continue to adhere to the principles of this wave), this wave focused on achieving equality for women with men and the development of opportunities for women without the constraints of gender expectations. A number of different feminist perspectives are part of second-wave feminism. Liberal, radical, and Marxist feminists are probably the most well known of these. *Liberal feminists* work for equality within the present system and aim to extend to women the rights already possessed by men. *Radical feminists* advocate the revolutionary transformation of society and the development of alternative social arrangements to those currently in place. *Marxist* or *socialist feminists* see capitalist economic structures at the root of women's oppression, while *lesbian feminists* see heterosexuality as a primary cornerstone of male supremacy and encourage women to create various kinds of identifications with one another.

Other kinds of feminists also are a part of second-wave feminism. *Cultural feminists* believe that women and men are different primarily because of the ways that culture shapes individuals and believe that women's traditional roles socialize women into behaviors that are nurturing and supportive. *Revalorists* are feminists who are committed to valuing traditionally feminine skills, activities, and perspectives that typically are marginalized. They seek to recover and accord value to women's unique contributions to culture. *Essentialist feminists* believe that biology is destiny and that biological differences between women and men determine their behaviors—behaviors that should be seen as equal even though different. According to this perspective, recognition of these differences and an equal valuation of them will enable women to achieve equality with men. *Womanists* are women of color who define themselves as feminists and who believe that an understanding of the intersection of race and gender is needed to address the oppression of women of color. *Ecofeminists* see the earth as characterized by a female essence or identity and link women's oppression to the destruction of the environment.

Third-wave feminists were born after 1960 and thus grew up with many advantages and freedoms that second-wave feminists struggled to achieve. Third-wave feminism, which began in the 1980s, challenges a universal definition of womanhood as predominantly middle class, white, able bodied, and heterosexual—a definition third-wave feminists see as their legacy from second-wave feminists. Third-wave feminists, then, include women and men from different races, religions, classes, sexualities, and abilities as part of feminist movement. Because of the diversity featured in this feminism, third-wave feminists focus on unique personal experiences, circumstances, and contexts as mechanisms for constructing an agenda of feminist activism.

Many types of feminism characterize third-wave feminism, just as they do the second wave. One group of third-wave feminists focuses on the intersection of various oppressions. Sometimes called *women-of-color feminists* or *third-world feminists,* these individuals define themselves and their activism in opposition to the racial exclusion that they see marking second-wave feminism. These feminists adopt standpoint theories and focus on the intersectionality of multiple identities and outsider-within locations as ways to understand and counter simultaneous oppressions based on varied aspects of identity. *Postfeminism* is sometimes defined by the media as anti-feminist or as a label that suggests that feminism no longer is needed. As a type of third-wave feminism, however, it expresses the intersection of feminism with postmodernism, poststructuralism, and postcolonialism and addresses the demand of marginalized, diasporic, and colonized cultures for a feminism capable of giving voice to local and indigenous feminisms.

Another type of third-wave feminists—often called *power feminists*—indict second-wave feminists on the grounds that they construct women as victims rather than empowering them. They suggest that when women focus on oppressive conditions and define themselves as victims, they begin to seek power through an identity of powerlessness. In contrast, power feminists suggest, women have personal responsibility for what happens to them. Power feminism asks "a woman to give to herself and seek what she needs, so she can give to others freely, without resentment," and it seeks "power and uses it responsibly, both for women as individuals and to make the world more fair to others." Power feminism has a "psychology of abundance" that wants all women to get "more of whatever it is they are not getting enough of because they are women: respect, self-respect, education, safety, health, representation, money."[6]

These myriad definitions of and perspectives on feminism suggest the diversity that characterizes feminism. Rather than confuse, this variety opens up choices and possibilities and speaks to the essence of feminism itself. Despite the differences between and within the second and third waves of feminism, feminists are united by a broadening of the scope of the term *feminism* to include the effort to eliminate relations of domination not just for women but for all people. Despite its origin in a movement designed to allow the contributions of women to be visible and valued, feminism now is generally seen as much larger than a commitment to achieve equality for women. A society that names white, heterosexual men as superior not only oppresses women but everyone else who does not fit into the category of white, male, and heterosexual. Thus, feminists are committed to eliminating relations of oppression and domination in general, whether of women, African Americans, old people, lesbians, gay men, or others.

Feminists do not believe that oppression and domination are worthy human values and seek to eradicate the ideology of domination that permeates Western culture. They want to transform relationships and the larger culture so that the patriarchal values and traits of alienation, competition, imperialism, elitism, control, and dehumanization that characterize interaction under an ideology of domination are disrupted. They seek instead to contribute to the development of relationships and cultures characterized by self-determination, equality, fairness, responsibility, affirmation, a valuing of others, acknowledgment of the interdependence of all life forms, and respect for others.[7]

Feminism is rooted, then, in choice and self-determination. Although they may go about it in different ways, what all feminists seek is the assumption of agency by all individuals, where all individuals are able to make their own choices for their lives. Assumption of agency means that people are unconstrained by the definitions or expectations of others or by material conditions that work to constrain their choices. Beth Kiyoko Jamieson articulates this notion of agency as the principle that "individuals have the right to make their own decisions about how to live their lives, that individuals must be assumed to be capable of making ethical decisions, and that social reprobation (well-intentioned or not) must not inhibit the decision-making process. Liberty demands that individuals be considered capable of directing the goals and means of their own lives."[8]

Concomitant with the assumption of agency by all individuals is allowing others to make their own choices. As Kiyoko Jamieson suggests, "If we allow social pressure to delineate which options are 'correct' and to enforce accordant behavior, liberty is threatened. Even if the external observers have good intentions and hope to help a woman in need, the imposition of their biases in unacceptable. A bully who means well is still a bully. And even feminists can be bullies."[9]

Feminist movement in general and the efforts of scholars to incorporate feminism into the communication field generated a feminist method of rhetorical criticism.[10] Pinpointing the time at which feminist perspectives began to enter the discipline of communication is difficult, but three essays stand out as important initiating texts. Karlyn Kohrs Campbell's essay "The Rhetoric of Women's Liberation," published in 1973, is an analysis of the contemporary women's movement. In this article, Campbell suggested that the movement is an oxymoron because its substantive and stylistic components are so different from traditional conceptions of rhetoric that it constitutes a unique rhetorical genre.[11] Campbell's essay was followed in 1974 by an essay by Cheris Kramarae (formerly Kramer) titled "Women's Speech: Separate but Unequal?" In this essay, Kramarae raised the possibility of "systems of co-occurring, sex-linked, linguistic signals" that point to linguistic sex differences between women and men.[12] Sally Miller Gearhart's "The Womanization of Rhetoric," published in 1979, challenged a fundamental tenet of rhetorical theory—the definition of rhetoric as persuasion. She indicted this definition on the grounds that any intent to persuade is an act of violence and proposed instead a female model of communication as an anti-dote to the violence that characterizes life on planet Earth.[13]

The works of these three scholars are important because of the trans-formative shifts they foreshadowed for rhetorical studies. Campbell's and Gearhart's essays were significant because, for the first time in print in the communication discipline, the argument was offered that feminism necessarily transforms rhetorical constructs and theories. These authors questioned fundamental assumptions about rhetoric, suggesting recon-ceptualizations of rhetorical studies grounded in the influence of feminist perspectives. The contributions made by Kramarae foreshadowed the emergence of another major focus of feminist work in communication—efforts to incorporate, value, and legitimate the study of women's com-munication practices in the discipline. The emphasis she placed on the process of incorporating women's language and rhetorical practices as data—thus making women's linguistic practices a subject of research in the discipline—laid the groundwork for the study of women's communi-cative practices from perspectives generated by women themselves.

A second major feminist contribution to rhetorical theory and criti-cism was scholarship dedicated to rhetorical analyses of the rhetoric of women and topics concerning women. Studies of women rhetors were, for the most part, studies of women who were political and social activ-ists, not unlike the men in positions of political and/or social power whose rhetorical practices were investigated by rhetorical scholars. The study of women not only pointed the way for considerations of gen-dered speaking styles, but, more important, once studies moved beyond white, middle- or upper-class men in positions of power, the study of diverse forms of expression, rhetors, and contexts became possible.

Another kind of critical study that brought women into rhetorical studies was the social movement study that focused on movements of particular relevance to women—the movement to secure passage of the Equal Rights Amendment to the U.S. Constitution, for example. Women also began to be included in the discipline through the study of debates on subjects of particular interest to women—issues such as abortion and sexual harassment—that traditionally had not been the focus of schol-arly investigation. Making topics of special concern to women the sub-ject of scholarship also suggested an expansion of interests on the part of rhetorical scholars as well as a legitimation of women that had not been seen earlier.

Recognition that women had been neglected by rhetorical studies led to various critiques of disciplinary traditions and practices. One of the first such critiques was provided by Kathryn Carter and Carole Spitzack's edited volume *Doing Research on Women's Communication*, published in 1989. In the introductory essay in this volume, Spitzack and Carter addressed what they referred to as the *blind spot* in the communi-cation discipline—the impact of gender on research practices. Contribu-tors questioned taken-for-granted assumptions about communication scholarship, identified publishing norms and practices that functioned to contain and subvert the radical nature of feminist research, and opened the way for rethinking communication concepts and scholarly practices.[14] A more recent example of such critique occurred in 1994, with the publication of an essay by Carole Blair, Julie R. Brown, and Leslie A. Baxter, "Disciplining the Feminine." The rejection from a journal of a feminist essay they had written earlier led them to write a new essay based on and analyzing as data the comments of the reviewers about the first essay. Reviewers questioned their status as scholars, accused them of being anti-science, and declared them to be members of an "extremist fringe of the so-called feminist movement" in their responses to the original essay. Blair, Brown, and Baxter used these reviews to highlight the problematic nature of the review process in communication journals.[15]

The emergence of rhetorical studies about women and women's issues and research on gender in all communication contexts raised the question of what constitutes a feminist perspective. Various institutional mechanisms, including caucuses and conferences, provided the space in which such efforts to define and clarify feminist perspectives could occur. These included the instigation of women's caucuses in the national and regional organizations of the communication discipline, including the Women's Caucus of the Speech Communication Association (now the National Communication Association), formed in 1971, and the Organization for Research on Women and Communication (ORWAC), affiliated with the Western States Communication Association, which started in 1976. Its publication of the journal *Women's Studies in Communication* began in 1977. The first conference to grapple with issues at the heart of feminist perspectives occurred in 1978 at Bowling Green State University. The conference spawned the Organization for the Study of Communication, Language, and Gender (OSCLG), which now publishes the journal *Women and Language*, another outlet for feminist scholarship in communication. The Conference on Gender and Communication, which began at Pennsylvania State University in 1984, offered yet another annual forum where feminist perspectives were worked out and debated. With the emergence, labeling, and clarification of feminist perspectives, there was a growing sense that feminist scholarship was not only tolerated but accepted as a legitimate perspective from which to approach communication.

Feminist scholars recognized that incorporating feminist perspectives into rhetorical studies could do nothing less than transform the discipline. Karen A. Foss and Sonja K. Foss, in their summary article in 1983, "The Status of Research on Women and Communication," pointed out that what was needed was "growth by revolution," whereby scholars question their presuppositions, replace them as appropriate, and create new conceptualizations that incorporate women's perspectives.[16] Similarly, in their 1987 typology of women in communication research, Spitzack and Carter argued that feminist scholars need to do more than fill in the gaps in existing research categories of women as communicators if women truly are to be integrated into the communication discipline. The process of reconceptualization, they suggested, will produce "novel theories, investigative strategies and topic areas" that will transform the discipline.[17] Many feminist scholars today use their research to transform or reconceptualize traditional rhetorical theory that was created by elite men to reflect more inclusive understandings of rhetoric.[18]

Feminist criticism has emerged as one method by which scholars engage in research designed to intervene in the ideology of domination. Feminist criticism is the analysis of rhetoric to discover how the rhetorical construction of gender is used as a means for domination and how that process can be challenged so that all people understand that they have the capacity to claim agency and act in the world as they choose. Gender is a culture's conception of the qualities considered desirable for women and men, a construction created and maintained through various forms of rhetoric. In feminist criticism, then, the focus is on the rhetorical process by which these qualities come to seem natural and ways in which that naturalness can be called into question.

Because the concern of feminist critics is with relationships of domination of all kinds, not simply those based on gender, feminist criticism can be used to analyze the construction of domination based on race, class, sexual orientation, or any other dimension of identity. I have chosen to call this criticism *feminist* because domination on the basis of sex, as bell hooks explains, "is the practice of domination most people experience, whether their role be that of discriminator or discriminated against, exploiter or exploited. It is the practice of domination most people are socialized to accept before they even know that other forms of group oppression exist."[10] I also have chosen to retain the *feminist* label because it acknowledges the scholars who first began to do this kind of criticism—feminists. Although the procedures outlined in the following sections are discussed in terms of gender and women, then, they could be used as well in the analysis of artifacts where the concern is primarily with race, class, or another variable on which domination may be based.

PROCEDURES

Using the feminist method of criticism, a critic analyzes an artifact in a four-step process: (1) selecting an artifact; (2) analyzing the artifact; (3) formulating a research question; and (4) writing the essay.

Selecting an Artifact

Artifacts that involve the rhetoric of typically marginalized or subordinate groups are good artifacts to analyze using feminist criticism. If you are acquainted with an artifact that depicts a difference that is often

denigrated—that presents a view of race, gender, class, sexual orientation, religion, ability, or any other aspect of identity—in a way that irri-
tates, angers, inspires, or challenges you—that artifact might be a good
one to use for a feminist critique. But because gender, race, class, and
other dimensions of identity are present in most artifacts, even when difference or the denigration of difference is not featured, almost any artifact can be used for feminist criticism. A football game, the construction
of the image of a president, or a building could be analyzed in feminist
criticism for the construction of gender (or other dimensions of identity)
that is implicit in these artifacts.

Analyzing the Artifact

Feminist criticism involves two basic steps: (1) analysis of the construction of gender—or whatever aspect of identity is your focus—in the
artifact studied; and (2) exploration of what the artifact suggests about
how the ideology of domination is constructed and maintained or how it
can be challenged and transformed.

Analysis of Gender

Feminist criticism begins with an analysis of how women and men,
femininity and masculinity, are depicted in an artifact, using as units of
analysis ones drawn from the artifact itself, ones discussed in other
chapters in this book, or any that provide clues to the construction of
gender in an artifact. Your concern is with discovering what the artifact
presents as standard, normal, desirable, and appropriate behavior for
women and men. Women and men are constructed in particular ways
through rhetorical artifacts, and your task is to discover the particular
nature of the construction in your artifact. You may discover that women
are portrayed in an artifact in ways that accord with particular forms of
male interest—they are depicted, for example, as sexual objects for men;
as primarily responsible for housework, childrearing, and caregiving; or
as weaker or secondary to men. Alternatively, women may be absent
from texts except as necessary devices to support the depiction of masculinity in artifacts, as in conventional Western and horror films.

A critic also may gain information about the construction of gender
by identifying how an artifact positions its audience. An artifact provides a preferred viewpoint from which to view the world of the artifact.
This is the position an audience member must occupy to participate in
the pleasures and meaning of the text. This position requires a particular
cultural experience to make sense of the artifact and is the result of the
structures of characters, meanings, aesthetic codes, attitudes, norms, and
values the rhetor projects into the text.

In many cases, the subject position offered to the audience is a gen-
dered one—feminine or masculine—that describes how the world looks
and feels to women or to men or describes a world rooted in ways of
understanding typically associated with women or men.[12] In many pop-

ular artifacts, a masculine position is structured for the subject, and audience members are asked to identify with a male protagonist who controls events and conveys a sense of omnipotence. Men's experiences are universalized so that the masculine is aligned with the universal; what happens to men or what men find desirable and appropriate is seen as applying to women. The female subject in such texts usually is positioned as the object rather than the subject of the action; she is displayed for the gaze and enjoyment of men. In artifacts in which the subject position is a masculine one, women are asked to identify with a male point of view, to think as men, and to accept as normal and legitimate that point of view.

An analysis of gender in an artifact also may depict various choices open to women and men in terms of their standpoints, the material conditions of their lives, the degree to which they assume agency, and even how they define the dominant system and their status vis-à-vis that system. Members of the same marginalized group can assume different standpoints concerning their material and social conditions, their identity, the degree to which they believe conditions control them, and the degree of agency they assume, and your analysis can focus on the standpoint a rhetor adopts.

Implications of the Construction of Gender

As a result of exploring the construction of gender in an artifact, a critic makes a judgment about the conceptions of femininity and masculinity in it and whose interests the conceptions seem to serve: Does the conception affirm and support the ideology of domination, or does it model other ways of being? At this point, you have two options. If your analysis of the artifact reveals that it depicts an ideology of domination, your next step is to use the analysis to help discover how domination is constructed and maintained through rhetoric. If your analysis of the artifact reveals that it departs from acceptance of an ideology of domination and challenges the status quo or creates a different ideology in which to operate, you will use the analysis to contribute to an understanding of how individuals can use rhetoric to claim agency and engage in acts of self-determination.

When you discover a text in which men's experiences are central and perhaps universalized, in which women are not taken into account, or in which values such as hierarchy are featured, you have an opportunity to use the artifact as a vehicle to study the ideology of domination and the rhetorical processes that create and sustain it. Use your analysis to describe rhetorical practices through which the existing ideology of domination is constructed and maintained through rhetoric. Such a description may include analyzing how power is exercised in the system through rhetoric and how the hegemony or dominance of particular groups is constructed and maintained in patriarchy. Hegemony is the imposition of the ideology of one group on other groups—it is the power to describe reality and to have that description accepted. It expresses the advantaged position of white, heterosexual men in a dominant culture, and a critic can describe how that advantaged position is maintained through particular rhetorical strategies. Other directions you might pursue are whose interests are marginalized, silenced, or excluded or how an artifact is able to draw audience members into its designs, providing satisfaction and pleasure, even to audiences of women.

Your analysis also can contribute to an understanding of the rhetorical strategies individuals use to construct their marginalization or subordination around a category of identity—gender or race, for example. Explication of the constraints and forces that encourage and facilitate an individual's adoption of a victim stance or a sense of powerlessness as a result of an aspect of identity or a particular material condition can help us understand the rhetorical operation of such self-definition and the absence of agency that follows. Discovery of the way in which an ideology of domination facilitates self-imposed marginalization, then, is another possible route to take in pursuing the implications of a particular construction of gender in an artifact.

If your artifact is one that affirms and reinforces the ideology of domination, then, use your analysis to contribute to an understanding of how those structures are constructed and maintained through rhetoric. Such an analysis provides a critical distance on existing gender relations, clearing a space in which existing gender arrangements can be evaluated and perhaps altered. By describing relationships that exist within the context of an ideology of domination, it calls them into question, opening the way for change and for new kinds of relations.

As a result of the analysis of gender in an artifact, you may find that the conception of gender encoded in the artifact suggests ways in which individuals claim agency, engage in acts of self-definition or self-determination, refuse to be confined by an ideology of domination, or transform dominating structures and relations in imaginative ways. In such a case, your next step is to discuss how the artifact facilitates the assumption of agency.

A critic may find that a text provides an opening for transformation by providing evidence of ways in which women can ignore ideologies of domination and do not allow themselves to be confined by them. An artifact, for example, may provide models for the ways in which women have managed to articulate their perspectives and have them heard in spite of the rhetorical forces that attempt to silence and exclude them. It may highlight women's acts of re-naming or re-definition or the creation of subject positions for women.

Another focus a critic may discover in an artifact that facilitates assumption of agency is to explore that artifact as a model worthy of emulation for creating nondominating structures and relationships. As a result of their particular experiences and insights, many women have developed alternative ways of communicating and espouse values that are different from those that typify the ideology of domination. Women often are taught to be nurturing, affiliative, and cooperative, for example—qualities that are contrary to values that mark the ideology of domination such as competition, domination, and hierarchy. An artifact, then, may offer themes, styles, values, forms of communication, and kinds of relationships that can serve as models for alternatives to the ideology of domination.

These are just a few of the ways in which an artifact may challenge and seek to transform the ideology of domination, provide openings for its transformation, or articulate a different mode of being altogether. By describing the experiences of women, ways in which their subordinate position is resisted, and ways in which their communication can serve as models for alternatives to an ideology of domination, artifacts can contribute to an understanding of how individuals assume agency and thus effectively trivialize or dismantle the ideology of domination.

Formulating a Research Question

In feminist criticism, a critic's primary interest is in the construction of domination and of alternatives to domination, often as these relate to gender. The research questions asked by feminist critics, then, are likely to be questions such as these: "How is gender (or race, class, sexual orientation, ability, religion, etc.) constructed in artifacts?" "What rhetorical strategies are used to construct and maintain the ideology of domination?" "How do members of marginalized groups construct ways of being independent of the ideology of domination?" "What rhetorical strategies are used by members of marginalized groups to challenge or transform the ideology of domination?" "How can the rhetorical practices of marginalized groups be used to reconceptualize rhetorical concepts to make them more inclusive?"[11]

Writing the Essay

After completing the analysis, you are ready to write your essay, which includes five major components: (1) an introduction, in which you discuss the research question, its contribution to rhetorical theory, and its significance; (2) a description of the artifact and its context; (3) a description of the method of criticism—in this case, feminist criticism; (4) a report of the findings of the analysis, in which you describe the conception of gender in the artifact and its implications; and (5) a discussion of the contribution the analysis makes to rhetorical theory.

Sample Essays

The essays that follow provide examples of different kinds of feminist criticism. The first essay exemplifies criticism in which the analysis of gender in an artifact contributes to an understanding of the ideology of domination. James Fredal analyzes a song from *Sesame Street* to answer the question, "How are patriarchal attitudes and beliefs engendered in artifacts directed at children?" Sonja K. Foss's analysis of a work of art by Judy Chicago—*The Dinner Party*—exemplifies criticism in which the analysis of gender in an artifact leads to contributions to the development of agency and the breaking free of the constraints of an ideology of domination. She seeks to answer the question, "What strategies do submerged groups use to legitimize their own perspectives?" Dara Krause, See Vang, and Shonagh Brent's essay analyzing the children's book *Daddy's Roommate* demonstrates feminist criticism applied to a difference that involves an aspect of identity other than gender. They analyze the depiction of gay parenting in the book to answer the question, "What rhetorical strategies can be used to normalize a construction of family that is non-hegemonic and controversial?"

Notes

[1] Mary MacNamara, "What is Feminism? Another View . . . ," *Wicca: "Wise Woman" Irish Feminist Magazine*, 21 (c. 1982), 6–7, qtd. in Cheris Kramarae, Paula A. Treichler, and Ann Russo, *A Feminist Dictionary* (Boston: Pandora, 1985), p. 159.

[2] Linda Aldoory and Elizabeth L. Toth, "The Complexities of Feminism in Communication Scholarship Today," *Communication Yearbook*, 24 (2001), 346.

[3] bell hooks, *Feminist Theory: From Margin to Center* (Boston: South End, 1984), p. 26.

[4] hooks, p. 24.

[5] This history is condensed from Amanda D. Lotz, "Communicating Third-Wave Feminism and New Social Movements: Challenges for the Next Century of Feminist Endeavor," *Women and Language*, 26 (Spring 2003), 2–9.

[6] Naomi Wolf, *Fire with Fire: The New Female Power and How it Will Change the 21st Century* (London: Chatto & Windus, 1993), pp. 150, 149, 151.

[7] hooks, p. 24.

[8] Beth Kiyoko Jamieson, *Real Choices: Feminism, Freedom, and the Limits of Law* (University Park: Pennsylvania State University Press, 2001), p. 226.

[9] Kiyoko Jamieson, pp. 226–27.

[10] This history is condensed from Sonja K. Foss, Karen A. Foss, and Cindy L. Griffin, *Feminist Rhetorical Theories* (Thousand Oaks, CA: Sage, 1999), 14–32.

[11] Karlyn Kohrs Campbell, "The Rhetoric of Women's Liberation: An Oxymoron," *Quarterly Journal of Speech*, 59 (February 1973), 74–86.

[12] Cheris Kramer, "Women's Speech: Separate but Unequal?" *Quarterly Journal of Speech*, 60 (February 1974), 14.

[13] Sally Miller Gearhart, "The Womanization of Rhetoric," *Women's Studies International Quarterly*, 2 (1979), 195–201.

[14] Carole Spitzack and Kathryn Carter, ed., *Doing Research on Women's Communication: Perspectives on Theory and Method* (Norwood, NJ: Ablex, 1989).

[15] Carole Blair, Julie R. Brown, and Leslie A. Baxter, "Disciplining the Feminine," *Quarterly Journal of Speech*, 80 (November 1994), 399.

[16] Karen A. Foss and Sonja K. Foss, "The Status of Research on Women and Communication," *Communication Quarterly*, 31 (Summer 1983), 202.

[17] Carole Spitzack and Kathryn Carter, "Women in Communication Studies: A Typology for Revision," *Quarterly Journal of Speech*, 73 (November 1987), 419.

[18] Samples of such feminist reconceptualizations include: Mary Rose Williams, "A Reconceptualization of Protest Rhetoric: Women's Quilts as Rhetorical Forms," *Women's Studies in Communication*, 17 (Fall 1994), 20–44; Sonja K. Foss and Cindy L. Griffin, "Beyond Persuasion: A Proposal for an Invitational Rhetoric," *Communication Monographs*, 62 (March 1995), 2–18; Candace West, "Women's Competence in Conversation," *Discourse and Society*, 6 (January 1995), 107–31; and Elizabeth J. DeGroot, "A Reconceptualization of the Enthymeme from a Feminist Perspective," Diss. University of Oregon 1990.

"Ladybug Picnic"
Engendering Pyrophobia and Promethean Desire
James Fredal

Patriarchy is not a monolith, nor is it ever finished. Like other ideologies and practices of domination, patriarchy constantly must be reproduced and maintained rhetorically. Those engaged in this maintenance rarely perceive themselves as reproducing the cultural forms that allow patriarchy to exist. More often, cultural products are seen simply as enacting what they proclaim for themselves: news programs simply report the news, advertisements simply sell, songs simply entertain. Rhetorical critics who question these ostensible functions, as feminist critics do, are said to be reading too much into an artifact or to be finding things that aren't really there. In fact, hegemonic practices rely on this resistance to criticism in order to maintain the appearance of naturalness that they construct.

The resistance is particularly noticeable and especially important in those arenas where the construction and maintenance of dominant ideologies, like patriarchy, are most needed. The substance of children's television programming, for example, resists serious critical attention as a relatively unimportant cultural activity at the same time that it is crucial for engendering in young girls and boys the attitudes and beliefs on which patriarchy relies for its survival. In this essay, I will examine one song from a children's program that is particularly adept at resisting serious attention in order to discover the ways in which it portrays and reinforces the attitudes and values characteristic of patriarchy.

"Ladybug Picnic" is a short, animated counting song on a *Sesame Street* video called *Silly Songs*. The song features twelve identical ladybugs in identical pink bonnets who engage in various picnicking activities. They run sack races, play jump rope, tell jokes, and finally sit around a campfire and talk while roasting marshmallows. Each refrain begins with the singer rhythmically counting up to twelve in groups of three as the ladybugs appear to enjoy their next game. The song is short, only one minute and fifteen seconds. It immediately follows the opening song on the video, "Honker Duckie Dinger Jamboree" and precedes the ever-popular "Jellyman Kelly." *Silly Songs* is just one of many *Sesame Street* videos, most of which are arranged thematically. Other videos include *Rock and Roll* and an animal-songs video called *Sing, Hoot and Howl*.

Sesame Street has been around for over twenty years. Its residents—Big Bird, Bert and Ernie, Oscar the Grouch, and Cookie Monster, among others—are some of the best-known television personages for children and adults alike. As a program broadcast by public television, *Sesame Street* enjoys a trust increasingly withheld from the networks. Thus, the many caveats about television sex and violence and the need for parents to "screen" shows not intended for young audiences typically are not applied to shows like *Sesame Street*. In this negative sense, then, it has earned the right to be overlooked by adults even more than network children's shows. *Sesame Street* is overlooked by children as well. Lewis Lapham's article in

This essay was written while James Fredal was a student in Sonja K. Foss's rhetorical criticism class at Ohio State University in 1994. Used by permission of the author.

the December, 1993, issue of *Harper's*, "Adieu, Big Bird: On the Terminal Irrele-vance of Public Television," argues that public broadcasts continue to lose audience share because they do nothing that cable channels and the networks don't do, only public television does it on a tighter budget. "Instead of offering an alternative to the Roman circus of commercial television," argues Lapham, public television "presents a show of slightly less expensive lions" (35). As more cable channels offer more sophisticated, action-oriented, high-tech entertainment, *Sesame Street* goes the way of other public television broadcasts: toward increasing marginalization.

Silly Songs is interesting because its very title further resists serious attention even by those children who do watch. In the unique parlance of parenting tod-dlers, *silly* is a useful term rich in meaning. More commonly used than in stan-dard English, *silly* refers to the non-serious and nonsensical, unreal, or pretend and frequently inappropriate behavior of children. In the never-ending battle to teach, model, and reinforce socially appropriate behavior, *silly* usually refers to the uninhibited, make-believe play that seems always on the verge of getting out of hand, especially in public. Thus, the term implies actions that are pretend, non-serious, or inconsequential (Lapham might call public television *silly*) as well as actions that are unethical, inappropriate, or incorrect (actions such as interrupting a group activity that does not include the child). *Silly Songs* thus announces itself to children and parents as a program that does not merit serious attention. The songs will not deal with "real" or socially appropriate behaviors or with serious content. As such, the video explicitly invites a sort of benign neglect. "You needn't pay attention too closely," the viewer is told, "we're just being silly."

ANALYSIS OF GENDER

"Ladybug Picnic," paradoxically, *is* an educational song and, to that extent, does have a serious message. The song teaches children their numbers, in this case the number twelve. The silliness of the song lies rather in its narrative con-tent, the details that fill out the number. These are, of course, the twelve ladybugs engaged in a thoroughly non-serious activity: a picnic. The ladybugs are indeed silly, finding themselves unable to engage in any activity to completion, much less any serious activity. Their first game, the sack race, is both competitive and active, requiring agility and strenuous effort. The race ends prematurely as the ladybugs all "fall on their backs and they fall on their faces." Wobbly but undaunted, the ladybugs proceed to a less demanding activity, jumping rope. More traditionally a "girl's game," jumping rope is noncompetitive but still requires substantial agility and energy to do well. Here, the ladybugs' failure is not one of physical ability (perhaps because this is what females are supposed to do well); rather, the rope breaks. Baffled by even this rudimentary mechanical problem (retying the rope), they opt for a game that is entirely noncompetitive and nonactive: telling knock-knock jokes.

Curiously, the ladybugs play this game by knocking their heads together, which is not the typical way that knock-knock jokes are told but perhaps appro-priate to this silly song. Head knocking often signifies stupidity or ineptitude and is often signified by knocking the head with the knuckles. This would be the equivalent of calling someone a *blockhead* or *thick headed*. Perhaps this is the best way to portray this silly bunch of bugs. Their doltishness matches their clumsy ineptitude well.

We are not told why they quit the joke telling, but they very quickly retire to the campfire, around which they begin to "chatter away." Maybe "chattering" is just what they enjoy. This is, after all, the traditional female pastime *par excellence*, a communal version of the back-fence gossip, where the ladybugs reach the pinnacle of silliness. As their heads turn this way and that, their mouths are all going at once. We can't hear the chatter over the song lyrics, but it's just as well since none of them seems to be listening, either. Their inconsequential, meaningless, and unceasing talk or "chatter," as the lyrics label it, revolves around such trivia as "the high price of furniture and rugs," typical domestic-commodity concerns. Unfortunately, the bugs' chatter is soon to be interrupted by their campfire, which is steadily growing out of control. As the topic turns from furniture and rugs to the high price of "fire insurance for ladybugs," the fire threatens their circle. They all (finally!) stop talking and jump back away from the fire.

The topic of fire insurance is an important one for this group since, as the traditional nursery rhyme tells us ("Ladybug, ladybug, fly away home/Your house is on fire, and your children have flown"), house fires are common for ladybugs, frequently resulting in the loss of their children. Such criminal neglect—mothers away from home while the house burns and the children flee—is to be expected from bugs as silly as these ladies. It plays upon the deepest of a mother's fears: the loss or death of her children, especially in her absence or because of her neglect. Curious, then, that this endemic specter, filial loss, and the attendant guilt, should spill into discourse just as the ladybugs' campfire roars larger without their noticing. Most likely, they were distracted by their own chatter. Their discussion of their fear concerning a topic of unanimous import (understandable, given how often the disastrous nursery rhyme is recited to them), their consequent guilt and self-deprecation, and their difficulty in purchasing insurance for their families prevent them from attending to the fire, which then proceeds, as though on purpose, to break out of its appointed bounds.

Language itself, then, seems to be the culprit responsible for the fire. But not just any language. Specifically, the discourse of ladybugs when they are together, especially when this language turns to serious topics, is to blame. Perhaps, in fact, the nursery rhyme got its start because of this calamitous tendency of ladybugs to chatter among themselves, as they might at a picnic. Discourse as picnic chatter leads ladybugs to ignore their domestic responsibilities and brings about familial ruin. As though to remind them of the dangers of ladybug chatter, the campfire re-enacts the very concern that they begin to discuss. Just as they become engrossed in ladybug talk, the fire threatens to engulf them, overtaking their discursive space even as it signifies the danger of their inflammatory chatter. Like a fire that breaks out of its bounds, ladybug chatter can become dangerous when it goes on too long, even or especially when it turns to topics of serious concern to the ladies themselves. Chatter may turn to commiseration and commiseration to resolve. Like fire for ladybugs is women's talk for men: something to be always feared and controlled.

Unable to control the fire themselves, these ladybugs are fortunate to have a firefighter show up just in time. He pulls out his firehose and douses the fire. The ladybugs cheer, saved from destruction. With the fire out, the picnic is over, and the ladybugs can return to their homes.

UNDERSTANDING PATRIARCHY

The task of cataloguing all video recordings that featured men or the relationships between men and women would be rather simple, since the deletions would be so few. The relationships that women share with each other probably have been overlooked more systematically than any other type of human relationship. What *Sesame Street* calls *silly* we might call *neglected, marginalized,* or *suppressed*. Films that do feature women's relationships with each other tend to do so along a very few lines. They compete with each other for a man, they share their attempts to win a man, or they are just silly. Women who attempt to build relationships outside the world of men typically either fail (as does the ladybugs' chatter) or die (as do Thelma and Louise).

The only masculine figure in this video is a dog dressed in a firefighter's hat and wielding a rather phallic looking firehose. This unmarked dog might not be male, but the role the dog plays has been a traditionally male one. This dog controls fire. Like a modern Prometheus, the firefighting dog controls technology (such as fire trucks) as much as fire, representing exactly what it did for Hesiod, Aeschylus, and Shelley: the domination of nature, including human nature. Mary Shelley observed, in her retelling of the Prometheus myth, that technological, scientific control over human nature was the modern equivalent of controlling fire, the ultimate goal of man's Promethean desire. In "Ladybug Picnic," the control over human nature takes a gender-specific turn. As an insect, she is an embodiment of nature, but, by nature, she is female. Ladybugs thus physically coalesce what men always have desired to control the most: wilderness and women.

We then might read the growth of the fire as the assertion of male prerogatives for dominance over the other. In the ladybugs, this other is both nature and woman. As the firedog arrives, we see the fire as man's best friend, breaking up the ladybugs' chatter before it leads to anything serious and then responding obediently to the master's tool. By controlling fire, this dog symbolically controls the ladybugs as well, since bug and flame are connected with each other through the fire-centered discourse. Both fire and women are of great domestic use when kept under control at home, yet both become dangerously inflammatory when unleashed, as at this picnic. As a fire's heat aids its own spread, so women's chatter feeds off itself, becomes all consuming and dangerous.

Of course, boys and girls watching "Ladybug Picnic" don't know Prometheus and wouldn't be likely to see in ladybugs a symbolic conflation of nature and the female. In an apparently innocuous song, however, one that resists serious attention (by being *silly* and by calling attention to ladybugs as sheer numbers), the story can so boldly be told about women failing in competitive and physical activities, about women's inability to play together, about women's attempts to talk together outside the world of men, and about the consequences of such attempts. Curious, too, is that such an apparently silly song can be so doubly damning of women's talk. The ladybugs' chatter about fire insurance was itself engendered by a children's rhyme that reproduced for them the tragic consequences of their being away from home, yet their attempts to discuss this concern are themselves out-shouted by the roar of the growing fire. As their fear of fire pushed its way into discourse, the fire pushed the words back into their mouths and sent them back home. These ladybugs could not keep quiet yet could not speak. The panoptic fire guarded them.

The silly stories we tell recreate for us a reality, a reality into which we are forced to fit ourselves. As a nursery rhyme constructed the ladybugs' fire-fear for them, shaping their emotional reality, their insurance bills, and their discourse, just so we would have to suppose that this silly song could narrate itself into real lives of the children who watch the video on which it is featured. We would have to find it warning young girls about what is inappropriate for them (mechanical prowess and exclusive girl-talk about serious matters), while it conscripts young boys to their roles as fire-masters (even if they prefer chatter).

Feminist critiques of rhetorical artifacts are important as clues to the ways in which women and men have been shaped by the largely male language with which we speak and important to overcoming those often invisible shaping forces. This song alerts us to the powerful messages that shape our conceptions of gender—of what is appropriate and what isn't—and suggests that we begin to take very seriously indeed artifacts that are seen to be, or claim themselves to be, unserious, inconsequential, and silly. This is particularly true of the discourse about, by, and for children. Because children are most open to the messages they see and hear, children's books, songs, and television shows deserve our close attention, the better to understand the places at which gender constructions begin and the better to resist the confines that children's texts construct.

Judy Chicago's *The Dinner Party*
Empowering of Women's Voice in Visual Art
Sonja K. Foss

With his notion of the discursive formation, Michel Foucault has focused attention on the lack of input into mainstream discourse by subordinate groups on the periphery of society. A discursive formation is the code of a culture that governs "its language, its schemas of perception, its exchanges, its techniques, its values, the hierarchy of its practices" (Foucault, 1970, p. xx). It is the characteristic system, structure, or network that defines the conditions for the possibility of knowledge or for the worldview of an age. Various rules govern who is allowed to speak and be heard in a discursive formation, the conditions under which they are allowed to speak, and the content and form their discourse must assume (Foucault, 1972, pp. 41–44, 56–67, 68, 224–225). Knowledge is generated by the discursive practices of a discursive formation so that those individuals who are not "heard" or allowed to participate in the dominant discourse do not have their knowledge incorporated into the common cultural knowledge.

Kramarae (1981) arrives at similar conclusions about the role of a submerged group's discourse in a culture in her discussion of the minority perspective on language. Minority groups in a culture, she asserts, tend to have little power because they have little control over their economic fortunes or social status. Consequently, they find that their speech is not evaluated highly by those in the predominant culture, they generally are not represented in decision-making or policy-making processes of that culture, and they thus are denied a voice in it. Samuel Beckett (1958) explained this inability to be heard particularly well: "I am walled round with their vociferations, none will ever know what I am, none will ever hear me say it, I won't say it, I can't say it, I have no language but theirs, . . ." (p. 52).

A prerequisite to having their voices heard in a discursive formation or the dominant culture is that members of a submerged group must develop their own authentic voice. They must develop knowledge and discourse out of their own experiences and interpret and label these experiences in their own terms. Perhaps even more important, they must come to see their experiences and discourse as legitimate and valuable. Developing this authenticity and attributing power to it are difficult for a submerged group, however, because their experience has been interpreted for them for so long by others and devalued by those others. The submerged group has been trained to see itself as represented in the dominant discourse of the culture and has come to subordinate even its authentic and potentially powerful voice to that culture (Schulz, 1984). Certainly, the submerged group faces difficulties following development and empowerment of its authentic voice—it must secure acknowledgment of its authority to speak by the dominant group. But empowerment cannot happen without a strong sense of identity within the submerged group apart from the dominant culture. Group members first must possess the "courage to be and to speak . . . . the Courage to Blas-

From *Women Communicating: Studies of Women's Talk*, ed. Barbara Bate and Anita Taylor (Norwood, NJ: Ablex, 1988), pp. 9-26. Used by permission of Ablex Publishing Corporation and the author.

pheme" (Daly, 1978, p. 264) the definitions of themselves as powerless that have been established by the dominant discourse.

My purpose in this essay is to identify some of the strategies that submerged groups use to empower their own perspective or to develop legitimacy for the knowledge and discourse that are available to them. I have chosen to examine the discourse of women as a case study of this process. In a male-dominated culture where "[p]atriarchy is itself the prevailing religion" (Daly, 1978, p. 39), women constitute a marginal group. They have been excluded in many ways from public life, and they occupy largely peripheral and powerless positions when they do enter that realm. Because of their different positions from men, women have experience that "is institutionally and linguistically structured in a way that is different from that of men" (Ferguson, 1984, p. 23). Yet, this experience, along with the knowledge and discourse it generates, is submerged, devalued, and generally not heard in the male-dominated culture. As Daly (1978) explains, "It is when women speak our own truth that incredulity comes from all sides" (p. 91). Women's words, because they do not conform to the rules of the dominant discursive formation, are treated as "officially worthless" (Daly, p. 92).

While numerous scholars have attempted to identify the characteristic qualities of women's perspective or voice as a result of their different experiences in the culture, I do not want to make a case either for or against particular qualities as representative of the female voice. Instead, my focus in this essay is on the process by which women come to see their symbols, rituals, and regular practices—the *content* of their experiences that tends to be overlooked in the male worldview—as legitimate.

I have selected for the study of strategies used to empower women's voice a work of visual art, Judy Chicago's *The Dinner Party* (a detailed description and photographs of the work can be found in Chicago, 1979). I chose this work for my object of study because of its richness of data. Because it incorporates both discursive and nondiscursive data—words, colors, lines, textures, and images—it may reveal strategies that would not be apparent in a work of discursive rhetoric alone. In addition, if, in fact, women's perspective is submerged in our culture, a work that is free to go beyond the bounds of the conventional language system, which gives voice largely to men, might demonstrate more clearly strategies used to empower that alternative perspective.

In selecting *The Dinner Party* as the data for my study, I am aware of a number of assumptions I require the reader to accept if this study is to be seen as capable of contributing to theory development in communication. First, of course, I am assuming that visual images are included in the scope of rhetoric or communication. As the conscious production or arrangement of colors, forms, images, textures, and other elements in a manner that affects or evokes a response, I see visual images as forms of rhetoric that attempt, as does discursive rhetoric, to influence others' "thinking and behavior through the strategic use of symbols" (Ehninger, 1972, p. 3).

I also recognize that works of art contain both rhetorical and aesthetic qualities. Experience of a work at an aesthetic level is the apprehension or perception of the sensory elements of the object—enjoyment of its colors or the valuing of its texture, for example. But when a viewer attributes meaning to those sensory elements and they begin to refer to images, emotions, and ideas beyond themselves, the response has become a rhetorical one—that with which I will be concerned here.

No one true meaning or interpretation can be made of an art object's function as a rhetorical symbol. To say that an art object has meaning for a viewer does not suggest that it signifies some fixed referent. Rather, meaning results from and requires a viewer's creation of an interpretation of the visual object. Different meanings are attributed to a work of art, then, by different viewers as a result of the differing endowments and experiences brought to the work.

The predominant role of the viewer in the establishment of the meaning for a work of art, however, does not mean that a viewer has total freedom to attribute any meaning at all to the work. A viewer's interpretation is limited by the actual object itself. Although that meaning is not an inherent part of the object, the solid physical presence of a work of art makes possible the work's aesthetic and rhetorical effects. More important, the physical characteristics render one rhetorical interpretation more likely to occur than another.

In my analysis of *The Dinner Party*, I will identify the physical or material properties of the work that a viewer is likely to use as the basis for attribution of meanings to it. While my description may seem anthropomorphic in that I will use phrases such as, "*The Dinner Party* provides" or "the work generates," this style was selected simply as a matter of convenience. I do not intend to suggest that the meaning of the work lies in these physical attributes or that *The Dinner Party* itself is a rhetor capable of producing purposive communication. Rather, I am suggesting that as the physical embodiment of its creator's intention, the work can be examined as containing particular characteristics that are likely to guide the viewer's interpretation in particular directions. The viewer is free to interpret *The Dinner Party* or create meaning for it according to her own experiences, as long as the meaning attributed is grounded somehow in the material form of the art object.

THE DINNER PARTY

The Dinner Party opened on March 14, 1979, at the San Francisco Museum of Modern Art. The show next traveled to the University of Houston in Clear Lake City, Texas, opening there on March 9, 1980. It was shown at the Boston Center for the Arts in July and August of 1980 and at the Brooklyn Museum in New York from October, 1980, through January, 1981. In July and August of 1981, *The Dinner Party* was on display in Cleveland Heights, Ohio, followed by its exhibition in Chicago from September, 1981, through February, 1982. It now is in storage until a permanent gallery space can be located for it.

The work itself is a room-size installation piece whose primary element is an open-centered, triangular table approximately 48 feet long on each side and 26 inches wide. Resting on the table are 39 sculptured plates, each representing a woman from history—from the mythical past through the present. The first wing of the table represents women from prehistory to the decline of Greco-Roman culture and includes plates representing women such as the Primordial Goddess; Kali, an ancient Indian goddess; Hatshepsut, an Egyptian pharaoh of the eighteenth dynasty; and Sappho, a Greek poet of about 600 B.C. The second wing of the table represents women from the period of Christianity to the Reformation and includes plates for such figures as Saint Bridget, a sixth-century Irish saint; Eleanor of Aquitaine, a French queen of the thirteenth century; and Petronilla de Meath, a woman who was burned as a witch in Ireland. The third wing represents

© Judy Chicago, 1979. Photograph by Michael Alexander.

the seventeenth through the twentieth centuries and includes plates for Anne Hutchinson, a seventeenth-century American Puritan and reformer; Caroline Herschel, a nineteenth-century German scientist; Sojourner Truth, an American abolitionist and feminist; and English writer Virginia Woolf.

Each place setting includes a ceramic or painted china plate, a gold-lined ceramic goblet, lustre flatware, a gold-edged napkin, and an elaborate needle-work runner that contains the name of the woman represented in gold script. The goblets, napkins, and flatware are the same for all the place settings, but each of the plates and runners is different.

The place setting representing Emily Dickinson, for example, contains a very feminine, pink plate with a vulva-like center surrounded by six rows of real lace that were dipped in liquid ceramic and then fired. The plate rests on a round pink-and-white lace "collar" or placemat, and the gold runner beneath it is edged in the same pink lace of the plate.

The plate that represents Susan B. Anthony also contains a center vaginal form—this time in a deep red color, edged by a fold of lighter red. Four molded, draped "wings" spread out from this center and curl up at the edges of the plate, suggesting a butterfly rising from the plate. The butterfly form is a luminescent red, which seems to vibrate against a beige background. The plate rests on a bright red triangle of sturdy woven fabric edged with fringe. Streaming out from behind this triangle are strips of white and black fabric, representing a "Memory

Quilt" for Anthony. Embroidered on each white strip is the name of a suffragist from Anthony's period, including Anna Howard Shaw, Harriot Stanton Blatch, and Paulina Wright Davis.

In the plate of Theodora, a Byzantine empress of the sixth century, the illusion of separate mosaic tiles in green, pink, and gold is created through a series of lines etched into the plate. While this plate is flat, in contrast to Dickinson's and Anthony's, it again features a butterfly form. The butterfly image is composed of circles, diamonds, and other forms that suggest traditional designs of stained-glass windows. Theodora's plate rests on a round, braided gold placemat on top of a gold satin runner. At the front of the runner, below Theodora's name, is a strip of purple satin edged with purple and gold lace and ribbon.

The table, containing 39 such place settings, rests on a raised triangular platform called the Heritage Floor. It is composed of more than 2,300 hand-cast white pearlescent triangular tiles. Written across the tiles in gold script are the names of 999 women, grouped by historical period around the woman's place at the table who represents that particular period.

The Dinner Party was the creation of artist Judy Chicago, born Judy Cohen in Chicago in 1939. She studied art at the University of California at Los Angeles,

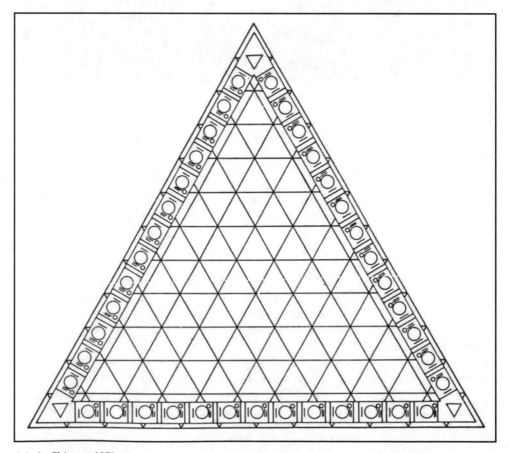

© Judy Chicago, 1979.

where the sexually feminine images she employed in her work were ridiculed by her male professors. She began to realize the need for more support for women artists and for recognition that the images produced by women artists would be different from those produced by men. She became known as a feminist artist and in 1969 renounced "all names imposed upon her through male social dominance" (Chicago, 1977, p. 63) and chose her own name: Judy Chicago.

While teaching at Fresno State, Chicago organized an art class for women. With the members of the class, she founded Womanspace, an exhibition space for women housed in an old mansion in Los Angeles. She went on to develop a Feminist Art Program at the California Institute of the Arts in Valencia, which led her to conclude that women artists need an entirely independent structure in which to work. She then organized the Feminist Studio Workshop in Los Angeles. In 1973, the Workshop, Womanspace, and other feminist galleries and organizations were incorporated into the Woman's Building in Los Angeles, which was designed to provide a feminist context for women artists.

Chicago worked on the execution of *The Dinner Party* by herself for three years, studying ceramics and china painting in order to learn the techniques necessary for the execution of the piece. In October, 1975, faced with the growing awareness that she could not complete a work of this magnitude alone, Chicago began taking on help. She obtained the assistance of a graduate student with experience in porcelain to work on the execution of the plates, an assistant to supervise the needlework on the runners, researchers to compile the biographies of the 3,000 women from which the names for the floor tiles were selected, and an assistant to supervise the casting and sanding of the floor tiles. Diane Gelon, an art historian, was added to coordinate the entire project and to serve as second-in-command to Chicago.

In addition to the five or six individuals who fully participated during the three-year cooperative period of the project, about 125 individuals were considered "members of the project," and another 300 assisted with smaller contributions of both work and ideas to the execution of the piece. The work was carried out in Chicago's Santa Monica studio, which had been remodeled with the assistance of a grant from the National Endowment for the Arts to include a ceramics studio, an electric kiln, a needlework loft, and a dust-free china painting room. Thus, although the piece was conceived and directed by Chicago, it incorporated the work and ideas of many others as well.

STRATEGIES OF EMPOWERMENT

Analysis of *The Dinner Party* reveals three primary strategies used in the work as means to empower and legitimize women's authentic voice: (a) The work is independent from male-created reality; (b) it creates new standards for evaluation of its own rhetoric; and (c) women are clearly labeled as agents.

Independence from Male-Created Reality

In *The Dinner Party*, the presentation of women's culture occurs entirely apart from the male-dominated world outside the setting of the exhibition. It is a separatist piece not only because it deals exclusively with women's culture but also because it lacks reference to anything male. Women's achievements are the sole focus of the work, and men are not referred to in any way in it. The work is formed entirely from women's traditional arts such as china painting and needlework, art forms not recognized as having value in the male-dominated art world. Further, female imagery predominates. The triangular shape of the table is a primitive symbol of the feminine; vaginal images appear in the centers of many plates; and the dinner-table setting suggests women's traditional concerns. *The Dinner Party*, then, encourages the viewer to focus only on women, a stance that has two consequences.

First, the work's independence from male culture defines women's culture as derived from women's positive experiences rather than in opposition to men's culture. It presents the creation or formation of a new, separate symbolic order for women that "does not essentially depend upon an enemy for its existence/becoming" (Daly, 1978, p. 320). Refusal to create in opposition to a male enemy allows the formulation of positive, affirming discourse in contrast to that created from a sense of inferiority.

The danger of focusing on an enemy as the basis for creation and empowerment of an authentic voice, explains Daly (1978), is that it does not allow that voice to grow and develop. It remains at the level of attacking the enemy. The individual who defines herself and her voice only in opposition "may become fixated upon the atrocities of andocracy, 'spinning her wheels' instead of spinning on her heel and facing in Other directions" (p. 320). Betty Friedan (1981) makes the same point, asserting that there is value in a fight "within, and against, and defined by that old structure of unequal, polarized male and female sex roles. But to continue reacting against that structure is still to be defined and limited by its terms" (p. 40). In contrast, in *The Dinner Party*, women's culture by itself is portrayed as rich, abundant, self-sufficient, and positive, with energy and worth arising from its own special qualities. It is seen as having authentic qualities that constitute a significant and valuable perspective in and of themselves.

Definition of women's culture totally apart from men's also enables *The Dinner Party* to present an alternative to the male-dominated view of the world more effectively. It creates this view not by comparing the female perspective to that of men but through presentation of an alternative vision on its own terms. Ferguson (1984) makes a strong case as to why empowerment of a dissenting voice will not result from the integration of the subordinate group into the existing structure. When members of a submerged group attack the system from within by integrating themselves into the system, climbing to the top, and then attempting to change it, they are doomed to fail. As Ferguson asks, after "internalizing and acting on the rules of [the dominant system] for most of their adult lives, how many . . . will be *able* to change? After succeeding in the system by using those rules, how many would be *willing* to change?" (p. 192). She continues: "It is hard to be a 'closet radical' when an inspection of the closets is part of the organization's daily routine" (p. 193). The dominant system, then, cannot be resisted on its own terms, since they are terms that render opposition invisible.

Ferguson (1984) explains how discourses of opposition must function in order to be effective: they must present their visions in terms other than those of the dominant structure. This task is accomplished by "unearthing/creating the specific language of women, and comprehending women's experience in terms of that linguistic framework rather than in terms of the dominant discourse" (p. 154). By creating a rhetoric in terms other than those of the dominant discourse, Ferguson explains, experiences are changed:

Just as our experience is defined by the intuitive and reflective awareness that our language makes available, our language in turn is circumscribed by our experience; to alter the terms of public discourse one must change the experiences people have, and to restructure experiences one must change the language available for making sense of those experiences. (p. 154)

The Dinner Party, then, frames a world and uses images and forms rooted in the female experience. Thus, it poses an alternative to the dominant discourse, the "old molds/models . . . by being itself an Other way of thinking/speaking" (Daly, 1978, p. xiii). *The Dinner Party*, through its presentation of women alone and lack of reference to men, suggests that women "eject, banish, depose the possessing language—spoken and written words, body language, architectural language, technological language, the language of symbols and of institutional structures" (Daly, 1978, p. 345), inspiriting and empowering their own vision of the world.

Creation of New Standards for Evaluation of Rhetoric

A second strategy used in *The Dinner Party* to authenticate the female experience is the development of new standards for judging women's rhetoric. Just as viewers are led, in *The Dinner Party*, to reject the male-dominated perspective as the only reality, so they are encouraged to develop new means of evaluating women's discourse. Rejection of male domination and focus on the creation of an independent women's reality frees participants from dependence on, as Daly (1978) names it, "Male Approval Desire" (p. 69)—male standards of evaluation. Thus, participants are able to construct their own expectations and criteria for evaluation derived from the authentic experiences of women's culture: "Depending less and less upon male approval, recognizing that such approval is more often than not a reward for weakness, we approve of our Selves. We prove our Selves" (Daly, 1978, pp. 341–342).

The evaluation typically accorded the discourse of a submerged group such as women tends to be negative. One of the earliest to express this view formally was Otto Jespersen in 1922, who described women's speech as an aberration of men's. He said women use less complex sentences, talk faster and with less thought, and have less extensive vocabularies than men. Studies that revealed that women's speech contained more hedges and qualifiers frequently were interpreted as suggesting women's lack of certainty and confidence, while nonverbal gestures sometimes described as characteristic of women, such as more frequent smiling and eye contact, were seen as suggesting powerlessness and submissiveness. These kinds of conclusions illustrate a view of women's speech as a deviation from "real speech." It is "non-standard" because it is different from the speech of men and does not conform to the norms of male speech; consequently, it is inferior. When women's rhetoric is judged negatively according to the standard of conformity to male rhetoric, it is accorded little status and is unable to affect, in any significant way, the dominant discourse (Kramarae, 1981, pp. 95–97).

In *The Dinner Party*, viewers are able to see a number of possibilities for new standards for judgment of women's discourse. They center not around the impact of women's rhetoric on the dominant discourse but rather around the effects of women's rhetoric on themselves. One standard that emerges is the degree to which the rhetoric corresponds to women's experiences, suggested from the focus in *The Dinner Party* on the dinner-table setting. The dinner-party setting is a traditional one for women. It points to the domestic role usually assumed by women, which includes setting tables, preparing meals, and giving dinner parties. The traditional art forms of needlework and china painting used in the work—traditional art forms for women—also are derived from women's experiences, as are the vaginally suggestive images of many of the plates, corresponding to women's biological and physical experiences.

A second standard suggested by *The Dinner Party* to use in assessing women's rhetoric is whether female imagery is presented as positive and valuable. Application of this standard suggests that images unique to or at least typical of the submerged group must not be demeaned, as they might be outside of the culture. In *The Dinner Party*, Chicago almost makes the feminine holy by elevating and celebrating female imagery and traditionally female arts to provide affirmative symbols for women. Because each woman represented at the table stands for one or more aspects of women's experiences and achievements, the viewer is led to see that women have achieved in many areas throughout history, which also points to the notion that the feminine is valuable. The idea is repeated in the sophistication and excellent craftsmanship of the plates and runners, suggesting that women's creations and women as creators are outstanding and certainly deserving of positive evaluations. The 13 place settings on each side of the table, which suggest the 13 individuals seated at the Last Supper, encourage the conclusion that this is a gathering of particular worth and significance, again suggesting the value of the female.

The Dinner Party has the potential capacity to evoke a number of strong emotions in its viewers, suggesting yet another standard by which to judge women's rhetoric—its capacity to evoke emotions. A submerged group develops authenticity and legitimacy only when its users are excited by that discourse and thus have

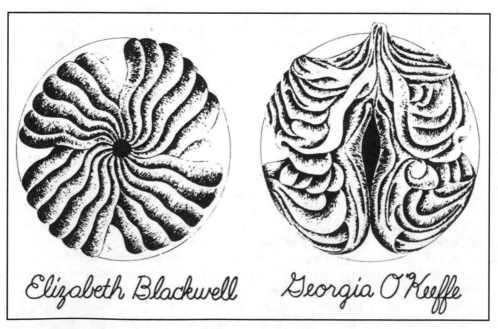

strong desires to use and maintain it. One emotion evoked by *The Dinner Party* is hope or optimism, which is generated by the work's presentation of steady progress in women's status and condition. This progress is suggested by the gradual rising of the butterfly images of the plates as they move from historical to contemporary times. The plates representing the contemporary women appear as though they may fly off the plates, suggesting continued growth and movement for women in their accomplishments and achievements. Viewers also are encouraged to feel the emotion of pride in the accomplishments of women through the numerous women represented in the work as well as anger that the many achievements of women presented in the piece have been ignored for so long. The variety and the brightness of the colors used in *The Dinner Party* also function to induce qualities of joy, celebration, and excitement in the female experience.

A fourth criterion offered in *The Dinner Party* by which women's rhetoric might be judged is whether or not the rhetoric provides a context in which it should be viewed. When rhetoric is presented apart from the dominant culture, it may appear disconnected, irrelevant, and perhaps even a bit absurd simply because it does not conform to the standards established in the dominant discourse. To avoid these negative perceptions, a new context is needed so that the users of the rhetoric understand it in a context in which it is significant and legitimate.

The provision of context can assume many forms. In *The Dinner Party*, context is provided for women's voice through a presentation of the history of that voice. Of particular importance to a submerged group is the need for knowledge of its history—usually a history that has been forgotten or suppressed by the dominant group. The recapturing of that history provides a basis for constructing current culture and generates a sense of pride in it. In *The Dinner Party*, women's history is re-created for viewers through the traditional women's art forms of needlework and china painting. It is also shown in the presentation of women's accomplishments from the past, both in the plates representing women and in the names of women on the Heritage Floor.

A second way in which context can be provided for a submerged group's discourse and knowledge is through presentation of a vision for that group in the future. Such a vision suggests to members of the group that their rhetoric will survive and that it will continue to create a version of reality that is authentic and strong. *The Dinner Party* helps viewers envision the future of women's culture, discourse, and knowledge in a number of ways. The butterfly image of many of the plates is a conventional symbol of flight and growth. As the butterflies lift farther off the plates as they progress through time, they indicate that women currently are capable of flying much farther than they have in numerous realms of endeavor. The table setting itself creates expectancy and anticipation in the viewer that women will continue to achieve and make valuable contributions. The table is ready, and food presumably has been prepared; the hosts now await the arrival of the guests, just as the viewer awaits further contributions by women.

The rhetoric of *The Dinner Party*, then, standing apart from the dominant discourse and the usual context it provides, creates its own context with a past and a future. Thus, the female voice gains greater authenticity as a legitimate alternative to that dominant discourse.

A final criterion for evaluation that emerges from *The Dinner Party* concerns a work's accessibility. If discourse is to have sufficient impact on its users to be given legitimacy as an authentic and powerful voice, it must be accessible to them. This requirement does not mean that all symbols used must be conventional and concrete and that nothing abstract or ambiguous can be included in the rhetoric of a submerged group. But major aspects of the rhetoric must be available to all participants—regardless of their stage of development as participants in their own culture. *The Dinner Party* exemplifies this accessibility in that it is a work of art that almost any viewer can understand. It relies heavily on conventional form—an everyday, familiar dinner-table setting—that is easily understood and accessible in its meaning. This form evokes expectations that have been learned from past experience with the dinner-table form and that the viewer brings with her to the work of art. Experience with the form, then, makes the image and thus the voice represented comfortable and familiar; the reactions of bewilderment and puzzlement that many viewers may have to contemporary art are not those accorded *The Dinner Party.*

Just as *The Dinner Party* rejects the view that male culture is normative by creating a culture apart from it and refusing interaction with it, so are male standards of the dominant discourse rejected for judging women's discourse. Instead, *The Dinner Party* suggests a new set of standards by which to judge rhetoric derived from the culture of a submerged group: The goodness of fit with the experiences of the submerged group; the degree to which the images of the submerged group are presented as positive; the rhetoric's capacity to evoke emotions; the capacity of the rhetoric to provide a context in which it is seen as appropriate and significant; and the degree to which the rhetoric is accessible to members of the submerged group.

Labeling of Agents

A prominent feature of *The Dinner Party* is that it specifically and clearly names who the agents are in the rhetoric it presents—who has the power and authority to act in the world presented. In contrast to rhetoric in which the agent who is communicating is not revealed, subjects of the rhetoric are clearly named in *The Dinner Party.* The women represented at the table and those whose names appear on the Heritage Floor are described in biographies available to viewers and in the images used to depict them in the plates and the runners. Viewers can learn a great deal about the women who serve as the subjects of *The Dinner Party.*

Simply viewing the place setting of Theodora, for example, tells a great deal about who she was. The tiny squares on her plate that create the illusion of mosaic work suggest her connection with churches. The placemat of gold embroidery that surrounds her plate suggests a gold halo and thus rule in the religious realm. The runner of gold and purple satin suggests royalty, as does the illuminated capital letter of her name on the runner. Thus, viewers of *The Dinner Party* leave the work with a sense of the individuality of these distinctive women's experiences and qualities.

Two consequences arise from this specific labeling of agents in *The Dinner Party.* First, it shows women how they can create and control the discourse and knowledge of their world. Total lack of control and responsibility is the result of rhetoric that mystifies, deletes, or hides the agents involved (Daly, 1978, pp. 120, 123–124). In such rhetoric, women are not able to control the world because that control belongs to some unknown authority that cannot be questioned and challenged simply because it is unknown.

In contrast, when agents are specifically named and described, as they are in *The Dinner Party,* women are able to question old authority and control structures. They are allowed to see that women have been and are active agents who have the capacity to control their lives; this control is not exerted by some unknown source. Thus, clear labeling of who the agents are and the nature of their qualities enables the viewers of *The Dinner Party* to begin to conceptualize about themselves as controllers in relation to one another and to the world.

A second consequence of the labeling of agents in *The Dinner Party* is that it allows and encourages a relationship to develop between the viewers and the subjects of the work. It suggests a reciprocity between the viewers and the women who are the subjects of the work by providing points of identification between the two parties. The agents, because they are made known in such detail, then, may begin to have an impact on the viewers and affect their existence so that viewers' and agents' lives become related. As the viewers investigate and analyze why the subjects made the decisions they did to follow particular paths, the women who are the subjects of *The Dinner Party* may perform the role of guides.

Viewers thus may find in the lives of these women qualities and models to make their own lives whole or more meaningful. A viewer of a place setting representing a woman who clearly was the architect of her own choices, for example, might experience confidence or uncertainty about her own choices or lack of them. Personal identifications may develop between subjects and viewers of *The Dinner Party* as the subjects offer their stories, encourage, and suggest new options for the viewers in their own lives. By understanding better the sources of their respective positions in the world and gaining a clearer sense of themselves from the subjects of *The Dinner Party,* viewers may become better able to see the legitimacy and value of their own discourse and knowledge.

The Dinner Party avoids naming the enemy in order that undue attention is not given to responding and reacting to that enemy. Instead, the focus of the work is on women themselves as subjects. These agents are specific women with concrete stories and personal qualities much like those of the work's viewers. *The Dinner Party* thus creates a strong sense of who women are and of their potential to control that definition, meeting a criterion essential to the development of a powerful and legitimate voice for women.

IMPLICATIONS FOR GENERATIVE THEORY

Investigation of the strategies used by submerged groups to develop an authentic voice and legitimize that voice in the face of a dominant discourse yields findings relevant to a number of research areas. One is the possibility it raises for the development of generative theory. A generative theory "is one that unsettles common assumptions within the culture and thereby opens new vistas for action" (Gergen, 1982, p. 133). It is a theory that has *"the capacity to challenge the guiding assumptions of the culture, to raise fundamental questions regarding contemporary social life, to foster reconsideration of that which is 'taken for granted,' and thereby to generate fresh alternatives for social action"* (Gergen, p. 109). A generative theory may accomplish these tasks by instigating doubt, generating doubt and implying alternative courses of action, or fully articulating alternatives to current investments (Gergen, p. 169). Certainly, some research in gender and communication already is contributing to the development of generative theory, but other research is done within the framework of the dominant discourse. What I am advocating is the development of theories about gender and communication that challenge that framework systematically, comprehensively, and consistently.

An investigation of the efforts of a submerged group to develop its own authentic discourse encourages the construction of generative theory in two ways. First, it provides a new set of data or "facts" from which to develop theory. While most researchers generally hold that theory should be premised on sound facts, what counts as a fact is determined by the theoretical framework in which the researcher is operating. When an investigator begins with the facts of how rhetoric operates in the dominant discourse, he or she already has incorporated the consensus of that framework, and "the potential for a generative outcome is thereby reduced" (Gergen, 1982, p. 135). But when an investigator views and collects as data the rhetoric of a submerged group that is not valued by or given input into the dominant discourse, a new theory of communication or implications for current theories may be discovered that encourage us to invent and study "new modes of Being/Speaking" (Daly, 1978, p. 33).

A second way in which this type of investigation may result in generative theory is through an examination of theory in its linguistic aspects. The chief products of research and inquiry are essentially word systems, and the theoretical language selected determines the function the language and thus the inquiry plays in the culture (Gergen, 1982, pp. 95, 98). Every theory or form of interpretation can be viewed as a potential form of social control, legitimizing and victimizing various groups by the conceptions expressed in the language of that theory. By formulating theory in the language of a submerged group, the linguistic context of research can be critically examined, suggesting new theoretical conceptions as a result.

When we develop generative theory, as the study of submerged rhetoric encourages, we will have the satisfaction of knowing that we have not necessarily or unjustly constricted our inquiry by neglecting alternative views of understanding, and we will not "place a range of significant restrictions over the kinds of theories that are likely to be developed and sustained" (Gergen, 1982, p. 133). Our central product of research, then, will not be simply an elaboration and extension of a singular worldview. Instead, we will have a clearer picture of the production and maintenance of the dominant order from which some of our biases about women's communication and their associated ideologies are derived and clear the air of "the conventions of the powerful solidified into universal truths" (Ascher, 1984, p. 101).

References

Ascher, C. (1984). On "clearing the air": My letter to Simone de Beauvoir. In C. Ascher, L. DeSalvo, & S. Ruddick (Eds.), *Between women* (pp. 84–103). Boston: Beacon.

Beckett, S. (1958). *The unnamable*. New York: Grove.

Chicago, J. (1977). *Through the flower: My struggle as a woman artist*. Garden City, NY: Anchor/Doubleday.

Chicago, J. (1979). *The Dinner Party: A symbol of our heritage*. Garden City, NY: Anchor/Doubleday.

Daly, M. (1978). *Gyn/ecology: The metaethics of radical feminism*. Boston: Beacon.

Ehninger, D. (Ed.). (1972). *Contemporary rhetoric: A reader's coursebook*. Glenview, IL: Scott, Foresman.

Ferguson, K. E. (1984). *The feminist case against bureaucracy.* Philadelphia: Temple University Press.

Foucault, M. (1970). *The order of things: An archaeology of the human sciences.* New York: Pantheon.

Foucault, M. (1972). *The archaeology of knowledge* (A. M. S. Smith, Trans.). New York: Pantheon.

Friedan, B. (1981). *The second stage.* New York: Summit.

Gergen, K. J. (1982). *Toward transformation in social knowledge.* New York: Springer-Verlag.

Jespersen, O. (1922). *Language: Its nature, development and origin.* London: George Allen & Unwin.

Kramarae, C. (1981). *Women and men speaking: Frameworks for analysis.* Rowley, MA: Newbury House.

Schulz, M. (1984). Minority writers: The struggle for authenticity and authority. In C. Kramarae, M. Schulz, & W. M. O'Barr (Eds.), *Language and power* (pp. 206–217). Beverly Hills: Sage.

Americanizing Gay Parents
A Feminist Analysis of *Daddy's Roommate*

Dara R. Krause, See Vang, and Shonagh L. Brent

Bell hooks defines feminism as "a struggle to eradicate the ideology of domination that pervades Western culture" (hooks 24) and a challenge to an entire system of domination of which patriarchy is part. Feminist critics can contribute to the eradication of the ideology of domination by analyzing artifacts that provide new models for living in which difference is not equated with inferiority. Our purpose in this essay is to analyze one such artifact—a children's book, *Daddy's Roommate*, by Michael Willhoite, published by Alyson Wonderland in 1990.

Sasha Alyson, founder of Alyson Wonderland, one of the country's first gay publishing companies, provides an anecdote about the impact of the book *Daddy's Roommate* on children: "Let's start with Nicholas, a 5-year-old with two gay fathers. For a week after he got the book, Nicholas carried 'Daddy's Roommate' everywhere. The book apparently made him feel included in a way the families he had seen on TV and in other books had not" (Alyson 1). The mission statement of the Alyson Wonderland series is that it "focuses on books for and about the children of lesbian and gay parents" (Willhoite 31). Alyson explains how children of gay men can be validated by a depiction of a family that counteracts hegemony and normalizes the child's controversial lifestyle.

Hegemony expresses the advantaged position of white, heterosexual men in a patriarchal system. *Daddy's Roommate* departs from hegemony in that it does not express a heterosexual perspective. Hegemony in this instance relates to the patriarchal standard of children having a married female mother and male father who fulfill the roles of nurturer and breadwinner, respectively. This hegemonic perspective suggests that gay men are not able to care effectively for children because they are selfish and oversexed, they do not provide the female figure required to provide a nurturing environment, and they subject children to the possibilities of harassment and emotional problems. In short, these reasons suggest, gay men who parent do not fit the patriarchal notion of living a "normal" life.

Daddy's Roommate is worthy of close examination because it is a teaching tool for children who need an alternative account of homosexuality. This tool needs to be comprehensible to children, exposing them to functional homosexual love. The young boy's admission of ignorance in the book probably applies to many of the book's readers: "At first I didn't know what [gay] meant. So [Mom] explained it" (25). Through its words and illustrations, *Daddy's Roommate* seems to make a conscious effort to acknowledge and challenge homosexual stereotypes for the reader who has become accustomed to hegemony.

DADDY'S ROOMMATE

Daddy's Roommate is a straightforward description of a young boy's interaction with one of his sets of parents—his father and his father's partner. The text is

This essay was written while Dara R. Krause, See Vang, and Shonagh L. Brent were students in Bernard J. Armada's rhetorical criticism class at the University of St. Thomas in 2003. Used by permission of the authors.

simple: a single sentence lines the bottom of each page and provides the caption for a picture, which suits the book's intended audience of young children. Publisher Alyson Wonderland describes *Daddy's Roommate* in this way: "This is the first book written for the children of gay men. The large, full-color illustrations depict a boy, his father, and the father's lover as they take part in activities familiar to all kinds of families: cleaning the house, shopping, playing games, fighting, and making up" (Alyson Wonderland 1). The Sexuality Information and Education Council of the United States, which affirms sexuality as a natural and healthy part of life no matter what one's orientation, adds, "Using simple language . . . this book is intended for very young children. The main character and narrator is a young boy who talks about his daddy and his daddy's roommate, Frank. He mentions all the fun activities the three do together . . ." (Lesbian 1). Though it was one of the 10 most challenged books of the 1990s (Greenblatt 1), it is also a Lambda Literary Award-winning pioneer book (Daddy's 1). This is evidence that although a work may garner literary merit, some believe it should be unconditionally rejected simply because it contains homosexual content. Such responses suggest the enormity of the task faced by *Daddy's Roommate* in trying to transform the hegemonic perspective on families with gay parents.

ANALYSIS

To analyze *Daddy's Roommate*, we will be using the feminist method of rhetorical criticism, which is designed to discover how the rhetorical construction of gender is used as a means of oppression and how that process can be challenged and resisted. Because the feminist critic is concerned with oppressive relationships of all kinds, feminist criticism can be used to analyze the construction and transformation of oppression based on race, class, sexual orientation, or any other dimension of identity. In this essay, we use feminist criticism to analyze a particular construction of sexual orientation, particularly as it is relevant to families.

We argue that the book *Daddy's Roommate* departs from heterosexual hegemony by presenting two gay men who are capable parent figures actively involved in the life of a child. The book thus seeks to transform American society's narrow, patriarchal construction of functional families through the unbiased perspective of a young boy, who discovers an alternative view of love and happiness through a gay relationship—"just one more kind of love" (26).

Daddy's Roommate challenges stereotypes about and encourages acceptance of gay parenting and lifestyles by situating the gay family squarely in the American dream. It does this in three ways. First, it marks the family as middle class, thus meeting the economic criteria for the dream. Second, it presents loving characters interacting in everyday roles and activities that mark the American dream and to which the audience thus can relate. Third, it shows the family as embodying traditional family values. The book thus expands the parameters of the American dream to include homosexual parents' participation in this dream.

Middle-Class Status

Daddy's Roommate depicts the two gay men in the book as embodying the middle-class values of the American dream. The cover sets the tone for the whole book in this regard. A middle-class setting is evident in the manicured landscaping, average household furnishings, contemporary interior design, and the characters' fashionable attire and possessions. The members of this family clearly live comfortable lives. The men dress in ways that reflect and are typical of middle-class economic status. They are clean cut and wear conservative, classy clothing that is often red, white, and blue. Frank reads *Time*, a signature household publication of America (2). He also plays baseball, the American pastime, with the boy (10), and they attend a ball game sporting team apparel (18). The men work in white-collar jobs and appear financially secure, evidenced by the professional business attire each man wears at one point in the book. Their professional occupations suggest both respectability as well as their ability to care for and spend quality time with the boy.

Loving and Familiar Characters

A second way in which *Daddy's Roommate* challenges stereotypes about and encourages acceptance of a new family form is through its depiction of characters. The characters of the book are loving individuals in familiar roles, making them accessible and appealing to the reader. The repetition of the word *together* as well as the depiction of the boy and the two fathers spending time together show the familial bond. The organization of the story starts with an explanation of what the father and Frank do together (live, work, eat, sleep, shave, fight, make up) and then describes what the men and the boy do together (go to ball games, the zoo, and the beach; work; shop; sing). These are very familiar roles for parents and children in families.

The family is socially well adjusted, as can be seen in the illustrations that portray the main characters fitting in with traditional families that do not seem to recognize their alternative lifestyle. A prime example of this is when Frank is rubbing sunscreen on the father while the boy talks with other people on the beach (20). No one pays attention to the gay relationship in this scene. The same apparent lack of recognition of the non-hegemonic nature of this family by others is evident when the three are at the ball game, the zoo, and the theater.

Another way in which the characters are seen as loving and normal is in the depiction of the boy's mother. Although the boy's father and mother get divorced at the beginning of the story, the mother is neither angry nor bitter. She seems to accept her former husband's relationship, even explaining it to her son as "just one more kind of love" (26). She clearly has no flaw that caused the divorce or the father's preference, evidenced in her wearing an apron with "world's best mom" imprinted on it as she spends time with and cares for her son.

Family Values

Daddy's Roommate also challenges the assumption that gay men cannot be nurturers and adequate parents by emphasizing common parental roles often associated with the ideal family that is part of the American dream. The men are in contact with the boy in 19 of 27 scenes, often in a one-to-one activity, which shows the cultivated individual relationship the boy shares with each of his father figures. They clearly are devoted to him. Each of the men plays both a traditional male and a female role in his relationship with the child, suggesting that both roles associated with traditional families are being met in this family. For instance, Frank helps the boy catch bugs (12). Two scenes later, he is making a "*great* peanut butter-and-jelly sandwich" (14). The fathers sing at the piano in the evenings with the boy (23) and comfort him when he has nightmares (15). Further, the decisions about the family and the boy are shared by the couple, illustrated when the men make a common decision that heterosexual couples routinely face with their children: whether to feed them healthy cereal or sugary cereal (22). The book challenges assumptions that men can fulfill only certain roles and that they are not fit to be nurturers. Clearly, they play the paternal and maternal roles simultaneously.

The book also counters the hegemonic perception that gay men are primarily focused on sex and thus cannot be focused on children, as is required for parenting. In this way, the book continues to make the men's relationship fit the parameters of the ideal American family, where sex between the mother and father is not a featured part of that ideal. The book downplays the sexual relationship between the two men in several ways. It is noteworthy that Frank unselfishly accepts the son; Frank is not in the relationship for his partner only. The relationship of the men to the child—and not to each other—is emphasized. The men's unselfishness is extended through an intimate bond that is not overtly sexual. The book takes "the sex out of homosexuality. These aren't books about sex or sex education. They're about families" (History 1). Of the eight scenes of the men alone, most of them are in neutral, nonsexual locations. In the more intimate scenes, there is no sexual tone. For instance, when the men are going to bed, the father is turning out the light, and Frank is already sleeping (6). In the making-up scene following a fight over clothing burned by an iron, the men are in close proximity, yet the only physical contact is a hand on the other's arm (9). The book thus violates a common misperception that homosexuals are exceedingly sexual. In fact, the issue of being gay does not arise until page 24 of 29. A mainstream lifestyle has been emphasized until this point, which increases the accessibility and likelihood of a positive reception for the revelation. Had the book started with "My daddy and Frank are gay," it would have risked audience shock and displeasure.

A final stereotype to which the book responds is that a gay father's relationship will negatively affect his son. Actually, the boy seems *positively* affected; the final two pages are displays of happiness that could be seen in traditional American families. The book shows the father and Frank enjoying popcorn and a movie together, captioned with the words, "Daddy and his roommate are very happy together." The final page is of the three males together, stating, "And I'm happy too!"

CONCLUSION

In *Daddy's Roommate*, the patriarchal ideal of the American dream is acknowledged and modified to assert that two gay men can be attentive and loving parents and thus meet the criteria for that dream. The book presents the middle-class, economically secure setting of the dream, the loving characters in familiar roles who populate the dream, and the typical family activities that mark the dream. The basic rhetorical strategy the book uses to induce acceptance of the controversial lifestyle of a marginalized group is to embed it within the ideal vision of the American dream. The book shows what many would consider to be an un-American family meeting the criteria for the economic status, characters, and activities that mark fulfillment of a very American dream. This strategy serves to normalize the counter-hegemonic perspective and positions readers and gay parents on the same side—the side of the American dream—so that the mentality of "us and them" becomes "we"—a common dream for a way of life.

WORKS CITED

Alyson, Sasha. "Children of the Rainbow." 30 Dec. 1992. 31 Mar. 2003
    <http://www.johnnyvalentine.com/ChildrenOfThe Rainbow.htm>.
"Alyson Wonderland Book Listing." 31 Mar. 2003
    <http://www/qrd.org/qrd/youth/1994/alyson.wonderland.books>.
"Daddy's Roommate—Written and Illustrated by Michael Willhoite." Gay-mart. 2002. 31 Mar. 2003
    <http://www.gaymart.com/shopbook/2item/i004570.html>.
Greenblatt, Ellen. "Barriers to GLBT Library Service in the Electronic Age." 2001. 2 Apr. 2003
    <http://library.cudenver.edu/libq/barriers.html>.
"History of Heather." 2000. 31 Mar. 2003
    <http://www.alyson.com/htm1/00_files/00_ednote/0400/0400heather10_03_int.html>.
hooks, belle. Feminist Theory: From Margin to Center. Boston: South End, 1984.
"Lesbian, Gay, Bisexual, and Transgender Sexuality and Related Issues." SIECUS. 2002. 2 Apr. 2003
    <http://www.siecus.org/pubs/biblio/bibs0005.html>.
Willhoite, Michael. Daddy's Roommate. Boston: Alyson Wonderland, 1990.

Additional Samples of Feminist Criticism

Acosta-Alzuru, Carolina. "'I'm Not a Feminist . . . I Only Defend Women as Human Beings': The Production, Representation, and Consumption of Feminism in a *Telenovela*." *Critical Studies in Media Communication*, 20 (September 2003), 269–94.

Anderson, Karrin Vasby. "Hillary Rodham Clinton as 'Madonna': The Role of Metaphor and Oxymoron in Image Restoration." *Women's Studies in Communication*, 25 (Spring 2002), 1–24.

Arthos, John, Jr. "'My Voice is Bound to the Mass of My Own Life': Private and Public Boundaries in Feminist Rhetoric." *Southern Communication Journal*, 63 (Winter 1998), 113–30.

Behling, Laura L. "Reification and Resistance: The Rhetoric of Black Womanhood at the Columbian Exposition, 1893." *Women's Studies in Communication*, 25 (Fall 2002), 173–96.

Biesecker, Barbara A. "Towards a Transactional View of Rhetorical and Feminist Theory: Rereading Helene Cixous's *The Laugh of the Medusa*." *Southern Communication Journal*, 57 (Winter 1992), 86–96.

Bineham, Jeffery L. "Theological Hegemony and Oppositional Interpretive Codes: The Case of Evangelical Christian Feminism." *Western Journal of Communication*, 57 (Fall 1993), 515–29.

Birmingham, Elizabeth. "Reframing the Ruins: Pruitt-Igoe, Structural Racism, and African American Rhetoric as a Space for Cultural Critique." *Western Journal of Communication*, 63 (Summer 1999), 291–309.

Borisoff, Deborah, and Dan F. Hahn. "Thinking with the Body: Sexual Metaphors." *Communication Quarterly*, 41 (Summer 1993), 253–60.

Bostdorff, Denise M. "Vice-Presidential Comedy and the Traditional Female Role: An Examination of the Rhetorical Characteristics of the Vice Presidency." *Western Journal of Speech Communication*, 55 (Winter 1991), 1–27.

Brinson, Susan L. "TV Rape: Television's Communication of Cultural Attitudes Toward Rape." *Women's Studies in Communication*, 12 (Fall 1989), 23–36.

Brummett, Barry, and Margaret Carlisle Duncan. "Toward a Discursive Ontology of Media." *Critical Studies in Mass Communication*, 9 (September 1992), 229–49.

Bybee, Carl R. "Constructing Women as Authorities: Local Journalism and the Microphysics of Power." *Critical Studies in Mass Communication*, 7 (September 1990), 197–214.

Cantor, Muriel G. "Prime-Time Fathers: A Study in Continuity and Change." *Critical Studies in Mass Communication*, 7 (September 1990), 275–85.

Carlson, A. Cheree. "Creative Casuistry and Feminist Consciousness: The Rhetoric of Moral Reform." *Quarterly Journal of Speech*, 78 (February 1992), 16–32.

Carlson, A. Cheree. "Defining Womanhood: Lucretia Coffin Mott and the Transformation of Femininity." *Western Journal of Communication*, 58 (Spring 1994), 85–97.

Carlson, A. Cheree. "Limitations on the Comic Frame: Some Witty American Women of the Nineteenth Century." *Quarterly Journal of Speech*, 74 (August 1988), 310–22.

Cooks, Leda M., Mark P. Orbe, and Carol S. Bruess. "The Fairy Tale Theme in Popular Culture: A Semiotic Analysis of *Pretty Woman*." *Women's Studies in Communication*, 16 (Fall 1993), 86–104.

Cooper, Brenda. "'Chick Flicks' as Feminist Texts: The Appropriation of the Male Gaze in *Thelma & Louise*." *Women's Studies in Communication*, 23 (Fall 2000), 277–306.

Daughton, Suzanne M. "The Fine Texture of Enactment: Iconicity as Empowerment in Angelina Grimké's Pennsylvania Hall Address." *Women's Studies in Communication*, 18 (Spring 1995), 19–43.

Daughton, Suzanne M. "Women's Issues, Women's Place: Gender-Related Problems in Presidential Campaigns." *Communication Quarterly,* 42 (Spring 1994), 106–19.

Demo, Anne Teresa. "The Guerilla Girls' Comic Politics of Subversion." *Women's Studies in Communication*, 23 (Spring 2000), *Women's Studies in Communication*, 23 (Spring 2000), 133–56.

Dow, Bonnie J. "Femininity and Feminism in Murphy Brown." *Southern Communication Journal*, 57 (Winter 1992), 143–55.

Dow, Bonnie J. "Hegemony, Feminist Criticism and *The Mary Tyler Moore Show.*" *Critical Studies in Mass Communication*, 7 (September 1990), 261–74.

Dow, Bonnie J. "Spectacle, Spectatorship, and Gender Anxiety in Television News Coverage of the 1970 Women's Strike for Equality." *Communication Studies*, 50 (Summer 1999), 143–57.

Dow, Bonnie J., and Mari Boor Tonn. "'Feminine Style' and Political Judgment in the Rhetoric of Ann Richards." *Quarterly Journal of Speech*, 79 (August 1993), 286–302.

Downey, Sharon D. "Feminine Empowerment in Disney's *Beauty and the Beast.*" *Women's Studies in Communication*, 19 (Summer 1996), 185–212.

Downey, Sharon D., and Karen Rasmussen. "The Irony of *Sophie's Choice.*" *Women's Studies in Communication*, 14 (Fall 1991), 1–23.

Fabj, Valeria. "Motherhood as Political Voice: The Rhetoric of the Mothers of Plaza de Mayo." *Communication Studies*, 44 (Spring 1993), 1–18.

Foss, Sonja K., and Karen A. Foss. "The Construction of Feminine Spectatorship in Garrison Keillor's Radio Monologues." *Quarterly Journal of Speech*, 80 (November 1994), 410–26.

Gayle, Barbara Mae, and Cindy L. Griffin. "Mary Ashton Rice Livermore's Relational Feminist Discourse: A Rhetorically Successful Feminist Model." *Women's Studies in Communication*, 21 (Spring 1998), 55–76.

Goldman, Robert, Deborah Heath, and Sharon L. Smith. "Commodity Feminism." *Critical Studies in Mass Communication*, 8 (September 1991), 333–51.

Griffin, Cindy L. "A Feminist Perspective on Age: Anne Noggle's Photographs of Women and Aging." *Women's Studies in Communication*, 16 (Fall 1993), 1–26.

Griffin, Cindy L. "Rhetoricizing Alienation: Mary Wollstonecraft and the Rhetorical Construction of Women's Oppression." *Quarterly Journal of Speech*, 80 (August 1994), 293–312.

Haaland, Bonnie A. "The Decontextualization of Abortion: An Analysis of 'The Silent Scream.'" *Women's Studies in Communication*, 12 (Fall 1989), 59–76.

Hanke, Robert. "Hegemony Masculinity in *thirtysomething.*" *Critical Studies in Mass Communication*, 7 (September 1990), 231–48.

Hanke, Robert. "The 'Mock-Macho' Situation Comedy: Hegemonic Masculinity and its Reiteration." *Western Journal of Communication*, 62 (Winter 1998), 74–93.

Hayashi, Reiko. "Helping!?: Images and Control in Japanese Women's Magazines." *Women's Studies in Communication*, 18 (Fall 1995), 189–98.

Hayden, Sara. "Negotiating Femininity and Power in the Early Twentieth Century West: Domestic ideology and Feminine Style in Jeannette Rankin's Suffrage Rhetoric." *Communication Studies*, 50 (Summer 1999), 83–102.

Hegde, Radha Sarma. "Recipes for Change: Weekly Help for Indian Women." *Women's Studies in Communication*, 18 (Fall 1995), 177–88.

Henke, Jill Birnie, Diane Zimmerman Umble, and Nancy J. Smith. "Construction of the Female Self: Feminist Readings of the Disney Heroine." *Women's Studies in Communication*, 19 (Summer 1996), 229–49.

Hoerrner, Keisha L. "Gender Roles in Disney Films: Analyzing Behaviors from Snow White to Simba." *Women's Studies in Communication*, 19 (Summer 1996), 211–28.

Illouz, Eva. "Reason Within Passion: Love in Women's Magazines." *Critical Studies in Mass Communication*, 8 (September 1991), 231–48.

Jablonski, Carol J. "Rhetoric, Paradox, and the Movement for Women's Ordination in the Roman Catholic Church." *Quarterly Journal of Speech*, 74 (May 1988), 164–83.

Jacobsen, Cheryl Rose. "Lifting the Curse of Eve: Women Writers and Advice Literature on Childbirth." *Women's Studies in Communication*, 18 (Fall 1995), 135–51.

Japp, Phyllis M. "Gender and Work in the 1980s: Television's Working Women as Displaced Persons." *Women's Studies in Communication*, 14 (Spring 1991), 49–74.

Jasinski, James. "The Feminization of Liberty, Domesticated Virtue, and the Reconstitution of Power and Authority in Early American Political Discourse." *Quarterly Journal of Speech*, 79 (May 1993), 146–64.

Jorgensen-Earp, Cheryl R. "The Lady, the Whore, and the Spinster: The Rhetorical Use of Victorian Images of Women." *Western Journal of Speech Communication*, 54 (Winter 1990), 82–98.

Jorgensen-Earp, Cheryl R. "'The Waning of the Light': The Forcible-Feeding of Jane Warton, Spinster." *Women's Studies in Communication*, 22 (Fall 1999), 125–51.

King, Janis L. "Justificatory Rhetoric for a Female Political Candidate: A Case Study of Wilma Mankiller." *Women's Studies in Communication*, 13 (Fall 1990), 21–38.

Kray, Susan. "Orientalization of an 'Almost White' Woman: The Interlocking Effects of Race, Class, Gender, and Ethnicity in American Mass Media." *Critical Studies in Mass Communication*, 10 (December 1993), 349–66.

Loeb, Jane Connelly. "Rhetorical and Ideological Conservatism in *thirtysomething*." *Critical Studies in Mass Communication*, 7 (September 1990), 249–60.

Lutfiyya, M. Nawal. "Critical Street Theorizing: A Case Study of Ladies Against Women, or, Comedy as Political Policy Development." *Women's Studies in Communication*, 15 (Spring 1992), 25–48.

Marston, Peter J., and Bambi Rockwell. "Charlotte Perkins Gilman's 'The Yellow Wallpaper': Rhetorical Subversion in Feminist Literature." *Women's Studies in Communication*, 14 (Fall 1991), 58–72.

Mattina, Anne F. "'Rights as Well as Duties': The Rhetoric of Leonora O'Reilly." *Communication Quarterly*, 42 (Spring 1994), 196–205.

McLaughlin, Lisa. "Discourses of Prostitution/Discourses of Sexuality." *Critical Studies in Mass Communication*, 8 (September 1991), 249–72.

McMullen, Wayne J., and Martha Solomon. "The Politics of Adaptation: Steven Spielberg's Appropriation of *The Color Purple*." *Text and Performance Quarterly*, 14 (April 1994), 158–74.

Miller, Shane. "The Woven Gender: Made for a Woman, but Stronger for a Man." *Southern Communication Journal*, 62 (Spring 1997), 217–28.

Myrick, Roger. "Making Women Visible through Health Communication: Representations of Gender in AIDS PSAs." *Women's Studies in Communication*, 22 (Spring 1999), 45–65.

O'Brien, Pamela Colby, "The Happiest Films on Earth: A Textual and Contextual Analysis of Walt Disney's *Cinderella* and *The Little Mermaid*." *Women's Studies in Communication*, 19 (Summer 1996), 155–83.

Orbe, Mark P. "Constructions of Reality on MTV's 'The Real World': An Analysis of the Restrictive Coding of Black Masculinity." *Southern Communication Journal*, 64 (Fall 1998), 32–47.

Perkins, Sally J. "The Dilemma of Identity: Theatrical Portrayals of a 16th Century Feminist." *Southern Communication Journal*, 59 (Spring 1994), 205–14.

Perkins, Sally J. "The Myth of the Matriarchy: Annulling Patriarchy through the Regeneration of Time." *Communication Studies*, 42 (Winter 1991), 371–82.

Perkins, Sally J. "The Rhetoric of Androgyny as Revealed in *The Feminine Mystique*." *Communication Studies*, 40 (Summer 1989), 69–80.

Perkins, Sally J. "*The Singular Life of Albert Nobbs*: Subversive Rhetoric and Feminist Ideology." *Women's Studies in Communication*, 16 (Spring 1993), 34–54.

Procter, David E., Roger C. Aden, and Phyllis Japp. "Gender/Issue Interaction in Political Identity Making: Nebraska's Woman vs. Woman Gubernatorial Campaign." *Central States Speech Journal*, 39 (Fall/Winter 1988), 190–203.

Ragan, Sandra L., and Victoria Aarons. "Women's Response to Men's Silence: A Fictional Analysis." *Women's Studies in Communication*, 9 (Fall 1986), 67–75.

Rasmussen, Karen. "*China Beach* and American Mythology of War." *Women's Studies in Communication*, 15 (Fall 1992), 22–50.

Rogers, Richard A. "Pleasure, Power and Consent: The Interplay of Race and Gender." *Women's Studies in Communication*, 16 (Fall 1993), 62–85.

Rushing, Janice Hocker. "Evolution of 'The New Frontier' in *Alien* and *Aliens*: Patriarchal Co-optation of the Feminine Archetype." *Quarterly Journal of Speech*, 75 (February 1989), 1–24.

Rushing, Janice Hocker. "Putting Away Childish Things: Looking at Diana's Funeral and Media Criticism." *Women's Studies in Communication*, 21 (Fall 1998), 150–67.

Rushing, Janice Hocker, and Thomas S. Frentz. "The Frankenstein Myth in Contemporary Cinema." *Critical Studies in Mass Communication*, 6 (March 1989), 61–80.

Schwichtenberg, Cathy. "Madonna's Postmodern Feminism: Bringing the Margins to the Center." *Southern Communication Journal*, 57 (Winter 1992), 120–31.

Sellnow, Deanna D. "Music as Persuasion: Refuting Hegemonic Masculinity in 'He Thinks He'll Keep Her.'" *Women's Studies in Communication*, 22 (Spring 1999), 66–84.

Sheckels, Jr., Theodore F. "Mikulski vs. Chavez for the Senate from Maryland in 1986 and the 'Rules' for Attack Politics." *Communication Quarterly*, 42 (Summer 1994), 311–26.

Sheckels, Theodore F. "The Rhetorical Use of Double-Voiced Discourse and Feminine Style: The U.S. Senate Debate over the Impact of Tailhook '91 on Admiral Frank B. Kelso II's Retirement Rank." *Southern Communication Journal*, 63 (Fall 1997), 56–68.

Shugart, Helene A. "Counterhegemonic Acts: Appropriation as a Feminist Rhetorical Strategy." *Quarterly Journal of Speech*, 83 (May 1997), 210–29.

Shugart, Helene A. "Reinventing Privilege: The New (Gay) Man in Contemporary Popular Media." *Critical Studies in Media Communication*, 20 (March 2003), 67–91.

Shugart, Helene A. "She Shoots, She Scores: Mediated Constructions of Contemporary Female Athletes in Coverage of the 1999 US Women's Soccer Team." *Western Journal of Communication*, 67 (Winter 2003), 1–31.

Stearney, Lynn M. "Feminism, Ecofeminism, and the Maternal Archetype: Motherhood as a Feminine Universal." *Communication Quarterly*, 42 (Spring 1994), 145–59.

Sullivan, Patricia A. "Women's Discourse and Political Communication: A Case Study of Congressperson Patricia Schroeder." *Western Journal of Communication*, 57 (Fall 1993), 530–45.

Sunderland, Jane. "Baby Entertainer, Bumbling Assistant and Line Manager: Discourses of Fatherhood in Parentcraft Texts." *Discourse & Society*, 11 (April 2000), 249–74.

Sutton, Jane. "The Taming of *Polos/Polis*: Rhetoric as an Achievement Without Woman." *Southern Communication Journal*, 57 (Winter 1992), 97–119.

Taylor, Bryan C. "Register of the Repressed: Women's Voice and Body in the Nuclear Weapons Organization." *Quarterly Journal of Speech*, 79 (August 1993), 267–85.

Triece, Mary E. "Framing Miss-Conduct: The Rhetoric of Paradox in the Struggle of Cleveland Conductorets During World War I." *Women's Studies in Communication*, 25 (Fall 2002), 197–22.

Torrens, Kathleen M. "All Dressed Up With No Place to Go: Rhetorical Dimensions of the Nineteenth Century Dress Reform Movement." *Women's Studies in Communication*, 20 (Fall 1997), 189–210.

Triece, Mary E. "Rhetoric and Social Change: Women's Struggles for Economic and Political Equality, 1900–1917." *Women's Studies in Communication*, 23 (Spring 2000), 238–60.

Trujillo, Nick. "Hegemonic Masculinity on the Mound: Media Representations of Nolan Ryan and American Sports Culture." *Critical Studies in Mass Communication*, 8 (September 1991), 290–308.

Trujillo, Nick. "In Search of Naunny's History: Reproducing Gender Ideology in Family Stories." *Women's Studies in Communication*, 25 (Spring 2002), 88–18.

Vande Berg, Leah R. "*China Beach*, Prime Time War in the Post-feminist Age: An Example of Patriarchy in a Different Voice." *Western Journal of Communication*, 57 (Summer 1993), 349–66.

White, Cindy L., and Catherine A. Dobris. "A Chorus of Discordant Voices: Radical Feminist Confrontations with Patriarchal Religion." *Southern Communication Journal*, 58 (Spring 1993), 239–46.

Williams, J. P. "Biology and Destiny: The Dynamics of Gender Crossing in *Quantum Leap*." *Women's Studies in Communication*, 19 (Fall 1996), 273–90.

Williams, Mary Rose. "A Reconceptualization of Protest Rhetoric: Women's Quilts as Rhetorical Forms." *Women's Studies in Communication*, 17 (Fall 1994), 20–44.

Wyman, Leah M., and George N. Dionisopoulos. "Transcending The Virgin/ Whore Dichotomy: Telling Mina's Story in *Bram Stoker's Dracula*." *Women's Studies in Communication*, 23 (Spring 2000), 209–37.

Xiao, Xiaoyu, and D. Ray Heisey. "Liberationist Populism in the Chinese Film *Tian Xian Pei*: A Feminist Critique." *Women's Studies in Communication*, 19 (Fall 1996), 313–33.

7

~~~

Generic Criticism

Generic criticism is rooted in the assumption that certain types of situations provoke similar needs and expectations among audiences and thus call for particular kinds of rhetoric. Rather than seeking to discover how one situation affects one particular rhetorical act, the generic critic seeks to discover commonalities in rhetorical patterns across recurring situations. The purpose of generic criticism is to understand rhetorical practices in different time periods and in different places by discerning the similarities in rhetorical situations and the rhetoric constructed in response to them—to discover "how people create individual instances of meaning and value within structured discursive fields."[1] The French word *genre* is the term used to refer to a distinct group, type, class, or category of artifacts that share important characteristics that differentiate it from other groups. As rhetors develop messages, genres influence them to shape their materials to create particular emphases, to generate particular ideas, and to adopt particular personae. Similarly, audience members' recognition of a particular artifact as belonging to a particular genre influences their strategies of comprehension and response.[2]

A rhetorical genre is a constellation, fusion, or clustering of three different kinds of elements so that a unique kind of artifact is created. One element is situational requirements or the perception of conditions in a situation that call forth particular kinds of rhetorical responses. A genre also contains substantive and stylistic characteristics of the rhetoric—features of the rhetoric chosen by the rhetor to respond to the perceived requirements of particular situations. Substantive characteristics are those that constitute the content of the rhetoric; stylistic characteristics constitute its form.[3] The third element of a rhetorical genre, the organizing principle, is the root term or notion that serves as an umbrella label for the various characteristic features of the rhetoric. It is the label for the internal dynamic of the constellation that is formed by the substantive, stylistic, and situational features of the genre.[4]

If there is a genre of eulogistic discourse, for example, then speeches of eulogy for Eleanor Roosevelt, George Harrison, the *Columbia* astronauts, and Charles Bronson should be similar in significant aspects. They should share stylistic and substantive strategies and the organizing principle that binds them together. While strategic responses and stylistic choices, in isolation, may appear in other rhetorical forms, what is distinctive about a genre of rhetoric is the recurrence of the forms together, unified by the same organizing principle. A genre, then, is not simply a set of features that characterizes various rhetorical acts but a set of interdependent features.

The roots of the notion of genre and of generic criticism can be traced to the writings of Aristotle and other classical rhetoricians. Much of classical rhetorical theory is based on the assumption that situations fall into general types, depending on the goal of the rhetoric. Classical rhetoricians divided rhetoric into three types of discourse—deliberative or political, forensic or legal, and epideictic or ceremonial. Each of these types has distinctive aims—expedience for deliberative speaking, justice for forensic speaking, and honor for epideictic speaking. They have distinctive strategies as well—exhortation and dissuasion for deliberative speaking, accusation and defense for forensic speaking, and praise and blame for epideictic speaking.[5] Thus, classification of discourse on the basis of similar characteristics and situations has been part of the tradition of the communication field since its inception.

The first person to use the term *generic criticism* in the communication discipline was Edwin Black, who used the term in his critique of neo-Aristotelianism in 1965. He proposed as an alternative to the traditional method of criticism a generic frame that included these tenets: (1) "there is a limited number of situations in which a rhetor can find himself"; (2) "there is a limited number of ways in which a rhetor can and will respond rhetorically to any given situational type"; and (3) "the recurrence of a given situational type through history will provide a critic with information on the rhetorical responses available in that situation."[6] Black suggested, then, that distinctive, recurrent situations exist in which discourse occurs and encouraged critics to analyze historical texts to describe their common features.

Lloyd F. Bitzer's notion of the rhetorical situation, presented in 1968, also contributed to the development of generic criticism. Bitzer's notion of recurring situations was particularly significant for generic criticism: "From day to day, year to year, comparable situations occur, prompting comparable responses; hence rhetorical forms are born and a special vocabulary, grammar, and style are established."[7] Although his notion of the rhetorical situation has generated controversy,[8] it further developed the theoretical base for generic criticism.

Yet another contribution to the development of generic criticism was a conference held in 1976 called "'Significant Form' in Rhetorical Criticism." Sponsored by the Speech Communication Association (now the National Communication Association) and the University of Kansas, the conference was organized around the notion of significant form, which referred to recurring patterns in discourse or action. These patterns include the "repeated use of images, metaphors, arguments, structural arrangements, configurations of language or a combination of such elements into what critics have termed 'genres' or 'rhetorics.'"[9] The result of the conference was a book, *Form and Genre: Shaping Rhetorical Action*, edited by Karlyn Kohrs Campbell and Kathleen Hall Jamieson, that provided theoretical discussions of the concept of genre and included samples of generic criticism.

Anthony Paré and Graham Smart expanded the study of genre by focusing specifically on rhetorical genres in organizational settings. They define genre as a distinctive profile of regularities across four dimensions: (1) textual features such as styles of texts and modes of argument; (2) regularities in the composing process such as information gathering and analysis of information; (3) regularities in reading practices such as where, when, and why a document is read; and (4) the social roles performed by writers and readers so that no matter who acts as social worker, judge, or project manager, the genre is enacted in much the same way. Paré and Smart believe this view of genres in organizations explains how the effective production of discourse and knowledge occurs within organizations.[10]

The work of Mikhail Bakhtin also has been influential in the development of genre studies. Bakhtin asserts that we "speak only in definite speech genres, that is, all our utterances have definite and relatively stable typical *forms of construction of the whole*. Our repertoire of oral (and written) speech genres is rich. We use them confidently and skillfully *in practice*, and it is quite possible for us not even to suspect their existence *in theory*." Bakhtin suggests that even "in the most free, the most unconstrained conversation, we cast our speech in definite generic forms, sometimes rigid and trite ones, sometimes more flexible, plastic, and creative ones." Among the speech genres that are widespread in everyday life are the various genres of greetings, farewells, congratulations, information about health, and the like. These genres have official, respectful forms as well as intimate, familiar ones.[11]

The Sydney School of genre studies, named after its primary institutional base in the University of Sydney's Department of Linguistics, offers another contribution to genre studies—the study of genres to effect social change. Michael Halliday, who once headed the department, sought to bring linguists and educators together to create a literacy pedagogy appropriate for a multicultural society.[12] The result was the use of generic analysis to probe systems of belief, ideologies, and values. The work of the members of this school encourages critics to ask questions about genres such as: How do some genres come to be valorized? In whose interest is such valorization? What kinds of social organization are put in place or kept in place by such valorization? What does participation in a genre do to and for an individual or a group? What opportunities do the relationships reflected in and structured by a genre afford for humane creative action or, alternatively, for the domination of others? Do genres empower some people while silencing others? What representations of the world are entailed in genres? These questions suggest as an agenda for the next phase of generic studies a critical examination of issues such as the nature of the sanctioned representations in genres and their implications for people's lives, the degree of accessibility of a genre to potential users, and genre maintenance as power maintenance. More generally, the Australian genre researchers contribute to generic criticism an explicit acknowledgment of the political dimensions of genres.[13]

PROCEDURES

Using generic criticism, a critic analyzes an artifact in a four-step process: (1) selecting an artifact; (2) analyzing the artifact; (3) formulating a research question; and (4) writing the essay.

Selecting an Artifact

Your choice of an artifact or artifacts for generic criticism depends on the kind of analysis you are doing. As explicated below, generic criticism involves three options—generic description, generic participation, and generic application. If you are interested in generic description, your artifacts should be a variety of texts that appear, on the surface, to share some rhetorical similarities. These artifacts can come from different time periods and be of various forms—speeches, essays, songs, works of art, and advertisements, for example—if they all seem similar in nature and function. If your goal is generic participation, choose an artifact that seems like it should belong to or has been assigned to a particular genre but does not seem to fit. If you are doing generic application, your artifact should be an artifact that you want to assess in terms of how well it conforms to the genre of which it is a part. This should be an artifact that, for some reason, leads you to question how it is functioning in the context of its genre.

Analyzing the Artifact

Generic criticism involves three different options for a critic, with each leading to a different contribution to the understanding of genres—

generic description, generic participation, and generic application.[14] The first option is generic description, where you examine several artifacts to determine if a genre exists. This is an inductive operation, in which you begin with a consideration of specific features of artifacts and move to a generalization about them in the naming of a genre. The second option, generic participation, is a deductive procedure in which you move from consideration of a general class of rhetoric to consideration of a specific artifact. Here, you test a specific artifact against a genre to discover if it participates in that genre. The third option is generic application—also a deductive procedure—that involves application of a generic model to particular artifacts in order to assess them.

Generic Description

In the attempt to describe a genre, a critic examines various artifacts to see if a genre exists. Your purpose in generic description is to define a genre and formulate theoretical constructs about its characteristics. Generic description involves four steps: (1) observing similarities in rhetorical responses to particular situations; (2) collecting artifacts that occur in similar situations; (3) analyzing the artifacts to discover if they share characteristics; and (4) formulating the organizing principle of the genre.

The first step of generic description is your observation that similar situations, removed from each other in time and place, seem to generate similar rhetorical responses. In other words, you speculate that a genre of rhetoric exists. Your suspicion of the presence of a genre is not to be confused with a preconceived framework that predicts or limits the defining characteristics of the genre. Rather, your hunch simply serves as a prod to begin an investigation to see if a genre exists and, if so, what elements characterize it. If your starting place is the idea that the messages produced in situations when someone announces the intention to run for public office seem to share characteristics, that idea does not dictate that you will discover certain characteristics. All you know at this point is that the situations seem similar, and the rhetoric in these situations also may share commonalities.

The second step is the collection of a varied sample of artifacts that may represent the genre. Identify rhetorical acts in which the perceived rhetorical situation appears similar or search out contexts that seem to be characterized by similar constraints of situation. If you suspect a genre of rhetoric may exist in which individuals announce their candidacy for office, for example, you would want to collect instances where individuals have announced their intention to run for office. A study by James S. Measell began in a similar fashion. He noticed that similar rhetorical situations were faced by Abraham Lincoln and William Pitt, the prime minister of England during the French Revolution. Both Lincoln and Pitt needed to justify "their administrative policy to withhold the privileges of habeas corpus,"[15] so the rhetoric of Lincoln and Pitt on the topic became the data for his study.

The third step in the process is close analysis of the artifacts collected to discover if there are substantive or stylistic features shared in the various artifacts you have collected. Here, you seek commonalities in how the rhetors dealt with the perceived problem in the situation. In the process of discovering similarities and differences among the rhetorical acts under study, you are not confined to looking for particular kinds of strategies or to using one critical method. Ideally, you allow the artifacts being studied to suggest the important similarities and differences, focusing on those elements that stand out as critical. These might be metaphors, images, sentence structure, failure to enact arguments, or an infinite variety of other elements. You may discover, for example, substantive strategies—those that deal primarily with content—such as use of metaphors dealing with family or the expression of self-sacrifice. Stylistic strategies—those that deal largely with form—may include elements such as adoption of a belligerent tone or use of ambiguous terminology. You may choose to focus on units of analysis suggested in other critical methods such as neo-Aristotelianism or fantasy-theme analysis. Neo-Aristotelian criticism could be used at this stage of generic description to discover similarities among the various artifacts in the use of emotional appeals, for example. Using fantasy-theme criticism, you could choose to search for commonalities in depictions of characters, settings, and actions.

In the process of textual analysis to discover rhetorical strategies, you may want to perform subsample comparisons of the artifacts you are investigating to identify subclasses of a genre. You may seek to determine, for example, if a genre of resignation rhetoric exists and, in the process, discover variants of resignation rhetoric, each characterized by a somewhat different set of rhetorical strategies. You may need to distinguish, then, among various characteristics, seeing some as paradigm cases of a genre, some as borderline cases, and some as characteristics of a subgenre.[16] B. L. Ware and Wil A. Linkugel's essay on speeches of apology is an example of the delineation of subgenres; they identify four different subgenres of apologetic discourse: absolutive, vindicative, explanative, and justificative.[17]

If sufficient similarities are noted to continue the search for a genre, the fourth step for a critic in the process of generic description is to formulate the organizing principle that captures the essence of the strategies common to the sample collected. In her analysis of *Seinfeld*, *Beavis and Butt-head*, and *The Howard Stern Show* as examples of a possible genre of humorous incivility, for example, Laura K. Hahn names as the organizing principle closure to new perspectives. What brings the shows' substantive and stylistic characteristics together, she suggests, is an active resistance to diverse perspectives.[18] This act of labeling the organizing principle actually may occur simultaneously with the delineation of substantive and stylistic strategies because the elements identified may come to your attention grouped around an obvious core or principle. Regardless of the order in which the steps occur, at the end of this process, you have formulated a list of rhetorical characteristics that appear to define a genre and an organizing principle that unites them.

You may have difficulty deciding whether or not a particular characteristic is a distinguishing feature of a genre. In such instances, the following questions may help you determine if it is one that contributes to a distinct genre:

- Can rules be identified with which other critics or observers can concur in identifying characteristics of rhetorical practice when they are confronted with the same examples? Not only must the distinguishing features of a genre be namable but so must the rules that are serving as guides for you in making distinctions among characteristics in different artifacts. These rules, of course, do not specify precisely how the rhetorical act is to be performed. A genre is not formulaic; there is always another strategy that a rhetor can use to meet the requirements of the situation. But a genre establishes bounded options for rhetors in situations, and naming the rules that define those options can help clarify whether a characteristic is part of a genre or not.[19]

- Are the similarities in substantive and stylistic strategies clearly rooted in the situations in which they were generated? In other words, does the way in which the situation is defined require the inclusion of an element like this in the artifact? Simply the appearance of one characteristic in several artifacts does not mean it was devised to deal with the same perceived situational constraints. Refer frequently to the description of the perceived situation to establish that the similarities are not simply coincidental but are grounded in some aspect of that situation.[20]

- Would the absence of the characteristic in question alter the nature of the artifact? A genre is created from a fusion of characteristics, and all are critical in the dynamic of that fusion. Simply saying that a certain element appears in all of the artifacts under study is not enough. A genre exists only if each element is fused to the other elements so its absence would alter the organizing principle. A genre is given its character by a fusion of forms and not by its individual elements.[21]

- Does the characteristic contribute to insight about a type of rhetoric or simply lead to the development of a classification scheme? The test of a genre is the degree of understanding it provides of the artifacts. Insight—and not neatness of a classification scheme—is your goal in generic description. If the discovery of similarities among artifacts classifies but does not clarify, it may not be particularly useful.[22]

Description of a genre, then, in which various artifacts are examined to see if a genre exists, is one option for the generic critic. This procedure involves examining a variety of artifacts that seem to be generated in similar situations to discover if they have in common substantive and stylistic strategies and an organizing principle that fuses those strategies. If, in fact, they do, you have developed a theory of the existence of a genre.

Generic Participation

A critic who engages in generic participation determines which artifacts participate in which genres. This involves a deductive process in which you test an instance of rhetoric against the characteristics of a genre. Generic participation involves three steps: (1) describing the perceived situational requirements, substantive and stylistic strategies, and organizing principle of a genre; (2) describing the situational requirements, substantive and stylistic strategies, and organizing principle of an artifact; and (3) comparing the characteristics of the artifact with those of the genre to discover if the artifact belongs in that genre. You then may use the findings to confirm the characteristics of the genre or to suggest modifications in it.

As an example of this process, let's assume you are interested in discovering if the rhetoric used by the director of the UFO museum in Roswell, New Mexico, constitutes conspiracy rhetoric. For a study of generic participation, you first would turn to earlier studies in which the characteristics of conspiracy rhetoric are delineated and then would see what elements characterize the speeches of the director. Comparison of the two sets of features would enable you to discover if those speeches participate in a genre of conspiratorial discourse.

Generic Application

A third option is open to a critic who is interested in studying genres—generic application. Rather than simply determining if a particular artifact belongs in a particular genre, you use the description of the genre to evaluate particular instances of rhetoric. Your task here is to apply the situational, stylistic, and substantive elements that characterize a genre to a specific artifact that has been defined as participating in that genre in order to assess it. On the basis of the application of the generic characteristics to the specific model, you are able to determine if the artifact is a good or poor example of the genre.

Four basic steps are involved in generic application (the first three are the same as the steps for generic participation): (1) describing the perceived situational requirements, substantive and stylistic strategies, and organizing principle of a genre; (2) identifying the perceived situational requirements, substantive and stylistic strategies, and organizing principle of an artifact that is representative of that genre; (3) comparing the characteristics of the artifact with those of the genre; and (4) evaluating the artifact according to its success in fulfilling the required characteristics of the genre.

In using generic features to evaluate an artifact, a critic draws critical insights about the effectiveness of a particular artifact in fulfilling perceived situational demands. When a generic form is used by a rhetor, it creates expectations in the audience members, who perceive and evaluate rhetoric in terms of generic classifications and expect a particular style and certain types of content from particular types of rhetoric. If the rhetoric does not fulfill these expectations, the audience is likely to be confused and to react negatively. Body art, for example, a form of visual and performance art, tends to violate the genre of visual art. Visitors to galleries expect to see art framed and hanging on walls—the generic form of visual art. Instead, they encounter works such as *Transfixed*, in which body artist Chris Burden had himself nailed to the roof of a Volkswagen bug and had the engine run at full speed for two minutes. While viewers may come to realize that the breaking of the generic frame is done intentionally by the artist/rhetor to encourage viewers to question the definition of art, simply the violation of generic expectations may create confusion, frustration, and rejection of the artwork by viewers—at least initially.[23]

A critic also may discover that generic violations increase an artifact's effectiveness, as is the case with Sergio Leone's film *Once Upon a Time in the West*. Viewers expect a film in the genre of the Western tradition but find many violations of the genre—in unusual costumes worn by the cowboys, comic characters, the slow unfolding of scenes, and difficulty telling the heroes from the villains. These violations, however, create an experience for the viewer that is positive rather than negative. Evaluation of artifacts, whether positive or negative, is made on the basis of the suasory impact of the artifacts that results from their fulfillment or violation of generic expectations.

Formulating a Research Question

Your research questions in generic criticism will vary according to whether you are engaged in generic description, participation, or application. In generic description, your research questions are: "Does a genre exist among a set of artifacts? If so, what are the characteristics of the genre?" In generic participation, your research question is: "Does this artifact participate in a particular genre?" In generic application, the question with which you are concerned is: "Is this artifact successful in fulfilling the required characteristics of its genre?"

Writing the Essay

After completing the analysis, you are ready to write your essay, which includes five major components: (1) an introduction, in which you discuss the research question, its contribution to rhetorical theory, and its significance; (2) a description of the artifact(s) and their contexts; (3) a description of the method of criticism—in this case, generic analysis and the specific type in which you are engaged—generic description, generic participation, or generic application; (4) a report of the findings of the analysis, in which you reveal the connections you have discovered between your artifact(s) and a genre; and (5) a discussion of the contribution the analysis makes to rhetorical theory.

SAMPLE ESSAYS

The three sample essays that follow illustrate some of the options open to a critic who engages in generic criticism. Sharon M. Varallo's essay is an example of generic description. She is interested in discovering if a genre of family photographs exists and is guided by the research question, "What rhetorical means do families use to construct themselves as a unit?" Danielle Montoya engages in an analysis of generic participation to discover if Ansel Adams's photograph *Discussion on Art* reflects attributes of Adams's artistic genre and, if so, how it participates in communicating the artist's perspective. John M. Murphy's essay on Robert Kennedy's speeches following the death of Martin Luther King, Jr. is a sample of both generic participation and generic application. He establishes that Kennedy's speeches fit the characteristics of the genre of the jeremiad, and he then uses the description of that genre to evaluate Kennedy's rhetoric. His primary research question is, "How does the jeremiad function in times of crisis?"

Notes

[1] Charles Bazerman, "Systems of Genres and the Enactment of Social Intentions," in *Genre and the New Rhetoric*, ed. Aviva Freedman and Peter Medway (London: Taylor & Francis, 1994), p. 79.

[2] Richard M. Coe, "'An Arousing and Fulfillment of Desires': The Rhetoric of Genre in the Process Era—and Beyond," in *Genre and the New Rhetoric*, ed. Aviva Freedman and Peter Medway (London: Taylor & Francis, 1994), p. 182.

[3] For a useful description of substance and form as they relate to genre, see Carolyn R. Miller, "Genre as Social Action," *Quarterly Journal of Speech*, 70 (May 1984), 159.

[4] For a discussion of strategies and organizing principle, see: Karlyn Kohrs Campbell and Kathleen Hall Jamieson, "Form and Genre in Rhetorical Criticism: An Introduction," in *Form and Genre: Shaping Rhetorical Action*, ed. Karlyn Kohrs Campbell and Kathleen Hall Jamieson (Falls Church, VA: Speech Communication Association, [1978]), pp. 18, 21, 25; Karlyn Kohrs Campbell and Kathleen Hall Jamieson, "Rhetorical Hybrids: Fusion of Generic Elements," *Quarterly Journal of Speech*, 68 (May 1982), 146; Jackson Harrell and Wil A. Linkugel, "On Rhetorical Genre: An Organizing Perspective," *Philosophy and Rhetoric*, 11 (Fall 1978), 263–64; and Robert L. Ivie, "Images of Savagery in American Justifications for War," *Communication Monographs*, 47 (November 1980), 282.

[5] Aristotle, *Rhetoric*, 1.5–10. For a more elaborate discussion of genre in the *Rhetoric*, see G. P. Mohrmann and Michael C. Leff, "Lincoln at Cooper Union: A Rationale for Neo-Classical Criticism," *Quarterly Journal of Speech*, 60 (December 1974), 463. For a discussion of differences between contemporary notions and Aristotle's notion of genre, see Thomas M. Conley, "Ancient Rhetoric and Modern Genre Criticism," *Communication Quarterly*, 27 (Fall 1979), 47–48.

[6] Edwin Black, *Rhetorical Criticism: A Study in Method* (Madison: University of Wisconsin Press, 1978), p. 133.

[7] Lloyd F. Bitzer, "The Rhetorical Situation," *Philosophy and Rhetoric*, 1 (Winter 1968), 13.

[8] Among the essays that deal with Bitzer's notion of the rhetorical situation are: Lloyd F. Bitzer, "The Rhetorical Situation," *Philosophy and Rhetoric*, 1 (Winter 1968), 1–14; Richard L. Larson, "Lloyd Bitzer's 'Rhetorical Situation' and the Classification of Discourse: Problems and Implications," *Philosophy and Rhetoric*, 3 (Summer 1970), 165–68; Arthur B. Miller, "Rhetorical Exigence," *Philosophy and Rhetoric*, 5 (Spring 1972), 111–18; Richard E. Vatz, "The Myth of the Rhetorical Situation," *Philosophy and Rhetoric*, 6 (Summer 1973), 154–61; Scott Consigny, "Rhetoric and Its Situations," *Philosophy and Rhetoric*, 7 (Summer 1974), 175–86; Barry Brummett, "Some Implications of 'Process' or 'Intersubjectivity': Postmodern Rhetoric," *Philosophy and Rhetoric*, 9 (Winter 1976), 21–51; David M. Hunsaker and Craig R. Smith, "The Nature of Issues: A Constructive Approach to Situational Rhetoric," *Western Speech Communication*, 40 (Summer 1976), 144–56; Lloyd F. Bitzer, "Functional Communication: A Situational Perspective," in *Rhetoric in Transition: Studies in the Nature and Uses of Rhetoric*, ed. Eugene E. White (University Park: Pennsylvania State University Press, 1980), pp. 21–38; and Richard A. Cherwitz and James W. Hikins, *Communication and Knowledge: An Investigation in Rhetorical Epistemology* (Columbia: University of South Carolina Press, 1986).

[9] Karlyn Kohrs Campbell and Kathleen Hall Jamieson, "Acknowledgements," in *Form and Genre: Shaping Rhetorical Action*, ed. Karlyn Kohrs Campbell and Kathleen Hall Jamieson (Falls Church, VA: Speech Communication Association, [1978]), p. 3.

[10] Anthony Paré and Graham Smart, "Observing Genres in Action: Towards a Research Methodology," in *Genres and the New Rhetoric*, ed. Aviva Freedman and Peter Medway (London: Taylor & Francis, 1994), pp. 146–54.

[11] M. M. Bakhtin, *Speech Genres and Other Late Essays*, trans. Vern W. McGee, ed. Caryl Emerson and Michael Holquist (Austin: University of Texas Press, 1986), pp. 78–79.

[12] Michael A. K. Halliday, *An Introduction to Functional Grammar* (London: Edward Arnold, 1985). For a history of the Sydney School, see Bill Cope, Mary Kalantzis, Gunther Kress, and Jim Martin, "Bibliographic Essay: Developing the Theory and Practice of Genre-Based Literacy," comp. Lorraine Murphy, in *The Powers of Literacy: A Genre Approach to Teaching Writing*, ed. Bill Cope and Mary Kalantzis (Pittsburgh: University of Pittsburgh Press, 1993), pp. 231–47.

[13] Many scholars continue to raise questions about and refine generic criticism. See, for example, Herbert W. Simons and Aram A. Aghazarian, *Form, Genre, and the Study of Political Discourse* (Columbia: University of South Carolina Press, 1986); Thomas Conley's essay in Simons and Aghazarian's volume: "The Linnaean Blues: Thoughts on the Genre Approach," pp. 59–78; and William L. Benoit, "Beyond Genre Theory: The Genesis of Rhetorical Action," *Communication Monographs*, 67 (June 2000), 178–92.

[14] These three options were suggested by Harrell and Linkugel, pp. 274–77.

[15] James S. Measell, "A Comparative Study of Prime Minister William Pitt and President Abraham Lincoln on Suspension of Habeas Corpus," in *Form and Genre: Shaping Rhetorical Action*, ed. Karlyn Kohrs Campbell and Kathleen Hall Jamieson (Falls Church, VA: Speech Communication Association, [1978]), p. 87.

[16] For more discussion of this process, see Herbert W. Simons, "'Genre-alizing' About Rhetoric: A Scientific Approach," in *Form and Genre: Shaping Rhetorical Action*, ed. Karlyn Kohrs Campbell and Kathleen Hall Jamieson (Falls Church, VA: Speech Communication Association, [1978]), p. 41.

[17] B. L. Ware and Wil A. Linkugel, "They Spoke in Defense of Themselves: On the Genre Criticism of Apologia," *Quarterly Journal of Speech*, 59 (October 1973), 282–83. They define the subgenres in this way: In the absolute subgenre, the speaker seeks acquittal; in the vindictive subgenre, preservation of the accused's reputation and recognition of the rhetor's worth as a human being relative to that of the accusers; in the explanative subgenre, understanding by the audience of the rhetor's motives, actions, or beliefs so it will be unable to condemn; and in the justificative subgenre, understanding and approval.

[18] Laura K. Hahn, "A Generic Analysis of the Rhetoric of Humorous Incivility in Popular Culture," Diss. Ohio State University 1999.

[19] For more on the notion of rules, see: Campbell and Jamieson, "Introduction," pp. 295–96; and Simons, p. 37.

[20] This notion receives some treatment in: Stephen E. Lucas, "Genre Criticism and Historical Context: The Case of George Washington's First Inaugural Address," *Southern Speech Communication Journal*, 51 (Summer 1986), 356–57; and Campbell and Jamieson, "Form and Genre in Rhetorical Criticism," p. 22.

[21] Campbell and Jamieson, "Form and Genre in Rhetorical Criticism," pp. 23–24.

[22] This notion was suggested by: Campbell and Jamieson, "Form and Genre in Rhetorical Criticism," p. 18; Walter R. Fisher, "Genre: Concepts and Applications in Rhetorical Criticism," *Western Journal of Speech Communication*, 44 (Fall 1980), 291; and Roderick P. Hart, "Contemporary Scholarship in Public Address: A Research Editorial," *Western Journal of Speech Communication*, 50 (Summer 1986), 292.

[23] For a discussion of body art and its function for an audience, see Sonja K. Foss, "Body Art: Insanity as Communication," *Central States Speech Journal*, 38 (Summer 1987), 122–31. For more discussion and examples of the impact of genres on audience expectations, see Kathleen M. Hall Jamieson, "Generic Constraints and the Rhetorical Situation," *Philosophy and* Rhetoric, 6 (Summer 1973), 166–67.

Family Photographs
A Generic Description
Sharon M. Varallo

In this essay, I will describe and analyze three photographs to determine if a genre of family photographs exists. I am interested in family communication and want to discover ways in which family members rhetorically construct themselves as a unit. Toward that end, I address the situational requirements necessary for a particular response, a description of the artifacts collected, an analysis of the substantive and stylistic features of the artifacts, and an overall pattern of organization for this genre.

SITUATIONAL REQUIREMENTS

The first step in generic description is the observation of similarities in rhetorical responses to particular situations. In other words, in order for an artifact to exist that might be called a *family photograph*, a number of elements must be present. The elements on which I briefly focus include the need for a family, a camera, a photographer, and an audience:

(1) The most obvious element required to be present is a family. The definition of *family* is much broader now than it has been in years past, as evidenced by new descriptors such as *blended families*, which did not exist a short time ago. The situational requirement, therefore, is a broadly defined one: whether the group members consider themselves to be traditional or nontraditional, the subjects being photographed must perceive themselves to be a family.

(2) The presence of a camera is necessary to the situation. Because many cameras are relatively inexpensive, they are accessible to the general population; people from almost every economic class, therefore, are able to present themselves as a family in front of a camera.

(3) A photographer must be present. Unless the photograph is taken with a camera with time-delay capability, family photos are taken with a non-family member as onlooker and producer.

(4) An audience is required. Why else would a family stop, pull together, smooth hair, and smile broadly at no one in particular? The family members know that the photograph will capture them in a particular moment, so they collect themselves enough to present themselves in ways that clearly show they are a family. The family itself could be the audience the photograph most persuades; in collecting family photos, we constantly reassure ourselves that we are members of the culturally valued group called a *family*.

DESCRIPTION OF ARTIFACTS

The artifacts I have chosen to analyze are three photographs of family groups. They include the Varallo family photograph, the Chryslee-Miller family photograph, and the Marty-Rhoades family photograph. All of the photographs are of immediate family members, and all of the families are white and middle class.

This essay was written while Sharon M. Varallo was a student in Sonja K. Foss's rhetorical criticism class at Ohio State University in 1994. Used by permission of the author.

The Varallo family photograph was taken in December, 1973, during the Christmas holiday season. The photograph shows a mother, father, son, and daughter standing in front of a Christmas tree. The tree, decorated with plastic confections, is positioned in front of a window covered with white patterned curtains. The children are standing in front of their parents. The father's arm is encircling his wife, who, in turn, is touching her daughter. The son stands independently. The females are wearing primarily red, and the males are dressed primarily in white.

The Chryslee-Miller family photograph was taken in May of 1992 prior to a graduation ceremony for the older son. The photograph includes a mother and father and two sons, one of whom is dressed in a graduation cap and gown. The family members are standing in a line, all in close proximity to one another, obviously convening around the graduating son. The mother has her arms around both her sons, the father has his arm around his older son, and the younger son has his arm around his mother. The photograph was taken in front of a tree in the family's backyard.

The Marty-Rhoades photograph was taken during a vacation trip to visit family in August, 1992. The photograph includes two women who are partners and co-parents and their seven-year-old daughter. This family is shown huddled on a rock that is jutting out into the ocean, and the background is of the water and shoreline reefs. Both women are touching their daughter, and she appears to be leaning against them. They all are wearing casual clothing.

SUBSTANTIVE AND STYLISTIC ELEMENTS

A substantive and stylistic analysis of the photographs uncovers the meanings present in the artifacts. In the case of non-discursive artifacts such as photo-

The Varallo family.

The Chryslee-Miller family.

The Marty-Rhoades family.

graphs, substantive and stylistic elements cannot be separated; thus, both will be discussed together. This stage of generic description finds the similarities in the artifacts and considers what those similar elements might signify. As similarities in the photographs are uncovered, their importance or unimportance to a genre of family photographs also is addressed.

First, the children tend to be positioned in front of and physically lower than the adults. In the Varallo and Marty-Rhoades photographs, the children are positioned in front of and physically lower than the adults; this positioning is not surprising given that the children are, after all, shorter than the parents. However, in many family photographs where the children are taller than the parents, the children often are positioned so they are shorter than the parents. Julia Hirsch (1981) discusses a possible reason for this feature of family photography:

> The authority of these conventions, like the hold of traditional family roles which still makes us want strong fathers and nurturing mothers, loving children and sheltering homes, is difficult for any of us to resist. Professional as well as amateur photographers still place families in poses that express and cater to these longings. (p. 12)

Hirsch's revelation of the family as a metaphor for all of humankind gives any representation of the family a much greater significance. Families pose for formal photographs to show themselves as a family *should* be. The positioning of the subjects to ensure the distinction between the matriarch/patriarch and the children seems necessary to the genre.

A second similarity is that all the people are sitting or standing in close proximity to one another. Perhaps some of this closeness is required for everyone to fit into the picture, but the picture could be taken from a distance to produce a longer shot, so the physical closeness is not a necessity for the photograph itself. This closeness clearly suggests to an onlooker that the family is one unit. By standing near one another, the family members create a distinct and distinguishable group. To fit into the genre of the ideal family photograph, the members should be standing close to one another.

A third similarity related to the first two is that the mothers touch their children, while the fathers are less likely to do so. The Marty-Rhoades mothers are connecting the most obviously with their daughter; their warmth and intimacy are apparent from their comfortable connection with one another. The other mothers also touch their children in "natural" ways that the fathers do not. The Chryslee-Miller father has his hand on his son's shoulder but otherwise does not appear to be touching him and is standing directly forward in an independent stance. The Varallo father is touching only his wife. The connections of the mothers to the daughters show nurturing and protective women, and the separation of the fathers and the sons shows independence and distance: both are the kinds of behaviors that fit within the traditional family mold addressed by Hirsch and are an element necessary to the ideal genre.

Fourth, women seem to have paid more attention to their appearance than the men and, overall, seem to have been concerned more with presenting a pleasing image. The Varallo woman has on make-up and a wig and has thin, finely plucked eyebrows, as was the fashion at that time. The Chryslee-Miller woman has coordinated accessories—a red belt and red earrings—to add flair to her dress. Albeit more subtly, the Rhoades and Marty women also have on jewelry, and the daughter is wearing small post earrings. In all the photographs, the women's dress closely matches that of the other women in the photograph, as if they coordinated their efforts: the Varallo females are wearing red, and the Rhoades and Marty women are dressed similarly in style—they are wearing comfortable, kick-about clothing. Finally, all the women are smiling broadly. These elements combine to present an image of women as, perhaps, the filler of a more nurturing role. After all, the Chryslee-Miller and Varallo fathers—and the adult Chryslee-Miller sons—did not feel the need to smile: they present themselves as more independent and more of what traditionally might be called *strong*. The women perhaps are showing the traditional roles expected of them as part of a family. Their concern with a pleasing image is both individual and group oriented and influences the showing of the entire family.

Yet another characteristic that distinguishes the photographs is their optimism. The Marty-Rhoades family members have open-mouthed smiles as if laughing in response to a joke. The Varallo photograph is of people smiling for the camera, seemingly on command. The Varallo father is the only unsmiling person, and, as such, he stands out. The Chryslee-Miller photograph evidences optimism in yet another way: it celebrates a family milestone as the members have gathered for a son's graduation. These observations coincide with Hirsch's: "Family photographs, so generous with views of darling babies and loving couples, do not show grades failed, jobs lost, opportunities missed . . . . The family pictures we like best are poignant—and optimistic" (p. 118). We are motivated to fit the image. Optimism, not realism, is important to family photographs.

A sixth characteristic feature of the photographs is that the pictures are posed. These photographs, although seemingly natural, are not candid. Everyone except the Chryslee-Miller graduate is looking directly at the camera, and each person seems acutely aware of being photographed. In this way, photographs present a kind of normalcy that is not normal: my family never stood that way unless we were getting our picture taken, and chances are the Chryslee-Miller and Marty-Rhoades families usually did not stand in that fashion on a normal day. This awareness and posing seem important to the genre as well.

The backgrounds in the photographs clearly were important and consciously chosen, perhaps to help represent the image of the family; this is a seventh characteristic of the photographs. All the photographs were taken during a special event, an event that is clear from an analysis of the background details. The Varallo photograph was snapped at Christmas time, and the family members positioned themselves in front of the Christmas tree. The Chryslee-Miller family stood in front of a tree in their backyard, gathered around a graduate. The Marty-Rhoades family, standing with the ocean as a backdrop, were clearly out of the ordinary settings of their usual lives. Part of the catalyst for taking the photographs seems to have been the event itself. Special events, therefore, also may be integral to the ideal family photograph.

The backgrounds in these particular photographs may offer insights into a critique of the genre of family photographs. The decorations on the Varallo tree, for instance, are sugar-coated, plastic candy ornaments. The Christmas tree was a pretend tree, the decorations were pretend confections, and our presentation of ourselves as the ideal family was pretend. We also stood in front of a window, perhaps symbolizing our desire for public approval, and the window is covered with curtains, perhaps symbolizing our need to hide the "real" family. The star on the Christmas tree is directly above the patriarch's head, crown like, giving the male a kingly air. The Chryslee-Miller photograph was taken in front of a tree in the backyard, and part of the house is visible in the background, serving to reinforce the representation of the traditional family. The most open background of all the photographs is in the photograph of the Marty-Rhoades family. Interestingly, their environment is natural. While the Varallo family seems limited to one way of showing a family, the Marty-Rhoades family is the most open of all, not just in background but in the family structure itself. As lesbian partners and parents, they present a family that likely would garner objection in traditional circles. Their family photograph, however, shows a more open, natural setting and clearly shows the most sincere warmth. Their smiles are genuine, while the others, though not necessarily fake, are obviously primarily for the camera.

That these photographs rarely capture the subjects' feet is an eighth characteristic of the genre of family photographs. Only upper torsos are visible in the Varallo and Chryslee-Miller photographs, and we barely see the feet of the Marty and Rhoades women. Although this photographic choice may have some symbolic significance, it does not appear vital to the genre.

Finally, similarities exist in the physical presentations of the photographs. The Marty-Rhoades photograph is enlarged and framed and usually sat on a table in the family's living room. The framing and public showing of the picture added to the impression that the family is special. The photograph was set apart, given a place of honor on a table, put out to be admired and to remind those who saw it most often—the two women and their daughter—that they were, indeed, a family. Although the framing and presentation of the photograph reinforces the ideal family it presents, that the photograph be framed is not vital to the genre. The other two photographs, for instance, are normal-sized photographs and have been in both private and public places, ranging from the "photo drawer" to a bulletin board; they still seem to qualify as participants in this genre.

ORGANIZING PRINCIPLES OF THE GENRE

In summary, the substantive and stylistic elements that seem vital to the genre include the presentation of:

(1) higher (status) positioning of the patriarch and/or matriarch

(2) close physical proximity of the family members

(3) mothers touching the children and touching more in general

(4) women more concerned with presenting a pleasing image

(5) optimism, usually evidenced in smiles

(6) a posed group

(7) backgrounds showing a special event

If all of these elements are present and the situational requirements are met, a photograph would seem to fit into a distinct category of family photography. From these observations, I conclude that there is, indeed, a genre of family photographs. The necessary elements noted in the previous section are substantial enough to warrant the inclusion of a new genre in the realm of generic criticism.

CONCLUSION

These photographs undoubtedly serve to convince and reinforce the "proper" family image to society at large and also to the families themselves. The photographs probably serve as a strong element of self-persuasion; in Hirsch's words, perhaps we are both seller and consumer of the idea of the ideal family. Formal family photography deals with character (Hirsch, p. 82), and few are willing to preserve for eternity a flawed image. None of the families evidenced in these photographs remains intact today—all three dissolved through divorce or separation of the parents. Nowhere, however, is family strife shown in any of these photographs. We all have our central identities at stake, and we therefore present ourselves as a unified family, the rules of which implicitly seem to be known.

Reference

Hirsch, J. (1981). *Family photographs*. New York: Oxford University Press.

Beauty in Conflict
Discussion on Art
Danielle Montoya

Artist Ansel Adams is known throughout the world for his landscape photographs set in the American West and Southwest. I received an Ansel Adams calendar for Christmas and found, among the works included, a photograph that seemed to violate the genre of the landscape photograph for which he is known. It is entitled *Discussion on Art* and was taken about 1936, during the time he was completing one of his most famous natural landscape portfolios, *Images 1920–1974*. Unlike any of his other photographs, this work depicts two men in what appears to be an unnatural or constructed setting, and it challenges the characteristic works of Adams through distinct choices of style, form, and composition.

Discussion on Art, 1936. Photograph by Ansel Adams. Used with permission of the Trustees of The Ansel Adams Publishing Rights Trust. All rights reserved.

This essay was written while Danielle Montoya was a student in Karen A. Foss's rhetorical criticism class at the University of New Mexico in 2002. Used by permission of the author.

The purpose of this analysis is to investigate the photograph *Discussion on Art* to discover if it reflects attributes of Ansel Adams's artistic genre and, if so, how the photograph participates in communicating the rhetor's artistic perspective. To explore the work's participation in the genre, I will apply the method of generic rhetorical criticism and, in particular, of generic participation.

I will analyze *Discussion on Art* and its participation in Ansel Adams's artistic genre according to three specific elements of rhetorical genres: (1) situational requirements—the contextual setting that evokes specific rhetorical responses; (2) substantive and stylistic characteristics—the unique features that constitute the content; and (3) the organizing principle—the dynamic formed by the situational and stylistic elements. In the interest of achieving a solid and representative understanding of the artistic genre of the photographs of Ansel Adams, I first analyze seven photographs from the *Images 1920–1974* collection: *Mount Resplendent*, Mount Roboson National Park, Canada, 1928; *Icicles*, Yosemite National Park, California, 1950; *Bicycle*, Yosemite National Park, California, 1937; *Granite Crags*, Sierra Nevada, California, 1927; *Statue and Oil Derricks*, Signal Hill, Long Beach, California, 1939; *Cape Royal from the South Rim*, Grand Canyon National Park, Arizona, c. 1947; and *Silverton, Colorado*, 1951.

DESCRIPTION OF THE ADAMS GENRE

In the collection of natural landscape photographs available in the seven photographs I analyzed, five patterns of situational and stylistic elements emerge: (1) contrast in natural settings; (2) contrast between light and dark, (3) contrast between high and low; (4) contrast between humans and nature; and (5) contrast between smooth and rough. Each of the seven works participates in all five patterns on some level. However, each composition is unique and individual in the emphasis of the elements of contrast and opposition and how they function in the work.

Contrast in Natural Settings

The primary defining feature of Ansel Adams's artistic genre is that all of the photographs focus on subjects in their natural settings. By *natural setting*, I do not mean that all of the photographs avoid and omit materials or settings that are humanly made; however, the works reflect physical contexts that have been undisturbed or unprovoked by the artist. The settings are free of affectation or artificiality. They are not altered or disguised and are photographed as the artist found them to exist in the physical world.

Each composition is created through the aesthetic contrast and opposition of elements found in the natural setting. For example, *Bicycle* exhibits a humanly made object, the bicycle, in opposition to the natural snow. The human presence is acknowledged but, at the same time, is contrasted with a statement of absence in the collection of snow. Neither the bicycle nor the snow has been altered, disguised, or manipulated by the artist. The composition and contrast exist in the natural, physical world without the influence of the artist.

Icicles found melting on a rock face provide another example of elements found in natural opposition. In *Icicles*, the color and texture of the icicles in the foreground are found in natural contrast with the color and texture of the rocks in the background. The image of contrast occurs naturally and is not altered or corrupted by the artist. Opposition and contrast are found and represented in the setting in which they were discovered by Adams.

Another setting that articulates a perspective of opposition is exposed by Adams in *Statue and Oil Derricks*. Nearly all elements in the composition are humanly created; however, the setting in which they are discovered and photographed is left unchanged and is represented as it exists without the influence of the artist. The natural medium in which the statue was created contrasts with the medium of the oil derricks and industrial park in the background. These two main elements of the work are in striking contrast as they existed and were found by Adams.

Adams chooses to photograph beauty found in the contrast he sees around him in the world, as it exists, without artistic influence, alteration, or manipulation apart from that involved in the selection of the photographic frame. He observes contrast within and between subjects and their environments, emphasizing those elements through his artistic compositions.

Contrast Between Light and Dark

A signature technique to the aesthetic composition of Adams's work is a focus on elements of light and dark. This stylistic practice creates a generic style that emphasizes the contrast and opposition he finds in natural settings. For example, *Mount Resplendent* depicts stark contrast between the layer of white snow and the huge mountain of black rock. Shadows caused by the terrain cause black striping to occur horizontally in the foreground, opposing the same effect that happens vertically in the background. The crevices, crags, and points in the mountain itself add depth and texture through the use of black and white. In the foreground, a chunky shadow is cast amid the smoothness of the horizontal plane of the snow leading to the sheer cliff at the top of the mountain. At the left side of the composition, the dark mountain is contrasted against the light of the sky, giving *Mount Resplendent* an ominous feel. It evokes an awe of the natural beauty contrasted with the stark danger and darkness of the mountain and its elements.

Adams uses the same stylistic technique in *Cape Royal from the South Rim* to capture the awe the viewer experiences in seeing the space, texture, and "grandness" of the Grand Canyon. In this piece, the light and shadow are caught playing on high plateaus and low valleys. The shadow and darkness emphasize the depth of the canyon and obscure the rocks below so that the observer is impressed with a sense of endlessness and void. The shadow and depth are contrasted with the light striking the inclining sides and flat tops of the plateaus. The light also brings focus to the texture of the higher land, detailing the sheer cliffs, jagged inclines, and the step-like layering of the two. Light and darkness are observed and captured as they articulate the contrast that emphasizes the beauty and complexity of the Grand Canyon. Adams articulates his perspective through the photograph, composing an image of contrast to attempt to enhance and accentuate the experience for the viewer.

Images of light and darkness aid in underscoring the opposition present in *Statue and Oil Derricks*. In this composition, the light color of the medium in which the statue was created is enhanced by direct sun on the largest open surface area, making the statue seem to radiate light. Light also enhances the soft curves of the statue, bringing attention to the gentle and feminine presence of the work. A shadow, in contrast, falls across the left side of the face of the image, accentuating the statue's contemplative, downcast, non-threatening air. The gentle, luminescent presence of the statue is contrasted with the darkness of the background. Strong black lines draw attention to the angular, sharp shape of the oil derricks. The strength of steel and the blackness of industry are in direct opposition to the statue. The dark shapes and the black of oil and industry create looming shadowy silhouettes. The statue at the center of the photograph, however, is highlighted by the sun and is a brighter, stronger, more present and powerful image than the opposing oil derricks. Images contrasted in dark and light create the gentle presence as more central to the composition and assist in creating mood and meaning around the statue and oil derricks.

In all of the seven photographs I analyzed, Adams uses elements of light and dark to emphasize and enhance. In the three works discussed, light and dark contribute significantly to the composition. In other works, tension between light and dark is still present but is not as important to the visual aesthetic or perspective of the compositions.

Contrast Between High and Low

Patterns in high and low contrast in Adams's photographs also work to define his artistic genre. *Statue and Oil Derricks* combines aspects of light and dark with aspects of high and low. The statue, higher in the composition, is in contrast with the oil derricks that are lower in the photograph, although the derricks would dwarf the statue if placed next to it. Adams uses height to create the statue as the dominant image and to subvert the appearance of the oil derricks. Levels of height assist the artist in communicating his perspective.

This skill is also employed in *Silverton, Colorado*. Low one-story houses in the foreground are contrasted with the height and mass of the mountains behind them. The low placement of the houses contributes to creating and enhancing the effect of the towering mountains. Although the houses are in the foreground and want to make their presence known, the height of the mountains behind them seems to overpower and overcome them. Portraying the relative height of the mountains and the houses helps to expound the significance and independence of the land and makes clear the view of the artist. Characteristics of high and low are also present and significant in *Cape Royal from the South Rim* and *Granite Crags*. The stylistic application of contrast between high and low helps to define the genre and to highlight significant aspects of the works. The elements of high and low are present in each of the seven photographs and are a qualifying characteristic of the genre. Like the other qualifying characteristics, this one varies across the photographs in emphasis and significance.

Contrast Between Humans and Nature

A tension or contrast between humans and nature is a recurring image and theme in all seven works. Although Adams often photographs landscapes devoid of human presence and undisturbed by human existence, his own presence is articulated through the existence of the photograph. In that sense, each photograph, specifically the most desolate and intimidating settings, is in conflict with the human presence of the artist. Several of the photographs, however, expressly address the contrast of the human presence with nature. *Silverton, Colorado*, for example, portrays the existence of humans as natural. The human presence, represented by houses in the foreground, is not obtrusive, and it does not deface or harm the power and beauty of the mountain behind it. The houses are simply a part of what is real; they are a part of the landscape and construct a natural contrast. The human presence is not destructive here—it just is.

The same presence is found in *Bicycle*. The bicycle indicates the human presence that is contrasted with the suggestion of human absence through the layer of snow that has collected. The existence of people and artificial objects is not seen as an intrusion on nature. They are not seen as blatant disruptions in the natural environment but actually have membership in it. The beauty is created in the contrast the two create as they exist together.

Contrast Between Smooth and Rough

The pattern of beauty in contrast is perpetuated through the stylistic elements of smooth and rough, soft and hard. *Bicycle*, for example, illustrates the contrast between the hard, smooth metal bicycle and the soft and textured snow cover. The contrast of textures underscores other elements of opposition that occur in the composition, such as those of light and dark and human and natural. The tension between textures is also exemplified in *Icicles*. The clear, white icicles are contrasted with the dark, solid, opaque rock beneath. The aesthetic opposition is enhanced by the competition of the textures. The smoothness of the sharp icicles in the foreground contradicts the rough, dull rock face in the background.

This same technique is evident in *Granite Crags*, where the jagged angular rocks cut into the soft cirrus clouds in the background, accentuating the harsh and stark qualities of the formation. Patterns of texture are clear in all seven works and are enhanced and elaborated with contrasts of light and dark, high and low, and human and nature.

All five recurring stylistic and situational characteristics combine to comprise Adams's photographic genre. Beauty and aesthetic appeal are found in natural contrasts the artist finds in the world, as it exists, without influence, alteration, or manipulation by the artist himself. The organizing principle that governs each composition and comprises the genre is beauty in natural opposition.

GENERIC COMPARISON WITH *DISCUSSION ON ART*

To determine the generic participation of *Discussion on Art* in Adams's genre, I applied each of the five stylistic and situational characteristics that typify his photographs to the photograph in question.

Contrast in Natural Settings

All seven works analyzed to investigate the generic qualities of Adams's work existed in a natural setting. Each photograph contained evidence of materials or objects created from the earth that exist with and in spite of the human presence. At first glance, *Discussion on Art* seems to stray from this qualifying characteristic. Upon a more careful investigation, however, the generic pattern of opposition in a natural setting is perpetuated.

The photograph suggests that humans in their natural settings are in conflict. As in the seven works definitive of the genre, the artist has found contrast in the world as it exists, without artistic influence, alteration, or manipulation. Adams has photographed what he wants the audience to believe is spontaneous. The work captures a scene that is unprovoked and undisturbed by the artist. In accordance with the generic quality, Adams observes contrast among subjects and between subjects and their environments, emphasizing those elements through the aesthetic composition.

Contrast Between Light and Dark

Elements of light and dark accentuate the natural opposition found in the photograph. The white flower is contrasted with the dark suit to emphasize the symbols of what is considered genteel and civilized. Just a few inches lower on the darkness of the suit is the contrast of the light hand beginning to grip the suit in an act that violates the social control implied by the suits and the flower. The light areas in the dark background also draw attention to the female figure positioned similarly to the impassioned man in the center. The contrast of light and dark that is carried through both figures opposes the gentle nurturing nature of the female and the aggressive threatening nature of the male. The contrast between man and woman in the work also underscores the contrast and opposition of the central action in the photograph. The light areas in the work are only the hands and faces of the characters in the composition. These areas, in contrast to the overall darkness of the work, highlight the placement of the faces in the photograph.

Contrast Between High and Low

Adams's use of light and dark aligns the faces of *Discussion on Art* on an incline from right to left. While the man on the left is confronted, he does not display intimidation by lowering himself to his aggressor; however, the aggressor is attempting to assert power by raising himself over and leaning into his opponent. The higher and lower positioning of the bodies in the composition highlights the conflict and activity in the center of the photograph. The figure highest in the composition, however, is the woman in the background. Her position asserts her importance, strength, and power as a central figure in the piece despite her placement in the background. The high and low visual aesthetics work in combination with contrasts of light and dark to emphasize the opposition taking place on many different levels in the work.

Contrast Between Humans and Nature

Light and dark and high and low also work to stress the conflict between humans and nature in the photograph. The conflict underscored in this stylistic pattern becomes the conflict between humans and their own nature. The setting implied by the title is an art museum, calling for a level of class, gentility, and civilization. The dark suits and accentuating flower highlight the push and desire for social control, propriety, and decency. These characteristics are contrasted with the nature of the humans embroiled in the conflict and unable to adhere to imposed social control. Although humans are perceived to be of a higher order, their baseness is the animalistic quality they cannot escape.

Contrast Between Smooth and Rough

The textures of civilized and uncivilized, refined and rough around the edges, are polarized facets of the same entity in *Discussion on Art*. Texture is elaborated not with what can be seen as visually tactile but occurs metaphorically between civilized and uncivilized, man and woman. The softness of the gentle and nurturing woman is a stark contrast to the rough and hard aggressive nature of the man. The texture is found in the language we construct around the nature of man, woman, and human nature. The aesthetic visual elements in the work underscore the evidence of natural opposition and contrast found in the setting and communicated through the work.

CONCLUDING OBSERVATIONS

Discussion on Art, seemingly not part of Ansel Adams's artistic genre, exhibits the recurring patterns of situational and stylistic qualities characteristic of that genre. Characteristics of all five elements of the genre are apparent in *Discussion on Art*, qualifying the work as a participant in Adams's aesthetic genre. Through this genre, the artist's insights and observations are communicated and perpetuated.

Beauty in natural opposition communicates the patriarchal idea that humans' natural setting is conflict. The nature of humans drives them to assert their personal perspective. As human beings, we constantly strive to have our perspectives and presence asserted and validated. We judge our value and worth by the acceptance of our ideas and opinions by others and, as history has shown, we turn to violence and conflict to force acceptance of our presence and perspective by others.

The participation of *Discussion on Art* in the genre of Adams's photography also communicates that we are in conflict with what we perceive to be the nature of humankind. Men are socially expected to be the aggressor, violent, in conflict, hard, and rough, while women are forced to ignore that which we name natural to humanity and remain soft, kind, and nurturing. Woman is asked to ignore the human tendency to assert her perspective and presence aggressively. She must stand in the background and accept her socially defined place and nature, just as man accepts his. Both sexes are in conflict with the culturally created social reality imposed on them. The beauty, then, is the contrast between the human nature and the expectations we place on ourselves that create the conflict and opposition, the natural shadows, the plateaus that we allow to surface, and the valleys we subvert.

As a rhetorical vehicle, Adams obscures and enlightens perspectives, beliefs, views, and opinions that emphasize and communicate beauty in conflict. Each of his masterpieces contributes to this perspective and functions as a medium that expresses the rhetor. The genre allows the artist to reinforce his perspective and presence through repetition in themes and style. The patterns that characterize the genre act as an echo to the social reality constructed and communicated by the artist, and we are able to see and appreciate the beauty in conflict.

"A Time of Shame and Sorrow"
Robert F. Kennedy and the American Jeremiad
John M. Murphy

On April 4, 1968, an assassin's bullet ended the life of Martin Luther King, Jr. In the next week, seventy-six American cities dealt with the consequences. Forty-six people died, all but five of them black, and 2,500 were injured. Nearly 30,000 people were arrested and 70,000 Federal and National Guard troops tried to cope with the disorder by turning many American cities into armed camps (Newfield 269–70). The White House worried that it might actually run out of troops (Kaiser 148). Readers of the *New York Times* awoke the Saturday after King's death to a front-page picture of American troops setting up machine guns to protect the Senate of the United States.

Public figures responded to King's death and the subsequent violence with rhetoric familiar to the American people. Some deplored the kind of nation that would allow such an act to occur, such as James Farmer's reaction: "Evil societies always destroy their consciences" (Van Gelder 1). On the opposite end of the political spectrum, some implied that King had brought on his own fate. Governor Ronald Reagan of California, polishing his conservative credentials for a presidential campaign, noted that this was the kind of "great tragedy that began when we began compromising with law and order, and people started choosing which laws they'd break" (Chester et al. 18). Governor John B. Connally replied in a similar vein, claiming that King had "contributed much to the chaos and the turbulence in this country but he did not deserve this fate" (Van Gelder 26). Three of the 1968 presidential candidates, with a more cautious approach, decided that the situation was too dangerous or difficult for extended public comment. Richard Nixon, Eugene McCarthy and George Wallace expressed their regret at the incident, although only Nixon and McCarthy chose to do so personally to Coretta King while attending the funeral (Van Gelder 26; Larner 66; Chester et al. 19; Hofmann 25).

Other political leaders attempted to give meaning to King's death by proposing legislation as an appropriate tribute to the man and his work. In other words, they chose to combine the epideictic aspects of a eulogy with deliberative strategies aimed at bringing about the passage of civil rights bills (Jamieson and Campbell). The President and the Vice-President issued statements using such strategies (Johnson 23; "Humphrey Appeals" 24), as did Governor Nelson Rockefeller in New York (Witkin 24). Such legislative reform, they hoped, would carry on King's work, ameliorate the injustices of racial prejudice, and end the turmoil. The *New York Times*, noting the power of such appeals, predicted that they would be successful (Hunter 25).

One powerful politician, however, specifically rejected a legislative response to King's death. Senator Robert F. Kennedy argued that the "question is not what programs we should seek to enact" ("Cleveland" 1). Perhaps recognizing the mood of a country that generally failed to see how previous legislation had

From *Quarterly Journal of Speech*, 76 (1990), 401-14. Used by permission of the Speech Communication Association [National Communication Association] and the author.

helped matters, Kennedy found the cause of King's death in America's toleration of "a rising level of violence that ignores our common humanity and our claims to civilization alike" ("Cleveland" 1). In a striking move for a presidential candidate, Kennedy called not for new policy initiatives, but rather he demanded that each American take individual responsibility for the disorder and work to "remove this sickness from our soul" ("Cleveland" 1).

This essay argues that, in order to interpret the meaning of the chaos around him, Senator Kennedy adopted the traditional rhetorical form of the jeremiad. His speeches on this occasion offer the opportunity to examine the function of the modern jeremiad as a means to restore social harmony in a time of crisis. Kennedy made an outstanding strategic choice by attempting to fashion the response of the audience so that they would seek to bring "good out of evil" (Bormann 1977, 1985). This case illustrates, however, that while rhetors employing the jeremiad may call for political change to end discord, the jeremiad limits the scope of reform and the depth of social criticism. Analysis of Robert Kennedy's discourse reveals the strengths and the limitations of the jeremiad as a response to social crisis.

Kennedy used the jeremiad to shape the audience's response to the tragedy of King's death and the resulting disorders. The epideictic exigency to eulogize King dominated the situation. In this case, then, the jeremiad can be viewed within what Celeste Condit has called the "macro-genre" of epideictic speaking (284). Condit argues that the most complete type of epideictic speeches, what she terms "communal definition" (291), performs a series of functions for the audience and for the speaker. They define the problems the community faces and enable the community to understand itself and its values. At the same time, the audience can judge the speaker's potential for leadership through evaluation of his or her eloquence and "humane vision" (Condit 291). The epideictic speech builds and creates a community for both speaker and audience, particularly, as Condit emphasizes, in times of crisis that threaten the society. Senator Kennedy used the jeremiad to interpret the problems that faced American society, to provide the audience with an understanding of events, and to suggest the way toward a brighter future.

Robert Kennedy's vision of the future, however, evolved from the interpretation of the American past inherent within the jeremiad. Kennedy's rhetoric serves as an example of the ways in which the jeremiad acts as a rhetoric of social control. I argue that jeremiadic strategies function to transform dissent and doubt about American society into a rededication to the principles of American culture. Such discourse aids in the traditional task of epideictic speakers: overcoming crisis and restoring social harmony. However, it also precludes a searching examination of the "Establishment" or the system: what James Q. Wilson recently labeled the "American Way" of structuring the government and social relationships (p. 34). The jeremiad deflects attention away from possible institutional or systemic flaws and toward considerations of individual sin. Redemption is achieved through the efforts of the American people, not through a change in the system itself.

Study of Kennedy's discourse also provides important insight into his success as a presidential candidate and into the continuing influence of his words today. In the week before King's death, the Kennedy campaign was drifting, shaken by the withdrawal of Lyndon Johnson and his new peace policies regarding Vietnam (Newfield 268). The eulogy Kennedy gave in Indianapolis and the speech he delivered the following day in Cleveland are regarded as the best of his public career and are widely reprinted today (Cook 292–93; Newfield 272; Schlesinger 939–43; "T.R.B." 1). The themes Kennedy discovered in those speeches helped him to redefine his campaign. By using the jeremiad, Kennedy could explain the troubles of the time while speaking for fundamental national values. His eloquence in this trying situation revealed important leadership qualities, indicating that variations on the jeremiad function well as campaign rhetoric. The balance of this essay will review the important features of the jeremiadic tradition in American public address, examine Senator Kennedy's remarks after the assassination in light of that tradition, and conclude with a discussion of the strengths and limitations of the modern American jeremiad.

THE AMERICAN JEREMIAD

Senator Kennedy's repeated emphasis on crisis and redemption as he spoke in Cleveland the day after the killing suggests that his rhetoric might profitably be examined within the American jeremiadic tradition. As a rhetorical type, the jeremiad began making its mark with the arrival of the Puritans in North America (Bercovitch 3–9). This "political sermon," which was delivered on ritualistic occasions, intertwined practical spiritual guidance with advice on public affairs. Identifying the Kingdom of God with the progress of the American settlements, these speeches assumed that the Puritans were God's chosen people with a special mission on earth to bring all people under His domain. With the passage of time and troubles, the vision expanded to include all American citizens by the time of the Revolution (Bercovitch 128–34).

The typical jeremiad in Puritan New England first explained the spiritual or Biblical precedent that served as the communal norm. The speech then would demonstrate in great detail the failure of the community to adhere to that norm and the catastrophes that have resulted. Finally, the minister would offer a prophetic vision of the utopia to come if only the people would repent and reform (Johannesen 158). Bercovitch emphasizes the importance of this vision of the future. Jeremiads went beyond cataloguing the evils of the audience. They combined lamentations with a firm optimism about the eventual fate of the community (Bercovitch 23). That vision of the "shining city on a hill" worked to unite the audience in pursuit of the goal and to reaffirm the values of the community.

Since fulfillment "was never quite there," Bercovitch argues that the function of the jeremiad "was to create a climate of anxiety that helped release the restless 'progressivist' energies required for the success of the venture" (23). Johannesen notes that the balance between lamentation and exultation was "in keeping with the historic Jeremiah's role of both castigating apostasy and of heralding a bright future" (159). After all, Jeremiah used discourse "to root out, to pull down, and to destroy, and to throw down, to build, and to plant" (Johannesen 159). Thus, the jeremiad emphasized the ways to "fetch good out of evil" and provided for renewal in a time of troubles (Bormann "Good Out of Evil" 132).

A number of critics have noted that the modern jeremiad still performs these functions for its audience. The civil religion of the American Dream now serves as the grounding for arguments (Johannesen 138; Ritter 158–59). Modern "Jeremiahs" assume that Americans are a chosen people with the special mission of establishing that "shining city on a hill." They point to the difficulties of the day as evidence that the people have failed to adhere to the values that made them special, to the great principles articulated by patriots such as Jefferson and Lincoln. The evils demonstrate the need to renew the American covenant and to restore the principles of the past so that the promised bright future can become a reality. From the speeches of presidential candidates to newspaper columns, the modern jeremiad has played a major role in recent American public address (Ritter; Johannesen).

But the restoration theme inherent in the jeremiad suggests that this rhetorical form has considerable limitations. While critics have documented its ability to unify and shape a community, traditional functions of epideictic speech, the jeremiad cannot serve as a vehicle for social criticism. This limitation is serious because jeremiads usually appear in a time of questioning and societal crisis that may well demand such examination. Instead of questioning American values, however, jeremiadic speakers urge a more stringent adherence to those values as a way to bring "good out of evil" and as a means to fulfill the prophecies of the past that assured the eventual success of America. Sacvan Bercovitch writes of the Puritan ministers: "Despite their insistent progressivism, the future they appealed to was necessarily limited, by the very prophecies they vaunted, to the ideals of the past" (179). The form of the jeremiad directs what might otherwise be a search for social and political alternatives into a celebration of the values of the culture and of change within the status quo. Bercovitch notes that a major rhetorical goal of colonial jeremiads was to "assert progress through continuity" (71). The difficulty of achieving social change by relying on the precepts of the past is particularly apparent when the issue is American racism.

1968

By early April of 1968, many Americans saw little hope of restoring the ideals of the American Dream. In fact, columnist Joseph Kraft wrote a column entitled "National Dissensus: Mental and Moral Decay is Eating Out the Vitals of the Country" (B7). In the first few months of the year, Americans endured the capture of the *Pueblo*, the Tet offensive, a crisis with the dollar, the Kerner Commission report on racism in America, the defeat and abdication of President Johnson, and the assassination of King with the subsequent disorders.

The Kerner Commission report and the polling data done by the University of Michigan Institute for Social Research help explain the depth of the bitterness in America and the extent of the disorders following King's death. Those reports indicated that the perceptions of whites and blacks on the state of the nation were diverging sharply. Increasing numbers of whites felt that enormous efforts had been made, much money had been spent, and extensive legislation had been passed, to no avail. Racial tensions and violence continued to increase. Meanwhile, blacks, young men in particular, saw far less change in America. True, "Jim Crow" laws had generally been eliminated. Most blacks, however, could not afford the restaurants to which they now had access. Conditions in the ghetto had not improved appreciably (Chester et al. 35–40). Dangerous unravelings in the national fabric were becoming apparent and these racial tensions, combined with all of the other crises in 1968, led to serious doubts about the country itself. No less a figure than James Reston concluded: "The main crisis is not in Vietnam itself, or in the cities, but in the feeling that the political system for dealing with these things has broken down" (Quoted in White 109). Through it all, Senator Robert Kennedy sought to define his role in the fluctuating political situation.

After months of indecision that sapped his credibility with the American people, Robert Kennedy declared his candidacy for the Presidency on March 16, 1968. Kennedy ran because he strongly opposed the President on Vietnam and on urban policy and felt "that we can change these disastrous, divisive policies only by changing the men who make them" ("Announcement of Candidacy" 1). From the start his campaign was in trouble. Kennedy entered after Eugene McCarthy's New Hampshire primary showing demonstrated that a candidacy opposing the war in Vietnam could succeed. Senator Kennedy's late entry, combined with his previous reputation for "ruthlessness," damaged his position (Witcover 85–90; "Robert Kennedy—His Public Image" 14). President Johnson's withdrawal from the race and his peace initiatives on March 31 robbed RFK of his two main issues: the war and the President's record. Disconcerted by these events and worried about the strength of Vice-President Humphrey and Senator McCarthy as rivals for the Democratic nomination, the Kennedy campaign sought to start anew in the Indiana primary.

April 4 marked the first day of speaking in the Hoosier state. The advance teams booked Kennedy into places of strong support, college campuses and poor areas, to begin with momentum. At Notre Dame and Ball State Universities, "the crowds were good, if not ecstatic" (Witcover 139). At Ball State, a black student challenged Kennedy, asking if he truly believed that white America wanted to help minorities. Kennedy responded: "Most people in America want to do the decent thing" (Witcover 139). On the plane to his appearance in the ghetto of Indianapolis, Kennedy learned of King's killing. Keeping to the schedule, he eulogized King in Indianapolis that night and then canceled all appearances save one speech the next day before the Cleveland City Club.

The circumstances facing Senator Kennedy created significant rhetorical obstacles. The fact of King's death meant that Kennedy chose to use epideictic strategies to define the American community in light of the assassination. These strategies included providing the audience with an understanding of this terrible event, shaping a new sense of the community in response to the loss, and submitting his vision of the nation for the judgment of the audience (Condit 288). These demands were particularly strong because of the disorder that, by the Cleveland speech, was occurring in most American cities and because of the growing doubt about the viability of the American system. King's death crystallized all of the concern about the country; if Martin Luther King, Jr. was to be killed for his efforts on behalf of nonviolence, the nation was at risk.

In addition, Robert Kennedy had particular expectations attached to his words. The King assassination inevitably reminded the country of Dallas, and, as a Kennedy, the Senator was uniquely situated to shape the nation's response to this crisis. More than any other speaker, Kennedy represented a fondly remembered past and yet, given his opposition to the President, stood apart from the problems of the present. More pragmatically, the Senator was also a presidential candidate. His reaction to King's death could help or hinder his cause enormously. The state of the country, the Kennedy persona, and Robert Kennedy's own ambitions all helped to create his unique response to the death of Martin Luther King, Jr.

Senator Kennedy's eulogy for Dr. King the night of April 4 in Indianapolis has been highly praised (Newfield 270; "T.R.B." 1). Before a crowd that did not know of King's death, by urging adherence to King's method of nonviolence and by revealing his feelings about his brother's death, Kennedy channeled the natural anger and sadness of the audience in a positive direction (Cook 294–306; David and David 307–08). While this extemporaneous speech, written by Kennedy himself on the way to the rally, was not a jeremiad, it opened a key question and introduced important themes that Kennedy would address the next day in Cleveland.

After quieting the crowd, Senator Kennedy began the speech with a simple acknowledgement of King's death. He memorialized King in the next sentence, noting that he had "dedicated his life to love and justice for his fellow human beings, and he died because of that effort" ("Eulogy" 292). This line honored King's sacrifice, but it raised a disturbing question for Kennedy and the audience. Why should a man die because he pursued love and justice? The body of the speech, however, did not address that query. Instead, Kennedy chose to examine "what kind of a nation we are and what direction we want to move in" ("Eulogy" 292).

In the first section of the speech, he noted that people could react with hatred and violence and discussed the natural reasons for such a response ("Eulogy" 292). In the second section of this brief address, Kennedy turned to the superior alternative, asking the crowd to "make an effort, as Martin Luther King did, to understand and comprehend" and to replace violence with love ("Eulogy" 292). He argued that he knew, after his brother's death, the desire for revenge, but concluded that "we have to make an effort to understand, to go beyond these rather difficult times" ("Eulogy" 292). Kennedy tried to assure the audience that their current pain would result in knowledge and rebirth, just as his loss had led him to a new life.

Not surprisingly, the speech then wove together these personal concerns and the fate of the nation. Kennedy completed the body of the address with a series of parallel constructions that focused on America, dismissing hatred as an alternative and telling people that the country needed love, wisdom, compassion "and a feeling of justice toward those who still suffer within our country, whether they be white or whether they be black" ("Eulogy" 292).

Senator Kennedy's eulogy served what Condit calls the "definition/understanding" function of epideictic address by explaining a disturbing event within the frame of values and beliefs accepted by the audience (288). Kennedy focused on the need for reconciliation and compassion in that terrible time. His use of himself as an example created identification with the audience and provided proof positive that death could lead to rebirth. While he beautifully fulfilled the traditional requirements for a eulogy (Cook 303–05; Jamieson and Campbell 147), he did not explain why a man who gave so much for the country should be killed for that effort. In that sense, this epideictic address was incomplete because there was no clear reason why the audience should follow King's path, in light of his fate. Kennedy needed to provide a deeper understanding of the troubles, one that could explain the violence and offer a road to redemption that would enact King's values while offering hope for success. His speech in Cleveland the following day offered that opportunity.

"A TIME OF SHAME AND SORROW"

Although Kennedy's first instinct had been to cancel all speaking engagements, he received calls from "concerned Negro leaders, some of whom wanted him to do something to help them discourage an outbreak of retaliatory violence" (Witcover 142). The Cleveland City Club speech on April 5 was a response to that plea, but the occasion also allowed Kennedy to provide a fuller analysis of the country's woes. Building on the themes suggested by the eulogy, Kennedy's speechwriters, primarily Adam Walinsky, Jeff Greenfield, and Ted Sorensen, constructed what Jack Newfield has called "the best written text of the campaign, and perhaps of Kennedy's public career" (Newfield 272).[1]

The speech reflected the overwhelming epideictic exigence of King's death and the resulting disorders. To meet those demands, Kennedy chose to interpret the events of the day through the lens of the jeremiad. Focusing on the moral actions of individual Americans, Kennedy argued that those sins were responsible for the national malaise. Thus, Kennedy first detailed the violations of American ideals, then traced the causes of the disorders to the sins of the people, and finally, called for a greater adherence to the values of American traditions as the way toward redemption. This logic shaped a view of the troubles that directed the attention of the audience toward individual transgressions against American ideology. The American value system was not the problem; it was the solution. Consequently, Kennedy could explain the difficulties of the time while reaffirming the nobility and vitality of the nation. America could still fulfill its "sacred destiny" as a beacon of democracy for the rest of the world if the people would live up to the traditional values of the American covenant.

Kennedy began his address by defining the time as one of "shame and sorrow" ("Cleveland" 1). He depicted the growing menace of violence and put a human face on the victims of violence. All were "human beings whom other human beings loved and needed" ("Cleveland" 1). Seeking to find the reasons behind the epidemic, he noted that, pragmatically, violence accomplished nothing: "No martyr's cause has ever been stilled by an assassin's bullet" ("Cleveland" 1). He then turned to the morality of the people as a reason for the disorder.

Kennedy began that moral study by condemning the cowardice and madness of violence. Significantly, he created a close connection between the violence of individuals and the welfare of the state. Consistent with the age-old pattern of the jeremiad, Kennedy argued that each individual carried the responsibility for the success of the American experiment, claiming that "whenever we tear at the fabric of life another man has painfully and clumsily woven for himself and his children, the whole nation is degraded" ("Cleveland" 1). Kennedy intertwined an individual's choices and the country's future. The metaphor of a "national fabric" created an inescapable bond between Americans and their nation. Kennedy emphasized the futility of violence, and the ensuing violation of the American covenant, by resorting to the authority of Lincoln: "Among free men there can be no successful appeal from the ballot to the bullet; and those who take such appeal are sure to lose their cause and pay the cost" ("Cleveland" 1).

Bercovitch maintains that New England ministers, in an effort to redefine the American settlements as the New Jerusalem, created a "legend of New England's golden age" which elevated the original emigrants "into a mythical tribe of heroes—a race of giants in an age of miracles" (67–68). Similarly, Kennedy, drawing on the myth of Lincoln as the President who reunited the country and called for compassion at the end of the Civil War, urged Americans to act as their ancestors had done. The community could renew "its conception of itself and what is good" through reliance on the lessons of history (Condit 289).

Why did the nation need this instruction? Robert Kennedy discovered the reasons in the sins of individual people. Americans tolerated "a rising level of violence." Pinpointing commonplace actions, Kennedy claimed that we "calmly accept" stories of "civilian slaughter in far-off lands." Movies and television "glorify killing" and "call it entertainment." Americans "make it easy for men of all shades of sanity to acquire whatever weapons and ammunition they desire." People even "honor swagger and bluster and the wielders of force" ("Cleveland" 1). As the Senator enumerated such examples, the argument became clear. Killings such as King's and John Kennedy's were shocking, but they happened because of the consistent individual acceptance, even admiration, of violent acts every day in America. As a Puritan minister might have done, Kennedy catalogued, in some detail, the sins of the people. This list focused attention on individual acts by every American rather than on any flaws with the country itself. As Senator Kennedy defined problems of the community, he shaped a view of the disorder in the country as a natural consequence of individual, not systemic, sins. Kennedy concluded this section of the speech by making the reason for the carnage clear and calling for a spiritual solution: "Some look for scapegoats, others look to conspiracies but this much is clear: violence breeds violence, repression brings retaliation, and only a cleaning of our whole society can remove this sickness from our soul" ("Cleveland" 1).

Quickly, Senator Kennedy made the extent of the national cleansing explicit. He contrasted the "violence of institutions" with the caring of individual people. Civil disorders, he argued, were not the entire problem. Institutions in America sinned through "indifference, inaction, and slow decay" ("Cleveland" 1). While Kennedy began to deal with systemic problems in this short section of the speech, he did so by personifying American institutions. He did not present them as different from individual Americans nor did he acknowledge that the crisis might be caused by the structure of American society. Instead, he focused on their current behavior as he did with individual sinners. Kennedy wanted all to live out the values they professed to uphold.

Rather than seeing the death of King and the violence in the cities as a product of the system, Kennedy shaped a view of these events as the natural results of Americans' violation of the tenets of the American way. The actions necessary for renewal, logically, could be found in the American heritage. Condit argues that, as epideictic speakers shape a sense of community in the face of tragedy, they rely heavily on the group's shared history. Indeed, the "reference to heritage is usually very explicit" (Condit 289). The first two sections of the speech defined the nation's problems in terms of the people's failure to live up to their heritage. Naturally, Kennedy also found that the road to renewal led through American history.

In his conclusion, Kennedy urged Americans to admit their difficulties, to face them honestly, and, again, to emulate the actions of Abraham Lincoln. Significantly, Kennedy linked this process to the idea of leadership: "The question is whether we can find in our own midst and in our own hearts the leadership of human purpose that will recognize the terrible truths of our existence" ("Cleveland" 2). Implicitly, Kennedy argued that the function of a leader was to act as he was acting. In that sense, Kennedy was laying the groundwork for his later presidential campaign rhetoric and asking the audience to judge his vision of the country, a function, Condit argues, necessary to epideictic rhetoric (290–91). The speech then ended with the admission that the work would be hard, but, in another allusion to Lincoln, Kennedy assured people that the covenant could be restored:

"Surely we can learn, at least, to look at those around us as fellow men and surely we can begin to work a little harder to bind up the wounds among us and to become in our hearts brothers and countrymen once again" ("Cleveland" 1).

This speech resembled a sermon more than a campaign address. Kennedy, detailing the horrors of the day, claimed that the nation was in terrible difficulty. The Lincoln quotation summarized the argument of the first half of the speech and served to remind the audience of the tragedy and waste of assassination. These words reinforced the notion that such violence had no place in the ideal of America. The principles of the society were not at fault. Why did violence occur then? Kennedy traced the cause to the sins of the people. They had departed from Lincoln's way and glorified killing in every way imaginable. From entertainment programming to Vietnam news reports, Americans welcomed violence into their homes every night. Kennedy made of all this death a seamless web. The only possible solution, in his view, was individual rebirth that could lead to a national revival. The nation could endure if the people would "bind up the wounds."

Robert Kennedy shaped perceptions of the King assassination and of violence in America in such a way as to absolve the system of blame. He explained the troubling events of the time as the natural consequence of individual failures to adhere to the values of the America covenant as articulated by men such as Abraham Lincoln. The jeremiad turns attention away from possible flaws in the covenant itself, such as institutionalized racism, and toward the failure of individuals to live out the appropriate values. The solution to the crisis lay in a greater dedication to the "ideals of the past."

RHETORICAL ASSESSMENT AND IMPLICATIONS

Jules Witcover has written that this "speech was, in a very real sense, a turning point in the presidential campaign of Robert Kennedy" (145). Witcover argues that Kennedy not only responded well to the death of King, but also discovered new themes for his struggling campaign. My analysis supports that conclusion. Robert Kennedy's use of the jeremiad held significant implications for his success as a speaker and candidate.

In the spring of 1968, the jeremiad, despite its problems, was a strategically apt choice for Kennedy because it allowed him to provide a coherent explanation for the rush of events. Ernest Bormann has written that the Puritan jeremiad "was a way of conceiving the inconceivable, of making intelligible order out of the transition from European to American experience" ("Good Out of Evil" 131). Kennedy sought to make intelligible the killing of King, the resultant disorders, and, in a broader sense, the long series of crises detailed earlier in this essay. The rhetorical form of the jeremiad allowed Kennedy to shape a plausible view of the situation for the American people, one that explained the crises, but assured the eventual triumph of the American system. The difficulties of the day could be understood and solved within the framework of American tradition. The balance between the terrible difficulty of the present and the promise of the future, as Bercovitch argues, released the energies necessary to make the changes to restore the covenant. The current crises became a test of the American character. The outcome was assured if the American people would respond with the spirit of their progenitors. The fact that Kennedy was a presidential candidate only made the possibility of reform that much more real and present. Kennedy offered himself to

Americans who would "find in our own midst and in our own hearts the leadership of human purpose" that could lead the way to the promised land.

Moreover, unlike other leaders who responded to the assassination, Senator Kennedy had the personal authority to inveigh against violence. As he stated in Indianapolis, he spoke as a victim, as a man who had suffered and survived. He served as proof that death could lead to a new beginning. Further, in a peculiar way, Kennedy himself represented a way to restore the balance. In the minds of many Americans, the disorder had begun with the death of John Kennedy. From that time on, the tumult increased every year while nostalgia and guilt colored perceptions of 1961–63. In fact, *Time* magazine wrote about this feeling as early as 1966: "In part, the phenomenon grows out of what Indiana's Senator Vance Hartke calls 'a national guilt complex' over the assassination, a sort of politics of expiation whose chief beneficiary is Bobby" ("The Shadow and the Substance" 33). As a political Jeremiah, Kennedy could point to the troubles of the time, pinpoint the acceptance of violence as the reason, and, through his presidential campaign, offer a uniquely attractive means for restoring the covenant. While I hesitate to delve too deeply into the psyche of the American people, the appeal is clear. More than any other leader, Kennedy incarnated the past, the values of the American covenant, and a beloved martyred President. By electing Robert Kennedy, Americans could atone for that "original sin" and begin the process of working "a little harder to bind up the wounds among us."

Kennedy articulated these themes throughout the rest of the campaign, in a change from his earlier campaign rhetoric (Murphy). For instance, in his first campaign speech, at Kansas State University, Kennedy focused on the spiritual problems of the country but attributed their existence to the Vietnam War. American involvement in the war had brought about the crisis in the nation and the end of that war would resolve the problems ("Landon Lecture"). After the Cleveland speech, Kennedy spoke of Vietnam as a symptom of the underlying appetite for violence in America and called for a reaffirmation of American values as the solution. Later in the Indiana campaign, he contended that the campaign was a "voyage of discovery, a search into the heart of the American past for the enduring principles, to guide us toward the uncertain future" ("Indiana Televised Interview" 7). In California, the day after his defeat in Oregon, he quoted the Preamble to the Constitution and argued: "We can only restore these ancient values through imagination and ideas to suit the conditions of the future. This is what the founding fathers believed when they said our liberty needs to be freshly restored in every generation, and that is just what I'm trying to do" ("Airport Statement" 2). He argued for a restoration and the jeremiad was admirably suited for this task. His campaign possessed considerable rhetorical coherence and force.

This analysis suggests that variations on the jeremiadic form are excellent strategies for campaign speakers. Prior analyses of jeremiadic speaking have argued that such rhetoric creates the unity and drive necessary to meet and overcome crises. What earlier critiques have often neglected is the fact that the "jeremiahs" gain in prestige and stature because they are perceived as speaking for fundamental national values. Ritter (1980), for instance, notes the social cohesion created by nomination-acceptance addresses that use variations on the jeremiad but does not discuss in detail the power of these strategies to raise the *ethos* of the candidate. The case of Robert Kennedy argues strongly for the utility of such tactics. Speakers using the jeremiad seem to understand why the problems of the day exist and can offer solutions without threatening the basic structure of the country. In that sense, they offer the "humane vision" that audiences demand of epideictic speakers (Condit 290–91). As Condit notes, audiences rightfully take eloquence as a sign of leadership. The jeremiad provides a vision of America's future that is deeply rooted in its most fundamental values. Even in times of greatest tension, as after the death of King, the jeremiad affirms the nobility of the American experiment. By speaking so consistently for the "American way" and the American people, even as they criticize specific aspects of the culture, these "jeremiahs" go far toward establishing themselves as people worthy to lead the country.

The jeremiad also has limitations, and these must be examined not only for future research on this rhetorical form but also to reach a full assessment of Kennedy's rhetorical choices. Robert Kennedy's speaking in this situation, however eloquent, ultimately served the purposes of the status quo. I do not mean to imply that Kennedy lacked concern for social progress. He justified that progress, however, through an appeal to the past and to the cause of "cultural revitalization" (Bercovitch 179). Kennedy's vision was confined "to the terms of the American myth" (Bercovitch 180). He sought to make the ideal America and the real America correspond but he could not propose policy alternatives or engage in social criticism outside of that ideal. His view of the ideal America restricted the changes he could propose for the real America.

In recent years, the study of the jeremiad has attracted the time and attention of a large number of critics. Their work details the ubiquity of the jeremiad, as this essay does, but the social and political consequences that undergird the jeremiad demand further examination. As the case of Kennedy demonstrates, the jeremiad calls for social change, but it also puts limits on reform. Bercovitch argues that one major contribution that the Whigs of post-Revolutionary America made to the rhetoric of the jeremiad was this insistence on control (134). When the founders contended that liberty needs to be "freshly restored" each generation, they meant that such "revolutions" would be within the confines of the American covenant. They saw the American Revolution itself as a continuation of the process begun by the Puritan emigration to a new land. Criticism and change served to restore and reaffirm basic American values not to overturn them. As Bercovitch notes:

> In the ritual of revolution [the Whigs] instituted, radicalism itself was socialized into an affirmation of order. If the condition of progress was continuing revolution, the condition of continuity (the Whig leaders insisted) was control of the revolutionary impulse. The social norms encouraged revolution, but the definition of revolution reinforced authority. (134)

The jeremiad, then, serves as a rhetoric of social control. In times of crisis, it functions to shape responses to the difficulties that reaffirm the viability and nobility of the American experiment. The jeremiad brings with it a definition of American history as a constant movement toward a special destiny, sanctioned by God, to establish that "shining city on a hill." By looking to the past through the jeremiad, Americans limit the kinds of choices they can make about the future. While reform within that tradition is possible, the jeremiad carries fundamental assumptions that make serious consideration of structural change difficult. Even though many Americans saw Robert Kennedy as a radical, he stood squarely within the American jeremiadic tradition. While he certainly spoke to and for radicals and outcasts in American society, he proposed that they enter American society on his terms. They would move up and out of poverty as Kennedy's family had done: by embracing the premises and values of the American Dream. The system itself did not need radical change.

During the Oregon primary, Eugene McCarthy used precisely these grounds to attack Kennedy on both urban policy and the philosophy of containment of Communism that led to the Vietnam War (Larner 94–110). On urban policy, for instance, McCarthy argued that Kennedy's proposals for ghetto revitalization could not possibly address the enormous economic and social problems faced by blacks and constituted a kind of "apartheid" (Larner 108). As indicated above, Kennedy felt that, with some governmental and private sector help, blacks could move up and out of the ghetto as the Irish before them had done. McCarthy responded that the basic racism of American society made such an analogy impossible and such a policy impracticable. If the country's problems inhered in its social structure, rather than in the sins of individuals, as McCarthy, James Farmer, and others argued in the wake of King's death, Kennedy could not step outside of the existing structure to propose appropriately radical solutions. The rhetorical form of the jeremiad clearly limits the range of political choices that are available even as it creates social cohesion. If the jeremiad is as pervasive as Bercovitch and others suggest, then rhetorical critics need to understand and explain both its strengths and its weaknesses.

These conclusions about the nature of the jeremiad also suggest that epideictic speaking itself may function in a similar manner to limit the political choices of the audience. Most research on epideictic speaking as a genre acknowledges its reliance on the values of the audience and on "*memoria*, or recollection of a shared past, . . . [as] an exceptionally important resource" (Condit; Campbell and Jamieson 204). Perelman and Olbrechts-Tyteca maintain that epideictic speeches, by emphasizing adherence to a particular system of values, may pave the way for policies that embody those values (49–52). While Condit does not accept that view as having explanatory power for all epideictic speaking, she acknowledges its relevance in some cases (286). If, in times of crisis, epideictic rhetoric is used to redefine the community in ways that reflect historically shared assumptions, then those values will restrict the range of political choices available to the audience. While this study can certainly come to no definitive conclusions on that matter, the deliberative ramifications of epideictic rhetoric need considerably more examination than they have yet received.

Senator Kennedy's assassination after the California primary has raised his presidential campaign to the status of myth and has often obscured a clear assessment of his rhetoric. In the wake of King's death, Robert Kennedy was one of the few national figures to attempt to bring "good out of evil." He deserves considerable praise for his persistent calls for compassion and for his strategically sound rhetorical choices. While Kennedy's rhetoric limited the means that he could offer the American people to reach those ends, it possessed the potential to unify the country behind a program of controlled progress, "the happy union of liberty and order" (Bercovitch 137). Whether such a policy could have met the needs of time is a question that remains unanswered.

Note

[1] Accounts of the speechwriting process indicate a situation of considerable confusion. The three writers worked throughout the night, with Sorensen phoning in his suggestions from New York. Greenfield fell asleep at his typewriter trying to finish the text at 3:30 in the morning and was put to bed by Kennedy. While the speech reflects themes Kennedy had discussed before, the speech was clearly a collaborative effort, hastily composed, among all of the principals (Newfield 272; Schlesinger 942).

Works Cited

Aarons, Leroy. "Kennedy Launches Indiana Campaign." *Washington Post* 5, April 1968, final ed.: A2.

Aarons, Leroy. "RFK, His Voice Quavering, Tells Rally 'Very Sad News.'" *Washington Post* 6, April 1968, final ed.: A2.

"America Come Home." Editorial. *New York Times* 6, April 1968, late ed.: 38.

Bercovitch, Sacvan. *The American Jeremiad*. Madison: University of Wisconsin Press, 1978.

Bormann, Ernest. "Fetching Good Out of Evil: A Rhetorical Use of Calamity." *Quarterly Journal of Speech* 63, (1977): 130–39.

Bormann, Ernest. *The Force of Fantasy: Restoring the American Dream*. Carbondale: Southern Illinois University Press, 1985.

Condit, Celeste. "The Function of Epideictic: The Boston Massacre Orations as Exemplar," *Communication Quarterly* 33, (1985): 284–98.

Cook, Roger. "'To Tame the Savageness of Man': Robert Kennedy's Eulogy of Martin Luther King, Jr." In Lloyd E. Rohler and Roger Cook (Eds.), *Great Speeches for Criticism and Analysis*. Greenwood, IN: Alistair Press, 1988.

David, Lester and Irene David. *Bobby Kennedy: The Making of a Folk Hero*. New York: Paperjacks, 1988.

Diffley, Kathleen. "'Erecting Anew the Standard of Freedom': Salmon P. Chase's 'Appeal of the Independent Democrats' and the Rise of the Republican Party." *Quarterly Journal of Speech* 74, (1988): 401–15.

Johannesen, Richard L. "The Jeremiad and Jenkin Lloyd Jones." *Communication Monographs* 52, (1985): 156–72.

Johannesen, Richard L. "Ronald Reagan's Economic Jeremiad." *Central States Speech Journal* 37, (1986): 79–89.

Johnson, Lyndon B. "Statement by the President." *New York Times* 6, April 1968, late ed.: 23.

Kaiser, Charles. *1968 In America*. New York: Weidenfeld and Nicolson, 1988.

Kennedy, Robert. "Announcement of Candidacy." 16 March 1968, *RFK Speeches and Press Releases Box #4*, John F. Kennedy Presidential Library and Museum.

Kennedy, Robert. "Cleveland City Club Speech." 5 April 1968, *RFK Speeches and Press Releases Box #4*, John F. Kennedy Presidential Library and Museum.

Kennedy, Robert. "Eulogy of Martin Luther King, Jr." In Lloyd E. Rohler and Roger Cook (Eds.), *Great Speeches for Criticism and Analysis*. Greenwood, IN: Alistair Press, 1988.

Kennedy, Robert. "Interview with Senator Robert F. Kennedy." 17 April 1968, *RFK Speeches and Press Releases Box #4*, John F. Kennedy Presidential Library and Museum.

Kennedy, Robert. "Statement of Senator Robert F. Kennedy: Press Conference, Los Angeles International Airport." 29 May 1968, *RFK Speeches and Press Releases Box #4*, John F. Kennedy Presidential Library and Museum.

Kennedy, Robert F. *To Seek A Newer World*. New York: Bantam Books, 1968.

Kraft, Joseph. "National Dissensus: Mental and Moral Decay Is Eating Out the Vitals of the Country." *Washington Post* 7, April 1968, final ed.

Larner, Jeremy. *Nobody Knows*. New York: The Macmillan Company, 1969.

Miller, Perry. *Errand Into The Wilderness*. Cambridge: Harvard University Press, 1964.

Miller, Perry. *The New England Mind: From Colony To Province*. Cambridge: Harvard University Press, 1953.

Murphy, John M. Renewing The National Covenant: The Presidential Campaign Rhetoric of Robert Kennedy. Diss. U. of Kansas, 1986.

Newfield, Jack. *Robert F. Kennedy: A Memoir*. New York: Berkley Publishing, 1978.

"RFK Denounces Slaying of Dr. King." *Washington Post* 6, April 1968, final ed.: A2.

Ritter, Kurt. "American Political Rhetoric and the Jeremiad Tradition: Presidential Nomination Acceptance Addresses, 1960–76." *Central States Speech Journal* 31 (1980): 153–71.

"Robert Kennedy—His Public Image." *Gallup Political Index Report No. 6*, Nov. 1965: 14.

Schlesinger, Arthur M. *Robert Kennedy and His Times*. New York: Random House, 1978.

"The Shadow and the Substance." *Time* 16 September 1966:33.

Strout, Richard. "T.R.B. From Washington." *New Republic* 13 April 1968: 1.

Van Gelder, Lawrence. "Dismay in Nation." *New York Times* 5 April 1968, late city ed.: 1.

Vanden Heuvel, William and Milton Gwirtzman. *On His Own: Robert F. Kennedy 1964–1968*. Garden City: Doubleday and Co., 1970.

White, Theodore H. *The Making of the President 1968*. New York: Atheneum Publishers, 1968.

Wills, Garry. *The Kennedy Imprisonment*. New York: Pocket Books, 1981, 1982.

Wilson, James Q. "The Newer Deal." *New Republic* 2 July 1990: 33.

Witcover, Jules. *85 Days: The last Campaign of Robert Kennedy*. New York: G.P. Putnam, 1969.

Speech on Martin Luther King, Jr.'s Death
Robert F. Kennedy
April 4, 1968

Ladies and Gentlemen,

I have some sad news for you, and I think sad news for all of our fellow citizens, and people who love peace all over the world, and that is that Martin Luther King was shot and was killed tonight.

Martin Luther King dedicated his life to love and to justice between fellow human beings, he died in the cause of that effort.

In this difficult day, in this difficult time for the United States, it is perhaps well to ask what kind of a nation we are and what direction we want to move in. For those of you who are black—considering the evidence evidently is that there were white people who were responsible—you can be filled with bitterness, and with hatred, and a desire for revenge. We can move in that direction as a country, in greater polarization—black people amongst blacks, and white amongst whites, filled with hatred toward one another.

Or we can make an effort, as Martin Luther King did, to understand and to comprehend, and replace that violence, that stain of bloodshed that has spread across our land, with an effort to understand compassion and love.

For those of you who are black and are tempted to be filled with hatred and distrust of the injustice of such an act, against all white people, I can only say that I feel in my own heart the same kind of feeling. I had a member of my family killed, but he was killed by a white man. But we have to make an effort in the United States, we have to make an effort to understand, to get beyond, to go beyond these rather difficult times.

My favorite poet was Aeschylus, and he once wrote: "In our sleep, pain which cannot forget falls drop by drop upon the heart, until in our own despair, against our will, comes wisdom through the awful grace of God."

What we need in the United States is not division; what we need in the United States is not hatred; what we need in the United States is not violence and lawlessness; but with love and wisdom, and compassion toward one another, and a feeling of justice toward those who still suffer within our country, whether they be white or whether they be black.

So I shall ask you tonight to return home, to say a prayer for the family of Martin Luther King, that's true, but more importantly to say a prayer for our own country, which all of us love—a prayer for understanding and that compassion of which I spoke.

We can do well in this country. We will have difficult times; we've had difficult times in the past; and we will have difficult times in the future. It is not the end of violence; it is not the end of lawlessness; and it's is not the end of disorder.

But the vast majority of white people and the vast majority of black people in this country want to live together, want to improve the quality of our life, and want justice for all human beings that abide in our land.

Let us dedicate to ourselves to what the Greeks wrote so many years ago: to tame the savageness of man and make gentle the life of this world.

Let us dedicate ourselves to that, and say a prayer for our country and for our people. Thank you very much.

A Time of Shame and Sorrow
Robert F. Kennedy
April 5, 1968

This is a time of shame and sorrow. It is not a day for politics. I have saved this one opportunity, my only event of today, to speak briefly to you about the mindless menace of violence in America which again stains our land and every one of our lives.

It is not the concern of any one race. The victims of the violence are black and white, rich and poor, young and old, famous and unknown. They are, most important of all, human beings whom other human beings loved and needed. No one—no matter where he lives or what he does—can be certain who will suffer from some senseless act of bloodshed. And yet it goes on and on and on in this country of ours.

Why? What has violence ever accomplished? What has it ever created? No martyr's cause has ever been stilled by an assassin's bullet.

No wrongs have ever been righted by riots and civil disorders. A sniper is only a coward, not a hero; and an uncontrolled, uncontrollable mob is only the voice of madness, not the voice of reason.

Whenever any American's life is taken by another American unnecessarily— whether it is done in the name of the law or in the defiance of the law, by one man or a gang, in cold blood or in passion, in an attack of violence or in response to violence— whenever we tear at the fabric of the life which another man has painfully and clumsily woven for himself and his children, the whole nation is degraded.

"Among free men," said Abraham Lincoln, "there can be no successful appeal from the ballot to the bullet; and those who take such appeal are sure to lose their cause and pay the costs."

Yet we seemingly tolerate a rising level of violence that ignores our common humanity and our claims to civilization alike. We calmly accept newspaper reports of civilian slaughter in far-off lands. We glorify killing on movie and television screens and call it entertainment. We make it easy for men of all shades of sanity to acquire whatever weapons and ammunition they desire.

Too often we honor swagger and bluster and wielders of force; too often we excuse those who are willing to build their own lives on the shattered dreams of others. Some Americans who preach non-violence abroad fail to practice it here at home. Some who accuse others of inciting riots have by their own conduct invited them.

Some look for scapegoats, others look for conspiracies, but this much is clear: violence breeds violence, repression brings retaliation, and only a cleansing of our whole society can remove this sickness from our soul.

For there is another kind of violence, slower but just as deadly destructive as the shot or the bomb in the night. This is the violence of institutions; indifference and inaction and slow decay. This is the violence that afflicts the poor, that poisons relations between men because their skin has different colors. This is the slow destruction of a child by hunger, and schools without books and homes without heat in the winter.

This is the breaking of a man's spirit by denying him the chance to stand as a father and as a man among other men. And this too afflicts us all.

I have not come here to propose a set of specific remedies nor is there a single set. For a broad and adequate outline we know what must be done. When you teach a man to hate and fear his brother, when you teach that he is a lesser man because of his color or his beliefs or the policies he pursues, when you teach that those who differ from you threaten your freedom or your job or your family, then you also learn to confront others not as fellow citizens but as enemies, to be met not with cooperation but with conquest; to be subjugated and mastered.

We learn, at the last, to look at our brothers as aliens, men with whom we share a city, but not a community; men bound to us in common dwelling, but not in common effort. We learn to share only a common fear, only a common desire to retreat from each other, only a common impulse to meet disagreement with force. For all this, there are no final answers.

Yet we know what we must do. It is to achieve true justice among our fellow citizens. The question is not what programs we should seek to enact. The question is whether we can find in our own midst and in our own hearts that leadership of humane purpose that will recognize the terrible truths of our existence.

We must admit the vanity of our false distinctions among men and learn to find our own advancement in the search for the advancement of others. We must admit in ourselves that our own children's future cannot be built on the misfortunes of others. We must recognize that this short life can neither be ennobled or enriched by hatred or revenge.

Our lives on this planet are too short and the work to be done too great to let this spirit flourish any longer in our land. Of course we cannot vanquish it with a program, nor with a resolution.

But we can perhaps remember, if only for a time, that those who live with us are our brothers, that they share with us the same short moment of life; that they seek, as do we, nothing but the chance to live out their lives in purpose and in happiness, winning what satisfaction and fulfillment they can.

Surely, this bond of common faith, this bond of common goal, can begin to teach us something. Surely, we can learn, at least, to look at those around us as fellow men, and surely we can begin to work a little harder to bind up the wounds among us and to become in our own hearts brothers and countrymen once again.

Additional Samples of Generic Criticism

Achter, Paul J. "Narrative, Intertextuality, and Apologia in Contemporary Political Scandals." *Southern Communication Journal*, 65 (Summer 2000), 318–33.

Aly, Bower. "The Gallows Speech: A Lost Genre." *Southern Speech Journal*, 34 (Spring 1969), 204–13.

Andrews, James R. "They Chose the Sword: Appeals to War in Nineteenth-Century American Public Address." *Today's Speech*, 17 (September 1969), 3–8.

Bass, Jeff D. "The Rhetorical Opposition to Controversial Wars: Rhetorical Timing as a Generic Consideration." *Western Journal of Speech Communication*, 43 (Summer 1979), 180–91.

Bennett, W. Lance. "Assessing Presidential Character: Degradation Rituals in Political Campaigns." *Quarterly Journal of Speech*, 67 (August 1981), 310–21.

Benoit, William L., and Susan L. Brinson. "AT&T": 'Apologies are not Enough.'" *Communication Quarterly*, 42 (Winter 1994), 75–88.

Benoit, William L., Paul Gulliform, and Daniel A. Panici. "President Reagan's Defensive Discourse on the Iran-Contra Affair." *Communication Studies*, 42 (Fall 1991), 272–94.

Benoit, William L., and Robert S. Hanczor. "The Tanya Harding Controversy: An Analysis of Image Restoration Strategies." *Communication Quarterly*, 42 (Fall 1994), 416–33.

Blair, Carole. "From 'All the President's Men' to Every Man for Himself: The Strategies of Post-Watergate Apologia." *Central States Speech Journal*, 35 (Winter 1984), 250–60.

Brown, Stephen H. "Generic Transformation and Political Action: A Textual Interpretation of Edmund Burke's Letter to William Elliot, Esq." *Communication Quarterly*, 38 (Winter 1990), 54–63.

Brummett, Barry. "Premillennial Apocalyptic as a Rhetorical Genre." *Central States Speech Journal*, 35 (Summer 1984), 84–93.

Brummett, Barry. *Rhetorical Dimensions of Popular Culture*. Tuscaloosa: University of Alabama Press, 1991, pp. 125–46, 147–71.

Bryant, Donald C. "The Speech on the Address in the Late Eighteenth-Century House of Commons." *Southern Speech Communication Journal*, 51 (Summer 1986), 344–53.

Butler, Sherry Devereaux. "The Apologia, 1971 Genre." *Southern Speech Communication Journal*, 37 (Spring 1972), 281–89.

Campbell, Karlyn Kohrs. "The Rhetoric of Women's Liberation: An Oxymoron." *Quarterly Journal of Speech*, 59 (February 1973), 74–86.

Campbell, Karlyn Kohrs, and Kathleen Hall Jamieson, eds. *Form and Genre: Shaping Rhetorical Action*. Falls Church, Virginia: Speech Communication Association [1978], several essays, pp. 75–161.

Carlson, A. Cheree. "John Quincy Adams' 'Amistad Address': Eloquence in a Generic Hybrid." *Western Journal of Speech Communication*, 49 (Winter 1985), 14–26.

Carlton, Charles. "The Rhetoric of Death: Scaffold Confessions in Early Modern England." *Southern Speech Communication Journal*, 49 (Fall 1983), 66–79.

Carpenter, Ronald H., and Robert V. Seltzer. "Situational Style and the Rotunda Eulogies." *Central States Speech Journal*, 22 (Spring 1971), 11–15.

Clark, Thomas D. "An Exploration of Generic Aspects of Contemporary American Campaign Orations." *Central States Speech Journal*, 30 (Summer 1979), 122–33.

Clark, Thomas D. "An Exploration of Generic Aspects of Contemporary American Christian Sermons." *Quarterly Journal of Speech*, 63 (December 1977), 384–94.

Connell, Ian, and Dariusz Galasiski. "Academic Mission Statements: An Exercise in Negotiation." *Discourse & Society*, 9 (October 1998), 457–79.

DeWitt, Jean Zaun. "The Rhetoric of Induction at the French Academy." *Quarterly Journal of Speech*, 69 (November 1983), 413–22.

Downey, Sharon D. "The Evolution of the Rhetorical Genre of Apologia." *Western Journal of Communication*, 57 (Winter 1993), 42–64.

Farrell, Thomas B. "Political Conventions as Legitimation Ritual." *Communication Monographs*, 45 (November 1978), 293–305.

Foss, Karen A. "Out from Underground: The Discourse of Emerging Fugitives." *Western Journal of Communication*, 56 (Spring 1992), 125–42.

Fulkerson, Richard. "*Newsweek* 'My Turn' Columns and the Concept of Rhetorical Genre: A Preliminary Study." In *Defining the New Rhetorics*. Ed. Theresa Enos and Stuart C. Brown. Newbury Park, CA: Sage, 1993, pp. 227–43.

Gold, Ellen Reid. "Political Apologia: The Ritual of Self-Defense." *Communication Monographs*, 45 (November 1978), 306–16.

Gronbeck, Bruce E. "The Rhetoric of Political Corruption: Sociolinguistic, Dialectical, and Ceremonial Processes." *Quarterly Journal of Speech*, 64 (April 1978), 155–72.

Hammerback, John C., and Richard J. Jensen. "Ethnic Heritage as Rhetorical Legacy: The Plan of Delano." *Quarterly Journal of Speech*, 80 (February 1994), 53–70.

Hearit, Keith Michael. "From 'We Didn't Do It' to 'It's Not Our Fault': The Use of Apologia in Public Relations Crises." In *Public Relations Inquiry as Rhetorical Criticism: Case Studies of Corporate Discourse and Social Influence*. Ed. William N. Elwood. Westport, CT: Praeger, 1995, pp. 117–31.

Hogben, Susan, and Justine Coupland. "Egg Seeks Sperm. End of Story . . .? Articulating Gay Parenting in Small Ads for Reproductive Partners." *Discourse & Society*, 11 (October 2000), 459–85.

Hoover, Judith D. "Big Boys Don't Cry: The Values Constraint in Apologia." *Southern Communication Journal*, 54 (Spring 1989), 235–52.

Ivie, Robert L. "Images of Savagery in American Justifications for War." *Communication Monographs*, 47 (November 1980), 279–94.

Jamieson, Kathleen Hall, and Karlyn Kohrs Campbell. "Rhetorical Hybrids: Fusions of Generic Elements." *Quarterly Journal of Speech*, 68 (May 1982), 146–57.

Johannesen, Richard L. "The Jeremiad and Jenkin Lloyd Jones." *Communication Monographs*, 52 (June 1985), 156–72.

Kahl, Mary. "Blind Ambition Culminates in Lost Honor: A Comparative Analysis of John Dean's Apologetic Strategies." *Central States Speech Journal*, 35 (Winter 1984), 239–50.

King, Janis L. "Justificatory Rhetoric for a Female Political Candidate: A Case Study of Wilma Mankiller." *Women's Studies in Communication*, 13 (Fall 1990), 21–38.

Kruse, Noreen Wales. "Apologia in Team Sport." *Quarterly Journal of Speech*, 67 (August 1981), 270–83.

Lucas, Stephen E. "Genre Criticism and Historical Context: The Case of George Washington's First Inaugural Address." *Southern Speech Communication Journal*, 51 (Summer 1986), 354–70.

Martin, Howard H. "A Generic Exploration: Staged Withdrawal, the Rhetoric of Resignation." *Central States Speech Journal*, 27 (Winter 1976), 247–57.

McMullen, Wayne J. "Gender and the American Dream in *Kramer vs. Kramer*." *Women's Studies in Communication*, 19 (Spring 1996), 29–54.

Miles, Edwin A. "The Keynote Speech at National Nominating Conventions." *Quarterly Journal of Speech*, 46 (February 1960), 26–31.

Nelson, Jeffrey. "The Defense of Billie Jean King." *Western Journal of Speech Communication*, 48 (Winter 1984), 92–102.

Olson, Kathryn M. "Completing the Picture: Replacing Generic Embodiments in the Historical Flow." *Communication Quarterly*, 41 (Summer 1993), 299–317.

Orr, C. Jack. "Reporters Confront the President: Sustaining a Counterpoised Situation." *Quarterly Journal of Speech*, 66 (February 1980), 17–32.

Pullum, Stephen J. "Sisters of the Spirit: The Rhetorical Methods of Female Faith Healers Aimee Semple McPherson, Kathryn Kuhlman, and Gloria Copeland." *Journal of Communication and Religion*, 16 (September 1993), 111–25.

Quimby, Rollin W. "Recurrent Themes and Purposes in the Sermons of the Union Army Chaplains." *Speech Monographs*, 31 (November 1964), 425–36.

Ritter, Kurt W. "American Political Rhetoric and the Jeremiad Tradition: Presidential Nomination Acceptance Addresses, 1960–1976." *Central States Speech Journal*, 31 (Fall 1980), 153–71.

Rodgers, Raymond S. "Generic Tendencies in Majority and Non-Majority Supreme Court Opinions: The Case of Justice Douglas." *Communication Quarterly*, 30 (Summer 1982), 232–36.

Sefcovic, E. M. I. "Stuck in the Middle: Representations of Middle-Aged Women in Three Popular Books About Menopause." *Women's Studies in Communication*, 19 (Spring 1996), 1–27.

Shaw, Punch. "Generic Refinement on the Fringe: The Game Show." *Southern Speech Communication Journal*, 52 (Summer 1987), 403–10.

Short, Brant. "Comic Book Apologia: The 'Paranoid' Rhetoric of Congressman George Hansen." *Western Journal of Speech Communication*, 51 (Spring 1987), 189–203.

Simons, Herbert W. "'Going Meta': Definition and Political Applications." *Quarterly Journal of Speech*, 80 (November 1994), 468–81.

Simons, Herbert W., and Aram A. Aghazarian, eds. *Form, Genre, and the Study of Political Discourse*. Columbia: University of South Carolina Press, 1986, numerous essays, pp. 203–77.

Stoda, Mark, and George N. Dionisopoulos. "Jeremiad at Harvard: Solzhenitsyn and 'The World Split Apart.'" *Western Journal of Communication*, 64 (Winter 2000), 28–52.

Valley, David B. "Significant Characteristics of Democratic Presidential Nomination Speeches." *Central States Speech Journal*, 25 (Spring 1974), 56–62.

Vande Berg, Leah R. Ekdom. "Dramedy: *Moonlighting* as an Emergent Generic Hybrid." *Communication Studies*, 40 (Spring 1989), 13–28.

Vartabedian, Robert A. "Nixon's Vietnam Rhetoric: A Case Study of Apologia as Generic Paradox." *Southern Speech Communication Journal*, 50 (Summer 1985), 366–81.

Ware, B. L., and Wil A. Linkugel. "They Spoke in Defense of Themselves: On the Generic Criticism of Apologia." *Quarterly Journal of Speech*, 59 (October 1973), 273–83.

Weaver, Ruth Ann. "Acknowledgment of Victory and Defeat: The Reciprocal Ritual." *Central States Speech Journal*, 33 (Fall 1982), 480–89.

White, Cindy L., and Catherine A. Dobris. "A Chorus of Discordant Voices: Radical Feminist Confrontations with Patriarchal Religion." *Southern Communication Journal*, 58 (Spring 1993), 239–46.

Wooten, Cecil W. "The Ambassador's Speech: A Particularly Hellenistic Genre of Oratory." *Quarterly Journal of Speech*, 59 (April 1973), 209–12.

For a more complete bibliography of genre studies, see: Fisher, Walter R. "Genre: Concepts and Applications in Rhetorical Criticism." *Western Journal of Speech Communication*, 44 (Fall 1980), 296–99; and Simons, Herbert W. and Aram A. Aghazarian, eds. *Form, Genre and the Study of Political Discourse*. Columbia: University of South Carolina Press, 1986, pp. 355–77.

8

~~~

Ideological Criticism

When rhetorical critics are interested in rhetoric primarily for what it suggests about beliefs and values, their focus is on ideology. An ideology is a pattern of beliefs that determines a group's interpretations of some aspect(s) of the world. It is a system of beliefs that reflects a group's "fundamental social, economic, political or cultural interests." It represents "who we are, what we stand for, what our values are, and what our relationships are with other groups"—particularly groups that oppose what we stand for, threaten our interests, and prevent us from accessing resources important to us.[1]

The primary components of an ideology are evaluative beliefs—beliefs about which there are possible alternative judgments.[2] We can see such an ideology in the following set of beliefs about the issue of immigration:

- Too many people come to our country.
- Immigrants only come here to live off welfare.
- Most immigrants are economic refugees.
- Immigrants fill up inexpensive housing and take jobs from people who need them.
- Immigrants face growing resentment in the inner cities.
- The government must send back illegal immigrants.
- Immigration has to be restricted to "real" refugees only.[3]

Beliefs such as these that comprise an ideology around immigration serve as the foundation for knowledge, attitudes, motives, and predilections of groups that adhere to this ideology.

Other examples of ideologies are patriotism, anti-Communism, Christianity, multiculturalism, conservatism, anti-terrorism, and survivalism. Ideologies can be less formal, though, as evidenced in those embedded in 12-step programs, reality-television shows, testing as the means for judging quality in education, and dieting. Each of these ideologies includes a set or pattern of beliefs that evaluates relevant issues and topics for a group, providing an interpretation of some domain of the world and encouraging particular attitudes and actions to it.

Ideologies are shared by groups whose members share a problem or desire, are mutually dependent—or at least know about other members of the group, and feel an affinity for the group. But not only formal groups have ideologies. Groups in which membership is less formal—such as the anti-war movement or believers in aliens from outer space—can have ideologies. Individuals may identify with an ideology although they are not formal members of any group associated with that ideology. In these cases, individuals are adopting, to a greater or lesser degree, the ideas of an ideology and are using fragments of that ideology to help organize their own knowledge, attitudes, and actions. They enact the ideology in various—and often idiosyncratic—ways in their everyday social practices.[4]

A number of scholars have contributed to the development of ideological criticism in the communication field, including Teun A. van Dijk,[5] Philip C. Wander,[6] Michael Calvin McGee,[7] Raymie E. McKerrow,[8] Janice Hocker Rushing, Thomas S. Frentz,[9] Lawrence Grossberg,[10] Celeste M. Condit,[11] and Omar Swartz.[12] These scholars have been influenced by a number of different perspectives and philosophies in their development of ideological approaches to criticism.

One perspective that informs ideological criticism is structuralism, a series of projects in which linguistics is used as a model for attempts to develop the "grammars" of systems such as myths, novels, and genres. The work of Claude Lévi-Strauss, who analyzes a wide range of myths in an effort to discover their structure or grammar, is representative of a structuralist approach.[13] By constructing such grammars—systematic inventories of elements and their relationships—structuralists gain insights into the ideologies of artifacts because the grammars embody and provide clues to those ideologies.

A form of structuralism that many ideological critics have found useful is semiotics or semiology, the science of signs. Developed by Ferdinand de Saussure[14] and Charles Sanders Peirce,[15] semiotics is a systematic attempt to understand what signs are and how they function. Signs are units that can be taken as substituting for something else and, consequently, have meaning. All sorts of things can function as signs—words, font styles, camera angles, colors, clothing, and gestures, for example. Semiotics provides a way to study components of an artifact as clues to its meaning and ideology. Among those who have contributed to the development of semiotics and its use in ideological criticism are Roland Barthes,[16] Arthur Asa Berger,[17] and Kaja Silverman.[18]

Marxism also informs the work of many ideological critics.[19] As an intellectual system, Marxism is a way of analyzing cultural products in terms of the social and economic practices and institutions that produce them. Although Marxist critics—such as Theodor Adorno,[20] Louis Althusser,[21] Walter Benjamin,[22] Bertolt Brecht,[23] Terry Eagleton,[24] Jürgen Habermas,[25] Georg Lukács,[26] and Herbert Marcuse[27]—differ in their interpretations and applications of Marxism, they are united by the belief that material conditions interact with and influence the symbols by which groups make sense of their worlds. Ideological forms are more than ideas, beliefs, and values, these scholars believe. They have a material existence and are embodied in cultural institutions such as schools, churches, and political parties and in artifacts such as paintings, novels, and speeches.

Yet another influence on ideological criticism is deconstructionism, which sometimes is called *poststructuralism* because it developed after and in response to structuralism. The philosophy and critical method of deconstructionism is most closely associated with Jacques Derrida,[28] and its foremost American exponent is Paul de Man.[29] The purpose of deconstructionism is to deconstruct the self-evidence of central concepts—to subject to critical analyses the basic structures and assumptions that govern texts and the development of knowledge. Methodologically, deconstruction is directed to the questioning of texts—taking apart and exposing their underlying meanings, biases, and preconceptions—and then transforming or reconceptualizing the conceptual fields of those texts.

Postmodernism, a theory of cultural, intellectual, and societal discontinuity, also influences much ideological criticism. Postmodern theories are based on the notion that our culture has moved into a new phase—one that follows the period of Modernism, which championed reason as the source of progress in society and privileged the foundation of systematic knowledge. The new form of society has been transformed radically by media and technology, which have introduced new forms of communication and representation into contemporary life. This postmodern society requires new concepts and theories to address the features that characterize the new era: Fragmentation of individuals and communities, a consumer lifestyle, a sense of alienation, and a destabilization of unifying discourses and principles. The postmodern project is useful to ideological critics in that it provides information about the context for many contemporary artifacts and suggests the exigence to which many of these artifacts and their ideologies respond. Among the primary contributors to theories of postmodernism are Jean-François Lyotard,[30] Jean Baudrillard,[31] and Fredric Jameson.[32]

Another source from which ideological critics draw is cultural studies, an interdisciplinary project directed at uncovering oppressive relations and discovering available forces with the potential to lead to liberation or emancipation. As a loosely unified movement, cultural studies dates to the Birmingham Centre for Contemporary Cultural

Studies in Great Britain, founded in 1964 by Richard Hoggart[33] and later headed by Stuart Hall.[34] Although theorists associated with cultural studies adopt diverse approaches, including Marxist, poststructuralist, postmodern, feminist, and Jungian perspectives, they tend to share some basic assumptions about culture. Culture, they believe, consists of everyday discursive practices, with these discursive practices both embodying and constructing a culture's ideology. They see artifacts of popular culture as legitimate data for critical analysis because they are places where struggles take place over which meanings and ideologies will dominate.

The ideological criticism that has developed from perspectives such as structuralism, semiotics, and Marxism is rooted in basic notions about ideologies and how they function. Primary is the notion that multiple ideologies—multiple patterns of belief—exist in any culture and have the potential to be manifest in rhetorical artifacts. Some ideologies, however, are privileged over others in a culture, and ideologies that present oppositional or alternative perspectives are sometimes repressed. The result is a dominant way of seeing the world or the development of a hegemonic ideology. Hegemony is the privileging of the ideology of one group over that of other groups. It thus constitutes a kind of social control, a means of symbolic coercion, or a form of domination of the more powerful groups over the ideologies of those with less power.[35] When an ideology becomes hegemonic in a culture, certain interests or groups are served by it more than others. The hegemonic ideology represents experience in ways that support the interests of those with more power.

When an ideology becomes hegemonic, it accumulates "the symbolic power to map or classify the world for others."[36] It invites "us to understand the world in certain ways, but not in others."[37] A dominant ideology controls what participants see as natural or obvious by establishing the norm. Normal discourse, then, maintains the ideology, and challenges to it seem abnormal. A hegemonic ideology provides a sense that things are the way they have to be as it asserts that its meanings are the real, natural ones. In a culture where the ideology of racism is hegemonic, for example, the privilege accorded to whites seems normal, as does the lack of opportunity accorded to individuals of other races. If practices in the culture concerning people of color are questioned, the questions are seen as abnormal.

The dominance of one group's ideology over others can be seen in the discourse around the Iraq War initiated by the United States in 2003. Although many perspectives and ideologies were involved in the discourse about whether the United States should invade Iraq—those of religious leaders, politicians, President George W. Bush, members of his cabinet, Iraqi citizens, military officers, pacifists, backers of the president, and skeptical citizens—the dominant perspective that emerged and functioned as hegemonic was that of the president and his cabinet members. In part because they were the ones with access to classified information about the situation in Iraq and terrorist activity, had the capacity to hide or release the information available to them, had the ability to converse with world leaders to try to enlist their support, and had guaranteed media coverage of their words and actions, their perspective became privileged over that of other perspectives.

To maintain a position of dominance, a hegemonic ideology must be renewed, reinforced, and defended continually through the use of rhetorical strategies and practices. Resistance to the dominant ideology is muted or contained and its impact is limited by a variety of sophisticated rhetorical strategies. Often, in fact, these strategies incorporate the resistance into the dominant discourse in such a way that the challenge will not contradict and even may support the dominant ideology. In a culture in which an ideology of racism is dominant, for example, questions about why people of color are not given equal opportunities may be muted by representations of these people as lacking in internal motivation. Thus, the argument that they are not given equal opportunities is seen as irrelevant and thus is unable to have any impact on the dominant ideology.

The rise to dominance of particular ideologies is not always as deliberate and conscious a process as the above description makes it seem. We all are subjected to dominant perspectives in the most mundane and ordinary activities of our lives. All of the institutions in which we participate embody particular ideologies. Our educational system, for example, shapes students in particular directions, teaching us as part of its complex ideology to obey orders and to follow rules. Religion, families, the media, the legal system, and popular culture perpetuate various ideologies and convince participants in a culture to accept those ideologies. Although, as individuals, we may adhere to ideologies different from the one that is hegemonic, we cannot help but participate in the hegemonic ideology as we participate in our culture through activities such as watching television, browsing through popular magazines, and attending school.

The primary goal of the ideological critic is to discover and make visible the dominant ideology or ideologies embedded in an artifact and the ideologies that are being muted in it. As a result of an ideological analysis, a critic seeks to explicate the role of communication in creating and sustaining an ideology and to give voice to those whose interests are not represented. The ultimate aim of an ideological critic is the emancipation of human potential that is being thwarted by an existing ideology or ideologies or a celebration of artifacts that facilitate this emancipation. In many ways, ideological criticism is not unlike feminist criticism in that both involve analyzing an artifact for a particular ideology and exploring its implications. Feminist criticism, however, focuses on artifacts associated with traditionally marginalized or subordinate groups as they function within one ideology—the ideology of domination. In ideological criticism, ideologies of various kinds are identified in many kinds of artifacts.

PROCEDURES

Using the ideological method of criticism, a critic analyzes an artifact in a four-step process: (1) selecting an artifact; (2) analyzing the artifact; (3) formulating a research question; and (4) writing the essay.

Selecting an Artifact

Virtually any artifact can serve as an artifact for ideological criticism because ideologies exist almost everywhere. Although you may be tempted to select a political text for an ideological analysis—and such texts certainly work well as data for this kind of analysis—other kinds of artifacts often can produce less obvious insights. Artifacts of popular culture such as advertisements, television shows, basketball games, concerts, coffee houses, lawn ornaments, or flash mobs are often sites where ideological conflicts are played out. Audiences are often less resistant to ideological messages in such artifacts because they do not expect to see them there.

Analyzing the Artifact

A critic who explores an artifact for the traces of ideology that are manifest in it does so in two steps: (1) identifying the nature of the ideology; and (2) identifying strategies in support of the ideology.

Identifying the Nature of the Ideology

The first step in an ideological analysis is to articulate the ideology that is embodied in the artifact. The following are typical components of an ideology, each of which functions to organize a number of beliefs. Answering the questions about each will provide you with a comprehensive view of the ideology in an artifact.

- *Membership.* Who are we? Where are we from? What do we look like? Who belongs to us? Who can become a member of our group?
- *Activities.* What do we do? What is expected of us? Why are we here?
- *Goals.* Why do we do this? What do we want to realize?
- *Values/norms.* What are our main values? How do we evaluate ourselves and others? What should (not) be done?
- *Position and group-relations.* What is our social position? Who are our enemies or opponents? Who is like us, and who is different?
- *Resources.* What are the essential social resources that our group has or needs to have?[38]

Although an ideology may contain beliefs that are clearly articulated in all six categories of membership, activities, goals, values/norms, position, and resources, you are likely to find that various groups focus their beliefs in one or a few areas of the schema. The ideology of feminism, for example, focuses primarily on a goal—to eliminate relations of oppression and domination in our culture. A Christian ideology focuses on values, while the ideology of capitalism focuses on the resource dimension and freedom of the market as the means to achieve resources.[39]

As a result of your articulation of the ideology embodied in the artifact, you should be able to answer these questions about the ideology: What is the preferred reading of the artifact? What does the artifact ask the audience to believe, understand, feel, or think about? What arguments are being made in the artifact and for what? What are the particular characteristics, roles, actions, or ways of seeing being commended in the artifact? What values or general conceptions of what is and is not good are suggested? What are the assumptions or premises of the artifact? What doesn't the artifact want the audience to think about? What ways of seeing does it ask the audience to avoid? What alternative interpretations of the world are possible to the one offered by the ideology in the artifact? What does the artifact suggest is unacceptable, negative, undesirable, marginal, or insignificant?

Identifying Strategies in Support of the Ideology

Thus far, in your ideological analysis, you have been using the rhetoric of an artifact as clues to its ideology. Now you want to focus on rhetoric in another way—to discover the rhetorical mechanisms used to advocate for and defend that ideology. The expression of ideology in rhetoric is usually more than a display of a set of beliefs; it also has a persuasive function. Rhetors who create artifacts that embody ideologies usually want to change the minds of their audiences in ways that are consistent with those ideologies. At this step, then, your focus is on rhetorical strategies used to persuade others to consider or adopt those ideologies and to defend them from those who offer alternative ideologies.

Virtually an infinite number of rhetorical strategies are available for promoting one ideology over another. To identify these strategies, pay attention to the following dimensions of the rhetoric and to the strategies within these dimensions that are likely to facilitate acceptance of an ideology by an audience.[40]

Nature of the ideology. Various factors give advantage to some groups over others in determining which ideologies come to dominate a culture. Of primary importance in this process is the possession by a group of a broad-based and coherent ideology that is able to attract support from some groups and at least passive assent from others. An ideology built on assumptions that are shared by many different groups in a culture—the importance of patriotism, for example—is accepted more readily by audiences than one built on more marginal beliefs—the legitimacy of polygamy, for example. Similarly, an ideology that is marked by obvious inconsistencies or contradictions in its beliefs will have a harder time being marketed to an audience.

Communicative genre. The genre to which the artifact belongs affects the persuasiveness of an artifact's ideology. Some genres typically function as persuasive expressions of opinions, while others have a lower level of ideological expression, implication, and function. An op-ed piece in a newspaper, a leaflet, a sermon, and a Congressional debate, for example, all belong to genres that we typically see as persuasive, while a conversation with a colleague on the weather, instructions for setting up your new computer, and a scholarly article on nonverbal communication do not. Similarly, we expect ideologically relevant opinions from specific individuals and not others. A politician, corporate executive, priest, or journalist speaking about an issue is more likely to be heard as expressing ideologically based opinions than a child or a homeless person, for example. The genre in which the ideology is presented, then, constitutes a strategy for supporting the ideology. Although contexts that are clearly ideological certainly can be persuasive in supporting an ideology, ideological communication may be most effective when audiences do not expect ideological implications—television news, textbooks, or warranties accompanying household appliances, for example.

Size of audience. A third feature that is crucial in the widespread acceptance of an ideology is the size of the audience to which it is presented. Mass-mediated or other kinds of public discourse are likely to have more serious ideological consequences than daily conversations with coworkers, for example, because they convey beliefs to many more ingroup and outgroup members. Moreover, public discourse—such as that of politics or the media—usually features institutional rhetors who have more authority and hence more credibility than rhetors known to smaller numbers of people. Much of the ideological consensus constructed in society would be difficult to obtain without coverage of rhetoric by the mass media. The larger the scope of a discourse, the greater the ideological effects. Numerical superiority, access to resources or technologies not available to others, alliances with other groups that increase their legitimacy or authority, and the backing of other powerful groups all tend to advantage groups in the process of gaining larger audiences for an ideology.[41]

Content. In presenting a set of beliefs about an issue, rhetors cannot include everything they know or understand about the issue. They choose to focus on some things rather than others, and their choices in terms of content can increase the persuasiveness of an artifact's ideology. Decisions about what content to highlight and feature and what to suppress tend to be made according to these principles: (1) express/emphasize information that is positive about Us; (2) express/emphasize information that is negative about Them; (3) suppress/de-emphasize information that is positive about Them; and (4) suppress/de-emphasize information that is negative about Us.

There are a number of ways in which artifacts can emphasize and de-emphasize information according to these principles. The major topics discussed or referenced are one way—they suggest what is most relevant or important for the rhetor. Artifacts also can emphasize and de-emphasize information in the level of detail they provide about a situation. They can provide a great deal of detail, much of which may be irrelevant to understanding an issue or event, if the details provide negative information about outgroups or reflect positively on the ingroup. Conversely, they may be more vague when the information being discussed reflects negatively on the ingroup and positively on the outgroup. Implicitness and explicitness may be used in a similar fashion. Presuppositions may be made explicit or left implicit as a function of the interests of group members. Negative properties attributed to an outgroup (such as drug abuse) are likely to be made explicit, while positive attributes (such as high motivation to succeed) are likely to remain implicit in an artifact's ideology.

Style. The form or style of an artifact is one of the most obvious means rhetors have to signal their ideological beliefs. As with content, style can be used to express positive and negative information about an outgroup and an ingroup. Active or passive voice, which can show individuals either as agents or objects of action, is one way. Word order is another stylistic mechanism that can put information in a more or less prominent position. Probably the most obvious ideological expression of style is found in the words chosen to express concepts. Outgroups usually are described in ideologies in neutral or negative terms and ingroups in neutral or positive terms, as in the distinction between the terms *terrorist* and *freedom fighter*. Other aspects of style that can affect the presentation of an ideology are pronunciation; graphics in a visual artifact; tone (formal, polite, familiar, friendly); the ideas that are repeated and thus emphasized; and figures of speech such as metaphors, rhyme, alliteration, euphemism, and understatement.

Interactional strategies. The ways in which interaction is managed also can play a role in securing acceptance for a particular ideology. Rhetors who suggest greater power through their bodily position, clothing, and facial expressions, for example, condition the way in which ideologies are accepted by others. Speakers who want to offer alternative ideologies may be prevented from doing so by other speakers who interrupt them, control turn taking, or respond by laughing or openly disagreeing.

In other cases, a dominant ideology prevails because there is little or no access for the public to alternative ideologies. In this case, there appear to be no strong popular alternatives to the dominant ideology, or these alternatives are unknown or marginalized. In the case of the Iraq War, for example, most coverage was of activities in support of the war, no matter how trivial. Thus, the media covered the renaming of French fries as *freedom fries* by restaurants in Washington, D.C., and the pouring of French wines down drains and toilets by American citizens to signal their unhappiness with France's opposition to the war.

Celebrities who spoke out against the war were likely to be met with smear campaigns and censorship. For example, Warner Bros. airbrushed the billboard advertising its film *What a Girl Wants* so that its star,

Amanda Bynes, was no longer flashing a peace sign. *The New York Post* began to publish a "Don't Aid These Saddam Lovers" list and urged a boycott of forthcoming movies, television shows, CDs, DVDs, and concerts of those on the list. Susan Sarandon and Tim Robbins were disinvited from events at which they were scheduled to appear in punishment for their anti-war opinions. The Baseball Hall of Fame, for example, cancelled the 15th anniversary celebration of the film *Bull Durham* to avoid the participation of the couple. When the Dixie Chicks singer Natalie Maines said at a concert in London, "We're ashamed that the president of the United States is from Texas," about half of the 148 country radio stations in the United States stopped playing their songs.[42]

Formulating a Research Question

One or more of the following questions are likely to serve as your research questions in ideological analysis: "What is the ideology manifest in this artifact?" "What is the preferred reading of the artifact?" "What rhetorical strategies provide support for this ideology?" "Who are the groups or voices whose interests are privileged or favored in the ideology?" "Whose interests are negated, unexpressed, or not represented in the ideology?"

Writing the Critical Essay

After completing the analysis, you are ready to write your essay, which includes five major components: (1) an introduction, in which you discuss the research question, its contribution to rhetorical theory, and its significance; (2) a description of the artifact and its context; (3) a description of the method of criticism—in this case, ideological analysis; (4) a report of the findings of the analysis, in which you identify the ideology manifest in the artifact and the rhetorical strategies that promote it over other ideologies; and (5) a discussion of the contribution the analysis makes to rhetorical theory.

SAMPLE ESSAYS

In the essays that follow, critics analyze a variety of artifacts to discover the ideologies they embody. Derek T. Buescher and Kent A. Ono analyze the Disney film *Pocahontas* to answer these questions: "What is the nature of the film's ideology concerning American colonial encounters with Native Americans?" and "How does the neocolonial ideology the film presents function within contemporary society?" In her analysis of the Web sites of three United Nations agencies, Khadidiatou Ndiaye seeks to answer the question: "How inclusive is the ideology of UNICEF, UNFPA, and UNAIDS as portrayed in these organizations' Web sites?" Anthony "Tony" N. Docan's ideological analysis of the vice presidential nomination acceptance speech of Winona LaDuke of the Green Party is designed to answer the questions: "What ideologies does LaDuke present in the speech?" and "What rhetorical strategies does she use to increase the appeal of an unfamiliar ideology?"

Notes

[1] Teun A. van Dijk, *Ideology: A Multidisciplinary Approach* (Thousand Oaks, CA: Sage, 1998), p. 69.

[2] For a more detailed explanation of beliefs and ideology, see van Dijk, *Ideology*, pp. 28–52.

[3] van Dijk, *Ideology*, p. 66.

[4] van Dijk, *Ideology*, pp. 141, 155–56.

[5] van Dijk, *Ideology*; Teun A. van Dijk, *Communicating Racism: Ethnic Prejudice in Thought and Talk* (Newbury Park, CA: Sage, 1987); Teun A. van Dijk, *News Analysis: Case Studies of International and National News in the Press* (Hillsdale, NJ: Erlbaum, 1988); and Teun A. van Dijk, *Elite Discourse and Racism* (Newbury Park, CA: Sage, 1993).

[6] Philip C. Wander, "Salvation Through Separation: The Image of the Negro in the American Colonization Society," *Quarterly Journal of Speech*, 57 (February 1971), 57–67; Philip C. Wander, "The John Birch and Martin Luther King Symbols in the Radical Right," *Western Speech*, 35 (Winter 1971), 4–14; Philip C. Wander, "The Savage Child: The Image of the Negro in the Pro-Slavery Movement," *Southern Speech Communication Journal*, 37 (Summer 1972), 335–60; Philip Wander and Steven Jenkins, "Rhetoric, Society, and the Critical Response," *Quarterly Journal of Speech*, 58 (December 1972), 441–50; Philip Wander, "'The Waltons': How Sweet It Was," *Journal of Communication*, 26 (Autumn 1976), 148–54; Philip Wander, "On the Meaning of 'Roots,'" *Journal of Communication*, 27 (Autumn 1977), 64–69; Philip Wander, "The Angst of the Upper Class," *Journal of Communication*, 29 (Autumn 1979), 85–88; Philip Wander, "Cultural Criticism," in *Handbook of Political Communication*, ed. Dan D. Nimmo and Keith R. Sanders (Beverly Hills: Sage, 1981), 497–528; Philip Wander, "The Ideological Turn in Modern Criticism," *Central States Speech Journal*, 34 (Spring 1983), 1–18; Philip Wander, "The Aesthetics of Fascism," *Journal of Communication*, 33 (Spring 1983), 70–78; Philip Wander, "The Rhetoric of American Foreign Policy," *Quarterly Journal of Speech*, 70 (November 1984), 339–61; Philip Wander, "The Third Persona: An Ideological Turn in Rhetorical Theory," *Central States Speech Journal*, 35 (Winter 1984), 197–216; Richard Morris and Philip Wander, "Native American Rhetoric: Dancing in the Shadows of the Ghost Dance," *Quarterly Journal of Speech*, 76 (May 1990), 164–91; and Philip C. Wander, "Introduction: Special Issue on Ideology," *Western Journal of Communication*, 57 (Spring 1993), 105–10.

[7] Michael C. McGee, "In Search of 'The People': A Rhetorical Alternative," *Quarterly Journal of Speech*, 61 (October 1975), 235–49; Michael C. McGee, "'Not Men, but Measures': The Origins and Import of an Ideological Principle," *Quarterly Journal of Speech*, 64 (April 1978), 141–54; Michael Calvin McGee, "The 'Ideograph': A Link Between Rhetoric and Ideology," *Quarterly Journal of Speech*, 66 (February 1980), 1–16; Michael Calvin McGee, "The Origins of 'Liberty': A Feminization of Power," *Communication Monographs*, 47 (March 1980), 23–45; Michael Calvin McGee and Martha Anne Martin, "Public Knowledge and Ideological Argumentation," *Communication Monographs*, 50 (March 1983), 47–65; Michael Calvin McGee, "Secular Humanism: A Radical Reading of 'Culture Industry' Productions," *Critical Studies in Mass Communication*, 1 (March 1984), 1–33; Michael Calvin McGee, "Another Philippic: Notes on the Ideological Turn in Criticism," *Central States Speech Journal*, 35 (Spring 1984), 43–50; Allen Scult, Michael Calvin McGee, and J. Kenneth Buntz, "Genesis and Power: An Analysis of the Biblical Story of Creation," *Quarterly Journal of Speech*, 72 (May 1986), 113–31; Michael Calvin McGee, "Power to the {People}," *Critical Studies in Mass Communication*, 4 (December 1987), 432–37; and Michael Calvin McGee, "Text, Context, and the Fragmentation of Contemporary Culture," *Western Journal of Speech Communication*, 54 (Summer 1990), 274–89.

[8] Raymie E. McKerrow, "Critical Rhetoric: Theory and Praxis," *Communication Monographs*, 56 (June 1989), 91–111; and Raymie E. McKerrow, "Critical Rhetoric in a Postmodern World," *Quarterly Journal of Speech*, 77 (February 1991), 75–78.

[9] Janice Hocker Rushing, "The Rhetoric of the American Western Myth," *Communication Monographs*, 50 (March 1983), 14–32; Janice Hocker Rushing, "E.T. as Rhetorical Transcendence," *Quarterly Journal of Speech*, 71 (May 1985), 188–203; Janice Hocker Rushing, "Mythic Evolution of 'The New Frontier' in Mass Mediated Rhetoric," *Critical Studies in Mass Communication*, 3 (September 1986), 265–96; Janice Hocker Rushing, "Ronald Reagan's 'Star Wars' Address: Mythic Containment of Technical Reasoning," *Quarterly Journal of Speech*, 72 (November 1986), 415–33; Janice Hocker Rushing, "Evolution of 'The New Frontier' in *Alien* and *Aliens*: Patriarchal Co-optation of the Feminine Archetype," *Quarterly Journal of Speech*, 75 (February 1989), 1–24; Janice Hocker Rushing, "Power, Other, and Spirit in Cultural Texts," *Western Journal of Communication*, 57 (Spring 1993), 159–68; Thomas S. Frentz and Thomas B. Farrell, "Conversion of America's Consciousness: The Rhetoric of *The Exorcist*," *Quarterly Journal of Speech*, 61 (February 1975), 40–47; Janice Hocker Rushing and Thomas S. Frentz, "The Frankenstein Myth in Contemporary Cinema," *Critical Studies in Mass Communication*, 6 (March 1989), 61–80; Janice Hocker Rushing and Thomas S. Frentz, "Integrating Ideology and Archetype in Rhetorical Criticism," *Quarterly Journal of Speech*, 77 (November 1991), 385–406; and Thomas S. Frentz and Janice Hocker Rushing, "Integrating Ideology and Archetype in Rhetorical Criticism, Part II: A Case Study of *Jaws*," *Quarterly Journal of Speech*, 79 (February 1993), 61–81.

[10] Lawrence Grossberg, "Marxist Dialectics and Rhetorical Criticism," *Quarterly Journal of Speech*, 65 (October 1979), 235–49; Lawrence Grossberg, "Is There Rock after Punk?" *Critical Studies in Mass Communication*, 3 (March 1986), 50–73; and Lawrence Grossberg, "Cultural Studies and/in New Worlds," *Critical Studies in Mass Communication*, 10 (March 1993), 1–22.

[11] Celeste Michelle Condit, "Hegemony in a Mass-Mediated Society: Concordance about Reproductive Technologies," *Critical Studies in Mass Communication*, 11 (September 1994), 205–30; and Celeste Michelle Condit, "The Rhetorical Limits of Polysemy," *Critical Studies in Mass Communication*, 6 (June 1989), 103–22.

[12] Omar Swartz, *Conducting Socially Responsible Research* (Thousand Oaks, CA: Sage, 1997); Omar Swartz, *The Rise of Rhetoric and Its Intersections with Contemporary Critical Thought* (Boulder, CO: Westview, 1998); and Omar Swartz, *The View from* On the Road: *The Rhetorical Vision of Jack Kerouac* (Carbondale: Southern Illinois University Press, 1999).

[13] See, for example, Claude Lévi-Strauss, *The Savage Mind* (Chicago: Chicago University Press, 1966); and Claude Lévi-Strauss, *Totemism*, trans. Rodney Needham (Boston: Beacon, 1963).

[14] See, for example, Ferdinand de Saussure, *Course in General Linguistics*, ed. Charles Bally, Albert Sechehaye, and Albert Reidlinger, trans. Roy Harris (London: Duckworth, 1983).

[15] See, for example, Charles Sanders Peirce, *Peirce on Signs: Writings on Semiotic*, ed. James Hoopes (Chapel Hill: University of North Carolina Press, 1991).

[16] See, for example, Roland Barthes, *Elements of Semiology*, trans. Annette Lavers and Colin Smith (1964; rpt. New York: Noonday, 1967); and Roland Barthes, *Mythologies*, trans. Annette Lavers (1957; rpt. New York: Noonday, 1972).

[17] See, for example, Arthur Asa Berger, *Signs in Contemporary Culture: An Introduction to Semiotics* (New York: Longman, 1984); and Arthur Asa Berger, *Media Analysis Techniques* (Newbury Park, CA: Sage, 1991).

[18] Kaja Silverman, *The Subject of Semiotics* (New York: Oxford University Press, 1983).

[19] See, for example, Karl Marx and Frederick Engels, *The German Ideology: Parts I and III*, ed. Roy Pascal (New York: International, 1947); and Karl Marx, *The Grundrisse*, ed. and trans. David McLellan (New York: Harper and Row, 1971).

[20] See, for example, Theodor Adorno, *Aesthetic Theory*, ed. Gretal Adorno and Rolf Tiedmann, trans. C. Lenhardt (London: Routledge and Kegan Paul, 1984); and Theodor Adorno, *The Jargon of Authenticity*, trans. Knut Tarnowski and Frederic Will (Evanston, IL: Northwestern University Press, 1973).

[21] See, for example, Louis Althusser, *For Marx*, trans. Ben Brewster (1965; rpt. London: Allen Lane, 1969); and Louis Althusser, *Lenin and Philosophy and Other Essays*, trans. Ben Brewster (New York: Monthly Review, 1971).

[22] See, for example, Walter Benjamin, *Illuminations*, ed. Hannah Arendt, trans. Harry Zahn (New York: Schocken, 1968); and Walter Benjamin, *Understanding Brecht*, trans. Anna Bostock (London: NLB, 1977).

[23] See, for example, Bertolt Brecht, *Brecht on Theatre*, ed. and trans. John Willett (New York: Hill and Wang, 1964).

[24] See, for example, Terry Eagleton, *Marxism and Literary Criticism* (Berkeley: University of California Press, 1976); and Terry Eagleton, *The Function of Criticism: From the Spectator to Post-Structuralism* (London: Verso, 1984).

[25] See, for example, Jürgen Habermas, *Communication and the Evolution of Society*, trans. Thomas McCarthy (Boston: Beacon, 1979); Jürgen Habermas, *The Theory of Communicative Action, Volume I: Reason and the Rationalization of Society*, trans. Thomas McCarthy (Boston: Beacon, 1984); and Jürgen Habermas, *The Theory of Communicative Action, Volume II: Lifeworld and System: A Critique of Functionalist Reason*, trans. Thomas McCarthy (Boston: Beacon, 1987).

[26] See, for example, Georg Lukács, *History and Class Consciousness*, trans. Rodney Livingston (London: Merlin, 1971); and Georg Lukács, *The Historical Novel*, trans. Hannah Mitchell and Stanley Mitchell (London: Merlin, 1962).

[27] See, for example, Herbert Marcuse, *An Essay on Liberation* (Boston: Beacon, 1969); and Herbert Marcuse, *Counterrevolution and Revolt* (Boston: Beacon, 1972).

[28] See, for example, Jacques Derrida, *Writing and Difference*, trans. Alan Bass (Chicago: University of Chicago Press, 1978); Jacques Derrida, *Margins of Philosophy*, trans. Alan Bass (Chicago: University of Chicago Press, 1982); and Jacques Derrida, "Structure, Sign, and Play," in *The Structuralist Controversy*, ed. Richard Macksey and Eugenio Donato (Baltimore: John Hopkins Press, 1972), pp. 247–72.

[29] See, for example, Paul de Man, *Blindness and Insight: Essays in the Rhetoric of Contemporary Criticism* (New York: Oxford University Press, 1971); and Paul de Man, *Allegories of Reading: Figural Language in Rousseau, Nietzsche, Rilke, and Proust* (New Haven: Yale University Press, 1979).

[30] See, for example, Jean-François Lyotard, *The Postmodern Condition: A Report on Knowledge*, trans. Geoff Bennington and Brian Massumi (1979; rpt. Minneapolis: University of Minnesota Press, 1984).

[31] See, for example, Jean Baudrillard, *Simulations* (1981; rpt. New York: Semiotext(e), 1983); and Jean Baudrillard, *The Mirror of Production*, trans. Mark Poster (St. Louis: Telos, 1975).

[32] See, for example, Fredric Jameson, *Postmodernism, or the Cultural Logic of Late Capitalism* (Durham, NC: Duke University Press, 1991); and Fredric Jameson, *The Geopolitical Aesthetic: Cinema and Space in the World System* (Bloomington: Indiana University Press, 1992).

[33] See, for example, Richard Hoggart, *The Uses of Literacy: Aspects of Working-Class Life, with Special Reference to Publications and Entertainments* (New York: Oxford University Press, 1970); and Richard Hoggart, *On Culture and Communication* (1971; rpt. New York: Oxford University Press, 1972).

[34] See, for example, Stuart Hall, "The Rediscovery of 'Ideology': Return of the Repressed in Media Studies," in *Culture, Society and the Media*, ed. Michael Gurevitch, Tony Bennett, James Curran, and Janet Woolacott (London: Methuen, 1982), pp. 56–90; Stuart Hall, "Encoding/Decoding," in *Culture, Media, Language*, ed. Stuart Hall, Dorothy Hobson, Andrew Lowe, and Paul Willis (London: Hutchinson, 1980), pp. 128–38; and Stuart Hall and Tony Jefferson, eds., *Resistance Through Rituals: Youth Subcultures in Post-War Britain* (London: Hutchinson, 1976).

[35] Antonio Gramsci is credited with the initial conceptualization of this notion of hegemony. See Antonio Gramsci, *Selections from the Prison Notebooks*, trans. and ed. Quintin Hoare and Geoffrey N. Smith (1971; rpt. New York: International, 1987).

[36] Stuart Hall, "The Toad in the Garden: Thatcherism Among the Theorists," in *Marxism and the Interpretation of Culture*, ed. Cary Nelson and Lawrence Grossberg (Urbana: University of Illinois Press, 1988), p. 44.

[37] Alan O'Connor, "Culture and Communication," in *Questioning the Media: A Critical Introduction*, ed. John Downing, Ali Mohammadi, and Annabelle Sreberny-Mohammadi (Newbury Park, CA: Sage, 1990), p. 36.

[38] van Dijk, *Ideology*, pp. 69-70.

[39] van Dijk, *Ideology*, p. 70.

[40] These factors come largely from van Dijk, *Ideology*, pp. 264–74.

[41] For a full description and illustration of this process, see Condit, "Hegemony in a Mass-Mediated Society."

[42] Ellen Hawkes, "Shock and Jaw: Climate of a New Blacklist? Garofalo Says No Thanks," *Ms.*, 13 (Summer 2003), 30–39.

Civilized Colonialism
Pocahontas as Neocolonial Rhetoric
Derek T. Buescher and Kent A. Ono

The year 1992 had tremendous symbolic importance for nationalists, educators, and indigenous peoples living in the U.S. The perception of Columbus as heroic founder of America changed as a result of commemorative events, books, articles, speeches, films, and other popular discourses about Columbus and his infamy. These public discourses questioned whether it made sense to say "Columbus discovered America." Thus, 1992 represents a key juncture within U.S. rhetorical history, for it marks a time when students of nationalist history, who believed themselves the beneficiaries of the legacy of colonialism, began to question on a system-wide basis the moral, political, and ethical choices of their "forebearers" as well as their own individual relationships to those decisions. At the same time, indigenous peoples protested pre-1992 conceptions of Columbus and the patriotic revelry associated with them.[1] As a result of protests by Native American peoples and allied political groups, many grade school teachers taught students to question the Columbus discovery story. In the face of new stories about Columbus and colonialism, students began to ask different questions such as "Well, why did he/we do it?"—"it" meaning slaughter indigenous peoples, ravage natural resources, and steal land and other material wealth: in a word, colonize.

One answer to that question appeared in the summer of 1995 in the form of Disney's film *Pocahontas*.[2] Parents and other adults may not have recognized, at first glance, the profound rhetorical significance of this film because Disney did not market the film to them. As with most of its films, especially animated ones like *Sleeping Beauty* (1959), *Cinderella* (1950), and *The Little Mermaid* (1989), Disney marketed *Pocahontas* to children, and especially to girls. Disney has long been known for creating fantasies, but this was the first time in Disney's long history of producing animated films that it turned a historical narrative into an animated fable—transforming the memory of a Native American woman into a "toon." The animated Pocahontas story Disney tells is more fun, more exciting than those kids may read in their history books, and certainly more exciting than the less popular films about Columbus shown three years before with a "PG-13" rating.[3] Disney makes history fun—or does Disney make fun of history? Call it artistic license or effective marketing, but Disney turned the 10- to 15-year-old Native American girl (depending on which history one reads), Pocahontas, into a woman; turned the middle-aged man, John Smith, into a young man; and turned their "supposed" meeting into a romance. And as we all know, especially Disney, romance sells.

We contend in this paper that *Pocahontas* rewrites the quincentennial story of Columbus and other colonizers' conquering of the Americas, and in its place tells the tale of a relatively peaceful, romantic encounter between colonizers and Native Americans. In this way, Disney helps audiences unlearn the infamous history of mass slaughter by replacing it with a cute, cuddly one, a memorable exception to the typical colonization narrative. Disney's *Pocahontas* narrative answers

From *Women's Studies in Communication*, 19 (Summer 1996), 127–53. Used by permission of the Organization for Research on Women and Communication and the authors.

the question, "Why did he/we do it?" by arguing that colonialists were searching for gold, and though they were willing to kill what they called "savages" to get it, when they found no hidden treasures, they opened their eyes and saw a beautiful land with friendly people—treasures of a different sort but even more valuable. In Disney's version of history, except for one errant "savage," most native people are nice and one woman actually is eager and willing to learn and to practice the colonial ideology, the English language, Western romantic rituals, and (hopefully) religion. The skeptical chief initially looks like a "savage" to the colonizers, but upon further acquaintance shows promising signs of good faith and potential acceptance of colonization. The chief personifies the wise Native American who *just might be converted too*. Upon leaving this newfound paradise—albeit without gold—colonizers would need to return, because the natives seemed almost civilized and therefore civilizable. *Pocahontas* presages events to come; it foretells the hazards Native American society could pose to colonialism's advancement in the Americas, but it shows that even those hazards eventually could be overcome.

We begin this essay by defining colonialism and distinguishing it from neocolonialism. Then we briefly describe a version of the historical way colonialism functions. Sketching the traditional colonial story and its conventions generates a better understanding of the differences between colonialism and neocolonialism and of how *Pocahontas* operates within a neocolonialist economy. Then we describe the film's narrative, addressing the film's construction of characters as symbolic figures within neocolonialist narratives. We provide an extended discussion of how this film "civilizes" colonialism through a contemporary neocolonialist rhetoric. Finally, we discuss how this form of neocolonialism functions within contemporary society.

In part because neither of us is Native American, our critique of dominant representations of Native Americans does not attempt to explain what Native American culture is or how it should be represented. Thus, while we argue against what we see as damaging depictions of Native Americans, we choose neither to "set the record straight" on the history of Pocahontas nor to tell the "real story." Instead, following Rosaldo (1993) who noticed that "a mood of nostalgia makes racial domination appear innocent and pure" (p. 68), we attempt to unmask the neocolonial narrative of one particular text in order to initiate further discussion.

A GENERIC COLONIAL STORY

Disney's *Pocahontas* holds together Anglo Euro-colonialism at the point where it begins to unravel. For children and adults starting to rethink the legitimacy of colonialist practices, it provides a tightly woven answer in the consumable form of an amiable, innocent, accepting, nurturing, and feminine cartoon figure: Pocahontas. *Pocahontas* transforms colonialism into a benevolent ideology of good will, proto-environmentalism, proto-feminism, and cross-cultural tolerance, a soothing tonic with which to heal public social ills. As such, *Pocahontas* is a neocolonialist text. It masks present-day colonialist relations inherited from the past and appropriates contemporary social issues such as feminism, environmentalism, and human freedom in order to justify both fear of people of color and beliefs of their inferiority.

Colonialist practices today operate for the most part under the conscious threshold of the contemporary popular imagination. Thus, neocolonialism is contemporary culture's willful blindness to the historical legacy of colonialism enacted in the present. Contemporary culture masks the *continuing* lived history of people disenfranchised by colonialism by failing to acknowledge colonialism's presence in the U.S. today. Whereas colonialists killed Native Americans and later justified it, neocolonialists depend on a history of successful colonialism, forgetfulness that colonialism continues, and the production of therapeutic public stories to quell any lingering dis-ease with continuing practices of disenfranchisement.

Colonialism in the United States was never overthrown; the Anglo-colonizer was never cast out, and native peoples never regained political control. Indeed, the ideology of colonialism was rewoven into the social fabric through popular cultural products such as movies, television, novels, radio, and consumer goods, as well as more pedagogical media: textbooks, military training manuals, and religious texts. Neocolonialism is the contemporary form that colonialism begat: a remodeled colonialist ideology for the present. Neocolonialism employs contemporary ideological and economic strategies to make racism, genocide, sexism, nationalism, and inequitable capital distribution appear necessary. Neocolonialism pretends to offer a kinder version of present global economics than past colonialism; hence, its presence may at times be quite subtle.

Pocahontas is a complex rhetorical object which offers a particular system of beliefs about the world. The film relies on historical representations and, thus, does not persuade audience members to accept a new ideology so much as it ratifies their unspoken, taken-for-granted attitudes and assumptions about colonialism's necessity. A critique of gender relations, narrative, or ideology alone would be insufficient to explain the complex racial dynamics, the specificity of representations of Native Americans, or the historical significance of colonialism in this film. However, a critique of neocolonialism combines these concerns in order to answer a series of difficult questions evoked by *Pocahontas*: What is the relationship between the construction of nature and of Native American women? How does the text differentiate between two colonialists: John Smith and Governor Ratcliffe? Why and how does the text contrast Powhatan to Kocoum? And, finally, how do these representations function within the larger symbolic and narrative economy of neocolonial film portrayals? This critique of neocolonialism, then, addresses the complex rhetorical functions of cinema's representations of women, gender relations, Native Americans, and history within *Pocahontas*, and in so doing offers an enhanced understanding of popular culture's strategic neocolonialist appropriations of environmentalism, feminism, and multiculturalism.

While little research in communication studies has addressed the questions we ask above,[4] recent scholarship in other academic disciplines does attempt to explain what happens when colonizers invade a geographic region and claim it as their own. To explain this practice of colonization which, with variations, repeats itself cross-culturally on an international scale, we rely heavily on Sharpe's (1993) *Allegories of Empire: The Figure of Woman in the Colonial Text*. In addition, we use the works of various writers (e.g., Ahmed, 1992; Malkki, 1992; and Shohat, 1991) who address colonialism within divergent but specific contexts to scrutinize the story of "civilization."

Colonization begins when colonizers appropriate land, conquer indigenous people, and found colonialist governments to oversee the efficient operation of property and labor. Once they conquer indigenous peoples—eliminating the most threatening and enslaving the rest—*the civilizing process* begins. They teach the colonized the language, logic, and history of the colonizer. Colonizers force colonized people to submit to the colonizer's moral standards, laws, principles, and often religion (Christianity in the case of U.S. colonizers). However, this is not meant to imply that the colonized simply accept or even participate willingly in the civilizing process. Some colonized peoples may purposefully refuse to learn the religion, morals, and laws of their oppressors; and those who do may choose not to abide by rules of language.

Despite resistances and protests made by colonized people, colonizers produce narratives, histories, and fables describing their successful conquests. In those stories, colonialists typically depict the oppressed as barbarians and themselves as beneficent peoples acting in the best interests of all involved (Sharpe, 1993). Colonialists subdue rebellions and protests by "barbarians" who have not been properly civilized and who therefore continuously must be retaught their proper positions, roles, and stations within colonialist society. Such colonialist narratives tell us that natives ultimately need colonialism (to "progress") and that, despite their uneducated opinions, native peoples deep down really do desire the superiority, control, reason, and order colonialism offers (Shohat, 1991).

Colonial narratives also argue that colonialism was needed to rescue native women from oppressive native men.[5] In the name of saving women, colonialism presented itself as a necessary and benevolent force. As Ahmed (1992) points out, "Colonial feminism, or feminism as used against other cultures in the service of colonialism, was shaped into a variety of constructs, each tailored to fit the particular culture that was the immediate target of domination" (pp. 150–151). Thus, feminism is used as a rhetorical trope in colonialist narratives to justify colonialist domination of native women and men as well as colonial women.

Colonialism holds up the banner of "freedom" *for some* to justify and legitimate the servitude of *others*. Sharpe (1993) writes, "The development of a racial argument in response to the attack on slavery shows that the fixing signification of race is intimately bound up with a humanist discourse of emancipation" (p. 5). As the self-chosen emancipator of women, the colonial man in these narratives invades land and native culture in order to preserve white women's virtues and womanhood, both of which he invented as "a colonial iconography of martyrdom" (p. 55) to justify the civilizing mission. Colonial women's rescue from the clutches of darkness restores the moral order. Colonialism utilizes feminism and the concept of emancipation to guide women out of oppressive relationships with men; it becomes the grounds for feminist individualism (p. 55). Thus, the emancipation of white women is a model for the emancipation for her "lesser" women counterparts.

The colonialist narrative constructs the audience as *a sympathizer with acts of vengeance*; the audience becomes an accomplice to the crime of colonialism, an enablement of social power. For example, in discussing the Abolition Act of 1829 in which the British occupying India banned *sati* ritual suicides of women, Sharpe (1993) writes, "the European is a moral agent. The magistrate positions the horrified onlooker who is sympathetic to the widow's plight as one who is morally superior to the cruel and unfeeling crowd enjoying the spectacle" (p. 52). *Pocahontas* positions the viewer in a similar manner. The film asks for the viewer's sympathy with Pocahontas's plight, her entrapment within a patriarchal order which demands that she marry a man she does not love. Each and every person who crosses the boundary to sympathize with Pocahontas and dreams of her union with John Smith reinforces the legitimacy of the neocolonial narrative because such a crossing requires the viewer to participate in the justification of colonialism for the emancipation of dark women by enlightened white men. As such, neocolonialist narratives incorporate liberation discourses in an attempt to justify both historical and contemporary colonial practices. In order to explain how the neocolonial narrative *Pocahontas* accomplishes this, we turn specifically to an analysis of the film's narrative.

THE *POCAHONTAS* NARRATIVE

Pocahontas uses feminism, environmentalism, and multiculturalism to argue for the benevolent colonialism signified by John Smith versus the malevolent colonialism typified by Governor Ratcliffe. Through a happy cross-cultural encounter and a sharing of gifts, *Pocahontas* suggests that colonialism was simply one manifestation of today's preferable multicultural world. Furthermore, colonialists emancipate Pocahontas from Native American patriarchy by figuring Pocahontas as a woman dreaming of a more exciting life, or, as her counterpart Belle in *Beauty and the Beast* (1991) sings, "more than this provincial life"; for Pocahontas, adventure is "just around the riverbend." By pitting the "natural" Pocahontas and John Smith against the greedy Governor Ratcliffe, who wreaks havoc on the environment, *Pocahontas* affirms environmentalism while eliminating only Ratcliffe's form of colonialism. Thus, the *Pocahontas* narrative argues that the colonialism represented by Smith, when done properly, is a benevolent emancipatory process.

Disney's movie *Pocahontas* opens with members of the Virginia Company (all white men), headed by Governor John Ratcliffe, setting sail for the Americas to find their fortune—gold and land—and glory. On the voyage the crew endures dangerous sea weather that almost kills a crew member, Thomas. They also talk and sing joyfully about killing savages. When the crew arrives on the mainland, Pocahontas, who has realized she wants more for her life than marrying the suitor (Kocoum) chosen by her father (Powhatan), sees the white sails of the incoming ship. John Smith, the experienced colonizer and all-around heroic figure, later spies Pocahontas through the sights of his gun. They meet and their evolving romance coincides with growing tensions between the native people and the colonizers, who have begun to build a camp and tear up the land in their search for gold.

The culmination of these tensions is the death of Kocoum, the suitor chosen for Pocahontas by her father. Thomas, the boy Smith rescued earlier from the clutches of the sea, shoots Kocoum. Thomas's shooting of Kocoum and the native peoples' (subsequent) "capture" of Smith leads to warfare between the Native Americans and colonialists. Pocahontas takes it upon herself to prevent further bloodshed. As the native people, led by Powhatan, approach the crest of a precipice where they intend to kill Smith, Pocahontas runs valiantly to rescue him. With the aid of the wind, eagle, and various other natural spirits, she jumps in front of the death blow her father is about to deliver to her suitor. The colonizers and the Powhatans suddenly realize the error of their warring ways and put their weapons down to "fight no more." However, the Governor, blinded by greed, turns on the Powhatans and, in an attempt to shoot Chief Powhatan, hits Smith instead. The colonialists then turn on the bloodthirsty governor and, finally convinced of his villainy, bind him in chains and gag him for the trip back to England.

Despite Smith's invitation, Pocahontas opts to remain with her people and bids Smith a sad farewell.

In the process of telling a story of romance, the film imbues each character and each relationship between characters with specific meanings. The film codes main characters with features, attributes, actions, and values typical of characters within the colonial narrative. As a result, each character represents a particular ideological position in the colonial world. However, by ornamenting these characters with certain details, the film not only creates possibilities for audience associations between the film and the neocolonialist narrative, but also gives each character greater ideological resonances with other characters.

Three sets of dialectical connections between characters help the film construct a neocolonial ideological economy. That is, neocolonial ideology establishes a series of relationships of power and maintains those relationships to allow for efficient operation of the colonialist logic. However, the colonialist narrative differs from the neocolonialist one in specific ways. Colonialism produces a rape threat in order to justify future insurgencies and past actions; neocolonialism cites, appropriates, and reinscribes past colonialism onto the present in order to produce a feminist heroine and privilege her romance over contemporary social problems. Moreover, whereas colonialism grounds its logic within a feminism that subscribes to a morality of virtues existing prior to the 1800s, contemporary neocolonialism utilizes a postfeminist rhetoric that assumes feminism happened, was successful, and no longer is necessary except to free colonized pre-feminist women from their masculine oppressors. This postfeminist rhetoric relies on the legacy of a 1960s modernist feminism of individualism to make its argument. Thus, both colonialism and neocolonialism rely on a kind of feminist discourse. However, neocolonialism strategically employs the rhetoric of contemporary social movements for liberation, such as environmentalism and multiculturalism. In contrast, colonialism safeguards morality by depicting woman-as-victim, thus producing the rape threat and justifying the grounds for saving her via invasion. Individual characters, especially as they contrast or align with other characters, symbolize allegorical ideological relationships within the neocolonialist textual economy.

Pocahontas/Nature

Pocahontas not only tells the story of a powerful Native American heroine, it also establishes a relationship between women and nature typical of colonialist narratives. While it might seem odd at first to suggest that nature functions as a character, in the context of a Disney animated film in which a tree has arms, a face, and speaks, it makes sense to do so. Indeed, Flit the bird and Meeko the raccoon not only make noises that imply rudimentary language skills, but also interrupt people, point to objects, and have distinct personalities. Powhatan and Kekata, the Powhatan shaman, define the wind as Pocahontas's mother, and the wind comforts her, carries messages to her, and helps her think, talk, walk, and paddle. Thus, the film inscribes human characteristics onto natural phenomena and, through this anthropomorphic lens, also cultures and genders nature.

Indeed, the film draws an essentialist connection between women and nature by implying that both require colonization. The film portrays Native American women as caretakers of nature and, in turn, depicts nature as caretaker of all people.[6] Thus, while men canoe, fraternize, and wage wars, Powhatan women, except for Pocahontas herself, plant corn and gather food. While for other women the corn fields represent work, for princess Pocahontas the cornfield represents the site of her romantic interludes with Smith. Pocahontas, who at one point picks one ear of corn but then stops, is more accurately the corn waiting to be picked.

Similarly, in *Pocahontas*, the landscape of the Americas is wide open, lush, pristine, beautiful, and full of "resources." Perhaps reading these descriptors as ideally feminine, the colonialists give the land a woman's name, Virginia,[7] and the Governor announces that the colonialists claim this land as Jamestown, the first settlement of Virginia, for King James. The depiction here of civilized masculinity settling on virgin female land enhances rather than detracts from the colonialist logic. As Shohat (1991) writes:

> the notion of "virginity," present for example in the etymology of Virginia, must be seen [in] diacritical relation to the metaphor of the (European) "motherland." A "virgin" land is implicitly available for defloration and fecundation. Implied to lack owners, it therefore becomes the property of its "discoverers" and cultivators . . . . A land already fecund, already producing for the indigenous peoples, and thus a "mother," is metaphorically projected as virgin, "untouched nature," and therefore as available and awaiting a master. (p. 47)

As Shohat (1991) intimates, the image of empty, pristine land awaiting colonization defines the film's central protagonist, Pocahontas, as well. The film depicts her as a young woman "coming of age." Although the film does not say this overtly, it invites us to understand her romance with Smith as her first relationship. Her closest friend, Nakoma, to whom she entrusts her secrets, makes no mention of anyone prior to him, even during moments when they are alone discussing men. Moreover, because the text lets us know that the Powhatans subscribe to the practice of arranged marriages, and because Powhatan announces Pocahontas's marriage to Kocoum, we are encouraged to assume she has had no prior suitors.

In addition to her portrayal as a virgin, the film also depicts Pocahontas in other ways associated with the land—specifically, as landscape and as animal. For instance, at the very beginning of the film when Pocahontas observes the ship approach the shore, she crawls up to the rock's precipice on all fours and flattens herself to blend in with the landscape in order to see without being seen. Similarly, when John Smith climbs the rock face, Pocahontas hides, crouching down low behind the bushes, and quiets the animals who might attract Smith's attention. Further, Smith's first vision of Pocahontas is her image reflected in the stream water he cups in his hands. In this first view, Smith sees her only as a reflection of and through nature. Not only does she bend low and double as the landscape itself, but one repeated shot in the film trailers shows her running and jumping off a cliff, doing a "swan dive" with wing-like suspension before disappearing into the water below. She not only is connected to the land, but through her movements begins to resemble it.

Unlike Pocahontas, who is able to walk, run, and float, and whose body is coded as natural and feminine, Grandmother Willow, the magical tree with whom Pocahontas secretly talks, remains rooted to the earth. Whereas Pocahontas *begins* to resemble the land, Grandmother Willow is indistinguishable from it. While Willow also is coded as a woman, this centuries-old tree is a bodiless but humanized caretaker of small wild animals and Powhatan women. In contrast to Pocahontas, Willow is more nature than human. Although she speaks, has a face, arms, and even a history, this "Grandmother" who tells Pocahontas of her own mother's past cannot ambulate, which means she receives no social contact unless people see fit to visit her. Apparently, women with too much nature tend toward paralysis.

Despite the fact that we learn that she gains pleasure from looking at John Smith's (hence men's) body when she tells Pocahontas that Smith is "handsome, too," Grandmother Willow has no human body to move toward romance. She merely supplies advice and information about romance. To illustrate the travails of romance, she tells Pocahontas about the marriage between Powhatan and Pocahontas's mother (nameless, except insofar as she is presented allegorically as "The Wind," as indicated in the credits). And while she finds matchmaking more fun, Willow's primary role as both nature and grandmother is that of caretaker. She is Pocahontas's spiritual guide and the protector of those incapable of taking care of themselves (i.e., the forest's small creatures). For example, when Lon and Ben, two members of the ship's crew to whom the film gives names and faces, come searching for Smith, Grandmother Willow hides Smith and Pocahontas. She then scares off Lon and Ben by lifting a root (leg) to trip them and snapping them with "vines," an action that both protects her granddaughter and fuels the English settlers' beliefs that this new land is mystical, haunted, and inhabited by savages—that they are, in fact, in alien territory.

The wind appears as an even less tangible form of femininity and nature than the nearly petrified Willow. As magical connector and mediator, the wind has no personality or voice; she is simply an ethereal spiritual guide, visible only as enveloping swirls of leaves and mystical symbols around Pocahontas. Her main purpose in the film is to lead Pocahontas to follow her heart, which is recognition of her love for John Smith.

Still, the wind has another important role in the film: she brings Smith to Pocahontas. In creating a tremendous storm at sea, the wind sets the stage for John Smith's heroic rescue of Thomas and fans the sails for the "new" world. During the storm in the Atlantic, the wind tosses the colonizers' ship, the *Susan Constant*. The wind's gusts and waves nearly swallow the boat and ultimately cast Thomas overboard. After John Smith saves Thomas and both are back on deck, the wind stops blowing. As an invisible, omniscient character, the wind witnesses John Smith's heroic act, an act which demonstrates his suitability for Pocahontas. Just as Powhatan ultimately offers gifts to John Smith, the wind brings John Smith to Pocahontas with a stamped seal of approval.

In addition to acting as Pocahontas's protector, the wind—as Pocahontas's benevolent mother—both accompanies and educates Pocahontas. Kekata, the shaman, enunciates the link between Pocahontas and the wind when he says, "You know Pocahontas. She has her mother's spirit. She goes wherever the wind takes her." At this moment the film cuts to Pocahontas standing high above her people while the wind and leaves circle around her. The wind embodies the spirit of her desire for freedom and adventure. While talking to Pocahontas, Powhatan says of her mother, "She is still with us. Whenever the wind moves through the trees, I feel her presence." Later, when Grandmother Willow tells Pocahontas to listen to the voice of the wind, she ultimately chooses the direction of the colonizer.

Smith/Ratcliffe

Unlike Pocahontas's identification with nature, John Smith gains identity in relation to other men. John Smith is a bit clumsy in nature, but as the Anglo victor he has the power to overcome natural obstacles and other men. On "her turf," John Smith not only spies on Pocahontas without her realizing his presence, but he also outruns and outclimbs her throughout the film. Symbolically, then, civilization overcomes nature. In scenes with John Smith and Pocahontas, the film often portrays their relationship as more of a friendly competition between hunter and hunted than as a simple tale of attraction between woman and man.

The film also contrasts Smith's comfortable relationship with nature/Pocahontas with the discomfort of Ratcliffe and shipmates. While Ratcliffe plunders nature without conscience, Ben and Lon express skepticism and fear toward nature when Grandmother Willow trips them. John Smith, however, shows no fear in the face of nature (Thomas's rescue), and indeed, sees nature as a cherished possession: a conquered love versus a conquered foe. Through a series of contrasts between Smith and other men, the film develops his superiority and the superiority of the values and world view he embodies.

John Smith and Governor John Ratcliffe offer two versions of the male colonialist—one friendly, the other villainous. The film invites audience members to choose between these contrasting representations of the colonialist by seeing Smith's kind of colonialism as heroic and good and Ratcliffe as exploitative and evil. If the film succeeds in gaining our compliance with its fantasy, it will convince us via the fallacious assertion that only two colonial alternatives exist that we must choose one. While one form of colonialism makes no sense, the other form *does*. The film encourages us to rationalize Smith's colonialist practices of befriending native peoples, educating them, and making them understand the benefits of colonialism over the only other alternative. Thus, when the other colonialist Ratcliffe shoots at Powhatan with a gun, the colonialist Smith jumps in front of Powhatan and takes the bullet. As a result of his bravery, Smith reveals Ratcliffe's sinister purpose, which renders Smith the hero not the traitor that the crew originally suspects him to be. Smith's successful differentiation from the villainous Ratcliffe earns him Pocahontas's love, the spectator's trust, and his fellows' admiration.

Indeed, Smith is so much the hero of the film that he threatens to upstage Pocahontas, the character for whom the film was titled. Smith's bright blond hair represents the white alternative to dark Native American masculinity; Smith is a pro-feminist alternative to Native American patriarchy. Smith smiles, laughs, and even gives biscuits and a compass to Meeko, the raccoon. Unlike Pocahontas's father, Smith relates to and understands Pocahontas as a person; he supports her efforts to liberate herself as a woman from the confines of what the film codes as oppressive Native American patriarchy and to embrace the good, woman-supportive patriarchy Smith symbolizes. He abides by and respects her decisions. Unlike Kocoum, whom Powhatan understatedly describes as "stable," Smith bends, as we see during Pocahontas's lessons to him about nature. For instance, when Smith points his gun at a bear, he lets her touch his rifle and push down gently.[8] Later, he watches her run home without following. And, at the end of the film, though he invites her to come with him, he abides by her decision to stay with her people in the Americas.

While the film feminizes Smith by making him the perfect understanding masculine companion for today's liberated (into couplist heterosexual romance) Pocahontas, the film simultaneously depicts him as the ultimate superior warrior. For instance, before his ship lands he boasts of killing "savages" and even brags to Thomas, "you just worry about that fortune of yours, Thomas, leave the savages to me." From there, we witness the moral transformation of his character from ruthless savage-killer to nonviolent lover. Although the film poses no verbal argument countering the white supremacist rhetoric he espouses before they set sail, he does later fall in love with Pocahontas and, in order to challenge his shipmates' racism, tells them of this affair.

Although Smith ends his conquest of Native Americans, he retains his fighting acumen, physical prowess, and agility. We witness his bravery when he dives headlong into the ocean to save Thomas during a raging storm. In London, he initially boards the ship by standing on a cannon being hoisted on a rope into the air; he later swings from branches, climbs rock faces, and builds bridges with tree logs lickety-split. Even after falling in love with Pocahontas he teaches the awkward Thomas how to shoot a gun. In the end, Powhatan rewards his bravery with baskets of possessions brought to him by compliant natives and dubs him a close (white) friend of the Powhatans. Though he retains his masculine prowess— jumping to take a bullet—he gains a "feminine sensitivity" for the liberated woman through flexibility that helps him learn from his encounter with Pocahontas and nature.

Through his flexibility and strength, Smith becomes the moral hero of the film. After Thomas kills Kocoum and the Powhatans capture Smith, a shot of Smith shows him with head bowed, on his knees, hands bound to a wooden post and crossbar. Condemned to die an "innocent" man, Smith tells Pocahontas— when she enters the tepee—that he is willing to sacrifice his life for the benefit of all. He says all he desires is to be remembered and that, through their memories, he will live on. As the embodied figure of Christ, Smith stands for a morally superior civilizing force. As Sharpe (1993) suggests, he takes on "the white man's burden that represents colonialism as an act of martyrdom" (p. 122).

The film not only depicts Smith as a martyr but also as a philanthropist. We learn in the opening scene that wealth does not interest him. He does not conduct his missions into the "hundreds of new worlds" for wealth but for adventure. Once he befriends Pocahontas, he begins to see what good civilization can bring and tells her that his people will bring order to and increase the quality of life for the technologically backward savages. As evidence of his generosity and intent to help, he helps her out of the water by offering his hand, saying, "let me help you out of there." In the role of the helping teacher who colonizes, Smith is a benevolent, moral missionary, not a ravaging, greedy, materialist, selfish proprietor— like Ratcliffe.

Whereas Smith is the virtuous hero of the film, Ratcliffe is its arch-villain. From the beginning of the film, when he underplays Smith's successful rescue of Thomas, Ratcliffe's role as antagonist is evident. Not unlike Jafar in *Aladdin* (1992), Ratcliffe is the supremely devilish "fall guy" whom audiences "just love to hate." The film presents him as an obese, gluttonous, pompous, greedy, and only marginally competent leader who promotes the white supremacy of the Virginia Company's men by waging a campaign of suspicion, anxiety, and fear against the Powhatans.

Not surprisingly, the film portrays Ratcliffe as Smith's alter ego. Whereas Smith is kind, generous, and caring, Ratcliffe is deceitful, unscrupulous, and abusive. Whereas Smith searches for adventure, Ratcliffe searches for gold; his underlying motive is not only to find it, but to take more than his share. Whereas Smith learns from his mistakes and stops killing savages, Ratcliffe remains unchanged in his assessment of Native Americans as "filthy little heathens." Self-absorbed, Ratcliffe relentlessly chases his dreams, despite the harm he does to others.

The tensions between Ratcliffe and Smith are hierarchical as well as ideological. Unlike the "lower class" Anglo employees who work for Ratcliffe, the well-groomed Smith prances off into the forest to meet Pocahontas at his will. Ever distrustful, Ratcliffe sends Thomas to spy on Smith when he leaves camp. As a result, Thomas not only tells Ratcliffe about Smith's actions and whereabouts, but intervenes in a fight between Smith and Kocoum, shooting and killing Kocoum. But while the film codes Thomas's shooting of Kocoum as naively following the orders of Ratcliffe, it depicts Ratcliffe as deliberately shooting Powhatan. Thus, when Smith intercedes, the crew turns on Ratcliffe and arrests him.

Through these contrasting portraits of Smith and Ratcliffe, the film shifts all guilt for colonialism's wrongs—racism, antipathy, and violence—onto the evil character of Ratcliffe. By positioning Ratcliffe as the scapegoat, the film grooms Smith as its hero. Throughout most of the movie, Ratcliffe successfully coerces naive settlers into accompanying him on quests for material wealth. The film portrays the settlers as witless common folk caught within the web of Ratcliffe's immoral and illicit scheme and, hence, as unknowing agents of colonialism. The movie excuses their actions and transfers their responsibility onto Ratcliffe, who bears the brunt of the burden of colonialism's wrongs.

In the end, the crew takes Ratcliffe and all of the evils of colonialism he represents back home to England.[9] Although the film does not elaborate on Ratcliffe's imprisonment and Smith's heroism, Smith nonetheless emerges as a wounded victor. He understands that his mission to liberate Pocahontas is a civilizing mission which first requires colonialism and then a magical romance to eliminate any mixed emotions about living on stolen land. Because he recognizes Pocahontas and civilization as the objects of his quest, instead of gold and conquest, he is the neocolonial counter to Ratcliffe's colonialism.

Powhatan/Kocoum

In contrast to Smith, Kocoum is portrayed as a rape threat to Pocahontas, and Powhatan symbolizes oppressive Native American patriarchy eventually transformed. While Ratcliffe suffers ignominy and Kocoum dies, Powhatan lives.

Powhatan represents the potential success of colonialism, the conversion of the chief from a competitor of colonialism to a thankful friend of kind, selfless colonialists. From the beginning of the film, Powhatan and Pocahontas do get along well, but Powhatan does not understand his daughter. Pocahontas's resemblance to his deceased wife gives the traditional Powhatan pleasure. Still, Powhatan sees Pocahontas duty-bound to wed whomever he chooses. The conversion of Powhatan from distant patriarchal ruler to caring and understanding parent parallels his growing friendship with colonialists. As a father who does not really understand his daughter, he also does not understand the benevolence of colonialism and, therefore, initially wants to wage war against the colonialists for having killed Kocoum. However, when Pocahontas puts her body on the line to save John Smith, Powhatan realizes he cannot club *her* to death and accepts his daughter's "wisdom," which he says is "beyond her years." Later, when Smith risks his own life to save Powhatan, Powhatan decides that Smith really is a friend to the Powhatan people and, in a gesture of friendship, gives Smith his fur coat saying, "Thank you, my brother."

Powhatan's transformation from pre- to post-feminist man, from warrior to "brother," allows him to understand and accept his daughter's desires and consequently the benevolence of colonialism. Kocoum, the "stable" one, never makes such a change. Because Kocoum steadfastly defies and threatens colonialism, he is the film's major obstacle to it. Hence, Kocoum's death signifies the elimination of the "Native" from "Native American."

By foregrounding certain traits, the film dehumanizes Kocoum, depicting him as "savage"—inscrutable, stoic, irrational, and animalistic. Kocoum wants only to preserve himself and his people by fighting and reproducing. As the masculine threat to colonialism, Kocoum represents the pre-feminist, anti-liberatory, and "uncivilized" native man, in contrast to Powhatan who is transformed into a postfeminist.

Kocoum wants Pocahontas as a possession, but expresses no love for her. Of course, we know from the outset that Kocoum will never possess Pocahontas. He is, as Pocahontas and Grandmother Willow tell us, "so serious," hence, unreformably inscrutable. Pocahontas dismisses Kocoum's advances and indicates that any attempt by him to "capture" her is unwanted and undesired. Although Powhatan states that Kocoum is the tribe's greatest warrior (hence, representing the "good" values of Disney's Native Americans), Pocahontas still does not see him as good enough for her. As a result, Kocoum represents the rape threat that justifies his elimination from the film.

In addition to his behavioral persona, Kocoum reinforces oppressive patriarchy through his words. Throughout the film he speaks for two reasons only. First, he argues at the council meeting that the tribe must fight the colonizers. Referring to the first scene in which we see Native Americans, who are returning from war, Kocoum states, "I will lead our warriors to the river and attack. We will destroy these invaders the way we destroyed the Massawomeks." While he distinguishes between native civilizations, Kocoum nonetheless speaks simplistically and unreasonably (a distinction Disney probably would not have acknowledged even ten years ago), incapable of recognizing the benevolence of colonialists.

Kocoum also speaks when he tells Nakoma that Pocahontas ought to stay close to the village and discontinue her adventuresome walks outside the village and his control. Kocoum's attempt to keep Pocahontas close to the hearth illustrates the patriarchal view that men must protect weak women who might endanger themselves. Through few words and actions, Kocoum enacts the stereotypical Hollywood representation of Native Americans: the stoic, silent, strong dark-skinned warrior always ready to kill. In several shots in the film, his chest sticks out, emphasizing the bear prints the shaman Kekata places on his pectorals, and foregrounding the excessive sexuality that makes him so frightening to the colonizers. Because Kocoum is such an ominous threat, both his death and the success of Smith as suitor are justified.

Smith represents civilization, whereas Kocoum embodies native peoples' lack of civility. Kocoum attacks John Smith not because he loves Pocahontas, but because his nature is war-like. He must fight. He cannot discuss; he does not speak the colonizer's tongue, so he must use weapons. He reacts impulsively and irrationally with violence.

Disney's depiction of Kocoum as a barbaric representative of an inferior animalistic race that requires the civilizing force of colonialism reverberates with the colonial narrative's conventional portrayal of non-white peoples as non-human. This image legitimates and justifies Kocoum's death, for as the uncivilizable native man, he threatens colonialism itself. In contrast, Powhatan, who speaks, discusses, and demonstrates the potential for civilization, can live.

*   *   *

Pocahontas links the colonial justification of taking land with its parallel justification of colonizing women through a definition of both as possessions. By depicting woman and nature, both and together, as objects, the film rationalizes colonialist domination as a "natural" effect of colonialist superiority. Colonization of land and women go hand in hand. The colonization (i.e., the physical occupation and *use*) of property and women in order to liberate them (from the danger of barbarous dark native males) is retold in the neocolonialist narrative of *Pocahontas*. The film tells the story of colonizers who survey and then produce a "new world" for their own purposes, who see land as a "natural" resource containing gold, and who gain access to it by eliminating Native Americans who challenge their right to take the land. In part, the film eliminates Native American claims by constructing them as backward, pre-scientific, and nonprogressive: because they have not *utilized* the land properly, exploited it to its fullest potential, they deserve to lose it to those who will.

The film defines the landscape as empty and Pocahontas as virgin in order to justify colonial invasion. While the opening shot of the film depicts a burgeoning urban London, the final shot of the film shows land and water comparatively "empty" of civilization. The visual strategy here displaces the indigenous peoples from the land, erases them, and portrays the land as a "new frontier" waiting to be conquered.[10] Like its images of land, the film depicts Pocahontas as mismanaged within Native American patriarchy; as a result, according to Disney, white colonizers justifiably vie for her as a sexual commodity.

In order to rationalize her as a possession to be taken, the film eroticizes and fetishizes Pocahontas. Pocahontas matters only insofar as she is a body, a form on which to play out the ravages of colonialism. She is an exotic creature capable of jumping off three hundred foot waterfalls, of conjuring up magical winds that give humans the ability to fly, and of painting "with all the colors of the wind." Disney constructs Pocahontas as a mystical, mist-shrouded object of desire for the heterosexual white colonizer Smith. The film endows her female body with the largest chest, the smallest feet and waist, the biggest almond-shaped eyes, and the longest hair of any character in the movie. Colonial narrative logic dictates that colonizers must protect women from barbaric men; thus, the discourse *objectifies women in the name of genocide*. As Sharpe (1993) argues, "The slippage between the violation of English women as the object of rape and the violation of colonialism as the object of rebellion permits the moral value of the domestic woman—her self-sacrifice, duty, and devotion—to be extended to the social mission of colonialism" (p. 68).

The construction of the colonialist man in two distinct forms—one good, one bad—functions strategically to limit the choices spectators of the film can make about the rationality of colonialism from a contemporary standpoint. The film constructs Smith as the blond hero who rightfully gains the affection of the film's female protagonist. By juxtaposing Smith against Ratcliffe, and then by constructing Smith as the representative of "good colonialism," the film recuperates other ideological implications of colonialism in the neocolonialist narrative. The film asserts the inherent superiority of the missionary over the ruthless, money-grubbing, narcissistic nationalist who colonizes. Thus, from a contemporary perspective, the film rationalizes colonialism by opting for the missionary who, while he once killed, comes to realize the importance of learning about others. Smith becomes an allegory for the present political situation that retains its colonialist history by rationalizing colonialism: eliminating the negative associations of colonialism with ruthless materialism and resignifying colonialism as a positive value in a multicultural world. Moreover, by limiting the spectator's choices, the film implies these are the only options available. Thus, by portraying two sides of colonialism as dichotomous, the film also suggests that they cannot both exist at the same time: one must die for the other to live.

Benevolent colonialism cannot win the day, however, without the concurrent elimination of the only other identifiable threat to its existence—the dark, colonized man. The film constructs a negative image of Native American masculinity as detrimental to the expansion of the civilized colonialist mission, and, thus, in need of eradication. The film uses Kocoum to implicate Native Americans in the colonial battle, and fashions Kocoum and Ratcliffe as two equal and opposite malevolent forces. Moreover, because Native American masculinity inheres in the character of Kocoum, the film must emasculate and then eliminate him so he can be seen neither as worthy of the affections of women nor as a threat to dominant colonialist masculinity. This is accomplished when Thomas, who has just learned how to use a gun, shoots Kocoum. Kocoum's powers as a warrior prove inadequate when compared with the technological advancement of civilized peoples. This implies that while technology may not always be desirable, the colonial subject must continue to acquire knowledge and power of technology in order to survive.[11]

Kocoum's death allegorically symbolizes the death of all Native Americans and allows the film to justify its construction of Native American history as a fable. In his place remain the transformed, civilized Pocahontas and Powhatan and, of course, the civilizer Smith and his heir apparent, Thomas, also the alleged name of the real life Pocahontas's and her husband John Rolfe's child.

CONCLUSION

The colonial narrative in Pocahontas attempts to answer the question of "why did he/we do it?" by arguing for the necessity of a civilizing mission. Although the film pretends to offer a more culturally sensitive text, it merely provides a more contemporary version of the colonial narrative—a neocolonial narrative. This narrative does three things: first, it establishes Pocahontas as contra-Native Americans; second, it demonstrates that she must be freed from her patriarchal people in order to gain freedom; third, because she remains part of nature and therefore backwards, it confirms that she must be educated into the ways of colonialism.

Although the film codes Pocahontas as a free spirit by relating her genealogically to the wind, the film represents her as a confined woman in her first encounter with her father. Pocahontas is imprisoned within a patriarchal society where arranged marriages are a cultural ritual. Having been betrothed to the strongest warrior against her will, Pocahontas protests her entrapment. She cringes and physically wilts, and the leaves and wind of her mother stop circling around her in the darkness of her father's lodge.

The film portrays Pocahontas as a prisoner, wrongfully and immorally trapped within a backward and pre-scientific culture. Typical of filmic representations of colonialist narratives, in *Pocahontas*,

> not only has the Western imaginary metaphorically rendered the colonized land as a female to be saved from her environ/mental disorder, it has also projected rather more literal narratives of rescue, specifically of Western and non-Western women—from African, Asian, Arab, or Native American men. The figure of the Arab assassin/rapist . . . helps produce the narrative and ideological role of the Western liberator as integral to the colonial rescue phantasy. (Shohat, 1991, pp. 62–63)

Disney depicts Pocahontas needing freedom from oppression, not simply because she is trapped within a patriarchal and savage community, but also because she is both free of and captive to her culture.

While Powhatan and Kocoum are obsessed with waging and winning war and protecting honor, Pocahontas dreams of liberation through romance. The two are logically connected: while free to choose Smith, Pocahontas could do no less; the narrative logic of colonialism, including the heterosexist patriarchal ideology of consensual marriage, necessitates that choice. The film depicts a woman's choice as a *fait accompli*. What Addison (1993) says about *Aladdin* applies equally well to Disney's newest animated film:

> *Aladdin* offers up, in the character of Jasmine, a pseudo-feminist image in service of a deeply racist film, a film which animatedly reinscribes at least two American cultural strategies. The first is a domestic strategy which shapes gender conceptions: the mystification of power through romantic love, and the packaging of romantic love as a freedom for women. (p. 19)

Like *Aladdin*, *Pocahontas* asks the viewer to "'free' her from the Arab-Islamic [Native American] social order. . . . Indeed, Aladdin [John Smith] seduces Jasmine [Pocahontas] by offering to show her 'a whole new world'" (Addison, 1993, p. 12). The difference here is that in *Pocahontas* the "new world" is literally "*the* new world*."

Pocahontas can "discover" true romance only outside Native American culture and in Western patterns of thought, which further justifies the colonial narrative. *Pocahontas* legitimizes colonialism and the continuing reproduction of a woman in need of rescue both from entrapment and the threat of rape. In order for Pocahontas to "find her way" out of her Native American entrapment, the ideology of colonialism offers her three tools: language, science and, ironically, fear of miscegenation.

Pocahontas uses language to relate to Smith and to gain understanding of the colonizer's civil culture. Pocahontas learns English through her connection to nature, the wind, and her "innate feminine" emotional desire to find true bourgeois romance "just around the riverbend." For example, when Smith helps Pocahontas out of the river, the wind and leaves flow around her and the voice of Grandmother Willow sings "Listen with your heart. You will understand." Magically, Pocahontas responds to Smith's question, "Who are you?" by closing her eyes, listening with her heart, and responding, "Pocahontas . . . . My name is Pocahontas." By listening to her pure heart and the wind, she comprehends and speaks English; the civilizing process does not require the arduous battle colonialists waged, but rather is an instantaneous effect of animated film production that civilizes Pocahontas magically.

When Pocahontas opens her mouth to tell Smith who she is, she also names herself in his English, "Pocahontas." Thus, she fully articulates her identity only within a linguistically constructed colonial subject position and in the context of being identified by Smith as an objectified other. *Pocahontas* celebrates the colonizers' practice of enforcing their language as the predominant tongue within the colonial relationship. Pocahontas, as the text's civilizable subject, takes part in this act without even thinking: *all she must do is listen to her heart and she will understand the path to freedom through colonization, the truth of scientific knowledge, and the irrationality of her own tongue.*

Yet, Pocahontas's choice of English is not an end in and of itself. Language, as an instrument of power and knowledge, also leads Pocahontas to a greater understanding of two other tools offered to her by the colonizer. Once she understands English, Pocahontas proves herself capable of understanding the logic of science and discovery—two central precepts of the colonial narrative. The film depicts scientific and geographical discovery through the compass. As a directional device, the compass points Pocahontas toward the "proper" suitor; it also points her toward truth and knowledge.

Even though Pocahontas seeks emotional clarity by speaking English, she still does not know how to act when she must save Smith's life. In this confusion, Meeko, the raccoon, brings Pocahontas Smith's compass. When we first see Pocahontas, Nakoma finds her contemplating a strange dream in which she sees an arrow. She tells Grandmother Willow: "as I look at it, it starts to spin . . . . It spins faster, and faster, and faster until suddenly, it stops." The arrow of Pocahontas's dream, as Grandmother Willow explains, "is pointing [Pocahontas] down [her] path." When Pocahontas asks her how she will find her path, Willow tells her to listen with her heart (i.e., to listen to romance). In this way, Pocahontas's dream and the compass also predetermine a path for Pocahontas, directing her to a heterosexual relationship with Smith. The compass places Pocahontas within both the colonial order and the stereotypical construction of woman as emotional. Pocahontas seeks understanding in the tools of science and discovery; the answers she receives help her better understand her emotional status rather than the typical rational world of understanding that enlightenment thinking offers.

While Pocahontas utilizes the compass to find her way in life (the more metaphorical use of the compass), explorers like John Smith use the compass to plot the lay of the land. When colonialists "discover" territory, the compass points to a *true* direction and makes it possible to map the territory for even further exploration and exploitation. The compass necessarily precedes the map. With compass and map in hand, the colonizers bring territory under their control and power. Because "maps are ineluctably a cultural system" (Harley, 1992, p. 232), they also indicate a particular cultural way of seeing. In *Pocahontas*, the compass represents the logic the colonized woman must be taught and is the means by which the land can be mapped. The film implies that without the compass the "new world" would still be "undiscovered" and Pocahontas's now-colonized world would never have been found. The compass is yet another tool for acquiring knowledge in the name of civilization and scientific discovery.

Scientific discovery provides the pretext for taming Pocahontas and nature, which are symbolically linked. Only through the Western concept of "discovery," which implies both action and agency, does Pocahontas learn the ways of peace and freedom. Shohat (1991) explains the relationships among femininity, nature, and discovery when she writes:

> The traditional discourse on nature as feminine—for example Francis Bacon's idea that insofar as we learn the laws of nature through science, we become her master, as we are now, in ignorance, "her thralls"—gains, within the colonial context, clear geopolitical implications. Bacon's search for expanding scientific knowledge is inseparable from the contemporaneous European geographical expansion. (p. 52)

The compass and scientific knowledge ultimately propel Pocahontas down the twin paths of what the film suggests are righteousness and truth while simultaneously opening up both territory and mind to future insurgencies. The arrow of Western logic points the way for the ever-expanding Western mind and its exploration into land conceptualized as property and femininity. The compass establishes the scientific link between women and nature that enables the colonizing mission to invade in the name of imperial expansion and Western freedom.

Even though colonialism manufactures the goal of freeing colonized women from colonized men's patriarchy, the romantic direction the compass alludes to between Smith and Pocahontas cannot be actualized. In today's neocolonial world, *Smith and Pocahontas's love must be extinguished in the name of racial preservation and anti-miscegenation*. Fear of miscegenation requires that the film portray the solitary Pocahontas returning to her people in order to spread the knowledge she learns from her benevolent colonial encounter. This knowledge is that the white colonizer presents a pure and moral civil world order where women are free to marry any man they desire as long as they assume the cultural identity of the colonizer through language, science, and anti-miscegenation.

Like Jasmine in *Aladdin*, Pocahontas "is captured by the American romance of coupling" (Addison, 1993, p. 19). However, in *Pocahontas* the coupling itself is averted because of the threat of miscegenation. Disney's *Pocahontas* masks interracial relationships by preventing the audience from witnessing the interracial affair. The film also prevents children from thinking about the eventual decimation and annihilation of most Native Americans as a result of colonization because anti-miscegenation represents another foundation of the colonial narrative. This racial threshold represents the fear and delight of miscegenation in Western form. In her relationship with Kocoum, *Pocahontas signifies the native woman requiring colonization as a means of freedom from the native man*.

Pocahontas is much more than an entertaining story for children and a light-hearted one for adults. *Pocahontas* enacts the colonialist narrative and in so doing legitimates a cultural framework rooted in racism, anti-miscegenation, patriarchy, and capitalism. This story cannot be separated from the cultural hegemony of colonialism. We believe the film is not merely, or even primarily, a cross-cultural love story of historical interest, but rather a colonialist narrative that rewrites the colonial expansion of 1492 to the present day as an allegedly necessary part in the process of liberating women from Native American men. The film employs the discourses of environmentalism, feminism, and multiculturalism to recuperate the colonial story. As a result, the film illustrates intersections of race, class, gender, and nature within neocolonial rhetoric, a newly told old story. In the end, Disney's *Pocahontas* answers the question "Why did he/we do it?" by maintaining the ideology of the ongoing civilizing mission in a contemporary form of neocolonialism.

Notes

[1] See, for example, two special issues of *American Indian Culture and Research Journal*; for a discussion of the Quincentenary in 1993, see Fixico (1993), Flynn (1993), Hale (1993), Hernandez-Reguant (1993), Morris (1993), and Riding In (1993).

[2] Disney's role in narrating neocolonialist narratives parallels its own colonization of mediated space. As Shohat (1991) suggests, "Western cinema not only inherited and disseminated colonial discourse, but also created a system of domination through monopolistic control of film distribution and exhibition in much of Asia, Africa, and Latin America" (p. 45). In addition to theme parks, Disney uses the airwaves as a kind of "imaginary homeland" (Anderson, 1983).

[3] *Christopher Columbus: The Discovery* (1992) and *1492: Conquest of Paradise* (1992) are examples.

[4] The closest example of analyses of communication and neocolonialism took place in a special issue of *Critical Studies in Mass Communication* called "Cultural Diversity" (1991). Three articles dedicated to discussing U.S. imperialism are authored by Schiller, Salwen, and Straubhaar. However, none of these articles addresses neocolonialism or the generic narrative as it relates to gender, race, nature, and history. Two exceptions that became available after this paper was written are a book by Rushing and Frentz (1995) and an article on postcolonialism and rhetoric by Shome (1996).

[5] See Addison's (1993) essay.

[6] This typical reading of Native Americans as closely bonded with nature takes place through a popular culture lens whose closest approximation of Native American spirituality is contemporary deep ecology. In fact, environmentalists tend to *utilize* the trope of Nature/Native American as either disappearing or dead. In this way, contemporary pop- and eco-discourses define Native Americans as a reference, strategy, or marker of an idealized politics.

[7] Naming initiates the process of taking possession of the land, of denying (an)other's claim to placement on a land and, therefore, of making that land into something for the colonizer and not for indigenous people.

[8] The film codes the gun throughout as men's access to masculinity, thereby linking masculinity to colonial power. In the beginning of the film, Smith rides a cannon onto the *Susan Constant*. After Ratcliffe spies some Powhatans, Thomas, an eager but novice marksperson, fires his gun between Ratcliffe's legs, startling him. After Ratcliffe shoots one of the Powhatan men, he chastises Thomas and says he will never be a man until he learns how to shoot a gun. Later in the film, in order to get Thomas to spy on Smith, Ratcliffe denigrates Thomas and tells him to shoot any native he sees. Eventually, Thomas does shoot his gun and kills Kocoum. One could argue, therefore, that Kocoum's death is directly related to the need for colonizing men to gain masculine approval from other colonial men.

[9] The film does not indicate whether any colonialists stay in "their" new settlement. Although Powhatan and his people bring gifts to the colonialists, the film remains ambiguous regarding the fate of the relationship between the Jamestown settlers and the Powhatan people.

[10] See, for example, Malkki's (1992) argument that people do not require physical removal from territory in order to be displaced from that space.

[11] See Rushing and Frentz (1995).

References

Addison, E. (1993). Saving other women from other men: Disney's *Aladdin*. *Camera Obscura*, *31*, 5–25.

Ahmed, L. (1992). *Women and gender in Islam*. New Haven, CT: Yale University Press.

Anderson, B. R. O. (1983). *Imagined communities: Reflections on the origin and spread of nationalism*. London: Verso.

Fixico, D. L. (1993). Encounter of two different worlds: The Columbus-Indian legacy of history. *American Indian Culture and Research Journal, 17*, 17–31.

Flynn, J. P. (1993). Christopher Columbus and the problems with history. *American Indian Culture and Research Journal, 17,* 11–16.

Hale, C. R. (1993). Documents related to the Quincentenary. *American Indian Culture and Research Journal, 17,* 229–240.

Harley, J. B. (1992). Deconstructing the map. In T. J. Barnes and J. S. Duncan (Eds.), *Writing worlds: Discourse, text and metaphor in the representation of landscape* (pp. 231–247). London: Routledge.

Hernandez-Reguant, A. (1993). The Columbus quincentenary and the politics of the "encounter." *American Indian Culture and Research Journal, 17,* 17–35.

Malkki, L. (1992). National Geographic: The rooting of peoples and the territorialization of national identity among scholars and refugees. *Cultural Anthropology, 7,* 24–44.

Morris, C. P. (1993). Who are these gentle people? *American Indian Culture and Research Journal, 17,* 1–15.

Riding In, J. (1993). The politics of the Columbus celebration: A perspective of myth and reality in United States society. *American Indian Culture and Research Journal, 17,* 1–9.

Rosaldo, R. (1993). *Culture and truth: The remaking of social analysis.* Boston: Beacon Press.

Rushing, J. H., & Frentz, T. S. (1995). *Projecting the shadow: The cyborg hero in American film.* Chicago: University of Chicago Press.

Salwen, M. (1991). Cultural imperialism: A media effects approach. *Critical Studies in Mass Communication, 8,* 13–28.

Schiller, H. I. (1991). Not yet the post-imperialist era. *Critical Studies in Mass Communication, 8,* 13–28.

Sharpe, J. (1993). *Allegories of empire: The figure of woman in the colonial text.* Minneapolis: University of Minnesota Press.

Shohat, E. (1991). Gender and culture of empire: Toward a feminist ethnography of the cinema. *Quarterly Review of Film and Video, 13,* 45–84.

Shome, R. (1996). Postcolonial interventions in the rhetorical canon: An "other" view. *Communication Theory, 6,* 40–59.

Straubhaar, J. D. (1991). Beyond media imperialism: Asymmetrical interdependence and cultural proximity. *Critical Studies in Mass Communication, 8,* 39–59.

Cyber Ideology
An Ideological Criticism of the
UNICEF, UNAIDS, and UNFPA Web Sites

Khadidiatou Ndiaye

The possibilities offered by the Internet have given people with the desire to make the world a global village the opportunity to make their dream a reality. The world is getting much closer because people everywhere now have an opportunity to share their beliefs, culture, and views online. Companies, agencies, and associations have seized the opportunity and are using the Internet to improve their accessibility and to allow people all over the world to read their messages.

As a global system representing 189 nations of the world, the United Nations (UN) can be considered the forum of the world, an organization that works to bring the world together to solve global issues. For such an organization, the Internet's potential for reaching populations all over the world is enormous, and UN officials were quick to tap into this potential. The foreword to *The Internet: An Introductory Guide for United Nations Organizations* addresses the importance of the Internet to the United Nations' work:

> The Internet is clearly a phenomenon of global significance. The implications for the United Nations family of organizations are tremendous. United Nations agencies have at their fingertips not only an effective tool for collaborative work, but also a far-reaching and popular mechanism for disseminating information to the entire global community. This works both ways: United Nations agencies become immediately accessible to a worldwide group of Internet users as well. (The U.N. joins the net, 1996, p. 1)

This global significance is due to the Internet's potential for erasing physical and social boundaries. Today, all agencies of the United Nations have structured Web sites.

In this essay, I offer an ideological criticism of the Web sites of the United Nations Children's Fund (UNICEF), the United Nations Populations Fund (UNFPA), and the Joint United Nations Programme on HIV/AIDS (UNAIDS). Using these three Web sites as artifacts for analysis, I will explore how inclusive the ideologies of UNICEF, UNFPA, and UNAIDS are as portrayed in these organizations' Web sites.

The question of inclusiveness is important in looking at the three Web sites because of the agencies' identity and public message. UNAIDS, UNFPA, and UNICEF are agencies of unity; they represent the world's efforts to fight relevant issues together. Because these agencies rely on the world's support to exist, they reinforce daily the principles of unity and talk often about working for all of the world's population. Analyzing the inclusiveness of the Web sites will allow us to see if they "practice what they preach." Looking at their Web sites is even more important if we consider the fact that the Internet is becoming one of the primary

This essay was written while Khadidiatou Ndiaye was a student in Karen A. Foss's rhetorical criticism class at the University of New Mexico in 2002. Used by permission of the author.

ways in which United Nations agencies communicate with the populations represented by the UN. Exploring the question of inclusiveness will make visible who is truly represented.

LOGGING ON: THE THREE WEB SITES AT A GLANCE

UNICEF, UNFPA, and UNAIDS are United Nations agencies dealing with social issues, including children's well-being, women, population concerns, and HIV/AIDS. The following descriptions of the Web sites of each of the agencies focus only on the main pages of the Web sites because these pages hold the central message provided by the agencies. That central message is the main vehicle through which the ideology is presented.

The United Nations Children's Fund (UNICEF) Web Site

The UNICEF Web site's main page is divided into four frames, one horizontal frame on top and three vertical frames. The UNICEF logo is placed in a prominent place on the top left of the page. The Web site is the most colorful of the three Web sites analyzed. The page uses two background colors, red as the main and orange for the top frame. Other colors are also used to separate the main points. There are three pictures on the page, with the first taking up considerable space. It features children wearing costumes and make-up, and all the children are carrying little boxes in forms of buses with the UNICEF inscription. The caption for this first picture reads: "It's time to Trick or Treat for UNICEF. This Halloween, children are collecting money to help children in developing countries." The children are all smiling, and most of the children look to be white, although discerning the race of two children is difficult because of the make-up they are wearing.

The second picture, which is much smaller, is of a young girl carrying an infant. The two children are looking directly at the camera; they are definitely not smiling and seem to be sad. We cannot tell how the two are dressed because the only clearly identified items are a scarf covering the young girl's head and a hat for the infant. On the bottom of the picture is the word "Afghanistan," suggesting that the two children are from that country.

The third picture is also small (the same size as the second one), and it captures the profile of a young girl. The young girl is white, is not smiling, and looks sad. There is no reference to her nationality, and at the bottom of the picture are the words "social monitor support."

There are also two images in the same frame with the small pictures. In the first image is a stack of books with the only words "our shared future" on the top and "Achebe-Morrison" on the bottom of the page. The last image has a map of Southern Africa and the words "updated" in small letters and "Southern African Crisis" in large capital letters. In the most prominent area of the page, the logo of UNICEF is used as a background with the words "United Nations Special Session on Children . . . Landmark goals for children . . . Click here for complete coverage" prominently placed in the middle of the box.

The Web page is interactive; the user sees additional topics just by placing the cursor on one of the main options. These options are "UNICEF in Action," "Highlights," "Information Resources," "Donations, Greeting Cards, & Gifts," "Press Centre," "Voices of Youth," and "About UNICEF."

The United Nations Population Fund (UNFPA) Web Site

The UNFPA Web site uses primarily three colors—dark blue, light blue, and white. There are three frames: one horizontal at the top of the page and two vertical, with the first vertical a margin frame. The UNFPA logo is located on the top left of the page with the dark blue background. There are two pictures on the page, one of which is very prominent and takes up almost the entire main frame. The picture depicts a woman carrying an infant in her arms. Both are looking directly at the camera with a grave—almost sad—expression. There is a series of phrases to the left of the picture: "UNFPA responds to Afghan Crisis" is written in large letters and "Relief Effort Aims to Save Women's Lives" and "How Can You Help" in smaller letters. The second picture is quite small and is located at the bottom of the page. The image is slightly faded and depicts a young woman staring directly into the camera with a neutral expression on her face. The caption below the picture is "UNFPA Initiative against Fistula."

The vertical margin frame is divided into three parts. The first part is called "Key Issues" and offers the following link topics: "Safe Motherhood," "Adolescent and Youth," "Gender Equity," "HIV/AIDS," "Population and Development Strategies," "Emergencies," and "Reproductive Health Commodities." The second part of the margin frame is titled "Global Reach," and its topics include "Africa, Arab States & Europe," "Asia & the Pacific," "Latin America & the Caribbean," and "Technical Support." The final frame is titled "Executive Board" and offers only one topic: "UNDP/UNFPA Executive Board."

Another important aspect of the UNFPA Web site is the "Latest News" feature, which offered three topics at the time of this analysis: "UNFPA Launches Two-Year Campaign to Fight Obstetric Fistula in Sub-Saharan Africa," "Afghan Health Officials to Learn from Iran's Experience," and "Malawi Food Crisis and Reproductive Health Concerns." In addition, the Web site has link options for journalists and information regarding a campaign titled "34 Millions Friend Campaign."

Joint United Nations Programme on HIV/AIDS (UNAIDS) Web Site

The third Web site used in this analysis is the UNAIDS Web site. Compared to the first two Web sites, the UNAIDS Web site is rather plain. No pictures are used, and the only image the Web site contains is the international symbol of AIDS, the red ribbon. The page has three vertical frames of equal size and one bottom frame. The logo of UNAIDS is located in the left in a prominent area. The content of the page is divided into topics, and red headings separate the topics links. The headings are "Latest News," which includes four separate topics. The first heading reads: "New education action plan launched," "Monitoring the declaration of the commitment on HIV/AIDS," and "AIDS fight under resourced." The second heading, "What's New," has 10 topics ranging from "UNAIDS report on the global HIV/AIDS epidemic" to "Cosponsor news." The "Upcoming Events" heading highlights an upcoming "Microcredit Summit," and the fourth heading, "Elsewhere on the Web," has one topic: "The Future of AIDS." The bottom frame has a library of information on the following topics: "For Journalists," "About UNAIDS," "Publications," "HIV/AIDS Info," and "Special Sections."

FROM SURFACE TO REAL IDEOLOGIES

An ideology is a pattern or set of ideas, assumptions, beliefs, values, or interpretations of the world by which a group operates. As a large organization with members all over the world, the United Nations has a very public and obvious ideology centered on globalization—bringing people all over the world together. "It's your world," its slogan states, suggesting that individuals should take ownership of the world and its problems.

The public ideology of bringing the world together to solve problems is the basis for the surface ideology of the three Web sites. Surface ideology, in this context, refers to the central message the Web sites want to convey or the message the Web sites' design teams believe they are presenting. I named this surface ideology "working for the world," and the strategies used to convey it are openness and action.

Openness as a strategy refers to the inviting aspect of the Web sites. The Web sites want the viewers to feel that they are welcome. Openness is a preliminary strategy in that viewers cannot see how the Web site is "working for the world" if they are not inclined to spend time exploring the Web site. By using openness as a strategy, the Web-site designers want to keep their audience interested long enough to see how the agencies are, indeed, working for the world.

The use of colors, clearly organized layouts, and pictures help present this openness. Pleasing colors are used in all three Web sites; the use of red, blue, and orange within the Web sites serves to limit users' potential apprehensions. These colors are almost playful and are designed to make users feel at ease.

The next element used to convey openness is clarity. Providing a simple and organized layout is a way to invite users to return to the Web site. Viewers who can easily find the information they need will be more likely to feel invited and to return to the Web site.

A final strategy for achieving openness is through the use of pictures. The pictures in the UNICEF and UNFPA Web sites reinforce this sense of an easily accessible Web site because the user can click on each of these pictures for further information. The openness strategy is designed to make viewers feel that they are part of these agencies and to invite them to log on to visit their Web sites so they can see how the agencies are working for them.

Once the viewers feel welcome enough to log on and visit the Web sites, then the Web sites work to show how the three agencies are "working for the world" using a strategy of action. All three Web sites use a considerable amount of space to describe the work the agencies are doing and to show the world they are working hard. This strategy allows them to show the viewer the extent to which they are "working for the world." The action strategy is presented primarily through the use of text. There are several headings referring to news on each page, and reports are emphasized in all three Web sites.

The surface ideology of "working for the world" fits well with the public message of unity and globalization. The designers of the Web sites use the strategies of openness and action to convey the ideology that the agencies work for everyone, enacting the United Nations' slogan, "It's your world." Through these Web sites, the agencies seem to add, "It's your Web site." After close analysis, however, this surface ideology turns out to be just that—a message that stops at the surface.

NOT-SO-GLOBAL IDEOLOGY: THE REAL IDEOLOGY

I will argue that, in spite of the UN's advocating unity around the world, the Web sites of the agencies analyzed are not inclusive. The ideology presented through these agencies' Web sites is not inclusive because Third World countries are presented as victims needing help, and the Web sites are more concerned with the images of the agencies than with meeting the needs of different groups.

Helper/Helped Ideology: Victims not Equal Partners

The pictures found in the UNICEF and UNFPA Web sites suggest an ideology of helper/helped, where people from developing nations need help, which is provided by people from the West. The strategies used to convey this ideology include pictures, captions, and type of information provided.

The pictures ask the audience to feel sorry for the people represented. The first picture that serves to convey this ideology is found in the UNFPA Web site. The picture of a woman carrying a child is a prominent one; it is large and is the first thing the viewer sees. The woman and child are looking directly at the camera, and they have grave facial expressions; the child looks downright sad. A second picture that uses the same technique is found on the UNICEF Web site. This picture features a young girl carrying a child; it is much smaller and not as prominent, but it still has the same effect. What this second picture lacks in size, it makes up for in emotional impact in that a young child carrying an infant evokes even more pity. The absence of the mother in this picture is another reason to feel sorry for these children—a young girl has to care for an infant who presumably has lost her mother.

The pictures in the UNICEF and UNFPA Web site may differ in size and prominence, but they use the same strategy to make the Web-site viewer feel sorry for these individuals. I call this technique the *pity appeal*. In this strategy, individuals from developing nations are portrayed as people for whom the audience should feel sorry. African author Aidoo (1995) provides a critique of this appeal to pity by describing the commonly used portrayals of African woman in Western media:

> She is breeding too many children, she cannot take care of, and for whom she should expect other people to pick up the tab. She is hungry and so are her children . . . she is half-naked, her drooped and withered breasts are well exposed; there are flies buzzing around the faces of her children; and she has a permanent begging bowl in her hand. (p. 39)

These stereotypes are not exclusively used for African women; they often apply to the representations of all individuals of developing nations. These individuals usually are depicted as people who need help, whose cause needs to be adopted, and whose misery needs to be erased.

The pity appeal is also used by organizations looking for donations such as World Vision, Children International, ChildReach, Save the Children, and Compassion International. The same style of pictures emphasizing a strategy of pity can be found at the Web sites of all five organizations.[1] The point is not to put on trial the strategies used by organizations such as Children International but to question what the UN agencies are suggesting to their audiences by using this technique. Unlike the United Nations, organizations such as Save the Children and Compassion International do not have as primary a mission to bring the world together; they are looking for financial assistance for children.

One can argue that by using pity as the basis for appeal, UNICEF and UNFPA are only suggesting that these countries also need help. They are asking people to participate in helping solve global problems. This argument would work if we did not notice the individuals who are the victims—the ones portrayed as needing help. The two pictures discussed earlier are clear as to the individuals they represent—they both refer to Afghanistan. In the UNICEF Web site, the other pictures presented work to complement this idea. First, in opposition to the picture of the sad young girls is the picture of laughing children dressed in Halloween costumes. Most of these children are white and, since they are celebrating Halloween, we can assume that they are from the West (Halloween is a Western holiday). This assumption is reinforced by the caption of the picture, "It's time to Trick or Treat for UNICEF. This Halloween, children are collecting money to help children in developing countries." Through this caption and the contrast of the pictures, a hierarchy of children is established. The happy smiling children of the West are working to help the poor, sad children in developing countries.

Other elements in the UNFPA Web site contribute to establishing this hierarchy of helped and helper. In addition to the pity appeal that the women and child pictured represent, the headlines also serve to reinforce this idea by providing only negative ideas of developing countries. The headlines talk about the Malawi food crisis, fighting obstetric fistula in Sub-Saharan Africa and yet another southern Africa crisis.

Also important to note is that the stories that deal with the developing world being helped and the West as a helper are clearly labeled so that the Web-site viewer can access these stories from the main page of the Web site. There are two Web-site elements with no links to a geographical area. The first is a picture showing the profile of a young white girl captioned with the words, "social monitor support." To understand what the picture was about, I clicked on its link and was surprised to see that it deals with the economic crisis in Western Europe. To understand that the picture dealt with this crisis, the viewer had to click on the link. This is not necessary for all the crises related to the developing world because they are clearly labeled. In other words, the one instance in which the West needs help is hidden on the Web site—those aspects that do not fit the helper/helped ideology are not visible. This is also true for a second element with no geographical ties—an image with the words "our shared future" and in smaller letters "Achebe-Morrison." The story deals with acclaimed African author Chinua Achebe working on a fiction series for children. This story of a citizen of the developing world serving as a helper is relegated to the second level of the Web site.

Using contrasting pictures, headlines, and the systematic placing of labels, the Web sites of UNICEF and UNFPA do not suggest an inclusive ideology where equal partners work together. Rather, they use strategies such as an appeal to pity and non-inclusion to present the developing world as the sad victim that requires help from the West.

The Web Site: A Place to Shine?

Another area that prevents the UNAIDS, UNICEF, and UNFPA Web sites from living up to their public ideology of bringing people together is their underlying tone. These Web sites do not invite the audience to think about their role in these global issues but rather to consider all that the agencies are doing. Priority is given to stories about what the agencies have done and all of the work in which they are involved. In other words, the Web sites serve to make the agencies look good by highlighting their participation in many projects. The strategy used to accomplish this is an emphasis on news and action reports.

Information related to news is highlighted in all three sites. It is not only placed in a prominent area of the site to catch the audience's attention, but it also is repeated. For example, two out of the three major headings of the UNAIDS Web site deal with news. The repetition is clear; the first heading is titled "Latest News" and the second "What's New." In the same Web site, there is a heading titled "For Journalists" that once again provides news. The other two Web sites also prioritize news. UNICEF has a press center option and a "What's New" option strategically placed at the top of the page. The third Web site—that of UNFPA—has three options for news: The main part of the page has "the latest news link," another option for "more news options or features," and another news link on the top of the page. I first saw this intensity and repetition of the news option as a positive aspect of the page. My opinion on this changed later as I explored in more depth the Web sites' ideology.

The news in these Web sites is not used to inform the audience and meet its needs; rather, it is a vehicle that serves the interests of the agencies. The news stories are all about what the agencies are doing, not what is important to the audience. For example, the most important news item for UNAIDS is "the education plan launched." UNFPA uses, interestingly enough, the same language and talks about "launching a campaign." UNICEF uses the largest part of the Web site to cover a special session on children, and the audience is asked to "click for complete coverage." These examples show that news is used in the Web sites to spotlight the agencies and not to inform people about relevant issues. The result of this desire to "shine"—to use the Web site as a vehicle for flaunting or boasting about the agency's work—is a suppression of voices. If what is important—what is newsworthy—is related to the agencies, then the voices of the people these agencies serve are not given a chance to be heard. The people from the 189 countries are not given the chance to use or be heard on these Web sites. These Web sites should not be places for the agencies to shine but rather an opportunity for their members to work together to solve problems related to children's lives, population, and AIDS.

THREE WEB SITES: THREE MISSED OPPORTUNITIES

The potential of the Internet for bringing unity and working together will continue to grow as cyber cafes open in even the most remote areas of the world. As agencies of the UN, the world's largest organization, UNICEF, UNFPA, and UNAIDS are vehicles for the ideology of bringing people together. A close examination of these agencies' Web sites, however, reveals a disturbing ideology. The ideology excludes people of developing nations by presenting them as victims—as people whose only role is to accept the help provided by the West. The Web sites lose the potential to provide a forum for people all over the world as they equate newsworthy with self-recognition. They do not allow for mutual help or true information exchange. In the end, what is clear is that the three Web sites analyzed are not inclusive and miss the opportunity to bring people together to make the lives of children better, to address population concerns, and to fight the ravages of AIDS.

Inclusiveness is increasingly common as an objective for communication in our global era. As we become aware of the richness that diverse perspectives provide in trying to solve the world's problems, rhetors are encouraged to use rhetorical strategies that invite diverse perspectives and to consider those perspectives seriously. This analysis suggests that this laudable objective is more difficult to achieve than we might have imagined. Despite apparently careful and creative efforts by the designers of the UN Web sites to communicate their inclusiveness and welcoming of myriad perspectives, many features of the Web sites divide and dismiss as much as they include. This analysis suggests that the construction of some groups as needy and others as agents, the featuring of the problems of one group and the hiding of the problems of another, and a focus on the organizational rhetor's own accomplishments rather than the accomplishments or interests of its members all belie the inclusiveness that the Web sites signal through their openness and their action orientation. Perhaps the contradiction is intentional; the organizations may be seeking to convey an image of one kind while genuinely harboring some ideological beliefs that contradict that. Another possibility is that, with the new technology of the Web, the many ways in which inconsistencies within messages can occur have not yet been explicated. Web sites are exciting new communicative sites with tremendous potential for community building, even at an international level, but whether this potential will be realized in true unity or in separation and division clearly is as yet unknown.

Note

[1] Web sites for the five organizations are (1) World Vision: http://www.worldvision.co.nz (2) Children International: http://www.children.org (3) ChildReach: http://www.childreach.com (4) Save the Children: http://www.savethechildre.net (5) Compassion International: http://www.ci.org

References

Aidoo, Ama A. (1995). The African women today. In O. Nnaemeka (Ed.), *Sisterhood, feminisms and power: From Africa to the Diaspora* (pp. 39–50). Trenton, NJ: Africa World Press.

The U.N. joins the net. *The Futurist*; Washington; Jan./Feb. 1996.

UNAIDS: Joint United Nations Programme on HIV/AIDS (n.d.). Retrieved October 29, 2002, from http://www.unaids.org.

UNFPA: United Nations Population Fund (n.d.). Retrieved October 29, 2002, from http://www.unfpa.org.

UNICEF: United Nations Children's Fund (n.d.). Retrieved October 29, 2002, from http://www.unicef.org.

A Tale of Two Ideologies
Winona LaDuke's Vice Presidential Nomination Acceptance Speech

Anthony "Tony" N. Docan

On July 22, 2000, Winona LaDuke gave an acceptance speech for her nomination for vice president of the United States of America. LaDuke, a member of the Green Party and an activist, announced that she would be Ralph Nader's vice presidential running mate for the 2000 election. LaDuke, an Anishinabe from the Makwa Dodaem (Bear Clan) of the Mississippi Band of the White Earth reservation in northern Minnesota (Porter, 1998), brings a nontraditional and often muted perspective to the political arena. I chose this speech as an artifact for ideological criticism because I am interested in how new ideologies are presented to allow new interests and beliefs to become visible. The purpose of this paper is to interpret LaDuke's speech by explicating two ideologies LaDuke presents, one of which is likely to be new to her audience. I also will explore the rhetorical strategies she uses to introduce this new ideology to an uninformed audience and to encourage its consideration of the ideology as its members make electoral and other choices.

BACKGROUND

The Green Party of the United States is an alternative political party that is concerned with environmentalism, nonviolence, social justice, and grassroots organizing. Their 10 key values are: grassroots democracy, social justice, equal opportunity, ecological wisdom, nonviolence, decentralization, community-based economics and economic justice, feminism and gender equity, respect for diversity, personal and global responsibility, and future focus and sustainability (Green Party, 2002).

The National Green Party's convention in 2000 was attended by over 1,200 people, and more than 200 reporters from 70 press organizations covered the convention (Green Pages, 2002). The convention took place in Denver, Colorado, and had the goals of (1) bringing the Green Party's message to Americans who never had heard of the Party; (2) demonstrating that the Green Party is an alternative to the two-party political system; and (3) and providing Green Party leaders with the opportunity to share their visions for the future (Green Party, 2002).

Winona LaDuke, a well-known Green Party member, activist, writer, and speaker, was nominated to run for vice president and thus had the opportunity to speak about numerous issues at the convention. She began her speech by announcing her acceptance of the vice presidential nomination and pointed out her interest in creating a "new model of electoral politics—not to run any campaign." She spoke about "reframing the debate on issues of this society" and that "decision making should not be the exclusive right of the privileged." LaDuke went on to discuss the importance of citizen activism and used herself as an

This essay was written while Anthony "Tony" N. Docan was a student in Karen A. Foss's rhetorical criticism class at the University of New Mexico in 2002. Used by permission of the author.

example. She addressed problems such as welfare-reform legislation and environmental policy while continually stressing that these issues need to be dealt with "over the long term." Furthermore, she discussed the culture of the people of the White Earth reservation, where she resides, and provided many examples of their struggles with employment, poverty, and environmental problems. Near the end of her speech, LaDuke spoke about "full human rights" and the environmental, social, and economic policies that must take future generations into consideration. LaDuke concluded her speech by stating that she was pleased to join with other citizen activists . . . to make this truly an inclusive and substantive dialogue on the future of this America."

IDEOLOGICAL CRITICISM

To analyze LaDuke's speech, I will use the method of ideological criticism, a method of rhetorical criticism that examines ideologies or "the beliefs, interests, and values that determine one's interpretations or judgments" (Maasik & Solomon, 2000, p. 805). An ideology is concerned with the ideas and assumptions of the world by which a group, such as a political party, operates. Geuss (1981) summarizes the concerns of ideologies as "the beliefs the members of the group hold, the concepts they use, the attitudes and psychological dispositions they exhibit, their motives, desires, [and] values" (p. 5).

Ideological criticism has been influenced by numerous scholars, philosophies, and perspectives, including structuralism, Marxism, deconstructionism, post-modernism, and cultural studies. Most pertinent to this analysis, cultural studies attempts to uncover oppressive relations and to discover the means by which individuals and communities can gain liberation, voice, and emancipation. These oppressive structures demonstrate the existence of hegemony, the process by which "particular groups struggle in many different ways, including ideologically, to win the consent of other groups and achieve a kind of ascendancy in both thought and practice over them" (Hall, 1997, p. 48).

Ideologies are usually not deliberately and consciously recognized. Rather, they gain momentum, salience, and strength from support in numbers, access to resources, and alliances with powerful groups that increase their legitimacy. When ideologies become hegemonic, they allow us to understand the world in particular, yet limited ways, while other viewpoints are less visible. As ideologies become a part of the mainstream, they seem natural, normal, and familiar. When this familiarity is resisted, it is often a limited resistance in which the challenge often does not contradict and even may support the dominant ideology.

In an ideological analysis, the critic identifies the nature of the ideology, interests included, and strategies used to support the ideology. To identify the nature of the ideology, the critic frequently examines the artifact for what it asks the audience to believe, understand, feel, or think by exploring assumptions, premises, and particular characteristics of the artifact. A second step is to examine the interests included in the artifact, looking for whose voices are included and excluded and whose interests are privileged, neglected, or oppressed. Finally, an identification of rhetorical strategies allows for an understanding of how rhetoric is used to create or support the ideology identified.

IDENTIFICATION OF IDEOLOGIES

LaDuke presents two major ideologies throughout her speech. One is the ideology of the current political system and its values, limitations, and problems. LaDuke also presents a new ideology to the audience, which is the main focus of her speech.

Mainstream Ideology

LaDuke spends a significant amount of time in her speech describing the current political system, thus painting an ideological picture of present-day politics in the minds of her audience. Two consistent ideological themes emerge as representative of this mainstream system: hierarchy and objective knowing.

Hierarchy

Throughout the speech, LaDuke boldly speaks about the "distribution of power and wealth," "the abuse of power and the rights of the natural world," and living in a society based on "conquest." She addresses decision making as something that currently is "the exclusive right of the privileged." Furthermore, LaDuke asks the rhetorical question, "Can men of privilege . . . actually have the compassion to make public policy that is reflective of the interests of others? At this point, I think not." From these statements referencing the nature of politics, an ideology that involves hierarchical structures becomes apparent. This hierarchical construction that LaDuke creates of the current political system invites the audience to consider politics as a unmistakably top-to-bottom proposition.

The top-down structure of politics is further emphasized by the amount of distance within the hierarchy. In the current system, LaDuke asserts, decisions are made by people from afar. She argues that "as small and rural as is my area of the north woods . . . the decisions made in Washington still affect me" and "that decisions made by others—people who have never seen my face . . . have come to impact me and my community." A few people on top of the hierarchy, then, make big decisions for small communities at the bottom of the hierarchy. LaDuke illuminates this unbalanced and hierarchical decision-making process when discussing poverty on American Indian reservations. She speaks about "impoverished conditions," "low income," "unemployment," and a lack of education on these reservations to demonstrate that the top-down and distant hierarchical structures of the U.S. political system damage the "quality of life in America."

Objective Knowing

Another characteristic of the mainstream ideology is the emphasis placed on the division between personal experience and logical, objective statistics. The assumption that objective knowledge exists is a part of Western cultural values. The notion that the "universe separates the knowing human from things to know" is evident throughout the speech (Multicultural Education, 2002). This idea posits that human beings and personal experiences should be a separate entity from things such as ideas, facts, and understandings and suggests that objective knowledge not only exists but is valuable. Objective knowing also implies that impartial, detached, and unbiased thinking, choosing, and acting actually can occur.

The notion of objective knowledge is apparent in the ideology that LaDuke presents. She uses many statistics in the speech, as, for example, in her statements,

"There are some 9 million children in this country in poverty," "Four out of 10 of the poorest counties in the nation are on Indian reservations," and "90 percent of the children in female-headed households live in impoverished conditions." Furthermore, when discussing environmental policy, she states that "900,000 logging trucks [are] full of trees," and "state and other officials refer to last year's wind shear on my reservation that took down over 200,000 acres of trees as a *natural disaster.*"

LaDuke's blunt and frequent use of statistics demonstrates the objective value and worth placed on accounts of events by the mainstream ideology. Instead of focusing on personal and unique accounts of the lived experiences of these people, they are described in numbers, creating a distance between the people and what is happening to them. This detached way of viewing the world is an important piece of the ideological duality that LaDuke presents.

Interests Served

Hierarchies and objective ways of knowing only benefit a select group of people, while other interests are left out of the picture. The "one percent of the population which has more wealth than the bottom 90 percent of the population" is clearly being served. The top of the hierarchy, such as the policy makers, politicians, and those with corporate interests, have control, power, privilege, and voice. Conversely, the poor, women, children, Native Americans, and impoverished are not represented in this ideology. Their interests are negated, unexpressed, and oppressed as a result.

Native American Ideology

LaDuke's presentation of the mainstream system works as a stepping stone to present the audience with an ideology new to many of them—a Native American ideology. This ideology is comprised of three recurring themes: the importance of time, respect for the natural world, and inclusiveness.

Consideration of the Seventh Generation

The first aspect of LaDuke's Native American ideology focuses on time and the seventh generation. Many Native American cultures believe that "each new generation is responsible to ensure the survival of the seventh generation. The prophecy given to us, tells us that what we do today will affect the seventh generation and because of this we must bear in mind our responsibility to them today and always" (IISD, 2002). Furthermore, the concept of the seventh generation ensures that individuals will assume responsibility for Mother Earth and for future generations.

The notion of the seventh generation appears throughout LaDuke's speech in statements such as, "we need to consider an amendment to the U.S. Constitution in which all decisions made today will be considered in light of their impact on the seventh generation from now." Furthermore, when LaDuke discusses Indian poverty, unemployment, and impoverished conditions, she states that "these problems will need to be addressed over the long term." When she speaks about environmental issues, she asks two questions: "Who's going to be there when all those trees are gone? Who will be there when there are no forests except for a monoculture popple and tree farms?" These questions demonstrate that LaDuke's notion of the future is of utmost importance, whereas the current ideology does not account for the future in responsible ways. To reiterate the value of the future, at the end of the speech, LaDuke states that we must "have an environmental, economic and social policy that is based on consideration of the impact on the seventh generation from now." There is a clear assumption here that the actions of today will influence the world of tomorrow. LaDuke's focus on the future is unique because she is not simply concerned with the immediate future; instead, she is concerned with a future she will likely not be alive to see. This future, however, can and will be impacted by the choices individuals make now.

Respect for the Natural World

LaDuke's altruistic and unselfish valuing of a distant future takes an array of aspects of life into consideration. One of the most important aspects on which LaDuke focuses is the relationship between people and nature. LaDuke speaks about being from a "forest culture" and explains that "[o]ur creation stories are about those forests, our ancestors are buried there. Our food, our medicinal plants, our relatives live in those forests."

Numerous other assumptions and values of a traditional Native American philosophy concerning the natural world emerge in LaDuke's speech as well. The notion that the "universe is one vast living organism, continually changing and impermanent" is apparent (Multicultural Education, 2002). The earth, similar to a human, is valued as a living organism and not as a tool, economic opportunity, or piece of property. The earth changes, is impermanent, and is affected by and affects others. In addition, the assumption that the "universe is one vast living organism of many interrelated forces and parts [and that] humans are a part of this life force" emerges within LaDuke's ideology (Multicultural Education, 2002). Here, we see the direct relationship between the natural world and how humans play a part in changing, shaping, hurting, or protecting this living organism. Therefore, to value, respect, care for, treat with dignity, and plan for the natural world through appropriate regulations is essential.

LaDuke further stresses the importance of the natural world when she discusses "fundamental rights to . . . land [and] natural resources." When LaDuke speaks about "reframing the debate on the issues of this society," she immediately references the "rights of the natural world." There is an assumption here that humans are not the only objects on this earth that should have rights. LaDuke sees the environment as an entity of utmost importance and therefore believes it should be protected, preserved, and respected in ways similar to how human beings should be treated.

Another component of LaDuke's ideology concerning the natural world speaks to quality of life. She speaks of "human rights and dignity," "quality of life issues," and "full human rights." LaDuke makes assertions such as, "all people have the right and responsibility to determine their destiny," and "we have fundamental rights to self-determination, to language, land, territory, natural resources and our children." To LaDuke, human rights and quality of life are of utmost importance to the U.S. When humans are allowed to have and realize self-determination, language, resources, and a sense of destiny, then one's natural motives, desires, and values have the possibility to be realized, recognized, and respected.

Voice for the Underrepresented

The notion of inclusiveness is also a part of LaDuke's new ideology, evident in her enactment of voice, the power of the collective, and citizen activism during the speech. Her inclusion is aimed at bringing in to her vision those who are typically underrepresented in politics at all levels. Gaining and using voice is demonstrated when LaDuke says that "those who are affected by policy . . . should be heard in the debate." In addition, she refuses to remain silent by saying, "I will not stand by mute." LaDuke also mentions language numerous times throughout her speech, illuminating how voice is communicated, understood, and used within this empowering ideology. She ends her speech by saying, "I am pleased to join with other[s] . . . to make this truly an inclusive and substantive dialogue on the future of this America." The notion of voice makes clear her commitment to hearing community members who typically are not heard in the dominant culture.

In addition to voice, LaDuke's Native American ideology incorporates the power of the collective. Voice is an essential characteristic that allows community members to gain a sense of unity and collectivity. She talks about "standing with others around this country," "becoming public citizens," and seeing "neighbors." She uses a great deal of "we" language in phrases such as "we are talking about," "we intend to stand," "we call them," "we are," "we have the challenge," and "we will still be living." LaDuke uses group-oriented language as well, as in "we can collectively say that we are talking about real economic and social benefits."

By using group-inclusive language and by promoting a sense of community and collectiveness, LaDuke not only includes all members of her audience and makes them feel welcomed and safe, but she also presents this inclusiveness as part of her proposed ideology. She also implicitly suggests that "human beings in collectivity behave and think differently than human beings in isolation" and that the collectivity has "'a mind of its own' distinct from the individual qua individual" (McGee, 2000, p. 456). When more minds are able to think, express, and have the outlet of language and voice, then the chances are increased for a brighter future.

With a sense of voice and collectivity instilled in her audience and envisioned ideology, LaDuke makes activism another component of her ideology. LaDuke speaks of "citizen activism and change" and states, "That is how I view myself, as a citizen activist." At the end of her speech, LaDuke says, "I consider myself a patriot—not to a flag—to a land. And in that spirit, I am pleased to join with other citizen activists." To LaDuke, once voice is gained and collectivity is realized, then action at the personal, community, and political levels can be taken to better the future. The new future is created, however, through the efforts of the underrepresented—those who usually are not seen as being efficacious in the political world.

Interests Served

Certain interests are included in LaDuke's Native American ideology that were not incorporated in the mainstream ideology discussed earlier. This ideology includes the voices of women, children, the poor, land-based cultures, and the underprivileged. These are the people who have an interest in using their time to better the natural world, make community-appropriate decisions, care for those in poverty, and focus on issues of quality of life. LaDuke's inclusive ideology incorporates the concerns of these people, who seek self-determination, desire, motivation, resources, and respect.

The objective-subjective dialectic LaDuke establishes works as an ideological divider in terms of the interests that are served. On one side, the frequent use of statistics demonstrates the objective value and worth placed on accounts of events by the mainstream ideology. Instead of focusing on personal and unique accounts of the lived experiences of these people, they are described in numbers, creating a distance between the people and what is happening to them. This detached way of viewing the world is an important piece of the mainstream ideology that LaDuke explicates. That LaDuke values the subjective is evident when she presents her belief concerning inclusiveness. This subjective ideological belief and who it benefits become more apparent when LaDuke's speech is examined for her rhetorical strategies.

RHETORICAL STRATEGIES TO SUPPORT LADUKE'S IDEOLOGY

LaDuke uses two rhetorical strategies throughout her speech to promote a Native American ideology over the mainstream ideology—perspective by incongruity and universalization. Both facilitate a consideration by non-Native audiences of an ideology that probably seems foreign and strange.

Perspective by Incongruity

A strategy explicated by Kenneth Burke (1965), perspective by incongruity is a juxtaposition of qualities or ideas that usually are seen as opposites or as belonging to different contexts (pp. 89–94). Using this strategy, opposing ideas are presented side by side, allowing different perspectives to be illuminated.

LaDuke uses perspective by incongruity by placing the two ideologies side by side. In particular, she places side by side two different ways of knowing that derive from the two ideologies. The first ideology largely consists of objective knowledge, created through and reliant on facts and statistics, which is placed next to LaDuke's ideology that features subjective knowledge, rooted in personal experience. An example that demonstrates LaDuke's use of perspective by incongruity is illuminated when she speaks about welfare reform legislation:

> This is the nation leading the world in terms of number of people in poverty. There are some 9 million children in this country in poverty. Welfare reform eliminates the safety net for those children. Now let me tell you about some real people. Native Americans are the poorest people in the country. Four out of 10 of the poorest counties in the nation are on Indian reservations. This is the same as White Earth. My daughter's entire third-grade class with few exceptions is below the poverty level. The only choice those parents have with any hope—with 45 percent unemployment—is to work at the casino at about six bucks an hour. Two parents working and paying child-care expenses make them ostensibly the working poor—not much different than being in poverty. So, my friends, a family of seven who live in a two-bedroom trailer down the road from me—a fifteen year old trailer—on AFDC have few options under the new welfare reform plan. I will not stand by mute as the safety net is taken away from those children and that third-grade class.

In this example, LaDuke begins by using statistics, which are taken to be objective facts, to discuss poverty. She immediately follows these statistics with a discussion of a specific group of people, Native Americans. She transitions further into a more subjective and personal arena when she discusses the parents and children of her daughter's third-grade class. LaDuke moves from what she sees as an outdated ideology, which uses and values objective knowledge, to an ideology that values subjectivity and personal experiences. The rapid and jarring switch from one ideology to the other serves to accentuate their differences.

In her discussion of environmental policy, LaDuke again uses perspective by incongruity:

> **Environmental policy.** WTI Incinerator is a hazardous incinerator in East Liverpool, Ohio, located less than 1,000 feet from a school. It was visited by Al Gore in 1992, where he pledged, if elected, it would not open. It did.
>
> **Endangered species.** Bill Clinton said in 1992 that he would not allow a weakening of the endangered species act, yet he signed an appropriations bill in 1994 that prohibits any funds to be used to unlist or list any species under the endangered species act. This put a freeze on any action on over 1000 species that are waiting to be listed under the act.
>
> **Our forests and the salvage rider.** Clinton vetoed the first version of this, then signed it the second time when it was attached to an appropriations bill for the Oklahoma City bombing victims, later claiming that he never thought the timber industry could use it to get around the laws.
>
> What is my experience in this? I come from a forest culture. Our creation stories are about those forests, our ancestors are buried there. Our food, our medicinal plants, our relatives live in those forests. We call them *forests*, but they are viewed by Potlatch, Blandin and Champion as board feet of timber.

In this example, LaDuke provides three examples of environmental tragedies caused in part by political decisions. These examples go beyond simply stating the lackadaisical environmental attitude held by many political leaders. These examples are objective in character and provide LaDuke with a stepping stone to then move to the subjective—her personal experiences—which allow her new ideology to be explained and considered. Furthermore, a different perspective is illuminated for her audience. Instead of simply placing value on hard-cold facts and the context surrounding them, LaDuke allows her audience to place value on personal experience—the experience of her culture in relation to the natural world. This strategy allows LaDuke to present objectively oriented information that still supports her surface-level argument, but, at the same time, she offers her audience a new perspective as to how political decisions should be made—that of the personal.

In another example of perspective by incongruity, LaDuke asserts: "As a human, I understand these issues, and as a woman, I ask why it is that I should be more concerned about the sugar content of breakfast cereal than the amount of mercury in my son's tissue from eating fish from Minnesota lakes." In this statement, LaDuke begins by presenting a general concern that is likely to be of interest to a sizable amount of the population and compares this to a more serious and life-threatening issue. She moves from the objective to the personal. On the surface level, she brings awareness to her audience about often-ignored issues, such as the dangers of eating fish from lakes. On the ideological level, LaDuke sets up the outdated way of looking at life and presents her ideological notion of making the political into the personal. Political decisions, regulations, and governances have been transformed into personal actions and effects.

In each of the prior examples, LaDuke allows new perspectives to emerge, giving the oppressed a sense of voice and even a strategy by which to accomplish their goals. She uses objective facts on the surface to support a point while also presenting an inclusive ideological perspective that the political is personal. This perspective allows subjective and personal needs and desires to be accounted for, respected, and valued. This perspective takes micro-level needs into consideration and makes appropriate decisions for community-level needs.

Universalization

LaDuke uses another strategy in the presentation of her ideology to increase its appeal. She universalizes her ideology by portraying the interests of particular groups as though they were general interests. Near the beginning of her speech, LaDuke moves from speaking about herself to her community to "all people." This example demonstrates how she portrays the interests of particular groups as if they were universal interests and concerns:

> As most of you probably know, I live and work on the White Earth reservation in Northern Minnesota, the largest reservation in the state in terms of population and land base. . . . Yet I find that as small and rural as is my area of the north woods, as small as my pond is, the decisions made in Washington still affect me. And it is that fact, that decisions made by others—people who have never seen my face, never seen our lakes, never tasted our wild rice or heard the cry of a child in Ponsford—have come to impact me and my community. I am here to say that all people have the right and responsibility to determine their destiny and I do not relinquish this right to PACs, to lobbyists and to decision makers who are far away.

In this paragraph, LaDuke generalizes about her experiences as a person, community member, and activist and moves to speaking about her Native American and rural community. She begins speaking about herself and moves to Native Americans and then to everyone by speaking about the rights of all people. This demonstrates how LaDuke depicts the interests of Native Americans as the collective interests of all people, a reversal of the typical view of Native Americans as marginalized and substantially different from other Americans. Here, Native Americans are functioning synecdochically for all Americans.

In another instance, LaDuke briefly speaks about her personal experiences with women in Mexico, their oppression, and the role of the U.S. in NAFTA:

> I have looked into the eyes of Tzotzil women in Chiapas, Mexico, whose eyes are all that show—women whose faces are covered in the tropics with ski masks because if the Mexican military or para-military see them, they will be killed if they are known. I've seen the U.S. military-supplied armored personnel carriers on small dirt roads in Chiapas and recognized the absence of human rights and dignity that is central to NAFTA. And I also recognize the impact of $250 million in U.S. military aid and trade to a country like Mexico—a country with no known enemies.
>
> American foreign policy is reflective of American economic policy and at best, both presently and historically, it makes refugees. That is the major reason we have the challenge of immigration.

In this example, LaDuke moves from speaking about her personal experiences with oppressed women and the absence of human rights and dignity and moves on to express these concerns as general interests to everyone. By doing so, LaDuke rhetorically universalizes the concerns and problems of the oppressed into an arrangement that portrays the interests of particular groups as though they were general interests.

Conclusions

In her acceptance speech, Winona LaDuke offers her audiences two ideologies. One is the standard ideology associated with politics and decision-making processes in America in general. It is characterized by hierarchy and objective knowing. The other ideology is rooted in Native American perspectives and includes the beliefs of consideration of the seventh generation, respect for the natural world, and voice for the underrepresented. LaDuke clearly would like her audience to understand, appreciate, and perhaps vote on the basis of the second ideology, and she uses two primary rhetorical strategies to garner support for it. Perspective by incongruity allows audiences to see the stark contrasts between the two ideologies, particularly in terms of the different ways of knowing they embody, and a universalization of the experience of herself and other Native Americans enables Native Americans to be placed at the cultural center, with other groups on the periphery. As a result, the Native American ideology is able to be seen as more acceptable and normal than it might otherwise be—it becomes an ideology that non-Natives can try out to see if it might not align with some of their individual beliefs.

Although Ralph Nader and Winona LaDuke did not win the election in 2000, their defeat should not be used to evaluate the effectiveness of LaDuke's rhetorical strategies in this speech. I suggest that, through the presentation of contrasting ideologies, perspective by incongruity, and universalization, LaDuke inserted into mainstream political thought some of the beliefs associated with Native American culture, thus facilitating their growth and impact in the future in ways that cannot yet be seen.

References

Burke, K. (1965). *Permanence and change*. Indianapolis: Bobbs-Merrill.
Geuss, R. (1981). *The idea of a critical theory: Habermas and the Frankfurt School*. New York: Cambridge University Press.
Green Pages. (2002). The Association of State Green Parties in 2000 and beyond. Retrieved October 26, 2002 from http://www.greenpages.ws/v5i1/asgp.html
Green Party. (2002). Green Party. Retrieved October 26, 2002 from http://www.greenpartyus.org/
Hall, S. (1997). *Representation: Cultural representations and signifying practices*. Thousand Oaks, CA: Sage.
IISD. (2002). Our Responsibility to the Seventh Generation. Retrieved November 2, 2002 from http://iisd1.iisd.ca/7thgen/
Maasik, S., & Solomon, J. (2000). *Signs of life in the U.S.A.: Readings on popular culture for writers* (3rd ed.). Boston, MA: Bedford/St. Martin's.
McGee, M. C. (2000). The "ideograph": A link between rhetoric and ideology. In Burgchardt (Ed.), *Readings in rhetorical criticism* (2nd ed.) (pp. 456–470). State College, Pennsylvania: Strata Publishing.
Multicultural Education. (2002). Summary of underlying values and assumptions. Retrieved October 30, 2002 from http://curry.edschool.virginia.edu/go/multicultural/
Porter, K. (1998). Voices from the gaps: Women writers of color. Retrieved October 26, 2002 from http://voices.cla.umn.edu/authors/WinonaLaduke.html

Acceptance Speech for Green Party's Nomination for Vice President of the United States of America

Winona LaDuke
July 22, 2000

Aniin indinawaymuginitook. Niin gagwe gitimaagis noongom. Beenaysikwe indigo, idash, Winona LaDuke indizhinikaaz, Makwa niin dodaem. Gahwah bah bahnikaag ishkonigi-niing indoojibaa. Miigwetch, Mazinnaggain ininiwug, Miigwetch indinawaymugunitook.

I am here to announce today that it is with great honor that I am joining with Ralph Nader and the Green Party in a national effort in this presidential campaign. I will be his vice presidential running mate.

As Mr. Nader has previously stated, we intend to stand with others around this country as the catalyst for the creation of a new model of electoral politics—not to run any campaign. This will be a campaign for democracy waged by private citizens who choose to become public citizens.

I am not inclined toward electoral politics. Yet, I am impacted by public policy. I am interested in reframing the debate on the issues of this society—the distribution of power and wealth, the abuse of power and the rights of the natural world, the environment and the need to consider an amendment to the U.S. Constitution in which all decisions made today will be considered in light of their impact on the seventh generation from now. That is, I believe, what sustainability is all about. These are vital subjects which are all too often neglected by the rhetoric of "major party" candidates and the media.

I believe that decision making should not be the exclusive right of the privileged—that those who are affected by policy—not those who by default often stand above it—should be heard in the debate. It is the absence of this voice which, unfortunately, has come to characterize American public policy and the American political system.

As most of you probably know, I live and work on the White Earth reservation in Northern Minnesota, the largest reservation in the state in terms of population and land base, and, as most of you know—in terms of recent political and legal struggles—the site of a great deal of citizen activism and change in recent months. That is how I view myself, as a citizen activist. Yet I find that as small and rural as is my area of the north woods, as small as my pond is, the decisions made in Washington still affect me. And it is that fact, that decisions made by others—people who have never seen my face, never seen our lakes, never tasted our wild rice or heard the cry of a child in Ponsford—have come to impact me and my community. I am here to say that all people have the right and responsibility to determine their destiny, and I do not relinquish this right to PACs, to lobbyists and to decision makers who are far away.

When you live in one of the poorest sections of the country and in the state of Minnesota, you are able to understand, perhaps better, the impact of public policy. It is indeed my contention that there is no real quality of life in America until there is quality of life in the poorest regions of this America.

For instance, over half of the American Indians on my reservation live in poverty. This represents five times the state average. Of particular concern is that nearly two thirds of the children on my reservation live in poverty. Also 90 percent of the children in female-headed households live in impoverished conditions. Median family income on my reservation is just slightly above half the state average for median income. Per capita income is at the same level. Unemployment on the reservation is at 49 percent, according to recent BIA statistics. And nearly one third of all Indians on the reservation have not attained a high school diploma. Finally, it is absolutely critical to note that approximately 50 percent of the population on the reservation is under 25 years of age, indicating that these problems will need to be addressed over the long term.

What does that mean in the larger picture? Let me give you some examples.

Welfare-reform legislation. This is the nation leading the world in terms of number of people in poverty. There are some 9 million children in this country in poverty. Welfare reform eliminates the safety net for those children. Now let me tell you about some real people. Native Americans are the poorest people in the country. Four out of 10 of the poorest counties in the nation are on Indian reservations. This is the same as White Earth. My daughter's entire third-grade class with few exceptions is below the poverty level. The only choice those parents have with any hope—with 45 percent unemployment—is to work at the casino at about six bucks an hour. Two parents working and paying child-care expenses make them ostensibly the working poor— not much different than being in poverty. So, my friends, a family of seven who live in a two-bedroom trailer down the road from me—a fifteen-year-old trailer—on AFDC have few options under the new welfare reform plan. I will not stand by mute as the safety net is taken away from those children and that third-grade class.

Environmental policy. WTI Incinerator is a hazardous incinerator in East Liverpool, Ohio, located less than 1,000 feet from a school. It was visited by Al Gore in 1992, where he pledged, if elected, it would not open. It did.

Endangered species. Bill Clinton said in 1992 that he would not allow a weakening of the endangered species act, yet he signed an appropriations bill in 1994 that prohibits any funds to be used to unlist or list any species under the endangered species act. This put a freeze on any action on over 1000 species that are waiting to be listed under the act.

Our forests and the salvage rider. Clinton vetoed the first version of this, then signed it the second time when it was attached to an appropriations bill for the Oklahoma City bombing victims, later claiming that he never thought the timber industry could use it to get around the laws. In total, salvage available for future harvest in the Northern Rockies alone is equivalent to 237,000 logging trucks full of trees—nationally, 900,000 logging trucks full of trees. Allowable cuts are now acceptable under headings like "winter injury," "poor vigor," "old age," and "to realize forest productivity"—broad and subjective terminology. This situation is, of course, mimicked in the Superior National Forest.

What is my experience in this? I come from a forest culture. Our creation stories are about those forests, our ancestors are buried there. Our food, our medicinal plants, our relatives live in those forests. We call them *forests*, but they are viewed by Potlatch, Blandin and Champion as board feet of timber.

Now let me ask you a question: How is it that when the people of the White Earth reservation ask the federal government for the return of the Tamarac National Wildlife Refuge or to manage the Tamarac National Wildlife Refuge—lands taken illegally from our people—we are refused or put off? Yet these same lands are basically given to Potlatch and Champion. Why is it that the state and other officials refer to last year's wind shear on my reservation that took down over 200,000 acres of trees as a *natural disaster*? Yet Potlatch expands present mills and they will be cutting a square mile of Minnesota's north woods daily—the equivalent of an eight-foot pile of logs piled across both the north and south bound lanes of 35W from Minneapolis to Duluth—and that is referred to as *economic growth*.

Who's going to be there when all those trees are gone? Who will be there when there are no forests except for a monoculture popple and tree farms? You can't eat money.

How about Indian policy? Lots of promises and no action. Two free lunches, some Kodak moments, and immense budget cuts. Indian policy has come far in America, there's no question. Until almost the end of the 19th century, Indians were dealt with by the Department of War. Since then, Indian people have been in the Department of Interior; we are the only humans in the Department of Interior treated as a natural resource. This is a problem in budget cuts. Literally, we are fighting with ducks over appropriations. Is that changing? Right now, in the international arena, the U.S. State Department is opposing the classification of indigenous peoples under international law as peoples. Peoples have rights under international law and those rights are not the sole and exclusive jurisdiction of member states. We are arguing that we have fundamental rights to self-determination, to language, land, territory, natural resources and our children. And the U.S. State Department is opposing our human rights.

Now a question you may ask me is: Can a person who lives in the north woods of Minnesota have thoughts big enough for national policy debate or international policy? I would argue yes. In fact, I would question the inverse. Can men of privilege— who do not feel the impact of policies on forests, children, or their ability to breastfeed their children—actually have the compassion to make public policy that is reflective of the interests of others? At this point, I think not.

I have seen my neighbors, small farmers in northern Minnesota, go under while corporate agriculture subsidies in the Sunbelt mount. I have seen dairy cows with x's on their foreheads for the dairy-termination program leave on cattle cars never to return, and I have been at too many farm auctions to feel that things are good on the farm. I know the difference between water quality on a small dairy farm and that on a 3,000- or 10,000-acre hog farm. As former Texas Agriculture Secretary Jim Hightower says: "Sometimes there's just too many pigs in the creek."

I have looked into the eyes of Tzotzil women in Chiapas, Mexico, whose eyes are all that show—women whose faces are covered in the tropics with ski masks because if the Mexican military or para-military see them, they will be killed if they are known. I've seen the U.S. military-supplied armored personnel carriers on small dirt roads in Chiapas and recognized the absence of human rights and dignity that is central to NAFTA. And I also recognize the impact of $250 million in U.S. military aid and trade to a country like Mexico—a country with no known enemies.

American foreign policy is reflective of American economic policy and, at best, both presently and historically, it makes refugees. That is the major reason we have the challenge of immigration. I congratulate Paul Wellstone on his principled stand on NAFTA, Colin Peterson's opposition to NAFTA, and ask one more time for Senator Rod Grams' office to return my calls. And while Dan Quayle could not spell potato I can. O-P-I-N-II-G. That's Ojibwe for potato. And that language is one of 187 endangered indigenous languages which do not benefit from English-only legislation.

As a human, I understand these issues, and as a woman, I ask why it is that I should be more concerned about the sugar content of breakfast cereal than the amount of mercury in my son's tissue from eating fish from Minnesota lakes.

In conclusion, until American domestic and foreign policy addresses quality of life issues for the poorest people in the country, we cannot say that there is quality of life. Until all of us are treated as peoples—with full human rights—we cannot tout a human rights record. Until policy decisions are made that do not benefit solely the one percent of the population which has more wealth than the bottom 90 percent of the population, I do not think that we can collectively say that we are talking about real economic and social benefits. And finally, until we have an environmental, economic and social policy that is based on consideration of the impact on the seventh generation from now, we will still be living in a society that is based on conquest—not one that is based on survival. I consider myself a patriot—not to a flag—to a land. And in that spirit, I am pleased to join with other citizen activists, with Cam Gordon, with Lee Ann TallBear, with Ralph Nader and the Green Party to make this truly an inclusive and substantive dialogue on the future of this America.

Miigwetch, Mi'iw.

Additional Samples of Ideological Criticism

Altman, Karen E. "Consuming Ideology: The Better Homes in America Campaign." *Critical Studies in Mass Communication*, 7 (September 1990), 286–307.

Bodroghkozy, Aniko. "'We're the Young Generation and We've Got Something to Say': A Gramscian Analysis of Entertainment Television and the Youth Rebellion of the 1960s." *Critical Studies in Mass Communication*, 8 (June 1991), 217–30.

Cloud, Dana L. "Operation Desert Comfort." In *Seeing Through the Media: The Persian Gulf War*. Ed. Lauren Rabinovitz and Susan Jeffords. New Brunswick, NJ: Rutgers University Press, 1994, pp. 155–70.

Cloud, Dana L. "The Rhetoric of <Family Values>: Scapegoating, Utopia, and the Privatization of Social Responsibility." *Western Journal of Communication*, 62 (Fall 1998), 387–419.

Condit, Celeste Michelle. "Hegemony in a Mass-Mediated Society: Concordance about Reproductive Technologies." *Critical Studies in Mass Communication*, 11 (September 1994), 205–30.

Cooks, Leda M., Mark P. Orbe, and Carol S. Bruess. "The Fairy Tale Theme in Popular Culture: A Semiotic Analysis of *Pretty Woman*." *Women's Studies in Communication*, 16 (Fall 1993), 86–104.

Coupland, Justine, and Angie Williams. "Conflicting Discourses, Shifting Ideologies: Pharmaceutical, 'Alternative' and Feminist Emancipatory Texts on the Menopause." *Discourse & Society*, 13 (July 2002), 419–45.

Delgado, Fernando Pedro. "Chicano Ideology Revisited: Rap Music and the (Re)articulation of Chicanismo." *Western Journal of Communication*, 62 (Spring 1998), 95–113.

Fang, Yew-Jin. "'Riots' and Demonstrations in the Chinese Press: A Case Study of Language and Ideology." *Discourse & Society*, 54 (October 1994), 463–81.

Flores, Lisa A., and Dreama G. Moon. "Rethinking Race, Revealing Dilemmas: Imagining a New Racial Subject in *Race Traitor*." *Western Journal of Communication*, 66 (Spring 2002), 181–207.

Franklin, Sarah. "Deconstructing 'Desperateness': The Social Construction of Infertility in Popular Representations of New Reproductive Technologies." In *The New Reproductive Technologies*. Ed. Maureen McNeil, Ian Varcoe, and Steven Yearley. London: MacMillan, 1990, pp. 200–29.

Frentz, Thomas S., and Thomas B. Farrell. "Conversion of America's Consciousness: The Rhetoric of *The Exorcist*." *Quarterly Journal of Speech*, 61 (February 1975), 40–47.

Frentz, Thomas S., and Janice Hocker Rushing. "Integrating Ideology and Archetype in Rhetorical Criticism, Part II: A Case Study of *Jaws*." *Quarterly Journal of Speech*, 79 (February 1993), 61–81.

German, Kathleen M. "Frank Capra's *Why We Fight* Series and the American Audience." *Western Journal of Speech Communication*, 54 (Spring 1990), 237–48.

Hackett, Robert A., and Zuezhi Zhao. "Challenging a Master Narrative: Peace Protest and Opinion/Editorial Discourse in the US Press During the Gulf War." *Discourse & Society*, 5 (October 1994), 509–41.

Haines, Harry W. "'What Kind of War?': An Analysis of the Vietnam Veterans Memorial." *Critical Studies in Mass Communication*, 3 (March 1986), 1–20.

Halualani, Rona Tamiko. "The Intersecting Hegemonic Discourses of an Asian Mail-Order Bride Catalog: Pilipina 'Oriental Butterfly' Dolls for Sale." *Women's Studies in Communication*, 18 (Spring 1995), 45–64.

Hariman, Robert, and John Louis Lucaites. "Public Identity and Collective Memory in U.S. Iconic Photography: The Image of 'Accidental Napalm.'" *Critical Studies in Media Communication,* 20 (March 2003), 35–66.

Hayden, Sara. "Teenage Bodies, Teenage Selves: Tracing the Implications of Bio-Power in Contemporary Sexuality Education Texts." *Women's Studies in Communication,* 24 (Spring 2001), 30–61.

LaFountain, Marc J. "Foucault and Dr. Ruth." *Critical Studies in Mass Communication,* 6 (June 1989), 123–37.

Lessl, Thomas M. "Science and the Sacred Cosmos: The Ideological Rhetoric of Carl Sagan." *Quarterly Journal of Speech,* 71 (May 1985), 175–87.

Lewis, Charles. "Hegemony in the Ideal: Wedding Photography, Consumerism, and Patriarchy." *Women's Studies in Communication,* 20 (Fall 1997), 167–87.

Marvin, Carolyn. "Theorizing the Flagbody: Symbolic Dimensions of the Flag Desecration Debate, or, Why the Bill of Rights Does Not Fly in the Ballpark." *Critical Studies in Mass Communication,* 8 (June 1991), 119–38.

McGee, Michael Calvin. "The Origins of 'Liberty': A Feminization of Power." *Communication Monographs,* 47 (March 1980), 23–45.

Moore, Stephen H. "Disinterring Ideology from a Corpus of Obituaries: A Critical Post Mortem." *Discourse & Society,* 13 (July 2002), 495–536.

Morris, Richard, and Philip Wander. "Native American Rhetoric: Dancing in the Shadows of the Ghost Dance." *Quarterly Journal of Speech,* 76 (May 1990), 164–91.

Murphy, John M. "Domesticating Dissent: The Kennedys and the Freedom Rides." *Communication Monographs,* 59 (March 1992), 61–78.

Nakayama, Thomas K. "Show/Down Time: 'Race,' Gender, Sexuality, and Popular Culture." *Critical Studies in Mass Communication,* 11 (June 1994), 162–79.

Nomai, Afsheen J., and George N. Dionisopoulos. "Framing the Cubas Narrative: The American Dream and the Capitalist Reality." *Communication Studies,* 53 (Summer 2002), 97–111.

Ott, Brian L., and Eric Aoki. "Popular Imagination and Identity Politics: Reading the Future in *Star Trek: The Next Generation.*" *Western Journal of Communication,* 65 (Fall 2001), 392–415.

Parry-Giles, Trevor. "Character, the Constitution, and the Ideological Embodiment of 'Civil Rights' in the 1967 Nomination of Thurgood Marshall to the Supreme Court." *Quarterly Journal of Speech,* 82 (November 1996), 364–82.

Parry-Giles, Trevor. "Ideological Anxiety and the Censored Text: Real Lives at the Edge of the Union." *Critical Studies in Mass Communication,* 11 (March 1994), 54–72.

Palmer, David L. "Virtuosity as Rhetoric: Agency and Transformation in Paganini's Mastery of the Violin." *Quarterly Journal of Speech,* 84 (August 1998), 341–57.

Rojo, Luisa Martin. "Division and Rejection: From the Personification of the Gulf Conflict to the Demonization of Saddam Hussein." *Discourse & Society,* 6 (January 1995), 49–80.

Rushing, Janice Hocker. "E. T. as Rhetorical Transcendence." *Quarterly Journal of Speech,* 71 (May 1985), 188–203.

Rushing, Janice Hocker. "Evolution of 'The New Frontier' in *Alien* and *Aliens*: Patriarchal Co-optation of the Feminine Archetype." *Quarterly Journal of Speech,* 75 (February 1989), 1–24.

Rushing, Janice Hocker. "Mythic Evolution of 'The New Frontier' in Mass Mediated Rhetoric." *Critical Studies in Mass Communication,* 3 (September 1986), 265–96.

Rushing, Janice Hocker. "The Rhetoric of the American Western Myth." *Communication Monographs*, 50 (March 1983), 14–32.

Rushing, Janice Hocker. "Ronald Reagan's 'Star Wars' Address: Mythic Containment of Technical Reasoning." *Quarterly Journal of Speech*, 72 (November 1986), 415–33.

Rushing, Janice Hocker, and Thomas S. Frentz. "The Frankenstein Myth in Contemporary Cinema." *Critical Studies in Mass Communication*, 6 (March 1989), 61–80.

Salvador, Michael. "The Rhetorical Subversion of Cultural Boundaries: The National Consumers' League." *Southern Communication Journal*, 59 (Summer 1994), 318–32.

Sanchez, Victoria E., and Mary E. Stuckey. "Coming of Age as a Culture: Emancipatory and Hegemonic Readings of *The Indian in the Cupboard*." *Western Journal of Communication*, 64 (Winter 2000), 78–91.

Scult, Allen, Michael Calvin McGee, and J. Kenneth Kuntz. "Genesis and Power: An Analysis of the Biblical Story of Creation." *Quarterly Journal of Speech*, 72 (May 1986), 113–31.

Shah, Hemant, and Michael C. Thornton. "Racial Ideology in U.S. Mainstream News Magazine Coverage of Black-Latino Interaction, 1980–1992." *Critical Studies in Mass Communication*, 11 (June 1994), 141–61.

Short, Brant. "'Reconstructed, But Unregenerate': *I'll Take My Stand*'s Rhetorical Vision of Progress." *Southern Communication Journal*, 59 (Winter 1994), 112–24.

Sloop, John M. "'Apology Made to Whoever Pleases': Cultural Discipline and the Grounds of Interpretation." *Communication Quarterly*, 42 (Fall 1994), 345–62.

Smith, Cynthia Duquette. "Discipline—It's a 'Good Thing': Rhetorical Constitution and Martha Stewart Living Omnimedia." *Women's Studies in Communication*, 23 (Fall 2000), 337–66.

Solomon, Martha. "'With Firmness in the Right': The Creation of Moral Hegemony in Lincoln's Second Inaugural." *Communication Reports*, 1 (Winter 1988), 32–37.

Stein, Sarah R. "The '1984' Macintosh Ad: Cinematic Icons and Constitutive Rhetoric in the Launch of a New Machine." *Quarterly Journal of Speech*, 88 (May 2002), 169–92.

Stormer, Nathan. "Embodying Normal Miracles." *Quarterly Journal of Speech*, 83 (May 1997), 172–91.

Taylor, Bryan C. "Fat Man and Little Boy: The Cinematic Representation of Interests in the Nuclear Weapons Organization." *Critical Studies in Mass Communication*, 10 (December 1993), 367–94.

Trujillo, Nick. "Interpreting (the Work and the Talk of) Baseball: Perspectives on Ballpark Culture." *Western Journal of Communication*, 56 (Fall 1992), 350–71.

Trujillo, Nick, and Leah R. Ekdom. "Sportswriting and American Cultural Values: The 1984 Chicago Cubs." *Critical Studies in Mass Communication*, 2 (September 1985), 262–81.

Wander, Philip. "The Aesthetics of Fascism." *Journal of Communication*, 33 (Spring 1983), 70–78.

Wander, Philip. "The Angst of the Upper Class." *Journal of Communication*, 29 (Autumn 1979), 85–88.

Wander, Philip C. "The John Birch and Martin Luther King Symbols in the Radical Right." *Western Speech*, 35 (Winter 1971), 4–14.

Wander, Philip. "On the Meaning of 'Roots.'" *Journal of Communication*, 27 (Autumn 1977), 64–69.

Wander, Philip. "The Rhetoric of American Foreign Policy." *Quarterly Journal of Speech*, 70 (November 1984), 339–61.

Wander, Philip C. "Salvation Through Separation: The Image of the Negro in the American Colonization Society." *Quarterly Journal of Speech*, 57 (February 1971), 57–67.

Wander, Philip C. "The Savage Child: The Image of the Negro in the Pro-Slavery Movement." *Southern Speech Communication Journal*, 37 (Summer 1972), 335–60.

Wander, Philip. "'The Waltons': How Sweet It Was." *Journal of Communication*, 26 (Autumn 1976), 148–54.

Watts, Eric K. "An Exploration of Spectacular Consumption: Gangsta Rap as Cultural Commodity." *Communication Studies*, 48 (Spring 1997), 42–58.

Weiss, Julie H. "Mothers as Others: The Construction of Race, Ethnicity, and Gender in Self-Help Literature of the 1940s." *Women's Studies in Communication*, 18 (Fall 1995), 153–63.

Wilson, Kirt H. "Towards a Discursive Theory of Racial Identity: *The Souls of Black Folk* as a Response to Nineteenth-Century Biological Determinism." *Western Journal of Communication*, 63 (Spring 1999), 193–215.

Xing, Lu. "An Ideological/Cultural Analysis of Political Slogans in Communist China." *Discourse & Society*, 10 (October 1999), 487–508.

Zagacki, Kenneth S. "The Rhetoric of American Decline: Paul Kennedy, Conservatives, and the Solvency Debate." *Western Journal of Communication*, 56 (Fall 1992), 372–93.

9

∿∿∿

Metaphor Criticism

Metaphors are nonliteral comparisons in which a word or phrase from one domain of experience is applied to another domain. Derived from the Greek words *meta*, meaning "over" and *phereras*, meaning "to carry," metaphor involves the process of transferring or carrying over aspects that apply to one object to a second object. When we describe an economic downturn in the Silicon Valley using metaphors such as "it has been in a tailspin," "Silicon Valley is the Mecca for startups," "the bottom fell out," "something will have to pick up the slack," and "the Web breathed new life into the Valley," we are describing an industry in terms from domains such as aviation, religion, and medicine.

A metaphor joins two terms normally regarded as belonging to different classes of experience. These two terms or the two parts of a metaphor are called the *tenor* and the *vehicle*. The tenor is the topic or subject that is being explained. The vehicle is the mechanism or lens through which the topic is viewed.[1] In the metaphor "My roommate is a pig," for example, the roommate is the tenor, the subject being addressed, and the pig is the vehicle or the lens being applied to the subject we are seeking to understand. The two terms are seen as related by a "system of associated commonplaces," entailments, or characteristics, and in their interaction to create a metaphor, the characteristics associated with the vehicle are used to organize conceptions of the tenor.[2] In the metaphor "My roommate is a pig," we use one system of commonplaces (those dealing with pigs) to filter or organize our conception of another system (that of the roommate). As the associated characteristics of the tenor and vehicle interact, some qualities are emphasized and others are suppressed. In addition, we recognize that there are both similarities and differences between the two systems of characteristics.[3]

The first extended treatment of metaphor was provided by Aristotle, who defined metaphor as "the transference of a name from the object to which it has a natural application."[4] Aristotle's definition set the direction for the study of metaphor as decoration or ornamentation. From this perspective, metaphor is seen as a figure of speech or linguistic embroidery that the rhetor uses only occasionally to give extra force to language. As Aristotle explains, metaphor "gives clearness, charm, and distinction to the style."[5] Cicero's view of metaphor is similar: "there is no mode of embellishment . . . that throws a greater lustre upon language."[6] To summarize this perspective on metaphor, metaphors "are not necessary, they are just nice."[7]

When metaphor is seen as decoration, it is regarded as a deviant form of language—as extraordinary rather than ordinary language. As Aristotle suggests, metaphors "create an unusual element in the diction by their not being in ordinary speech."[8] Thomas Hobbes, writing in the sixteenth and seventeenth centuries, echoes this notion, suggesting that metaphor frustrates the process of communicating thoughts and knowledge. He considers metaphor to be one of four abuses of speech because we "deceive others" when we use metaphor.[9] Richard Whately expresses a similar view of metaphor, suggesting that the use of metaphor departs "from the plain and strictly appropriate Style."[10]

When metaphor is seen as linguistic embellishment that makes it different from the typical use of language, rules are needed to limit its use in effective rhetoric. Throughout the history of the treatment of metaphor, strong warnings have been given against the improper use of metaphor. Although Aristotle states that metaphor is not something that can be taught,[11] he provides guidelines for its proper use. A metaphor, for example, should not be "ridiculous," "too grand," "too much in the vein of tragedy," or "far-fetched."[12] Cicero's writings on metaphor provide another illustration of the kinds of rules offered for its proper use. A metaphor must bear some resemblance to what it pictures, and it should give clarity to a point rather than confuse it.[13]

In contrast to the view of metaphor as decoration, metaphor now is seen as a major way in which we constitute reality. We do not perceive reality and then interpret or give it meaning. Rather, we experience reality through the language by which we describe it; it is whatever we describe it *as*. Metaphor is a basic way by which the process of using symbols to construct reality occurs. It serves as a structuring principle, focusing on particular aspects of a phenomenon and hiding others; thus, each metaphor produces a different description of the "same" reality. In Max Black's words: "Suppose I look at the night sky through a piece of heavily smoked glass on which certain lines have been left clear. Then I shall see only the stars that can be made to lie on the lines previously prepared upon the screen, and the stars I do see will be seen as organized by the screen's structure. We can think of a metaphor as such a screen."[14]

The metaphor that "time is money" illustrates how the use of a particular metaphor can affect our thought and experience of reality. This metaphor, reflected in common expressions in our culture such as, "This gadget will *save* you hours," "I've *invested* a lot of time in her," and "You need to *budget* your time," leads us to experience the reality of time in a particular way. Because we conceive of time as money, we understand and experience it as something that can be spent, budgeted, wasted, and saved. Long-distance telephone charges, hotel-room rates, yearly budgets, and interest on loans are examples of how time is experienced as money.

Yet another case of how our selection of a particular metaphor affects our perception of reality is the metaphor that "argument is war." That we tend to see an argument through the metaphor of war is evidenced in such expressions as, "He *attacked* my argument," "I *demolished* her argument," "I *won* the argument," and "He *shot down* all of my arguments." As a consequence of the war metaphor, we experience an argument as something we can win or lose. We view the person with whom we engage in the argument as an opponent. We may find a position indefensible and thus abandon it and adopt a new line of attack. In contrast, if we used a different metaphor on argument—"argument is a dance," for example—participants would be seen as partners. Their goals would be to perform in a balanced, harmonious, and aesthetically pleasing way; to collaborate to produce a finely coordinated performance; and to continue working until the dance was perfected. With the selection of a different metaphor, we would view and experience arguments differently.[15]

By organizing reality in particular ways, our selected metaphors also prescribe how to act. Metaphors contain implicit assumptions, points of view, and evaluations. They organize attitudes toward whatever they describe and provide motives for acting in certain ways. Because of the metaphor that time is money, for example, we expect particular actions from others. We expect to be paid according to amount of time worked, and we decide whether to engage in certain activities according to whether the time spent will be sufficiently valuable. Similarly, once a metaphor of *blighted area*—a metaphor of disease—is used to describe a community, we are motivated to remove the blight and thus cure the disease. Were the same area to be labeled a *neighborhood*, our evaluation of it would be positive and would focus on its homeyness, stability, and informal networks of support. We then would be motivated to preserve the community as it is. Whatever metaphor is used to label and experience a phenomenon, then, suggests evaluations of it and appropriate behavior in response.

When metaphor is seen as a way of knowing the world, it plays a particular role in argumentation. Metaphor does not simply provide support for an argument; instead, the structure of the metaphor itself argues. The metaphor explicates the appropriateness of the associated characteristics of one term to those of another term and thus invites an audience to adopt the resulting perspective. If the audience finds the associated characteristics acceptable and sees the appropriateness of linking the two systems of characteristics, the audience accepts the argument the metaphor offers.[16]

Steven Perry explains how metaphor constitutes argument in his study of the infestation metaphor in Hitler's rhetoric: "Hitler's critique of the Jew's status as a cultural being . . . is not illustrated by the metaphor of parasitism; it is *constituted* by this metaphor."[17] The figurative language is not supplementary or subordinate to the argument; it is itself Hitler's argument. The listener or reader who does not reject the interaction of the characteristics of *infestation* and *Jews* has accepted a claim about what the facts are and the evaluation expressed in the metaphor. A metaphor, then, argues just as typical argumentative structures do, but it usually does so more efficiently and comprehensively.[18]

A number of theorists in various fields have helped to develop the perspective that metaphor is a primary means by which phenomena in the world become objects of reality or knowledge for us.[19] George Lakoff and Mark Johnson were instrumental in introducing the notion that metaphor is pervasive in everyday language and thought. [20] Kenneth Burke takes a similar view, suggesting that metaphor plays a critical role "in the discovery and description of 'the truth.'"[21] "If we employ the word 'character' as a general term for whatever can be thought of as distinct (any thing, pattern, situation, structure, nature, person, object, act, rôle, process, event, etc.)," he explains, "then we could say that metaphor tells us something about one character as considered from the point of view of another character. And to consider A from the point of view of B is, of course, to use B as a *perspective* upon A."[22] In the communication field, Michael Osborn[23] and Robert L. Ivie[24] have been instrumental in theorizing and applying this perspective on metaphor.

PROCEDURES

Using the metaphor method of criticism, a critic analyzes an artifact in a four-step process: (1) selecting an artifact; (2) analyzing the artifact; (3) formulating a research question; and (4) writing the essay.

Selecting an Artifact

Choose an artifact for metaphor criticism that contains some explicit metaphors. At one level, of course, all language is metaphoric, but you will find metaphor criticism easier and more useful if you apply it to artifacts that contain some surface metaphors.

Analyzing the Artifact

In criticism in which metaphors are used as units of analysis, a critic analyzes an artifact in four steps: (1) examining the artifact for a general sense of its dimensions and context; (2) isolating the metaphors in the artifact; (3) sorting the metaphors into groups according to vehicle or tenor; and (4) discovering an explanation for the artifact.[25]

Examining the Artifact as a Whole

The first step for a critic is to become familiar with the text or elements of the artifact and its context to gain a sense of the complete experience of the artifact. Attention to the context is particularly important because, although some metaphors generally are understood in particular ways without attention to the context in which they are used, the meaning of most metaphors must be reconstructed from clues in the setting, occasion, audience, and rhetor. The meaning of calling a person a *pig*, for example, would be different when applied to a police officer by a crowd yelling "racist pig" than if applied to a teenager in her messy room. Information about the context of the artifact can be gathered in a variety of ways, including a review of rhetoric contemporaneous with the artifact, the audience's reactions to the artifact, and historical treatments of the context.

Isolating the Metaphors

The second step in a metaphor analysis is to isolate the metaphors employed by the rhetor. A brief selection from Martin Luther King, Jr.'s speech, "I Have a Dream," illustrates the procedure for isolating metaphors in an artifact. The introduction of King's speech includes this passage: "Five score years ago, a great American, in whose symbolic shadow we stand today, signed the Emancipation Proclamation. This momentous decree came as a great beacon light of hope to millions of Negro slaves, who had been seared in the flames of withering injustice. It came as a joyous daybreak to end the long night of their captivity." Six metaphors can be found in this passage: *in whose symbolic shadow we stand, great beacon light of hope, seared in the flames of withering injustice, daybreak,* and *long night of their captivity.* Although, in many artifacts, only the vehicle is actually present in metaphors and the tenor is implied, in this passage, King includes both tenor and vehicle in most of his metaphors. The tenor of hope is seen through the vehicle of a beacon light, injustice is flame, the Emancipation Proclamation is daybreak, and captivity is the long night. His metaphor of standing in the symbolic shadow of Lincoln, however, does not explicitly include a tenor. Implied is a tenor of history and past struggles that cast their shadow and lend their spirit to the current situation. In the process of isolating metaphors in your artifact, look for metaphors where both tenor and vehicle are present and for those where only the vehicle is stated. At the end of this process, you have reduced the artifact to a list of metaphors.

Sorting the Metaphors

The next step of the process involves sorting the metaphors you have identified into groups, looking for patterns in metaphor use. The metaphors are sorted or grouped according to either vehicle or tenor, depending on your interest and the kinds of insights that are emerging for each in the analysis. If you want to discover how a rhetor conceptualizes a particular subject, group together all of the vehicles used to depict that subject. For example, if you note that a rhetor describes a workplace using terms such as *zoo*, *asylum*, *snake pit*, *jungle*, and *firestorm*, you are sorting the metaphors according to vehicles, and the tenor remains the same.

If you are interested in a rhetor's general worldview, identify all of the metaphors you find in the artifact. You are likely to discover a number of different tenors or topics and a number of different vehicles used to frame those topics. The major tenors and vehicles that appear in a text serve as an index to how the rhetor sees the world. In this case, you are sorting metaphors around the tenors in the artifact. In Martin Luther King, Jr.'s speech, for example, the metaphors used by King can be grouped into tenors that deal with blacks, the Constitution, and America.

Discovering an Explanation for the Artifact

In this step, the groups of metaphors—metaphors organized around either tenors or vehicles—are analyzed to develop an explanation for your artifact. You probably chose to analyze your artifact because there is some aspect of the artifact that doesn't fit or that you cannot explain. Perhaps you like the artifact and cannot explain its appeal for you. Perhaps it disturbs you, but you don't know why. Perhaps it seems unusual in some way. Your coding of the metaphors, in which some aspects of tenors, vehicles, or both are revealed as significant, can provide an explanation for your initial reactions.

Use the principles of frequency and intensity to discover what is significant about the metaphors and provide an explanation of your artifact. If vehicles from the same category are used repeatedly to describe many different tenors, for example, this is a pattern that might suggest an important insight about the artifact. If your analysis reveals that a particular tenor is described using a very unusual vehicle, you would note that as significant on the basis of intensity. Those metaphors that stand out because of frequency and intensity in tenors and/or vehicles, then, suggest areas where something is going on that can help explain the artifact.

The significant features that emerge from your metaphor analysis may suggest various kinds of explanations for your artifact. An explanation, for example, may deal with the image the vehicles convey of the topics discussed by the rhetor, the ideas that are highlighted and masked as a result of the metaphors used, the attitudes and values for which the metaphors argue, or the effects the particular metaphors are likely to have on the audience. Your explanation also might lie in how the rhetor's identity or actions are shaped by the metaphors selected.

Formulating a Research Question

Your research question for a metaphor analysis depends on whether your explanation of the artifact features tenor or vehicle. If you are featuring a particular tenor and are interested in the vehicles used to describe the tenor, your question would be about the tenor or topic and the implications of the selection of the particular vehicles for the rhetor's worldview, the audience's perception of the topic, or the way in which debates or controversies about the topic might play out in the world. If your analysis features the vehicles used by a rhetor to discuss many different tenors or topics, your research question would be about the implications of constructing a world as the rhetor has done for the rhetor, the audience, or a public controversy.

Writing the Essay

After completing the analysis, you are ready to write your essay, which includes five major components: (1) an introduction, in which you discuss the research question, its contribution to rhetorical theory, and its significance; (2) a description of the artifact and its context; (3) a description of the method of criticism—in this case, metaphor analysis; (4) a report of the findings of the analysis, in which you reveal the metaphors, their patterns, and their function in the artifact; and (5) a discussion of the contribution the analysis makes to rhetorical theory.

SAMPLE ESSAYS

The following essays provide samples of criticism in which metaphors are used as units of analysis to answer various research questions. In Gerald V. O'Brien's essay on metaphors used in the debate concerning the restriction of immigration in the early 1900s, he is guided by the implicit research question, "How can the selection of metaphors affect policy debates?" In his analysis of an essay by Allan Gurganus on his experience as a soldier in Vietnam, Ryan H. Blum asks the research question, "How can marginalized groups express resistance to a hegemonic rhetoric?" Marla Kanengieter-Wildeson's essay analyzing a building by architect Michael Graves focuses on visual metaphors, and her analysis is directed toward answering the research question, "How are ideologies subverted through the use of visual metaphors?" She combines ideological and metaphor criticism to answer this question.

Notes

[1] The terms *tenor* and *vehicle* were suggested by I. A. Richards, *The Philosophy of Rhetoric* (London: Oxford University Press, 1936), p. 96. David Douglass discusses confusion over these terms in "Issues in the Use of I. A. Richards' Tenor-Vehicle Model of Metaphor," *Western Journal of Communication*, 64 (Fall 2000), 405–24.

[2] The term *associated commonplaces* was suggested by Max Black, *Models and Metaphors: Studies in Language and Philosophy* (Ithaca, NY: Cornell University Press, 1962), p. 40; *entailments* was suggested by George Lakoff and Mark Johnson, *Metaphors We Live By* (Chicago: University of Chicago Press, 1980), p. 9.

[3] For more on the notion of differences in the operation of metaphor, see Richards, p. 127.

[4] Aristotle, *Poetics*, 21.

[5] Aristotle, *Rhetoric*, 3.2.

[6] Cicero, *On Oratory and Orators*, 3.41.

[7] Andrew Ortony, "Metaphor: A Multidimensional Problem," in *Metaphor and Thought*, ed. Andrew Ortony (Cambridge: Cambridge University Press, 1979), p. 3.

[8] Aristotle, *Poetics*, 22.

[9] Thomas Hobbes, *Leviathan*, ed. C. B. MacPherson (1651; rpt. New York: Penguin, 1951), pt. 1, chpt. 4, p. 102.

[10] Richard Whately, *Elements of Rhetoric* (New York: Harper, 1864), pt. 3, chpt. 2.3.

[11] Aristotle, *Poetics*, 22.

[12] Aristotle, *Rhetoric*, 3.34.

[13] Cicero, 3.39.

[14] Black, p. 41.

[15] Lakoff and Johnson, pp. 4, 7–9.

[16] Steven Perry, "Rhetorical Functions of the Infestation Metaphor in Hitler's Rhetoric," *Central States Speech Journal*, 34 (Winter 1983), p. 230; and Carroll C. Arnold, *Criticism of Oral Rhetoric* (Columbus, OH: Charles E. Merrill, 1974), p. 203.

[17] Perry, p. 230.

[18] Michael Leff, "I. Topical Invention and Metaphoric Interaction," *Southern Speech Communication Journal*, 48 (Spring 1983), 226.

[19] For summaries of the history of the treatment of metaphor, see: Michael M. Osborn, "The Evolution of the Theory of Metaphor in Rhetoric," *Western Speech*, 31 (Spring 1967), 121–32; and Mark Johnson, "Introduction: Metaphor in the Philosophical Tradition," in *Philosophical Perspectives on Metaphor*, ed. Mark Johnson (Minneapolis: University of Minnesota Press, 1981), pp. 3–47.

[20] Lakoff and Johnson.

[21] Kenneth Burke, *A Grammar of Motives* (1945; rpt. Berkeley: University of California Press, 1969), p. 503.

[22] Burke, pp. 503–04.

[23] Michael M. Osborn and Douglas Ehninger, "The Metaphor in Public Address," *Communication Monographs*, 29 (August 1962), 223–34; John Waite Bowers and Michael M. Osborn, "Attitudinal Effects of Selected Types of Concluding Metaphors in Persuasive Speeches," *Communication Monographs*, 33 (June 1966), 147–55; Michael Osborn, "Archetypal Metaphor in Rhetoric: The Light-Dark Family," *Quarterly Journal of Speech*, 53 (April 1967), 115–26; Osborn, "The Evolution of the Theory of Metaphor in Rhetoric"; and Michael Osborn, "The Evolution of the Archetypal Sea in Rhetoric and Poetic," *Quarterly Journal of Speech*, 63 (December 1977), 347–63.

[24] Robert L. Ivie, "The Metaphor of Force in Prowar Discourse: The Case of 1812," *Quarterly Journal of Speech*, 68 (August 1982), 240–53; Robert L. Ivie, "Speaking 'Common Sense' About the Soviet Threat: Reagan's Rhetorical Stance," *Western Journal of Communication*, 48 (Winter 1984), 39–50; Robert L. Ivie, "Literalizing the Metaphor of Soviet Savagery: President Truman's Plain Style," *Southern Communication Journal*, 51 (Winter 1986), 91–105; and Robert L. Ivie, "Metaphor and the Rhetorical Invention of Cold War 'Idealists,'" *Communication Monographs*, 54 (June 1987), 165–82.

[25] These steps in the process of metaphor criticism came largely from Ivie, "Metaphor and the Rhetorical Invention of Cold War 'Idealists,'" pp. 167–68.

Indigestible Food, Conquering Hordes, and Waste Materials

Metaphors of Immigrants and the Early Immigration Restriction Debate in the United States

Gerald V. O'Brien

As President George W. Bush discovered shortly after he referred to the "war on terrorism" as a "crusade," metaphors and other rhetoric can have a great amount of importance in the policy arena. Whether describing social problems, the proposed response to them, or even the players and groups involved, even a single word can be a potent vehicle for enhancing or diminishing support for one's position (Lakoff, 1995). It is not merely coincidental that political debate is often peppered with such picturesque terminology. As Donald Schön (1979) noted, problem setting, or the formation of how social problems are perceived, may be a more important policy issue than problem solving, and problems are framed in large part through the employment of metaphors (p. 255). To quote Krohn (1987), "those who attempt to defend questionable word choices by claiming 'it's only semantics' fail to understand that much more is involved than mere vocalization" (p. 142).

This article describes metaphoric themes that were employed during the immigration restriction debate of early 20th century. This debate led to the most sweeping immigration restriction policies in U.S. history, in the Immigration Acts of 1921 and 1924. Since a brief overview of the immigration restriction debate itself is important in providing a context for metaphor use, the article begins with this. Following the overview, the major metaphoric themes will be described, with the article concluding with a section discussing the implications of this study for metaphor scholars.

EARLY IMMIGRATION RESTRICTION LEGISLATION

In the United States, fear and denigration of immigrants was present throughout the 19th century. Organized opposition to foreigners, however, did not reach a fever pitch until the decades immediately preceding and following the turn of the century. Between 1880 and 1920 the number of new immigrants into the country increased greatly, in some years exceeding a million per year. Whether the country could adequately assimilate such a large number of persons was a predominant concern.

Much of the anxiety surrounding immigration resulted from the geographic distribution of immigrants by homeland. Following the 1880s, those entering the United States were, in general, coming not from the Western and Northern European nations that had earlier populated the land, but more so from Eastern and Southern European nations such as Russia, Hungary, and Italy (Garis, 1924;

From *Metaphor and Symbol*, 18 (2003), 33-47. Used by permission of Lawrence Erlbaum Associates, Inc. and the author.

Young, 1922). These groups would be described in the writings of immigration restriction advocates as, respectively, the "old" and the "new" immigration.

The most pressing concern about the new immigrants was that they were regarded as physically, mentally, and morally inferior to the older immigrant class. Studies purported to show that immigrants were populating the prisons and mental institutions in much greater percentages than native stocks, and that the intelligence quotient of Southern and Eastern European immigrants was markedly lower than their peers from the North and West (Brigham, 1923; McLaughlin, 1903; Young, 1922). The nation, many argued, needed to focus on quality and not quantity in its immigrant class (Ward, 1910).

Although the number and presumed quality of the "new" immigration were primary rationales for restricting entrance into the nation, many other fears magnified the threat. These included concerns that they threatened the jobs of Americans, that they depressed pay scales, that their votes could easily be bought by corrupt politicians, and that their congregation in large urban areas would change the power structure through bloc voting (Calavita, 1984; Garis, 1924; McLaughlin, 1903).

With the exception of anti-Chinese legislation, early immigration restriction policies in the United States focused not on race or nationality, but rather on keeping out those immigrants who possessed "undesirable" characteristics, such as various disabling conditions, infectious diseases, pauperism, and anarchistic tendencies (Calavita, 1984; Fairchild, 1926). In 1917, the literacy test was signed into law, requiring immigrants be able to read either English or their native language (Calavita, 1984; Hall, 1913).

The 1921 immigration restriction act was passed in response to the ostensible need to legislate a more sweeping policy. This temporary act, which became permanent and more restrictive in 1924, was the most significant immigration restriction policy in American history. The primary component of the 1921 law was the development of a national origin quota. By means of this quota, annual immigration from specific countries would be limited to 3% of the total number of foreign-born persons from that country that were in the United States according to the 1910 census. Because of the nature of the national quotas, immigration from "undesirable" nations of Southern and Eastern Europe was drastically reduced (Calavita, 1984; Hutchinson, 1981).

PATTERNS OF METAPHOR USE IN DESCRIBING THE "NEW" IMMIGRATION

Those who wrote in public forums in favor of restrictive immigration measures were apt to depict the threats that were posed by an "open door" policy through the extensive employment of metaphors. The following themes include examples of metaphoric language that were designed to denigrate immigrants. Also important in the analysis, however, is consideration of what Lakoff (1995) called "conceptual" metaphors, or what Allbritton (1995) termed "metaphor-based schemas." Although metaphors are usually described, Allbritton wrote, as "figurative expressions" or utterances, they can also be understood as a more global means of viewing the "target domain," or that which is described through the metaphor (pp. 36–37). Take, for example, the object metaphor. The phrase "waste material" is a clear metaphorical expression describing the target domain, in this case many of the new immigrants, as disposable objects. The more sweeping "IMMIGRANT AS OBJECT" conceptual metaphor, on the other hand, may be reinforced in a large variety of ways, many of them nonlinguistic. Indentured servitude, ethnic stereotyping, and the replacement of immigrants by machinery in the workplace are only a few of the nonverbal methods by which the conceptual metaphor is supported. Although most of the following examples demonstrate the linguistic use of metaphors, the conceptual aspects of the metaphors will also be discussed.

Organism Metaphor

The organism metaphor was a particularly apt means of describing the presumed adverse impact of immigrants on the nation. Described by Levine (1995), the central feature of the organism metaphor as a conceptual metaphor is that the social community is viewed as analogous to a physical body. Just as the integrity of our own bodies may be threatened by contaminating external elements, so too is the social body vulnerable to corruption by invading sub-groups. Although linguistic metaphors related to disease are most often used to describe the negative impact of the marginalized group on society, metaphors that relate to discomfort or disfigurement may also be included within the organism metaphor. An example of the former is the depiction of the immigrant as indigestible food causing digestive pains, while an example of the latter would be the portrayal of the immigrant or the immigrant's home or business as a blight on the neighborhood.

Many elements of a country are analogous to bodily elements, and we often speak, for example, of the "body of the nation." In addition, immigration became an issue of concern in conjunction with the rapid increase in disease prevention and the public health profession. Infection- and disease-related metaphors were very much in keeping with the thinking of immigration restrictionists, and provided a rhetorically picturesque means of sharing these fears publicly. Moreover, immigrants have always been rightly feared as carriers of disease, and thus the public was conditioned to think of them in such a way. The earliest immigration restriction policies were passed in response to the very real fear of the spread of disease from incoming foreigners (Abbott, 1924; "'The Pestilence at the Gate," 1921). Once the connection between disease and immigrants was formed, it became linguistically easy to describe all immigrants as potentially diseased organisms who threatened the integrity of the nation.

A principle concern of the new immigration from Southern and Eastern Europe was its massing together within large urban settings such as New York and Chicago—or, in the case of Japanese and Chinese immigrants, California—rather than being dispersed throughout the country. This clustering of immigrants in "alien communities" within the nation's borders was a source of fear not only because these groups were depicted as crowding out the "native" population and taking over the cities, but also because such clustering was taken to have an adverse impact on assimilation.

Organism metaphors that were particularly apt to be used in conjunction with assimilation included "digestion" and "absorption." Just as the food we ingest benefits us in large part because it is distributed throughout the body, that which is not easily digested by or absorbed within the body is viewed as discomforting or even a threat to health (Fairchild, 1926). This is just as true of the social body as it is of the individual organism. Americans, Roberts (1924) wrote in support of 1924 immigration legislation, wanted "a law that will . . . give America a chance to digest the millions of unassimilated, unwelcome and unwanted aliens that rest so heavily in her" prior to taking on a great many more (p. 58). Americans had discovered, French Strother noted (1923), that "the stomach of the body politic [was] filled to bursting with peoples swallowed whole whom our digestive juices do not digest" (p. 634). A 1912 article in the *Literary Digest* stated that the immigrant "settles into masses, indigestible, with almost no chance for American influences—even for knowledge of America—to touch him" ("Making the immigrant unwelcome," 1912, p. 36). Edwin Conklin (1921) provided an extended description of the organism metaphor, noting that:

> We talk euphemistically about the "assimilation" of foreign peoples, as if they were so much food material that could be digested, absorbed, and built into our own organization without in any way changing that organization except to make it larger. . . . But the only way in which we could "assimilate" alien races, that is, convert them into our own life and not be converted into theirs, would be by eating and digesting them, thus destroying their protoplasm, hereditary traits, instincts, and cultures, and out of the elements of these building up our own organization. (p. 357)

In describing the rapid increase in immigration, especially from Southern and Eastern Europe, Cannon (1923) focused on the disease element of the organism metaphor when he warned that "we have begun to gag a bit over the size and quality of the dose." "Is it simply," he wondered, "that the food is strange and alien, or does it possibly contain poisons against which we have no antidote" (p. 325)? Metaphors depicting the immigrant as a source of contagion were especially apt to be used in conjunction with those groups that were viewed as posing a threat to American democracy. Shortly after the turn of the century McLaughlin (1903) wrote that "the law-abiding citizen fears from the immigrant, not only the germ of bodily disease, but the germ of anarchy and also favorable media for its growth" (p. 231). During the Red Scare that followed World War I and the Russian Revolution, an article in the *Washington Post* warned that the nation was being threatened by "a flood of undesirables inoculated with the virus of Bolshevism and Communism" (cited in "An Alien Antidumping Bill," 1921, p. 13). Frazer added (1923b) that Socialist publications supporting unionization were "cheap inflammatory rot, as poisonous and destructive in its effects as typhus germs in a run-down system" (p. 88). Such organism metaphors would obviously become a staple of the McCarthy era vision of the communist as a burrowing figure bent on contaminating others with his venomous ideals and fostering spiritual and political decay of the national organism.

The organism metaphor was particularly descriptive of the connection between the human bloodstream and early perceptions of the "gene pool" or the racial composition of the community. "Until the foreign blood we have is absorbed so that it is made American," insisted a commentary in the Washington *Herald*, "a further transfusion is anything but desirable" (cited in "The Threatened Inundation from Europe, 1920, p. 9). Immigrants were said to be a "stream of impurity" that needed to be thoroughly filtered, a "tide of pollution" that had to be purified, and a "turgid stream of undesirable and unassimilable human 'off-scourings'" (Ellis, 1923, p. 80; "Keep America 'White'"!, 1923, p. 399; "Making the immigrant unwelcome," 1912, p. 13).

The "IMMIGRANT AS DISEASED ORGANISM" conceptual metaphor was fostered by the perception that immigrants were increasing exponentially, both through the large number of new arrivals and their great fecundity (Hendrick, 1907; Phelan, 1919; Rowell, 1920). They would eventually, many believed, take over communities and eventually the nation itself. Although the following quote includes some linguistic metaphors, it is more important in its overall presentation of the immigrant population as a potentially infectious cancerous growth:

> In every city the tendency of the foreigners is to colonization. The units cohere, the mass crystallizes, and stands apart from other elements of the population. It is a process of segregation. A nucleus comes from Europe and takes up a house; other groups, coming from the same village or province, gather around this center; it grows, pushing out the former occupants of the block, working ever from the inner courts and alleys out to the main streets or avenues, until at length the block becomes preponderatingly foreign, and stands there, as related to the city, like a flint surrounded by a bed of chalk. (Roberts, 1914, p. 160)

Central to the "IMMIGRANT AS DISEASED ORGANISM" conceptual metaphor are fears of spread, contamination, and decomposition. These elements were often reinforced even when linguistic metaphors were not employed. As with more recent "white flight," writers shared stories of previously "pristine" neighborhoods that were taken over by marginalized groups, which supposedly led to degeneration and decay of the area. Immigrants were a threat, James Davis (1922) wrote, because the United States was a "new and clean country," whereas "life in foreign lands among filth and dirt brought upon the countries of the Old World great plagues of typhus, cholera, leprosy, tuberculosis, and many other diseases" (p. 257).

It was generally accepted that new immigrant groups came from unsanitary corners of the globe, traveled in disease-ridden ships, and, even in America, lived in cramped unhygienic tenements where disease was prevalent. One of the hallmarks of the organism metaphor is that its targets often find themselves living in conditions where they develop diseases at much higher rates than the "normal" population. Jewish ghettoes, mental institutions, massive public housing projects, and other such "stigmatized" environments serve to make the metaphorical real, and thus solidify the use of disease metaphors as an apt means of portraying the group in question.

Object Metaphor

The objectification of immigrants was accomplished in part through the substantial use of race, class, and ethnic stereotypes and demographic statistics to describe immigration-related problems and trends. The terms that were used to describe newcomers, however, also fostered the view that such persons were largely impersonal or interchangeable objects. Throughout the primary literature, immigrants were repeatedly represented as "MATERIAL" whose distinctive characteristic was in their value to the nation as cheap labor. An argument for the 1921 restriction bill was that it would "stimulate the inflow from countries which yield much more assimilable material" (cited in "Inviting Immigration," 1921, p. 8). Another opponent of open immigration sarcastically wrote that "practically all of the material brought into the Children's Court for remoulding is a gift from Europe" (Coulter, 1904, p. 731).

The unfinished nature of the immigrant was such that the immigrant was often described as "raw material" (Fairchild, 1926, p. 396). Although the raw material metaphor at least held out the hope that the immigrant—or more likely, his/her descendents—could be fashioned into a productive American citizen, in many cases the undesirable newcomer was characterized as waste material, or "cargoes of human flotsam" (*Congressional Record*, 1921, p. 1438). Many writers were especially concerned about "supported" immigration, whereby other countries would force their criminals or other undesirable citizens to emigrate to the U.S. In response to this practice, restrictionists contended that the country was becoming the "'dumping ground' of the refuse material of the Old World," and implored Americans to do something about "the dumping of Europe's human refuse at our doors" ("Keep America 'White'"!, 1923, p. 400; Weber, 1892, p. 424). "It is obvious to me," Leon Whitney (1926) wrote, "that Europe has regarded America as a human garbage can" (p. 4).

The "IMMIGRANT AS MATERIAL" metaphor was especially pertinent for describing the "melting pot" theory of assimilation (Garis, 1924, p. 366; Ward, 1913, p. 100). James Davis, the Secretary of Labor, said (1922) that the congregation of immigrants prevented the melting pot from blending them together. Recommending that incoming immigrants be distributed throughout the nation, he wrote that "We have got to take out the lumps or break them up and smooth out the mass" (p. 257). This view of immigrants as "ingredients" obviously grades over into the organism metaphor and the view of the immigrant as an entity to be "absorbed" or "digested." The much-quoted words from Israel Zangwill's play *The Melting Pot* includes both organism and object metaphors:

> There she lies, the great Melting Pot—listen! Can't you hear the roaring and the bubbling? There gapes her mouth—the harbor where a thousand mammoth feeders come from the ends of the world to pour in their human freight. Ah, what a stirring and a seething! Celt and Latin, Slav and Teuton, Greek and Syrian—black and yellow . . . how the great Alchemist melts and fuses them with his purging flame. (1917, pp. 184–185)

The objectification of the immigrant was also fostered by "trade" rhetoric that compared immigrants to other forms of commerce. The *Washington Post* noted that just as Congress passed

> emergency legislation to protect commerce and industry by preventing the dumping of foreign goods upon the American market, . . . the opponents of the [1921] immigration bill would deny like protection to the working-people and would permit the dumping of foreign labor in unlimited quantities upon the American market. . . . Why should this nation become a dumping-ground of human material any more than a dumping ground of cheap-labor goods? (cited in "Making the Immigrant Unwelcome," 1912, p. 13)

Roy Garis noted in 1924 that "today the immigrant's labor is considered no more than any other commodity to be bought at the lowest price" (p. 67). Eugenicist and immigration restrictionist Harry Laughlin, in his influential report before Congress on the need for restrictive measures, noted that with any other commodity the "importer of goods" passed judgement on articles prior to agreeing to accept them. We should, he added, have the same attitude toward immigrants ("Europe as an Emigrant-Exporting," 1924, 1239). Ellis Island physician Dr. Victor Stafford contended "it is a no more difficult task to detect poorly built, defective or broken down human beings than to recognize a cheap or defective automobile" (cited in Kraut, 1994, p. 63).

The "IMMIGRANT AS OBJECT" conceptual metaphor was fostered by the large size of the immigrant population, their segregation from the rest of the community, and the perception that many of them refused to assimilate to American life. As objects of labor, immigrants were welcomed when low-wage work was needed, but, as with the Chinese who helped to build the railroads, once their labor was completed their utility was marginal. That immigrants were replaceable by new machinery also bolstered the conceptual metaphor of the immigrant as an object of labor (Collins, 1924).

Due to the general belief that many of the new immigrants embraced their native as opposed to their adapted homeland, restrictionists contended that it was appropriate to view them simply as interchangeable members of their "racial" group. General DeWitt's famous statement that "A Jap's a Jap" pertained both to Americans of Japanese descent as well as the foreign enemies of America during World War II (Ogawa, 1971, p. 11). American anti-Semitic writings of the day also presented Jewish immigrants as a separate people who could not become Americans. Even if they attempted to assimilate or even "pass" as gentiles, many advocates of restriction argued that Jews were destined to always maintain their "Jewish essence."

Natural Catastrophe and War Metaphors

As the number of immigrants per year increased to a million or more, the surge was portrayed by many restrictions as a natural catastrophe or enemy invasion. Obviously one of the most frequently used terms that described the growing immigrant population was "FLOOD." The flood metaphor was especially likely to be used in conjunction with the threat to American character that was posed by the overwhelming rush of immigrants (Ellis, 1923; Ward, 1913). Whether perceived as a poison coursing through the blood veins of the nation or an engulfing flood, liquid metaphors were an important element of restrictionist writings, and served as an apt means of portraying a group of persons who arrived over the water.

Thomas Darlington wrote in the *North American Review* in 1906 that the "incoming tide threatens to overwhelm us with the magnitude and ceaseless oncoming of its flood" (p.1266). If, restrictionists warned, limitations were not increased, "the flood gates will be down and a turgid sea of aliens will inundate our seaports" ("Guarding the Gates," 1924, p. 401). Two years after passage of the 1921 legislation, James Davis noted that this policy had "effectively dammed a rising tide of immigration from Europe" (1923, p. 134). One House Member expressed concern that the restriction acts necessitated increased vigilance at the Canadian and Mexican borders. "Now that we are tightening the restrictions and trying to partially dam the stream," he wrote, "the pressure at the weak points will be greater" (*Congressional Record*, May 13, 1921, p. 1436). Describing the fears of unrestricted Asian immigration, another writer warned that for the government to refuse to maintain policies establishing different immigration standards for Europeans and Orientals would be to "undermine the dike that keeps out the infinite ocean" (Rowell, 1920, p. 65). Elizabeth Frazer (1923c) was particularly picturesque in her description of immigrants:

> It's a ceaseless ebb and flow, a vast tidal river of labor, of homeless peasantry,
> surging in, surging out, backing up a bit in winters and slack seasons, and boil-

ing out again like a massive sheet of water over a dam at the onset of prosperity in the spring. (p. 14)

Related to the natural catastrophe metaphor was the war metaphor. An us-against-them imperative arose not only because of the alien nature of the immigrant, but also due to their presumed deficiencies and refusal to assimilate. These groups of undesirable foreigners were bent on engaging in, even without their knowledge, a bloodless takeover of the nation. Numerous advocates of restrictive measures depicted the "new" immigration as an "invasion" of the country. Comparing immigration to the nation's involvement in World War I, Conklin (1921) wrote that "armies equal in size to the one we sent to France land every two years on our shores" (p. 353). According to Warne (1913), the foreign invasion of the United States was "equal to one hundred and fifty full regiments of one thousand each." Therefore, he continued ominously, these foreigners "were double the entire fighting strength of the United States Army" (p. 2). Is it necessary, he queried, that "the invader should come in warships instead of in the steerage hold of steam vessels before the migration can be called an invasion" (p. 7)? The immigration problem was so serious, Cannon (1923) said, that "like the hordes of old they are destined to conquer us in the end, unless by some miracle of human contriving we conquer them first" (p. 330). Restrictive immigration laws, intoned a former New York congressman in 1892, "were more necessary than forts and ships against hostile invasions" (cited in Curran, 1975, p. 118).

Many writers contended that immigrant groups had already taken over many sections of the country. James Phelan, a California politician who spearheaded the anti-Japanese movement in the state, wrote in 1919 that there were "upwards of eighty thousand Japanese in California, and they are as much a tributary colony of Japan as though the flag of Nippon had supplanted the Stars and Stripes" (p. 324). Writers spoke of urban areas where large numbers of new immigrants settled as "foreign cities" within the nation (Frazer, 1923a, 1923b, 1923c; Roberts, 1924).

The "IMMIGRANT AS INVADER" conceptual metaphor was supported not only by the large number of immigrants and their massing together, but in addition by the fact that the characteristics, traditions and values of many new immigrant groups were not the same as those of the older immigrant population. A substantial percentage of the new immigration, for example, was from Catholic (Italy and Ireland) and Jewish (Russia and Eastern Europe) countries. Many early restrictionists viewed this "invasion" by religious minorities as a direct and imminent threat to the religious traditions and moral underpinnings of the nation.

A more insidious threat related to the fear that the new immigrants would overwhelm the racial integrity of the nation. New immigrants were portrayed not only as an enemy force, but also as an adversary that was not even aware of the damage that it was likely to inflict on the nation. The arguments of early racial anthropologists such as Arthur de Gobineau and Houston Stewart Chamberlain were regurgitated in the writings of many immigration restrictionists. Greece, Rome, and other seminal cultures, they argued, did not die out because of invasions from without, but rather from race degeneration that arose through miscegenation and "race suicide" (Chamberlain, 1913; De Gobineau, 1966; Grant, 1916). It did little good to protect the nation through armies and munitions, they intoned, when an unseen, but more deadly, internal enemy was corrupting America from within.

Animal and Subhuman Metaphors

The dehumanization of "out-groups" is often fostered through widespread use of animalistic metaphors to describe group members. Although such metaphors were less prevalent in the immigration restriction debate than organism, object, natural catastrophe, and war metaphors, they were invoked periodically. Animal metaphors were often used when the particular characteristic of an animal was seemingly descriptive of the threat posed by the immigrant group. Foreigners congregated in colonies, "like a swarming ball of bees upon a tree branch" (Frazer, 1923a, p. 6), and transatlantic stowaways were like "a wiggling, squirming mass of humanity [which] lay exposed . . . like a nest of venomous snakes" (Weiss, 1921, p. 40). In an extended portrayal, Owen Wister (1921) said that immigrants were cuckoos that had flown "into the open windows and doors" of Uncle Sam's house. The cuckoo, he wrote, "never builds its own nest, but always lays its egg in the nest of some other bird." Eventually, of course, the cuckoo would take over the nest from its original inhabitants. Wister warned that although the American eagle was mightier than any cuckoo, it was "not larger than a million cuckoos," and its future was thus threatened (p. 47).

Groups that are targeted for control are often compared to parasites or "low animals" capable of infection and contamination. This image combines the animal and the organism metaphor (Keen, 1986; Lowenthal & Guterman, 1970). Feri Weiss (1921) wrote that those who populated "'Little Italy, 'Little Ghetto,' 'Little Hungary,' or any other 'little' colony in New York or Kalamazoo" were "parasites on the oak of national prosperity, and should be eradicated" (pp. 200–201). Immigrants of "inferior quality" were also referred to as "white ants" who were "eating away the political structure" of the nation and "a big swarm of mosquitoes, infested with malaria and yellow fever germs" ("The Harm of Immigration," 1893, p. 43; Weiss, 1921, p. 207). In her 1923 *Saturday Evening Post* series, Frazer (1923a) described her study of immigrants in medical terminology, stating that her intention was to "investigate the foreign colonies imbedded in the fair physical corpus of New York." What would we see, the author asked, "if we put an actual wriggling cross-section of life under the microscope and took a squint through the lens" (p. 6)?

The "IMMIGRANT AS ANIMAL OR SUBHUMAN ENTITY" conceptual metaphor was reinforced by writings that seemed to demonstrate that new immigrants reflected a less evolved state of civilization than "native" Americans and the older immigrant population. In the writings of many immigration restrictionists, the level or complexity of one's native civilization was directly related to one's "humanness." Elizabeth Frazer described the primitive nature of "new" immigrants in wording that echoed the eugenicists of the day. In their native lands, she noted, they led

> A serene, tranquil, backwater existence untroubled by any wild, turbulent questions of that intelligence which, by its fermenting through the ages, has reared up man on his legs as an adventurous biped instead of continuing a foursome existence alongside his quadruped brethren. In these villages, intellectually speaking, a kind of noble, passive vacuum prevails. . . . It is from stagnant reservoirs like this that many of our morons derive. (Frazer, 1923e, 105)

Frazer's earlier installment in the series (1923b), on immigrants in Pittsburgh, noted that not much should be expected of Russian peasants, since they "simply haven't climbed up that far yet on the racial family tree" (p. 85). The perception that devalued immigrant groups symbolized an atavistic species was made clear too by Cannon (1923):

> Some of them represent types insensitive to the stimuli of cultural civilization. In the animal world the amoeba must have existed unchanged for millions of years. It is not a degenerate type for there is nothing more primitive in the animal creation, but it has remained untouched by the influences that have played upon it from the beginning. Our knowledge of man covers too brief a period to allow us to dogmatize, but there are certain races that show a somewhat similar incapacity for growth and development, even under conditions which produce marked alterations in other races. (p. 331).

DISCUSSION

The metaphors that were employed to denigrate immigrants reinforced both conscious and subliminal fears that were particularly ominous because of the rapidly changing culture of the time. Industrialization, urban expansion, unionization, the war in Europe, medical advances and the growth in the public health system were just a few elements of cultural reorganization, and all related in important ways to immigration. The challenge of those who advocated restrictive measures during the first decades of the twentieth century was to convince the descendents of immigrants that their own ancestors were different, in crucial ways, than those who were now coming to America. This was accomplished with the aid of metaphors that served to set the latter group apart as profoundly divergent from those who "built the country."

This is not to say that immigration restriction itself was inappropriate or wrong. Judging the actions of the past against contemporary moral standards is, of course, extremely problematic. Much of the fear of immigration during the first quarter of the century was justifiable, especially considering the large numbers of immigrants, and their congregation in large urban areas. The Immigration Acts of 1921 and 1924, however, focused not just on the quantity of immigration but also on the quality, and tied the latter issue to race, ethnicity and social class-related fears. Dehumanizing and menacing metaphors were primarily invoked to underscore these fears, and create the vision of a great and healthy nation whose very survival was threatened by corrupting, infectious, and violent outside elements.

Writings that depict marginalized groups as less than human or a threat to society constitute an important and possibly essential precursor to inhumane or adverse social policies. This is especially true in a democratic nation that purportedly values egalitarianism, individual rights and due process. Justification for limiting the rights of minority groups requires the development of negative social images of these groups in question—images that are often fostered through the use of both linguistic and conceptual metaphors. When the public at large accepts these pejorative metaphorical depictions as an accurate means of perceiving group members, regressive policies may be forthcoming. Brennan (1995), Keen (1986), Noël (1994), O'Brien, (1999), Wolfensberger (1972) and others have noted that pejorative metaphors often serve to frame public debates that relate to marginalized community groups. Such framing often leads directly to presumptions about both the cause of social problems and the most effective policy response to them (Elwood, 1995; Lakoff, 1995; Schön, 1979). If marginalized groups can be depicted as being less than fully human, members do not require the full range of human rights. If members seem to pose a threat to the community, public action against them can be justified as measures of self-defense (Brennan, 1995).

The importance of an analysis of metaphoric themes that were employed to fashion a negative image of immigrants, moreover, extends beyond this single target domain or historical period. Similar themes cut across different time periods and relate to a wide variety of target groups. The birth differential argument, for example, has been employed at various times to augment societal fear of African- and Hispanic-Americans, persons with feeble-mindedness, the rural poor, "welfare" recipients and other groups. Metaphors that undergird this argument, such as the rapidly reproducing animal, micro-organism or bacteria, may remain fairly constant across a span of time, or only change in superficial ways (Brennan, 1995; Lowenthal & Guterman, 1970; Wolfensberger, 1972).

Academicians and others with an interest in metaphor and rhetoric may play an extremely valuable role in the policy arena by calling attention to metaphoric themes that have the effect of supporting repressive public policies against marginalized groups, analyzing these themes, and countering the development of social myths at their root. Even in a society that values individual freedom and minority rights, there are obviously valid rationales for social control measures. We should all be concerned, however, when such measures gain support because of rhetorical devices and social myths as opposed to a factual understanding of the threat that is posed by those who are primarily impacted by such laws. Many metaphors, especially those that touch our subconscious fears and disgust, do not exist in a historical vacuum. They arise time and again to provide credence to those feelings, often by giving them a human face.

References

Abbott, E. (1924). *Immigration: Selected documents and case records*. Chicago: University of Chicago Press.

Allbritton, D. W. (1995). When metaphors function as schemas: Some cognitive effects of conceptual metaphors. *Metaphor and Symbolic Activity, 10,* 33–46.

An alien antidumping bill. (1921, May 7). *Literary Digest, 69*(6),12–13.

Brennan, W. (1995). *Dehumanizing the vulnerable: When word games take lives*. Chicago: Loyola University Press.

Brigham, C. C. (1923). *A study of American intelligence*. Princeton, NJ: Princeton University Press.

Calavita, K. (1984). *U.S. immigration law and the control of labor: 1820–1924*. London: Academic Press, Inc.

Cannon, C. J. (1923). Selecting citizens. *The North American Review, 217,* 325–333.

Chamberlain, H. S. (1913). *Foundations of the nineteenth century* (J. Lees, Trans.). New York: John Lane Co.

Collins, J. H. (1924, September 6). Who will do our dirty work now? *The Saturday Evening Post, 197,* 6(10), 122, 125, 129–130.

Congressional Record. (May 13, 1921). Volume 61, Part 2, 67th Congress, 1st Session, 1434–1443.

Conklin, E. G. (1921). Some biological aspects of immigration. *Scribner's Magazine, 69,* 352–359.

Coulter, E. K. (1904). Alien colonies and the children's court. *The North American Review, 576,* 731–740.

Curran, T. J. (1975). *Xenophobia and immigration, 1820–1930*. Boston: Twayne Publishers.

Darlington, T. (1906). The medico-economic aspect of the immigration problem. *The North American Review, 183,* 1262–1271.

Davis. J. J. (1922). Immigration and naturalization. *The Outlook, 131,* 256–260.

Davis, J. J. (1923, December 1). Jail—or a passport: Some facts and views of immigration. *The Saturday Evening Post, 196*(22), 23, 134, 137.

De Gobineau, A. (1966). *The inequality of human races* (A. Collins, Trans.). Los Angeles: Noontide Press.

Ellis, W. T. (August 25,1923). Americans on guard. *The Saturday Evening Post, 196*(8), 23, 80, 83, 86.

Elwood, W. N. (1995). Declaring war on the home front: Metaphor, presidents, and the war on drugs. *Metaphor and Symbolic Activity, 10,* 93–114.

Europe as an emigrant-exporting continent and the United States as an immigrant receiving nation. U.S. House of Representatives, Committee on Immigration and Naturalization. Testimony of Harry H. Laughlin. March 8, 1924, 1231–1318.

Fairchild, H. P. (1926). *Immigration: A world movement and its American significance.* New York: The MacMillan Company.

Frazer, E. F. (1923a, June 16). Our foreign cities: New York. *The Saturday Evening Post, 1953*(51), 6–7, 136–138, 141–142.

Frazer, E. F. (1923b, June 30). Our foreign cities: Pittsburgh. *The Saturday Evening Post 195*(53), 23, 85, 88, 91, 94.

Frazer, E. F. (1923c, August 25). Our foreign cities: Chicago. *The Saturday Evening Post, 196*(8), 14–15, 102, 105.

Garis, R. L. (1924). America's immigration policy. *The North American Review, 220,* 63–77.

Grant, M. (1916). *The passing of the great race.* New York: Charles Scribner's Sons.

Guarding the gates against undesirables. (1924). *Current Opinion, 76,* 400–401.

Hall, P. F. (1913). The recent history of immigration and immigration restriction. *Journal of Political Economy, 21,* 735–751.

The harm of immigration. (1893). *The Nation, 56,* 42–43.

Hendrick, B. J. (1907). The great Jewish invasion. *McClure's Magazine, 28,* 307–321.

Hutchinson, E. P. (1981). *Legislative history of American immigration policy 1798–1965.* Philadelphia: University of Pennsylvania Press.

Inviting immigration from Northwestern Europe. (1921, February 26). *The Literary Digest, 68*(9), 7–8.

Keen, S. (1986). *Faces of the enemy.* New York: Harper and Row.

Keep America "White"! (1923). *Current Opinion, 74,* 399–401.

Kraut, A. M. (1994). *Silent travelers: Germs, genes and the "immigrant menace."* New York: Basic Books.

Krohn, F. B. (1987). Military metaphors: Semantic pollution of the market place. *Et Cetera, 44,* 141–145.

Lakoff, G. (1995). Metaphor, morality, and politics, or, why conservatives have left liberals in the dust. *Social Research, 62,* 177–213.

Levine, D. N. (1995). The organism metaphor in sociology. *Social Research, 62,* 239–265.

Lowenthal, L., & Guterman, N. (1970). *Prophets of deceit: A study of techniques of the American agitator.* Palo Alto, CA: Pacific Books.

Making the immigrant unwelcome. (1921, April 30). *Literary Digest, 69*(5), 34–35.

McLaughlin, A. J. (1903). The American's distrust of the immigrant. *Popular Science Monthly, 62,* 230–236.

Noël, L. (1994). *Intolerance: A general survey* (A. Bennet, Trans.). Montreal & Kingston: McGill-Queen's University Press.

O'Brien, G. V. (1999). Protecting the social body: Use of the organism metaphor in fighting the "menace of the feeble-minded." *Mental Retardation, 37,* 188–200.

Ogawa, D. M. (1971). *From Japs to Japanese: An evolution of Japanese-American stereotypes.* Berkeley, CA: McCutchan Publishing Company.

The pestilence at the gate. (1921, February 26). *The Literary Digest, 68*(9), 13.

Phelan, J. D. (1919). The Japanese evil in California. *The North American Review, 323*–328.

Roberts, K. (1924, February 2). Slow poison. *The Saturday Evening Post, 196*(31), 8–9, 54, 58.

Roberts. P. (1914). *The new immigration*. New York: The MacMillan Company.

Rowell, C. H. (1920). California and the Japanese problem. *The New Republic, 24*, 64–65.

Schön, D. A. (1979). Generative metaphor: A perspective on problem-setting in social policy. In A. Ortony (Ed.), *Metaphor and thought* (pp. 254–283). New York: Cambridge University Press.

Strother, F. (1923). The immigration peril. *The World's Work, 46*, 633–637.

The threatened inundation from Europe. (1920). *The Literary Digest, 67*(12), 7–9.

Ward, R. D. (1910). Natural eugenics in relation to immigration. *The North American Review, 192*, 56–67.

Ward, R. D. (1913). Eugenic immigration. *American Breeders Magazine, 4*(12), 96–102.

Warne, F. J. (1971). *The immigrant invasion*. New York: Jerome S. Ozer. (Original work published 1913.)

Weber, J. B. (1892). Our national dumping-ground: A study of immigration. *The North American Review, 325*, 424–430.

Weiss, F. F. (1921). *The sieve*. Boston: The Page Co.

Whitney, L. F. (1926). *The source of crime*. New Haven, CT: The American Eugenics Society, Inc.

Wister, O. (1921). Shall we let the cuckoos crowd us out of our nest? *American Magazine, 91*, 47.

Wolfensberger, W. (1972). *Normalization*. Toronto: National Institute on Mental Retardation.

Young, K. (1922). Intelligence tests of certain immigrant groups. *The Scientific Monthly, 15*, 417–434.

Zangwill, I. (1917). *The melting pot*. New York: The MacMillan Company.

Making the Familiar Foreign
Dissent and Metaphor Surrounding the Iraq War
Ryan H. Blum

In his article "Captive Audience," which appeared in the April 6, 2003, issue of *The New York Times Magazine*, Allan Gurganus links his experiences as a Vietnam veteran with his concern over the conflict in Iraq. In so doing, he makes the case that the portrayal of war is far removed from the brutal reality of active combat and that the role of the wartime soldier irreparably alters the life of a young person. The author's concern for the conflict in Iraq stems from his lost youth, which is attributed to a reluctant participation in the Vietnam conflict.

Gurganus's is a cautionary tale, one that on its face seeks to undermine the communication that has emerged from the popular media and the Bush administration. The success of this piece is found neither in its motives nor intentions. Rather, clues to the strength of the article are found in its stylistic details—those metaphors that move the piece beyond the polemic into the artistic and provide the reader with a corrective to the comforting rhetoric surrounding the U.S. conflict in Iraq. His essay thus offers one strategy to counteract the rhetorical influence of a dominant group. In particular, I explore the question of how marginalized groups express resistance to a hegemonic rhetoric—in this case, a rhetoric that has been strengthened and personalized by the close relationship between the media and a presidential administration.

Metaphoric criticism is a method of rhetorical criticism rooted in the assumption that stylistic details like metaphors are not superfluous. Instead, they are seen as crucial elements in forwarding the rhetorical vision of a rhetor. Although short in length, "Captive Audience" contains a number of effective metaphors that further an introspective sentiment eschewed by the dominant ideology.

Undertaking an exploration of metaphors in a given work can take two forms—an analysis of tenor (the primary subject) or an analysis of vehicle (frame). In the case of Gurganus's essay, readers are offered a wide variety of vehicles, and the relationships between them are not immediately evident. I begin my exploration of Gurganus's metaphors with a sampling of the metaphors based on their tenor.

The first group of metaphors relates to a soldier's inability to articulate an involvement in Vietnam. For instance, readers are offered the colloquial expression for being gay—"coming out"—as a metaphor for admitting that one is a Vietnam veteran. Then there is the pairing of a "lead-lined meat locker" with the unshared memories of combatants. At another point, Gurganus captures the idea of a soldier's inability to make sense of the politics behind the conflict in the metaphorical phrase, "don't speak the local language."

Other metaphors are assigned to the experience of being a soldier and the duties that must be performed in that role: "Heavy lifting" is defined as the work of military personnel, as is the term "killing chores." The metaphor "trapped boys" stands in for the soldiers themselves, while the Vietnam experience is a

This essay was written while Ryan H. Blum was a student in Sonja K. Foss's rhetorical criticism class at the University of Colorado at Denver in 2003. Used by permission of the author.

"Children's Crusade." Similarly, "Dante's 11th circle" is equated with the experience of armed conflict.

Another tenor is related to the identities of the individuals involved in the war experience, both at home and abroad. For instance, "the old guys" are politicians and generals. In addition, the name "Larry" is used as a metaphor for the average soldier, and "Al" is a metaphor for the father of the average soldier. Linking "Uncle Sam" with the draft board continues this sort of familial metaphor.

As compelling as these metaphorical tenors are, a more insightful glimpse into Gurganus's rhetorical strategy is available through a focus on the associations entailed by the vehicles themselves. I now turn my attention to the vehicles used to explain how Gurganus's article opposes the rhetoric of the Bush administration and mainstream media. In doing so, I focus on the attributes surrounding three primary groupings of metaphorical vehicles: unappealing locations, uncomfortable actions, and seemingly familiar but unknown others.

The first category of vehicles—unappealing locations—contains items like the "lead-lined meat locker," "Dante's 11th circle," and "booths without doors." Even on their faces, each of these imaginary places offers no comfort. There is a palpable sense of pain or vulnerability associated with these phrases that unsettles the placidity of the reader. Moreover, the horror that we are to imagine is undefined; we lack further description or experience to envision the scene. This is the first in a series of depersonalizations that characterize the process by which Gurganus begins to overturn the rhetorical devices of those in power—the familiar, the personal, the comforting—with the frightening unfamiliarity of chaos that constitutes military activity.

The second associative frame consists of actions that are uncomfortable. The vehicles that develop this sentiment are "heavy lifting," "killing chores," negotiating "a learning curve," admitting difference/"coming out," "thawing," muteness/"an inability to speak the local language," and a "crusade of children." Acting in any one of these ways, much less all of them, would be distressing. Such distress acts as a foil to the rhetoric of those in favor of military activity in Iraq. When the United States began its invasion, both the secretary of state and the vice president made comments regarding the effortlessness with which American success would be achieved. The metaphorical associations created by the author dissipate the illusion of comfort provided by the popular media and the Bush administration.

The final vehicular association—seemingly familiar but unknown people—is a grouping of names that employs the guise of familiarity to achieve its ends. The characters provided to the readers, "Al," "Larry," "Uncle Sam," "the old guys," and the "Burger King," seem to profess a degree of acquaintance. Upon reflection, however, these are individuals with whom we never will become intimate. Even though we know their names, Al and Larry are as much of a mystery as those old guys and the Burger King. Unlike the dominant political communication emerging from our leaders and the media, where reporters are "embedded" with units so that we learn the names of grunts, platoon leaders, and generals, the world created by Gurganus sounds familiar while making us feel foreign. Here, a name may be printed upon a uniform, but the person behind it is camouflaged. This disorientation serves to make the reader feel alienated and out of place, creating an opportunity for introspection.

Considering the sentiment generated through these three categories, a more cohesive understanding of the metaphorical terrain is possible. Readers are provided with an unappealing montage of locations, places distant from the comforts assured by the administration. There is also a list of actions that individuals are not likely to enjoy, which moves readers farther from a desired sense of security. Finally, readers are presented with characters who appear familiar but are mysterious and possibly threatening (old, avuncular, and hierarchical). Taken together, readers are placed in the position of being strangers in a strange land.

The disassociation rendered by these metaphors explains how a marginalized rhetor—a war protestor—may overturn the reassuring vision created by a presidential administration and a sympathetic or cooperative media. The communication coming from those in power is decidedly positive, familiar, and comforting. Through his efforts, Gurganus takes readers' assumptions of place, activity, and person and throws them into chaos. Once an audience becomes unsure of these rhetorical elements, doubts about the claims of the dominant group may surface. This promise of resistance can explain how a marginalized group may overcome the close relationship between the media and those in control of political activity.

Captive Audience

Allan Gurganus
The New York Times Magazine
April 6, 2003

From 1966 to 1970, I disappeared from snapshots. I hid, even from my parents' camera. See, I was ashamed, of the uniform. I'd tried for "conscientious objector" in my Carolina county and was laughed out of the office. So, avoiding six years in a federal pen, I spent four in bell-bottoms, floating just off Southeast Asia. Buddies wore their caps cocked, making this assigned life feel more personal. I wore my uniform as a prisoner wears his. Why am I finally "coming out" about all this? I never ever speak of it. The new war drives me. My "service" years I freeze-dried. Till last week, I kept them stashed in the dark rear corner of a lead-lined meat locker. Now they're thawing—fact is, "My name is Allan and I am secretly . . . B-32-37-38." Name, hometown and serial number, that's what Iraqi captors ask of our latest P.O.W.'s. These kids' faces are banged up, squinty. Eyes shocked and awed at gunpoint, they recall me to myself. Such dulled innocence drives me to confess.

If you live long enough, you can become your own parent. I am now that to me, even a granddad. Against the Defense Department, I so long to defend my former grandson self and all these other kids. A graying 55-year-old homeowner can see just how young 18 really is! I served in another such Children's Crusade. I'm qualified to call it a disaster. Even the generals who were in charge back then admit that now. The same guys are helping plan this new one. I was a kid enlisted, against his will, to do the heavy lifting for a nation launched on a mission botched from the start. The entrance imperative: all macho force. The exit strategy? None whatever. Only very young kids would be fool enough to go that far and do as told. Some claim they didn't even mind. I myself remember. And, for me, and for this new crop, I mind. I'm watching.

I know these trapped boys from the inside. Perfect physical specimens, they are cocksure about absolutely everything because they know next to nothing. From a commander's perspective, of course, that's very good. These kids signed up mostly to get some education. Their parents couldn't swing the loans. No college otherwise. All they know of war is from Dolby-deafening action movies. Mainly these kids rage in the fist of the hormonal, the impulsive, the puppy-playful. Girl-crazy, full of stock-car lore and vague dreams of executive glory—great soldier material.

It's spring here, and my jonquils have never been more plentiful and lush, but I walk around as if hooked by black extension cord to CNN, memories de-icing. It comes from my feelings for them. For those idiotic gung-ho kids who really believe they are making up the rules, who consider they are rugged individualists (and therefore take orders beautifully). Many probably never had a plane ride before (it sure was long!), only to sleep all night under a tarp in a sandstorm sitting up against some truck (nobody my age could walk for a week after doing that). And already they write home: "Don't worry about me, Mom. We'll straighten out this mess fast. Just keep my Camaro washed good." I also sent such letters. It is reassuring to reassure. Love becomes a kind of sedative for whatever killing chores you're forced to do tomorrow.

I want to tell you, I have never known a loneliness like it. It's Dante's 11th circle, to be dressed in ugly clothes exactly like 4,000 others, to be called by a number, to be stuck among men who will brag and scrap and fight but never admit to any terror, any need. To sleep in bunks stacked five high, to defecate in booths without doors, you sitting with knees almost meeting the knees of a hunched stranger. To know that you are so much smarter than the jobs assigned, to guess that you are serving in a struggle you can neither approve nor ever understand because the old guys in charge—guys whose sons are safe, golfing at home—they don't speak the local language, either.

During the soldiers' first week, except for blowing sand, it might all seem a lark. Decisions are made by others who give you enough trigger-finger wiggle room so that you can feel a bit expressive, as baby-faced as terrifying. Such volunteers are as intentionally cut off from the effects of their killing as any placated 8-year-old glazed over the lethal thumb work of his Gameboy. These G.I.'s imagine glory, girlfriends waiting at home. The geopolitical picture is as far beyond their reach as the notion that learning a Kurdish dialect just might save their lives.

After my own tour of duty ended, I slouched home and simply sat there for six days, scared to leave my parents' house, too tired to drive a car. "So . . . what are your plans?"—my father saw my state yet chose to treat me with all the tender care of a corporate job interviewer. But Mom must have noticed that the family album featured no photos of me since the draft. So she gathered up my medals, awards for nothing more than my offering my body as another vote against the Cong. Mom assembled these little trophies I was meant to care about. A pretty red-and-yellow ribbon and its bronze coin called the Vietnam Expeditionary. Mom bought a craft-shop shadow box, a nice one too, real wood, and lined with red velvet-like plush for displaying family heirlooms. She arranged my citations under glass, protecting them. But I'd won too few to make a really pleasing pattern. So Mom dipped into my old Boy Scout badges, fleshing out my history with the brass of "God and Country." Then she added my childhood Sunday School pin for perfect attendance. "You see? Impressive." She handed it over. I thanked her and sat staring down at it. Whenever my folks visited, I would get it out and prop it up somewhere until they left. It usually stayed in the attic, where it dwells, I guess, today. In some cardboard box stacked with letters I've really been meaning to answer since '79 or so. But thanks anyway, Mom. Not your fault. Not mine. But whose then?

The latest captured Americans from a downed helicopter squat here on camera, and you see their inexperience in how they're big-eyed scared as kids at their first horror flick. Boys hang their heads with a shame almost sexual. They're blaming themselves for crashing, guilty at how sand can spoil the rotor blades of our most costly chopper. These kids mainly "volunteered," to get ahead. And now, this learning curve. They are prisoners because to start at Burger King, even for a go-getter like Larry here, would get him to only assistant manager in, say, three or four years, and you can't do too darn much on 12 grand a year, can you? These are the ambitious kids, the "good kids," the ones who wanted to make something useful and shapely of their lives.

Now they know that Mom will see them, captured, on "Alive at Five." They know she'll cover her mouth while screaming: "Al, come quick. It's Larry! They got our Larry!"

My parents believed in honor, duty and rendering up firstborns to Uncle Sam. For them Sam was at least as real as Santa. Avuncular, if somewhat overdressed in stripes and gambler's goatee, he tended to look stern and to point right out at you. So when he knocked at our door and said he wanted me, my folks grinned: "He's hiding in the back bedroom, writing essays for the draft board all about peace and Quaker stuff. Though, fact is, he grew up Presbyterian. We'll go get him. Won't take a sec. You comfortable there?"

This week's young captives might just be released. Some will come home, back to their folks' ghetto stoops or trailers or tract houses strung with computer-generated welcomes, personalized, too. Their college years are still ahead of them. So look on the bright side. Bones that young knit fast. And, after a while, even after all the pain and not knowing why they did it, they will get to call this "their" war. And, of course, the medals will be splendid.

Architectural Metaphor as Subversion
The Portland Building
Maria Kanengieter-Wildeson

Susanne Langer described the role and function of architecture as shaping a culture's image by creating a human environment that expresses "characteristic rhythmic patterns within that culture."[1] She explains:

> Such patterns are the alternations of sleep and waking, venture and safety, emotion and calm, austerity and abandon, the tempo and the smoothness or abruptness of life; the simple forms of childhood and the complexities of full moral stature, the sacramental and the capricious moods that mark a social order.[2]

As these rhythmic patterns transform and shift within a specific culture, so do the symbols, icons, and monuments built by its members. Whether its language is the ideal symmetry of Greek *arete* expressed by the builders of the Parthenon or the sterility of Orwell's *1984* raised by the technocrats of steel and glass boxes, architecture relies on a poetic process—a process characterized by the use of metaphor.

In this essay, I will argue that, through the use of metaphor, architectural forms can subvert or reaffirm existing ideologies, and I will demonstrate this process in architect Michael Graves' Portland Building. In 1980, the city of Portland, Oregon, chose Michael Graves' design for its new public service building. Completed in 1982, the building sits on a 200-foot-square block between the City Hall on the east, the County Courthouse on the west, a public transit mall on the north, and a park on the west. Since its construction, the Portland Building remains an enigma in American architecture. Some have called the building's design "offensive rather than open and inviting,"[3] "a joke,"[4] and "dangerous,"[5] while others have proclaimed that it "would be a landmark from inception"[6] and "brings some not-so-old but almost forgotten American traditions to life."[7] That the Portland Building has influenced the landscape of architectural design and caused people to think and talk about their environment is clear.

I suggest that Graves, through his use of metaphor, has molded a carefully articulated statement that reshapes traditional notions about government institutions. His non-discursive message reaffirms the belief that humans play an intrinsic role in civic affairs and concurrently subverts the conventional assumption that efficient governmental bureaucracies are imperious, inelegant, and immutable rather than hospitable and humane.

The first metaphor Graves incorporates in the Portland Building is the metaphor of the building as toy. He associates various dimensions of the building with children's toys and activities, thus extending toy-like images to a building that is supposed to be the epitome of efficiency. For example, many geometric shapes—trapezoidal figures, squares, and rectangles—flippantly decorate the facade, with the shapes fitting together much like a three-dimensional puzzle. The toy metaphor also is characterized by the shape of the building—a truncated jack-in-the-box—flanked on four sides by small, square, blackened windows, evoking images

This essay was written while Marla Kanengieter-Wildeson was a student in Sonja K. Foss's rhetorical criticism class at the University of Oregon in 1989. Used by permission of the author.

of small building blocks used by children in their play. Approaching the Fourth Avenue entrance, the building reveals the features of a robotic face, complete with two eyes (two inverted, three-dimensional triangles) staring out in wide-eyed wonder. Across the top of the columns on one side of the building are bas-relief "ribbons," reminiscent of colorful streamers on May poles. The two-dimensional quality of these ribbons is cartoonish, and, as one reviewer notes, the building "looks as though it just won first prize at the county fair."[8] Thus, these playful accoutrements serve as facetious caricatures of the red tape usually associated with government.

The building's anthropomorphic quality is the second metaphor Graves uses to engage viewers. Richard Sennett underscores the prevalence of the human form in the history of architecture when he argues that in "the course of urban development master images of 'the body' have frequently been used, in transfigured form, to define what a building or an entire city should look like."[9] The building as human is seen in the Portland Building's three-part structure—a structure like that of a human body—legs (the base of the building is weighted in green), torso (the middle section is painted a parchment color), and head (coiffed in a receding tier). The context in which these images occur invites the metaphor of the body politic. By endowing the building with human form, Graves takes the bite out of Portland's political machine. Instead of an austere, looming edifice housing cynical politicians, nameless workers, or, in the words of T. S. Eliot, "hollow men," the Portland Building is shaped into a humane structure—one that reflects the kind of citizens visitors hope work inside. The building's humanlike characteristics celebrate the role of humans, not machines, in civic affairs.

The third metaphor Graves employs is a metaphor of building as romance. The Portland Building embraces a feeling of sensuality rather than utility. Citizens generally assume that a public service building first and foremost is functional. They have been conditioned to think that, in such buildings, walls are gray, furniture is brown, and lighting is fluorescent. Instead of the colorless neutrality of black, gray, and shiny steel dominant in virtually every streamlined slab of the modernist style, however, the Portland Building is dipped in a soft color scheme of pastels—maroon, blue, and green. The colors and the way in which they interact with light suggest the ambience of a Maxwell Parrish painting. By integrating color, form, light, and shadow, Graves erases the mundane and replaces it with a careful mixture of the sublime and the sensuous—with romance.

Although viewers and users of the Portland Building may appreciate it from an aesthetic perspective, my concern as a rhetorical critic is to understand how Graves' metaphors work in generating particular rhetorical responses to the building. The metaphors Graves selected work to encourage a transformation of viewers' usual attitudes toward government because they are rooted in and strongly linked to various positive patterns of experience. Graves references and articulates specific images and experiences that tend to generate positive emotions and to be associated with desirable and valued dimensions of human life (childhood memories, the joy of human contact, and romance). By juxtaposing these with equally strong but negative referents connected with government (bureaucracy, political machinery, sterility, and red tape), Graves gives visitors an opportunity to reconstruct their frame of reference for the offices and processes the building houses. The Portland Building's metaphors create a dialogue with visitors, encouraging them to readjust their perceived order—giving them an opportunity to reconstruct that order in a more positive way. The Portland Building, then, subverts the existing ideology of bureaucracy and invites citizens to revise their perspectives when approaching their city governmental structures—adopting a perspective of optimism, humor, and perhaps even delight.

I suggest that non-discursive metaphors often play a major role in the environment created by architecture; thus, such metaphors deserve the attention of rhetorical critics. Such non-discursive metaphors suggest that buildings are more than aesthetic sites upon which verbal discourse takes place; rather, through the metaphors they suggest, they can become, literally, a ground of ideology and argument, reaffirming conventional perspectives or, as in the case of the Portland Building, inviting viewers to apprehend, experience, and interpret their worlds in new ways.

Notes

[1] Susanne Langer, *Feeling and Form* (New York: Charles Scribner's, 1953) 96.

[2] Langer 96.

[3] Gary Clark, letter, *Oregonian* 4 Mar. 1980: B6.

[4] Robert K. Schroeder, letter, *Oregonian* 16 Mar. 1980: D2.

[5] Wolf von Eckhardt, "A Pied Piper of Hobbit Land," *Time* 23 Aug. 1983: 62.

[6] Steve Jenning, "Architects Favor Temple Design for City Office Building," *Oregonian* 18 Feb. 1980: B1.

[7] Vincent Scully, "Michael Graves' Allusive Architecture," *Michael Graves Building and Projects 1966–1981*, ed. Karen Vogel Wheeler, Peter Arnell, and Ted Bickford (New York: Rizzoli, 1982) 297.

[8] John Pastier, "First Monument of a Loosely Defined Style," *AIA Journal*, 72 (May 1983): 236.

[9] Richard Sennett, *Flesh and Stone, the Body and the City in Western Civilization* (New York: W. W. Norton, 1994) 24.

The Portland Building, Portland, Oregon, 1989. Photograph by Mary Rose Williams.

Additional Samples of Metaphoric Criticism

Adams, John Charles. "Linguistic Values and Religious Experience: An Analysis of the Clothing Metaphors in Alexander Richardson's Ramist-Puritan Lectures on Speech." *Quarterly Journal of Speech*, 9 (February 1990), 58–68.

Aden, Roger C. "Back to the Garden: Therapeutic Place Metaphor in Field of Dreams." *Southern Communication Journal*, 59 (Summer 1994), 307–17.

Aden, Roger C. "Entrapment and Escape: Inventional Metaphors in Ronald Reagan's Economic Rhetoric." *Southern Communication Journal*, 54 (Summer 1989), 384–400.

Aden, Roger C., and Christina L. Reynolds. "Lost and Found in America: The Function of Place Metaphor in *Sports Illustrated*." *Southern Communication Journal*, 59 (Fall 1993), 1–14.

Akioye, Akin A. "The Rhetorical Construction of Radical Africanism at the United Nations: Metaphoric Cluster as Strategy." *Discourse & Society*, 5 (January 1995), 7–31.

Benoit, William L. "Framing Through Temporal Metaphor: The 'Bridges' of Bob Dole and Bill Clinton in their 1996 Acceptance Addresses." *Communication Studies*, 52 (Spring 2001), 70–84.

Blankenship, Jane. "The Search for the 1972 Democratic Nomination: A Metaphorical Perspective." In *Methods of Rhetorical Criticism: A Twentieth-Century Perspective*, ed. Bernard L. Brock and Robert L. Scott (Detroit: Wayne State University Press, 1980), pp. 321–45.

Brown, Richard Harvey. "Rhetoric and the Science of History: The Debate Between Evolutionism and Empiricism as a Conflict in Metaphors." *Quarterly Journal of Speech*, 72 (May 1986), 148–61.

Brummett, Barry. "The Representative Anecdote as a Burkean Method, Applied to Evangelical Rhetoric." *Southern Speech Communication Journal*, 50 (Fall 1984), 1–23.

Carpenter, Ronald H. "America's Tragic Metaphor: Our Twentieth-Century Combatants as Frontiersmen." *Quarterly Journal of Speech*, 76 (February 1990), 1–22.

Cooper, Brenda, and David Descutner. "Strategic Silences and Transgressive Metaphors in *Out of Africa*: Isak Dinesen's Double-Voiced Rhetoric of Complicity and Subversion." *Southern Communication Journal*, 62 (Summer 1997), 333–43.

Daughton, Suzanne M. "Metaphorical Transcendence: Images of the Holy War in Franklin Roosevelt's First Inaugural." *Quarterly Journal of Speech*, 79 (November 1993), 427–46.

Farrell, Thomas B., and G. Thomas Goodnight. "Accidental Rhetoric: The Root Metaphors of Three Mile Island." *Communication Monographs*, 48 (December 1981), 271–300.

Fitzgibbon, Jane E., and Matthew W. Seeger. "Audiences and Metaphors of Globalization in the DaimlerChryslerAG Merger." *Communication Studies*, 53 (Spring 2002), 40–55.

Foss, Sonja K., and Anthony J. Radich. "Metaphors in 'Treasures of Tutankhamen': Implications for Aesthetic Education." *Art Education*, 37 (January 1984), 6–11.

Graves, Michael P. "Functions of Key Metaphors in Early Quaker Sermons, 1671–1700." *Quarterly Journal of Speech*, 69 (November 1983), 364–78.

Gribbin, William. "The Juggernaut Metaphor in American Rhetoric." *Quarterly Journal of Speech*, 59 (October 1973), 297–303.

Ivie, Robert L. "Literalizing the Metaphor of Soviet Savagery: President Truman's Plain Style." *Southern Speech Communication Journal*, 51 (Winter 1986), 91–105.

Ivie, Robert L. "Metaphor and the Rhetorical Invention of Cold War 'Idealists.'" *Communication Monographs*, 54 (June 1987), 165–82.

Ivie, Robert L. "The Metaphor of Force in Prowar Discourse: The Case of 1912." *Quarterly Journal of Speech*, 68 (August 1982), 240–53.

Jamieson, Kathleen Hall. "The Metaphoric Cluster in the Rhetoric of Pope Paul VI and Edmund G. Brown, Jr." *Quarterly Journal of Speech*, 66 (February 1980), 51–72.

Jensen, J. Vernon. "British Voices on the Eve of the American Revolution: Trapped by the Family Metaphor." *Quarterly Journal of Speech*, 63 (February 1977), 43–50.

Kaplan, Stuart Jay. "Visual Metaphors in the Representation of Communication Technology." *Critical Studies in Mass Communication*, 7 (March 1990), 37–47.

Koch, Susan, and Stanley Deetz. "Metaphor Analysis of Social Reality in Organizations." *Journal of Applied Communication Research*, 9 (Spring 1981), 1–15.

Koller, Veronika. "'A Shotgun Wedding': Co-occurrence of War and Marriage Metaphors in Mergers and Acquisitions Discourse." *Metaphor and Symbol*, 17 (2002), 179–203.

Kuusisto, Riikka. "Heroic Tale, Game, and Business Deal? Western Metaphors in Action in Kosovo." *Quarterly Journal of Speech*, 88 (February 2002), 50–68.

Mechling, Elizabeth Walker, and Jay Mechling. "The Jung and the Restless: The Mythopoetic Men's Movement." *Southern Communication Journal*, 59 (Winter 1994), 97–111.

Osborn, Michael. "Archetypal Metaphor in Rhetoric: The Light-Dark Family." *Quarterly Journal of Speech*, 53 (April 1967), 115–26.

Osborn, Michael, and John Bakke. "The Melodramas of Memphis: Contending Narratives During the Sanitation Strike of 1968." *Southern Communication Journal*, 63 (Spring 1998), 220–34.

Owen, William Foster. "Thematic Metaphors in Relational Communication: A Conceptual Framework." *Western Journal of Speech Communication*, 49 (Winter 1985), 1–13.

Patthey-Chavez, G. Genevieve, Lindsay Clare, and Madeleine Youmans. "Watery Passion: The Struggle Between Hegemony and Sexual Liberation in Erotic Fiction for Women." *Discourse & Society*, 7 (January 1996), 77–106.

Perry, Stephen. "Rhetorical Functions of the Infestation Metaphor in Hitler's Rhetoric." *Central States Speech Journal*, 34 (Winter 1983), 229–35.

Ritchie, David. "Monastery or Economic Enterprise: Opposing or Complementary Metaphors of Higher Education?" *Metaphor and Symbol* 17 (2002), 45–55.

Santa Ana, Otto. "'Like an Animal I was Treated': Anti-Immigrant Metaphor in US Public Discourse." *Discourse & Society*, 10 (April 1999), pp. 191–224.

Semino, Elena, and Michela Masci. "Politics is Football: Metaphor in the Discourse of Silvio Berlusconi in Italy." *Discourse & Society*, 7 (April 1996), 243–69.

Smith, Ruth C., and Eric M. Eisenberg. "Conflict at Disneyland: A Root-Metaphor Analysis." *Communication Monographs*, 54 (December 1987), 367–80.

Solomon, Martha. "Covenanted Rights: The Metaphoric Matrix of 'I Have a Dream.'" In *Martin Luther King., Jr., and the Sermonic Power of Public Discourse*. Ed. Carolyn Calloway-Thomas and John Louis Lucaites. Tuscaloosa: University of Alabama Press, 1993, pp. 66–84.

Stelzner, Hermann G. "Analysis by Metaphor." *Quarterly Journal of Speech*, 51 (February 1965), 52–61.

Stelzner, Hermann G. "Ford's War on Inflation: A Metaphor that Did Not Cross." *Communication Monographs*, 44 (November 1977), 284–97.

Straehle, Carolyn, Gilbert Weiss, Ruth Wodak, Peter Muntigl, and Maria Sedlak. "Struggle as Metaphor in European Union Discourses on Unemployment." *Discourse & Society*, 10 (January 1999), 67–99.

van Teefelen, Toine. "Racism and Metaphor: The Palestinian-Israeli Conflict in Popular Literature." *Discourse & Society*, 5 (July 1994), 381–405.

10

Narrative Criticism

Alasdair MacIntyre has described the human being as "essentially a story-telling animal."[1] Narratives organize the stimuli of our experience so that we can make sense of the people, places, events, and actions of our lives. They allow us to interpret reality because they help us decide what a particular experience "is about" and how the various elements of our experience are connected.[2] Narratives also play a critical role in decision making and policy making in our institutional lives. Narratives are integral to the functioning of institutions such as courts of law, corporations, and government and nonprofit agencies. Narratives induce us to make certain decisions in the context of these institutions and also help us justify those decisions.

Contributions to the study of narrative can be traced to classical Greece and Rome, where both Aristotle and Quintilian wrote about narration.[3] In the communication discipline, the work of Walter R. Fisher has been most influential in developing our understanding of the narrative paradigm.[4] The performance perspective on communication, in which human beings and cultures are seen as constituting themselves through performances of various kinds, including stories, is another component of the study of narrative. This approach is represented by the work of Victor Turner,[5] Clifford Geertz,[6] Richard Bauman,[7] and Dwight Conquergood.[8]

Narratives are found in many different kinds of artifacts. They constitute the basic form of most short stories, novels, comic strips, comic books, films, and songs. They also can occur in rhetoric that is less obviously narrative—conversations with friends, interviews, speeches, and even visual artifacts such as paintings and quilts.[9]

Narratives are distinguished from other rhetorical forms by four characteristics. A primary defining feature of narrative discourse is that it is comprised of events that may be either active (expressing action) or stative (expressing a state or condition). "The mice ran after the farmer's wife" expresses action and thus is an active event, while "the mice were blind" expresses a state or condition and thus is a stative event. A narrative must include at least two such events. "The blind mice ran after the farmer's wife" is not a narrative because it includes only one event—the mice running after the farmer's wife. "The blind mice ran after the farmer's wife, who cut off their tails with a carving knife" is a narrative because it involves two events.

A second characteristic of a narrative is that the events in it are organized by time order. A narrative is not simply a series of events arranged randomly; it is at least a sequence of events. The order does not have to be chronological and may involve devices like flashbacks and flashforwards, but at least the narrative tells in some way how the events relate temporally to one another. "The girl swam, the girl ate breakfast, the girl did homework, and the girl went to a movie" lacks a clear temporal order because the order in which these events occurred is not clear. This sentence thus is not a narrative. "The girl swam before breakfast, spent the day doing homework, and went to a movie in the evening," however, is a narrative because the order of events the statement recounts is clear.

A third requirement for a narrative is that it must include some kind of causal or contributing relationship among events in a story. Narratives depict change of some sort, and this third requirement defines the nature of that change by stipulating the relationship between earlier and later events in the story. Sometimes, in narratives, an earlier event is shown as causing a later event, as when a woman burns a letter that sets off a forest fire. In other narratives, an earlier event cannot be said to have caused a later event, but the earlier event is necessary for the later event to occur. For example, in a story in which a student is trying to gain admission to law school, the student's application is a necessary condition for either of the later events of admission or rejection, although it did not cause either of them. Some kind of causal or contributing relationship between early and late events in a story, then, defines a narrative.

A fourth requirement for a narrative is that it must be about a unified subject. "Elvis recorded his first hit record, Bob Hope died, the soldiers fought the Iraqis near Baghdad, John Hickenlooper won the election for mayor of Denver, and Jane Austin wrote novels" is not a narrative because it is about disconnected subjects. At a minimum, there must be one unified subject for a narrative.[10]

PROCEDURES

Using the narrative method of criticism, a critic analyzes an artifact in a four-step process: (1) selecting an artifact; (2) analyzing the artifact; (3) formulating a research question; and (4) writing the essay.

Selecting an Artifact

Any artifact that is a narrative or includes a story or narrative within it is appropriate for the application of a narrative analysis if it meets the four criteria for a narrative. It should contain at least two events and/or states of affairs that are temporally ordered, and the earlier events in the sequence should be at least causally necessary conditions for later events. The artifact also should be one where at least one unified subject is present. Possible artifacts include children's books, short stories, novels, films, monologues by comedians, letters, interviews in which individuals tell stories, or speeches. You can use nondiscursive artifacts for narrative analysis, but they may require more creativity in your application of the narrative method than discursive texts do.

Analyzing the Artifact

The basic procedure for conducting narrative criticism involves two steps: (1) identifying the dimensions of the narrative; and (2) discovering an explanation for the narrative. The first step involves examining the narrative in detail to gain a comprehensive understanding of it as a whole. The second involves focusing on those aspects of the narrative that are of most interest to you and that allow you to provide the best explanation for the artifact.

Identifying the Dimensions of the Narrative

The following questions allow you to explore the primary features of the narrative in detail:

Setting. What is the setting or scene—the details external to the character—in the narrative? Is there a change in setting over the course of the narrative? How does the setting relate to the plot and characters? How is the particular setting created? Is the setting textually prominent—highly developed and detailed—or negligible?[11]

Characters. Who are the main characters in the narrative? Are some of the characters nonhuman or inanimate phenomena, described as thinking and speaking beings? What are the physical and mental traits of the characters? In what actions do the characters engage? Do the traits or actions of the characters change over the course of the narrative?

How are the characters presented? Are they flat or round? A flat character has one or just a few dominating traits, making the behavior of the character highly predictable. Round characters, in contrast, possess a variety of traits, some of them conflicting or even contradictory. Their behavior is less predictable than that of flat characters because they are likely to change and to continue to reveal previously unknown traits.[12]

Narrator. Is the narrative presented directly to the audience, or is it mediated by a narrator? In direct presentation of the narrative, the audience directly witnesses the action, and the voice speaking of events, characters, and setting is hidden from the audience. In a narrative mediated by a narrator, the audience is told about events and characters by a narrator whose presence is more or less audible. If a narrator is audible, what in the narrative creates a sense of the narrator's presence? What makes the narrator intrusive or not?

What kind of person is the narrator? A narrator who apologizes, defends, and pleads is different from one who evaluates, criticizes, and preaches. What kind of vocabulary does the narrator use? Does the narrator favor certain types of words, sentence structures, metaphors, or types of arguments? Is the narrator wordy and verbose or straightforward and direct? Does the narrator adequately connect the various elements of the narrative to one another to create a cogent and meaningful narrative? What is the narrator's attitude toward the story being told, the subject matter of the story, the audience, and him- or herself?

If the narrative is being presented orally, what characterizes the narrator's pitch, pauses, tone of voice, gestures, emphasis, pronunciation, and other features of speech? Style also may be visual in narratives that are predominantly or exclusively visual, accomplished through such elements as types of shots in video or film, motions in dance, or styles of painting.

What kinds of powers are available to the narrator? What kind of authority does the narrator claim?[13] What is the point of view adopted by the narrator? Point of view is the perceptual and psychological point of view in the presentation of the narrative. Is the narrator omniscient, knowing the outcome of every event and the nature of every character and setting? Does the narrator tell the story from a god-like vantage point? Is the narrator omnipresent—able to skip from one locale to another in the narrative? Is the narrator allowed to range into the past or future or restricted to the contemporary story moment? Does the narrator engage in time and space summarizing, a process in which vast panoramas and large groups of people are seen from the narrator's exalted position? Does the narrator go beyond describing to engage in commentary such as interpretation and evaluation? Does the narrator engage in metanarrative discourse—discourse in which the narrative itself is discussed and elements in the narrative are commented on explicitly—such as definitions of terms or translations of foreign words? How does the narrator report characters' discourse? Does the narrator use direct forms of representation, in which the exact words of the characters are reported? Does the narrator use indirect forms, in which the characters' speech and thought are paraphrased, suggesting more intervention by the narrator?

How reliable is the narrator? In unreliable narration, the narrator's account is at odds with the audience's inferences and judgments about the story. The audience concludes that the events and characters depicted by the narrator could not have been as the narrator describes them. What seems to be the cause of the narrator's unreliability—gullibility, innocence, or a desire to mislead?[14]

4. Events: What are the major and minor events—plotlines, happenings, or changes of state—in the narrative? Major events in a story are called *kernels*. These are events that suggest critical points in the narrative and that force movement in particular directions. They cannot be left out of a narrative without destroying its coherence and meaning. Minor plot events, called *satellites*, are the development or working out of the choices made at the kernels. Their function is to fill out, elaborate, and complete the kernels. Satellites are not crucial to the narrative and can be deleted without disturbing the basic story line of the narrative, although their omission would affect the form of the narrative and the form's rhetorical effects.[15]

How are the events presented? Are they characterized by particular qualities? How fully are the kernels developed by satellites? How do the satellites affect the nature of the kernels? Are the events active (expressing action) or stative (expressing a state or condition)?[16]

5. Temporal Relations: What are the temporal relationships among the events recounted in the narrative? Do events occur in a brief period of time or over many years? What is the relationship between the natural order of the events as they occurred and the order of their presentation in the telling of the narrative? Does the narrator use flashbacks and flashforwards, common devices to reorder events as they are narrated?[17] How is the story that is told located in time with respect to the act of narrating it? Is the telling of the story subsequent to what it tells—a predictive or prophetic form? Is the telling in present tense, simultaneous or interspersed with the action depicted? Is the narration in the past tense, coming after the events recounted?[18]

What is the speed of the narrative? Speed is the relationship between the length of time the events in the narrative go on and the length of the narrative. Are particular events and characters narrated with higher speed than others? Does use of speed emphasize some events and characters over others?[19]

6. Causal Relations: What cause-and-effect relationships are established in the narrative? How are connections made between causes and effects? Is cause presented prior to effect or after it? How clearly and strongly are the connections between cause and effect made? Which receives the most emphasis—the cause or the effect? What kinds of causes are dominant in the narration? Are events caused largely by human action, accident, or forces of nature? In how much detail are the causes and effects described?

7. Audience: Who is the person or people to whom the narrative is addressed? Is it addressed to an individual, a group, or the narrator him-

or herself? Is the audience a participant in the events recounted? What are the signs of the audience in the narrative? What can be inferred about the audience's attitudes, knowledge, or situation from the narrative? Is the audience represented in a detailed or sketchy manner? What seems to be the narrator's evaluation of the audience's knowledge, personality, and abilities?[20]

8. Theme: What is the major theme of the narrative? A theme is a general idea illustrated by the narrative. It is what a narrative means or is about and points to the significance and meaning of the action. Themes are ideas such as "good triumphs over evil," "everyone can succeed with hard work," "kindness is a virtue," and "violence is sometimes justified." How is the theme articulated in the narrative? How obvious and clear is the theme?[21]

As a result of an examination of the elements of the narrative suggested by these questions and other elements you notice while investigating the narrative, you develop a comprehensive picture of the narrative. All of this information, however, is not included in your essay. What you include is developed in the second step of the process of narrative criticism, where you focus on a particular feature or features of the narrative.

Discovering an Explanation for the Narrative

Your task now is to identify which of the features of the narrative are most interesting and significant and have the most explanatory value for your artifact. You probably chose to analyze your artifact because there is some aspect of the artifact that doesn't fit or that you cannot explain. Perhaps you like the artifact and cannot explain its appeal for you. Perhaps it disturbs you, but you don't know why. Perhaps it seems unusual in some way. Your coding of the narrative, which revealed some dimensions as significant, can provide an explanation for your initial reactions.

Use the principles of frequency and intensity to discover what is significant about the narrative and can provide an explanation for it. For example, if you are analyzing the narrative of an animal-rights activist who fought against inhumane treatment for animals, you might discover that the setting, characters, events, and temporal relations presented in his story are constructed in such a way that inhumane conditions are seen as determining and controlling. You might surmise that this construction is a critical component of his worldview that might explain what interested you about the narrative. This would be a case where frequency—or a pattern you observe in which the same feature recurs—suggests an important insight about the narrative. A major revelation also might emerge from just one of the dimensions of the narrative, and you might choose this as a dimension on which to focus in explaining the narrative. If your coding reveals, for example, that the activist's description of himself in the narrative points to agency as residing in the collective group and not in the individual activist himself, you would note that as significant on the basis of intensity. Those aspects of the narrative that stand out because of frequency and intensity, then, suggest areas where something is going on that can help explain the artifact. In some cases, these will be substantive or content dimensions of the story. In other instances, elements of form may emerge as most significant.[22] Because of the interconnection of form and content, however, elements of both may emerge together as significant features of a narrative.

The significant features that emerge from your narrative analysis may suggest various kinds of explanations for your artifact. An explanation, for example, may deal with how the narrative directs the interpretation of a situation. A narrative, as a frame upon experience, functions as an argument to view and understand the world in a particular way; the features that emerge as significant in a narrative can help you understand the argument being made. What emerges as significant from your narrative also might reveal something important about an individual's identity. Because stories have to do with how their tellers interpret events and attribute meaning to them, they provide clues to the subjectivity of individuals. Similarly, the stories commonly told in a culture provide glimpses into that culture—the meanings attributed to particular events, the aspects of the culture that are privileged and repressed, and the values of the culture. The explanation of your artifact may lie in how the narrative can help you understand a particular culture.

Perhaps what emerges as significant in the narrative suggests that the explanation for your artifact lies in an evaluation of whether or not the narrative is a good one. Some narratives are better than others, so you might want to focus on particular findings from the analysis that allow you to make judgments about the quality of the story you are analyzing. Criteria you can use to judge narratives are discussed below.

Does the narrative embody and advocate values that you see as desirable and worthwhile? All narratives express values—conceptions of the good—whether implicitly or explicitly. Using this criterion for judgment, your focus is on the elements of the narrative that serve as an index to the values embedded in the narrative.

What ethical standards does the narrative suggest? Here, your primary concern is with degrees of rightness and wrongness in human behavior. To use ethics as a criterion for assessing a narrative, identify the ethical standards that it embodies or advocates. Numerous ethical systems have been proposed to apply to human behavior, including political perspectives, human-nature perspectives, dialogic perspectives, situational perspectives, and legal perspectives.[23] If ethics is your interest, your focus at this stage of the narrative analysis is on those dimensions of the narrative that point to an ethical code.[24]

How readily can the narrative be refuted? A third criterion for assessing a narrative is how easily it can be refuted by the audience to which it is addressed. Using this criterion, ask how someone with an opposing narrative—one that presents an alternative perspective on the world—could go about refuting the narrative presented for the same audience. What kinds of events, characters, settings, and so on would the narrative have to incorporate to refute the original narrative persuasively? In this kind of analysis, your attention is focused on the aspects of the narrative that make it more or less compelling.

Is the narrative coherent? You may be interested less in the ways in which the narrative functions in the world and more in the internal characteristics of the narrative form. The criterion of coherency concerns whether the narrative hangs together, has internal consistency, or has adequate connections within it. To examine the coherence of a narrative, you may want to ask such questions as: Is there a unified subject in the narrative? Are the various elements of the narrative adequately connected to one another to create a cogent and meaningful narrative? Do the elements of the story fall into the range of possibilities opened by earlier events in the story?[25] In this case, your focus in your analysis is on those dimensions of the narrative that point to coherence or suggest a lack of it.

Does the narrative demonstrate fidelity? Fidelity is the truth quality of the narrative—whether it represents accurate assertions about reality or rings true with what you know to be true. If the story is not about actual people and situations that have occurred in the world, the criterion of fidelity is whether the narrative is true to life—whether what it depicts actually could have happened.[26] Fidelity as a standard for the evaluation of narrative can be problematic because frequent disagreement occurs among audience members in determining what corresponds to actual reality and is "true" in anecdotes, legends, tall tales, and personal narratives.[27] A view of fidelity as correspondence to the facts of the real world might better be replaced, then, with correspondence to facts within the community or the context in which the narrative is told.[28]

Does the narrative fulfill the purpose of its creators? This criterion suggests an interest in whether the particular choices made by rhetors in creating the stories accomplish their purposes for telling the stories. Stories are told to accomplish particular objectives, and with this criterion, you judge the story according to how well it meets these objectives—perhaps to build community, to seek adherence for a view or policy, or to offer a perspective.

Does the narrative provide useful ideas for living your life? Rhetoric offers commands or instructions of some kind, helping us maneuver through life and feel more at home in the world. Because rhetoric is an individual's solution to perceived exigences, it constitutes "equipment for living"—a chart, formula, manual, or map that an audience may consult in trying to decide on various courses of action.[29] Stories can give us ideas for living our own lives, and we can use them to discover a course of action or to explore the consequences of a course of action we are considering. Using this criterion, your focus in your analysis is on those aspects of the narrative that constitute guides for thought and action.

As a result of identifying features that provide the best explanation for what intrigued or puzzled you about the narrative, you have the focus for your essay. This focus becomes the research question in the next step of the process of narrative analysis.

Formulating a Research Question

Many different kinds of research questions can be formulated for a narrative analysis because of the open-ended nature of the method. The significant features of a narrative that emerge from your analysis may suggest explanations of the narrative that turn into questions about how the construction of a narrative directs the interpretation of a situation, what a narrative reveals about an individual's identity, what a narrative suggests about the values of a culture, or an assessment of the narrative.

Writing the Essay

After completing the analysis, you are ready to write your essay, which includes five major components: (1) an introduction, in which you discuss the research question, its contribution to rhetorical theory, and its significance; (2) a description of the artifact and its context; (3) a description of the method of criticism—in this case, narrative criticism; (4) a report of the findings of the analysis, in which you reveal the dimensions of the narrative that are most significant; and (5) a discussion of the contribution the analysis makes to rhetorical theory.

SAMPLE ESSAYS

In the following samples of narrative criticism, narratives are used to answer a variety of research questions. In the essay by Thomas A. Hollihan and Patricia Riley, the focus is on the substantive themes of the narratives as they ask the research questions, "What is the nature of therapeutic narratives told in support groups?" "What in these narratives accounts for their appeal?" and "What are the impacts of these narratives on their audiences?" Yuko Kawai uses narrative analysis to analyze two articles published in 1966 on Asian Americans as the model minority to answer the question, "How do narratives create perceptions about race?" In Ryan Bruss's analysis of the film *Toy Story 2*, he asks two questions, "What are the gender roles depicted in *Toy Story 2*?" and "What are the narrative strategies used to construct these roles?" You will recognize elements of feminist criticism in Ryan's essay in that he applies aspects of both narrative and feminist methods to the film.

Notes

1 Alasdair MacIntyre, *After Virtue: A Study in Moral Theory* (1981; rpt. Notre Dame, IN: Notre Dame University Press, 1984), p. 216.

2 W. Lance Bennett, "Storytelling in Criminal Trials: A Model of Social Judgment," *Quarterly Journal of Speech*, 64 (February 1978), 1–22; and Catherine Kohler Riessman, *Narrative Analysis* (Newbury Park, CA: Sage, 1993), pp. 1–4.

3 For a good summary of Aristotle's and Quintilian's discussions of narrative, see John Louis Lucaites and Celeste Michelle Condit, "Re-constructing Narrative Theory: A Functional Perspective," *Journal of Communication*, 35 (Autumn 1985), 90–108.

4 Walter R. Fisher, *Human Communication as Narration: Toward a Philosophy of Reason, Value, and Action* (Columbia: University of South Carolina Press, 1987). For responses to Fisher, see: Barbara Warnick, "The Narrative Paradigm: Another Story," *Quarterly Journal of Speech*, 73 (May 1987), 172–82; Robert C. Rowland, "Narrative: Mode of Discourse or Paradigm?" *Communication Monographs*, 54 (September 1987), 264–75; and Michael Calvin McGee and John S. Nelson, "Narrative Reason in Public Argument," *Journal of Communication*, 35 (Autumn 1985), 139–55.

5 See, for example, Victor W. Turner and Edward M. Bruner, eds., *The Anthropology of Performance* (Urbana: University of Illinois Press, 1986).

6 See, for example, Clifford Geertz, *The Interpretation of Cultures* (New York: Basic, 1973).

7 See, for example, Richard Bauman, *Verbal Art as Performance* (Prospect Heights, IL: Waveland Press, 1977).

8 See, for example, Dwight Conquergood, "Between Experience and Meaning: Performance as a Paradigm for Meaningful Action," in *Renewal and Revision: The Future of Interpretation*, ed. Ted Colson (Denton, TX: Omega, 1986), pp. 26–59.

9 Some theorists distinguish among various kinds of communication and see narrative as functioning differently in each, but I am not making such distinctions. See, for example, Lucaites and Condit; and Thomas B. Farrell, "Narrative in Natural Discourse: On Conversation and Rhetoric," *Journal of Communication*, 35 (Autumn 1985), 109–27.

10 This is the definition of narrative proposed by Noël Carroll, "On the Narrative Connection," in *New Perspectives on Narrative Perspective*, ed. Willie van Peer and Seymour Chatman (Albany: State University of New York Press, 2001), pp. 22–34.

11 For more on setting, see Seymour Chatman, *Story and Discourse: Narrative Structure in Fiction and Film* (Ithaca, NY: Cornell University Press, 1978), pp. 101–07, 138–45; Robert Liddell, *A Treatise on the Novel* (London: Jonathan Cape, 1947), pp. 110–28; and Gerald Prince, *Narratology: The Form and Functioning of Narrative* (New York: Mouton, 1982), pp. 73–74.

12 For more on characters, see Chatman, *Story and Discourse*, pp. 119–38, 198–209; Prince, pp. 13–16, 47–48, 71–73; and Gérard Genette, *Narrative Discourse: An Essay in Method*, trans. Jane E. Lewin (Ithaca, NY: Cornell University Press, 1980), pp. 169–85.

13 Susan Sniader Lanser suggests that a narrator's authority arises from three features: status, a function of the narrator's credibility, sincerity, and storytelling skill; contact, the pattern of the narrator's relationship with the audience; and stance, the narrator's relationship to the story being told. Susan Sniader Lanser, *The Narrative Act: Point of View in Prose Fiction* (Princeton, NJ: Princeton University Press, 1981), pp. 85–94.

14 For more on the narrator, see Chatman, *Story and Discourse*, pp. 146–262; Prince, 7–16, 33–47, 50–54, 115–28; Genette, pp. 185–211; and Bauman, pp. 61–79.

15 For more on kernel and satellite events, see Chatman, *Story and Discourse*, pp. 53, 54; and Prince, pp. 83–92.

16 Active and stative events are discussed by Prince, pp. 62–63.

17 For more on temporal relations, see Prince, pp. 48–50, 64–65; and Seymour Chatman, "What Novels Can Do That Films Can't (and Vice Versa)," in *On Narrative*, ed. W. J. T. Mitchell (Chicago: University of Chicago Press, 1980), p. 118.

18 For more on the relationship between story time and narrating time, see Paul Ricoeur, "Narrative Time," in *On Narrative*, ed. W. J. T. Mitchell (Chicago: University of Chicago Press, 1980), pp. 165–86; Chatman, *Story and Discourse*, pp. 63–84; and Genette, pp. 33–160, 215–27. Genette distinguishes among three categories of relations: order (the order in which the events of the story are presented), duration (the relation of the time it takes to read out the narrative to the time the story-events themselves lasted), and frequency (number of representations of story moments).

19 For more on speed of the narrative, see Prince, pp. 54–59.

20 For more on the audience, see Prince, pp. 16–26; and Genette, pp. 259–60.

21 For more on theme, see Prince, p. 74.

[22] Seymour Chatman, *Story and Discourse*, p. 19; and Prince, p. 7. Some narrative theorists suggest that a narrative contains three parts rather than two: story, narrative, and narrating. The story is the sequence of events related or the content of the story; the narrative is the narrative text in which the story is manifest or the statement of the story in a particular medium such as a novel, myth, or film; and the narrating is the telling of the story or the act of narrating. See, for example, Genette, p. 27; and Edward M. Bruner, p. 145.

[23] For an overview of various ethical perspectives, see Richard L. Johannesen, *Ethics in Human Communication*, 2nd ed. (Prospect Heights, IL: Waveland, 1983).

[24] An ethic of narrative was suggested by Farrell, p. 125.

[25] Carroll, p. 37.

[26] Fisher, pp. 88, 105.

[27] Herbert Halpert, "Definition and Variation in Folk Legend," in *American Folk Legend: A Symposium*, ed. Wayland D. Hand (Berkeley: University of California Press, 1971), p. 51.

[28] This view of fidelity was suggested by: Richard Bauman, *Story, Performance, and Event: Cotextual Studies of Oral narrative* (New York: Cambridge University Press, 1986), p. 12; William F. Lewis, "Telling America's Story: Narrative Form and the Reagan Presidency," *Quarterly Journal of Speech*, 73 (August 1987), 288-89; and Farrell, pp. 122, 123.

[29] Kenneth Burke, *The Philosophy of Literary Form: Studies in Symbolic Action* (1941; rpt. Berkeley: University of California Press, 1973), pp. 293–304.

The Rhetorical Power of a Compelling Story
A Critique of a "Toughlove" Parental Support Group
Thomas A. Hollihan and Patricia Riley

> It has recently been said that almost the bitterest and most hopeless tragedies
> of all are the tragedies of parents with bad children. The tragedy of children
> with bad parents is no less acute. . . .
>   R. Cowell, *Cicero and the Roman Republic*, 1967, p. 298.

Families through the ages have been troubled by misbehaving and, at times,
delinquent children. In 49 B.C., Cicero blamed his brother for his nephew Quintus'
treacheries saying: "His father has always spoilt him but his indulgence is not
responsible for his being untruthful or grasping or wanting in affection for his
family, though it perhaps does make him headstrong and self-willed as well as
aggressive" (Cicero, cited in Cowell, 1967, p. 299). Twenty centuries later, contemporary researchers, practitioners, and theorists continue to investigate the exceedingly complex interaction of parental actions, societal and cultural pressures,
genetic predispositions, and children's behavioral choices that too often culmi-
nate in disaster or despair. Such studies still reflect Cicero's penchant for locating
blame for juvenile delinquency in parental actions: e.g., parents who drink too
much (Morehouse and Richards, 1982); parental relationships characterized by a
great deal of conflict (Emery, 1982); parents who are lax in discipline (Fischer,
1983); abusive parents (Paperny and Deisher, 1983); or parents who fail to provide
good nutritious food for their children (Stasiak, 1982).

Rather than suffer the disparagement of neighbors and relatives, or the accu-
sations of teachers and counseling professionals, many parents try to cope with
their problem children alone (Nemy, 1982). Recently, a program called
"Toughlove" has begun to provide parents of delinquent children with emotional
support and hope for solutions to their common problems. "Toughlove" prosely-
tizes that it is not the parents who are failing, it is their children. Founded by Phyllis and David York, the Toughlove groups promote highly disciplined child
rearing practices in an attempt to stop unruly teenagers from controlling households, to rid parents of guilt feelings, and to enable parents and non-problem children to lead a normal family life (Nemy, 1982).

The Toughlove approach has attracted a great deal of national attention. It
was endorsed by Ann Landers (1981), reported in *Time* ("Getting Tough," 1981),
People ("David and Phyllis," 1981), *Ms.* (Wohl, 1985), and the *New York Times*
(Nemy, 1982), and was featured on the *Phil Donohue Show* and ABC's *20/20*. Par-
tially as a result of this publicity, there are currently more than four-hundred
Toughlove groups in the United States and Canada (Nemy, 1982).

A recent Gallup Poll reported that 37 percent of the respondents felt that the
main problem with parents today was that they did not give their children sufficient discipline (cited in Wohl, 1985). The increased popularity of the Toughlove
program has undoubtedly been a response to these sentiments. Toughlove has

From *Communication Quarterly*, 35 (Winter 1987), 13–25. Used by permission of the Eastern Communication Association and the authors.

been credited with having sparked a series of books advising parents on how to discipline their children (Wohl, 1985; Bodenhamer, 1984; Sanderson, 1983; and Bartocci, 1984).

Toughlove, like Alcoholics Anonymous, operates primarily through a system of self-help groups that attempt to better people's lives, help them cope with crises, and teach them their own limitations (Alibrandi, 1982; Pattison, 1982; and Pomerleau, 1982). A rhetorical study of Toughlove should give insight into the appeal of this group and into the process that similar self-help groups use to become support systems. More importantly, the study of Toughlove will permit researchers to focus on how members are acculturated into the Toughlove philosophy, and how this philosophy guides their lives.

This study involved the observation of a series of Toughlove group meetings and an analysis of the flow of messages during these meetings. The form of these messages can best be described as the telling of individual stories, and ultimately the development of a shared group story. The study is grounded in the notion that these shared stories give insight into the group members' beliefs, actions, and worldviews, and into the process through which they attempt to change their lives. This perspective is best explicated in Walter R. Fisher's (1984) notion of the "narrative paradigm."

In developing the "narrative paradigm," Fisher (1984) asserted that human beings were essentially storytelling creatures and that the dominant mode of human decision making involved the sharing of these stories. Such stories contained "good reasons" which provided insight into the proper courses of human action. According to this perspective, the world consists of a set of stories from which people must choose. People are thus constantly engaged in storytelling and in evaluating the stories they are told (Fisher, 1984, pp. 7–8).

Where the rational world paradigm would expect individuals (advocates) to possess knowledge of subject matter and of the requirements of argumentative form—thereby creating experts with a capability for argument beyond that possessed by naive advocates—the narrative paradigm presumes that all persons have the capacity to be rational. Rationality is thus a function of the "narrative probability" and "narrative fidelity" of a given story—the degree to which stories hang together, their ability to make sense of encountered experience, and whether they corroborate previously accepted stories (Fisher, 1984).

Shared stories play an important role in the lives of those who tell them, for they are a way for people to capture and relate their experiences in the world. These stories respond to people's sense of reason and emotion, to their intellects and imagination, to the facts as they perceive them, and to their values. People search for stories which justify their efforts and resolve the tensions and problems in their lives, and desire stories that resolve their dissonance and are psychologically satisfying.

Those who do not share in the storytelling—those whose life experiences demand different types of stories—might view particular stories as mere rationalization, but this is to miss the very nature of the storytelling process. In this framework, one person's life story is another's rationalization, but if a story serves a useful purpose to those who tell it or listen to it, that story likely will be retold in the generative process of narrative understanding.

This study has three major goals: (1) to operationalize Fisher's narrative paradigm through actual observations; (2) to identify the Toughlove story; and (3) to critique the appeal of that story and discuss its possible consequences.

METHOD

A Toughlove group in a Los Angeles suburb was observed during four consecutive, three-hour meetings. Two researchers attended the meetings and took extensive notes, each attempting to copy down as many of the participants' comments as possible in order to capture the essence of the discussion. We were not allowed to tape record the sessions because the group leaders feared that the presence of taping equipment might "chill" the participants and prevent them from talking in detail about their problems.

The group leaders (two women who founded the group after experiencing difficulties with their own children) were briefed about the nature of the study prior to the first observation. One of the leaders introduced us before our first meeting with the group and asked if anyone objected to our presence. No one objected. We explained to the group that we were interested in watching real-life groups as a part of a small group research project underway at a local university. After each meeting, the Toughlove group leaders were asked if the group's participants had behaved differently due to our presence. On each occasion, the leaders indicated that there appeared to be no differences in the group members' interactions. After the last observation we conducted interviews with several randomly selected group members. Each interviewee was asked if they felt the observation affected the group in any way. Again, no differences were reported.

Following the final observation, each observer's notes were prepared for analysis. While it would have been preferable to have access to complete transcripts of the group meetings, we discovered that our written notes were quite detailed and provided us with a great deal of rhetoric for analysis. We proceeded by first, comparing our notes and eliminating issues of disagreement, and second, subdividing the information into actual remarks made by group members and our own comments about the group's process. We next subdivided the group members' statements into three categories that emerged from the notes: (1) story-lines ("Story-lines have beginnings, middles, and ends which give individual actions meanings, provide unity and self-definition to individual lives . . ." (Frentz, 1985, p. 5); (2) questions or comments to other parents; and (3) procedural issues (mainly leader comments).

Our approach is similar to a "mini-ethnography" where the observers are also the message analysts (Knapp, 1979). This perspective ensures that the highly emotional tone of the meeting, together with the dramatic nature of narrative fiction, are captured in the analysis. After the study was completed, the group as a whole was debriefed.

THE GROUP

The group had been in existence for just over one year when the observations took place. While the group had a nucleus of eight parents who always attended the meetings, the group's size increased significantly during the observation period. Twelve persons attended the first observed meeting, but by the fourth meeting there were more than thirty parents. The growing attendance may have resulted from a story on the group which appeared in a local newspaper. Following the last observed meeting the group split into two smaller groups in order to maintain the close personal atmosphere necessary for the highly emotional, self-disclosive discussions. All of the participating parents had experienced, or were in the midst of experiencing, a family crisis precipitated by their child's (or children's) behavior.

Parents came from a variety of occupational and sociocultural backgrounds, but they were predominantly from middle-class, blue-collar families. They were also primarily Caucasian (one Hispanic couple attended, but no Blacks or Asians). Several couples attended, but most of the members were women. Many were single parents—mothers and fathers—and the vast majority of the women worked outside of the home.

The problems faced by these parents were generally quite serious, including simple acts of rebellion, physical assaults, and threats of murder. The most common problems were drug and alcohol abuse. To illustrate the kinds of behavioral problems discussed by the group, a description of some of the children follows (all names are fictitious):

> Ellen—A 13-year-old female who skips school, steals from her parents, and during the time of the observation had run away from home.

> Bill—A 15-year-old male who struck his father's head against the headboard of his bed while he was asleep.

> Mark—An 18-year-old male who had been arrested for theft, breaking and entering, assault, and selling drugs. At the time of the observations, he was serving a one-year sentence in a juvenile correction facility.

> Angie—A 15-year-old female who carried a knife, had physical altercations with her mother, threatened her father by describing a dream in which she murders him, and was involved in a youth gang.

> John—A 16-year-old male who had beaten his mother with a baseball bat, assaulted her with a knife, and painted "fuck the fat ugly bitch" on their living room wall.

> Maria—A 12-year-old female who had run away from home and who was, during the time of observation, a prostitute.

> Keith—A 24-year-old male who had no job, refused to leave home, and who threatened to beat his mother because she refused to allow him to smoke marijuana in their living room.

Analysis of the parents' stories showed drug or alcohol abuse to be present in slightly more than two-thirds of the cases. The remainder of the cases seemed to reflect either problems of general disobedience or psychological/emotional disturbances. It was not uncommon for parents to come to group meetings with blackened eyes or other visible bruises from violent confrontations with their children. Many parents reported that they were terrified of their own children and, in several cases, parents claimed that their children had threatened them with violence merely because they planned to attend the Toughlove meeting.

THE SHARING OF THE TOUGHLOVE STORY

In each meeting, individual tales of fear and helplessness were transformed into hope and perseverance as these stories were woven into shared narrative fiction. If parents truly loved their children, they could not let them destroy themselves or their families; they had to be tough—this was the Toughlove story.

The meetings can best be described as extended storytelling sessions where the members, together, created a powerful, compelling, and cohesive story. Numerous sagas of their children's triumphs over drugs or alcohol were often repeated as part of the "ritual" acculturation of the new members. This was far more than imparting information to the newcomers; the retelling was always a highly emotional experience for the parents, often tearful at the start, ending in the quiet determination that they had regained control over their lives. Through the storytelling, the parents transformed their lives into a moral drama, suffused with righteousness, that absolved them of their guilt and restored orderliness and discipline to their lives. The retelling of these stories provided examples that Toughlove parents could survive and even conquer crises, kept members involved in the day-to-day life of the group, and preserved a sense of community among the members.

The Toughlove story promised a new beginning. The group's regular members described their desperation before they discovered Toughlove, and contrasted these feelings with the solace they felt once they embraced the Toughlove way of life. Although new members initially may have been reticent to tell their tales in the presence of strangers, their need to talk to someone was apparent as they blurted out their stories in a torrent of emotions.

In this drama, the parents left forever their roles as weak victimized players whose offspring tyrannized them and wreaked havoc on society. The Toughlove narrative empowered them to take charge of their families and demand the respect due them as elders. They would never again be failures, for only their children could lose in the Toughlove story. As one parent declared: "You have not failed—it is your children who are failing. Kids have to learn the consequences of their own actions." Still another added: "We made it easy for them, we covered the sharp edges so they would not bump into things when they learned to walk. We made it too easy—they never had to fight—we went to battle for them. Now they know how to push buttons and use us." Thus if their children were delinquent, they *chose* to be that way, and there are times when there is nothing that parents can do to modify their children's behavior. One group member asserted: "Sometimes you have to realize that your kid is a loser and that there isn't a damn thing that you can do about it." Group members nodded their assent.

THEMATIC ANALYSIS

The narrative fiction created by this Toughlove group contained several key themes. First, individual tales were interwoven to explain the "good reasons" for abandoning the predominant rival story—the modern approach to child-rearing. In their drama, the old-fashioned values, characterized by strict discipline, were purported to be superior to today's methods of raising children. The group members often blamed "TLC" (tender loving care) for the problems they had with their children. One father observed: "While TLC works for some kids it is a bust with others." Another father chimed in, "The best way to raise kids is with discipline—strict discipline—that's how our parents did it and we sure didn't cause them these kinds of problems." Several group members claimed that they had tried to use the modern approach in raising their own children but that it had failed. These same parents expressed pride that they now had the courage to condemn these modern approaches. As one mother adamantly claimed: "Everything we are learning here in Toughlove is contrary to Dr. Spock." The other members readily agreed.

This call for a return to traditional values had fidelity because it resonated with stories from the parents' youth, and because the loss of the old ways accounted for the traumas they had experienced. In this sense, the Toughlove narrative was one of historical renewal, a promise that the past could be recreated and the security and comfort of a bygone era recaptured (Bass, 1983). Parents frequently told stories from their own childhood—about how it felt to "go to the woodshed." They commented that they had feared their own parents at times, but they also respected them. Their own children, they sadly agreed, neither feared nor respected them. As one mother noted: "We raised our kids like they did on TV and not the way we were raised. It always worked on TV. It sure didn't work in my house."

These parents believed they were good people who had been misled. The Toughlove narrative was appealing because it confirmed their self-perceptions and absolved them of their failures. They may have been too kind, too lenient, not tough enough, but it was their children who had really failed because they took advantage of their parents' kindness.

A second major theme of the Toughlove narrative was the parents' disdain for the child service professionals. The professionals became villains in the story for two primary reasons. First, the parents claimed these professionals were too quick to blame them for the failures of their offspring. Virtually all of the parents attending the meetings complained that they had been told by counselors, teachers, principals, and others that they were responsible for their children's behavioral problems. Second, these professionals were condemned as highly vocal proponents of the "modern" approaches to child-rearing. Thus they were spokespersons for the dominant rival story—a story which, for the parents, lacked narrative coherence and fidelity, and a story which reflected an unrealistic approach to raising children. Accounts of visits to counselors were always a central part of an evening's storytelling. These "experts" were portrayed as naïve—"book smart" but "experience dumb"—and many group members related tales of their children "snowing" or "hoodwinking" the experts and bragging about it on their way home. Thus the professionals were depicted as part of the problem rather than as part of the solution.

Toughlove parents viewed the child-care professionals' rival story as detrimental because it suggested that parents and children shared the responsibility for the problems in the home. The parents believed that this story gave their children an excuse to continue misbehaving. As adherents to the Toughlove narrative, the parents discounted the possibility that they were partially to blame for the problems in their homes. Several parents recalled that counselors had mentioned their drinking problems or marital difficulties as potential causes for their children's misdeeds, but they claimed that it was "just a cop out" for kids to blame their parents for these problems. The Toughlove story, however, allowed parents to blame their children for their own problems, and doing so did not seem to make this story any less probable. On several occasions parents asserted: "This problem with my son is destroying my marriage." Or, "My daughter's behavior is causing me to drink too much."

In their role as experts on juvenile problems, supplanting the professionals, Toughlove parents placed most of the blame on their children and external factors. The enemies in the drama became the professionals, the media, the permissiveness of society, their children's friends, the lack of discipline in the schools, or modern approaches to child-rearing. If they as parents could be faulted at all, it was only that they had relied on the rival story and in so doing had become estranged from the "old-fashioned" values with which they had been raised.

The third central theme of the Toughlove narrative was that the system is pro-child, and that they could best cope with their problem children by depending on, and supporting, each other. The Toughlove group meeting was exalted as the one place where parents knew there would be people willing to listen to their problems without judging them. Group members consistently reported that the social service agencies, the schools, the police and the juvenile courts were of little help. The consensus of the group members was that "the laws protect kids, but it is parents who need protection."

The parents agreed that neither teachers nor police were helpful. The consistent story-line was that the schools did not teach, teachers could not control their students, and students were permitted to use drugs right on the school grounds. The police refused to come when they were called, and if they did come, they generally took the teenager's side in the dispute. One woman recalled that after her daughter was arrested for selling drugs the police picked her up to take her to a juvenile facility. On the way the officer was kind enough to stop by a friend's house so the girl could pick up her hairdryer.

The tales which recounted the utter helplessness these parents felt in coping with their past crises played an important part in the development of the group's shared story. If parents could not trust "the system" to resolve their problems, then they were all the more dependent on their fellow group members.

In this narrative fiction, the police and the juvenile system were both materially and symbolically anti-parent. The group members discussed how important it was to learn to protect themselves from the law. Several parents explained that their children had filed complaints against them, alleging child neglect or abuse, while their offspring were in fact destroying all harmony in the home and terrorizing their families. The group also discussed in great detail their responsibilities in providing for minor children. One woman insisted: "All parents are required by law to provide is a roof over their head and minimally sufficient clothing." Another mother told the group how she left home to escape from her son, leaving him only a loaf of bread and a jar of peanut butter to eat. The common thread running through most of these stories was the declaration that the police and the courts did not take these complaints seriously and failed to realize that these children represented a genuine threat to their parents and siblings. One angry mother related how the police told her that they could do nothing even though her son, whom she had thrown out, had returned to steal her possessions and destroy her furniture. The police refused to act because her house was still considered the boy's home, and, according to the officer, "A kid can't steal from himself, and can destroy his own house if he wants to."

Consistent with this theme, group members jointly developed language strategies to convince the police to arrest their children the next time they were called to the house. Several parents explained that the police would not take a teenager away the first, second, or even the third time they were summoned, but after that, if you labeled your child "incorrigible" you will have "hit upon the right legal mumbo-jumbo" to get him/her arrested. Other valuable information was given via stories—one mother explained that parents can report their kid missing after he leaves the house, "then after the police find him and bring him to the station you can refuse to pick him up, not accept custody. Then they have no choice, they have to put him somewhere else. That's what I did." She was upset because her son had been selling drugs in her house.

In contrast to the lack of help available from more conventional sources, the Toughlove narrative dramatized that if parents needed assistance they could always call upon another group member. As one of the group leaders recalled: "Crises don't happen between 8 A.M. and 5 P.M. when the social workers are willing to help. But if you are having trouble with your kid, even if it is midnight, you can call another Toughlove mom or dad. We will come by. These folks have come to my house when I needed help. And I've gone to theirs." Another member declared: "Kids have always had gangs. Now we have one too." Thus the Toughlove narrative encouraged parents to take heart—they had formed their own social services system, a support group that could circumvent or beat the system if necessary.

The fourth, and last, prominent theme in the narrative called for parents to put Toughlove into action by setting "bottom lines" for their children. These were the rules their children had to obey if they wanted to live with their family. The key to this strategy was that parents had to enforce their bottom lines, no matter what. The bottom lines set by individual parents were frequently discussed during the meetings. They included: you will not drink, you will not use drugs, you will attend school, you will meet this curfew, you will clean up after yourself, you will not entertain someone of the opposite sex in your bedroom, etc. By spelling out the behaviors appropriate for each of their children, and enforcing them, the Toughlove parents reinforced the shared group story that strict discipline was the answer to their troubles. Youths who did not meet their bottom lines were told they could no longer live at home. Although ejecting a son/daughter from the house was to occur only as a last resort, several parents in this group had forced their children to leave home even though they had nowhere else to go. Two other parents managed to have their children detained in Juvenile Hall, a county detention facility, and one had committed her son to a private detoxification center. The group's leader said the message contained in these stories was a simple one: "Set rules for your kids. If they don't follow them, tell them, 'don't let the door hit you on your way out.'" The Toughlove story thus characterized even these very unhappy outcomes as positive developments. It was presumed better to be rid of these problem children than it was to have to endure the profound disruptions that they caused in the home.

Newcomers were warned that instituting the bottom lines was no easy task, as the group leaders and regulars related anecdotes regarding their children's initial difficulties when the new rules were set. One woman recalled that her daughter kept breaking the rules, so she refused to prepare her meals. Since her daughter could not even find the can opener in the kitchen, the mother found that she gained the girl's cooperation fairly quickly. One father told the group that his daughter's bottom line was to do well in school. To make up for lost time, she had to attend classes regularly, go straight home after school and not have visitors, do her homework, and also help keep the house clean. He discovered that all she did was talk on the phone all afternoon, so he removed the phones from his home every morning and locked them in the trunk of his car so that she could not contact her friends during the day. New Toughlove members quickly understood that they were being prepared for a different type of battle than they were accustomed to, but one that they could hope to win.

During each meeting the group went through the reinforcing ritual of calling upon individual parents and asking them to describe what happened in their homes during the past week. Parents were asked to list the bottom lines they had set, and report whether or not their children had lived up to these rules. If a parent reported that one or more of the rules had been violated, the other group members cross-examined him/her to determine if the offending child had been suitably punished. Parents who showed signs of weakness were criticized, and parents who claimed they had been tough in enforcing the rules were praised by the other group members. This "grilling" of the parents allowed the Toughlove oldtimers to give encouragement to parents who were not used to standing firm. The Toughlove narrative left little room for "extenuating circumstances."

During this segment of storytelling, numerous parents exclaimed that their children were now behaving very differently as a result of the Toughlove program. Several expressed the conviction that they had finally managed to "win the respect" of their children—now that they could no longer be pushed around. These parents, furthermore, noted that while their children initially rebelled against the rules, they ultimately accepted them, because "children want and need discipline." The narrative was additionally strengthened when several parents commented that their children were happy that they had found Toughlove.

Most parents would leave the meeting after the story-telling/testimonial session appearing more relaxed than when they arrived, imbued with the Toughlove spirit, and vowing to spread the word. Others, battered by recent crises, would remain to exchange sorrows, advice, hugs, and telephone numbers before braving the trip home.

IMPLICATIONS OF THE TOUGHLOVE STORY

The Toughlove narrative proved to be comforting, engaging, predictable, and persuasive. Parents joined the group during times of crisis, many feeling as if they had failed because they had been unable to instill socially appropriate values and attitudes in their children. Shamed by the reactions of friends, relatives, and child-care experts, and resentful of a system that could not help and only blamed them for allowing such a disgraceful state of affairs to exist, they readily embraced the Toughlove narrative as an alternative for their problems.

Human communication works by identification, and these parents discovered that no one else understood life with delinquent children except other parents in similar circumstances. The rational world, with its scientific notions of child psychology and "Dr. Spock type experts," could not "speak" to them. The experts' story, which blamed them for their children's conduct, denied their own experiences and did not contain the formal or substantive features necessary for adherence. The Toughlove narrative met their needs and fulfilled the requirements for a good story, narrative probability—what constitutes a coherent story—

and narrative fidelity—that a story rings true with a hearer's experience (Fisher, 1984). The story was probable because it was based on old fashioned values, it restored the social order, and it placed blame where it belonged, on the shoulders of their disobedient and abusive offspring. The rival story which placed at least partial blame on the parents for their children's conduct was viewed as less probable. The story met the test of narrative fidelity because it resonated with their own feelings that they were essentially good people whose only failing had been that they were too permissive and not as tough as their own parents had been.

The Toughlove story was compelling because it so completely absolved parents of their guilt and relieved their sense of failure. The story also provided parents with a course of action that, at best, showed their children who was in charge and established rules they had to follow to remain part of the family, and at worst, allowed the remainder of the household to lead normal lives after the delinquent youth was "shown the door."

Despite the obvious appeal of these new "tough" approaches to childrearing, however, they are not without risk. The dimension of the Toughlove story which holds that children who do not adhere to their bottom lines should be ejected from the house is especially controversial. There is, of course, great danger that the ejected child may be unprepared to face life on his/her own and may in fact become a real threat to him/herself and to society. For instance, John Hinckley's parents were following the Toughlove philosophy when they insisted that their son become financially independent by March 20, 1982, precisely the day that he shot President Reagan and three other men ("Hinckley's Family," 1984).

Hinckley's father has since embarked on a national speaking tour to warn parents of the dangers in the Toughlove approach, declaring: "For heaven's sake don't kick somebody out of the house when they can't cope. But I'd never heard that before, and it (kicking John out of the house) seemed to me to make a lot of sense at the time" ("Hinckley's Family," 1984, p. 12). Hinckley's parents now urge other parents who are told to eject their children from home to be sure to seek the advice of those experts they had been told could not be trusted ("Hinckley's Family," 1984). This warning seems reasonable enough: parents should not take drastic steps when a more conservative means for disciplining children might work equally well—they should always proceed with caution.

Before this or any other rival story is likely to capture the trust and attention of the Toughlove parents, however, it needs to accommodate them as the hopeful, newly self-confident, bearers of old-fashioned values which they have become. If a rival story cannot capture people's self-conceptions, it does not matter whether or not it is "fact." Fisher noted that, "Any story, any form of rhetorical communication, not only says something about the world, it also implies an audience, persons who conceive of themselves in very specific ways" (Fisher, 1984, p. 14). Parents who do not have "problem children" may find the Toughlove story objectionable, but to those parents in the midst of a crisis the story has obvious appeal. The advocates of any rival story can win adherents only by "telling stories that do not negate the self-conceptions people hold of themselves" (Fisher, 1984, p. 14).

The other great danger in the Toughlove story is that it can be readily adapted to fit all children and all situations. For example, during our observation we noted that if parents told the group that they did not believe drugs or alcohol were responsible for their children's bizarre behavior, they were given a lecture on how to substantiate these abuses. Other potential reasons for their children's erratic or destructive behavior, including emotional or psychological disturbances, were dismissed without consideration. The Toughlove story thus proved quite elastic and was easily stretched to permit the conclusion that "bad drugs" or a "bad crowd" caused all behavior problems and, therefore, all required the same remedy.

The pressure to enact the Toughlove story was great; all parents had to play the "enforcer" role that ritualistically proved their faith and imbued them with the credibility and unquestioned support granted only to other Toughlove moms and dads. While the group leaders seemed to be aware of the danger that parents might seek to get a quick-fix to their problems by ejecting their children from the house when far less drastic actions would be more appropriate, the potential danger from such decisions (as characterized by the Hinckley example) never appeared as imminent to the Toughlove parents as was the impending end to the chaos in their lives.

The truth or falsity of the Toughlove story is not really at issue in this study. What is important is that through an analysis we can come to understand the appeal of stories and perhaps even learn how to avoid the creation of stories which might precipitate harmful consequences. Perhaps the most useful outcome of such study is that child-care professionals and social service agencies can learn how to create *better* stories—stories which affirm parents' self-worth, but also help them to deal with the crises in their homes without the risk of worsening those crises by reacting without careful deliberation.

References

Alibrandi, L. A. (1982). The Fellowship of Alcoholics Anonymous. In E. M. Pattison & E. Kaufman (Eds.), *Encyclopedic handbook of alcoholism* (pp. 979–986). New York: Gardner Press.

Bartocci, B. (1984). *My angry son: Sometimes love is not enough*. New York: Donald I. Fine.

Bass, J. D. (1983). Becoming the past: The rationale of renewal and the annulment of history. In D. Zarefsky, M. Sillars & J. Rhodes (Eds.), *Argument in transition: Proceedings of the Third Summer Conference on Argumentation* (pp. 305–318). Annandale, VA: Speech Communication Association.

Bodenhamer, G. (1984). *Back in control: How to get your children to behave*. Englewood Cliffs: Prentice-Hall.

Cowell, F. R. (1967). *Cicero and the Roman Republic* (4th ed.). Baltimore: Penguin Books.

David and Phyllis York treat problem teenagers with a stiff dose of "Toughlove." (1981, November 16). *People*, p. 101.

Emery, R. E. (1982). Intraparental conflict and the children of discord and divorce. *Psychological Bulletin, 92*, 310–330.

Fischer, D. G. (1983). Parental supervision and delinquency. *Perceptual and Motor Skills, 56*, 635–640.

Fisher, W. R. (1984). Narration as a human communication paradigm: The case of public moral argument. *Communication Monographs, 51*, 1–22.

Frentz, T. S. (1985). Rhetorical conversation, time, and moral action. *Quarterly Journal of Speech, 71*, 1–18.

Getting tough with teens. (1981, June 8). *Time*, p. 47.

Hinckley, J. & Hinckley, J. A. (1985). *Breaking Points*. Grand Rapids, MI: Zondervan.

Hinckleys: Family on a crusade. (1984, February 23). *Los Angeles Times*, p. 12.

Knapp, M. S. (1979). Ethnographic contributions to evaluation research: The experimental schools program evaluation and some alternatives. In T. D. Cook & C. S. Reichardt (Eds.), *Qualitative and quantitative methods in evaluation research* (pp. 118–139). Beverly Hills: Sage.

Landers, A. (1981, November). Giving kids "Tough" love. *Family Circle*, p. 34.

Loeber, R. & Dishion, T. (1983). Early predictors of male delinquency: A review. *Psychological Bulletin, 94*, 68–99.

Morehouse, E. & Richards, T. (1982). An examination of dysfunctional latency age children of alcoholic parents and problems in intervention. *Journal of Children in Contemporary Society, 15*, 21–33.

Nemy, E. (1982, April 26). For problem teen-agers: Love, toughness. *New York Times*, p. B12.

Paperny, D. M. & Deisher, R. W. (1983). Maltreatment of adolescents: The relationship to a predisposition toward violent behavior and delinquency. *Adolescence, 18*, 499–506.

Pattison, E. M. (1982). A systems approach to alcoholism treatment. In E. M. Pattison & E. Kaufman (Eds.), *Encyclopedic handbook of alcoholism* (pp. 1080–1108). New York: Gardner Press.

Pomerleau, O. F. (1982). Current behavioral theories in the treatment of alcoholism. In E. M. Pattison & E. Kaufman (Eds.), *Encyclopedic handbook of alcoholism* (pp. 1054–1067). New York: Gardner Press.

Sanderson, J. (1983). *How to raise your kids to stand on their own two feet*. New York: Congdon & Weed.

Stasiak, E. A. (1982). Nutritional approaches to altering criminal behavior. *Corrective and Social Psychiatry and the Journal of Behavioral Technology, Methods and Therapy, 28*, 110–115.

Wohl, L. C. (1985, May). The parent-training game—from "Toughlove" to perfect manners. *Ms.*, p. 40.

York, P. & York, D. (1980). *Toughlove*. Sellersville, PA: Community Service Foundation.

The Model Minority Myth of Asian Americans in 1966
A Narrative Criticism
Yuko Kawai

In the middle of the 1960s, at the latter stage of the civil rights movement, in which African Americans and other racial minority groups were fighting against racism in search of equal rights with whites, a new stereotype for Asian Americans—the model minority—emerged. Prior to the 1960s, Asians in the United States were represented as undesirable aliens who polluted the white land of the United States, coolies who took away Americans' jobs by working for low wages, and the embodiment of the yellow peril (Lee, 1999).

Two articles, published in 1966 by the mainstream media, are said to be responsible for the construction of the model minority myth of Asian Americans (Lee, 1999; Zia, 2000). On January 9, an article titled "Success Story, Japanese-American Style" appeared in *The New York Times Magazine*. On December 26, *U.S. News and World Report* published a similar article, "Success Story of One Minority Group in U.S.," this time focusing on Chinese Americans. The articles celebrated Asian Americans as the model minority group that successfully raised its socioeconomic status in U.S. society despite its non-white racial background. Since 1966, *Newsweek, Time, Fortune, The New York Times, The Washington Post*, and other mainstream media have featured other Asian Americans, such as Koreans, Vietnamese, and Asian Indians, as the model minority (Osajima, 2000; Takaki, 1989; Wu, 2002). The articles typically state that Asian Americans exceed whites in academic performance, achieve an income level equivalent to or higher than whites, and generally realize a high socioeconomic status in the United States.

The model minority myth is not just a stereotype of Asian Americans. It is a racial and political discourse that promotes a particular view about race relations and racism in the United States. In this essay, I analyze the two articles of the model minority myth published in *The New York Times Magazine* and *U.S. News and World Report* in 1966 to discover how the narrative is structured to create the model minority myth. The titles of both articles—"Success Story, Japanese-American Style" and "Success Story of One Minority Group in U.S."—use the word *story*. A narrative perspective provides an appropriate way to examine the model minority myth represented because the articles, through telling a particular story or narrative about Asian Americans, present a story about particular race relations.

THE MODEL MINORITY MYTH AND THE IDEOLOGY OF COLORBLINDNESS

The model minority myth has been criticized because it is an oversimplification and does not tell a story close to the lived reality of Asian Americans (e.g., Osajima, 2000; Takaki, 1989; Wu, 2002). The high income level of Asian Americans

This essay was written while Yuko Kawai was a student in Karen A. Foss's rhetorical criticism class at the University of New Mexico in 2002. A revised version of this essay was published in *Kaleidoscope: A Graduate Journal of Qualitative Communication Research*, 2 (Fall 2003). Used by permission of *Kaleidoscope* and the author.

is simply because the Asian American population concentrates in particular states and metropolitan areas in which living expenses are relatively higher than other areas, with about 50 percent of Asian Americans residing in the states of California, New York, and Hawaii (U.S. Census Bureau, 2002). Asian Americans live inside the central part of metropolitan areas twice as much as white people do (U.S. Census Bureau, 2001) and have more persons working per household than whites (Takaki, 1989). In addition, Asian Americans do not constitute a heterogeneous group; a serious income gap exists among various groups of Asian Americans. For example, people who came to the United States recently as refugees from countries such as Vietnam, Cambodia, and Laos live below the poverty line in far greater percentages than the general population (Wang & Wu, 1996). The educational level of Asian Americans may be high, but in comparison with whites at the equal educational level, Asian Americans earn less money (Wu, 2002).

The model minority myth is a racially and thus politically motivated discourse that involves all racial groups. It was not an accident that the mainstream media published the two articles representing the Asian American as the model minority in the middle of the 1960s (Wu, 2002). During this time, the Black Power movement, claiming that "America was fundamentally a racist society" (Osajima, 2000, p. 451), demanded the structural change of U.S. society far more radically than the civil rights movement. The model minority myth was a political message that targeted the Black Power movement (Osajima, 2000) because, by celebrating Asian Americans as the model minority that moved ahead despite its racial background, it asserted that U.S. society was fair enough to allow racial minority groups to succeed socially and economically.

Critical race theory provides a useful theoretical lens by which to understand the model minority myth as a racial and political discourse. Critical race theorists argue that colorblindness disguises actual racial inequality by promoting formal equality (e.g., Bell, 1992; Lawrence & Matsuda, 1997). The ideology of colorblindness abstracts individuals and contexts and regards the consequences of racial inequality as an individual rather than a social and institutional problem (Guinier & Torres, 2002). Colorblindness is a racial and political discourse that denies the existence of institutional racism by atomizing individuals and detaching them from historical, economic, political, and social contexts. By doing so, racism is framed as the problem of racial minority groups rather than the problem of the dominant group, and the former is considered to be responsible for the consequences of racial inequality. Critical race theorists attack the concept of race as a formal and neutral category and, at the same time, advocate the importance of race because institutional racism is still real. Not talking about race, these theorists assert, does not lead to a society free of racism (Guinier & Torres, 2002).

The model minority myth exemplifies a "stock story" (Guinier & Torres, 2002) for colorblindness. The model minority myth tells a particular story about Asian Americans and, at the same time, offers a way of viewing the world in which race does not matter, racial minority groups can advance if they make an effort, and any lack of success is their problem. Understanding the narrative structure of the initial two articles of the model minority myth is important to challenge the ideology of colorblindness. The two articles are significant not only because they demonstrate the prototype of the myth but also because they elucidate the context in which the myth first was constructed.

The first article, "Success Story, Japanese-American Style," was written by William Petersen, a professor of sociology at the University of California at Berkeley and published in *The New York Times Magazine* on January 9, 1966. This eight-page article, focusing on Japanese Americans, reports their past and present experiences in the United States. The second article, "Success Story of One Minority Group in U.S.," does not include an author's name; it appeared on December 26, 1966, in *U.S. News and World Report*. This three-page article discusses how well Chinese Americans are doing without resorting to social welfare.

I use narrative criticism as a method to examine how the two articles are structured to create the model minority myth and thereby understand what kind of worldview the narrative offers its audience. Narrative is a way of ordering and presenting a view of the world through a description of a situation involving such dimensions as characters, actions, settings, narrator, audience, theme, temporal relations, and causal relations. Through the examination of the various narrative dimensions, an understanding emerges of the kind of world the articles attempt to demonstrate and the strategies they use to induce readers to believe in the model minority myth.

ANALYSIS

The two articles of the model minority myth are structured very similarly. Settings, characters, temporal relations, and spatial relations are the most significant dimensions of the narrative in the two articles.

Settings

The two articles share four identical settings: historical setting, educational setting, familial setting, and criminal setting. In the historical setting, both articles trace the history of Japanese and Chinese immigrants from the nineteenth century, when these groups began to arrive in the United States, until the 1960s. The historical settings for both Japanese and Chinese Americans are filled with anti-Asian prejudice and discrimination: They are denied basic civil rights and targeted by racially motivated violence. *The New York Times Magazine* article depicts Japanese Americans as people who were subjected to "the vast mass of anti-Japanese agitation in the first decades of this century," "assaulted on the streets," "denied access to any urban professions," "denied citizenship," and "denied the ownership of the land" (Petersen, 1966, p. 21). "Japanese businesses were picketed" before the exclusion law targeting the Japanese American was enacted (p. 21). After World War II broke out, Japanese Americans were "subjected in rapid succession to a curfew" and suffered from the "forced transfer of an entire population to concentration camps, where they lived surrounded by barbed wire and watched by armed guards" (p. 33).

Likewise, the *U.S. News and World Report* article describes the historical setting for the Chinese American as a space full of hardships and racial discrimination. In California, "the first legislature slapped foreign miners with a tax aimed at getting Chinese out of the gold mining business," "Chinese could not testify against whites in court," "Chinese-Americans could not own land in California, and no corporation or public agency could employ them" ("Success Story," 1966, p. 73). They "worked in mines, on railroads, and in other hard labor" and after "moving into cities, where the best occupations were closed to them, large numbers became laundrymen and cooks because of the shortage of women in the

West" (p. 73). In 1871, "white mobs raged through the Chinese section," and "twenty-three Chinese were hanged, beaten, shot or stabbed to death" (p. 76).

In the educational setting, education is described as a way for Japanese and Chinese Americans to move ahead in U.S. society. In this setting, Japanese and Chinese Americans are represented as people who are extremely serious about education, which lifts their social status by enabling them to secure middle or lower level white-collar jobs. *The New York Times Magazine* article introduces a Japanese American high school boy who "used to read his texts, underlining important passages, then read and underline again, then read and underline a third time" (Petersen, 1966, p. 38). Japanese Americans choose to study "business administration, optometry, engineering or some other middle-level profession" because they see "their education as a means of acquiring a stable skill" (p. 40). For Japanese Americans, education is "conducted like a military campaign against a hostile world: with intelligent planning and tenacity, they fought for certain limited positions and won them" (p. 40).

The *U.S. News and World Report* article states that "Chinese American children are expected to attend school faithfully, work hard at their studies—and stay out of trouble" ("Success Story," 1966, p. 73). Chinese American parents' "supervision and verbal discipline are strict," so if they are informed that their children's school performance is poor, "there is an immediate improvement" (p. 73). Chinese American parents "always watch out for the children, train them, send them to school and make them stay home after school to study" (p. 76). Thus, school teachers compete "for posts in schools with large numbers of Chinese American children" (p. 73). In addition to the regular school, Chinese Americans "send their youngsters to Chinese schools for one or two hours a day so they can learn Chinese history, culture, and—in some cases—language" (p. 76).

In the familial setting, family is portrayed as the most important entity that shapes and disciplines Japanese and Chinese Americans. The articles emphasize the authority of parents and loyalty to family and the traditional Chinese and Japanese notion of family. Japanese Americans have "greater attachment to family," and "the wishes of any individual counted for far less than the good reputation of his family name, which was worshipped through his ancestors" (Petersen, 1966, p. 41). Parents have enormous power over their children, these articles report, and children learn to honor their "obligations to parents and avoid bringing them shame" by memorizing the *shushin* or maxims at Japanese language schools (p. 41).

The Chinese American group is depicted as "a big family" ("Success Story," 1966, p. 73). When members of this group are in need, they do not need to turn to welfare because "if someone has trouble, usually it can be solved within the family," and "within a tight network of family and clan loyalties, relatives continue to help each other" (p. 73). A Chinese American banker in New York is quoted as saying, "there are at least 60 associates here whose main purpose is to help our own people" (p. 76). The articles introduce the traditional Chinese idea of family by quoting a local judge: "Traditionally, the family patriarch ruled the household, and the other members of the family obeyed and followed without questioning his authority" (p. 76). The Chinese follow "the custom of being good to . . . relatives," and thus a man who came from China was "looked after by his sister's family" until he "opened a small restaurant of his own" (p. 74).

The criminal setting emphasizes the low crime rates among Japanese and Chinese Americans despite their overcrowded and overpopulated living environments. In the article on Japanese Americans, although the first and second generations of Japanese Americans "have lived in neighborhoods, characterized by overcrowding, poverty, dilapidated housing, and other 'causes' of crime," their low crime rate is "exceptional" (Petersen, 1966, p. 40). The article continues to argue that "in such a slum environment, even though surrounded by ethnic groups with high crime rates, they have been exceptionally law-abiding" (p. 40). It also mentions that "in Los Angeles today, while the general crime rate is rising, for Japanese adults it is continuing to fall" (p. 40).

Chinese American children do not cause trouble due to "strict parental supervision" ("Success Story," 1966, p. 76). Chinatowns are "islands of peace and stability" and "the safest place in the city" (p. 73), despite the fact that "it [Chinatown in San Francisco] is one of the most densely populated neighborhoods in the United States" and "the housing shortage here [Chinatown in New York] is worse than in Harlem" (p. 76). In 1965, for example, "not one San Francisco Chinese—young or old—was charged with murder, manslaughter, rape or an offense against wife or children" (p. 76). The article quotes a New York City police lieutenant who says, "you don't find any Chinese locked up for robbery, rape, or vagrancy" (p. 76).

Characters

The narrative of both articles is structured by a comparison between the main characters, the Japanese American and the Chinese American, and a supporting character, the African American. Without the presence of the supporting character, this narrative is not possible. The two articles start *and* end with a comparison between the Japanese/Chinese American and the African American.

The first paragraph of *The New York Times Magazine* article argues, "Asked which of the country's ethnic minorities has been subjected to the most discrimination and the worst injustices, very few persons would even think of answering: 'The Japanese American.' Yet, if the question refers to persons alive today, that may well be the correct reply" (Petersen, 1966, p. 20). Immediately after this, the article states that, "like the Negroes, the Japanese have been the object of color prejudice" (p. 20). What is different between the African American and the Japanese American is that the Japanese American "has risen above even prejudiced criticism . . . by their own almost totally unaided effort," whereas "for all the well-meaning programs and countless scholarly studies now focused on the Negro, we barely know how to repair the damage that the slave traders started" (p. 21).

The New York Times Magazine article ends with a discussion of the importance of minority groups' cultural ties with their homelands, comparing the Japanese American and the African American. It argues that the African American, "with the least meaningful ties to an overseas fatherland . . . has no refuge when the United States rejects him," whereas "the Japanese could climb over the highest barriers our racists were able to fashion in part because of their meaningful links with an alien culture" (Petersen, 1966, p. 43). Japanese Americans can survive racial prejudices and climb the social ladder because they retain Japanese culture. Japanese Americans can count on their culture to support their self-esteem when they are rejected by the mainstream U.S. society. African Americans, because they have lost their home culture, do not have something to which to turn when they are discriminated against because of their race.

The same comparison is employed in the *U.S. News and World Report* article on the Chinese American. The article begins by arguing that "at a time when it is being proposed that hundreds of billions be spent to uplift Negroes and other minorities, the nation's 300,000 Chinese Americans are moving ahead on their own—with no help from anyone else" ("Success Story," 1966, p. 73). The article also claims that the Chinese American's history is "a story of adversity and prejudice that would shock those now complaining about the hardships endured by today's Negroes" (p. 73).

The article ends with a comparison of racial prejudice against Chinese Americans and that against African Americans. It asserts that Asian Americans faced racial prejudices more than African Americans. By quoting a social worker in Los Angeles, the article contends that "it must be recognized that the Chinese and other Orientals in California were faced with even more prejudice than faces the Negro today. We haven't stuck Negroes in concentration camps, for instance, as we did the Japanese in World War II" ("Success Story," 1966, p. 76).

The two articles, by comparing Asian Americans and African Americans, attempt to construct an idea that Asian Americans have experienced racial prejudice and discrimination as much as or even more than African Americans. Asian Americans have elevated themselves "by their own totally unaided effort or on their own—with no help from anyone else" ("Success Story," 1966, p. 73)—whereas African Americans have not. The strategy is twofold: (1) To make Asian Americans equivalent to African Americans to be able to compare them; and (2) To place Asian Americans above African Americans by using Asian Americans as an example that racial minority groups can achieve success without help. The first part of the strategy requires the revision of the received view regarding racial minority groups' history. *The New York Times Magazine* article insists that Japanese Americans have been "subjected to the most discrimination and the worse injustices" (Petersen, 1966, p. 20), although "few persons would even think of answering" (p. 20) the question this way. The *U.S. News and World Report* article similarly states that Chinese Americans' experience of racial discrimination "would shock those now complaining about the hardships endured by today's Negroes" ("Success Story," 1966, p. 73). What these two statements imply is that people do not believe Asian Americans have faced racial discrimination similar to or worse than African Americans. The two articles, however, undertake to revise this view and replace it with the belief that Asian Americans have been racially discriminated against more than African Americans. In short, what the articles argue is this: If Asian Americans, who went through similar or worse racial discrimination, can move ahead in U.S. society without any help, why can't African Americans do the same? The articles attempt to create an idea of a U.S. society in which race does not matter and racial minority groups can raise their social and economic status if they try hard.

Influence of Character Relations on Settings

Because the narrative is structured along the comparison between Asian Americans and African Americans, everything discussed in the articles is read as a comparison even when the two groups are not directly compared. In the four settings shared by the two articles—historical, educational, criminal, and familial—the articles talk only about Japanese and Chinese Americans. African Americans barely appear in the historical, educational, familial, and criminal settings.

Because of the significant narrative structure, the articles produce the comparison between them covertly even when the comparison is not directly conducted. By discussing that Japanese and Chinese Americans perform well at school, have solid family ties, and commit very few crimes, the articles simultaneously indicate the opposite for African Americans: African Americans do not perform well at school, do not have solid families, and commit crimes more frequently.

Said (1979) contends that the concept of the Occident or the West cannot exist without the creation of the Orient. Likewise, the model minority requires the "problem minority." As the discussion of the Orient necessarily relates to the discussion of what is not the Orient, asserting that Asian Americans are the model minority simultaneously implies that other racial minority groups are not. Because the narrative of the two articles is structured by a comparison with African Americans, they are constantly situated as the opposite of the model minority. In other words, "each commendation of Asian Americans is paired off against a reprimand of African Americans" (Wu, 2002, p. 62).

The absence of the historical setting for African Americans and the presence of the historical setting for Asian Americans magnify the idea that Asian Americans do well despite their experience of racism, and thus there must be something wrong with African Americans. The historical setting for Asian Americans claims that Asian Americans have encountered racial prejudice and discrimination similar to or worse than African Americans. It is true that Asian Americans were targeted by racially motivated violence, denied citizenship and other basic human rights, and endured hardships because of racism, but Asian Americans were not slaves. African Americans were forced to come to America and had been enslaved for centuries, whereas most Asian Americans, except for Southeast Asian refugees, were voluntary immigrants to the United States like white people were, although they were not treated like whites. Prior to the 1965 immigration act that reopened the door for Asian immigration to the United States, immigrants from Asia were selected people from the upper or middle classes of their homelands. For example, the Japanese government screened emigrants and sent those who were literate and educated because they were regarded as Japan's "representative to the world" (Zia, 2000, p. 29).

In addition, in order to come to the United States from Asia, emigrants needed at least to have financial means to sail across the Pacific Ocean. As Wu (2002) posits, "in Asia, there are millions of urban and rural poor who do not have the means to travel out of the city or the village, much less to the United States" (p. 53). Financial, social, and cultural capital need to be accumulated for generations. Unlike African Americans, who were uprooted from their homelands, Asian Americans could take this capital with them when they came to the United States. By offering the historical setting only for Asian Americans but not for African Americans and yet comparing Asian Americans with African Americans, the articles obscure the historical context for African Americans and construct a colorblind worldview.

CONCLUSIONS

The two articles on the model minority myth shared identical settings and characters. The relationships between the main and the supporting characters in both articles also are identical. The significant structure of the myth is the comparison between the main characters, the Chinese and the Japanese American, and a supporting character, the African American. Due to this prime narrative structure, even when only the main characters perform in the four common settings—historical, educational, familial, and criminal—the supporting actor is "present." These significant dimensions of the narrative are systematically selected based on the ideology of colorblindness for the purpose of generating a colorblind worldview. Since the two articles were published, the model minority myth has been (re)constructed, incorporating other Asian Americans under different political, economic, and social contexts. The ideology of colorblindness still continues to be relevant in those different stories of the model minority myth.

Guinier and Torres (2002) suggest three major flaws in the discourse of colorblindness: "(1) it assumes that racial inequality is a problem of individuals; (2) in so doing, it masks entrenched racial inequality; and (3) it acts as a brake on grassroots organizing" (p. 43). The model minority myth as a colorblind discourse triggers similar implications. One is that the model minority myth creates a worldview in which racism is not U.S. society's problem but the problem of minority groups; it has to be overcome by their effort. Elevating Asian Americans as the model minority who succeeds in U.S. society despite racial prejudice and discrimination simultaneously entails the idea that racial minorities are responsible if they are still stuck with poverty and menial jobs. The *U.S. News and World Report* article is very explicit about this point. In the article, Chinese Americans are commended because "few Chinese Americans are getting welfare handouts—or even want them" ("Success Story," 1966, p. 73) or because Chinese Americans still follow "the old idea that people should depend on their own efforts—not a welfare check—in order to reach America's 'promised land'" ("Success Story," 1966, p. 73). By contending that America's promised land can be reached through racial minorities' own efforts, the model minority myth (thus colorblind discourse) functions to illustrate the mainstream U.S. society as a neutral, fair, and open space; it thereby sustains white privilege (Kim, 1999).

A second consequence of the model minority myth is that it splits racial minority groups and prevents them from forming an interracial solidarity to fight racism. The model minority myth played a role in the 1992 Los Angeles riot in which African Americans and Latinos attacked Korean American businesses and other Asian Americans. The riot occurred after the "not guilty" verdict was announced for the white police officer charged with beating Rodney King, an African American. Prior to this case, in 1991, a Korean American storeowner Soon Ja Du shot to death a 15-year-old African American girl, Latasha Harling, over an unpaid $1.79 bottle of orange juice. Superior Court Judge Karlin put Du on probation with a $500 fine and 400 hours of community service (Park, 1999). This extremely light sentence angered the African American community in South Central Los Angeles. Gotanda (1995) argues that Judge Karlin's sentence was based on the model minority myth with which the judge stereotyped Du as a hardworking and law-abiding "model" immigrant who was "harassed" by Harling, an African American whom the judge associated with crime and gangs. Du, with model minority privilege, was "judicially treated as a white" (Park, 1999, p. 66). In the 1992 riot, African Americans and Latinos regarded Asian Americans as "surrogate whites" and forced them to pay the price for the civil rights violation committed by white Americans.

The narrative of the model minority myth represents colorblindness. The comparison between Asian Americans and African Americans is possible only by abstracting their different backgrounds and contexts as racial minority groups. If the comparison is not possible, the myth itself is not possible. Kim (2000–2001), contending that minority groups are not equivalent, postulates that throughout U.S. history, Asian Americans have been more privileged than African Americans. Thus, to summarize all racial minority groups under the term *minority* without discussing interminority differences serves to nullify "certain Black claims and grievances" (p. 38). To refute the model minority myth by arguing that Asian Americans are not advantaged, as the myth claims, is not effective because it simply provides Asian Americans with "*bona fide* minority group" status (Kim, 2000–2001, p. 44). Asian Americans have been used to "prove" that racial minority groups can move ahead in U.S. society. Asian Americans, however, cannot be employed as evidence for such a claim if their relative privilege and advantage are addressed. Granting that a huge gap exists among various Asian American ethnic groups in terms of education and income level, Asian Americans as a racial group have access to racial privileging, as Soon Ja Du's case exemplifies.

Not discussing the different contexts in which whites and racial minority groups are situated is a way of sustaining colorblind ideology and white privilege. Not discussing the different contexts in which racial minority groups are situated and summarizing them all as one minority group is another way of promoting colorblindness. Recognizing privilege and changing the social structure that grants the privilege are necessary to resist colorblind ideology and create a just society.

References

Bell, D. (1992). *Faces at the bottom of the well: The permanence of racism*. New York: Basic.

Gotanda, N. (1995). Re-producing the model minority stereotype: Judge Joyce Karlin's sentencing colloquy in *People vs. Soon Ja Du*. In W. L. Ng, S. Chin, J. S. Moy & G. Y. Okihiro (Eds.), *Reviewing Asian America: Locating diversity* (pp. 87–106). Pullman: Washington State University Press.

Guinier, L., & Torres, G. (2002). *The miner's canary: Enlisting race, resisting power, transforming democracy*. Cambridge, MA: Harvard University Press.

Kim, C. J. (1999). The racial triangulation of Asian Americans. *Politics & Society, 27*(1), 105–38.

Kim, C. J. (2000–2001). Playing the racial trump card: Asian Americans in contemporary U.S. politics. *Amerasia Journal, 26* (3), 35–65.

Lawrence, C. R., & Matsuda, M. J. (1997). *We won't go back: Making the case for affirmative action*. New York: Houghton Mifflin.

Lee, R. G. (1999). *Orientals: Asian Americans in popular culture*. Philadelphia: Temple University Press.

Osajima, K. (2000). Asian Americans as the model minority: An analysis of the popular press image in the 1960s and 1980s. In M. Zhou & J. V. Gatewood (Eds.), *Contemporary Asian America: A multidisciplinary reader* (pp. 449–458). New York: New York University Press.

Park, K. (1999). Use and abuse of race and culture: Black-Korean tension in America. In K. C. Kim (Ed.), *Koreans in the hood: Conflict with African Americans* (pp. 60–74). Baltimore: Johns Hopkins University Press.

Petersen, W. (1966, January 9). Success story, Japanese-American style. *The New York Times Magazine*, pp. 20, 21, 33, 36, 38, 40, 41, 43.

Said, E. (1978). *Orientalism*. New York: Vintage.

Success story of one minority group in U.S. (1966, December 26). *U.S. News and World Report*, pp. 73–74, 76.

Takaki, R. (1989). *Strangers from a different shore: A history of Asian Americans*. New York: Penguin.

U.S. Census Bureau. (2001). *The Asian and Pacific Islander population in the United States. Table 21. Population by Metropolitan and Nonmetropolitan Residence, Sex, Race and Hispanic Origin: March 2000*. Retrieved November 30, 2002, from the U.S. Census Bureau Web site: http://www.census.gov/population/socdemo/race/api/ppl-146/tab21.pdf.

U.S. Census Bureau. (2002). *The Asian population: 2000*. Retrieved November 30, 2002, from the U.S. Census Bureau Web site: http://www.census.gov/prod/2002pubs/c2kbr01-16.pdf.

Wang, T. H., & Wu, F. H. (1996). Beyond the model minority myth. In G. E. Curry (Ed.), *The affirmative action debate* (pp. 191–207). Reading, MA: Addison-Wesley.

Wu, F. H. (2002). *Yellow: Race in America beyond black and white*. New York: Basic.

Zia, H. (2000). *Asian American dreams: The emergence of an American people*. New York: Farrar, Straus, and Giroux.

Success Story, Japanese-American Style

William Petersen
The New York Times Magazine
January 9, 1996

Asked which of the country's ethnic minorities has been subjected to the most discrimination and the worst injustices, very few persons would even think of answering: "The Japanese Americans." Yet, if the question refers to persons alive today, that may well be the correct reply. Like the Negroes, the Japanese have been the object of color prejudice. Like the Jews, they have been feared and hated as hyperefficient competitors. And, more than any other group, they have been seen as the agents of an overseas enemy. Conservatives, liberals and radicals, local sheriffs, the Federal Government and the Supreme Court have cooperated in denying them their elementary rights—most notoriously in their World War II evacuation to internment camps.

Generally this kind of treatment, as we all know these days, creates what might be termed "problem minorities." Each of a number of interrelated factors—poor health, poor education, low income, high crime rate, unstable family pattern, and so on and on—reinforces all of the others, and together they make up the reality of slum life. And by the "principle of cumulation," as Gunnar Myrdal termed it in "An American Dilemma," this social reality reinforces our prejudices and is reinforced by them. When whites defined Negroes as inherently less intelligent, for example, and therefore furnished them with inferior schools, the products of these schools often validated the original stereotype.

Once the cumulative degradation has gone far enough, it is notoriously difficult to reverse the trend. When new opportunities, even equal opportunities, are opened up, the minority's reaction to them is likely to be negative—either self-defeating apathy or a hatred so all-consuming as to be self-destructive. For all the well-meaning programs and countless scholarly studies now focused on the Negro, we barely know how to repair the damage that the slave traders started.

The history of Japanese Americans, however, challenges every such generalization about ethnic minorities, and for this reason alone deserves far more attention than it has been given. Barely more than 20 years after the end of the wartime camps, this is a minority that has risen above even prejudiced criticism. By any criterion of good citizenship that we choose, the Japanese Americans are better than any other group in our society, including native-born whites. They have established this remarkable record, moreover, by their own almost totally unaided effort. Every attempt to hamper their progress resulted only in enhancing their determination to succeed. Even in a country whose patron saint is the Horatio Alger hero, there is no parallel to this success story.

From only 148 in 1880 to almost 140,000 in 1930 the number of Japanese in the United States grew steadily and then remained almost constant for two decades. Then in 1960, with the more than 200,000 Japanese in Hawaii added to the national population, the total reached not quite 475,000. In other words, in prewar years Japanese Americans constituted slightly more than 0.1 per cent of the national population. Even in California, where then as now most of the mainland Japanese lived, they made up only 2.1 per cent of the state's population in 1920.

Against the perspective of these minuscule percentages, it is difficult to recapture the paranoiac flavor of the vast mass of anti-Japanese agitation in the first decades of this century. Prejudice recognized no boundaries of social class: the labor-dominated Asiatic Exclusion League lived in strange fellowship with the large California landowners. The rest of the nation gradually adopted what was termed "the California position" in opposing "the Yellow Peril" until finally Asians were totally excluded by the immigration laws of the nineteen-twenties.

Until the exclusion law was enacted, Japanese businesses were picketed. In San Francisco, Japanese were assaulted on the streets and, if they tried to protect themselves, were arrested for disturbing the peace. Since marriage across racial lines was prohibited in most Western states, many Japanese lived for years with no normal family life (there were almost 25 males to one female in 1900, still seven to one in 1910, two to one in 1920). Until 1952 no Japanese could be naturalized, and as noncitizens they were denied access to any urban professions that required a license and to the ownership of agricultural land.

But no degradation affected this people as might have been expected. Denied citizenship, the Japanese were exceptionally law-abiding alien residents. Often unable to marry for many years, they developed a family life both strong and flexible enough to help their children cross a wide cultural gap. Denied access to many urban jobs, both white-collar and manual, they undertook menial tasks with such perseverance that they achieved a modest success. Denied ownership of the land, they acquired control through one or another subterfuge and by intensive cultivation of their small plots, helped convert the California desert into a fabulous agricultural land.

Then, on Feb. 9, 1942, a bit more than two months after war was declared, President Roosevelt issued Executive Order 9066, giving military commanders authority to exclude any or all persons from designated military areas. The following day, Lieut. Gen. John L. DeWitt, head of the Western Defense Command, defined the relevant area as major portions of Washington, Oregon, Idaho, Montana, California, Nevada and Utah.

In this whole vast area all alien Japanese and native-born citizens of any degree of Japanese descent—117,116 persons in all—were subjected in rapid succession to a curfew, assembly in temporary camps within the zone and evacuation from the zone to "relocation centers." Men, women and children of all ages were uprooted, a total of 24,712 families. Nearly two-thirds were citizens, because they had been born in this country; the remainder were aliens, barred from citizenship.

"Some lost everything they had; many lost most of what they had," said the official report of the War Relocation Authority. The total property left behind by evacuees, according to the preliminary W.R.A. estimate, was worth $200 million. After the war, the Government repaid perhaps as much as 30 or 40 cents on the dollar. The last claim was settled only in November, 1965, after two out of the three original plaintiffs had died.

What conceivable reason could there have been for this forced transfer of an entire population to concentration camps, where they lived surrounded by barbed wire and watched by armed guards? The official explanation was that "the evacuation was impelled by military necessity," for fear of a fifth column. As General DeWitt said: "A Jap's a Jap. It makes no difference whether he is an American citizen or not. . . . They are a dangerous element, whether loyal or not."

The cases of injustice are too numerous to count. One of the more flagrant was that of the so-called renunciants. After years of harassment, a number of Japanese Americans requested repatriation to Japan, and they were all segregated in the camp at Tule Lake, Calif. On July 1, 1944, Congress passed a special law by which Japanese Americans might renounce their American citizenship, and the camp authorities permitted tough Japanese nationalists seeking converts to proselytize and terrorize the other inmates. Partly as a consequence, 5,371 American-born citizens signed applications renouncing their citizenship. Many of them were minors who were pressured by their distraught and disillusioned parents; their applications were illegally accepted by the Attorney General: A small number of the renunciants were removed to Japan and chose to acquire Japanese citizenship. A few cases are still pending, more than 20 years after the event. For the large majority, the renunciation was voided by the U.S. District Court in San Francisco after five years of litigation.

Who are the Japanese Americans; what manner of people were subjected to these injustices? Seen from the outside, they strike the white observer as a solidly unitary group, but even a casual acquaintanceship reveals deep fissures along every dimension.

The division between generations, important for every immigrant group, was crucial in their case. That the issei, the generation born in Japan, were blocked from citizenship and many of the occupational routes into American life meant that their relations were especially difficult with the nisei, their native-born sons and daughters. Between these first and second generations there was often a whole generation missing, for many of the issei married so late in life that in age they might have been their children's grandparents. This was the combination that faced General DeWitt's forces—men well along in years, with no political power and few ties to the general community, and a multitude of school children and youths of whom the oldest had barely reached 30.

The kibei, American-born Japanese who had spent some time as teen-agers being educated in Japan, were featured in racist writings as an especially ominous group. For some, it is true, the sojourn in the land of their fathers fashioned their parents' sentimental nostalgia into committed nationalism. In many instances, however, the effect of sending a provincial boy alone into Tokyo's tumultuous student life was the contrary. Back in the United States, may kibei taught in the Army language schools or worked for the O.S.S. and other intelligence services.

Camp life was given a special poignancy by the Defense Department's changing policy concerning nisei. Until June, 1942, Japanese Americans were eligible for military service on the same basis as other young men. Then, with the evacuation completed and the label of disloyal thus given official sanction, all nisei were put in class IV-C—enemy aliens. The Japanese American Citizens League (J.A.C.L.), the group's main political voice, fought for the right of the American citizens it represented to volunteer, and by the end of the year won its point.

Most of the volunteers went into a segregated unit, the 442d Infantry Combat Team, which absorbed the more famous 100th Battalion. In the bloody battles of Italy, this battalion alone collected more than 1,000 Purple Hearts, 11 Distinguished Service Crosses, 44 Silver Stars, 31 Bronze Stars and three Legion of Merit ribbons. It was one of the most decorated units in all three services.

With this extraordinary record building up, the Secretary of War announced another change of policy: the nisei in camps became subject to the draft. As District Judge Louis Goodman declared, it was "shocking to the conscience that an American citizen be confined on the ground of disloyalty, and then while so under duress and restraint, be compelled to serve in the armed forces or be prosecuted for not yielding to such compulsion." He released 26 nisei tried in his court for refusing to report for induction.

The Government's varying policy posed dilemmas for every young man it affected. Faced with unreasoning prejudice and gross discrimination, some nisei reacted as one would expect. Thus, several hundred young men who had served in the armed forces from 1940 to 1942 and then had been discharged because of their race were among the renunciants at Tule Lake. But most accepted as their lot the overwhelming odds against them and bet their lives, determined to win even in a crooked game.

In John Okada's novel *No-No Boy*, written by a veteran of the Pacific war about a nisei who refused to accept the draft, the issue is sharply drawn. The hero's mother, who had raised him to be a Japanese nationalist, turns out to be paranoid. Back in Seattle from the prison where he served his time (he was not tried in Judge Goodman's court), the hero struggles to find his way to the America that rejected him and that he had rejected. A nisei friend who has returned from the war with a wound that eventually kills him is pictured as relatively well-off. In short, in contrast to the works of James Baldwin, this is a novel of revolt against revolt.

The key to success in the United States, for Japanese or anyone else, is education. Among persons aged 14 years or over in 1960, the median years of schooling completed by the Japanese were 12.2, compared with 11.1 years by Chinese, 11.0 by whites, 9.2 by Filipinos, 8.6 by Negroes and 8.4 by Indians. In the nineteen-thirties, when even members of favored ethnic groups often could find no jobs, the nisei went to school and avidly prepared for that one chance in a thousand. One high school boy used to read his texts, underlining important passages, then read and underline again, then read and underline a third time, "I'm not smart," he would explain, "so if I am to go to college, I have to work three times as hard."

From their files, one can derive a composite picture of the nisei who have gone through the Berkeley placement center of the University of California over the past 10 years or so. Their marks were good to excellent but, apart from outstanding individuals, this was not a group that would succeed solely because of extraordinary academic worth. The extracurricular activities they listed were prosaic—the Nisei Student Club, various fraternities, field sports, only occasionally anything even as slightly off the beaten track as jazz music.

Their dependence on the broader Japanese community was suggested in a number of ways: Students had personal references from nisei professors in totally unrelated fields, and the part-time jobs they held (almost all had to work their way through college) were typically in plant nurseries, retail stores and other traditionally Japanese business establishments.

Their degrees were almost never in liberal arts but in business administration, optometry, engineering, or some other middle-level profession. They obviously saw their education as a means of acquiring a salable skill that could be used either in the general commercial world or, if that remained closed to Japanese, in a small personal enterprise. Asked to designate the beginning salary they wanted, the applicants generally gave either precisely the one they got in their first professional job or something under that.

To sum up, these nisei were squares. If they had any doubt about the transcendental values of American middle-class life, it did not reduce their determination to achieve at least that level of security and comfort. Their education was conducted like a military campaign against a whole world; with intelligent planning and tenacity, they fought for certain limited positions and won them.

The victory is still limited: Japanese are now employed in most fields but not at the highest levels. In 1960, Japanese males had a much higher occupational level than whites—56 per cent in white-collar jobs as compared with 42.1 per cent of whites, 26.1 per cent classified as professionals or technicians as compared with 12.5 per cent of whites, and so on. Yet the 1959 median income of Japanese males was only $4,306, a little less than the $4,338 earned by white males.

For all types of social pathology about which there are usable data, the incidence is lower for Japanese than for any other ethnic group in the American population. It is true that the statistics are not very satisfactory, but they are generally good enough for gross comparisons. The most annoying limitation is that data are often reported only for the meaninglessly generalized category of "nonwhites."

In 1964, according to the F.B.I.'s "Uniform Crime Reports," three Japanese in the whole country were arrested for murder and three for manslaughter. Two were arrested for rape and 20 for assault. The low incidence holds also for crimes against property: 20 arrests for robbery, 192 for breaking and entering, 83 for auto theft, 251 for larceny.

So far as one can tell from the few available studies, the Japanese have been exceptional in this respect since their arrival in this country. Like most immigrant groups, nisei generally have lived in neighborhoods characterized by overcrowding, poverty, dilapidated housing, and other "causes" of crime. In such a slum environment, even though surrounded by ethnic groups with high crime rates, they have been exceptionally law-abiding.

Prof. Harry Kitano of U.C.L.A. has collated the probation records of the Japanese in Los Angeles County. Adult crime rates rose there from 1920 to a peak in 1940 and then declined sharply to 1960; but throughout those 40 years the rate was consistently under that for non-Japanese. In Los Angeles today, while the general crime rate is rising, for Japanese adults it is continuing to fall.

According to California life tables for 1959–61, Japanese Americans in the state had a life expectation of 74.5 years (males) and 81.2 years (females). This is six to seven years longer than that of California whites, a relatively favored group by national standards. So far as I know, this is the first time that any population anywhere has attained an average longevity of more than 80 years.

For the sansei—the third generation, the children of nisei—the camp experience is either a half-forgotten childhood memory or something not quite believable that happened to their parents. They have grown up, most of them, in relatively comfortable circumstances, with the American element of their composite subculture becoming more and more dominant. As these young people adapt to the general patterns, will they also—as many of their parents fear—take over more of the faults of American society? The delinquency rate among Japanese youth today is both higher than it used to be and is rising—though it still remains lower than that of any other group.

Frank Chuman, a. Los Angeles lawyer, has been the counsel for close to 200 young Japanese offenders charged with everything from petty theft to murder. Some were organized into gangs of 10 to 15 members, of whom a few were sometimes Negroes or Mexicans. Nothing obvious in their background accounts for their delinquency. Typically, they lived at home with solid middle-class families in pleasant neighborhoods; their brothers and sisters were not in trouble. Yori Wada, a nisei member of the California Youth Authority, believes that some of these young people are in revolt against the narrow confines of the nisei subculture while being unable to accept white society.

In one extreme instance, a sansei charged with assault with the intent to commit murder was a member of the Black Muslims, seeking an identity among those extremist Negro nationalists.

In Sacramento, a number of sansei teen-agers were arrested for shoplifting—something new in the Japanese community but, according to the police, "nothing to be alarmed at." The parents disagreed. Last spring, the head of the local J.A.C.L. called a conference, at which a larger meeting was organized. Between 400 and 500 persons—a majority of the Japanese adults in the Sacramento area—came to hear the advice of such professionals as a psychiatrist and a probation officer. A permanent council was established, chaired jointly by a minister and an optometrist, to arrange for whatever services might seem appropriate when parents were themselves unable (or unwilling) to control their offspring. According to several prominent Sacramento nisei, the publicity alone was salutary, for it brought parents back to a sense of their responsibility. In the Japanese communities of San Francisco and San Jose, there were similar responses to a smaller number of delinquent acts.

Apart from the anomalous delinquents, what is happening to typical Japanese Americans of the rising generation? A dozen members of the Japanese student club on the Berkeley campus submitted to several hours of my questioning, and later I was one of the judges in a contest for the club queen.

I found little that is newsworthy about these young people. On a campus where to be a bohemian slob is a mark of distinction, they wash themselves and dress with unostentatious neatness. They are mostly good students, no longer concentrated in the utilitarian subjects their fathers studied but often majoring in liberal arts. Most can speak a little Japanese, but very few can read more than a few words. Some are opposed to intermarriage, some not; but all accept the American principle that it is love between the partners that makes for a good family. Conscious of their minority status, they are seeking a means both of preserving elements of the Japanese culture and of reconciling it fully with the American one; but their effort lacks the poignant tragedy of the earlier counterpart.

Only four sansei were among the 779 arrested in the Berkeley student riots, and they are as atypical as the Sacramento delinquents. One, the daughter of a man who 20 years ago was an officer of a Communist front, is no more a symbol of generational revolt than the more publicized Bettina Aptheker.

It was my impression that these few extremists constitute a special moral problem for many of the sansei students. Brazenly to break the law invites retribution against the whole community, and thus is doubly wrong. But such acts, however one judges them on other grounds, also symbolize an escape from the persistent concern over "the Japanese image." Under the easygoing middle-class life, in short, there lurks still a wariness born of their parents' experience as well as a hope that they really will be able to make it in a sense that as yet has not been possible.

The history of the United States, it is sometimes forgotten, is the history of the diverse groups that make up our population, and thus of their frequent discord and usual eventual cooperation. Each new nationality that arrived from Europe was typically met with such hostility as, for example, the anti-German riots in the Middle West a century ago, the American Protective Association to fight the Irish, the national quota laws to keep out Italians, Poles and Jews. Yet in one generation or two, each white minority took advantage of the public schools, the free labor market and America's political democracy; it climbed out of the slums, took on better-paying occupations and acquired social respect and dignity.

This is not true (or, at best, less true) of such "nonwhites" as Negroes, Indians, Mexicans, Chinese and Filipinos. The reason usually given for the difference is that color prejudice is so great in this country that a person who carries this visible stigma has little or no possibility of rising. There is obviously a good deal of truth in the theory, and the Japanese case is of general interest precisely because it constitutes the outstanding exception.

What made the Japanese Americans different? What gave them the strength to thrive on adversity? To say that it was their "national character" or "the Japanese subculture" or some paraphrase of these terms is merely to give a label to our ignorance. But it is true that we must look for the persistent pattern these terms imply, rather than for isolated factors.

The issei who came to America were catapulted out of a homeland undergoing rapid change—Meiji Japan, which remains the one country of Asia to have achieved modernization. We can learn from such a work as Robert Bellah's "Tokugawa Religion" that diligence in work, combined with simple frugality, had an almost religious imperative, similar to what has been called "the Protestant ethic" in Western culture. And as such researchers as Prof. George DeVos at Berkeley have shown, today the Japanese in Japan and Japanese Americans respond similarly to psychological tests of "achievement orientation," and both are in sharp contrast to lower-class Americans, whether white or Negro.

The two vehicles that transmitted such values from one generation to the next, the family and religion, have been so intimately linked as to reinforce each other. By Japanese tradition, the wishes of any individual counted for far less than the good reputation of his family name, which was worshiped through his ancestors. Most nisei attended Japanese-language schools either one hour each weekday or all Saturday morning, and of all the *shushin*, or maxims, that they memorized there, none was more important than: "Honor your obligations to parents and avoid bringing them shame." Some rural parents enforced such commandments by what was called the *moxa* treatment—a bit of incense burned on the child's skin. Later, group ridicule and ostracism, in which the peers of a naughty child or a rebellious teen-ager joined, became the usual, very effective control.

This respect for authority is strongly reinforced in the Japanese-American churches, whether Buddhist or Christian. The underlying similarity among the various denominations is suggested by the fact that parents who object strongly to the marriage of their offspring to persons of other races (including, and sometimes even especially, to Chinese) are more or less indifferent to interreligious marriages within the Japanese groups. Buddhist churches have adapted to the American scene by introducing Sunday schools, Boy Scouts, a promotional effort around the theme "Our Family Attends Church Regularly," and similar practices quite alien to the old-country tradition.

On the other hand, as I was told not only by Buddhists but also by nisei Christian ministers, Japanese Americans of whatever faith are distinguished by their greater attachment to family, their greater respect for parental and other authority. Underlying the complex religious life, that is to say, there seems to be an adaptation to American institutional forms with a considerable persistence of Buddhist moral values.

It is too easy however, to explain after the fact what has happened to Japanese Americans. After all, the subordination of the individual to the group and the dominance of the husband-father typified the family life of most immigrants from Southern or Eastern Europe.

Indeed, sociologists have fashioned a plausible theory to explain why the rate of delinquency was usually high among these nationalities' second generation, the counterpart of the nisei. The American-born child speaks English without an accent, the thesis goes, and is probably preparing for a better job and thus a higher status than his father's. His father, therefore, finds it difficult to retain his authority, and as the young man comes to view him with contempt or shame, he generalizes this perception into a rejection of all authority.

Not only would the theory seem to hold for Japanese Americans but, in some respects, their particular life circumstances aggravated the typical tensions. The extreme differences between American and Japanese cultures separated the generations more than in any population derived from Europe. As one issei mother remarked to the anthropologist John Embree: "I feel like a chicken that has hatched duck's eggs."

Each artificial restriction on the issei—that they could not become citizens, could not own land, could not represent the camp population to the administrators—meant that the nisei had to assume adult roles early in life, while yet remaining subject to parental control that by American standards was extremely onerous. This kind of contrast between responsibility and lack of authority is always galling; by the best theories that sociologists have developed we might have expected not merely a high delinquency rate among nisei but the highest. The best theories, in other words, do not apply.

One difficulty, I believe, is that we have accepted too readily the common-sense notion that the minority whose subculture most closely approximates the general American culture is the most likely to adjust successfully. Acculturation is a bridge, and by this view the shorter the span the easier it is to cross it. But like most metaphors drawn from the physical world, this one affords only a partial truth about social reality.

The minority most thoroughly imbedded in American culture, with the least meaningful ties to an overseas fatherland, is the American Negro. As those Negro intellectuals who have visited Africa have discovered, their links to "negritude" are usually too artificial to survive a close association with this—to them, as to other Americans—strange and fascinating continent. But a Negro who knows no other homeland, who is as thoroughly American as any Daughter of the American Revolution, has no refuge when the United States rejects him. Placed at the bottom of this country's scale, he finds it difficult to salvage his ego by measuring his worth in another currency.

The Japanese, on the contrary, could climb over the highest barriers our racists were able to fashion in part because of their meaningful links with an alien culture. Pride in their heritage and shame for any reduction in its only partly legendary glory—these were sufficient to carry the group through its travail. And I do not believe that their effectiveness will lessen during our lifetime, in spite of the sansei's exploratory ventures into new corners of the wider American world. The group's cohesion is maintained by its well-grounded distrust of any but that small group of whites—a few church organizations, some professors, and particularly the A.C.L.U. in California—that dared go against the conservative-liberal-radical coalition that built, or defended, America's concentration camps.

The Chinese in California, I am told, read the newspapers these days with a particular apprehension. They wonder whether it could happen here—again.

Success Story of One Minority Group in U.S.
U.S. News & World Report
December 26, 1966

Visit "Chinatown U.S.A." and you find an important racial minority pulling itself up from hardship and discrimination to become a model of self-respect and achievement in today's America.

At a time when it is being proposed that hundreds of billions be spent to uplift Negroes and other minorities, the nation's 300,000 Chinese-Americans are moving ahead on their own—with no help from anyone else.

LOW RATE OF CRIME

In crime-ridden cities, Chinese districts turn up as islands of peace and stability.

Of 4.7 million arrests reported to the Federal Bureau of Investigation in 1965, only 1,293 involved persons of Chinese ancestry. A Protestant pastor in New York City's Chinatown said: "This is the safest place in the city."

Few Chinese-Americans are getting welfare handouts—or even want them. Within a tight network of family and clan loyalties, relatives continue to help each other. Mrs. Jean Ma, publisher of a Chinese language newspaper in Los Angeles, explained: "We're a big family. If someone has trouble, usually it can be solved within the family. There is no need to bother someone else. And nobody will respect any member of the family who does not work and who just plays around."

Today, Chinese-American parents are worrying somewhat about their young people. Yet, in every city, delinquency in Chinatown is minor compared with what goes on around it.

STRICT DISCIPLINE

Even in the age of television and fast automobiles, Chinese-American children are expected to attend school faithfully, work hard at their studies—and stay out of trouble. Spanking is seldom used, but supervision and verbal discipline are strict.

A study of San Francisco's Chinatown noted that "if school performance is poor and the parents are told, there is an immediate improvement." And, in New York City, schoolteachers reportedly are competing for posts in schools with large numbers of Chinese-American children.

Recently Dr. Richard T. Sollenberger, professor of psychology at Mount Holyoke College, made a study of New York City's Chinatown and concluded: "There's a strong incentive for young people to behave. As one informant said, 'When you walk around the streets of Chinatown, you have a hundred cousins watching you.'"

What you find, back of this remarkable group of Americans, is a story of adversity and prejudice that would shock those now complaining about the hardships endured by today's Negroes.

It was during California's gold rush that large numbers of Chinese began coming to America.

On the developing frontier, they worked in mines, on railroads and in other hard labor. Moving into cities, where the best occupations were closed to them, large numbers became laundrymen and cooks because of the shortage of women in the West.

PAST HANDICAPS

High value was placed on Chinese willingness to work long hours for low pay. Yet Congress, in 1882, passed an Exclusion Act denying naturalization to Chinese immigrants and forbidding further influx of laborers. A similar act in 1924, aimed primarily at the Japanese, prohibited laborers from bringing in wives.

In California, the first legislature slapped foreign miners with a tax aimed at getting Chinese out of the gold-mining business. That State's highest court ruled Chinese could not testify against whites in court.

Chinese-Americans could not own land in California, and no corporation or public agency could employ them.

These curbs, in general, applied also to Japanese-Americans, another Oriental minority that has survived discrimination to win a solid place in the nation.

The curbs, themselves, have been discarded in the last quarter century. And, in recent years, immigration quotas have been enlarged, with 8,800 Chinese allowed to enter the country this year.

As a result, the number of persons of Chinese ancestry living in the United States is believed to have almost doubled since 1950.

Today, as in the past, most Chinese are to be found in Hawaii, California and New York. Because of ancient emphasis on family and village, most of those on the U.S. mainland trace their ancestry to communities southwest of Canton.

HOW CHINESE GET AHEAD

Not all Chinese-Americans are rich. Many, especially recent arrivals from Hong Kong, are poor and cannot speak English. But the large majority are moving ahead by applying the traditional virtues of hard work, thrift and morality.

Success stories have been recorded in business, science, architecture, politics and other professions. Dr. Sollenberger said of New York's Chinatown: "The Chinese people here will work at anything. I know of some who were scholars in China and are now working as waiters in restaurants. That's a stopgap for them, of course, but the point is that they're willing to do something—they don't sit around moaning."

The biggest and most publicized of all Chinatowns is in San Francisco.

Since 1960, the inflow of immigrants has raised the Chinese share of San Francisco's population from 4.9 per cent to 5.7 per cent. Altogether 42,600 residents of Chinese ancestry were reported in San Francisco last year.

SHIFT TO SUBURBS

As Chinese-Americans gain in affluence, many move to the suburbs. But about 30,000 persons live in the 25 blocks of San Francisco's Chinatown. Sixty-three per cent of these are foreign-born, including many who are being indoctrinated by relatives in the American way of life.

Irvin Lum, an official of the San Francisco Federal Savings and Loan Community House, said: "We follow the custom of being good to our relatives. There is not a very serious problem with our immigrants. We are a people of ability, adaptable and easy to satisfy in material wants. I know of a man coming here from China who was looked after by his sister's family, worked in Chinatown for two years, then opened a small restaurant of his own."

Problems among newcomers stir worries, however. A minister said: "Many are in debt when they arrive. They have a language problem. They are used to a rural culture, and they have a false kind of expectation."

A youth gang of foreign-born Chinese known as "the Bugs" or "Tong San Tsai," clashes occasionally with a gang of Chinese-American youngsters. And one group of Chinese-American teen-agers was broken up after stealing as much as $5,800 a week in burglaries this year.

Yet San Francisco has seen no revival of the "tong wars" or opium dens that led to the organizing of a "Chinese squad" of policemen in 1875. The last trouble between Chinese clans or "tongs" was before World War II. The special squad was abolished in 1956.

"Streets Are Safer"

A University of California team making a three-year study of Chinatown in San Francisco reported its impression "that Chinatown streets are safer than most other parts of the city" despite the fact that it is one of the most densely populated neighborhoods in the United States.

In 1965, not one San Francisco Chinese—young or old—was charged with murder, manslaughter, rape or an offense against wife or children. Chinese accounted for only two adult cases out of 252 of assault with a deadly weapon.

Only one of San Francisco's Chinese youths, who comprise 17 per cent of the city's high-school enrollment, was among 118 juveniles arrested last year for assault with a deadly weapon. Meantime, 25 per cent of the city's semifinalists in the California State scholarship competition were Chinese.

Most Chinese-Americans continue to send their youngsters to Chinese schools for one or two hours a day so they can learn Chinese history, culture and—in some cases—language. A businessman said: "I feel my kids are Americans, which is a tremendous asset. But they're also Chinese, which is another great asset. I want them to have and keep the best of both cultures."

Much the same picture is found in mainland America's other big Chinatowns—Los Angeles and New York.

Riots of 1871

Los Angeles has a memory of riots in 1871 when white mobs raged through the Chinese section. Twenty-three Chinese were hanged, beaten, shot or stabbed to death.

Today, 25,000 persons of Chinese ancestry live in Los Angeles County—20,000 in the city itself. About 5,000 alien Chinese from Hong Kong and Formosa are believed to be in southern California.

In Los Angeles, as elsewhere, Chinese-Americans are worrying about their children. Superior Judge Delbert E. Wong said: "Traditionally, the family patriarch ruled the household, and the other members of the family obeyed and followed without questioning his authority. "As the Chinese become more Westernized, women leave the home to work and the younger generation finds greater mobility in seeking employment, we see greater problems within the family unit—and a corresponding increase in crime and divorce."

A Chinese-American clergyman complained that "the second- and third-generation Chinese feel more at home with Caucasians. They don't know how to act around the older Chinese any more because they don't understand them."

The Family Unit

On the other hand, Victor Wong, president of the Chinese Consolidated Benevolent Association in Los Angeles, said: "Basically, the Chinese are good citizens. The parents always watch out for the children, train them, send them to school and make them stay home after school to study. When they go visiting, it is as a family group. A young Chinese doesn't have much chance to go out on his own and get into trouble."

A high-ranking police official in Los Angeles found little evidence of growing trouble among Chinese. He reported: "Our problems with the Chinese are at a minimum. This probably is due to strict parental supervision. There is still a tradition of respect for parents."

New York City, in 1960, had a population of 32,831 persons of Chinese ancestry. Estimates today run considerably higher, with immigrants coming in at the rate of 200 or 300 a month.

Many Chinese have moved to various parts of the city and to the suburbs. But newcomers tend to settle in Chinatown, and families of eight and 10 have been found living in two-room apartments.

"The housing shortage here is worse than in Harlem," one Chinese-American said. Altogether, about 20,000 persons are believed living in the eight-block area of New York's Chinatown at present.

The head of the Chinatown Planning Council said recently that, while most Chinese are still reluctant to accept public welfare, somewhat more are applying for it than in the past. "We are trying to let Chinese know that accepting public welfare is not necessarily the worst thing in the world," he said.

However, a Chinese-American banker in New York took this view: "There are at least 60 associations here whose main purpose is to help our own people. We believe welfare should be used only as a last resort."

A sizable number of Chinese-Americans who could move out if they wanted to are staying in New York's Chinatown—not because of fears of discrimination on the outside, but because they prefer their own people and culture. And Chinatown, despite its proximity to the Bowery, remains a haven of law and order. Dr. Sollenberger said: "If I had a daughter, I'd rather have her live in Chinatown than any place else in New York City."

A police lieutenant said: "You don't find any Chinese locked up for robbery, rape or vagrancy."

There has been some rise in Chinese-American delinquency in recent years. In part, this is attributed to the fact that the ratio of children in Chinatown's total population is going up as more women arrive and more families are started.

Even so, the proportion of Chinese American youngsters getting into difficulty remains low. School buildings used by large numbers of Chinese are described as the cleanest in New York. Public recreational facilities amount to only one small park, but few complaints are heard.

EFFORTS OF PROGRESS

Over all, what observers are finding in America's Chinatowns are a thrifty, law-abiding and industrious people—ambitious to make progress on their own.

In Los Angeles, a social worker said: "If you had several hundred thousand Chinese-Americans subjected to the same economic and social pressures that confront Negroes in major cities you would have a good deal of unrest among them. At the same time, it must be recognized that the Chinese and other Orientals in California were faced with even more prejudice than faces the Negro today. We haven't stuck Negroes in concentration camps, for instance, as we did the Japanese in World War II. The Orientals came back, and today they have established themselves as strong contributors to the health of the whole community."

Boy Story 2
A Narrative Analysis
Ryan Bruss

The general populace usually sees Disney stories—fantastic adventures through which children can live vicariously—as positive and beneficial for children. Beneath the fluff of their adorable tales, though, hide some troubling messages that are being offered to children. Traditionally, Disney cartoons feature dominant male characters such as Mickey Mouse, Donald Duck, Aladdin, and Simba, who steal the show, leaving the female characters to support them in token roles. There are some exceptions (*Beauty and the Beast* and *The Little Mermaid*, for example); however, even in the rare cases where female characters are featured, they are still dependent on males. One such installment in the line of Disney animation films is *Toy Story 2*, which hit theaters on November 21, 1999, and grossed over $240 million.

Toy Story 2 takes off where the first movie, *Toy Story*, ended, with Andy heading off to Cowboy Camp, leaving his toys behind. An obsessive toy collector, Al McWhiggin, owner of Al's Toy Barn, kidnaps Woody. In Al's apartment, Woody discovers he is a valuable collectible from a 1950s' TV show called *Woody's Roundup*. He meets the other toys from the show—Jessie, the cowgirl; Bullseye, the horse; and Stinky Pete, the prospector. Woody's friends from Andy's room get into many predicaments as they rescue Woody from life as a museum piece before Andy's return. Among the actors who provide the voices for the characters in the film are Tom Hanks (as Woody), Tim Allen (as Buzz Lightyear), Joan Cusak (as Jessie), Don Rickles (as Mr. Potato Head), and Wallace Shawn (as Rex).

In this essay, I analyze *Toy Story 2* using narrative analysis to investigate the gender roles in the film and to discover the narrative strategies used to construct these roles. I use as my method of analysis narrative criticism, which involves a comprehensive examination of elements of the narrative, including setting, characters, narrator, events, temporal relations, and theme. In the case of *Toy Story 2*, characters and the settings are the critical elements of the narrative that convey idealized gender roles, so these are the focus of my analysis. I will argue that, through the male and female roles of toys, this animated film teaches children and adults that the role of the male is to dominate and that the role of the female is to be subordinate.

THE CHARACTERS

Every character in *Toy Story 2* reflects the idea that the male is dominant and the female is passive. The male protagonists in the film can be divided into three types of flat stereotypes: strong leaders, supporting comics, and villains. The first group is represented by Buzz Lightyear and Woody, the two heroes. Buzz, a space-ranger toy, and Woody, a cowboy, are honest, loyal, strong, and self-sacrificing. Leaders among the other toys, they symbolize everything that is good in a toy

This essay was written while Ryan Bruss was a student in Robert Trapp's rhetorical criticism class at Willamette University in 2000. Used by permission of the author.

and are the two favorite playthings of their owner, Andy. Woody is the toy in charge of all the activities of the toys. He looks after them and organizes meetings and informational presentations on topics such as "what to do if one of your parts is swallowed." If a toy is in trouble, Woody is the one to whom the other toys go, and he has earned the respect of them all. Buzz, on the other hand, is not a leader so much in what he says but in what he does. He leads by his strength as a space ranger. Where others are too scared or too weak, Buzz marches ahead. Strong, smart, and aggressive, Buzz is the American male prototype. The combination of these aspects makes him the second leader of Andy's toys.

A second group of male characters, the comics, is made up of Rex, a dinosaur; Hamm, a piggybank; Slinky Dog, Woody's dog; and Mr. Potato Head. These are the supporting characters to Buzz and Woody. They go with them on their adventures. They are valuable companions, provide comic relief, and function to advance the plot.

A third group, the villains, includes Al McWhiggin, Stinky Pete, and Emperor Zurg. Al is the owner of a toy shop and is Woody's kidnapper. He is defined by his desire for money, a desire that makes him evil and causes trouble for the toys. Stinky Pete tries to thwart Woody's attempt at escaping the clutches of Al, and Zurg is the evil archenemy of Buzz Lightyear. All of these villains are portrayed as scheming, devious, and powerful.

All of the male characters, whether they are comics, villains, or good leaders, are vital characters to the progression of the story. Particularly as villains and as leaders, the males clearly are the ones who hold the power, knowledge, and willpower.

The female protagonists consist of three characters: Mrs. Potato Head, Bo Peep, and Jessie. Mrs. Potato Head is a minor character who supports her husband and addresses his needs. She worries about him and fusses over him and is defined by being Mr. Potato Head's companion. Bo Peep is also defined by her relationship to a male figure, Woody. From her very appearance, this definition is obvious. She is dressed in a puffy pink dress, a perfect traditional symbol of the meek, mild female. Her job is to take care of the flock while Woody is gone on his adventures. When he comes back, she is there waiting for him. She never shows any feelings or emotions other than affection toward Woody. When she sees Woody has a little scar, she says, "I like it. It makes you look tough." His well-being is Bo Peep's only concern.

The third female character, Jessie, seems different at first from her meek and mild female companions. Although strong willed, even she is presented as subordinate to Woody. In the television show in which they both starred, Jessie had the distinctly lower role. She was Woody's yodeling sidekick who had to be saved. In the plotline of the film, Jessie is dependent on Woody for her freedom, even though she can be rambunctious and wild at times. He represents her salvation, and only he can decide whether or not she returns to storage or goes to the museum. Thus, her wild side is controlled by the male character. Furthermore, Jessie is presented as rather dimwitted in comparison to Woody. She has overly emotional reactions and poor grammar. When Jessie finds out that Woody is going to return to Andy's room, she pouts and storms off, while Stinky Pete and Woody's horse Bullseye—two male characters—are disappointed but calm. Woody goes over and comforts Jessie, playing the strong male role by rescuing Jessie from her emotions.

Through the comparison of the characteristics of the primary male and female characters, a clear message is communicated. The male role is that of the leader and decision maker; he is the strong and smart one. The female, on the other hand, is docile and supportive and should not be allowed to get out of hand, for she is neither smart nor strong enough to act independently and choose her own destiny.

THE EVENTS

The two main events in the plot also support the role of the dominating male. The first event is Woody's rescue. Woody has been captured by the evil toy store owner Al. The rescue mission—the story's kernel—is led by Buzz, and all of the members of the rescue team are other male characters—Hamm, Rex, Slinky Dog, and Mr. Potato Head. The binary relationship between the dominant male and passive female is again seen in this mission. The males undertake the adventure, while the females prepare things for the males—Mrs. Potato Head stuffs Mr. Potato Head's head back with extra shoes and angry eyes. When the males are ready to set off, their women see them off at the window's edge. The male heroes march off into the sunset, set on their mission.

Along the way, smaller events or satellites occur that again highlight the binary gender relationship. The most blatant of these is when the heroes encounter a group of Barbie dolls in a toy store. The dolls are prancing about, diving into pools and doing the limbo. When Mr. Potato Head comments that he wishes he were a bachelor, Hamm tells him to "make way for the bachelor." In this sequence, we see the female toys as silly sexual objects for male stimulation. The heroes act, while the Barbies are acted upon.

The subsequent kernel is the saving of Jessie. Jessie gets swept away and is put on a plane to Japan. Jessie, a helpless female, needs to be saved by the heroic Woody. Although Jessie is the strongest female presented in the film, even she needs to be rescued by a male. Woody, through a series of difficult and improbable challenges, saves Jessie and brings her to safety. "Come on, it is time to take you home," he says to the wide-eyed, helpless Jessie. As they try to escape from the plane while it takes off, Woody is the one who takes charge and makes all the decisions. She follows him faithfully, and he leads her to safety below, where Buzz catches them. Once again, the binary relationship of male to female is realized. The two males—strong, smart, and brave—win against adversity and save the weak female who cannot fend for herself.

CONCLUSION

Disney, through its use of characters and events, creates a clear conception of male and female gender roles for its viewers. As seen in the two male heroes, Buzz and Woody, males are something special. They are the space rangers and cowboys of the world. Righting wrongs as they do takes intelligence, courage, and strength. The female identity is defined as unimportant. The significance of women derives from their association with the males. Jessie is important because of Woody and his role as the leader of the *Roundup* gang. Mrs. Potato Head and Bo Peep rely on their respective male counterparts for identity and significance. The message that is sent is simple: in terms of strength, intellect, ability, and potential, the male role is one of dominance, and the role of the female is one of subordination. *Toy Story 2*, given the findings of this narrative analysis, is more appropriately titled *Boy Story 2*, for it truly takes the role of male dominance within Disney films to infinity and beyond.

This analysis of *Toy Story 2* suggests ways in which films and other mediated communication use particular strategies to create a perspective that seems natural and ordinary. In this case, the particular nature of characters and events alone is sufficient to develop an overwhelming impression for audiences of stereotypical and limiting gender roles as appropriate and natural. The power of stories magnifies these impacts of the characters and events, creating a rhetorical form that young children would find difficult to resist.

Additional Samples of Narrative Criticism

Bass, Jeff. "The Appeal to Efficiency as Narrative Closure: Lyndon Johnson and the Dominican Crisis, 1965." *Southern Speech Communication Journal*, 50 (Winter 1985), 103–20.

Brown, William J. "The Persuasive Appeal of Mediated Terrorism: The Case of the TWA Flight 847 Hijacking." *Western Journal of Speech Communication*, 54 (Spring 1990), 219–36.

Burgchardt, Carl R. "Discovering Rhetorical Imprints: La Follette, 'Iago,' and the Melodramatic Scenario." *Quarterly Journal of Speech*, 71 (November 1985), 441–56.

Carlson, A. Cheree. "The Role of Character in Public Moral Argument: Henry Ward Beecher and the Brooklyn Scandal." *Quarterly Journal of Speech*, 77 (February 1991), 38–52.

Carpenter, Ronald H. "Admiral Mahan, 'Narrative Fidelity,' and the Japanese Attack on Pearl Harbor." *Quarterly Journal of Speech*, 72 (August 1986), 290–305.

Collins, Catherine A., and Jeanne E. Clark. "A Structural Narrative Analysis of *Nightline*'s 'This Week in the Holy Land.'" *Critical Studies in Mass Communication*, 9 (March 1992), 25–43.

Deming, Caren J. "*Hill Street Blues* as Narrative." *Critical Studies in Mass Communication*, 2 (March 1985), 1–22.

Dobkin, Bethami A. "Paper Tigers and Video Postcards: The Rhetorical Dimensions of Narrative Form in ABC News Coverage of Terrorism." *Western Journal of Communication*, 56 (Spring 1992), 143–60.

Fisher, Walter R. *Human Communication as Narration: Toward a Philosophy of Reason, Value, and Action*. Columbia: University of South Carolina Press, 1987, several essays, pp. 143–91.

Gerland, Oliver. "Brecht and the Courtroom: Alienating Evidence in the 'Rodney King' Trials." *Text and Performance Quarterly*, 14 (October 1994), 305–18.

Griffin, Charles J. G. "The Rhetoric of Form in Conversion Narratives." *Quarterly Journal of Speech*, 76 (May 1990), 152–63.

Griffin, Charles J. G. "The 'Washingtonian Revival': Narrative and the Moral Transformation of Temperance Reform in Antebellum America." *Southern Communication Journal*, 66 (Fall 2000), 67–78.

Gross, Daniel G. "A Teachers' Strike, Rival Stories and Narrative Agreement." *Nebraska Speech Communication Association Journal*, 31 (Spring/Summer 1992), 47–56.

Hollihan, Thomas A. "The Public Controversy Over the Panama Canal Treaties: An Analysis of American Foreign Policy Rhetoric." *Western Journal of Speech Communication*, 50 (Fall 1986), 368–87.

Jasinski, James. "(Re)constituting Community through Narrative Argument: *Eros* and *Philia* in *The Big Chill*." *Quarterly Journal of Speech*, 79 (November 1993), 467–86.

Katriel, Tamar, and Aliza Shenhar. "Tower and Stockade: Dialogic Narration in Israeli Settlement Ethos." *Quarterly Journal of Speech*, 76 (November 1990), 359–80.

Kirkwood, William G. "Storytelling and Self-Confrontation: Parables as Communication Strategies." *Quarterly Journal of Speech*, 69 (February 1983), 58–74.

Kramer, Michael W., and Julie E. Berman. "Making Sense of a University's Culture: An Examination of Undergraduate Students' Stories." *Southern Communication Journal*, 66 (Summer 2001), 297–311.

Lewis, William F. "Telling America's Story: Narrative Form and the Reagan Presidency." *Quarterly Journal of Speech*, 73 (August 1987), 280–302.

Mandelbaum, Jennifer. "Couples Sharing Stories." *Communication Quarterly*, 35 (Spring 1987), 144–70.

Mumby, Dennis K. "The Political Function of Narrative in Organizations." *Communication Monographs*, 54 (June 1987), 113–27.

Olson, Scott R. "Meta-television: Popular Postmodernism." *Critical Studies in Mass Communication*, 4 (September 1987), 284–300.

Owen, A. Susan. "Oppositional Voices in *China Beach*: Narrative Configurations of Gender and War." In *Narrative and Social Control*. Ed. Dennis K. Mumby. Newbury Park, CA: Sage, 1993, pp. 207–31.

Peterson, Tarla Rai. "Telling the Farmers' Story: Competing Responses to Soil Conservation Rhetoric." *Quarterly Journal of Speech*, 77 (August 1991), 289–308.

Poulakos, Takis. "Isocrates' Use of Narrative in the *Evagoras*: Epideictic Rhetoric and Moral Action." *Quarterly Journal of Speech*, 73 (August 1987), 317–28.

Ritter, Kurt. "Drama and Legal Rhetoric: The Perjury Trials of Alger Hiss." *Western Journal of Speech Communication*, 49 (Spring 1985), 83–102.

Rosteck, Thomas. "Narrative in Martin Luther King's *I've Been to the Mountaintop*." *Southern Communication Journal*, 58 (Fall 1992), 22–32.

Rowland, Robert C., and Robert Strain. "Social Function, Polysemy and Narrative-Dramatic Form: A Case Study of *Do the Right Thing*." *Communication Quarterly*, 42 (Summer 1994), 213–28.

Rushing, Janice Hocker. "Mythic Evolution of 'The New Frontier' in Mass Mediated Rhetoric." *Critical Studies in Mass Communication*, 3 (September 1986), 265–96.

Rushing, Janice Hocker. "Ronald Reagan's 'Star Wars' Address: Mythic Containment of Technical Reasoning." *Quarterly Journal of Speech*, 72 (November 1986), 415–33.

Salvador, Michael. "The Rhetorical Genesis of Ralph Nader: A Functional Exploration of Narrative and Argument in Public Discourse." *Southern Communication Journal*, 59 (Spring 1994), 227–39.

Schely-Newman, Esther. "Finding One's Place: Locale Narratives in an Israeli *Moshav*." *Quarterly Journal of Speech*, 83 (November 1997), 401–15.

Sefcovic, Enid M. I., and Celeste M. Condit. "Narrative and Social Change: A Case Study of the Wagner Act of 1935." *Communication Studies*, 52 (Winter 2001), 284–301.

Smith, Larry David. "Convention Oratory as Institutional Discourse: A Narrative Synthesis of the Democrats and Republicans of 1988." *Communication Studies*, 41 (Spring 1990), 19–34.

Smith, Larry David. "A Narrative Analysis of the Party Platforms: The Democrats and Republicans of 1984." *Communication Quarterly*, 37 (Spring 1989), 91–99.

Smith, Larry David. "Narrative Styles in Network Coverage of the 1984 Nominating Conventions." *Western Journal of Speech Communication*, 52 (Winter 1988), 63–74.

Solomon, Martha. "Autobiographies as Rhetorical Narratives: Elizabeth Cady Stanton and Anna Howard Shaw as 'New Women.'" *Communication Studies*, 42 (Winter 1991), 354–70.

Stuckey, Mary E. "Anecdotes and Conversations: The Narrational and Dialogic Styles of Modern Presidential Communication." *Communication Quarterly*, 40 (Winter 1992), 45–55.

Zelizer, Barbie. "Achieving Journalistic Authority through Narrative." *Critical Studies in Mass Communication*, 7 (December 1990), 366–76.

11

Pentadic Criticism

Pentadic criticism is rooted in the work of Kenneth Burke, who made significant contributions to our understanding of how and why human beings use rhetoric and to what effect. Although many of his ideas have been used as critical methods (see, for example, cluster criticism in chapter 4), in this chapter, the focus is pentadic criticism, derived from Burke's notion of the pentad.

Pentadic criticism is rooted in Burke's notion of *dramatism*, the label Burke gives to the analysis of human motivation through terms derived from the study of drama.[1] Two basic assumptions underlie dramatism. One is that language use constitutes action, not motion. Motion corresponds to the biological or animal aspect of the human being, which is concerned with bodily processes such as growth, digestion, respiration, and the requirements for the maintenance of these processes—food, shelter, and rest, for example. The biological level does not involve the use of symbols and thus is nonsymbolic.

In contrast, action corresponds to the neurological aspect of the human being, which Burke defines as the ability of an organism to acquire language or a symbol system. This is the realm of action or the symbolic. Some of our motives are derived from our animality—as when we seek food to sustain our bodies—but others originate in our symbolicity. When we strive to reach goals in arenas such as education, politics, religion, or finance, we are motivated by our symbolicity. Even our desires in such arenas arise from our symbol system. [2]

Burke elaborates on his notion of action at the heart of dramatism by establishing three conditions for action. One is that action must involve freedom or choice. If we cannot make a choice, we are not acting but are being moved, like a ball hit with a racket—we are behaving mechanically. Of course, we never can be completely free, but implicit in the idea of action is some choice. A second condition necessary for action is purpose. Either consciously or unconsciously, we must select or will a choice—we must choose one option over others. Motion is a third requirement for action. While motion can exist without action (as when an object falls, through the force of gravity, to the ground), action cannot exist without motion. Symbolic activity or action is grounded in the realm of the nonsymbolic.[3]

The distinction Burke proposes between motion and action is largely a theoretical one because once organisms acquire a symbol system, we are virtually unable to do anything purely in the realm of motion. Once we have a symbol system, everything we do is interpreted through the lens of that symbol system. To cook a meal, for example, may be considered motion because it satisfies the biological need for food. Yet, creating a meal is impossible without the involvement of our symbolic conceptions of eating. As we choose foods our family members or friends like and set the table and arrange the food on plates in aesthetically pleasing ways, the simple act of eating to sustain ourselves is transformed into symbolically laden messages about ourselves, our friends, and food. Preparing a meal, which has a biological basis, becomes an action.

A second assumption of dramatism is that humans develop and present messages in much the same way that a play is presented. We use rhetoric to constitute and present a particular view of our situation, just as a play creates and presents a certain world or situation inhabited by characters in the play. Through rhetoric, we size up a situation and name its structure and outstanding ingredients. How we describe a situation indicates how we are perceiving it, the choices we see available to us, and the action we are likely to take in that situation. Our language, then, provides clues to our motives or why we do what we do. A rhetor who perceives that one person is the cause of a particular problem, for example, will use rhetoric that names that perception. She will describe the situation in such a way as to feature that person's characteristics and to downplay other elements that may be contributing to the problem. Once you know how rhetors have described situations, you are able to discover their motives for action in the situations—how they justify, explain, and account for their actions.[4]

As rhetors describe their situations, they do so using the five basic elements of a drama—*act, agent, agency, scene,* and *purpose.* These five terms constitute what Burke calls the *pentad,* and they are used as principles or a "grammar" for describing any symbolic act fully: "you must have some word that names the *act* (names what took place, in thought or deed), and another that names the *scene* (the background of the act, the situation in which it occurred); also you must indicate what person or kind of person (*agent*) performed the act, what means or instruments he used (*agency*), and the *purpose*."[5] If you are acquainted with journalistic writing, you will recognize these terms as the five questions a journalist must answer to write an adequate story about an act or event: who? (agent), what? (act), why? (purpose), when? and where? (scene). Agency is an additional concern—how the act was done.

In addition to terms for act, scene, agent, agency, and purpose, Burke sometimes includes attitude as an element to be considered in an analysis of motivation. Attitude designates the manner in which particular means are employed. The act of cultivating a garden is done through specific agencies such as seeds, plants, and water. To cultivate with extraordinary diligence and care, however, involves an attitude or a "how." Burke states that "on later occasions I have regretted that I had not turned the pentad into a hexad, with "attitude as the sixth term."[6] Because he did not, he includes attitude as a part of agent: "in its character as a state of mind that may or may not lead to an act, it is quite clearly to be classed under the head of agent."[7]

Burke uses ratios that link the five terms in pairs as the mechanism for discovering the rhetor's motive in an artifact. A ratio is a pairing of two of the key terms that allows a critic to investigate how the first term in the pair affects the second. Explication of the ratios suggests which term controls the other terms, and in this term, Burke suggests, motive is located.

PROCEDURES

Using the pentadic method of criticism, a critic analyzes an artifact through a four-step process: (1) selecting an artifact; (2) analyzing the artifact; (3) formulating a research question; and (4) writing the essay.

Selecting an Artifact

Virtually any artifact is appropriate for a pentadic analysis. Discursive and nondiscursive artifacts work equally well, and the length and complexity of the artifacts generally do not matter in an application of the pentadic method.

Analyzing the Artifact

In criticism in which the terms of the pentad are used as units of analysis, two operations are performed by a critic: (1) labeling the five terms of *agent*, *act*, *scene*, *purpose*, and *agency* in the artifact; and (2) applying the ratios to identify the dominant term.

Labeling Terms

The first step in a pentadic analysis is to identify the five terms in the artifact from the perspective of the rhetor. Identification of the *agent* involves naming the group or individual who is the protagonist or main character of the situation as it is presented by the rhetor.[8] The agent could be the rhetor himself or another person or group. In a presentation to the jury at a murder trial, for example, a lawyer—the rhetor—could choose as the agent the murderer, the murder victim, or the victim's family. The agent in a speech by the president of the United States is the person, group, or institution that is the primary subject of the speech—perhaps Congress, the CIA, or the president's mother. The naming of the agent also may involve descriptions of what the agent is like—for example, kind, vicious, unscrupulous, dangerous, or generous.

The *act* is the rhetor's presentation of the major action taken by the protagonist or agent.[9] A critic who is studying the speeches of a United States president, for example, may find that the act is the effort to accomplish health-care reform, with the president serving as the agent. In a speech honoring someone for his community service, the act might be the creation of a literacy program by the person being honored. If the artifact you are studying is the work of an artist, you may find that, in a particular painting, the act is bathing a child, with the agent the woman who is shown doing the bathing.

The means the rhetor says are used to perform the act or the instruments used to accomplish it are labeled the *agency*.[10] In a speech about health-care reform, for example, a president might depict the agency as hard work, careful compromise, or futile attempts to gain the cooperation of the opposing party. In a song about love gone wrong, the agency for the lover's departure might be explained as callous disregard for the protagonist's feelings and needs.

Scene is the ground, location, or situation in which the rhetor says the act takes place—the kind of stage the rhetor sets when describing physical conditions, social and cultural influences, or historical causes.[11] In an inaugural address, for example, a president might describe a scene of division and hatred among Americans. In an environmentalist's testimony before a city council on the impact of a proposed policy on the local environment, the advocate might describe a scene of abundant nature in harmony and balance.

The *purpose* of the act is what the rhetor suggests the agent intends to accomplish by performing the act.[12] It is the rhetor's account of the protagonist's intentions or reason for an action. The purpose for a Native American's protest speech at a Columbus Day celebration, for example, might be to gain recognition for Native Americans' primary role in the creation of American civilization and culture. The purpose attributed to a community volunteer's actions might be to repay the support he received from others early in his life. Purpose is not synonymous with motive. Purpose is the reason for action by the agent that is specified by the rhetor for the agent. Motive is the larger explanation for the rhetor's action, manifest in the rhetorical artifact as a whole.

Identification of the five pentadic terms results in an overview of the rhetor's view of a particular situation. A critic may discover, for example, that a hijacker's statement to the FBI reveals these five terms: the agent is the United States, the act is the United States's imprisonment of her friend for a crime he did not commit; the agency is denial of basic rights to an American citizen; the purpose is to publicize her friend's imprisonment; and the scene is conditions of injustice and cover-up. Such a naming of the situation helps explain the hijacking by pointing to the hijacker's conception of the situation. This same hijacker, of course, has virtually an unlimited number of options she can use to describe her situation, and each description constitutes a different vocabulary of motives. She could name, for example, the agent as herself, the act as a heroic act of desperation she took only after she had exhausted all legal options, the agency as bravery and heroism, her purpose of saving her innocent friend from life in prison, and the scene as one of battle and perhaps martyrdom.

Applying the Ratios to Identify the Dominant Term

The naming of the five terms of the pentad is the first step in the application of the pentadic method of criticism. The next step is to discover which of the five elements identified dominates or is featured in the rhetoric. Discovery of the dominant term provides insight into what dimension of the situation the rhetor privileges or sees as most important.

Ratios are used to discover the dominant pentadic element. Application of the ratios involves the systematic pairing of the elements in the pentad to discover the relationship between them and the nature of the influence each has on the other. Each of the five elements, then, may be put together with each of the others to form these 20 ratios: scene-act, scene-agent, scene-agency, scene-purpose, act-scene, act-agent, act-agency, act-purpose, agent-scene, agent-act, agent-agency, agent-purpose, agency-scene, agency-act, agency-agent, agency-purpose, purpose-scene, purpose-act, purpose-agent, and purpose-agency.

Application of the ratios involves pairing two terms from those identified in the pentad for your artifact. There is no right ratio with which to begin this process; simply select two of the terms to pair. With each ratio, look for the relationship between these two terms in the rhetor's description of the situation, trying to discover whether the first term influences or directs the nature of the second term.

You may begin, for example, by putting together scene and act in a scene-act ratio. This ratio involves asking whether the nature of the scene, as described by the rhetor, affects the nature of the act the rhetor describes. To determine the answer to the question implied by the ratio, you might ask questions such as, "Does the first term in the ratio somehow require that the second term be a certain way?" or "Is there something in the first term that determines the nature of the second term in this ratio?" An act-scene ratio, in contrast, would explore whether the nature of the act dominates—whether the act, as it is described, directs, determines, or shapes the nature of the scene. You may discover that there is a significant relationship between the two terms in a ratio, or you may find that the first term in the ratio has little impact or effect on the second. Let's say the rhetor describes the scene as a country in which oppressive and dangerous conditions exist, freedom is being repressed, and citizens are being denied the opportunity for self-determination. The act is described as the heroic invasion of that country. In a scene-act ratio, the scene is portrayed by the rhetor as the precipitating event that generates the act of heroism; there would be no need to perform acts of heroism without the dangerous scene. Thus, the scene dominates over act in this ratio.

If a critic discovers, on the other hand, that the rhetor describes a scene in which people are content and benefit from a country's political structure and names as the act the invasion of the country by another country, the outcome of an exploration of the scene-act ratio would be different. In this case, the scene seems to have little influence on the act, but neither does the act have much effect on the scene. A critic probably would find, after investigating other ratios, that the dominant term of the rhetoric is something other than scene or act—perhaps agent (the nature of the invading country as a domineering, imperialist power) or purpose (the invading country's goal is to impose its will on other countries to bolster its influence in the world).

Continue to pair terms in ratios to discover if one term seems to affect or require the nature and character of another. For each of the 20 ratios, note "yes," "no," or "unclear" as the answer to the question of whether the first term in the ratio determines the second. You might have, for example, at the end of this process, a list that looks like this:

scene-act: no
scene-agent: no
scene-agency: no
scene-purpose: yes

act-scene: no
act-agent: no
act-agency: no
act-purpose: no

agent-scene: yes
agent-act: yes
agent-agency: yes
agent-purpose: no

agency-scene: no
agency-act: unclear
agency-agent: no
agency-purpose: unclear

purpose-scene: yes
purpose-act: no
purpose-agent: no
purpose-agency: no

A review of the ratios in this manner produces a pattern that points to the dominant term—the term that receives the most "yes" answers to the question of whether the first term directs or requires the second. In this case, agent is the dominant term because it is controls the second term of the ratio more than any of the other terms do.

This process of applying the ratios to discover which term influences the others is not included in the essay of criticism you produce. This is work you do behind the scenes prior to writing the essay. In your essay, you identify the featured or dominant term and provide support for it. This support usually takes the form of a discussion of how the term you propose as dominant influences or requires the other terms of the rhetor's description of the situation.

Burke provides a suggestion for gaining a more in-depth view of a rhetor's definition of a situation once you have discovered the dominant term of the pentad. The dominant term can be used to identify the philosophical system to which it corresponds, with that system generating ideas about the definition of a situation, its meaning for rhetors and audiences, and its possible consequences. If act is featured in the pentad, Burke suggests, the corresponding philosophy is realism, the doctrine that universal principles are more real than objects as they are physically sensed. This philosophical position is opposite that of nominalism, the doctrine that abstract concepts, general terms, or universals have no objective reference but exist only as names. If scene is featured, the philosophy that corresponds is materialism—the system that regards all facts and reality as explainable in terms of matter and motion or physical laws. If agent is featured, the corresponding philosophy is idealism, the system that views the mind or spirit as each person experiences it as fundamentally real, with the universe seen as mind or spirit in its essence.

The remaining terms are equated with other philosophical systems. If agency is featured, the pragmatic philosophy is the applicable philosophical school. Pragmatism is the means necessary for the attainment of a goal—instrumentalism or concern with consequences, function, and what something is "good for." In this doctrine, the meaning of a proposition or course of action lies in its observable consequences, and the sum of these consequences constitutes its meaning. If purpose is featured, the corresponding philosophy is mysticism. In mysticism, the element of unity is emphasized to the point that individuality disappears. Identification often becomes so strong that the individual is unified with some cosmic or universal purpose.[13]

In a speech by an anti-abortion advocate on the appropriateness of killing doctors who perform abortions, for example, the rhetor may describe the agent—himself—as a heroic savior, the act as stopping murder, the agency as any means necessary to stop murder, the purpose as saving innocent lives, and the scene as one of desperation in which legal tactics to stop murder have been unsuccessful. A critic may discover, as a result of application of the ratios, that the dominant term is purpose—to save innocent lives. With purpose featured, those who are persuaded by his argument accept a definition of the situation centered on purpose. The corresponding philosophy is mysticism, which features identification with a cosmic or universal purpose. You then could speculate that the motivating force for the rhetor and those who share his definition of the situation is a belief that they are representatives of divine will, doing God's work of honoring human life. The sacredness of this mission allows whatever acts are necessary to fulfill it.

Formulating a Research Question

Knowing a rhetor's worldview can be the basis for understanding many different rhetorical processes, so the research questions asked by critics using the pentadic method of criticism vary widely. You can ask questions about, for example, the significance of a particular term as controlling, the nature of a message in which a particular term is controlling, or the implications of particular constructions of the world and motive for rhetorical processes or public controversies.

Writing the Essay

After completing the analysis, you are ready to write your essay, which includes five major components: (1) an introduction, in which you discuss the research question, its contribution to rhetorical theory, and its significance; (2) a description of the artifact and its context; (3) a description of the method of criticism—in this case, pentadic analysis; (4) a report of the findings of the analysis, in which you identify the five pentadic terms in your artifact and suggest which one is dominant; and (5) a discussion of the contribution the analysis makes to rhetorical theory.

SAMPLE ESSAYS

Following are three sample essays in which pentadic analysis is used to discover the ways in which rhetors have chosen to describe their situations. David A. Ling uses the terms of the pentad to explore and evaluate Edward Kennedy's efforts to persuade an audience to see him as the victim of rather than responsible for an accident. The implicit research question that guides Ling's analysis is, "What types of definitions of situations are effective in enabling rhetors to regain credibility?" In her pentadic analysis of Project Prevention, Kimberly C. Elliott seeks to answer the question, "What strategies can be used to appeal to multiple and diverse audiences?" In the third sample, Diana Brown Sheridan uses pentadic elements as units of analysis to explore an act of protest, guided by the research questions, "How are personal symbols used in public protests?" and "What characteristics of the symbols make their use effective?"

Notes

[1] For a discussion of dramatism, see: Kenneth Burke, *Language as Symbolic Action: Essays on Life, Literature, and Method* (Berkeley: University of California Press, 1966), p. 54; Kenneth Burke, *The Philosophy of Literary Form* (1941; rpt. Berkeley: University of California Press, 1973), p. 103; Kenneth Burke, *A Grammar of Motives* (1945; rpt. Berkeley: University of California Press, 1969), pp. xxii, 60; Kenneth Burke, "The Five Master Terms: Their Place in a 'Dramatistic' Grammar of Motives," *View*, 2 (June 1943), 50–52; Kenneth Burke, "Dramatism," in *International Encyclopedia of the Social Sciences*, ed. David L. Sills ([New York]: Macmillan/Free, 1968), VII, 445–52; and Kenneth Burke, "Rhetoric, Poetics, and Philosophy," in *Rhetoric, Philosophy, and Literature: An Exploration*, ed. Don M. Burks (West Lafayette: Purdue University Press, 1978), pp. 32–33.

[2] The distinction between action and motion is discussed in: Burke, "Dramatism," p. 445; Kenneth Burke, *Permanence and Change: An Anatomy of Purpose* (1954; rpt. Indianapolis: Bobbs-Merrill, 1965), pp. 162, 215; Burke, *Language as Symbolic Action*, pp. 28, 53, 63, 67, 482; and Kenneth Burke, *The Rhetoric of Religion: Studies in Logology* (Berkeley: University of California Press, 1970), pp. 16, 274.

[3] Burke discusses conditions required for action in: *The Rhetoric of Religion*, pp. 39, 188, 281; *A Grammar of Motives*, pp. 14, 276; *The Philosophy of Literary Form*, p. xvi; and "Dramatism," p. 447.

[4] For more on the process of sizing up a situation through rhetoric, see Burke, *The Philosophy of Literary Form*, pp. 1, 6, 109, 298, 304.

[5] Burke, *A Grammar of Motives*, p. xv.

[6] Kenneth Burke, *Dramatism and Development* (Barre, MA: Clark University Press, 1972), p. 23.

[7] Burke, *A Grammar of Motives*, p. 20.

[8] For a discussion of agent, see Burke, *A Grammar of Motives*, pp. 20, 171–226.

[9] For a discussion of act, see Burke, *A Grammar of Motives*, pp. 227–74.

[10] Agency is discussed in Burke, *A Grammar of Motives*, pp. 275–320.

[11] Scene is discussed in: Burke, *A Grammar of Motives*, pp. xvi, 12, 77, 84, 85, 90; Burke, *The Rhetoric of Religion*, p. 26; and Burke, *Language as Symbolic Action*, p. 360.

[12] For a discussion of purpose, see Burke, *A Grammar of Motives*, pp. 275–320.

[13] Burke, *A Grammar of Motives*, pp. 128–30.

A Pentadic Analysis of Senator Edward Kennedy's Address to the People of Massachusetts July 25, 1969

David A. Ling

On July 25, 1969 Senator Edward Kennedy addressed the people of the state of Massachusetts for the purpose of describing the events surrounding the death of Miss Mary Jo Kopechne. The broadcasting networks provided prime time coverage of Senator Kennedy's address, and a national audience listened as Kennedy recounted the events of the previous week. The impact of that incident and Kennedy's subsequent explanation have been a subject of continuing comment ever since.

This paper will examine some of the rhetorical choices Kennedy made either consciously or unconsciously in his address of July 25th. It will then speculate on the possible impact that those choices may have on audience response to the speech. The principal tool used for this investigation will be the "Dramatistic Pentad" found in the writings of Kenneth Burke.

THE PENTAD AND HUMAN MOTIVATION

The pentad evolved out of Burke's attempts to understand the bases of human conduct and motivation. Burke argues that "human conduct being in the realm of action and end . . . is most directly discussible in dramatistic terms."[1] He maintains that, in a broad sense, history can be viewed as a play, and, just as there are a limited number of basic plots available to the author, so also there are a limited number of situations that occur to man. It, therefore, seems appropriate to talk about situations that occur to man in the language of the stage. As man sees these similar situations (or dramas) occurring, he develops strategies to explain what is happening. When man uses language, according to Burke, he indicates his strategies for dealing with these situations. That is, as man speaks he indicates how he perceives the world around him.

Burke argues that whenever a man describes a situation he provides answers to five questions: "What was done (act), when or where it was done (scene), who did it (agent), how he did it (agency), and why (purpose)."[2] Act, scene, agent, agency, and purpose are the five terms that constitute the "Dramatistic Pentad." As man describes the situation around him, he orders these five elements to reflect his view of that situation.

Perhaps the clearest way to explain how the pentad functions is to examine Burke's own use of the concept in *The Grammar of Motives*.[3] In that work, Burke argues that various philosophical schools feature different elements of the human situation. For example, the materialist school adopts a vocabulary that focuses on the scene as the central element in any situation. The agent, act, agency and purpose are viewed as functions of the scene. On the other hand, the idealist school views the agent (or individual) as central and subordinates the other elements to

From *Central States Speech Journal*, 21 (Summer, 1970), 81–86. Used by permission of the Central States Speech Association and the author.

the agent. Thus, both the materialist and the idealist, looking at the same situation, would describe the same five elements as existing in that situation. However, each views a different element as central and controlling. In Burke's own analysis he further suggests philosophical schools that relate to the other three elements of the pentad: the act, agency and purpose. What is important in this analysis is not which philosophical schools are related to the featuring of each element. What is important is that as one describes a situation his ordering of the five elements will suggest which of the several different views of that situation he has, depending on which element he describes as controlling.

This use of the pentad suggests two conclusions. First, the pentad functions as a tool for content analysis. The five terms provide a method of determining how a speaker views the world. Indeed, this is what Burke means when he says that the pentad provides "a synoptic way to talk about their [man's] talk-about [his world]."[4]

A second conclusion that results from this analysis is that man's description of a situation reveals what he regards as the appropriate response to various human situations. For example, the speaker who views the agent as the cause of a problem will reflect by his language not only what Burke would call an idealist philosophy, but he will be limited to proposing solutions that attempt to limit the actions of the agent or to remove the agent completely. The speaker who finds the agent to be the victim of the scene not only reflects a materialist philosophy but will propose solutions that would change the scene. Thus, an individual who describes the problem of slums as largely a matter of man's unwillingness to change his environment will propose self-help as the answer to the problem. The person who, looking at the same situation, describes man as a victim of his environment will propose that the slums be razed and its inhabitants be relocated into a more conducive environment. The way in which a speaker describes a situation reflects his perception of reality and indicates what choices of action are available to him.

THE PENTAD AND RHETORICAL CRITICISM

But what has all this to do with rhetoric? If persuasion is viewed as the attempt of one man to get another to accept his view of reality as the correct one, then the pentad can be used as a means of examining how the persuader has attempted to achieve the restructuring of the audience's view of reality. Burke suggests how such an analysis might take place when he says in *The Grammar*: "Indeed, though our concern here is with the Grammar of Motives, we may note a related resource of Rhetoric: one may deflect attention from scenic matters by situating the motives of an act in the agent (as were one to account for wars purely on the basis of a "warlike instinct" in people): or conversely, one may deflect attention from criticism of personal motives by deriving an act or attitude not from traits of the agent but from the nature of the situation."[5]

Thus beginning with the language of the stage, the Pentad, it is possible to examine a speaker's discourse to determine what view of the world he would have an audience accept. One may then make a judgment as to both the appropriateness and adequacy of the description the speaker has presented.

EDWARD KENNEDY'S JULY 25TH ADDRESS

Having suggested the methodology we now turn to a consideration of Senator Edward Kennedy's address of July 25th to the people of Massachusetts. The analysis will attempt to establish two conclusions. First, the speech functioned to minimize Kennedy's responsibility for his actions after the death of Miss Kopechne. Second, the speech was also intended to place responsibility for Kennedy's future on the shoulders of the people of Massachusetts. These conclusions are the direct antithesis of statements made by Kennedy during the speech. Halfway through the presentation, Kennedy commented: "I do not seek to escape responsibility for my actions by placing blame either on the physical, emotional trauma brought on by the accident or on anyone else. I regard as indefensible the fact that I did not report the accident to the police immediately."[6] Late in the speech, in discussing the decision on whether or not to remain in the Senate, Kennedy stated that "this is a decision that I will have finally to make on my own." These statements indicated that Kennedy accepted both the blame for the events of that evening and the responsibility for the decision regarding his future. However, the description of reality presented by Kennedy in this speech forced the audience to reject these two conclusions.

Edward Kennedy—Victim of the Scene

The speech can best be examined in two parts. The first is the narrative in which Kennedy explained what occurred on the evening of July 18th. The second part of the speech involved Kennedy's concern over remaining in the U.S. Senate.

In Kennedy's statement concerning the events of July 18th we can identify these elements:

The scene (the events surrounding the death of Miss Kopechne)
The agent (Kennedy)
The act (Kennedy's failure to report immediately the accident)
The agency (whatever methods were available to make such a report)
The purpose (To fulfill his legal and moral responsibilities)

In describing this situation, Kennedy ordered the elements of the situation in such a way that the scene became controlling. In Kennedy's description of the events of that evening, he began with statements that were, in essence, simple denials of any illicit relationship between Miss Kopechne and himself. "There is no truth, no truth whatever to the widely circulated suspicions of immoral conduct that have been leveled at my behavior and hers regarding that night. There has never been a private relationship between us of any kind." Kennedy further denied that he was "driving under the influence of liquor." These statements function rhetorically to minimize his role as agent in this situation. That is, the statements suggest an agent whose actions were both moral and rational prior to the accident. Kennedy then turned to a description of the accident itself: "Little over a mile away the car that I was driving on an *unlit* road went off a *narrow bridge* which had *no guard rails* and was built on a *left angle* to the road. The car overturned into a *deep pond* and immediately filled with water." (Emphasis mine) Such a statement placed Kennedy in the position of an agent caught in a situation not of his own making. It suggests the scene as the controlling element.

Even in Kennedy's description of his escape from the car, there is the implicit assumption that his survival was more a result of chance or fate than of his own actions. He commented: "I remember thinking as the cold water rushed in around my head that I was for certain drowning. Then water entered my lungs and I actually felt the sensation of drowning. But somehow I struggled to the surface alive." The suggestion in Kennedy's statement was that he was in fact at the mercy of the situation and that his survival was not the result of his own calculated actions. As an agent he was not in control of the scene, but rather its helpless victim.

After reaching the surface of the pond, Kennedy said that he "made repeated efforts to save Mary Jo." However, the "strong" and "murky" tide not only prevented him from accomplishing the rescue, but only succeeded in "increasing [his] state of utter exhaustion and alarm." The situation described is, then, one of an agent totally at the mercy of a scene that he cannot control. Added to this was Kennedy's statement that his physicians verified a cerebral concussion. If the audience accepted this entire description, it cannot conclude that Kennedy's actions during the next few hours were "indefensible." The audience rather must conclude that Kennedy was the victim of a tragic set of circumstances.

At this point in the speech Senator Kennedy commented on the confused and irrational nature of his thoughts, thoughts which he "would not have seriously entertained under normal circumstances." But, as Kennedy described them, these were not normal circumstances, and this was *not* a situation over which he had control.

Kennedy provided an even broader context for viewing him as the victim when he expressed the concern that "some awful curse did actually hang over the Kennedys." What greater justification could be provided for concluding that an agent is not responsible for his acts than to suggest that the agent is, in fact, the victim of some tragic fate.

Thus, in spite of his conclusion that his actions were "indefensible," the description of reality presented by Kennedy suggested that he, as agent, was the victim of a situation (the scene) over which he had no control.

Kennedy's Senate Seat: In the Hands of the People

In the second part and much shorter development of the speech, the situation changes. Here we can identify the following elements:

The scene (current reaction to the events of July 18th)
The agent (the people of Massachusetts)
The act (Kennedy's decision on whether to resign)
The agency (statement of resignation)
The purpose (to remove Kennedy from office)

Here, again, Kennedy described himself as having little control over the situation. However, it was not the scene that was controlling, but rather it was agents other than Kennedy. That is, Kennedy's decision on whether or not he will continue in the Senate was not to be based on the "whispers" and "innuendo" that constitute the scene. Rather, his decision would be based on whether or not the people of Massachusetts believed those whispers.

Kennedy commented: "If at any time the citizens of Massachusetts should lack confidence in their senator's character or his ability, with or without justification, he could not, in my opinion, adequately perform his duties and should not continue in office." Thus, were Kennedy to decide not to remain in the Senate it would be because the people of Massachusetts had lost confidence in him; responsibility in the situation rests with agents other than Kennedy.

This analysis suggests that Kennedy presented descriptions of reality which, if accepted, would lead the audience to two conclusions:

1. Kennedy was a tragic victim of a scene he could not control.
2. His future depended, not on his own decision, but on whether or not the people of Massachusetts accepted the whispers and innuendo that constituted the immediate scene.

Acceptance of the first conclusion would, in essence, constitute a rejection of any real guilt on the part of Kennedy. Acceptance of the second conclusion meant that responsibility for Kennedy's future was dependent on whether or not the people of Massachusetts believed Kennedy's description of what happened on the evening of July 18th, or if they would believe "whispers and innuendo."

RHETORICAL CHOICE AND AUDIENCE RESPONSE

If this analysis is correct, then it suggests some tentative implications concerning the effect of the speech. First, the positive response of the people of Massachusetts was virtually assured. During the next few days thousands of letters of support poured into Kennedy's office. The overwhelming endorsement was as much an act of purification for the people of that state as it was of Kennedy. That is, the citizenry was saying, "We choose not to believe whispers and innuendo. Therefore, there is no reason for Ted Kennedy to resign." Support also indicated that the audience accepted his description of reality rather than his conclusion that he was responsible for his actions. Guilt has, therefore, shifted from Kennedy to the people of Massachusetts. Having presented a description of the events of July 18th which restricts his responsibility for those events, Kennedy suggested that the real "sin" would be for the people to believe that the "whispers and innuendoes" were true. As James Reston has commented, "What he [Kennedy] has really asked the people of Massachusetts is whether they want to kick a man when he is down, and clearly they are not going to do that to this doom-ridden and battered family."[7] The act of writing a letter of support becomes the means by which the people "absolve" themselves of guilt. The speech functioned to place responsibility for Kennedy's future as a Senator in the hands of the people and then provided a description that limited them to only one realistic alternative.

While the speech seemed to secure, at least temporarily, Kennedy's Senate seat, its effect on his national future appeared negligible, if not detrimental. There are three reasons for this conclusion. First, Kennedy's description of the events of July 18th presented him as a normal agent who was overcome by an extraordinary scene. However, the myth that has always surrounded the office of the President is that it must be held by an agent who can make clear, rational decisions in an extraordinary scene. Kennedy, in this speech was, at least in part, conceding that he may not be able to handle such situations. This may explain why 57 percent of those who responded to a CBS poll were still favorably impressed by Kennedy after his speech, but 87 percent thought his chances of becoming President had been hurt by the incident.[8]

A second reason why the speech may not have had a positive influence on Kennedy's national future was the way in which the speech was prepared. Prior to the presentation of Kennedy's speech, important Kennedy advisers were summoned to Hyannis Port, among them Robert McNamara and Theodore Sorensen.

It was common knowledge that these advisers played an important role in the preparation of that presentation. Such an approach to the formulation was rhetorically inconsistent with the description of reality Kennedy presented. If Kennedy was the simple victim of the scene he could not control, then, in the minds of the audience that should be a simple matter to convey. However, the vision of professionals "manipulating" the speech suggested in the minds of his audience that Kennedy may have been hiding his true role as agent. Here was an instance of an agent trying to control the scene. But given Kennedy's description of what occurred on July 18th such "manipulation" appeared unnecessary and inappropriate. The result was a credibility gap between Kennedy and his audience.

A third factor that may have mitigated against the success of this speech was the lack of detail in Kennedy's description. A number of questions relating to the incident were left unanswered: Why the wrong turn? What was the purpose of the trip, etc.? These were questions that had been voiced in the media and by the general public during the week preceding Senator Kennedy's address. Kennedy's failure to mention these details raised the speculation in the minds of some columnists and citizens that Kennedy may, in fact, have been responsible for the situation having occurred: the agent may have determined the scene. If this was not the case, then Kennedy's lack of important detail may have been a mistake rhetorically. Thus, while Kennedy's speech resulted in the kind of immediate and overt response necessary to secure his seat in the Senate, the speech and the conditions under which it was prepared appear to have done little to enhance Kennedy's chances for the Presidency.

CONCLUSION

Much of the analysis of the effect of this speech has been speculative. Judging the response of an audience to a speech is a difficult matter; judging the reasons for that response is even more precarious. The methodology employed here has suggested two conclusions. First, in spite of his statements to the contrary, Kennedy's presentation portrayed him, in the first instance, as a victim of the scene and in the second, the possible victim of other agents. Second, the pentad, in suggesting that only five elements exist in the description of a situation, indicated what alternative descriptions were available to Kennedy. Given those choices, an attempt was made to suggest some of the possible implications of the choices Kennedy made.

Notes

[1] Kenneth Burke, *Permanence and Change* (Los Altos, CA: Hermes Publications, 1954), p. 274.
[2] Kenneth Burke, *A Grammar of Motives and A Rhetoric of Motives* (Cleveland: The World Publishing Company, 1962), p. xvii.
[3] *Ibid.*, pp. 127–320.
[4] *Ibid.*, p. 56.
[5] *Ibid.*, p. 17.
[6] This and all subsequent references to the text of Senator Edward Kennedy's speech of July 25, 1969 are taken from *The New York Times*, CXVII (July 26, 1969), p. 10.
[7] James Reston, "Senator Kennedy's Impossible Question," *The New York Times*, CXVII (July 27, 1969), section 4, p. 24.
[8] *CBS Evening News*, CBS Telecast, July 31, 1969.

Chappaquiddick Speech
Edward M. Kennedy
July 25, 1969

My fellow citizens:

I have requested this opportunity to talk to the people of Massachusetts about the tragedy which happened last Friday evening. This morning I entered a plea of guilty to the charge of leaving the scene of an accident. Prior to my appearance in court it would have been improper for me to comment on these matters. But tonight I am free to tell you what happened and to say what it means to me.

On the weekend of July 18, I was on Martha's Vineyard Island participating with my nephew, Joe Kennedy—as for thirty years my family has participated—in the annual Edgartown Sailing Regatta. Only reasons of health prevented my wife from accompanying me.

On Chappaquiddick Island, off Martha's Vineyard, I attended, on Friday evening, July 18, a cook-out I had encouraged and helped sponsor for a devoted group of Kennedy campaign secretaries. When I left the party, around 11:15 P.M., I was accompanied by one of these girls, Miss Mary Jo Kopechne. Mary Jo was one of the most devoted members of the staff of Senator Robert Kennedy. She worked for him for four years and was broken up over his death. For this reason, and because she was such a gentle, kind, and idealistic person, all of us tried to help her feel that she still had a home with the Kennedy family.

There is no truth, no truth whatever, to the widely circulated suspicions of immoral conduct that have been leveled at my behavior and hers regarding that evening. There has never been a private relationship between us of any kind. I know of nothing in Mary Jo's conduct on that or any other occasion—the same is true of the other girls at that party—that would lend any substance to such ugly speculation about their character.

Nor was I driving under the influence of liquor.

Little over one mile away, the car that I was driving on the unlit road went off a narrow bridge which had no guard rails and was built on a left angle to the road. The car overturned in a deep pond and immediately filled with water. I remember thinking as the cold water rushed in around my head that I was for certain drowning. Then water entered my lungs and I actually felt the sensation of drowning. But somehow I struggled to the surface alive.

I made immediate and repeated efforts to save Mary Jo by diving into strong and murky current, but succeeded only in increasing my state of utter exhaustion and alarm. My conduct and conversations during the next several hours, to the extent that I can remember them, make no sense to me at all.

Although my doctors informed me that I suffered a cerebral concussion, as well as shock, I do not seek to escape responsibility for my actions by placing the blame either in the physical, emotional trauma brought on by the accident, or on anyone else. I regard as indefensible the fact that I did not report the accident to the police immediately.

Instead of looking directly for a telephone after lying exhausted in the grass for an undetermined time, I walked back to the cottage where the party was being held and requested the help of two friends, my cousin, Joseph Gargan and Phil Markham, and directed them to return immediately to the scene with me—this was sometime after midnight—in order to undertake a new effort to dive down and locate Miss Kopechne. Their strenuous efforts, undertaken at some risk to their own lives, also proved futile.

All kinds of scrambled thoughts—all of them confused, some of them irrational, many of them which I cannot recall, and some of which I would not have seriously entertained under normal circumstances—went through my mind during this period. They were reflected in the various inexplicable, inconsistent, and inconclusive things I said and did, including such questions as whether the girl might still be alive some-where out of that immediate area, whether some awful curse did actually hang over all the Kennedys, whether there was some justifiable reason for me to doubt what had happened and to delay my report, whether somehow the awful weight of this incredible incident might, in some way, pass from my shoulders. I was overcome, I'm frank to say, by a jumble of emotions, grief, fear, doubt, exhaustion, panic, confusion and shock.

Instructing Gargan and Markham not to alarm Mary Jo's friends that night, I had them take me to the ferry crossing. The ferry having shut down for the night, I sud-denly jumped into the water and impulsively swam across, nearly drowning once again in the effort, and returned to my hotel about 2 A.M. and collapsed in my room.

I remember going out at one point and saying something to the room clerk.

In the morning, with my mind somewhat more lucid, I made an effort to call a family legal advisor, Burke Marshall, from a public telephone on the Chappaquiddick side of the ferry and belatedly reported the accident to the Martha's Vineyard police.

Today, as I mentioned, I felt morally obligated to plead guilty to the charge of leaving the scene of an accident. No words on my part can possibly express the terri-ble pain and suffering I feel over this tragic incident. This last week has been an ago-nizing one for me and for the members of my family, and the grief we feel over the loss of a wonderful friend will remain with us the rest of our lives.

These events, the publicity, innuendo, and whispers which have surrounded them and my admission of guilt this morning raises the question in my mind of whether my standing among the people of my state has been so impaired that I should resign my seat in the United States Senate. If at any time the citizens of Massa-chusetts should lack confidence in their Senator's character or his ability, with or with-out justification, he could not in my opinion adequately perform his duty and should not continue in office.

The people of this State—the State which sent John Quincy Adams and Daniel Webster and Charles Sumner and Henry Cabot Lodge and John Kennedy to the United States Senate—are entitled to representation in that body by men who inspire their utmost confidence. For this reason, I would understand full well why some might think it right for me to resign. For me this will be a difficult decision to make.

It has been seven years since my first election to the Senate. You and I share many memories—some of them have been glorious, some have been very sad. The opportu-nity to work with you and serve Massachusetts has made my life worthwhile.

And so I ask you tonight, the people of Massachusetts, to think this through with me. In facing this decision, I seek your advice and opinion. In making it, I seek your prayers—for this is a decision that I will have finally to make on my own.

It has been written a man does what he must in spite of personal consequences, in spite of obstacles, and dangers, and pressures, and that is the basis of human morality. Whatever may be the sacrifices he faces, if he follows his conscience—the loss of his friends, his fortune, his contentment, even the esteem of his fellow man—each man must decide for himself the course he will follow. The stories of the past courage can-not supply courage itself. For this, each man must look into his own soul.

I pray that I can have the courage to make the right decision. Whatever is decided and whatever the future holds for me, I hope that I shall have been able to put this most recent tragedy behind me and make some further contribution to our state and mankind, whether it be in public or private life.

Thank you and good night.

A Pentadic Analysis of the CRACK Web Site
Kimberly C. Elliott

CRACK is the acronym for "Children Requiring a Caring Kommunity," the original name of a nonprofit organization that now is called *Project Prevention*. It is a five-year-old, growing grassroots effort to prevent pregnancies among drug- and alcohol-addicted women by paying them to be sterilized or to use long-term birth control. Although CRACK also will pay addicted men to get vasectomies, fewer than 4% of its participants, to date, have been men.

In its first five years, the organization has raised $2 million, grown from a California home office to a staffed office and 28 other offices across the country, and paid almost 1,000 women to be sterilized or to use long-term birth control. Its founder is Barbara Harris, a woman who, with her husband, adopted the fifth, sixth, seventh, and eighth babies born to a drug-addicted mother. Her experience as an adoptive parent of drug-addicted infants inspired her to try to get a bill passed in California to define the birth of an addicted baby as a crime committed by its mother. The legislation also would have mandated long-term birth control for those mothers. After that legislative effort failed, Harris started CRACK.

Supporters and critics of the project abound. Supporters agree with Harris that her efforts are appropriate and effective. Critics deride a solution that fails to address the addiction that underlies the problem. Some view the organization as coercive, in part because it pays participants $200 to become sterilized or to use long-term birth control. Judging by Harris's original effort to help by making criminals of and imposing birth control upon mothers who give birth to addicted babies, one might surmise that Harris believes those mothers are responsible for exposing fetuses to drugs and alcohol and that an appropriate punishment for that behavior is state-imposed sterilization or birth control. Her current effort, however, seeks to appeal to participants by paying them to do as she wishes, rather than physically forcing them into compliance. Project Prevention also seeks to appeal to potential donors for financial support.

In this paper, I will analyze the discourse presented on the organization's Web site to identify the dramas it creates to both facilitate and mask its motivation while appealing to its two major audiences: drug and alcohol addicts and potential cash donors. I will use this example to consider how a rhetor might construct and concurrently present multiple dramas that function to influence multiple audiences that otherwise might reject its message.

THE ARTIFACT

Project Prevention's Web site, at cashforbirthcontrol.com, includes on every page photographs of happy, healthy looking children and documents filed under five headings: *The Cause, The Program, The Reasons, How to Help,* and *About Us. The Cause* includes a statement of organizational objectives, news, and testimonials. *The Program* includes a document titled *How We Help the Children,* a modest list of health-care providers and frequently asked questions (with answers). *The Reasons*

This essay was written while Kimberly C. Elliott was a student in Sonja K. Foss's rhetorical criticism class at the University of Colorado at Denver in 2003. Used by permission of the author.

section includes a document titled *The Sad Reality*, statistics, and photos of leaders in the organization. *How to Help* and *About Us* offer information about project leaders and ways to participate in the project or provide financial support.

Two documents within the Web site describe what Project Prevention does and its stated rationale. One is titled *Objectives* and the other *How We Help the Children*. Other documents, including *The Sad Reality*, which presents two case studies of drug-addicted infants, and *Statistics* offer support for the arguments in *How We Help the Children* and *Objectives*.

Project Prevention's "main objective is to offer effective preventive measures to reduce the tragedy of numerous drug-affected pregnancies." The *Objectives* document describes the problem of "drug-addicted pregnancies" as one that often causes children to suffer and taxpayers to spend "over a million dollars per child." Children may suffer from developmental and health problems and/or from being "bounced around the foster care system."

Within its objectives, the organization says that it will "support" the decision to use birth control while using drugs but that Project Prevention is not concerned with addressing "all problems for addicts," including drug-use prevention and rehabilitation. It adds, "our mission is to reduce the number of drug- and alcohol-related pregnancies to zero. Unlike incarceration, Project Prevention is extremely cost effective and does not punish the participants."

The *How We Help the Children* document explains that participation in the program is voluntary. It asserts, "most participants who choose permanent birth control are those who have already had far more children than most people have in a lifetime." This is the sole mention of children in the text of *How We Help the Children*.

The process for signing up and getting paid $200 is described. This document lists the brands of long-term birth-control products and the sterilization procedures for which participants may be paid. For example, tubal ligations and vasectomies warrant one-time $200 payments, while using Depo Provera for a full year pays $200 each year for participants who can prove they are and remain drug or alcohol addicted.

One paragraph in *How We Help the Children* contemplates how participants spend their $200. It asks, "what does she do with the money she has earned from us?" Although this wording suggests that participants work for and earn their $200, another suggests it is a gift or charity: "we do not monitor where our money is spent." Still another description used for the cash is "a $200 incentive," suggesting the cash is neither compensation earned nor a gift received but a tool used to persuade drug addicts to participate in the program.

PENTADIC ANALYSIS

I will analyze this artifact using the dramatist pentad, as conceived by Kenneth Burke, for the purpose of understanding a rhetor's motivation by analyzing the drama(s) a rhetor creates when telling a story. The elements of the pentad—act, agent, agency, scene, and purpose—are the units of analysis I will use.

THE KEY AND DOMINANT ELEMENTS

My analysis of Project Prevention's Web site yielded several pentads partially or fully developed within the rhetoric. Some pentads are internally inconsistent and/or poorly developed. For example, the key elements in one pentad are:

Agent: the organization (Project Prevention)
Act: paying $200 to drug- and alcohol-addicted people to become steril-
           ized or to use long-term methods of birth control
Scene: the presence of drug- and alcohol-addicted pregnancies
Purpose: to help children
Agency: preventing drug- and alcohol-addicted pregnancies

An internal inconsistency in this pentad is in the claim of helping children by preventing them from being born. Clearly, helping children cannot be CRACK's real purpose in this drama; it only can be its stated purpose, for the children it purports to help do not/will not exist, and those who never exist cannot be helped. One wonders who the happy and healthy looking children pictured on the Web site are. Are they the children who will never live?

An example of a poorly developed pentad within the Project Prevention rhetoric is one in which pregnancy is personified to serve as an agent. The key elements in that pentad are:

Agent: drug- and alcohol-addicted pregnancies/substance-exposed preg-
           nancies
Act: cause children to suffer, cost taxpayers, and strain the foster care
           system
Scene: where people use drugs
Purpose: (none offered)
Agency: expose children to substances

This incomplete pentad lacks a purpose. Because the agent (drug-addicted pregnancy) is both fictitious and inanimate, it is on at least two counts incapable of having a purpose for doing anything. In statements like "drug-addicted pregnancies are a two-tiered problem" and "awareness and concern are also growing about the hundreds of thousands of substance-exposed pregnancies that occur each year," the rhetor describes pregnancies that are addicted or exposed rather than addicted women who are pregnant and fetuses that are exposed to substances. Pregnancy, obviously, cannot be addicted to drugs or alcohol, and it does not exist independent of women, but this linguistic construct suggests otherwise. Also, the Project does not seek to stop drug-addicted women from becoming pregnant; rather, it wants to "reduce the tragedy of numerous drug-affected pregnancies."

There are no people in these linguistic constructs. Instead, the agent causing children to suffer, costing taxpayers, and straining the foster care system is pregnancy. Pregnancy clearly cannot act with intent, so this pentad lacks a key term for purpose. This pentad also reveals the implausibility and inconsistency of the drama by asserting that pregnancies expose children to drugs and alcohol, rather than identifying the real agents who might do so.

In my analysis, three complete, consistent, and interacting pentads emerged. Their common thread is prostitution as a metaphor. I have named the three pentads for the roles their agents play in the dramas created rhetorically by Project Prevention:

1. The Pimp
Agent: Project Prevention
Act: solicits financial support and expands the organization
Scene: capitalist, free-market economy
Purpose: to enrich itself, increase its power and influence

Agency: offers a product to donors (the johns), recruits addicts (the prostitutes) and pays them a portion of what it collects for the product
(control of their bodies)

2. The Johns
Agent: financial donors
Act: anonymously buy control of someone else's body
Scene: capitalist, free-market economy
Purpose: gratification through influencing/controlling others
Agency: pay Project Prevention (the pimp)

3. The Prostitutes
Agent: addicts
Act: modify their bodies in exchange for a fee
Scene: capitalist, free-market economy
Purpose: compensation, survival
Agency: according to instructions specified by Project Prevention (the pimp)

In the first pentad, act—soliciting funds and expanding the organization—is
the dominant term. The act dominates the dependent agent, makes the agency
possible and relevant, and facilitates the purpose. The scene and the act interact
symbiotically because the act both benefits from and becomes a part of the scene.
Neither term in the act-scene ratio dominates the other.

Agency fully dominates all other terms in the second pentad. Paying Project
Prevention is what renders one a financial donor (agent) in this drama, so agency
dominates the agency-act ratio by defining the agent. The agency dominates and
transcends the scene because it both makes use of the scene and lacks reliance
upon it. This agency can be used in any economic system, but it is particularly
effective in a capitalist economy in which participants readily enter into agreed-
upon (and arguably exploitative) exchanges. In the rhetor's construction of this
drama, the specified agency uniquely accommodates the agent's purpose, so
agency dominates purpose, too. Similarly, agency dominates act because the act
relies upon the agency of paying Project Prevention.

Agency is the dominant term in the third pentad. In the rhetor's drama,
addicts are able to collect a fee for being sterilized or using long-term birth control
only if they do so according to the instructions specified by Project Prevention, so
agency dominates in the agency-act ratio. Because the act can facilitate the purpose only if the agent employs the prescribed agency, the purpose also is dominated by the agency. Neither term is dominant in the agency-agent ratio because,
while the agent is influenced by the agency, the agency is not possible for any
agent other than addicts. Completion of the act relies upon the agency, so agency
dominates the agency-act ratio. Agency dominates the scene by making use of the
features of a free-market economy that encourages such agreed-upon exchanges
and makes them legal.

The least influential term in the third pentad is purpose. The purpose of
receiving compensation to survive is common to a variety of agents, not just
addicts, so the agent dominates the purpose-agent ratio. Compensation and survival do not require an agent to modify her or his body in exchange for a fee, so
purpose does not dominate the purpose-act ratio. The scene dominates the purpose because a capitalist economy mandates that people seek compensation to

facilitate their own survival. Finally, agency dominates purpose because the agency is a determinant in whether the purpose is served in this drama.

CONCLUSION

The prostitution metaphor in the three pentads in which the agents are cast in the roles of pimps, johns, or prostitutes serves as a multifaceted link among the dramas. Some constants exist. For example, each of the three dramas is set in the same scene. The metaphor also identifies a hierarchy of agents and illuminates an emergent hierarchy of pentads.

The rhetor/pimp/agent is the most powerful of the three agents, acting as a determinant in several elements of the other agents' dramas. For example, even the dominant term in the prostitutes' drama, agency, is as prescribed by the rhetor/pimp/agent from another drama. In the pentad in which the johns are the agent, the dominant term, agency, directly facilitates the dominant term (act) in the pimp's pentad. In other words, when the johns pay the pimp, the pimp's act of soliciting financial support and expanding is accomplished.

All of the dramas identified in the three pentads ultimately serve the rhetor/ pimp/agent. It appears that no elements would be allowed in the johns' or the prostitutes' pentads if they in any way undermined the elements of the pimp's drama, in which the rhetor's purpose is served. As revealed in the pentadic analysis, the least powerful element in what I have identified as the least powerful pentad is the prostitutes'/agents' purpose. Although Project Prevention makes some effort to appeal to addicts by offering them compensation, the addict's purpose clearly is of little importance to Project Prevention.

Because these three pentads tell much of the rhetor's story, it is notable that no children appear in any of these dramas. Despite Project Prevention's repetitious claims that its purpose is to "help the children," its entire drama can be performed without the appearance of any children. This is possible because Project Prevention's mission is to prevent the children it "helps" from existing and therefore from appearing anywhere. Indeed, the Web page titled *How We Help The Children* offers no explanation for how Project Prevention helps children. Instead, the page summarizes the agency (the dominant term) in the prostitutes' pentad—the procedures with which an addict must comply to be paid for becoming sterilized or using long-term birth control. The claim that children are central characters in Project Prevention's drama is a deception revealed by this pentadic analysis.

Finally, the prostitution metaphor underscores an exploitation of and the assumed desperation of some drug- and alcohol-addicted women. While some of Project Prevention's rhetoric suggests that it seeks to compensate both women and men for being sterilized, most of its rhetoric is directed at addicted women. Participating women have been paid by an organization to alter their bodies in prescribed ways. If women are influenced to do so by the promised payment of compensation to them and their interest in that compensation is motivated by their need to survive, then they are being exploited. Pimps don't sell exploitation, and neither does Project Prevention. They both sell fantasy and endeavor to hide the desperation motivating women to sell any brand of control over their bodies.

Because Project Prevention plays the role of a pimp in its own drama, it is engaged in promoting that which attracts and hiding that which does not. The three pentads presented within a prostitution metaphor are masked in the organization's Web-site rhetoric by the fictional and incomplete pentad in which "helping children" is the purpose. This universally appealing purpose is one of three prominent constructs the rhetor uses to appeal to and avoid offending members of its two major audiences: potential or current donors and drug- and alcohol-addicted women.

Another effort to avoid offending potential addict/participants, although inconsistently applied, is the use of language suggesting that Project Prevention is not targeting women. In a third major construct that functions to avoid offending potential addicts/participants, the rhetor avoids any suggestion that drug-using women and men who conceive a child are responsible for causing their children to suffer while maintaining that such children do suffer. By separating parents, particularly mothers, from pregnancies with language such as "drug-addicted pregnancies," the organization suggests that pregnancies victimize children. A logical extension of this construct is that pregnancies should be prevented (or ended), but Project Prevention makes no suggestion that terminating a pregnancy is advisable or even possible. Abortion is not even mentioned and therefore does not exist in Project Prevention's drama.

Because pregnancy is described as the problem, rather than parents, drugs, alcohol, substance abuse or addiction, any effort to help parents for the benefit of children is irrelevant and dismissed. As Project Prevention states on the *Objectives* page of its Web site, "we do not have the resources to solve all problems for addicts including housing, nutrition, education and rehabilitation." Thus, redirecting responsibility for exposing a fetus to alcohol or drugs from parents to pregnancy, whether drug-addicted, substance-exposed, drug-affected, or drug- and alcohol-related, serves both to relieve potential participants of responsibility for their actions and legitimate the organization's dismissal of all the needs of addicts.

Project Prevention's literature employs a varied methodology in attempting both to mask and facilitate its motivation while appealing to at least two very different audiences. It demonstrates how a rhetor might mask its function, character, and motive by creating and presenting fictional dramas, as the rhetor does with its claimed purpose of helping children by preventing them from living. Some such fictional dramas are incomplete, such as the rhetor's construction of pregnancies as agents that victimize children without a purpose.

The rhetoric in Project Prevention's Web site demonstrates how a rhetor might present a creative collection of pentads that alternately clash and coordinate with one another for the purpose of appealing to multiple audiences with multiple motivations. The rhetor may further demonstrate, with this method, reliance upon the notion that audiences will absorb the messages they find most relevant to themselves and overlook or dismiss the others.

Teddy Bears at Greenham Common
Diana Brown Sheridan

At Greenham Common Royal Air Force Base in Newbury, Great Britain, nine miles of chain-link fence divide two worlds. The fence straddles what was once an idyllic English park, Greenham Common, purchased in 1938 for the enjoyment of local people. On one side are the wildflowers, gorse, heather, and silver birches of the park; on the other is an air base, jointly constructed by the United States and Great Britain. The base contains silos built from enormous mounds of concrete and movable offensive launching vehicles that can roam the countryside with cruise missiles of incomprehensible destruction.

In response to the construction of this military complex, 40 Women for Life on Earth walked the 110 miles from South Wales to this new base in August of 1981. Balking at society's enactment of military power and its incursions on the well-being of the human race, these women started the protest that came to be known as the Women's Peace Camp at Greenham Common, a 12-year testimony to women's commitment to waging peace. Although the Camp closed in 1993 with the end of the Cold War, the legacy of the women's life-affirming visions continues to affect the consciousness of those who work for peace around the world.

The fence, separating the protest and military groups, enshrouds a plethora of intense symbols that reflect the protesting women's intentions to soften the hard and sharp contours and angles that represent the unwavering persistence of military power. Over the years, women decorated, painted, encircled, climbed over, and cut through the fence in an effort to transform it into a celebration of life and beauty in contrast to its intended pronouncement of sterility and fear. They attached balloons, posters, baby clothes, stuffed animals, and photographs of children and loved ones. Weaving yarn, string, and ribbon in and out of the links in the fence, the women tried to revise the concept of the fence as an imprisoning chain, reformulating an image of repression into multiple webs, representing women's interconnectedness with all of life.

My purpose in this essay is to examine one personal form of expression that appeared on the fence in order to determine how personal symbols operate rhetorically in public protest action. I have chosen as my rhetorical artifact a pair of small, dark, furry-looking teddy bears adorning the fence. One is perched a bit higher on the fence than the other and has a small bow around its neck, arms hanging by its side, and ears bent forward slightly. The other is wearing a pair of light-colored overalls, has white hands and eyes, and its ears are perked up.

In a pentadic criticism of the pair of teddy bears, I have identified as the five terms:

Act: Hanging objects on the fence at Greenham Common
Scene: Fence surrounding the missile base at Greenham Common
Agent: Protesting women at Greenham Common
Agency: Pair of teddy bears that are soft, cuddly, lovable, and endearing
Purpose: To protest the placement of missiles at Greenham Common

This essay was written while Diana Brown Sheridan was a student in Sonja K. Foss's rhetorical criticism class at the University of Oregon in 1988. Used by permission of the author.

After examining the ratios, I suggest that *agency*—the teddy bears' soft, enduring, and human qualities—stands out as the most significant element in the pentad. The bears' soft, cub-like characteristics serve to transform the *scene* of the fence from a hardened barrier to an animated playground of action. The snugly qualities of the bears make the protest *act* of hanging bears a reminder of motherly devotion to the often playful nurturing of children, a nurturing that well might cease if the missiles are ever put into action. The lovable qualities of the bears determine that the Greenham women, as *agents*, are imbued with the same essence of softness and life-affirming affection that distinguishes the teddy bears, in contrast to the hardness and lack of emotionality that define weaponry. The distinctiveness of the bears alters the women's *purpose* by turning a commonly shared feeling—fondness for a favorite childhood memory—into a humanizing and personal element in their protest against an apparently inhuman and brute military force.

An emphasis on agency leads me to conclude that the symbol of the teddy bears on the fence creates a new vision of the slogan, "the personal is political." By using beloved teddy bears, the women are tapping into a commonly shared and cherished memory of childhood that they transfer from the private arena of home to the public setting of antimilitarist protest. They use a gentle toy of childhood to show the folly of such grown-up and fearful toys as missiles. The bears are cuddly, reminiscent of the human condition; they are innocent, signifying an untainted world; and they are endearing and lasting, epitomizing the continuity of the human experience.

In full view of patrolling soldiers and protesting women, a pair of tiny teddy bears becomes the humanized symbol for the kind of armor required to protect the human race. Qualities such as endearing softness are needed, according to the women, to replace the oppressive and hard characteristics of huge weapons capable of destroying the earth. In addition, the teddy bears personify the connectedness of shared childhood, making the women's action one of inclusiveness, in contrast to the exclusiveness of an impersonal weapon system.

The function of the teddy bears on the fence, revealed in a pentadic analysis, suggests that when a personal symbol of humanity and connectedness is made public, the political no longer remains beyond the scope of everyday life for most people. What is personal becomes political—as a means of action, a new form of armor, and a context for creating a changed reality. The observable consequence of absorbing the teddy bears' qualities, therefore, becomes a pragmatic one in which new meaning is constituted through the women's protest action. The qualities of the personal symbol are brought into the public sphere, providing a source of power for action for those who previously felt they lacked agency and power in that sphere.

Additional Samples of Pentadic Criticism

Appel, Edward C. "The Perfected Drama of Reverend Jerry Falwell." *Communication Quarterly*, 35 (Winter 1987), 26–38.

Birdsell, David S. "Ronald Reagan on Lebanon and Grenada: Flexibility and Interpretation in the Application of Kenneth Burke's Pentad." *Quarterly Journal of Speech*, 73 (August 1987), 267–79.

Blankenship, Jane, Marlene G. Fine, and Leslie K. Davis. "The 1980 Republican Primary Debates: The Transformation of Actor to Scene." *Quarterly Journal of Speech*, 69 (February 1983), 25–36.

Brown, Janet. "Kenneth Burke and *The Mod Donna*: The Dramatistic Method Applied to Feminist Criticism." *Central States Speech Journal*, 29 (Summer 1978), 138–46.

Brummett, Barry. "A Pentadic Analysis of Ideologies in Two Gay Rights Controversies." *Central States Speech Journal*, 30 (Fall 1979), 250–61.

Cali, Dennis D. "Chiara Lubich's 1977 Templeton Prize Acceptance Speech: Case Study in the Mystical Narrative." *Communication Studies*, 44 (Summer 1993), 132–43.

Carlson, A. Cheree. "Narrative as the Philosopher's Stone: How Russell H. Conwell Changed Lead into Diamonds." *Western Journal of Speech Communication*, 53 (Fall 1989), 342–55.

Cooks, Leda, and David Descutner. "Different Paths from Powerlessness to Empowerment: A Dramatistic Analysis of Two Eating Disorder Therapies." *Western Journal of Communication*, 57 (Fall 1993), 494–514.

Fisher, Jeanne Y. "A Burkean Analysis of the Rhetorical Dimensions of a Multiple Murder and Suicide." *Quarterly Journal of Speech*, 60 (April 1974), 175–89.

Hahn, Dan F., and Anne Morlando. "A Burkean Analysis of Lincoln's Second Inaugural Address." *Presidential Studies Quarterly*, 9 (Fall 1979), 376–89.

Hayden, Sara. "Reversing the Discourse of Sexology: Margaret Higgins Sanger's *What Every Girl Should Know*." *Southern Communication Journal*, 64 (Summer 1999), 288–306.

Ivie, Robert L. "Presidential Motives for War." *Quarterly Journal of Speech*, 60 (October 1974), 337–45.

Kelley, Colleen E. "The 1984 Campaign Rhetoric of Representative George Hansen: A Pentadic Analysis." *Western Journal of Speech Communication*, 51 (Spring 1987), 204–17.

Nelson, Jeffrey, and Mary Ann Flannery. "The Sanctuary Movement: A Study in Religious Confrontation." *Southern Communication Journal*, 55 (Summer 1990), 372–87.

Peterson, Tarla Rai. "The Will to Conservation: A Burkeian Analysis of Dust Bowl Rhetoric and American Farming Motives." *Southern Speech Communication Journal*, 52 (Fall 1986), 1–21.

Procter, David E. "The Rescue Mission: Assigning Guilt to a Chaotic Scene." *Western Journal of Speech Communication*, 51 (Summer 1987), 245–55.

Rushing, Janice Hocker. "Mythic Evolution of 'The New Frontier' in Mass Mediated Rhetoric." *Critical Studies in Mass Communication*, 3 (September 1986), 265–96.

Rushing, Janice Hocker. "Ronald Reagan's 'Star Wars' Address: Mythic Containment of Technical Reasoning." *Quarterly Journal of Speech*, 72 (November 1986), 415–33.

Stewart, Charles J. "The Internal Rhetoric of the Knights of Labor." *Communication Studies*, 42 (Spring 1991), 67–82.

Tonn, Mari Boor, Valerie A. Endress, and John N. Diamond. "Hunting and Heritage on Trial: A Dramatistic Debate Over Tragedy, Tradition, and Territory." *Quarterly Journal of Speech*, 79 (May 1993), 165–81.

Yingling, Julie. "Women's Advocacy: Pragmatic Feminism in the YWCA." *Women's Studies in Communication*, 6 (Spring 1983), 1–11.

Zulick, Margaret D. "The Agon of Jeremiah: On the Dialogic Invention of Prophetic Ethos." *Quarterly Journal of Speech*, 78 (May 1992), 125–48.

12

Generative Criticism

The previous chapters in this book have provided you with an approach to doing criticism when your starting point is a particular method of criticism. Starting with a method produces some good insights and is a comfortable way to begin doing criticism if you are an inexperienced critic. Most seasoned rhetorical critics, however, engage in rhetorical criticism using a different process, and that process is the subject of this chapter. As useful as the formal methods of criticism are for discovering insights into rhetoric, they do not always allow what is most interesting and significant in an artifact to be captured and explained. In most cases, then, you will want to analyze artifacts without following any formal method of criticism. This kind of criticism is generative in that you generate units of analysis or an explanation from your artifact rather than from previously developed, formal methods of criticism.

A critic who engages in generative criticism analyzes an artifact in a nine-step process: (1) encountering a curious artifact; (2) coding the artifact in general; (3) searching for an explanation; (4) creating an explanatory schema; (5) formulating a research question; (6) coding the artifact in detail; (7) searching the literature; (8) framing the study; and (9) writing the essay.[1]

ENCOUNTERING A CURIOUS ARTIFACT

Critics sometimes begin the process of criticism with a question they want to answer. If you are interested in finding out about a particular

411

aspect of a rhetorical process and have in mind a specific question that inquires into that process, you could choose an artifact to analyze that allows you to investigate the question. You may be interested, for example, in how rhetors design messages for audiences they know will be hostile. You might choose to study, for example, a speech by the Pope to a group of U.S. nuns who want to be priests or a pro-union essay speech by a union organizer to an anti-union audience.

But most rhetorical critics do not begin with a research question that interests them. The act of criticism usually begins when you encounter an artifact that raises questions for you. You discover a rhetorical artifact that is appealing to you; generates a sense of uneasiness, intrigue, or amazement; or seems unusual in some way. You discover that, for some reason, an object is prompting you to think about some ideas, and you want to try "to understand both the object and [your] interest in it."[2]

Most professional rhetorical critics report that they begin the process of criticism with an artifact they want to study. Thomas S. Frentz and Janice Hocker Rushing, for example, explain such an impetus for criticism in this way: "For us, criticism typically starts as this kind of gut-level, unexamined intuitive feeling about a text(s). If we don't feel intensely about it one way or another—it can be hate, love, disgust, surprise, fear, awe, perplexity—we don't write."[3] Roderick P. Hart uses the term *curious text* to describe his initial interest in a particular artifact and suggests that many "critical projects begin because the critic is baffled." A curious text also can result when you encounter an incomplete argument. You read someone's book or essay and think there is more to the book or essay than has been told.[4]

Critics Elizabeth Walker Mechling and Jay Mechling also explain that "the puzzling texts present themselves first. We do not begin with a theory or method or hypotheses and then search for a case study to demonstrate or illuminate the theory."[5] Their description of how they decided to analyze the civil defense campaigns of the 1950s illustrates particularly well the process of encountering a text as the impetus for criticism. They both remember their parents' absurd efforts to protect their families from nuclear attack, including their development of a plan to evacuate the children from school and the creation of a bomb shelter out of a closet, complete with mattress shoved against the door. As they explain, this

> is the madness we sought to understand. How could our parents, perfectly reasonable people, act in this way? How could we, cynical pre-adolescents then, also take this world as "natural"? How were we so easily socialized into . . . "nuclear culture"? How did some people in the 1950s resist the socialization, even to the point of creating social movements engaging in civil disobedience meant to thwart civil defense planning? The questions were real and troubling. . . . The stakes of self-understanding were high, both in retrospect for understanding our nuclear socialization, and in prospect

for understanding what possibly pathological worldviews have become normal, "naturalized," for us [now]. These questions led us to settle upon the civil defense campaigns and resistances as the texts we would analyze.[6]

As the critics' descriptions suggest, the defining characteristic of an artifact that intrigues and interests you is likely to be something that doesn't fit or that breaks a pattern. Perhaps you like an artifact and can't explain its appeal for you. Perhaps you can't figure out why an artifact had the impact on an audience that it did. Perhaps you encounter an artifact that seems to violate much of what you know about communication, but it seems to be effective anyway. Perhaps an artifact disturbs or angers you, but you don't know why.

I recently confronted a curious text. With two friends, I went to see the German film *Run Lola Run*, a film about Lola, who gets a phone call from her boyfriend, Manni, telling her he needs a huge sum of money within 20 minutes or he will be killed by his mobster boss. Lola takes off running to try to get the money and makes three such runs, encountering the same people in different ways and with dramatically different outcomes for each run. We went to *Run Lola Run* to be entertained and had no intention of writing an essay of criticism about the film. When it was over, however, we knew we really liked the film, but we couldn't say why it resonated with us as it did. We knew that the three runs represented three different perspectives on something, but we couldn't figure out what. We also couldn't get the film out of our heads—it continued to nag at us until we finally gave in to its demands and began the process of rhetorical criticism.[7]

CODING THE ARTIFACT

After encountering an artifact that you cannot adequately explain, your next step in generative criticism is to do an initial broad-brush coding of the artifact to discover its central features. *Coding* here means that you notice and interpret the major features of the artifact. The features you notice should include some of the major dimensions or components of the artifact that would have to fit into whatever explanation you develop to understand the artifact. As part of this process, think about what you immediately remember about the artifact after encountering it only once. As you examine the artifact, look for what topics are treated and the order in which they appear, the lengths of various segments, and the significant words and images that mark the artifact. If you are analyzing a film, television ad, or music video, you might want to watch it without sound to focus your attention on the visual aspects of the artifact. Listen to it again without the pictures to focus attention on the sound.

In this process of identifying major features of the artifact, use *intensity* and *frequency* as your selection criteria. Intensity guides you to look for aspects of the artifact that seem important or significant—those aspects that stand out in the artifact. Also pay attention to frequency and look for patterns in the artifact—things that are repeated in the artifact and show up with some regularity. Because these recur, you might guess that they are somehow important in the artifact. Code the artifact according to intensity and frequency several times. Each examination will produce more information about the artifact's major elements, how they change over the course of the artifact, and the relationships and contradictions among the elements.

In our initial coding of *Run Lola Run*, my fellow critics and I watched the film on video several times and, as we watched, we wrote down images, dialogue, and events that seemed to stand out—features that met the criterion of intensity. We guessed, for example, that the fact that Lola makes three runs is important (and of course, in this case, the three runs also constitute a pattern that we would notice as we paid attention to frequency). We noticed that Lola encounters several people along her runs and thought these various characters might be important, so we noted who they were and what they did in each run. Time seemed to be very important because Manni only has 20 minutes to produce the required money, so we noted that. At the beginning of the film is a scene involving a soccer game, so we also included the game in our coding, thinking it might be significant, especially since a game of roulette appears in the third run. We noted that Lola and Manni seem to be on the outside of mainstream society because they do not have regular jobs, have little money, and dress in Eurotrash clothing.

We also noticed patterns in the film where the same objects, events, or qualities appear repeatedly, and we wrote these down, coding for frequency. The color red seems important in the film: Lola's hair is red, the telephone she answers at the beginning of the film is red, and the liminal bedroom scenes between the runs are filmed through a red filter. The color red appeared to constitute a pattern. Guns used in various ways also seem to be a pattern. A gun shows up in Manni and Lola's robbery of a grocery story in the first run, in Lola's effort to get money from her father in the second run, and in Manni's effort to retrieve his lost money from a tramp in the third run. We noted these and other patterns in the film.

After identifying the major features of the artifact, the next part of the coding process is to interpret them. Write a paraphrase, phrase, or label that describes what you are seeing in a passage, quotation, or image or what it might mean. You can write your codes in the margin of a discursive text or on another piece of paper if what you are analyzing is a film, video, television program, or visual image. The exact label you use as you code does not have to be very precise at this time. These labels are just general indicators of what you are seeing and probably will not be used in your actual essay. Our coding of the first run of *Run Lola Run*, for example, produced the following features and interpretations:

1. *Feature:* Menacing-looking clock. *Interpretation:* Time as a monster.
2. *Feature:* Tick-tock sound on the sound track. *Interpretation:* Urgency, time passing.
3. *Feature:* Cartoon Lola runs through a clock surrounded by teeth. *Interpretation:* Time as a monster.
4. *Feature:* Manni taunts Lola and claims she can't help him. *Interpretation:* Asking help of those who can't help.
5. *Feature:* Lola's father shakes his head "no" as she mentally reviews people she can ask for money. *Interpretation:* Asking help of those who can't help.
6. *Feature:* Manni turns down an offer of 500 marks from a friend. *Interpretation:* Refuses resources.
7. *Feature:* Lola stops for men carrying a pane of glass. *Interpretation:* Glass ceiling, obstacle.
8. *Feature:* Lola kneels before her father to ask him for the money. *Interpretation:* Adoption of low-status position.
9. *Feature:* Lola rejects invitation to buy a bike. *Interpretation:* Refuses resources.
10. *Feature:* Lola passes the tramp who has Manni's money and doesn't see him. *Interpretation:* Blind to resources.
11. *Feature:* Lola screams in fear at a dog on the stairs. *Interpretation:* Fearful for no reason.
12. *Feature:* Guard at bank says, "Little Miss wants to see Big Daddy." *Interpretation:* Construction of Lola as subordinate.
13. *Feature:* Lola and Manni rob a grocery store. *Interpretation:* Illegal means, employment of a strategy likely to fail.
14. *Feature:* Lola is shot by a police officer. *Interpretation:* Death of something, punishment.

As you develop your interpretations of the features, try not to bring in other people's theories—stay focused on the data of your artifact. Obviously, you cannot clear your mind of everything you know about communication as you code. As much as possible, let the data reveal insights to you independent of any preconceived theories. This will insure the originality of the explanation you develop. Be careful about coding according to what you want to find or what you are certain you will find. If you know what you are going to find, you already have your explanation for the artifact.

Remember that you will have to explain how you came to your interpretation of the data of the artifact. Your interpretive claims will have to make sense to someone else, so frequently ask yourself the question, "Could I explain this to someone else so they would be able to see how I moved from my observations of a feature to the interpretation I've given it?" For example, we see Lola's kneeling before her father to ask him for money as evidence for her adoption of a stance of inferiority and low power in the first run. If someone were to ask us how we came to this interpretation from this gesture in the film, we could explain that low-status people tend to engage in nonverbal behavior that suggests their low power, and kneeling is a classic sign of that stance. We also could argue that the person who is physically located above another tends to be the one with higher status. You do not need to go through this process with every interpretation of every feature of your artifact because much of this happens intuitively and almost automatically, but this is the process you should be able to do for a reader.

Many critics find writing or typing notes in a list helpful during the interpretation process. Leave some space between each observation/interpretation that you make. Physically cut the observations you have made apart so that each idea or observation is on a separate strip of paper. Then group the strips that are about the same thing and put them in one pile; group those that are about another topic and put them in another pile. Give labels to your piles—name them with a word or phrase that captures what you are seeing in the codes that made you want to group them together. In our case, for example, after we cut our codings apart and began putting them together in piles that seemed to reflect the same principle or idea, we had a number of categories:

1. *Material conditions as threats and obstacles*
   Menacing-looking clock.
   Tick-tock sound on the sound track.
   Cartoon Lola runs through a clock surrounded by teeth.
   Lola stops for men carrying a pane of glass.
   Lola screams in fear at a dog on the stairs.

2. *Refusing help*
   Manni taunts Lola and claims she can't help him.
   Manni turns down an offer of 500 marks from a friend.
   Lola rejects invitation to buy a bike.
   Lola passes the tramp who has Manni's money and doesn't see him.

3. *Rhetorical strategies doomed to fail*
   Lola's father shakes his head "no" as she mentally reviews people she can ask for money.
   Lola and Manni rob a grocery store.
   Lola is shot by a police officer.

4. *Assumption of inferior position*
   Lola kneels before her father to ask him for money.
   Guard at the bank says, "Little Miss wants to see Big Daddy."

The categories will enable you to begin to see the general themes that characterize the artifact. At the end of this initial coding process, you have a set of broad features, ideas, or topics that you believe might serve as clues to an explanation of the artifact. Something seems to be going on in the artifact in terms of these features that you believe will help explain the artifact. At this point, however, you do not yet see a pattern that puts the features together. We ended our initial coding process thinking that *Run Lola Run* might have something to do with feminism, gender, relationships between marginalized and dominant groups, rhetorical strategies used by subordinate groups, agency, time, and games because our initial coding produced piles of observations/interpretations in these categories.

At this point, you might want to mark in some way which slips of papers are in which piles so you could recreate them if you want to and mix them all up and sort them again to force yourself to come up with another way of organizing your interpretations. You might want to feature different ideas, downplay others, interpret features differently, and try to capture different kinds of possible relationships among the codes. What this process does is encourage you to stretch beyond an initial, obvious way of categorizing the observations/interpretations and to open up other possibilities for seeing your data. There are many other categories in which we could have grouped our observations/interpretations of the first run in *Run Lola Run*. A different category, for example, from the data noted above, might have been a label such as *lack of support for others*, which could include the codes of Lola's father shaking his head "no," Manni taunting Lola, and Manni turning down a friend's offer of money.

SEARCHING FOR AN EXPLANATION

Your next task is to search for an already existing or conventional way to explain the artifact. An explanation is likely to come in the form of a theory about an aspect of rhetoric or a construct from a theory. If you have been a student of communication for a while, you will bring to an artifact a repertoire of ideas and tools that can serve as possible explanations. If you are not yet very familiar with the communication discipline and its theories, you might want to do a miniature literature review at this time to discover if theories or concepts exist that can explain to your satisfaction your curiosity about your artifact. In addition, theories and concepts from outside the communication discipline may be relevant in your search for an explanation. Investigate journal articles and books related to the categories of themes your coding of the artifact revealed. Research that has been done on the artifact or on similar artifacts by others also might offer useful explanations. You may discover in an artifact, for example, elements that suggest to you Karlyn Kohrs Campbell's theory of a feminine rhetorical style. You then would look in the artifact for features of a feminine rhetorical style and construct your explanation from this application.

When you analyze an artifact using already existing concepts or theories, the temptation often is to engage in what is sometimes called *cookie-cutter criticism*, where all artifacts studied through the lens of the same method or theory come out looking exactly the same. For example, if you decide that what is going on in a speech by Bill Clinton that is most significant has something to do with his use of the characteristics of a feminine style, you will focus your analysis on the components of Campbell's notion of a feminine style—a personal tone; use of personal experience, anecdote, and examples as evidence; an inductive structure; audience participation; and identification between speaker and audience. Likewise, if you are analyzing a poem by Maya Angelou and something in the poem suggests that a feminine style may be part of your explanation for what intrigues you about it, again you would analyze the poem for those five components. You may not find the same things are going on in terms of the precise enactment of a feminine style in the two artifacts, but you would have molded your artifact into one where what is significant about it must fit into those five components. When you do this, you risk missing more significant and interesting things in your artifact. In addition, when the data are made to fit the theory, your essay of criticism sometimes illustrates the theory more than it illuminates your artifact. With such an approach, you usually are not encouraged to go beyond the confines of those concepts or theories for an explanation for your artifact.

But what usually happens is that your search for a conventional explanation does not produce one that satisfactorily explains the artifact. Gilbert B. Rodman provides an excellent example of a search for—and rejection of—conventional explanations for a curious artifact. He noticed that, for "a dead man, Elvis Presley is awfully noisy. His body may have failed him in 1977, but today his spirit, his image, and his myths do more than live on: they flourish, they thrive, they multiply."[8] He asks the questions: "Why is Elvis Presley so ubiquitous a presence in U.S. culture? Why does he continue to enjoy a cultural prominence that would be the envy of the most heavily publicized living celebrities?" He tries out a number of explanations—capitalism, fandom, and postmodernism— and suggests that none of them

> manages to provide a compelling or convincing account of why Elvis enjoys the current cultural ubiquity he does. . . . What the approaches . . . ultimately do is explain how Elvis is just like any (and every) other star and how his story can be stitched back into the larger fabric of media, culture, and society. The problem here, however, is not that there are no similarities between Elvis and other stars, but that the phenomenon at hand is only interesting because it *exceeds* the normal expectations of capitalism, fandom, and postmodernism. In the end, then, these potential solutions to the puzzle of Elvis's contemporary ubiquity don't explain the phenomenon so much as they explain it away; transforming a unique and unusual range of texts and practices into just another example of a supposedly already understood cultural phenomenon.[9]

We thought for a while that *Run Lola Run* could be explained by the three views of love/rhetoric in Plato's *Phaedrus*. But we not only discovered that these three views of rhetoric did not begin to explain what was going on in the film but also that an analysis built on this theory largely would have illustrated Plato's theory, would not have added anything new to it, and would have restricted our insights about the artifact. As an explanation, the theory, in other words, felt laminated onto the film instead of derived from it and its unique features.

What is most likely to happen after searching for an explanation of your artifact is that you will find a theory or construct that explains some pieces of your artifact but not all of them. It might explain one aspect or dimension of the artifact, but it does not account for all of the major dimensions you noticed in your initial coding. In this case, you do not yet have an adequate and satisfactory explanation of the artifact.

CREATING AN EXPLANATORY SCHEMA

If a conventional explanation for your artifact does not exist, you must develop your own explanatory schema for it—an explanation that comes from your thinking about the data of your artifact. Your objective in generating an explanatory schema is to discover a better explanation for your artifact than what was offered by the theories and constructs you tried out on your artifact in your search for a conventional explanation.[10] An explanatory schema is a framework for organizing your insights about the artifact in a coherent and insightful way. It is an explanation of what is going on in the artifact derived from an analysis of the artifact itself. It connects all or most of the features that emerged from your broad-brush coding of the artifact. An explanatory schema also can be thought of as a theory—the components of the schema are concepts in the theory, and the patterns among the concepts in the schema are statements of relationship in the theory. An explanatory schema, then, will be about some things—some constructs or concepts—and it will explain how those constructs or concepts relate to one another.

The explanation we developed for *Run Lola Run* is an example of an explanatory schema. Our explanation for the film is that it presents three different interpretive stances toward experience by marginalized groups that produce widely varying standpoints, available rhetorical strategies, and outcomes for rhetors. We suggest that, in each run, Lola experiences and understands her conditions in different ways and acts on her interpretations differently, resulting in three different standpoints, which we tentatively have labeled *victim, supplicant*, and *creator*. Each of these standpoints varies in its view of material conditions, rhetorical options, and degree of agency.

An explanatory schema does more than provide an explanation for what is intriguing to you about an artifact. It also serves as the structure of the essay you will write to present your analysis. Its component parts are the headings and subheadings of the findings or analysis section of your essay. In the case of our analysis of *Run Lola Run*, for example, we are likely to organize our analysis section around the headings of *victim*, *supplicant*, and *creator* when we write up our analysis and probably will divide each of those into subsections of *material conditions*, *rhetorical options*, and *agency*.

Although you can formulate an explanatory schema just by sitting alone at your desk and thinking, three techniques can be useful in your efforts to develop this schema. They speed up the process of developing a schema by providing sparks or prompts that can move you in new directions so that you are able to think in creative and insightful ways about your artifact. The three techniques are: (1) cutting and sorting codes; (2) engaging in a conceptualizing conversation; and (3) brainstorming.

Cutting and Sorting Codes

One technique that can help in the development of an explanatory schema makes use of the notes you made about the artifact in the initial coding step. If you wrote your codes in a list, cut the codes apart, and sorted your codes into piles according to topic, you can make use of them again to help you create an explanatory schema. The strips of paper that contain your codings and the groupings of them into different categories can be used to encourage you to try out all sorts of ideas that might function as explanations. Some of our piles for *Run Lola Run*, for example, were *material conditions as threats and obstacles, refusing help, rhetorical strategies doomed to fail,* and *assumption of inferior position*. List the labels you have given the piles and cut them apart so that each label is on a separate strip of paper. You then can move the labels (which represent features/interpretations) around to see how you can put them in relation to one another in a way that provides an explanation for your artifact. When we listed our labels on a piece of paper, cut them apart, and began to play around with how they could be connected to provide an explanatory schema for *Run Lola Run*, we asked questions such as: "Is there something that all these have in common?" "What picture do these present of Lola in this run?" "Are there inconsistencies among the themes/labels?" "To what ideas do all of these point?"

Engaging in a Conceptualizing Conversation

A second technique that facilitates the process of formulating an explanatory schema is to have a conversation with someone else or even a small group of people about your artifact. Your task in this conversation is to talk about the initial coding you did, explain what you are seeing in the artifact, clarify terms, and explain what in the artifact you find intriguing or baffling. Also describe what was unexplained by the previous theories you tried out as explanations for the artifact. Encourage your conversational partner to ask exploratory, open-ended, defining, doubting, connecting, and probing questions. The only requirements for good conversational partners are that they are patient, genuinely willing to listen, ask questions when they do not understand what you are saying, are curious, have little investment in being right or wrong themselves, and are individuals whose ideas you respect.

Even someone who knows nothing about communication or your topic can be a useful conversational partner and, in fact, these people often make better partners in this effort than people who are trained in communication. Those who know a lot about communication are most likely to help you find explanations for your artifact from conventions, drawing on theories they know about and particularly on theories that resonate with them. They may be less likely to allow an explanation to be generated from the artifact itself. Often, people without a knowledge of the communication discipline ask excellent questions and generate good ideas simply because they don't share your assumptions about communication and are less confined by a specific body of knowledge.

Set aside a significant amount of time for a conceptualizing conversation—it often takes several hours—and hold the conversation someplace where you won't be interrupted. You might want to tape the conversation so that insights you have along the way can be recaptured easily. Although notes on the conversation would be useful, note taking as you are talking and exploring ideas can be difficult to do.

Brainstorming

A third technique that is useful for developing an explanatory schema is to use formal techniques designed to facilitate creative and original thinking.[11] You might try techniques like those described below to prompt your thinking about your artifact and to help you come to a possible explanation for it. You can use these techniques either alone or in conversation with someone else.

Introducing Random Stimulation

Using this technique, you deliberately introduce apparently irrelevant and unconnected information into your thinking about the artifact. This can be done in a variety of ways. You can open a dictionary, point to a word, and then relate that word to your artifact in as many ways as you can. Another way is to look around the room and select an object. Create as many connections as you can between that object and your topic.

I used this technique to discover an explanation for a group of artworks that intrigued me—works of art known as *body art* that were popular in the 1970s and involved artists using their physical bodies as their medium of expression. These artists, for example, might bite themselves all over their bodies and then apply paint to the bites. I looked up from the desk where I was trying to create an explanatory schema and saw a picture of a clown on the wall, so I began connecting the clown to body art in as many ways as I could. After just a few minutes, I had my explanatory schema: The clown was not the explanation I was seeking, but the insane person was. I constructed an explanation around the notion of insanity, in which the viewer adopts the role of a therapist to make sense of the works. I never would have developed that schema without the image of the clown as a prompt.[12]

Shifting Focus

We are able to pay only limited attention to the things in our world, and we have a choice about where to focus our attention. Because our attention usually settles over the most obvious areas, a slight shift in attention by itself may suggest an explanation for an artifact. In shifting focus, you deliberately turn away from your natural attention areas to see what happens if you pay attention to something else in the artifact. If you are interested in George W. Bush's appeals to Latino/a voters at the Republican convention, for example, your likely attention is to the kinds of appeals the campaign made to these voters. The deliberate selection of a different, less obvious point of attention—the real intended audience for the appeals—might suggest an explanation you had not thought about before. Perhaps the appeals really are directed at white moderate and undecided voters and not at Latinos/as at all.[13]

Three perspectives can be particularly useful for exploring an artifact to discover possible options for a shift in focus. The terms are borrowed from physics—viewing the artifact as a particle, a wave, or a field. A view of the artifact as a particle assumes the artifact is an isolated, static entity or an irreducible constituent of matter. From this perspective, try to name the unique identifying features that differentiate your artifact from similar things. Taking a perspective on the artifact as a wave—a disturbance or an oscillation—you can see the artifact as a dynamic object or event and ask how the artifact is changing, noting movement in time, space, or conceptually. When you explore the artifact as a field, you see it not existing in isolation but as occupying a place in a larger system or network of some kind. You might ask how the components of the artifact are organized in relation to one another and what its position is in a larger system.

For an analysis of the Portland Building, located in Portland, Oregon, and designed by architect Michael Graves, you might generate ideas using this approach in the following ways.

1. Portland Building as a *particle*. What are its constituent units—materials, colors, structure, height, arrangement of rooms, placement on the lot?

2. Portland Building as a *wave*. How does the effect of the Portland Building on its users change as the building ages, the landscape around it changes, and it is used in ways other than those for which it was designed? How does the building evoke different responses according to the time of day and season in which it is viewed? How have judgments about the building changed over

time and according to changing architectural styles? How does the building direct the movement of users within it?

3. Portland Building as part of a *field*. How does the building function as part of the larger field of architecture, the field of Graves's buildings or the items he designs for Target, or the field of the city of Portland? How does the building constitute a system itself, composed of interrelated subsystems? What relationships order the parts of the building and connect them to other units within larger systems?

Obviously, some of these ideas would be able to be developed into an explanation of the Portland Building, and others would not, but the technique of shifting focus provides a way to generate possible explanations. (For a picture of the Portland Building and an analysis of it, see chapter 9).

Applying the Topics

If you have studied classical rhetoric, you are likely to be familiar with an ancient system that can be used to generate ideas for a conceptual schema for an artifact—Aristotle's *topoi* or topics. In his book the *Rhetoric*, Aristotle suggested various topics or places to go to discover ideas for arguments, including definition, comparison, contrast, cause and effect, opposites, relation of parts to whole, and conflicting facts. Three of the topics are used below to illustrate how they might generate ideas for explaining the rhetoric of Arnold Schwarzenegger as he campaigned for the governorship of California prior to the recall election of Governor Gray Davis in 2003:

1. Definition: How can Schwarzenegger's rhetoric be defined? Can it be defined as an effort to achieve credibility—an effort to diminish his careers of bodybuilding and acting? Can it be defined as acting? Can it be defined as building a political body? Can it be defined as a sequel in some way?

2. Comparison and contrast: How was Schwarzenegger's rhetoric like or unlike that of Ronald Reagan, another actor who began his political career by winning the governorship of California? Were the similarities and differences significant? How was his rhetoric like or unlike that of Gray Davis and the other 132 candidates?

3. Cause and effect: What effects might Schwarzenegger's rhetoric have on the perceptions of politics by Americans and others? Did the election of wrestler Jesse Ventura as governor of Minnesota a few years earlier create an environment in which Schwarzenegger's candidacy was taken more seriously? Is Schwarzenegger an effect of Ventura's success? What might the effects of Schwarzenegger's governorship be on the Republican Party?

Reversing

Using the reversal technique, you deliberately move away from what you know about the artifact (or believe you have figured out) and pursue an opposite direction or opposite qualities. Take things as they are in the artifact and turn them around, inside out, upside down, and back to front to see if the reversal generates ideas for an explanation. Reversal would generate thinking about *Run Lola Run* by encouraging us to ask questions such as: Lola is running to save Manni's life; is there a way in which Manni is saving Lola's life? The security guard stands at the entrance to the bank where Lola goes to ask her banker father for the money. Is there something that Lola guards? What does her father guard? Manni's boss demands money by noon. What does the money demand that the boss do? In one of the runs, Manni is killed by an ambulance. If the ambulance doesn't save Manni, who or what does it save?

Questioning

Questioning, or the why technique, provides an opportunity to challenge assumptions you might be holding about an artifact and to pursue various aspects of it in depth. This technique is similar to the child's habit of asking "why?" all the time. The difference is that, in this process, you are likely to know the answer to the questions you are asking. The asking simply encourages you to explore the possibilities and dimensions of the artifact in more detail. Perhaps you are studying flash mobs and observed a flash mob where people showed up at a downtown mall, received instructions from people carrying red balloons, and were directed to play an imaginary game of ping pong. Using the questioning technique, you might ask why the group would play pretend ping pong. You might answer that this activity is fun and playful. You would ask "why?" again. Your answer this time might be that the activities of flash mobs cannot be dangerous or threatening because that would keep many people from participating. You would ask "why?" again, noting that people often participate in dangerous activities in groups. Why is feeling safe rather than being provoked or stimulated important for flash mobs? And so on. At some point, an answer may suggest an explanation or part of an explanation for your artifact.

Whatever the means you use to arrive at it, at this time, you have an explanatory schema—an idea for an explanation of your artifact. The next step is to evaluate whether this explanatory schema will work as an explanation for your artifact. When you have a schema that explains the artifact well, you will know it in two ways. One is that the schema explains all the pieces of the artifact—nothing major about the artifact is left hanging or unexplained. Everything fits. The features you coded earlier as a result of frequency and intensity in the artifact should fit into or be able to be explained by the proposed schema.

A second criterion for judging your schema is whether it feels right. This undoubtedly seems like a strange way to judge an explanatory schema, but a schema that really explains your artifact produces a "got it!" or "ah ha!" feeling. When you come up with an explanation that addresses what intrigued or baffled you about the artifact, you will know this explanation is the one. Admittedly, at the beginning of your career as a rhetorical critic, almost any schema you devise is probably going to feel pretty good. To counter this possibility, try out two different possible explanatory schemas for your artifact. If they both have about the same amount of explanatory value and neither one seems particularly better than the other, you know you probably do not have the best schema you could develop for explaining your artifact.

When you are trying to create an explanatory schema from an artifact, the process often is difficult, frustrating, and takes time. You know something of rhetorical significance is occurring in the artifact but are not yet able to articulate and explain it. Be patient. My coauthor, Karen A. Foss, and I went through three dramatically different schemas for our analysis of Garrison Keillor's monologues on the radio program *A Prairie Home Companion* over the course of several years before we found the one we knew explained the appeal of the monologues for us.[14] Sufficient time and energy spent exploring the artifact eventually will yield an explanation that will enable you to understand the particular artifact better and also to contribute to rhetorical theory.

FORMULATING A RESEARCH QUESTION

When you are have constructed an explanatory schema that you believe provides an insightful explanation of your artifact and answers the questions that led you initially into an exploration of the artifact, you are ready to construct your research question. You want to be able to state clearly what your research question is, although you probably will turn the question into a purpose statement in the essay you write. Use the principle behind the TV show *Jeopardy* to create a question for which the explanatory schema you have developed is the answer. For example, the explanatory schema my coauthors and I developed for *Run Lola Run* is that the three runs in the film represent different ways of interpreting material conditions from a marginalized perspective. As a result of this schema, our research question became, "What is the mediating role that interpretation plays in the development of standpoints for marginalized rhetors?"

CODING THE ARTIFACT IN DETAIL

Following the formulation of your research question, code your artifact again, using the component elements of your explanatory schema. You are doing more in-depth coding here than what you did originally because you are testing your proposed schema against the data of your artifact and developing your schema further. Your research question now guides your coding, so as you analyze the artifact, you are looking for dimensions and qualities pertinent to answering it. As in the initial coding process, you are identifying features of the artifact and interpreting them.

When you have finished the detailed coding of your artifact, make another copy of your observations or codings. Save one copy of the coded artifact for future reference, and physically cut apart the notes or codes on the other copy. In a process much like the one you might have used in your initial coding of the artifact, sort the coded data into piles according to topics, putting all the strips of paper that have to do with the same topic together. Label the piles with a word or phrase that describes what is common to all the observations in that pile. If you can, create a space where you can lay the piles out and keep them out while you write your essay. If you do not have this kind of space, put the piles into separate envelopes and label the envelopes with the labels you put on the piles.

As you did with your initial coding, make a list of the labels of the piles. Cut the labels on this list apart. Play around with the labels, which represent your piles and major ideas, to see how they relate to one another and provide the explanation that is the answer to your research question. You are working to discover what is subordinate to what, what are the overarching categories, and so on. As you engage in this process, you are developing the explanatory schema you have seen until now only in general terms, working out kinks, conceptualizing aspects of it you did not think through before, refining it, and extending it.

When you have your explanatory schema fully developed and you know how the concepts captured by the piles of strips of paper are going to work together in your schema, create the actual labels you will use to name the various components of your schema. Choose these conceptual labels carefully because the components of your schema become the concepts of your theory and the subheadings in the body of your essay. If possible, name the components with labels that are original and not conventional—labels that do not come from existing literature, if possible. Clearly, if some part of your schema is a well-known rhetorical process with a known label, you want to use that label, but not everything in your schema should repeat what is already known. If you have new observations and insights, they should produce new labels.

Make your labels parallel with one another and at the same level of abstraction to contribute to your theory's coherence. The labels we tentatively have given to the three positions Lola adopts in *Run Lola Run*— *victim*, *supplicant*, and *creator*—although common words, have not been used before to describe options in interpreting material conditions. Thus, they are new in that no theory we know about puts them together in this way.

Searching the Literature

When you have an explanatory schema that explains your artifact in comprehensive and insightful ways, do a miniature literature review of the key concepts in the schema. The purpose for the literature review at this stage is to relate the literature to your explanatory schema so that you can enter conversations in the communication field about the ideas covered by the schema. See if literature exists that can help you elaborate on ideas in your schema, that points you to ways in which you can elaborate on an existing theory, or that makes visible a point of contention where you take issue with a way in which a construct is conceptualized. You are checking concepts and relationships from the literature against your actual data, looking for evidence of whether or not they apply to the artifact you are analyzing and, if so, the form they take in your artifact. In the case of our analysis of *Run Lola Run*, we reviewed literature on the topics of standpoint theory, agency, material conditions, and marginalized groups' modes of interacting with the dominant culture.

Searching the literature in this way probably is a different way to use literature from the way to which you are accustomed, where you do a literature review at the start of your study to help you design the study. In rhetorical criticism, new ideas should emerge that neither you nor anyone else has thought about previously. If you review all relevant literature before you analyze your artifact, you will be so steeped in the literature that your creative ideas will be constrained and stifled. Because discovery of new ideas is your purpose, you do not want to have knowledge of all the categories relevant to your theory at the beginning of your analysis. Only after a topic has emerged as pertinent to a possible explanation for your artifact do you want to go back to the literature to see if this topic has been studied and, if so, what others have said about it.

You may find yourself facing two common problems when you survey the literature. One is that the literature seems overwhelming because there is so much of it to cover that you have no idea how to begin. A second problem is keeping track of everything you read so you can make use of it effectively. You may find that you have highlighted passages or have stuck post-it notes on virtually every page of every book and article you have relevant to your subject. The following system of "coding" the literature addresses these problems and enables you to engage the literature in an efficient and manageable fashion.

Coding the literature means gleaning the ideas that are relevant and useful for your project from the literature. Do this coding the first time you read a book or an article instead of reading it first and then doing this kind of coding. When your literature is gathered and is stacked before you, sit at your computer and take each book or article in turn.

Review it for ideas that have a direct bearing on your explanatory schema. When you find such an idea, take notes about it on the computer. Type in single space either a direct quote or a summary of the idea you find useful, and include the source and page number for each note you take. Double or triple space between notes.

Using this system, you are likely to be able to read and code a book in an hour. This is possible because you do not read every word of the book. Use all the clues the book provides to discover what is relevant for your explanatory schema—the table of contents, chapter titles, headings, and the index. For each chapter that seems relevant to your explanatory schema, ask: "Is this chapter relevant for my study?" If it isn't, don't read it, and don't code it. When you come upon a relevant chapter, review it heading by heading and subheading by subheading. Ask at each heading, "Is this section relevant for my explanatory schema?" If it isn't, skip it. When you find something relevant, type a note about it.

If you are not a fast keyboarder, there is another way to code literature that may work better for you. As you read a book or an article, mark in the margin each excerpt or passage that is relevant to your explanatory schema. When you have finished reading a book or an article, take it to a copy machine and make a copy of each page where you marked a passage or passages. On the copied pages, write the source and page in the margin by each passage you have marked.

After you have coded all of the literature, print out two copies of the notes you took during your coding. Keep one as it is for future reference and cut the notes on the other copy apart. If you copied actual pages from books and journals, cut out the passages from each copied page that you have marked. At the end of this process, then, each note or marked passage is on a separate strip of paper, along with a shorthand reference to the source and page number from which the note came.

The next step of the process is to sort the strips into piles according to subject, putting everything that is about the same topic in the same pile. For example, all the strips of paper in one pile might have to do with power, those in another pile with gender, those in another pile with agency, and those in another pile with a disagreement in the communication field about the role that material conditions play in rhetoric. These piles should correspond to the major areas of your explanatory schema because you are only reading literature that is relevant to your explanatory schema.

If you cut apart your codings of your artifact, you now have two types of piles—piles of concepts that came from coding your artifact and piles of notes from your literature review that should be about the same topics as those in your data piles. Compare the ideas about the topics that emerged from the literature review with the insights that you have created in your explanatory schema. Use ideas from the literature as you write up your findings to elaborate on and extend your ideas in the schema. When we explain, for example, in our presentation of our analysis of *Run Lola Run* how mortification, or self-inflicted punishment, is a rhetorical strategy the characters choose in the first run, we probably will want to bring in some of Kenneth Burke's ideas about mortification. He provides elaboration for our notion because he suggests that mortification is designed to slay characteristics, impulses, or aspects of the self, an idea that fits perfectly with and supports our analysis because we are suggesting that what is being slayed in the first run of the film is agency.

FRAMING THE STUDY

The last step of analysis before you begin to write your essay is to decide how to frame your explanatory schema so that it can contribute to a significant conversation in the communication discipline. Your research question may explicitly suggest what this frame is, but in many cases, you can contribute to numerous theoretical conversations with the same research question. If your research question asks a question about how political leaders justify unpopular wars, for example, you can frame your essay as a contribution to an understanding of political discourse, an understanding of war rhetoric, or an understanding of justificatory rhetoric. In the case of our analysis of *Run Lola Run*, we are tentatively framing our explanatory schema concerning material conditions in terms of feminist standpoint theory and are suggesting that one piece of that theory is undertheorized and not adequately explained—what happens to standpoint when individuals interpret their material conditions in different ways. But we also could have framed our essay, for example, in terms of communication between marginalized and dominant groups and means for gaining access to the resources of the dominant culture.

WRITING THE ESSAY

After completing your analysis, you are ready to write your essay of criticism. The components of this essay are the same as those for an essay when you begin criticism with a method: (1) an introduction, in which you discuss the research question, its contribution to rhetorical theory, and its significance; (2) a description of the artifact and its context; (3) a brief description of the generative process used to analyze your artifact; (4) a report of the findings of the analysis—in this case, your explanatory schema or theory; and (5) a discussion of the contribution the analysis makes to rhetorical theory.

SAMPLE ESSAYS

Two sample essays that were developed using the generative method of criticism follow. Karen A. Foss and Kathy L. Domenici analyze the Argentine women who gather in the Plaza de Mayo in Buenos Aires to protest their disappeared children to answer the research question, "How does synedoche function in protest movements?" In her essay on a children's book *Star of Fear, Star of Hope*, Marcia S. Van't Hof analyzes her artifact to answer the question, "What are rhetorical strategies that are effective in introducing children to frightening historical realities?"

A list of additional samples that model generative criticism is not provided following the sample essays, as it was in the previous chapters. Most criticism published in communication journals today uses the generative method, so samples of it are readily available and accessible.

Notes

[1] My thanks to William J. C. Waters, who co-created these steps of the process.

[2] Philip Wander and Steven Jenkins, "Rhetoric, Society, and the Critical Response," *Quarterly Journal of Speech*, 58 (December 1972), 441.

[3] Janice Hocker Rushing and Thomas S. Frentz, "The Frankenstein Myth in Contemporary Cinema: Commentary," in *Critical Questions: Invention, Creativity, and the Criticism of Discourse and Media*, ed. William L. Nothstine, Carole Blair, and Gary A. Copeland (New York: St. Martin's, 1994), p. 155.

[4] Roderick P. Hart, "Wandering with Rhetorical Criticism," in *Critical Questions: Invention, Creativity, and the Criticism of Discourse and Media*, ed. William L. Nothstine, Carole Blair, and Gary A. Copeland (New York: St. Martin's, 1994), pp. 78, 80.

[5] Elizabeth Walker Mechling and Jay Mechling, "The Campaign for Civil Defense: Commentary," in *Critical Questions: Invention, Creativity, and the Criticism of Discourse and Media*, ed. William L. Nothstine, Carole Blair, and Gary A. Copeland (New York: St. Martin's, 1994), p. 120.

[6] Mechling and Mechling, p. 119.

[7] My coauthors on this project are William J. C. Waters and Bernard J. Armada.

[8] Gilbert B. Rodman, *Elvis after Elvis: The Posthumous Career of a Living Legend* (New York: Routledge, 1996), p. 1.

[9] Rodman, pp. 18–19.

[10] This process is much like the grounded-theory approach to analyzing data. See Barney G. Glaser and Anselm L. Strauss, *The Discovery of Grounded Theory: Strategies of Qualitative Research* (Chicago: Aldine, 1967); Anselm Strauss and Juliet Corbin, *Basics of Qualitative Research: Grounded Theory Procedures and Techniques* (Newbury Park, CA: Sage, 1990); and Barney G. Glaser, *Doing Grounded Theory: Issues and Discussions* (Mill Valley, CA: Sociology, 1998).

[11] See, for example, Edward de Bono, *Lateral Thinking: Creativity Step by Step* (New York: Harper Colophon, 1970).

[12] Sonja K. Foss, "Body Art: Insanity as Communication," *Central States Speech Journal*, 38 (Summer 1987), 122–31.

[13] Thanks to Richard D. Pineda for this example.

[14] Sonja K. Foss and Karen A. Foss, "The Construction of Feminine Spectatorship in Garrison Keillor's Radio Monologues," *Quarterly Journal of Speech*, 80 (November 1994), 410–26.

Haunting Argentina
Synecdoche in the Protests of the Mothers of the Plaza de Mayo

Karen A. Foss & Kathy L. Domenici

In April 1977, fourteen Argentine women gathered in the Plaza de Mayo in Buenos Aires to demand information about their disappeared children—why they had been taken, where they were being held, and whether they were alive or dead. The disappearances began when three Argentine military officers seized power in 1976 from the Peronist government. The term *disappearance* initially was used to describe the vanishing of people "without a trace" in Guatemala in 1966, although it has a worldwide history antedating its name (Gordon, 1997, p. 72). In Argentina, this brand of repression, which continued until 1983, was designed to eradicate subversive elements that the junta believed to be a threat to national security. The junta saw itself as the "natural ruling caste of Argentina, the guardian of the nation's values" (Bouvard, 1994, p. 23) and its mission as akin to a holy war (Agosin, 1990; Bouvard, 1994; Fabj, 1993; Fisher, 1989). What the junta termed the "Dirty War" (Bouvard, 1994, p. 23) produced thousands of disappeared Argentine citizens. The estimates vary, ranging from 30,000 to more than 45,000— and these figures do not include cases where entire families were taken, leaving no one to come forward with a claim (Bouvard, 1994, pp. 31–32).

The protests of the Mothers of the Plaza de Mayo culminated in 1979 in their constitution as an actual organization, Asociación Madres de Plaza de Mayo [Association of Mothers of the Plaza de Mayo], and they began to engage in a variety of activities to force the government to release information about the disappeared. These ranged from circulating petitions to contacting officials in other countries for assistance. It was their signature activity, however—circling the Plaza de Mayo every Thursday at 3:30—that made them unique at a time when public demonstrations were forbidden. That they were, for the most part, housewives who did not work outside the home and had not previously engaged in political struggle made their defiance of the junta even more remarkable (Agosin, 1990; Fisher, 1989). Furthermore, their protests were made even more powerful because they were virtually alone in them; groups that usually support populist causes—the Catholic church, the trade unions, the press—remained silent about the disappeared, the Mothers, and their demands.[1] The Mothers, then, overcame diverse backgrounds—different geographic origins, social and economic classes, religious and political orientations; gender conditioning; and lack of support (Fisher, 1989)—to insist upon the truth about their children. For the Mothers, the existence of the disappeared was a unifying catalyst for activism.

The authorities, not surprisingly, attempted to deflect the Mothers' actions by various means. Government officials made sporadic efforts to appease the Mothers by addressing human-rights violations, calling them "isolated 'errors' or 'excesses'"; in reality, however, such efforts were designed to distract—to direct

From *Quarterly Journal of Speech*, 87 (August 2001), 237–258. Used by permission of Taylor & Francis Ltd. and the authors.

attention away from the organized, systematic, and ongoing nature of the repression (Fisher, 1989, p. 72). One example of this tactic occurred in 1978, when Argentina hosted the World Cup—an event the Mothers believed was an opportunity to take their case to the outside world. The government, however, presented a carefully controlled image of Argentina that effectively prevented the Mothers from being heard. Thus, rather than publicizing the Mothers' cause, the World Cup celebration, in fact, provided the cover for a sharp increase in kidnappings (Fisher, 1989, p. 72).

After the collapse of the military government and the election of Raúl Alfonsín as president in 1983 (Bouvard, 1994, p. 125), human rights abuses still did not take center stage. In fact, the junta collapsed not because of its activities of repression but because of its economic record. Thus, despite the return of democracy to Argentina, the Mothers do not yet have the information they seek and continue to demand *"verdad, justicia, y memoria"*—the truth about the disappeared, justice for the perpetrators, and the need for Argentina to remember the disappeared (Asociación Madres, Línea Fundadora, n.d.). In fact, the passage of three laws after the return of democracy have protected the perpetrators, and the Mothers continue to seek repeal of these laws: (1) the law that frees all officials who perpetrated crimes while following orders [known as *Obediencia Debida*]; (2) the law that limits the charges against the military dictatorship [referred to as *Punto Final*]; and (3) the amnesty decree through which all those who were convicted were set free (Vanished Gallery, 2000).

In 1986, disputes about different organizational approaches, values, and foci led to the founding of a second Mothers' group, which calls itself the Madres de Plaza de Mayo—Línea Fundadora or Founding Line (Asociación Madres, Línea Fundadora, n.d.). The two groups of Mothers repeatedly emphasize that they are not opponents but simply have differences in approach and emphasis. In fact, members of both groups try not to focus on those differences so that they can be "in agreement on things that matter" (Domenici, 1999b).[2]

The Founding Line presents itself as a non-hierarchical, non-violent interest group that attempts to work with the government to find answers to the fate of the disappeared. These Mothers are interested in identifying and discovering the particular cause of death for each individual killed in the Dirty War. To search for remains—even to the point of exhuming bodies—is, for them, "a way of recovering the evidence of committed crimes" as well as providing "the chance to place a flower upon the final resting place of a loved one" (Asociación Madres, Línea Fundadora, n.d.).[3] Their diaper headscarves read *"Que pasó con nuestros hijos detenidos-desaparecidos?"* [What Happened to our Detained/Disappeared Children?].

In contrast, the original group of Mothers[4] is more hierarchical in its organizational structure, with Hebe de Bonafini as the first and only president (Bouvard, 1994, p. 95). These Mothers are perceived as the more radical group of the two, preferring to remember the disappeared collectively (Asociación Madres, 1995; Domenici, 1999b). This means that these Mothers are not interested in exhuming bodies to assign individual identities to the dead but prefer to concentrate on preserving the cultural memory about the Dirty War and demanding answers for the atrocities committed. In fact, they continue to insist that their children "are not dead. They live on in the struggle, the dreams and the revolutionary commitment of other young people." They reject economic reparations for the disappeared, saying that "a human life can't be given a monetary value," and posthumous tributes, plaques, and monuments because "this signifies the burial of the dead." For the Mothers, the only possible tribute "is to raise their banners of struggle and follow their path" (Asociación Madres, 1999). Their scarves read *"Aparición con Vida"* [Bring Them Back Alive].

In addition, the Mothers' work is supported by other groups that have formed related to the search for the disappeared. These include the Abuelas de Plaza de Mayo [Grandmothers] and HIJOS [Children]. The Grandmothers concentrate on locating the grandchildren of the disappeared and restoring them to their legitimate families as well as working to guarantee children's rights so that the removal of children from their parents will not happen again.[5] HIJOS is a human-rights organization that unites the children of the disappeared, and the members of this group are particularly interested in fighting the laws that grant protection to those involved in the disappearances as well as in maintaining "the spirit of struggle of their parents and other victims" (Vanished Gallery, 2000).

With the election of a new president, Fernando de la Rua, in October 1999, there may be greater possibility for resolution of the issues around the disappeared than previously has been the case. Rua talks of "leaving behind our confrontations and divisions" and wants his administration to be "transparent"— without secrecy or corruption: "This is why I will promote a dialogue with all the social and political sectors, with the opposition . . . and with all the good-willed men and women who want to build with us a better Argentina" (World Media Watch, 1999). The members of the Founding Line as well as the Grandmothers and HIJOS have chosen to collaborate with the new government while the Mothers have not, believing the new openness simply will cover up rather than provide any real information, justice, or vindication for the disappeared (World Media Watch, 1999).

Additional progress toward resolution of the issues involved in the Dirty War is evident in various trials of military officers from the Dirty War—both in Argentina and abroad. While perpetrators were granted amnesty for crimes linked to state terrorism such as assassination, disappearance, torture, rape, and theft, they can be tried on lesser charges such as abducting and changing the identities of the children taken from the disappeared. One such case occurred in January 2000, when Argentine Federal Judge Maria Servini ordered the arrest of six retired navy officers suspected of taking 12 babies from political prisoners held at a navy base (World Wide News, 2000). As an example of what is occurring outside of Argentina, in October 1999, the Italian government tried seven military officers in absentia for the disappearance of eight Italian nationals during the Dirty War (Vanished Gallery, 2000).

The work of the Mothers, then, continues on several fronts and with support from other organizations and other nations. The promised openness of the new administration may provide the Mothers with the greatest hope yet of resolution of the issues around the disappeared (Vanished Gallery, 2000). Though they realize that most of the Mothers themselves will not see the "end result," they continue to sow "ideals so that others can reap dreams and hopes in a world with more justice and solidarity" (Asociación Madres, Línea Fundadora, 1999).

Scholarly research about the Mothers of the Plaza de Mayo has concentrated on the role of motherhood in the practices, tactics, and effectiveness of the Mothers. Certainly, their status as mothers is extremely important to the Mothers themselves, and they conceptualize their activities within this frame:

> They were compelled to act not on moral or political grounds or out of concern for gross human rights' violations, as in the case of other groups, but because they were mothers. Their refusal to acquiesce in the loss of their children was not an act out of character, but a coherent expression of their socialization. (Navarro, 1989, p. 256)

The interests of the Mothers have broadened over time to include all kinds of human rights' issues;[6] nonetheless, the Mothers still see their mothering role as a primary motive for their actions: "'We are *mothers*, not women'" (Schirmer, 1988, p. 68). Their appeals are grounded in family and motherhood as part of a natural order that was disrupted in Argentina by the practice of disappearing citizens.[7]

Fabj (1993) suggests that the power of the Mothers came from their use of *marianismo*, the cult of feminine spiritual superiority and self-sacrifice that makes for an ideal wife and mother within the Latin American tradition.[8] The cultural mystique of *marianismo* provides one explanation for why the Mothers were allowed to march when political gatherings and demonstrations of all kinds were prohibited: the cultural glorification and respect accorded motherhood made the Mothers somewhat "untouchable" (Feijoo & Gogna, 1990, p. 90). But *marianismo* also made the Mothers less threatening to the government because women were not expected to violate traditional gender norms by engaging in serious political action. The women themselves recognized the contempt and dismissal in the actions of officials: "'We know perfectly well that they look down on us: they think of us as those mad old women'" (Feijoo & Gogna, 1990, p. 90). As "*Las Locas*," the Mothers' actions and requests were seen as irrational and without political import and thus as easily dismissed (Bouvard, 1994, p. 79; Schirmer, 1988).

While the role of "mother" is central to the identity and effectiveness of the Mothers of the Plaza de Mayo, it is not the only frame in which their activities can be examined and understood. In this essay, we argue that the metaphor of haunting provides a useful rhetorical frame in which to understand the Mothers' actions. By *haunting*, we refer to an experiencing of the presence of a disembodied spirit in a form that transcends boundaries of time and space. We are not suggesting that the Mothers consciously adopted this metaphor as part of a strategic rhetorical plan; however, in the choice of their symbols, common characteristics associated with a "haunted" place and experience emerge.

In fact, the Mothers' insistence that disappearance is a state of being provides the crucial condition for or starting point for the haunting metaphor: Disappearance "exists and is living with us, doing things to us, scaring us, driving us from our homes into exile, making us inconsolably lonely, or crazy, or unable to see what is right in front of our faces" (Gordon, 1997, p. 113). Gordon (1997) argues, in fact, that one of the Mothers' unique contributions is their understanding of haunting and its place in a society in which state-sponsored disappearances occur. The Mothers understand "what it means to be *connected* to the disappeared." They understand this connection because of "a special contact with loss and with what was missing but overwhelmingly present"—a contact that manifested itself in

> the responsibility the Mothers took for them [the disappeared], their attempt to communicate with them and to locate them, showing their faces, eyes, and

mouths in public, and the Mothers' extraordinary absence of fear of trafficking
in and with the haunting remains of state terror. (Gordon, 1997, p. 112)

Haunting at its base, then, demands a willingness to engage the ghost, and the
Mothers continually have asserted not only their willingness to do so but an insistence that it be done.

A second connection with the notion of haunting for the Mothers is evident in
the word *haunting* itself. The verb *to haunt* comes from the same root as the word
for *house*, suggesting the Mothers' primary identities as caretakers of children and
home. Yet the Mothers are very much uprooted from the home, both in the physical sense of having to leave it to search for their children and in the more metaphorical meaning of home as a sense of place that functions to provide a source of
personal, social, and cultural identity (Aden, 1995, p. 21). For the Mothers,
"home" clearly functioned as an important site of meanings that the disappearances ripped away. Unlike many situations of disorientation, where there is some
kind of ultimate resolution if not restoration of security and identity, such is not
the case for the Mothers.[9] The lack of resolution makes the haunting metaphor an
ideal frame because it contains the imagery of home but also its disruption. The
home has become the site of unsettled and contested meanings, each of which
functions as ghosts do, as a reminder of what is still in flux and unresolved.

The disruption to the home that the haunting metaphor captures further is
realized in the limbo in which the Mothers exist as women who have lost children.
As such, they are subject to negative attributions and the accompanying guilt
about their performance of the motherhood role. To put it bluntly, they are considered bad mothers because they have violated the fundamental task of mothering—
to raise a child and shape his or her growth in acceptable ways to adulthood—and
have failed in what Trebilcot (1984, p. 215) calls the "preservative interest."

With government officials declaring the children to be subversives, the Mothers had yet another reason for self-doubt and guilt—perhaps they were responsible for their children's disappearances because they raised them to be politically
and socially aware. From the perspective of many in Argentina, who believe the
disappearances indeed functioned to rid the country of subversive elements, the
Mothers are "bad" from another angle as well: not only did they raise their children to oppose their country's policies, but they are "bad" because they simply
will not admit this fact (Domenici, 1999b). The loss of their children and the powerful social and personal implications construct a limbo state, then, that is aptly
captured by the haunting metaphor. Elgin suggests that the lack of a term to
describe someone who has lost a child only exacerbates this limbo: while we have
the terms *widow, widower,* and *orphan* to describe particular relational losses, the
"fact that there is no name for the one who has lost a child is of enormous consequence: The nameless live in a kind of limbo" (2000, p. 3).

The metaphor of haunting cannot be considered apart from the notion of
trauma, since the appearance of most other-worldly apparitions is attributed to
some unresolved trauma in life. A traumatic experience is a repetitious reliving of
a difficult event; the trauma sufferer essentially is haunted or possessed by an
event or experience that is repeatedly imposing itself on the psyche (Caruth, 1991,
1995; Morgenstern, 1996; van der Kolk & van der Hart, 1991). Unlike a simple historical memory, the traumatic event remains powerful because it is simulta-

neously true and incomprehensible, and it is remembered as if still taking place in the present. The inability of the brain to contextualize or historicize the event makes that experience strangely senseless in the present, difficult to access on demand, and difficult to cope with or heal from. The traumatic, as a set of reactions to something highly disturbing, "threatens the very structures by which meaning is made of the world" (Brogan, 1998, p. 71), in part because of the necessary creation of what is essentially a parallel reality—the reality of ordinary life and the realm governed by trauma (Brogan, 1998, p. 73).

Janet (1976) suggests the importance of narrative memory as a means of translating the traumatic into something speakable, knowable, and manageable. The narrative memory is intentional and can be revised, and the act of undertaking its revision—the act of telling the story—also affords agency and a sense of control. We see connections between the trauma experienced by the Mothers upon their children's disappearances, the reliving of these experiences as a kind of haunting, and the rhetorical co-optation of the traumatic narrative as personal and political strategy.[10] We believe the features embedded in the concept of haunting make possible a reading of the Mothers' activism that can account for the effectiveness of their tactics and the personal and social transformations they were able to accomplish as well as suggesting the rhetorical limitations of the notion of haunting.

We suggest that the concept of haunting functions as what Burke calls a "representative anecdote," or representation that directs and compels the terminology contained within it. According to Burke (1969, p. 60), a representative anecdote must be sufficiently broad or representative enough to cover the conditions it contains but also sufficiently simple "in that it is broadly a reduction of the subject matter." A representative anecdote is "a *summation*, containing implicitly what the system that is developed from it contains explicitly" (Burke, 1969, p. 60). We maintain that the concept of haunting meets these conditions of the representative anecdote as it plays out in the symbols used by the Mothers. More specifically, we argue that it does so through the use of synecdoche, the process by which a part stands for the whole, as when we speak of *daily bread* to refer to food or call for all *hands* to be on deck.

Burke makes synecdoche one of his four Master tropes because of its powerful ability to affect perception, to abbreviate a situation or context, and to sum up its essence. Synecdoche is the trope that deals with representation. Thus, not only does the word represent or function as the sign of the thing, the thing or object also becomes the sign of the essence of that thing. Burke elaborates: "We might say that representation (synecdoche) stresses a *relationship* or *connectedness* between two sides of an equation, a connectedness that, like a road, extends in either direction" (Burke, 1969, p. 509).

While part to whole is the most common form of synecdoche, it also functions when the whole is used to refer to the part, as when genus is substituted for the species—creature for human, arms for rifles, vehicle for car (Corbett, 1971, p. 480). Implicit in synecdoche is what Burke calls a "relationship of convertibility" between the two terms, where ideally each is the "perfect paradigm or prototype for all lesser usages" (1969, p. 508). For Burke, this prototype or "noblest synecdoche" is, in fact, the case in which the whole can represent the part, and the part simultaneously represents the whole. Metaphysical doctrines in which the individual is considered a "replica of the universe, and vice versa" exemplify such a synecdoche since one could "look through the remotest astronomical distances to the 'truth within,' or could look within to learn the 'truth in all the universe without'" (Burke, 1969, p. 508). Each term, in other words, "'can be identified with'" the other to the degree that a perfect correspondence between the two is achieved (Burke, 1969, p. 508).

Because of the convertibility or identification between terms in a synecdochic or representative pair, Burke also raises the possibility of synecdochic reversals, in which certain relationships simultaneously represent but also contain the accompanying concept:

> I would want deliberately to "coach" the concept of the synecdochic by extending it to cover such relations (and their reversals) as: before for after, implicit for explicit, temporal sequence for logical sequence, name for narrative, disease for cure, hero for villain, active for passive. (Burke, 1969, p. 509)

As an example of the latter—active for passive—Burke cites the case of *Moby Dick*, in which Ahab's actions in pursuit of the whale are his passion, and his passion dictates his actions (1969, p. 509). Either side of the equation is taken as a sign, symbol, or symptom of the other, capturing, naming, or summing up the essence of the situation. Another example Burke offers is when a disease functions to perfect the cure or the cure functions to perpetuate the influence of the disease: each term helps produce and sustain the other (Burke, 1969, p. 512). We maintain that the metaphor of haunting not only contains synecdochic relationships but also creates the possibilities of their convertibility and reversal, leading to both advantages and limitations for social protest.

The study of synecdoche as rhetorical strategy in social movements is not new. Moore has been a primary contributor to this literature in communication, suggesting how divergent synecdochic forms construct competing realities in both the spotted-owl controversy (1993) and the hand-gun debate (1994). His work demonstrates how powerfully synecdoche can function to frame the terms of a conflict and dictate the kinds of solutions the conflict contains. As another example and, on a lighter note, Brummett (1981) discusses how what politicians eat functions as synecdoche to define their public images. There is considerable precedent, then, for the application of synecdoche to political contexts and controversies. Ironically, the trope of synecdoche may be especially relevant to understanding the Mothers' symbolic actions because state-sponsored disappearances are at core a "problem of representation." The disappeared have lost all of the usual forms by which social and political identity are represented: "no bureaucratic records, no funerals, no memorials, no bodies, nobody" (Gordon, 1997, p. 80).

We extend the work on synecdoche by suggesting its role in the protests of the Mothers of the Plaza de Mayo. To describe the synecdochic representations provided by the metaphor of haunting, we will focus on four symbolic forms prominent in the actions of the Mothers: diapers as kerchiefs, slogans and sayings, circling the Plaza de Mayo, and marches with silhouetted and photographed representations of the disappeared. Each of these symbols represents and elaborates the haunting terminology as it has played out in the protests of the Mothers of the Plaza de Mayo. These symbols, we suggest, result in a particularly effective set of rhetorical strategies for the Mothers by which to manage their personal trauma and create awareness of the issue but less effective options for achieving resolution of the political conflict. Because the origins of symbols can reveal much about how they come to function, we will focus on basic symbols used from the earliest days of the Mothers' activities. Thus, we will concentrate on those used by the Mothers before the group split and the Founding Line was formed. This analysis, we believe, not only can shed light on how haunting functions rhetorically as a representative anecdote but adds to our understanding of the powers and limits of synecdoche as a rhetorical strategy.

Symbolic Hauntings

The Diaper

The first symbol adopted by the Mothers remains one of the group's most identifiable and powerful—the diaper as headscarf. The Mothers' adoption of a white headscarf originally was designed to make themselves identifiable to one another. The most often told account has this symbol originating during a religious procession from Buenos Aires to the cathedral of Luján in September 1977. Because people talk with one another to pass the time during this procession, the Mothers believed it was a good opportunity to "explain their cause" (Bouvard, 1994, p. 74). Not all Mothers would be able to walk the entire way, however; some would join the procession at various points along the route. One of the Mothers suggested they wear something distinctive so they could recognize one another during the walk, and someone suggested a mantilla. Not everyone had a mantilla, however, so another Mother proposed a "'gauze shawl, a diaper? It will make us feel closer to our children'" (Bouvard, 1994, p. 74).

Another version of the story is that the kerchiefs first were worn when U.S. Ambassador Cyrus Vance approached the Foreign Office with a list of disappeared persons, seeking information about them. The Mothers gathered outside the office, but wanted "something so that we could recognize each other just in case some of us were detained" (Mellibovsky, 1997, p. 88). They discussed wearing a head-band in the Vietnamese style, but settled on a white handkerchief, "which everybody carried in her hand bag. . . . From then on the kerchief became an irreplaceable item" (Mellibovsky, 1997, p. 88).

The response to the Mothers in their signifying white diapers, whatever the origins of this symbol, not only served to identify the women to one another but also to create interest among those who saw the headscarves. Some passersby came up to say that they, too, had lost children; others, who knew nothing about the disappearances, learned about the government's activities by seeing the Mothers' headwear and initiating conversations about it out of curiosity. Consequently, the Mothers decided to make the diapers their identifying sign and began to make scarves out of cotton fabric rather than continuing to use regular diapers because "gauze was too flimsy and would not last" (Bouvard, 1994, p. 75).

Functioning synecdochically, the diaper provides the foundation for the metaphor of haunting. The diaper, of course, offers a superficial association with the ghostly: ghosts often are portrayed in white, flowing garments, and the gauze diaper shawls stand in for the ghosts, hinting at vestiges of such attire. More substantively, however, the diaper might be considered one of Burke's prototypic representational forms because of its ability to efficiently and simultaneously contain and generate the relationship between the Mothers and their missing children. First, diapers contain, represent, and communicate the most material and basic emotional, physical, and psychological bonds between mother and child. They call up Burke's Demonic or Body Trinity of the fecal, urinary, and genital, which he sees as a highly motivational source of "cathartic imagery" (Burke, 1966, p. 340). Standing for the primary relationship between mother and child, the diaper conjures up strong, almost "preconscious" imagery and identification for the Mothers and their audiences (Burke, 1966, p. 341).[11]

In referencing materiality in its most basic form, the diaper headscarves also encompass the intangible presence of the adults the infants could/could have become. The materiality of the diapers suggests the presence of the next generation of Argentines by simple virtue of the fact that children are the physical symbols of life continued. Yet that generation has disappeared; those individuals no longer exist in any material form—either as persons or as corpses and graves. Burke suggests that the "human body, world's body, and body politic" (Burke, 1966, p. 343) each imply the other, and this certainly is the case with the diaper as synecdoche. Not only does the diaper suggest basic humanness, but it refers to the larger universe in which children stand for the future of the world; that they are no longer material hints at the disruptive role of the body politic in a natural process.

The physicality of the diaper as headscarf accomplishes a repudiation of the body politic by means of reversal. The Mothers were told that their children were "subversives" and a danger to the state or that they had simply run off with lovers.[12] By putting the diapers on their heads, the Mothers efficiently renounced that position by asserting an alternative explanation: the disappeared were children—indeed, the next generation—who had been disappeared by a regime that wanted to exercise the most extreme forms of control over its citizens. The Mothers reinforce the disruption of the natural life cycle with a saying, *"En todo el mundo la gente nace y muere; en la Argentina la gente nace, desaparece, o muere"* [All over the world, people are born and people die. In Argentina, people are born, disappear, or die] (Domenici, 1999b).

The Mothers, then, turned the government's response on its head, just as they had turned the diaper into headgear rather than bottom wear. As synecdoche, the diaper is able to not only encompass and represent the most basic of human bonds but also a missing generation. The condensation of this symbol (Kaufer & Carley, 1993), with the diaper standing in for the disappeared child as well as symbolizing basic bonds of family and community, constructed the diaper into a kind of agent that haunted those who saw it with its clarity and complexity. Kaufer and Carley (1993, p. 222) suggest that symbols that are highly emblematic, as is the diaper, have high consensus, and thus contain the power to clarify different "camps" and "summon friends and foes to battle." The diaper signifies the missing children and brings them into focus as a ghostly presence in ways others symbols might not have been able to do.

Slogans and Sayings

A second ghostly vestige—the slogan, *"Aparición con Vida"* or "Bring Them Back Alive"—was embroidered on the diaper kerchiefs along with the date of disappearances of their children. The slogan itself, adopted in 1984, interjects an actual reference to the ghostly, since the Spanish word *aparición* simultaneously means *appearance* and *apparition*. While many considered the slogan ridiculous, since it was accepted that the disappeared were dead, to the Mothers it functions as a way of saying that "no one has taken responsibility for their deaths because no one has said who killed them, who gave the order" (Fisher 1989, p. 128). The Mothers argue that if their children were taken without being charged with crimes, those who killed them should be found and brought to justice: to admit and acknowledge their children's deaths excuses those responsible. Thus, many Mothers still refuse to talk about their children as dead (Agosin, 1990, p. 68; Bouvard, 1994, p. 138).[13]

"Aparición con Vida" functions as synecdoche, standing for a state of limbo in which the disappeared remain. The slogan's paradoxical force conjures up a realm between the living and the dead, maintaining for the disappeared a presence, an existence, that the government sought to deny. This slogan demands that the disappeared continue to live until a full accounting is offered for their deaths, effectively turning the disappeared into ghosts whose role it is to haunt the national consciousness. The victims are accorded presence and power through this synecdoche that simultaneously acknowledges and denies death (Brogan, 1998, p. 20).

The Mothers use other sayings to help construct the limbo state in which they and their children reside. Oxymoronic sayings such as "permanently pregnant" (Bouvard, 1994, p. 15) and "accumulated youth" (Domenici, 1999b) capture the sense of waiting that characterizes their relationship with their disappeared children. To use the word "pregnancy" to capture a state of waiting vividly pinpoints the situation of the disappeared and of the mother-child bond; to modify that state by the word "permanently" suggests a natural process stopped in its tracks until answers are found. This phrase allows the Mothers to simultaneously assert their motherhood while suggesting that they will not let go of the desire to find out what happened to their children. The phrase stands for an entire context that contains not only the mother-child bond of pregnancy but the notion of an unending patience and ability to wait. Furthermore, the Mothers present themselves—literally and figuratively—as the mothers of the next generation of Argentineans. Positioning themselves simultaneously in a state of permanent waiting to birth their own children and also as the progenitors of the next generation heightens the sense of a haunted condition: they, their children, and the future of Argentina are poised between birth and eternity.

Another way the Mothers employ the pregnancy synecdoche is when describing their children as having given birth to them. Their children's own activism—a likely reason for their disappearances (Bouvard, 1994, p. 82)—in turn has given birth to the Mothers' activism in a reversal of parent/child roles. The Mothers explain: "Our children begot us. . . . You stop being a conventional mother when you give birth to children who think and work for something beyond their narrow personal goals" (Bouvard, 1994, p. 178). Another Mother stated, "It is as if he had given birth to me and not me to him" to describe how her son's sense of social justice had inspired such interests for her as well (Munoz & Portillo, 1985). In employing such synecdochic reversal, the Mothers construct a world in which children become the agents of their mothers' activism. The synecdoche extends perfectly in either direction, with both mother and child having agency.

Another expression that sustains the haunted metaphor is "accumulated youth." Even though many of the Mothers are of advanced age, they are energetic and constantly busy on behalf of their children, whose disappearances give them the vitality necessary to continue their work (Domenici, 1999b). The notion of accumulation suggests a building up, an amassing, and an increasing of their youth, contrary to how normal time operates. They have the accumulated youth of their children who did not get to move into adulthood, and the incompleteness of the cycle means that youthfulness and vigor wait; they have nowhere to go. The Mothers see themselves not only as preserved in youthfulness but also as the keepers of the undeveloped lives of their children. The phrase "accumulated youth" positions the Mothers between the endpoints of young and old, accumulation and passage of time, representing the timelessness of the haunted condition in which they find themselves. By means of their slogans and sayings, then, the Mothers call attention to the absence of their children and the disruption of the natural life cycle. Their sayings function synecdochically to create a limbo state in which they wait for some resolution in regard to the disappeared.

Circling the Plaza de Mayo

Another powerful symbol that fits within the haunting motif is that of circling the Plaza de Mayo (Bouvard, 1994, p. 2). As with most of the Mothers' other symbols, the decision to walk around the Plaza was not a conscious choice; in fact, the Mothers first met at the entrance to a church a couple of blocks from the Plaza (Mellibovsky, 1997, p. 83). They often moved to the Plaza, however, to collect signatures on letters or to present a petition at the government offices located on the Plaza. The presence of the women became increasingly obvious to police, however, when the group grew to 30 or 40 women, and such gatherings clearly were in violation of public-meeting and loitering laws. The police then told the women they would need to move on, to "circulate." One Mother described the process: "And so we started to walk. . . . We could not stop, because when we tried to stop, they made us keep on walking" (Mellibovsky, 1997, pp. 83–84).

That the Mothers came to walk in the Plaza de Mayo, surrounded by the important sites of government, commerce, and religion, has strong synecdochic value. They walked in clear and obvious violation of laws against public demonstrations, "unprotected in that enormous place" (Munoz & Portillo, 1985), and their actions stood for as well as challenged the junta's power. Looking back, they acknowledge how difficult the decision to continue circling was; one Mother said, "Somebody in the place has got to have the courage to risk everything," even though "at the moment everyone was terrorized" (Munoz & Portillo, 1985). They have claimed the Plaza de Mayo as their space for over twenty years in full view of those whom they oppose, and the territory is now tacitly acknowledged to belong to the Mothers. They are essentially untouchable there, after some initial attempts to scare or dislodge them (Bouvard, 1994, p. 98), not unlike apparitions who cannot be touched in the space they claim.

The Mothers have constructed the Plaza as a place that contains the sense of presence of what is not physically there—from their disappeared children, to the knowledge about their disappearances, and even the kind of government in which disappearance as a political tool does not exist. The meaning of the Plaza de Mayo, then, placed where it is within Buenos Aires and as appropriated by the Mothers, conjures up both the invisibility and the continuity of the disappeared and the narrative that has been constructed about them.[14]

The circle, too, has other synecdochic meanings as well. In many cultures, the circle stands for eternal life. The unending circle of the wedding band, for instance, signifies an unbroken commitment and relationship. For many Native American tribes, the circle is a powerful symbol of atemporality that unites the past, present, and future as well as serving as the root metaphor of existence; the circle stands for life emerging from death and life winning out over death (Lake, 1991, p. 132). The circle takes on these connotations for the Mothers, for whom the quest to find answers about their children is timeless and never-ending. A poem by Pedro Orgambida, titled "Circulate," captures the circle's origins for the Mothers and the various ways it functions symbolically for the Mothers and for Argentina:

> Circulate, the policeman said,
> and they started to march on that Thursday
> like blind hens in a circle
> or birds from the South, in Summer whirlwinds
> Circulate, he said
> and didn't know he was winding up an endless dance
> a circle of love over death
> a wedding ring with time
> a ring around his own neck. (Mellibovsky, 1997, p. 81)

The circle can function synecdochically in yet another way, however. One of the meanings embedded within the notion of "walking in circles" is a sense of craziness; when someone is going crazy, they are literally going in circles—trapped in a logic that is not grounded in consensual perceptions of reality. The gesture of cir-

Mothers of the Plaza de Mayo, Buenos Aires, Argentina, 1998. Photograph by Karen A. Foss.

cling the ear sometimes is used to suggest "going crazy," an appropriate visual for a concept of spiraling in a world of one's own. Not surprisingly, many Mothers described themselves as going crazy when their children disappeared. They tell of "walking around like a zombie" (Mellibovsky, 1997, p. 142); of feeling immobilized by anguish to the point of being unable to leave their beds but also unable to sleep; of being "tormented" by memories of their children; fearful about what was happening to them; and guilty about how they had raised them or treated them when they were growing up (Bouvard, 1994, p. 67; Mellibovsky, 1997, p. 116). The netherworld in which they lived when their children "vanished into thin air" (Mellibovsky, 1997, p. 121) was indeed one that was crazy making: not knowing whether their children were dead or alive and being unable to resolve the situation created an endless circle of fear, doubt, grief, and hope over which they had little control.

The endless psychological and emotional torment was compounded by their circling of the city, as the Mothers endlessly made the rounds of government offices, army facilities, police stations, and prisons to seek answers about their children. They often waited for hours without food, water, or sanitary facilities, only to be told to "Come back tomorrow" (Bouvard, 1994, p. 66). The never-ending cycle of activity in which they engaged in their obsession to have their children returned, however, produced no more results than their inner struggles to understand and come to terms with the disappearances.

For the Mothers, participating in the gatherings at the Plaza de Mayo provided some release from the crazy-making limbo in which they found themselves. There, too, they circled, but at least, there were others with whom they could talk who understood their trauma and grief and with whom they could strategize about possible tactics for locating the disappeared. The Mothers served as an audience for each other, able to preserve the "unassimiable" form of their trauma while also managing it by translating it into historical narrative (Hansen, 1997, p. 114). Interestingly, telling their individual stories remains of paramount importance to the Mothers, even after over twenty years. When interviewed, their most common response to any question is to return to telling their stories (Domenici, 1999b). The stories not only make the trauma accessible to others but also provide structures through which the Mothers themselves can recast their traumas; the memories come to "guide, rather than overwhelm" (Brogan, 1998, p. 19). Croft (1999) notes the collaborative nature of storytelling and its ability to both "recreate" and "create experience" (p. 344). For the Mothers, the stories that emerged from their circling recreate the trauma but also create a shared community that fosters a new, larger set of narratives that transcend individual stories.

The Mothers' endless circling of the Plaza, every Thursday at 3:30 since 1977, then, works to maintain the limbo or haunted state first experienced by the women when their children were disappeared. The circle is a reminder that the craziness is not over—that the answers have not been found—and its public manifestation in the Plaza de Mayo is a way of keeping the ambiguity of the limbo state before the nation. The Mothers, in fact, continue to proclaim the appropriateness of the label, "*Las Locas*," because going crazy is the most appropriate response to having one's children disappeared. The ongoing circling of the Plaza, then, not only serves as a reminder of the craziness Argentina has endured but is a way of keeping the wounds open and festering rather than resolved and forgotten. Bouvard (1994, p. 151) explains:

> Contrary to the normal process of grieving, during which the agony of loss slowly moves away from the center of one's concerns, the Mothers have made a deliberate decision to keep the wounds open, in order to help them maintain their purpose and momentum.

The circle is another synecdochic symbol that not only represents but also reverses the various facets of the Mothers' lives and protests; it contains their craziness and their defiance, but also their hope. It is a symbol that is complex enough to encompass the symbolic situation fully, and it supports the haunting metaphor as well by sustaining the limbo in which the Mothers live.

Silhouettes and Photographs

Other symbols selected by the Mothers over the years for use in special marches, called Marches of Resistance, also extend the metaphor of a haunted place and the perseverance of a traumatized state through the trope of synecdoche. The Marches of Resistance began in 1981 when the Mothers decided to march for twenty-four hours in what has become a yearly tradition. Marching with white silhouettes of the disappeared was a new strategy for the third March of Resistance, organized to coincide with Students' Day on September 21, 1983 (Mellibovsky, 1997, pp. 128–129).

The idea for drawing faceless silhouettes of the disappeared was the inspiration of a group of artists who arrived for the march with life-sized cardboard cut-outs in the form of men, women, and children (Bouvard, 1994, p. 125). For twenty-four hours, people cut out and painted silhouettes and glued them to walls, buildings, and trees around the city: "There they are by each tree, each column, by the pyramid, on the Cathedral walls, and even beyond, penetrating all the streets of the city" (Mellibovsky, 1997, p. 131). One of the artists involved in the project described the results: "'The silhouettes didn't fill the emptiness, they only gave it shape. And quantity. Thousands of people made thousands of silhouettes of thousands of people'" (Mellibovsky, 1997, p. 132). The effect was that of the disappeared protesting:

> Thousands of women and men and kids and the newborn and those not yet born, stood fiercely upright, accusing the torturers, the assassins, the corrupt, those who today still spit in our faces, demanding, threatening, a shameful forgetfulness. . . . The disappeared. Wherever they might be, they haven't stopped struggling for a minute. They are more alive than us. (Mellibovsky, 1997, pp. 131–132)

Like the diapers, the slogans, and circling the plaza, the silhouettes are synecdoches that represent and give material form and presence to the disappeared, haunting the streets of Buenos Aires as a means of concretizing and coming to terms with an incomprehensible experience. The silhouettes stood in for the disappeared, making them manifest in very real ways.

The March of the Posters, though not a March of Resistance, was an equally powerful vehicle for making real the disappeared in a world that either denied or was ignorant about their disappearances (Mellibovsky, 1997, p. 133). For this march, each Mother carried a poster with an enlarged photograph of her disappeared child/children and the name, age, and date of disappearance. The youthfulness and immobility of those in the photographs had a powerful impact on those who saw them, described by one Mother this way:

> Their eyes remained fixed on the eyes in the photos; the posters remained
> immobile; immobile also the faces of the passersby. They looked at each other.
> Because the photos were not simply portraits. They demonstrated an unques-
> tionable existence that had to be restored. (Mellibovsky, 1997, p. 134)

The photographs made real the people who had disappeared as well as the fact of
the disappearances themselves. Their effectiveness lay in their ability to access a
different reality, to repossess what had been taken away. Through their public presentation, the Mothers provided "specific reference" to what was absent: "They
have been here once. They should be here now. Where are they" (Gordon, 1997, p.
109)? The sense of life experienced by those who saw the march is captured by the
Mother who said: "It was the first time that our kids had come out in the streets
with us to march since their disappearance" (Mellibovsky, 1997, p. 133). Another
Mother echoed this sentiment: "I believe that for the first time our children's
strong presence—which we feel all the time—was shared by the rest of the people" (Mellibovsky, 1997, p. 134).[15]

The presence of the children reasserted itself during a second poster march
when the Mothers braved a rainstorm and faced a "wall of men in uniform, lined
against the Pink House" [the Argentine White House] to march with their photographs. Neither the storm nor the soldiers deterred the women, and they "stayed
on without giving up one inch of their Plaza, and from their portraits their children continued to outface them, indestructible in spite of the deluge" (Mellibovsky, 1997, p. 135). The photographs constructed a powerful representation of
the disappeared whose presence was strong enough to face down the police, containing the sense of the disappeared as simultaneously present and absent.

But the photographs did not simply refer back to the disappeared; they created a relationship between the disappeared and those who saw them. Barthes
(1981) suggests the power of the photograph to convey to viewers the existence of
something so profoundly that it comes to matter to the viewer. He calls the element of the photograph that has the power to animate, break, punctuate, trigger,
or arouse the *punctum*; it is "the punctuation mark of an affectively moving epi-
sode" and has the capacity to make the referent come alive (Gordon, 1997, p. 107).
The photographs and silhouettes, then, provoked a reaction from the audience, an
"animation" that not only summoned the missing presence of the disappeared
but also a whole host of issues for the viewers: what does it mean to lose what I
thought was secure? What kind of society am I living in that not only sanctions
but initiates these kinds of losses (Gordon, 1997, p. 105)?

The use of silhouettes and photographs gave public presence to the disappeared
and created a relationship with those who saw them, enabling Argentines removed
from the experience to acknowledge if not identify with the trauma of the disappeared. Haunted by their children, the Mothers managed to publicly achieve Weinstein's "proper mourning" by establishing "a continuing sense of the deceased"
(1998, p. 98)[16] through a haunting of the nation's conscience with these concrete representations of the disappeared. The Mothers' appearances with the actual images of
the disappeared made public the hidden dimensions of the act of disappearance—
that it is a public kind of secret that haunts the population into submission by the
very fact of its fear. The Mothers' actions, however, revealed that the ghosts that
remain from such a process cannot be "completely managed" (Gordon, 1997, p. 127);
indeed, they remain as living reminders of what has been and still is unresolved.[17]

RHETORICAL CONSEQUENCES

From hindsight, the efforts of the Mothers of the Plaza de Mayo might appear to be a well-coordinated effort to move from the personal to the political, from the private to the public, and from coping with individual grief to creating shared solidarity. Yet only by coincidence did these symbols come together to create a space apart—a haunted space—that has maintained the salience of the disappeared as an issue. In concert, the symbols functioned synecdochically to achieve powerful results.

The ability of the symbols as synecdoche to extend in both directions is one explanation for the effectiveness of the Mothers' symbols. The diaper as synecdoche extends downward to encompass the most material of substances but also upward to refer to and represent the future generations of Argentines—an articulation made even more obvious by the use of the diapers as headwear. The slogans, sayings, and photographs extend similarly: they at once call to mind the historical events of birth and growth—basic processes of life—but also suggest a timeless attention to and standing still until the issues of the disappeared are resolved. The circle, too, functions as synecdoche, standing for the worst of the Mothers' craziness but also the possibilities and power of their collective action.

By their expansiveness, convertibility, and possibilities of reversal, the symbols enabled the Mothers to dismiss, refute, and eventually transform the meanings offered by the junta. The Mothers reversed the government's messages—that they really were just crazy, that they were inconsequential because they were "just mothers," or that their children were subversives—by using synecdochic symbols to articulate an opposing reality. These "crazy mothers" acted extremely rationally in following orders to keep walking around the Plaza—and ultimately created a subversive and very public presence the government could not dislodge. In taking something every Mother carried—a kerchief, a diaper—that could be dismissed because of its ordinariness, they created a potent reminder of a lost generation. Carrying photographs and silhouettes of disappeared children gave their children a vitality that continually confronted the government's explanations for the disappearances. The capacity of these symbols to so fully encompass a situation and to effect a reversal of and resistance to governmental rhetoric accounts in large part for their effectiveness.

Through the use of synecdoche, too, the Mothers imbue simple symbols with "essence" and "spirit" (Burke, 1966, p. 342), constructing and enacting a haunted state. In fact, the haunting metaphor may be one of the few metaphors powerful enough to encompass the Mothers' symbolic activity. Each of the symbols—the diaper, the slogans and sayings, photographs and silhouettes, and the circling—construct a world of the material and the intangible, the absent and the present. The result is a limbo space in which both the disappeared and the Mothers reside. The diaper symbol, for example, captures the physicality of the mother-child bond, making the material especially visible—and this in turn highlights the intangibility of the disappeared. The photographs and silhouettes point to children who once lived but who now are profoundly absent. A limbo state—a "betweeness" (Bell, 1997, p. 815)—emerges in the Mothers' symbols to persistently provide the grounds for their actions.

While the existence of the haunting metaphor in the Mothers' discourse is useful in and of itself for explaining and exploring the Mothers' worldview, we suggest that it also has important pragmatic functions for the Mothers as well as suggesting some limitations for their rhetorical approach. Gordon (1997) suggests that ghosts are "just the sign" that a haunting is taking place, and that more important than the haunting itself is the function the ghost serves for the future. He suggests that the ghost be treated as a "social figure" (p. 8) that "has its own desires" (p. 183); in other words, the force of the ghost is not simply that it stands as a negative reference to the past but that it offers the potential for something to be done in the future. Haunting, then, can be thought of as a precursor to new insights or actions because it is about moving from being troubled and traumatized to "doing something else" (Gordon, 1997, p. 202). It is about managing the present in a new way by bringing to bear the insights and illuminations of history that the ghost offers.

In the case of Argentina, the haunting made it possible for the Mothers to simultaneously process their own trauma and to articulate that trauma for the nation as a whole. The symbols they adopted allowed them to move from being the ones haunted—trapped in their homes by immobility over their children's disappearances—to producing visions with which to haunt the national consciousness. The symbols they chose allowed them to achieve a sense of "ego function" (Gregg, 1971), enabling them to see themselves as agents of political action. Arthurs (1992) describes the process by which liberation theology has been used to create conscientization, a process designed to alter the egos of the oppressed through self-rhetoric. We believe a similar process occurred with the Mothers. The symbols they selected, quite unconsciously, nevertheless functioned as "rhetorical wedges" (Arthurs, 1992, p. 5) that jarred the Mothers into critical self-awareness. They no longer thought of themselves as simply wives and mothers; at the moment when they put diapers on their heads, they essentially turned that role upside down. They were no longer simply "mothers of dead children" whom the military could dismiss; their persistent circling of the Plaza in front of the Argentine institutions of power created awareness of political options that previously had not been salient for them.[18]

That their symbols had such strong convertibility, extending simultaneously toward the concrete and toward the abstract, facilitated a personal and political transformation. The Mothers effected what Vivian calls the "politics of seeing and being seen" (1999, p. 133), appropriating symbols that not only brought their cause to the attention of others but brought a sense of self-awareness and political possibility to the Mothers themselves as well. At the same time that the symbols created a sense of ego-function for the Mothers, then, they created a state of limbo, a state of waiting for Argentina—an expectation that something needed to happen to resolve the issue of the disappeared. The convertibility of the symbols allowed the Mothers to move outside of themselves and their individual losses to create a space that could be accessed by others who did not know about the disappeared.

The synecdochic approach and its culmination in a haunting metaphor, however, is not without its limitations—and these limitations explain in part the lackluster outcomes of the Mothers' protests. First, the fact that synecdochic symbols manifest in the Mothers' discourse are convertible, with each whole containing the part and the part the whole, creates a closed system from which escape is difficult. The strength of the symbols alone means they are hard to let go of. For the Mothers, for whom identity and ego are so completely entwined with these prototypic symbols, giving them up may mean—or at least feel like—giving up the disappeared. The Mothers are locked in by their powerful symbols, moving back and forth between the symbol and the devastating experience for which it stands with a persistence that many a ghost would envy. The haunted construction that accompanies these synecdochic symbols makes even more difficult such an escape because of what a haunting is: it is a limbo, a stasis, a standing still between materiality and intangibility, presence and absence, poised in eternity. Again, there is movement between endpoints but little emphasis on moving above or out.

This state of stasis reminds us that synecdoche is the trope of representation—not perspective.[19] To put it another way, synecdoche, in dealing with representations, has a hard time leaving them behind because, as Burke (1966) notes, representation is always a reduction, a narrowing down, rather than a moving up. Thus, synecdoche does not have the capacity to see with the big lens. In fact, the representational focus of synecdoche, which demands attention to what stands for what rather than to any transformative possibility the symbols might contain, may make such a move virtually impossible.

The outcome of synecdoche, then, is state of limbo; while this allegedly is a state the Mothers want to overcome, it is also a world they know intimately—and it is a world that permeates all of Argentina. Perhaps the clearest example of this is how the Mothers and the country as a whole deal with issues of information about the disappeared. This has been one of the Mothers' major interests and demands—to find out what happened to the disappeared. Yet the Mothers themselves are divided on whether or not to exhume bodies—a process that can indeed reveal a great deal of information.[20] The nation also simultaneously asks for and resists information. On one hand, the Argentine Congress approved the creation of a reparations fund to enable the Grandmothers to continue searching for their grandchildren, many of whom were adopted by those in charge of the disappearances.[21] On the other hand, when those involved in the Dirty War confess—which might help the Mothers, Grandmothers, and HIJOS in their searches—the government discourages other similar confessions. This was the reaction when three high-ranking officers confessed about their roles in the disappearances; the response of then-President Carlos Menem urged others so inclined "not to make public confessions to avoid 'rubbing salt in old wounds'" (Vanished Gallery, 2000). The country seems to be in an information limbo, a state of stasis, desiring to know but simultaneously resisting the information that is offered.

The uneasy limbo that still exists in terms of how to handle those known to be responsible for the disappearances also attests to the difficulty Argentina as a nation may have in moving out of the state of limbo to which the Mothers' discourse contributes. The perpetrators were granted amnesty for crimes linked to state terrorism so when they are brought to trial in Argentina, it is only on lesser charges. Yet, even those who are convicted often are granted presidential pardons, essentially negating the convictions. The only other way to try the perpetrators of crimes linked to the disappearances themselves is to intercept the individuals abroad and try them in absentia in those foreign countries. The ground available for resolution is very much a world in between. In the end, that this is a world in limbo may help explain the reluctance of many Argentines to talk about the disappearances and the Mothers, even today.[22] The world the Mothers have created, despite their powerful symbols, is a confusing one where contradictory messages characterize the limbo state as well as help maintain it.[23]

The fact that synecdoche does not provide the possibilities of perspective also may account for some of the difficulties the Mothers encounter when they attempt to get involved in other causes around the world. When Tupac Amaru guerrillas seized the Japanese ambassador's residence in Lima, Peru, in 1996, taking hundreds of hostages, a group of Mothers flew to Peru and offered themselves as mediators, an offer that was ignored.[24] At a recent meeting of the Food and Agriculture Organization (FAO)[25] in Rome, when Argentina's Justice Minister Raul Enrique Castillo was speaking, the Mothers could not simply be ignored but had to be forcibly removed. They snuck into the meeting, unfurled banners, and shouted Castillo down, saying he had "no right to speak here because there are still human rights abuses and tortures" (Inter Press Service, 2000). After being removed from the premises and told that the Mothers henceforth would not be allowed in the United Nations, Mothers' president Hebe de Bonafini said, "After 21 years of suffering and struggle, we are denied a voice and are now being thrown from the United Nations" (Inter Press Service, 2000). Seemingly unaware that other actions were possible, the Mothers chose to create a context in which they themselves lost their place and voice within the United Nations—an outcome that in itself is a kind of metaphorical "disappearance."[26]

The recent millennium celebrations around the world offer another case in point of the Mothers as so enmeshed in their own cause that they did/could not consider the overall impact of their actions. While television viewers in the United States were presented with a collage of scenes showing cities and countries around the world ushering in the new year in joyful and celebratory ways, the Mothers were shown disrupting the new year's celebrations in the Plaza de Mayo and ultimately causing their cancellation. It was the only place in the world where public protest of that scale characterized the move from one century to the next.

The Mothers seem unable to recognize that they themselves have established a repressive system with their discourse in which virtually all other parties except for the Mothers are dismissed because of their inattention to or inaction in terms of the disappeared. The Mothers' discourse in essence denies the other, much as Argentina has denied the existence of the disappeared. Again, the closed system created by the synecdochic form, coupled with the stasis of the haunting metaphor, facilitates this undoubtedly unconscious process. Rather than seek reconciliation, healing, and resolution, the Mothers' symbols perpetuate an ongoing uneasiness, repression, and dismissal.[27]

The use of synecdoche in the Mothers' protests to establish a haunted state may be an effective strategy for the beginning of a social movement but less effective as the movement endures. Both the reductionist nature of synecdoche and the "betweeness" of the haunted state may keep transformative rhetorical possibilities from emerging. This case study of the Mothers' symbols suggests that rhetorical scholars need to look beyond simply the use of synecdoche in social movements to the long-term impact and effectiveness of this trope. We suggest that while the trope of synecdoche is useful for setting up and calling attention to an issue, it does not necessarily contain or facilitate a creative range of rhetorical options necessary for later stages.

In the end, despite the success of their symbols in creating awareness about the disappeared and moving the Mothers themselves from personal trauma to political action, the limitations of synecdoche may be what remain. In circling within a closed system of representation, the Mothers may be unwilling to assume the risks of moving forward because that would mean, quite literally, giving up their ghosts. It may be that there will be no serious progress in terms of resolving the issues of the disappeared for Argentina until the Mothers are gone, and those with less investment in the trauma of the disappeared—such as the Grandmothers, the HIJOS, and to some extent, the Mothers of the Founding Line—can embark on new directions. This is not to negate the impact of the Mothers and their symbols. Their choice of symbols and their representational power not only facilitated their own processing of grief but also brought the issue of the disappeared to Argentina as a whole. That the symbols have persisted with such intensity for almost twenty-five years is testament alone to their power but also to the burdensome task that still confronts Argentina:

> To look for lessons about haunting when there are thousands of ghosts; when entire societies become haunted by terrible deeds that are systematically occurring and are simultaneously denied by every public organ of governance and communication; when the whole purpose of the verbal denial is to ensure that everyone knows just enough to scare normalization into a state of nervous exhaustion; . . . when the whole situation cries out for clearly distinguishing between truth and lies, between what is known and what is unknown, between the real and the unthinkable and yet that is what is precisely impossible; when people you know or love are there one minute and gone the next; . . . when an ordinary building you pass every day harbors the facade separating the scream of its terroristic activities from the hushed talk of fearful conversations; when the whole of life has become so enmeshed in the traffic of the dead and the living dead . . . (Gordon, 1997, p. 64)

Notes

[1] The Catholic Church had a close relationship with the junta and denied victims of repression support (Fisher, 1989). The trade unions collaborated in the silencing as well, again because of government connections: while the unions largely were working class, and a large number of the disappeared were from this class, the leadership of the trade union bureaucracy was virtually untouched (Agosin, 1990, p. 161; Fisher, 1989). The press, too, was fearful of government reprisal, and refused, with one or two exceptions, to publicize the Mothers' statements or activities (Fisher, 1989). It is estimated that the disappeared came from the following occupations: blue-collar workers, 30.2%, students 21%, white-collar workers 17.9%, professionals 10.7%, teachers 5.7%, self-employed 5.0%, housewives 3.8%, military and security 2.5%, journalists 1.6%, actors and performers 1.3%, and nuns and priests .3% (Vanished Gallery, 2000).

[2] During a business trip to Buenos Aires, Kathy Domenici spent a day talking to Mothers of the Founding Line as well as Grandmothers of the Plaza de Mayo. She first met with about 8 Mothers, several feminist scholars, and conflict-management leaders, a meeting arranged by the individuals with whom she was working in Argentina. She then went to the office of the Mothers of the Founding Line, where she spoke with another group of 8–10 women. After a visit to the Plaza, where the Mothers had gathered for their 3:30 march, she visited the Grandmothers' office, where she spoke with 5 or 6 Grandmothers. Both authors visited the Plaza de Mayo the previous year and saw the Mothers marching; that visit was the catalyst for this research.

[3] Recent developments in anthropology have aided these recovery efforts considerably. The Argentine Forensics Anthropology Team, founded in 1984 to assist with the investigation and exhumation of grave sites in Argentina, consists of a pathologist, radiologist, ballistic expert, and archaeologist and uses the most up-to-date anthropological techniques to determine the facts about an individual's identity and death. See Gross (2000).

4 We will henceforth refer to the original group as the *Mothers*; references to the Mothers of the Founding Line will be identified as *Mothers, Founding Line.*

5 At the time of this writing, 58 children have been returned to or have located their biological families (Abuelas, 1999; Domenici, 1999a).

6 The Mothers' general focus is human rights, especially "the right to liberty, to equality, to not being discriminated against, to health, to education and culture, to respectable accommodations, to work, to just pay, and to a dignified retirement" (Asociación Madres, Línea Fundadora, n.d.).

7 While it is tempting to view the Mothers' actions in feminist terms, this is not a position or identity with which the Mothers themselves identify strongly.

8 For a general discussion of motherhood as a universal and enduring archetype closely associated with women's identity, see Stearney (1994).

9 Aden (1995), for example, discusses one such resolution in nostalgia, which can function to provide a temporary kind of escape and restoration—something not available to the Mothers.

10 The evidence of a traumatized population—at least in part—raises issues about the role of psychology in the management of this repression. Ironically, while the psychological profession in Argentina at the time of the Dirty War was the fourth largest such community in the world, its members generally stayed away from dealing with the disappearances and the trauma they provoked, preferring instead a "cautious professionalism" focused on "developing technique" and maintaining "professional neutrality." The result was a "depoliticized understanding of trauma" that "provided a kind of social sedative as it assuaged the anxieties of the middle class reclining on its couches" (Gordon, 1997, p. 91).

11 "Wright (1993) echoes Burke's interest in the possibilities of the preconscious, suggesting that preconscious imagery, and especially preconscious physical sequences, can serve as the basis for the formation of shared human images. Such imagery functions archetypally and can create identification in discourse even though participants themselves do not understand the source or full impact of the imagery. The diaper symbol may function in this way for the Mothers' audiences.

12 These are not uncommon beliefs, even among Argentines today (Domenici, 1999b).

13 Interestingly, Amnesty International suggests that the term *disappearances* is a misnomer because, in fact, the individuals who are disappeared are not lost or vanished. Gordon (1997, p. 75, 1981) elaborates: "Living or dead, each is in a very real place as a result of a real series of decisions taken and implemented by real people. *Someone* does know and, more importantly, is responsible." The slogan "*Aparición con Vida*" captures the sense of limbo that is crucial here—that the disappeared are someplace and someone is accountable for them.

14 Bell (1997) argues that a "common feature of the human experience of place" is the presence of those not physically there. According to Bell, places are "personed," and these ghosts—both living and dead—"haunt the places of our lives." The importance he gives to the ghosts that constitute a place seems quite appropriate for the Mothers and the Plaza de Mayo, where not only the Mothers but the presence of the disappeared simultaneously possess and conjure up the space.

15 Many Mothers recount feeling the presence of their children with them continuously—a kind of personal haunting. Typical is this Mother's account of the presence of her daughter, Graciela: "And thus, without intending it, I feel you are so near me that when I turn around, I hear you breathing. I feel that you are encouraging me with a smile . . . giving me courage so that I dare to go on . . . I don't know what else to do to find you. And I don't want to lose your image. I know I am wide awake. How can this happen? . . . I'm afraid to turn around. I am afraid to look at you; but if you are not here, how am I going to survive?" (Mellibovsky, 1994, pp. 29–30).

16 In contradiction to traditional literature on grief, which suggests that the bereaved should be helped to "move on" after a death, Weinstein suggests that, in fact, coming to a "fuller and more enduring sense of the person who has died" is the final task of grief work. He discovered that following grief counseling, clients often report an increase rather than a decrease of thoughts and memories about the deceased—and that these memories are "comforting and sustaining" (1998, p.100). This is certainly the case with the Mothers, who not only seek to perpetuate the ongoing presence of the disappeared but also find comfort in the presence of the disappeared that their photographs and silhouettes make public.

17 When presented with the haunting metaphor, its appropriateness resonated with many of the Mothers of the Founding Line, with whom Domenici spoke. At the same time, the Mothers mentioned that keeping ghosts alive is "dangerous" because it means insisting that society remain fearful and defensive in the presence of these ghosts. For a society to maintain such an unsettled position over the long term has unforeseen consequences (Domenici, 1999b).

[18] Burke discusses how much self-persuasion may be "preconscious" (1966, p. 330), and this certainly seems to be the case with the Mothers' process of conscientization. They did not set out to implement a social movement, their symbols came together by accident, and only after an enhanced ego sense provoked in large part by their own symbols did they see larger possibilities for and perspectives on their actions.

[19] For Burke (1966), representation and perspective signify two different Master tropes; synecdoche deals with representation and metaphor with perspective.

[20] While information is important, also easy to understand is why some of the Mothers do not find physical evidence at all useful in providing this information. As Gordon suggests: "A bag of bones tells us nothing about disappearance. A bag of bones is not justice. A bag of bones is knowledge without acknowledgment" (1997, p. 115).

[21] The reparations fund, in the amount of $25,000 per month for two years, will allow the Grandmothers to complete a National Bank of Genetic Data in order to track the disappeared and their offspring (Domenici, 1999a; Vanished Gallery, 2000).

[22] Domenici encountered this situation several times after she had spent the day with the Mothers in Argentina and then went on to present several workshops in Buenos Aires. She was asked explicitly not to mention the Mothers or the fact that she had talked with them during her workshop presentations.

[23] In all fairness, this world of limbo may be changing with the election of President Rua. He seems determined to create a different society for Argentina, a "new path" that offers "justice for all, so that we can recover our dignity and can grow in an atmosphere of equality" (World Media Watch, 1999). Whether he can serve as a catalyst for Argentina to transition out of a closed society into a more open one will be interesting to watch.

[24] President Hebe de Bonafini and several other Mothers flew to Lima after sending a letter to President Alberto Fujimori, asking "to be allowed to participate in the search for a solution to end the captivity of the 72 hostages." The Mothers, however, were not given authorization to enter the residence, and their requests for participation were essentially ignored. See British Broadcasting Corporation (1997).

[25] The FAO is the largest autonomous agency within the United Nations system. Its mandate is to raise levels of nutrition and standards of living and to improve agricultural productivity around the world.

[26] All of these incidents were the work of the Mothers, not those of the Mothers, Founding Line. The members of the Founding Line are more willing to cooperate with others and may, in fact, have an easier time moving out of the limbo of their symbols than the Mothers per se.

[27] Compare this situation with the end of apartheid in South Africa and the establishment of the Truth and Reconciliation Commission, headed by Archbishop Desmond Tutu. The Commission offered amnesty in exchange for the truth, a process that encouraged accountability, a culture of respect and forgiveness, and healing that facilitated the two races coming together rather than remaining apart. See Tutu (1999).

References

Abuelas de Plaza de Mayo. (1999, September 27). *Abducted children in Argentina* [On-line]. Available: www.wamani.apc.org/abuelas.

Aden, R. C. (1995). Nostalgic communication as temporal escape: *When It Was a Game*'s reconstruction of a baseball/work community. *Western Journal of Communication 59*, 20–38.

Agosin, M. (1990). *The Mothers of Plaza de Mayo (Linea Fundadora): The story of Renée Epelbaum, 1976–1985*. Trans. J. Molloy. Trenton, NJ: Red Sea Press.

Arthurs, J. D. (1992). The ego-function of conscientization as employed by small groups of the liberation theology movement. *Journal of Communication and Religion 15*, 1–14.

Asociación Madres de Plaza de Mayo. (1995). *Historia de las Madres de Plaza de Mayo*. Buenos Aires: Ediciones Asociación Madres de Plaza de Mayo.

Asociación Madres de Plaza de Mayo. (1999, September 27). *Our demands* [On-line]. Available: www.madres.org.

Asociación Madres de Plaza de Mayo, Línea Fundadora (n.d.). *Open letter to the people*.

Barthes, R. (1981). *Camera lucida: Reflections on photography*. New York: Noonday Press.

Bell, M. M. (1997). The ghosts of place. *Theory and Society 26*, 813–836.

Bouvard, M. G. (1994). *Revolutionizing motherhood: The Mothers of the Plaza de Mayo*. Wilmington, DE: Scholarly Resources.

British Broadcasting Corporation. (1997, February 25). BBC summary of world broadcasts [On-line]. Available: Lexis-Nexis/news/Mothers/Peru.

Brogan, K. (1998). *Cultural haunting: Ghosts and ethnicity in recent American literature*. Charlottesville: University Press of Virginia.

Burke, K. B. (1966). *Language as symbolic action: Essays on life, literature, and method*. Berkeley: University of California Press.

Burke, K. B. (1969). *A grammar of motives*. Berkeley: University of California Press.

Brummett, B. (1981). Gastronomic reference, synecdoche, and political images. *Quarterly Journal of Speech 67*,138–145.

Caruth, C. (1991). Introduction. *American Image 48*, 1–12.

Caruth, C. (1995). *Unclaimed experience: Trauma, narrative, and history*. Baltimore: Johns Hopkins.

Corbett, E. P. J. (1971). *Classical rhetoric for the modern student*. 2nd ed. New York: Oxford University Press.

Croft, S. E. (1999). Creating locales through storytelling: An ethnography of a group home for men with mental retardation. *Western Journal of Communication 63*, 329–347.

Domenici, K. (1999a, 29 April). Personal interviews with Grandmothers of the Plaza de Mayo, Buenos Aires, Argentina.

Domenici, K. (1999b, 29 April). Personal interviews with Mothers of the Plaza de Mayo, Founding Line, Buenos Aires, Argentina.

Elgin, S. H. (2000, May/June). Quotes and comments. *The Women & Language Newsletter 1*.

Fabj, V. (1993). Motherhood as political voice: The rhetoric of the Mothers of Plaza de Mayo. *Communication Studies 44*, 1–18.

Feijoo, M., & Gogna, M. (1990). Women in the transition to democracy. In *Women and social change in Latin America* (pp. 79–114). Atlantic Highlands, NJ: Zed.

Fisher, J. (1989). *Mothers of the disappeared*. Boston: South End.

Gordon, A. F. (1997). *Ghostly matters: Haunting and the sociological imagination*. Minneapolis: University of Minnesota Press.

Gregg, R. B. (1971). The ego-function of the rhetoric of protest. *Philosophy and Rhetoric 4*, 71–91.

Gross, T. (Host). (2000, February 8). *Fresh Air*. Philadelphia: National Public Radio.

Hansen, E. T. (1997). *Mother without child: Contemporary fiction and the crisis of motherhood*. Berkeley: University of California Press.

Inter Press Service. (2000, February 14). Madres thrown out after disrupting Argentina speech [On-line]. Available: www.ips.org.

Janet, P. (1976). *Psychological healing: A historical and clinical study*. Trans. E. Paul and C. Paul. New York: Arno.

Kaufer, D. S., & Carley, K. M. (1993). Condensation symbols: Their variety and rhetorical function in political discourse. *Philosophy and Rhetoric 26*, 201–226.

Lake, R. A. (1991). Between myth and history: Enacting time in Native American protest rhetoric. *Quarterly Journal of Speech 77*, 123–151.

Mellibovsky, M. (1997). *Circle of love over death: Testimonies of the Mothers of the Plaza de Mayo*. Trans. M. Proser & M. Proser. Willimantic, CT: Curbstone.

Moore, M. P. (1993). Constructing irreconcilable conflict: The function of synecdoche in the spotted owl controversy. *Communication Monographs 60*, 258–274.

Moore, M. P. (1994). Life, liberty, and the handgun: The function of synecdoche in the Brady bill debate. *Communication Quarterly 42*, 434–447.

Morgenstern, N. (1996). Mother's milk and sister's blood: Trauma and the neo-slave narrative. *Differences: A Journal of Feminist Cultural Studies 8*, 101–126.

Muñoz, S., & Portillo, L. (Producers). (1985). *Las Madres de Plaza de Mayo*. [Video]. Available: The American Documentary, 1776 Broadway, New York, NY 10017.

Navarro, M. (1989). The person is political: Las Madres de Plaza de Mayo. In S. Eckstein (Ed.), *Power and popular protest: Latin American social movements* (pp. 241–258). Berkeley: University of California Press.

Schirmer, J. G. (1988). "Those who die for life cannot be called dead": Women and human rights protest in Latin America. *Harvard Human Rights Yearbook 1*. Cambridge: Harvard Law School.

Stearney, L. M. (1994). Feminism, ecofeminism, and the maternal archetype: Motherhood as a feminine universal. *Communication Quarterly 42*, 145–159.

Trebilcot, J. (1984). *Mothering: Essays in feminist theory*. Totowa, NJ: Rowman & Allanheld.

Tutu, D. M. (1999). *No future without forgiveness*. New York: Doubleday.

van der Kolk, B. A., & van der Hart, O. (1991). The intrusive past: The flexibility of memory and the engraving of trauma. *American Image 48*, 425–454.

Vanished Gallery. (2000, February 12). *Further reading* [On-line]. Available: www.yendor.com/vanished.

Vivian, B. (1999). The veil and the visible. *Western Journal of Communication 63*, 115–139.

Weinstein, J. (1998). "A proper haunting": The need in mourning to maintain a continuing relationship with the dead. *Journal of Social Work Practice 12*, 93–102.

World Media Watch. (1999, October 29). [On-line]. Available: http://news2.thls.bbc.co.uk.

World Wide News. (2000, January). [On-line]. Available: www.yendor.com/vanished.

Wright, M. H. (1993). Identification and the preconscious. *Communication Studies 44*, 144–156.

Star of Fear, Star of Hope
North Star to Reach Reality
Marcia S. Van't Hof

An article in the November 27, 2000, edition of *The Denver Post* included the headline "Holocaust program helps teach tolerance." The feature that followed outlined the dilemma faced by high school teachers: How to teach the teenagers of today about one of the most terrifying historical events of history—the Holocaust. Much pedagogy simply does not connect with teens. Thus, the brutality becomes yet another set of statistics to memorize, or the genocide is presented so graphically that high-school students turn away in simple revulsion. The pedagogy discussed in the *Post* feature involved Teaching Tolerance Trunks "filled with $1,200 worth of books, CD-ROMs, posters, videos, maps, novels and teaching guides" that circulated among Colorado high schools. The trunks were intended to equip teachers "with the materials needed to explain the critical lessons of prejudice, greed, genocide, conformity and injustice" (p. 1A). The need indicated by the Teaching Tolerance Trunks is a need faced by teachers and parents everywhere—how to present the harsh reality of history to young people so that they may begin to process its contemporary lessons.

My analysis in this essay takes up this issue as it applies to an artifact designed for young children. The artifact is a children's picture book, *Star of Fear, Star of Hope*, that has won at least five international awards for children's literature. Written by Jo Hoestlandt and illustrated by Johanna Kang, the book was published in France in 1993, translated by Mark Polizzotti, and published in the United States in 1995. In this essay, I explore how this text employs rhetorical strategies—both visual and verbal—to introduce children to a frightening historical reality.

Star of Fear, Star of Hope is 28 pages long: A first-person narrative illustrated with simple drawings in sepia tones. The narrator is an old woman, Helen, who says that she does not want the world to forget her friend Lydia, so she tells the story that happened years earlier when her friend disappeared. Helen was looking forward to her ninth birthday in July of 1942, and she asked her Jewish friend Lydia to sleep over as part of the celebration. The two friends were telling scary stories before they went to sleep, wanting "to see if our hair would stand on end, like in the comic books" (p. 3). Their stories were interrupted by actual, rather than imagined, frights—the signs and sounds of two frantic, sanctuary-seeking Jewish strangers in the hallway. The two children listened breathlessly as the two called out their code names—"Madame Eleven O'clock" and the "Midnight Ghost"—and scratched and pounded at the apartment doors. After the danger passed, Lydia told Helen's parents that she wanted to go home. Helen's parents complied, and Helen was furious. How could her good friend desert her on the eve of her birthday? But Lydia left her present and went. Helen never saw her again.

The next morning, the streets resounded with shouts, footsteps, and whistles. Out her window, Helen could see a line of marchers guarded by soldiers. The

This essay was written while Marcia S. Van't Hof was a student in Sonja K. Foss's rhetorical criticism class at the University of Colorado at Denver in 2000. Used by permission of the author.

marchers were wearing yellow stars, and they included families like her own. Helen was mystified. "'They didn't look like robbers,' she thought" (p. 19). When Helen opened the present that Lydia had left, she found a handmade paper doll that had a cut-out of Lydia's face pasted on the doll's head. Lydia had made several outfits for the doll, including "a little coat on which she had even drawn a star" (p. 25). Helen wrote Lydia's name on the back of the doll. As the days, weeks, and years passed without Lydia, Helen still held onto the hope that Lydia had lived to become a grandmother like herself, a grandmother who might read *Star of Fear, Star of Hope* to her grandchildren, recognize herself, and call her friend Helen. The elliptical last sentence of the text reads, "I'll always have hope . . . (p. 27).

ANALYSIS

The unit for analysis for my exploration of *Star of Fear, Star of Hope* is generated by the research question itself. I will scrutinize the traces within the book that provide elements of realism, elements of comfort, and elements of discomfort. An artifact that seeks to introduce children to harsh reality in an effective manner must establish the *reality* of the narrative, allow for the *comfort* of the reading child, and yet introduce the *discomfort* of the harsh reality.

Reality

The story establishes itself as reality rather than fantasy. If children are to begin comprehending the Holocaust, they must understand that these events really happened; they are not the stuff of fantasies or dreams. Hoestlandt accomplishes this effect by her sensory details that signal believable experiences in real life. Lydia's mother breaks with her teeth the thread she is using for the Jewish star (p. 2); Madam Eleven O'clock scratches like a cat on the apartment door (p. 5); the Midnight Ghost has a red face and low voice (p. 7); the two girls, hearts pounding, stand frightened with bare feet on the cold tile floor (p. 7); Helen feels her heart squeeze when she realizes Lydia is gone (p. 23); and she falls asleep cuddled next to her parents (p. 17). With strong sensory details such as these, *Star of Fear, Star of Hope* signals that its narrative takes place in the common reality of children and their families rather than in an imaginary world such as those populated by beasts and fairies. As a real-world story, it invites readers to feel along with the characters as they see, hear, and touch one of the harshest realities two friends will ever face.

In addition, the narrative establishes its place in reality using details of childhood experience to which children easily can relate. For example, Helen says that when her parents came home for the evening, the two girls pretended to be asleep, fearing punishment if they were found up so late (p. 9). The emotions Helen feels when Lydia seemingly deserts her are ones that child readers probably find believable. Helen is so angry with her friend for leaving during her birthday celebration that she does not kiss her goodbye, even when her mother does (p. 13). Helen does not understand her friend's fear, so when Lydia hands her the homemade present and says, "I hope you like it," Helen responds with spiteful words: "I don't care! You're not my friend anymore!" (pp. 13–14). Any child can relate to hasty words spoken in the angry fit of a selfish tantrum. A child also may relate to the cozy security of a parent's bed, a place where Helen is allowed to spend the rest of the night. That such a privilege is unusual for Helen is evident when she says, "Some pretty strange things were happening that night" (p. 17). Because the narrative gives believable details about a child's experience, child readers may be able to accept that "some pretty strange things"—some harsh reality, in this case—really are possible within the circumference of their world.

The illustrations of *Star of Fear, Star of Hope* also signal the reality of the narrative. The characters are realistically and simply drawn; no one is in caricature or larger-than-life form. The sepia tones suggest old photographs, the kind that perhaps child readers have seen of their ancestors. Children may know by the time they read *Star of Fear, Star of Hope* that these photos portray real people who lived in the past. And yet the sepia tones are interrupted, as if to say that the people in this story are not peacefully departed and thus relegated to dusty memory. The interrupting element to the golden brown color scheme is the color red (appearing in the curtain, p. 4; on Lydia's doll, pp. 8, 28; on Lydia's dress, pp. 14-15; and on the paper-doll dress, p. 26). The color red, which is not found in the standard sepia palette, is strongly associated with Lydia and alerts readers to the importance and reality of Lydia as a person.

Child readers are invited to participate in the reality of *Star of Fear, Star of Hope* through yet another visual element. When the text pauses and pictures fill both pages (pp. 15–16 and 21–22), readers need to play out the words of the story in their own imaginations. They "fill in the blanks" at critical moments in the story: Lydia's departure and the marching Jewish families. When children thus accept an invitation to participate in the reality of the story, they will be more likely to incorporate it successfully into their own experience.

Comfort

In addition to the elements of reality employed by *Star of Fear, Star of Hope*, elements of comfort or security are replete in the narrative. For children to accept harsh reality, such elements are necessary to buffer the blow.

The narrative structure itself provides a secure framework upon which other elements of comfort may be built. The narrator, with whom the child reader will relate most readily, is not Lydia herself (a much more frightening perspective) but Helen, a girl-become-woman who happily survived the fearful events of the Holocaust. The plot structure, too, is comfortably familiar. Child readers are introduced to characters, the characters face a problem, the problem is resolved, and order is restored. The "I'll always have hope" ending (with its accompanying cheerful illustration of the two girls) is as close as any Holocaust story can get to the "happily ever after" that children expect.

In addition to the narrative structure itself, smaller scale verbal elements serve as elements of comfort. The story is written simply, with many sentences of three to five words. Nothing is threatening or complex within the vocabulary or syntax. The recurring thematic saying about stars ("Stars at morning, better take warning. Stars at night, hope is in sight") provides a cheerful, familiar element for a children's story—rhyme—whether or not the child knows the rhyme's original context.

Furthermore, *Star of Fear, Star of Hope* makes effective use of the principle of particularization as an element of comfort. Particularization in this narrative allows the story of the Holocaust to be introduced without a child's sensibilities needing to grapple with the whole horror: six million Jews systematically murdered in a national act of racially motivated brutality. *Star of Fear, Star of Hope* focuses its lens not on six million people but on one friendship involving two girls and two families on one day of their lives. The parents featured—Helen's—are close to each other, kind to their daughter, and sympathetic to the plight of the Jews. The other parents—Lydia's—are so dear to Lydia that she retreats into their care when the night at Helen's house becomes scary. A child reading this story does not need to make the emotional and intellectual leap into the entire horror of the Holocaust; the story's particularization simply invites identification with two children and their loving families.

Another element of comfort in *Star of Fear, Star of Hope* is the agency of the narrator. At the beginning of the story, Helen says that neither "the war nor the Germans could keep Lydia and me from going to school, or playing together, or getting into fights and making up, the way friends do all over the world" (p. 2). Even when she loses her friend, Helen is able to write Lydia's name on the doll her friend has left behind (p. 25), and eventually she is able to write the story that tells about her friend so that people still will remember Lydia. Ultimately, the narrator chooses to retain hope. She therefore retains agency and, by logical transfer, readers may retain agency as well. The comfort of some element of control over one's destiny remains.

Finally, the element of comfort that is crucial to any child is clearly present in *Star of Fear, Star of Hope*—a logical explanation for evil. True, children are used to reading stories in which evil is explained by the ugliness of the monsters or the meanness of a bully. This time, the explanation is more complex, but it is a clear and plausible one for child readers. A respected character, Helen's mother, offers it. When Helen offers the explanation for evil that assumes bad luck, Helen's mother sternly replies, "Bad luck almost never comes from the stars above, Helen. And this bad luck certainly doesn't. Unfortunately, it comes from people, from the wickedness of some and the weakness of others. Sometimes it can be so hard to live together" (p. 23). This clear, forceful declaration about the source of evil serves as a foundation upon which a child's more sophisticated understanding may be built. It is a starting place suitable for a child's emotional and intellectual capacities. It is an element of comfort.

The verbal elements of comfort are reinforced by the visual ones. The soft outlines of the human forms are emphasized by the open space, the sharp angles drawn in the background, and the glowingly golden sepia tones. The simple illustrations bring forward the actions and emotions of the human characters. The atmosphere is uncluttered and warm—a strong element of comfort in the face of discomfiting truth.

Discomfort

Sadly, the discomfiting truth must be told, and here we see *Star of Fear, Star of Hope* bringing forward clear elements of discomfort designed to introduce harsh reality to children. These elements do not predominate numerically; just a small dose of frightfulness will suffice. The narrative structure, though basically traditional and therefore comforting, inserts elements of painful mystery. At the very beginning of the story, Lydia's mother denied that the star she is sewing onto Lydia's coat is merely "pretty" but instead says: "The place for stars is in the sky. . . . When people take them down from the sky and sew them on their clothes, it only brings trouble" (p. 2). Helen does not understand what Lydia's mother is saying, but she decides to stop thinking about the stars (p. 3). But disquieting thoughts persist when the girls' playful scary stories turn to scary reality. They hear two fearful strangers in the hallway, strangers with fearful names. Mysterious, frightening events happen in quick succession: Lydia's departure, Madame Eleven O'clock's arrival to stay overnight, the march of Jews watched by armed police, and Lydia's family's empty apartment. Through the lens of a child's consciousness, these events are all difficult to understand. The dawning of comprehension comes gradually to both the narrator and to the child reader. Unreality becomes reality as these frightful, mysterious plot elements unfold. By the end of the story, the falling action is only happy in a limited sense. Even though the narrator has hope, the child reader may realize that Lydia and all those people who were marched down the street probably met a terrible fate.

Additional elements also contribute to discomfort. Several sentences end in ellipses, creating an insecurity about finality, completeness of thought, or satisfying answers. The mostly emotionless faces and dark black lines in the illustrations create a mysterious, foreboding effect. In all, the evil of the Holocaust is not buffered entirely by the narrative's elements of comfort. The disquieting, painful mystery of genocide gradually takes hold through a variety of elements of discomfort employed by the author and illustrator.

CONCLUSION

Perhaps the Colorado teachers using the Teaching Tolerance Trunks could take a lesson from *Star of Fear, Star of Hope*. The children's text employs a potent triad of elements involving realism, comfort, and discomfort. Whether young learners are seven or seventeen, they need to recognize that harsh reality is indeed real, that it is truly harsh, and yet that some sort of security is possible. Children need to grow into adults who face the full brunt of harsh reality and yet cling to hope. A better world requires the hard work of people who have grappled with evil guided by the assistance of such works as *Star of Fear, Star of Hope*.